ENGLAND ON TOUR

A Record of
All England Cricket
Tours Overseas, with Accounts,
Results and Statistics

ENGLAND ON TOUR

A Record of
All England Cricket
Tours Overseas, with Accounts,
Results and Statistics

Peter
Wynne-Thomas

HAMLYN
London · New York
Sydney · Toronto

Published by
The Hamlyn Publishing Group Limited
London · New York · Sydney · Toronto
Astronaut House, Hounslow Road,
Feltham, Middlesex, England

© Copyright The Hamlyn Publishing
Group Limited 1982

ISBN 0 600 34690 0

Printed in Italy

Introduction

The first tour by English cricketers overseas should have taken place in 1789 to Paris. The visit was arranged in conjunction with the Duke of Dorset, Britain's ambassador in Paris, and the Duke of Leeds, who was the Foreign Secretary. The team travelled to Dover to board the cross Channel ferry, but before they could begin the voyage, they were met by the Duke of Dorset, fleeing from the French Revolution.

Politics had clashed with cricket and the former, not for the last time, had won the day! This first tour has intrigued and baffled historians ever since records of it were unearthed. The question, which should rank among the world's great mysteries, is: who were the English cricketers going to play when they arrived in Paris? If this present volume does nothing more than prompt historians to delve for the answer, the author, at least, will be satisfied.

The story of the adventures and misadventures of English cricketers on tour is in essence the history of the development of the game outside the British Isles. It traces the steady improvement in cricketers overseas and sadly in a few instances the decline of those cricketers. The latter fact is immediately apparent from the first tour which did actually take place. In the late summer of 1859, the pick of England's cricketers crossed the Atlantic to play in the United States and Canada, for North America was regarded as the strongest home of the game outside England – the first cricket international, Canada versus the United States, had been staged as early as 1844. The 1859 English cricketers were overwhelmingly successful, but no more so than they proved to be on their initial visits to other countries. The slow collapse of cricket in North America can be seen as the teams sent from England got progressively weaker.

English cricketers first travelled to Australia in 1861-62, but it was not until 1876-77 that an Australian team was capable of challenging the tourists on even terms – before this the local sides had fielded anything up to 22 players against the English Eleven. The fact that the Australian team actually beat the English cricketers on even terms in 1876-77 meant that the 'Test Match' was born, though it was some years before the 'statisticians' and pressmen concocted the 'Test Match Records', with which everyone is familiar, and at the same time acclaimed England's defeat in 1876-77 as the 'First Test'.

The English tourists who went to Australia in the early days also visited New Zealand on several occasions, but the opposition there was much too weak to challenge the tourists on even terms.

In 1888-89 Major Warton, who had been stationed in South Africa for several years, pioneered the first English tour of that country and his team played South Africa on even terms in two matches, both of which are now described as 'Test Matches', though in reality they have no right to that august title. In the first instance, the English team beat the South Africans with ease, and in the second the English team was not even intended to be representative of England at full strength. To make the position of these Tests even more ludicrous, when the might of South Africa came to England in 1894, the visitors were not considered good enough to feature in the first-class averages. Cricket in South Africa however made great strides in the next few years and soon remedied this slight.

Six years after Major Warton's venture, R. S. Lucas took the first English team to the West Indies. The team were all amateurs and the visit was as much a social one as a cricketing tour, but it did serve to encourage cricket in the West Indies, as G. F. Vernon's adventure had done in India in 1888-89. The important factor of the visits to both India and West Indies was that the native populations were becoming fascinated by the game. In so many other countries where English teams toured, cricket was confined to expatriates. The supreme example of this is in South America. Lord Hawke took a side there in 1911-12 and tours have gone out quite regularly since, but in Argentina, Brazil, Chile and Peru cricket has remained the game of the English, and the decline of the English community in those countries parallels the decline of cricket also. A similar decline occurred in Egypt, where the large presence of English soldiers, sailors and civil servants created a team which was of first-class standard between the wars. Here at least a native Egyptian side was created but it has since fallen on hard times.

The improvement of the game in India, the West Indies and New Zealand and indeed in Pakistan and Sri Lanka has created its own problems. As late as 1929-30, the M.C.C. were content to leave the best English cricketers at home for the winter and still send out simultaneously 'representative' teams to both West Indies and New Zealand – by some historical quirk both these tours had 'Test Matches'. In the 1950s it became obvious that England could not continue to dispatch the second best to everywhere except Australia and South Africa. The opponents not only beat the weak English team, but were insulted by it.

The solution has yet to be found and politics which cancelled that very first tour very rarely stay in the background. Air travel and the development of one-day matches are two other influences that are changing the traditional pattern of major tours abroad, and the trials of George Parr and his companions on the tour of 1859 are at once completely different yet somehow the same as those met by English cricketers today – the problems of travel, of an alien climate and of opponents whose love of the game is as strong as the tourists.

Scope of Work

This book contains every English overseas tour involving first-class matches and a few other tours by good class English cricketers which the author considers worthy of note.

Tours which are made by 'Commonwealth' or 'International' teams, even though in some instances the majority of the players are from England, are not included, except for the 1967-68 'International' team to Africa and Asia, since this was entirely composed of English County cricketers. Details of the 1981-82 M.C.C. tours to Singapore and Hong Kong and to East Africa were not to hand at the time of going to press.

When southern hemisphere countries are toured, the years given to the tour in the headings and elsewhere relate to the season in which the tour is considered to have taken place. Thus tours of Australia and the West Indies will be described by a winter date, e.g. 1970-71, even though the entire tour might have taken place within one calendar year.

Definition of a First-class Match

There is not, nor has there ever been, an authority with powers to rule on the status of matches on a world-wide basis. Dealing with the matches given in this work, there are broadly two areas in which there is no clearly defined ruling on the status of matches. The first involves the early tours to each of the major cricketing countries, prior to those countries having competent 'Boards of Control' to rule on matches. The second involves the non-Test playing countries – the United States, Canada, Argentina, East Africa, Egypt, Malaya, etc. – in which first-class English sides have played three-day 11-a-side matches against representative teams.

The Association of Cricket Statisticians has been working on the problem of first-class status for the last ten years and is in the process of issuing 'Guides' to first-class matches in each country. At the present time 'Guides' to matches in the British Isles, Australia, South Africa and New Zealand have been published and this present book adheres to the rulings given in these Guides. So far as the other countries' matches are concerned, the status allotted to each is the considered opinion of the author.

In the summaries of results for each tour, Test Match results are printed in **bold type**, first-class matches are in ordinary Roman type, and other matches are in *italic type*.

Acknowledgements

The books used in the research for this work are so numerous that a bibliography is impractical. Apart from Wisden's Cricketers' Almanack, the two Lillywhite annuals, the magazines *Cricket, The Cricketer, Wisden Cricket Monthly, Playfair Cricket Monthly* and the various overseas annuals, extensive use has been made of the principal tour books and players' biographies.

The author is indebted to Philip Bailey for providing the first-class averages, to Philip Thorn and Keith Warsop for checking through the manuscript, to Dennis Lambert for providing scores of 1974-75 West Indian tours, to Peter Arnold for his advice and assistance throughout, and also to the various publications of the Association of Cricket Statisticians.

Summary of tours

t Denotes tied match included in draws * Tours with Test matches
Matches with no play at all are not included

	To	Organiser	Captain	All matches				First class			
				P	W	L	D	P	W	L	D
1859	North America	W. P. Pickering	G. Parr	5	5	0	0	Nil			
1861-62	Australia	Spiers and Pond	H. H. Stephenson	12	6	2	4	Nil			
1863-64	Australia and New Zealand	Melbourne C.C.	G. Parr	16	10	0	6	Nil			
1868	North America	North American Cricket	E. Willsher	6	5	0	1	Nil			
1872	North America	M.C.C.	R. A. Fitzgerald	8	7	0	1	Nil			
1873-74	Australia	Melbourne C.C.	W. G. Grace	15	10	3	2	Nil			
*1876-77	Australia and New Zealand	J. Lillywhite	J. Lillywhite	23	11	4	8	3	1	1	1
*1878-79	Australia, New Zealand and USA	Melbourne C.C.	Lord Harris	15	6	3	6	5	2	3	0
1879	North America	J. P. Ford	R. Daft	12	9	0	3	Nil			
*1881-82	USA, Australia and New Zealand	Lillywhite/Shaw/Shrewsbury	A. Shaw	30	15	3	12	7	3	2	2
*1882-83	Ceylon, Australia	Melbourne C.C.	Hon Ivo Bligh	18	9	3	6	7	4	3	0
*1884-85	Egypt, Australia	Lillywhite/Shaw/Shrewsbury	A. Shrewsbury	34	16	2	16	8	6	2	0
1885	North America	E. J. Sanders	R. T. Thornton	8	6	1	1	4	3	1	0
1886	North America	E. J. Sanders	W. E. Roller	9	8	0	1	3	3	0	0

	To	Organiser	Captain	All matches				First class			
				P	W	L	D	P	W	L	D
*1886-87	Australia	Lillywhite/Shaw/ Shrewsbury	A. Shrewsbury	29	12	2	15	10	6	2	2
1887-88	Australia	Melbourne C.C. (known as G. F. Vernon's Team)	Lord Hawke	26	11	1	14	8	6	1	1
1887-88	Australia and New Zealand	Lillywhite/Shaw/ Shrewsbury	C. A. Smith	25	14	2	9	7	5	2	0
*1887-88	Australia	Combined Teams	W. W. Read	1	1	0	0	1	1	0	0
*1888-89	South Africa	Major R. G. Warton	C. A. Smith	19	13	4	2	2	2	0	0
1889-90	Ceylon, India	G. F. Vernon	G. F. Vernon	13	10	1	2	Nil			
1891	North America	Lord Hawke	Lord Hawke	8	6	1	1	2	1	1	0
*1891-92	Malta, Ceylon, Australia	Lord Sheffield	W. G. Grace	29	12	2	15	8	6	2	0
*1891-92	South Africa	W. W. Read	W. W. Read	21	14	0	7	1	1	0	0
1892-93	Ceylon, India	Lord Hawke	Lord Hawke	23	15	2	6	8	4	2	2
1894	North America	Philadelphia	Lord Hawke	5	3	0	2	3	2	0	1
*1894-95	Ceylon, Australia	Australia	A. E. Stoddart	24	10	4	10	12	8	4	0
1894-95	West Indies	Lord Stamford	R. S. Lucas	16	10	4	2	7	3	3	1
1895	North America	Philadelphia	F. Mitchell	5	2	2	1	4	2	2	0
1895-96	South Africa	South Africa	Lord Hawke	18	7	3	8	4	3	0	1
1896-97	West Indies	West Indies	Lord Hawke	14	9	2	3	7	3	2	2
1896-97	West Indies	Jamaica	A. Priestley	16	10	5	1	9	4	5	0
1897	USA	Philadelphia	P. F. Warner	6	2	1	3	3	2	1	0
*1897-98	Australia	Australia	A. E. Stoddart	22	6	5	11	12	4	5	3
1898	North America	Philadelphia	P. F. Warner	8	6	0	2	3	3	0	0
*1898-99	South Africa	J. D. Logan	Lord Hawke	17	15	0	2	5	5	0	0
1899	North America	Philadelphia	K. S. Ranjitsinhji	5	3	0	2	2	2	0	0
1901	North America	Philadelphia	B. J. T. Bosanquet	5	3	2	0	2	1	1	0
*1901-02	Australia	Australia	A. C. MacLaren	22	8	6	8	11	5	6	0
1901-02	West Indies	West Indies	R. A. Bennett	19	13	5	1	13	8	5	0
1902-03	USA, New Zealand and Australia	New Zealand C.C. (known as Lord Hawke's Team)	P. F. Warner	22	19	2	1	10	7	2	1
1902-03	India	OUA and Calcutta	K. J. Key	19	12	2	5	6	2	2	2
1903	USA	Kent C.C.C.	J. R. Mason	4	4	0	0	2	2	0	0
*1903-04	Australia	M.C.C.	P. F. Warner	20	10	2	8	14	9	2	3
1904-05	West Indies	Lord Brackley	Lord Brackley	20	11	3	6	10	6	3	1
1905	North America	M.C.C.	E. W. Mann	8	5	1	2	2	1	1	0
*1905-06	South Africa	M.C.C.	P. F. Warner	26	17	5	4	12	7	5	0
1906-07	South Africa, New Zealand	M.C.C.	E. G. Wynyard	17	11	2	4	11	6	2	3
1907	North America	M.C.C.	H. K. Hesketh-Prichard	5	1	0	4	2	0	0	2
*1907-08	Australia	M.C.C.	A. O. Jones	19	7	4	8	18	7	4	7
1909	Egypt	M.C.C.	G. H. Simpson-Hayward	8	7	1	0	Nil			
*1909-10	South Africa	M.C.C.	H. D. G. Leveson-Gower	18	9	4	5	13	7	4	2
1910-11	West Indies	M.C.C.	A. W. F. Somerset	12	4	4	4t	11	3	4	4t
*1911-12	Ceylon, Australia	M.C.C.	P. F. Warner	19	13	1	5	14	11	1	2
1911-12	Argentine	M.C.C.	Lord Hawke	9	6	1	2	3	2	1	0
1912-13	West Indies	M.C.C.	A. W. F. Somerset	9	5	3	1	9	5	3	1
1913	USA	Incogniti	C. E. Greenway	6	4	1	1	2	1	1	0
*1913-14	South Africa	M.C.C.	J. W. H. T. Douglas	22	12	1	9	18	9	1	8
1920	North America	Incogniti	E. J. Metcalfe	9	7	0	2	Nil			
*1920-21	Ceylon, Australia	M.C.C.	J. W. H. T. Douglas	23	9	6	8	13	5	6	2
*1922-23	South Africa	M.C.C.	F. T. Mann	22	14	1	7	14	10	1	3
1922-23	Ceylon, Australia and New Zealand	M.C.C.	A. C. MacLaren	23	11	3	9	15	6	3	6
1923	Canada	Free Foresters	E. G. Wynyard	7	6	0	1	Nil			
1924	USA	Incogniti	E. J. Metcalfe	7	2	0	5	Nil			
*1924-25	Ceylon, Australia	M.C.C.	A. E. R. Gilligan	24	8	6	10	17	7	6	4
1924-25	South Africa	S. B. Joel	Hon L. H. Tennyson	21	8	2	11	14	5	2	7
1925-26	West Indies	M.C.C.	Hon F. S. Gough-Calthorpe	13	2	1	10	12	2	1	9
1926-27	India, Burma, Ceylon	M.C.C.	A. E. R. Gilligan	34	11	0	23	30	10	0	20
1926-27	South America	M.C.C.	P. F. Warner	10	6	1	3	5	3	1	1
1926-27	Jamaica	Hon L. H. Tennyson	Hon L. H. Tennyson	7	1	0	6	3	0	0	3
*1927-28	South Africa	M.C.C.	R. T. Stanyforth	18	7	2	9	16	7	2	7
1927-28	Jamaica	Hon L. H. Tennyson	Hon L. H. Tennyson	5	1	2	2	3	0	2	1
*1928-29	Ceylon, Australia	M.C.C.	A. P. F. Chapman	25	11	1	13	17	8	1	8

	To	Organiser	Captain	All matches				First class			
				P	W	L	D	P	W	L	D
1928-29	Jamaica	J. Cahn	J. Cahn	6	1	2	3	3	0	2	1
1929	Egypt	H. M. Martineau	H. M. Martineau	5	1	0	4	2	1	0	1
*1929-30	Ceylon, Australia and New Zealand	M.C.C.	A. H. H. Gilligan	23	11	2	10	13	4	2	7
*1929-30	West Indies	M.C.C.	Hon F. S. Gough-Calthorpe	13	4	2	7	12	4	2	6
1929-30	Argentine	Sir J. Cahn	Sir J. Cahn	6	2	1	3	3	1	0	2
1930	Egypt	H. M. Martineau	H. M. Martineau	5	1	1	3	2	1	0	1
*1930-31	South Africa	M.C.C.	A. P. F. Chapman	20	7	1	12	16	5	1	10
1931	Egypt	H. M. Martineau	H. M. Martineau	5	3	0	2	2	2	0	0
1931-32	Jamaica	Lord Tennyson	Lord Tennyson	6	1	3	2	3	0	3	0
1932	Egypt	H. M. Martineau	H. M. Martineau	7	3	4	0	2	0	2	0
*1932-33	Ceylon, Australia and New Zealand	M.C.C.	D. R. Jardine	26	10	1	15t	20	10	1	9t
1933	Egypt	H. M. Martineau	H. M. Martineau	8	4	1	3	2	2	0	0
1933	N. America, Bermuda	Sir J. Cahn	Sir J. Cahn	20	16	0	4	Nil			
*1933-34	India, Ceylon	M.C.C.	D. R. Jardine	34	17	1	16	18	10	1	7
1934	Egypt	H. M. Martineau	H. M. Martineau	10	9	1	0	2	2	0	0
*1934-35	West Indies	M.C.C.	R. E. S. Wyatt	12	2	2	8	12	2	2	8
1935	Egypt	H. M. Martineau	H. M. Martineau	10	3	4	3	2	0	2	0
1935-36	Ceylon, Australia and New Zealand	M.C.C.	E. R. T. Holmes	25	8	2	15	14	5	2	7
1935-36	Jamaica	Yorkshire C.C.C.	P. A. Gibb	6	1	0	5	3	1	0	2
1936	Egypt	H. M. Martineau	H. M. Martineau	10	8	1	1	2	2	0	0
*1936-37	Ceylon, Australia and New Zealand	M.C.C.	G. O. B. Allen	29	9	5	15	20	6	5	9
1936-37	Ceylon, Malaya	Sir J. Cahn	Sir J. Cahn	9	3	0	6	1	1	0	0
1937	Egypt	H. M. Martineau	H. M. Martineau	11	6	1	4	2	1	1	0
1937	Canada	M.C.C.	G. C. Newman	19	12	1	6	Nil			
1937-38	India	Lord Tennyson	Lord Tennyson	24	8	5	11	15	4	5	6
1937-38	South America	Sir T. E. W. Brinckman	Sir T. E. W. Brinckman	11	5	1	5	3	1	1	1
1938	Egypt	H. M. Martineau	H. M. Martineau	12	10	1	1	2	2	0	0
1938-39	Jamaica	Universities	E. J. H. Dixon	7	2	1	4	2	0	1	1
*1938-39	South Africa	M.C.C.	W. R. Hammond	18	9	0	9	17	8	0	9
1938-39	New Zealand	Sir J. Cahn	Sir J. Cahn	10	4	0	6	1	0	0	1
1939	Egypt	H. M. Martineau	H. M. Martineau	10	7	0	3	2	2	0	0
*1946-47	Australia and New Zealand	M.C.C.	W. R. Hammond	29	6	3	20	21	3	3	15
*1947-48	West Indies	M.C.C.	G. O. B. Allen	11	0	2	9	11	0	2	9
*1948-49	South Africa	M.C.C.	F. G. Mann	23	11	0	12	20	9	0	11
*1950-51	Ceylon, Australia and New Zealand	M.C.C.	F. R. Brown	30	10	4	16	20	8	4	8
1951	Canada	M.C.C.	R. W. V. Robins	22	18	2	2	1	1	0	0
*1951-52	India, Pakistan, Ceylon	M.C.C.	N. D. Howard	27	10	3	14	23	7	3	13
*1953-54	West Indies, Bermuda	M.C.C.	L. Hutton	17	8	2	7	10	6	2	2
*1954-55	Ceylon, Australia and New Zealand	M.C.C.	L. Hutton	28	17	2	9	21	12	2	7
1955-56	Pakistan	M.C.C.	D. B. Carr	16	7	2	7	14	7	2	5
1955-56	West Indies, Bermuda	E. W. Swanton	M. J. Cowdrey	7	3	2	2	4	1	2	1
*1956-57	South Africa	M.C.C.	P. B. H. May	22	13	3	6	20	11	3	6
1956-57	Jamaica	Duke of Norfolk	E. D. R. Eagar	10	4	0	6	3	2	0	1
1956-57	India	C. G. Howard	W. J. Edrich	2	1	1	0	2	1	1	0
1957-58	Tanganyika, Kenya, Uganda	M.C.C.	F. R. Brown	9	3	1	5	Nil			
*1958-59	Ceylon, Australia and New Zealand	M.C.C.	P. B. H. May	26	10	4	12	22	7	4	11
1958-59	South America	M.C.C.	G. H. G. Doggart	11	9	0	2	Nil			
1959	North America	M.C.C.	D. R. W. Silk	25	21	0	4	Nil			
1959-60	Rhodesia	Surrey C.C.C.	W. S. Surridge	2	0	1	1	2	0	1	1
*1959-60	West Indies, Honduras	M.C.C.	P. B. H. May	17	6	1	10	13	4	1	8
1960-61	New Zealand	M.C.C.	D. R. W. Silk	21	12	1	8	10	4	1	5
1961	Bermuda	Bermuda C.A.	W. S. Surridge	12	5	0	7	Nil			
1961	Tanganyika, Kenya, Uganda	F. R. Brown	F. R. Brown	7	4	0	3	Nil			
*1961-62	Pakistan, India, Ceylon	M.C.C.	E. R. Dexter	24	8	2	14	22	7	2	13

	To	Organiser	Captain	All matches				First class			
				P	W	L	D	P	W	L	D
1962	Bermuda	Gloucestershire C.C.C.	C. T. M. Pugh	9	3	3	3	Nil			
*1962-63	Ceylon, Australia and New Zealand	M.C.C.	E. R. Dexter	32	16	3	13	20	8	3	9
1963-64	Tanganyika, Kenya, Uganda	M.C.C.	M. J. K. Smith	11	7	0	4	2	1	0	1
*1963-64	India	M.C.C.	M. J. K. Smith	10	1	0	9	10	1	0	9
1963-64	Jamaica	Cavaliers	D. C. S. Compton	5	3	0	2	3	2	0	1
1964	N. America, Bermuda	Yorkshire	D. B. Close	12	9	0	3	Nil			
1964-65	West Indies	Cavaliers	T. E. Bailey	7	1	1	5	4	0	1	3
1964-65	World Tour	Worcestershire C.C.C.	D. Kenyon	14	8	1	5	2	1	1	0
1964-65	South America	M.C.C.	A. C. Smith	15	14	0	1	Nil			
*1964-65	South Africa	M.C.C.	M. J. K. Smith	19	11	0	8	17	10	0	7
*1965-66	Ceylon, Australia, New Zealand, Hong Kong	M.C.C.	M. J. K. Smith	31	14	2	15	19	5	2	12
1965-66	Jamaica	Worcestershire C.C.C.	D. Kenyon	5	0	0	5	1	0	0	1
1966-67	Pakistan	M.C.C.	J. M. Brearley	8	4	0	4	7	4	0	3
1966-67	Barbados	Arabs C.C.	A. C. D. Ingleby-Mackenzie	9	4	4	1	Nil			
1967	N. America	M.C.C.	D. R. W. Silk	25	21	0	4	Nil			
*1967-68	West Indies	M.C.C.	M. C. Cowdrey	16	4	0	12	12	3	0	9
1967-68	Africa, Asia	International	M. J. Stewart	21	15	0	6	5	4	0	1
1967-68	Kenya, Uganda	Warwickshire C.C.C.	M. J. K. Smith	9	2	0	7	1	0	0	1
*1968-69	Ceylon, Pakistan	M.C.C.	M. C. Cowdrey	10	2	1	7	7	0	0	7
1968-69	South Africa	R. J. McAlpine	R. J. McAlpine	14	4	5	5	Nil			
1969-70	West Indies	Duke of Norfolk	M. C. Cowdrey	9	5	2	2	3	1	1	1
1969-70	West Indies	Glamorgan C.C.C.	A. R. Lewis	6	1	1	4	2	0	0	2
1969-70	Ceylon, Far East	M.C.C.	A. R. Lewis	8	6	0	2	1	1	0	0
*1970-71	Australia and New Zealand	M.C.C.	R. Illingworth	29	13	3	13	16	4	1	11
1971-72	Zambia	Gloucestershire C.C.C.	A. S. Brown	5	3	0	2	Nil			
1972-73	West Indies	Kent C.C.C.	B. W. Luckhurst	11	4	0	7	Nil			
1972-73	South Africa	D. H. Robins	D. J. Brown	10	4	4	2	6	1	3	2
1972-73	Malaysia, Singapore	Oxford and Cambridge Universities	P. C. H. Jones	10	8	0	2	Nil			
*1972-73	India, Pakistan, Sri Lanka	M.C.C.	A. R. Lewis	17	4	2	11	16	3	2	11
1973-74	South Africa	D. H. Robins	D. B. Close	13	8	1	4	7	2	1	4
1973-74	Kenya, Zambia, Tanzania	M.C.C.	J. M. Brearley	8	5	0	3	1	1	0	0
*1973-74	West Indies	M.C.C.	M. H. Denness	16	3	3	10	12	2	2	8
1973-74	Barbados	Arabs C.C.	A. R. Lewis	9	3	1	5	Nil			
*1974-75	Australia, New Zealand, Hong Kong	M.C.C.	M. H. Denness	30	11	6	13	18	6	5	7
1974-75	West Indies	English Counties	J. H. Hampshire	7	3	0	4	Nil			
1974-75	South Africa	D. H. Robins	D. B. Close	8	2	3	3	5	0	2	3
1974-75	West Indies	D. H. Robins	J. A. Jameson	12	6	4	2	Nil			
1975-76	South Africa	D. H. Robins	D. Lloyd	11	5	3	3	4	2	2	0
1975-76	West Africa	M.C.C.	E. A. Clark	10	8	0	2	Nil			
1976	Canada	D. H. Robins	P. H. Parfitt	15	14	0	1	Nil			
*1976-77	India, Sri Lanka, Australia	M.C.C.	A. W. Greig	19	5	3	11	16	4	2	10
1976-77	Bangladesh	M.C.C.	E. A. Clark	4	1	0	3	Nil			
1977-78	Far East	D. H. Robins	M. H. Denness	13	7	0	6	1	0	0	1
*1977-78	Pakistan, New Zealand	England	J. M. Brearley	21	8	3	10t	15	4	1	10t
1977-78	Kenya	Minor Counties	D. Bailey	6	5	1	0	Nil			
1978-79	Bangladesh	M.C.C.	E. A. Clark	6	2	0	4	Nil			
*1978-79	Australia	England	J. M. Brearley	26	17	4	5	13	8	2	3
1978-79	South America	D. H. Robins	C. S. Cowdrey	13	13	0	0	Nil			
1979-80	Australia, New Zealand	D. H. Robins	C. S. Cowdrey	15	7	2	6	2	0	0	2
*1979-80	Australia, India	England	J. M. Brearley	21	11	7	3	9	4	3	2
*1980-81	West Indies	England	I. T. Botham	14	5	4	5	9	2	2	5
1980-81	Zimbabwe	Middlesex	J. M. Brearley	6	3	1	2t	3	1	1	1
1980-81	Zimbabwe	Leicestershire C.C.C.	R. W. Tolchard	5	1	1	3	3	0	0	3
*1981-82	India, Sri Lanka	England	K. W. R. Fletcher	22	6	5	11	15	3	1	11
1981-82	South Africa	S.A.B.	G. A. Gooch	8	0	4	4	4	0	1	3

1859: the first England cricket tour overseas

'Jemmy Grundy declared we should never see land again; poor George Parr was nearly out of his mind; old Jackson dropped to his knees; and indeed our situation was rather a critical one. Our jib-boom was broken and one poor old sailor had both his legs broken while he and some of the crew were endeavouring to set matters right.' That was William Caffyn's description of part of the homeward journey made by the pioneer English tourists of 1859. Apart from the terrible voyages across the Atlantic however, the tour was a tremendous success. The English team consisted of twelve professionals: H. H. Stephenson, Julius Caesar, Tom Lockyer and William Caffyn of Surrey, George Parr, Jemmy Grundy and John Jackson of Notts, Tom Hayward, R. Carpenter and A. J. Diver of Cambridgeshire, John Wisden and John Lillywhite of Sussex. Fred Lillywhite accompanied the team as reporter and took along his printing-press and scoring-tent.

The side was exceedingly strong, Parr, Carpenter and Hayward being the best batsmen in England at the time, whilst in Jackson and Wisden it possessed the best bowlers of the day. Caffyn, Diver, Grundy and Stephenson were all-rounders and Lockyer the main wicket-keeper. Parr, the Notts captain, led the twelve.

It took a little over a fortnight to cross from Liverpool to Quebec and the side were then taken by special train to Montreal for their first game. Despite poor weather several thousands turned out to watch Twenty-two of Lower Canada oppose the English Eleven and it soon became obvious that the home cricketers were no match for the fast bowling of Jackson, as the score fell to 12 for the loss of 6 wickets. Not that the batsmen found George Parr's under-arm lobs any easier, and in fact the captain ended the match with the splendid figures of 16 wickets for 27 runs. It proved to be the start of a triumphant tour, culminating in a final match—again with odds of twenty-two against eleven—versus a combined United States and Canadian side at Rochester.

Off the cricket field the team were royally welcomed and entertained, the only blot on the itinerary being Fred Lillywhite's printing equipment—at one stage George Parr lost his patience with Fred and in very forthright language consigned both Fred and his baggage to an 'unmentionable region'.

The tour was organised by W. P. Pickering, an old Cambridge Blue and an original member of Surrey County Cricket Club, who had emigrated to Montreal. He obtained guarantees amounting to £1,300 from various sponsors in both Canada and the United States and arranged the fixtures for the tour. After paying out all the expenses, each of the twelve cricketers took home about £90. The team had left England on 7 September and landed back in Liverpool on 11 November.

1859: G. Parr's Team to North America

1st Match: v XXII of Lower Canada (Montreal)   Sept 24, 26.
Lower Canada 85 (J. Jackson 7-21, G. Parr 6-8) & 63 (G. Parr 10-19, J. Jackson 6-20) lost to England 117 (G. Parr 24, Fisher 5-53) & 32-2 by 8 wkts.

2nd Match: v U.E.E. v A.E.E. Exhibition Game (Montreal)   Sept 27, 28, 29, 30.
U.E.E. 188 (John Lillywhite 53) beat A.E.E. 90 (W. Caffyn 5-34) & 44 (J. Wisden 5-18) by an inns & 54 runs.

3rd Match: v XXII of U.S.A. (Hoboken)   Oct 3, 4, 5.
U.S.A. 38 (J. Jackson 10-10, G. Parr 9-26) & 54 (W. Caffyn 16-24) lost to England 156 (Hallis 6-45) by an inns & 62 runs.
4th Match: T. Lockyer's XI v H. H. Stephenson's XI. Exhibition Game (Hoboken) Oct 6, 7, 8.
T. Lockyer's XI 163 (J. Caesar 52) & 90 (G. Parr 36, H. H. Stephenson 5-29) beat H. H. Stephenson's XI 93 (R. Carpenter 52, J. Grundy 5-21) & 86 (J. Wisden 8-45) by 74 runs.*

5th Match: v XXII of Philadelphia (Philadelphia)   Oct 10, 12, 13, 14.
Philadelphia 94 (J. Jackson 8-37) & 60 (J. Wisden 8-39) lost to England 126 (T. Hayward 34) & 29-3 by 7 wkts.

6th Match: North v South. Exhibition Game   Oct 14.
South 59 drew with North 120-6 (T. Hayward 60).

7th Match: v XXII of Hamilton (Hamilton)   Oct 17, 18, 19.
Hamilton 66 (H. H. Stephenson 7-19) & 53 (J. Wisden 14-24) lost to England 79 (W. Caffyn 25) & 41-0 by 10 wkts.

8th Match: v XXII of Canada & U.S.A. (Rochester)   Oct 21, 22, 24
Canada & U.S.A. 39 (J. Wisden 16-17) & 64 (J. Wisden 13-43) lost to England 171 (T. Hayward 50) by an inns & 68 runs.

The first cricket tourists from England, George Parr's side to America in 1859, photographed on board ship at Liverpool on 7 September 1859. Back row: R. Carpenter, W. Caffyn, T. Lockyer, J. Wisden, H. H. Stephenson, G. Parr, J. Grundy, J. Caesar, T. Hayward, J. Jackson. Front row: A. J. Diver, John Lillywhite.

1861-62: the first tour to Australia a great success

The success of the trip to North America persuaded the catering firm of Spiers and Pond that a similar tour to Australia would prove financially profitable, and in 1861 they sent their agent, Mr Mallam, to England in an attempt to sign up the best English professionals. He offered each player £150 plus first-class travelling expenses and this proposal was put to the players during the North v South match at Aston Park, Birmingham, in early September. George Parr and the Notts players immediately stated that the offer was not good enough, but after further discussion Mr Mallam persuaded the leading Surrey cricketers to accept, with H. H. Stephenson acting as captain. The party was made up of H. H. Stephenson, W. Mortlock, G. Griffith, Tom Sewell, Charles Lawrence, W. Caffyn and W. Mudie of Surrey, Tom Hearne of Middlesex, 'Tiny' Wells of Sussex, George Bennett of Kent and two Yorkshiremen – Roger Iddison and E. Stephenson. As no less than ten cricketers had refused terms – Daft, Parr, Jackson, Willsher, Lockyer, Hayward, Carpenter, Grundy, Anderson and Caesar – the party was in no way representative of England, but nevertheless was a reasonably strong combination. 'Tiny' Wells, who was accompanied by his wife, left England first, and the other eleven sailed from Liverpool in the *Great Britain* on 20 October. Unlike the 1859 trip, when storms were encountered in the Atlantic, the voyage to Australia met with calm seas, but it took over two months to reach Melbourne and the team found life on shipboard very tedious.

Over 10,000 people gathered to welcome the English cricketers as they came ashore and the coach in which they were conveyed to the restaurant owned by the sponsors was followed by a crowd of well-wishers – so great was the interest in the tour, that the ground selected for practice had to be kept secret.

In the first match, played against Eighteen of Victoria at Melbourne, each of the English eleven was issued with a hat with a ribbon and also a coloured sash, each man having a different colour and these colours were printed against each player's name on the scorecard. About 15,000 spectators watched the opening day's play, which commenced with the playing of the National Anthem as the England team entered the field. As in America the home team – although receiving odds – proved no match for the Tourists, who won by an innings. The second match involved a journey of about 200 miles by a coach drawn by 5 horses, and although the rough road made the travelling very tiring, the English team again won by an innings – the match ended early, so Griffith challenged 11 of the locals single handed. He bowled all eleven out, without a single one of them scoring a run!

The third match was against virtually the best twenty-two cricketers in Australia and proved to be an even draw. Leaving Victoria after a match at Geelong, the side went by ship to Sydney and again vast crowds turned out to greet the team as it landed. Somewhere between 15,000 and 20,000 people watched the game against New South Wales and the players were given a grand banquet attended by the Governor of the Colony.

The team met with its first defeat – by a Combined Twenty-Two of New South Wales and Victoria at Sydney. The English batting failed, possibly due more to the off-the-field activities than to any skill on the part of the Australian bowlers – scarcely a day passed whilst they were in Sydney without the tourists being entertained to champagne breakfasts, luncheons and dinners. Leaving New South Wales, the Englishmen boarded ship for Tasmania, where they again received a wonderful reception. A match was played at Hobart against Twenty-Two locals, followed by an exhibition game, before they sailed back to Melbourne.

The final match was played on 20, 21 and 22 March and proved an even draw, and each member of the English team then planted an elm tree to commemorate the tour. The sponsors offered the cricketers an extra £1,200 to stay another month, but since many of them had engagements to fulfil in England this was declined. Charlie Lawrence however accepted a post with the Albert Club in Sydney and did not return to England.

From every aspect the tour proved successful and both the sponsors and the cricketers made much more money than they had expected. The voyage home was as calm as the outward journey and the team reached England on 12 May. The Surrey Club gave them a complimentary dinner and they also received a benefit at Weston's Music Hall in Holborn.

1861-62: H. H. Stephenson's Team to Australia

1st Match: v XVIII of Victoria (Melbourne)   January 1, 2, 3, 4.
Victoria 118 (G. Griffith 7-30, G. Bennett 7-53) & 91 (T. Sewell 7-20) lost to England 305 (W. Caffyn 79, G. Griffith 61) by an inns & 96 runs.

2nd Match: v XXII of the Ovens (Beechworth)   January 9, 10.
England 264 (G. Griffith 46) beat Ovens 20 (G. Bennett 11-10, W. Caffyn 9-9) & 53 (G. Wells 8-10, C. Lawrence 11-38) by an inns & 191 runs.

3rd Match: v XXII of New South Wales & Victoria (Melbourne)   Jan 17, 18.
N.S.W. & Victoria 153 (W. Caffyn 7-27) & 144 drew with England 111 & 10-0.

4th Match: v XXII of Geelong (Geelong)   Jan 20, 21, 22
Geelong 111 (W. Caffyn 10-37) & 80 (T. Sewell 15-27) lost to England 128 & 64-1 by 9 wkts.

5th Match: v XXII of New South Wales (Domain, Sydney)   Jan 29, 30, 31, Feb 1.
England 175 (W. Mortlock 76) & 66 beat New South Wales 127 (T. Sewell 9-28) & 65 (G. Griffith 11-22) by 49 runs.

6th Match: v XXII of Bathurst (Bathurst)   Feb 6, 7.
Bathurst 49 & 25-6 drew with England 211 (G. Griffith 35).

7th Match: v XXII of New South Wales & Victoria (Domain, Sydney)   Feb 13, 14, 15
England 60 & 75 (G. Griffith 38, G. Moore 6-29) lost to N.S.W. & Victoria (C. Lawrence 9-36) & 35-9 by 13 wkts.

8th Match: v XXII of Tasmania (Hobart)   Feb 21, 22, 24.
Tasmania 107 (R. Iddison 8-32) & 141 (Whitesides 50, R. Iddison 11-63) lost to England 176 (E. Stephenson 60, Spicer 5-60) & 75-6 by 4 wkts.

9th Match: E. Stephenson's XI v H. H. Stephenson's XI. Exhibition Game   Feb 24.
E. Stephenson's XI 86 (R. Iddison 7-52) & 22-5 drew with H. H. Stephenson's XI 100 (T. Sewell 5-47).

10th Match: Surrey v The World XI (Melbourne). Exhibition Game   March 1, 3, 4.
The World 211 (G. Bennett 72, G. Griffith 5-52) & 86-4 beat Surrey 115 (G. Bennett 7-30) & 179 (W. Caffyn 75*, G. Bennett 8-85) by 6 wkts.

11th Match: v XXII of Ballarat (Ballarat)   March 6, 7, 8.
Ballarat 122 & 107 (R. Iddison 7-50) drew with England 155 (T. Hearne 37*).

12th Match: v XXII of Bendigo (Bendigo)   March 11, 12, 13.
England 246 (W. Caffyn 57, G. Bennett 56) beat Bendigo 81 (G. Bennett 13-40) & 102 (G. Bennett 10-41) by an inns & 63 runs.

13th Match: v XXII of Castlemaine (Castlemaine)   March 14, 15, 17.
England 80 (J. W. Amos 7-13) & 68 (Brooker 6-6) lost to Castlemaine 54 (G. Griffith 13-18) & 96-18 (G. Griffith 9-28) by 3 wkts.

14th Match: v XXII of Victoria (Melbourne)   March 20, 21, 22.
Victoria 140 (R. Iddison 9-37) & 151 (R. Iddison 13-168) drew with England 218 (W. Mortlock 53, W. Caffyn 45) & 63-7.

Opposite *The fifth match of H. H. Stephenson's tour of Australia in 1861-62, against twenty-two of New South Wales. The England eleven won by 49 runs before an attendance on the first day of 15,000 to 20,000 spectators.*

Below *The first tourists to Australia, taken just before their departure in October 1861. From left: W. Mortlock, W. Mudie, G. Bennett, C. Lawrence, H. H. Stephenson, Mr W. B. Mallam (the agent of the Australian sponsors), W. Caffyn, G. Griffith, T. Hearne, R. Iddison, T. Sewell, E. Stephenson.*

1863-64: George Parr's men play twenty-two a time in Australia and New Zealand

The Melbourne Club did not have the same problems as Spiers and Pond when it came to persuading the leading English cricketers to make a second tour to Australia. This time George Parr was appointed captain and asked to select a team to accompany him. Parr chose two other Notts players – J. Jackson and R. C. Tinley, four Surrey men – Julius Caesar, Tom Lockyer, William Mortlock and William Caffyn; the great Cambridgeshire players, T. Hayward, R. Carpenter and G. Tarrant; George Anderson of Yorkshire and a little known Gloucestershire amateur, Dr E. M. Grace. Mortlock, in fact, altered his mind and his place was taken by Alfred Clarke, the son of the man who founded Trent Bridge Cricket Ground.

The Twelve was thoroughly representative of England and far superior to its predecessor of 1861-62, only Caffyn being a member of both parties. The voyage from Liverpool lasted 61 days and Melbourne was reached on 16 December. Although rougher than the outward trip of 1861, it was a pleasant journey, but George Anderson proved a poor sailor and suffered a great deal from sea-sickness. The team had a fortnight's practice in Melbourne before the first match against Twenty-two of Victoria – it was estimated that about 40,000 watched the contest over the four days, the English team needing nine to win with 6 wickets in hand when stumps were drawn. There followed four up-country matches against local Twenty-twos and 'Spider' Tinley totally baffled the home batsmen with his lobs, his tally of wickets for the four matches being 27, 23, 26, 22 – 98 in all!

On 25 January, the tourists left Victoria by ship for New Zealand, arriving at Port Chalmers after six days, here they were presented to the local Maori chief, who took a special liking to George Parr and followed him everywhere, much to the captain's alarm. From Port Chalmers the team travelled in a coach-and-six, driven by a famous coachman, 'Cabbage-Tree Ned', to Dunedin, where the first match was played. As in Australia the tourists proved too good for the home sides and Tinley continued his success as a lob bowler. As well as Dunedin, matches were played at Christchurch and an athletics contest was also staged. Getting back to Australia, the team went to Castlemaine, whom they beat

by an innings, and each cricketer was presented with a scarf-pin as a memento of the game. On their visit to Sydney, the tourists met Charlie Lawrence, who had stayed behind after the 1861 visit – he scored the most runs for the home team in a match which lasted nine days – several of them being lost due to rain. The most exciting contest of the tour was the third against Twenty-two of New South Wales, the English team winning by just one wicket. After this game the side set sail to return to Melbourne, but a few miles out from Sydney the ship collided with another vessel which sank almost at once. George Parr was paralysed with alarm, whilst Tarrant quite lost his head, rushed down to get his valuables and then tried to jump into the life boat which was being lowered to pick up the survivors from the sunken boat. John Jackson, who had done himself extra well at the farewell lunch before they left, slept soundly through all the confusion. The damage to the team's boat was such that the captain was forced to return to Sydney for repairs and this caused the next fixture – against Geelong – to be delayed by a day. After an exhibition game at Maryborough, Dr Grace challenged any six local players – the challenge was accepted, but the locals could not dismiss the Doctor, who was 106 not out at the end of the day.

The final match against Twenty-two of Victoria took place on 21, 22 and 23 April and due to rain had to be drawn. On 26 April, the team, less Dr Grace, who stayed on to visit friends, and Caffyn, who accepted an engagement in Melbourne, boarded the Bombay steamer for home, arriving at Dover on 13 June.

The tour – not a match lost – was even more successful than the 1861 trip and each player cleared about £250 after expenses, double the amount made previously.

Above *The team for the tour of Australia in 1863-64. The players are, back: J. Caesar, A. Clarke, G. Tarrant, G. Parr, E. M. Grace, R. Carpenter, G. Anderson, W. Caffyn. Front: R. C. Tinley, T. Lockyer, T. Hayward, J. Jackson.*

Right *The match at Melbourne between England and Australia in 1864.*

1863-64: G. Parr's Team to Australia and New Zealand

1st Match: v XXII of Victoria (Melbourne) Jan 1, 2, 4, 5.
Victoria 146 (R. C. Tinley 11-52) & 143 (R. C. Tinley 8-63) drew with England 176 (T. Hayward 61, R. Carpenter 59, J. M. Bryant 6-43) & 105-4.

2nd Match: v XXII of Bendigo (Bendigo) Jan 7, 8, 9.
England 85 (T. W. S. Wills 6-35) & 178 beat Bendigo 74 (R. C. Tinley 13-35) & 45 (R. C. Tinley 14-22) by 144 runs.

3rd Match: v XXII of Ballarat (Ballarat) Jan 11, 12, 13.
Ballarat 82 (R. C. Tinley 13-20) & 94 (T. W. S. Wills 32, R. C. Tinley 10-50) lost to England 188 (J. Caesar 40) by an inns & 12 runs.

4th Match: v XXII of Ararat (Ararat) Jan 14, 15, 16.
England 137 (R. Carpenter 35, T. W. S. Wills 6-57) beat Ararat 35 (R. C. Tinley 14-22) & 34 (R. C. Tinley 12-23) by an inns & 68 runs.

5th Match: v XXII of Maryborough (Maryborough) Jan 19, 20, 21.
Maryborough 72 (R. C. Tinley 11-24) & 74 (R. C. Tinley 11-48) lost to England 223 (E. M. Grace 44, T. W. S. Wills 5-82) by an inns & 77 runs.

6th Match: v XXII of Otago (Dunedin) Feb 2, 3, 4.
Otago 71 (T. Hayward 15-34) & 83 (T. Hayward 9-36) lost to England 99 & 58-1 by 9 wkts.

7th Match: v XXII of Canterbury & Otago (Dunedin) Feb 4, 5.
Canterbury & Otago 91 (R. C. Tinley 13-49) & 66 (R. C. Tinley 13 wkts) drew with England 73 (E. M. Grace 42).

8th Match: v XXII of Canterbury (Christchurch) Feb 8, 9.
Canterbury 30 (R. C. Tinley 13-18) & 105 (R. C. Tinley 12-68) lost to England 137 (T. W. S. Wills 6-55) by an inns & 2 runs.

9th Match: G. Parr's XI v G. Anderson's XI. Exhibition Game. (Christchurch) Feb 9, 10.
G. Parr's XI 64 & 89 beat G. Anderson's XI 71 & 75 by 7 runs.

10th Match: v XXII of Otago (Dunedin) Feb 16, 17, 18.
England 198 (W. Caffyn 43, T. Hayward 40) beat Otago 98 (J. Jackson 10-21) & 49 (R. C. Tinley 11 wkts) by an inns & 51 runs.

11th Match: v XXII of Castlemaine (Campbell's Creek) March 2, 3, 4.
England 137 beat Castlemaine 54 (R. C. Tinley 9-28) & 46 (R. C. Tinley 12-28) by an inns & 37 runs.

12th Match: G. Parr's XI v G. Anderson's XI. Exhibition Match. (Melbourne) March 6, 7, 8, 9.
G. Parr's XI 153 (E. M. Grace 5-33) & 129 (W. Caffyn 40) lost to G. Anderson's XI 168 (T. Lockyer 44, R. C. Tinley 7-76) & 115-6 by 4 wkts.

13th Match: v XXII of New South Wales (Sydney) March 16, 17, 18, 24.
New South Wales 137 & 50 (J. Jackson 9-20) lost to England 128 (W. Caffyn 25) & 60-6 by 4 wkts.

14th Match: v XXII of New South Wales (Sydney) March 26, 28, 29.
New South Wales 102 (C. Lawrence 25) & 3-1 drew with England 114 (G. H. B. Gilbert 5-58).

15th Match: v XXII of New South Wales (Sydney) April 2, 4.
New South Wales 68 & 83 (R. C. Tinley 10-33) lost to England 75 (O. H. Lewis 5-14) & 77-9 (C. Lawrence 6-48) by 1 wkt.

16th Match: v XXII of Geelong (Geelong) April 12, 13.
Geelong 103 (R. C. Tinley 9-38) & 64-9 drew with England 135 (G. Tarrant 41).

17th Match: G. Parr's XI v G. Anderson's XI (Maryborough). Exhibition Game. April 14, 15.
G. Anderson's XI 164 (G. Tarrant 35) & 74 (T. Hayward 5-34) beat G. Parr's XI 112 (J. Jackson 45, R. C. Tinley 6-59) & 70 (J. Caesar 6-31) by 56 runs.

18th Match: v XXII of Ballarat (Ballarat) April 18, 19, 20.
England 310 (R. Carpenter 121, G. Parr 65) drew with Ballarat 128 (R. C. Tinley 8-72) & 48-15 (R. C. Tinley 10-28).

19th Match: v XXII of Victoria (Melbourne) April 21, 22, 23.
Victoria 150 (J. Jackson 10-34) & 83-17 (G. Tarrant 12-29) drew with England 131.

1868: another visit to Canada and the United States

Nine years had elapsed since the first English team crossed the Atlantic, and in the interval the bitter war between the Northern and Southern United States had taken place, also the popularity of baseball had outstripped that of cricket. Still several supporters of the game in North America had invited V. E. Walker, the Middlesex cricketer, to select a team and play a series of six matches. Several of the best English players, including R. Daft, T. Hayward, R. Carpenter and G. Wootton declined to take part and the twelve eventually consisted of Edgar Willsher (captain) from Kent, T. Humphrey, G. Griffith, H. Jupp and E. Pooley from Surrey, James Lillywhite and H. R. J. Charlwood of Sussex, Joseph Rowbotham and George Freeman of Yorkshire, John Smith and George Tarrant of Cambridgeshire and Alfred Shaw of Notts. It was a very fair side, Freeman and Willsher being the leading bowlers, whilst Jupp and Humphrey were the best bats.

After a crossing of ten days, the team arrived at the mouth of the Hudson on 13 September. The first fixture was in New York and the local Twenty-two were bowled out twice by Willsher, Freeman and Shaw, only one man reaching double figures. From New York the cricketers travelled via Niagara Falls to Montreal. The Canadians proved a very poor match for the English side. The whole Twenty-two of 'All Canada' could score but 28 against the bowling of Freeman and Willsher, then the tourists did what they liked with the home bowling, but rain on two of the four days caused the game to be drawn. After the one contest in Canada the

---

1868: E. Willsher's Team to North America

1st Match: v XXII of St George's C.C. (Hoboken)   Sept 16, 17, 18.
England 175 (F. Norley 6-67) beat St George's C.C. 61 (E. Willsher 14-23) & 88 (A. Shaw 9-21) by an inns & 26 runs.

2nd Match: v XXII of Canada (Montreal)   Sept 22, 23, 24, 25.
Canada 28 (G. Freeman 13-12) drew with England 310-9 (G. Griffith 69, H. Jupp 53).

3rd Match: v XXII of Boston (Boston)   Sept 28, 29, 30.
England 109 (C. Newhall 6-52) & 71 beat Boston 39 (G. Freeman 13-16) & 37 (G. Tarrant 12-16) by 104 runs.

4th Match: v XXII of Philadelphia (Germantown)   Oct 3, 5, 6.
Philadelphia 88 (G. Freeman 14-15) & 35 (G. Freeman 13-9) lost to England 92 (C. Newhall 6-48) & 32-8 (C. Newhall 5-21) by 2 wkts.

5th Match: v XXII of United States (Germantown)   Oct 8, 9, 10.
England 117 (C. Newhall 8-57) & 64 (C. Newhall 6-30) beat United States 47 (E. Willsher 8-18) & 62 (G. Freeman 9-17) by 72 runs.

6th Match: v XXII of America (Hoboken)   Oct 13, 14, 15, 16.
America 70 (E. Willsher 11-27) & 65 (G. Freeman 12-27) lost to England 143 (F. Norley 6-46) by an inns & 8 runs.

---

tour continued with a match at Boston on a pitch described as the worst ever encountered. 'The wicket was laid with thick, coarse, grassy turf, with holes in it big enough to lose the ball. In addition, as it had rained almost without stopping for five days previously, the outsides were covered with water and mud.'

The best match of the tour took place at Germantown against Twenty-two of Philadelphia and the English team just won by two wickets – this fine game was almost ruined by the American umpire whose decisions became so bad that he was eventually replaced.

Apart from the six cricket matches the side took part in several baseball matches, all of which were won by the Americans. The party arrived back in Liverpool on 3 November after another ten-day crossing of the Atlantic.

1872: W. G. Grace spreads the gospel in North America

The fifth major tour to leave England was the first one to be composed of amateur cricketers. In 1871, the secretary of the M.C.C., R. A. Fitzgerald, was asked to select an amateur side to visit North America and the following agreed to make the trip: V. E. Walker, R. D. Walker, R. A. H. Mitchell, J. W. Dale, W. G. Grace, W. H. Hadow, A. Appleby, A. N. Hornby, A. Lubbock, W. M. Rose and the Hon G. R. C. Harris. Between selection and departure, Mitchell, Dale and the two Walkers had to drop out and C. J. Ottaway, C. K. Francis, F. P. U. Pickering and E. Lubbock took their places. The side was therefore not really representative of the amateur strength of English cricket, let alone the full strength, but in W. G. Grace it possessed the greatest exponent of the game.

Leaving England about a month earlier than either of the other two tours to America, the team landed at Point Levi on 17 August after a rough passage and the first match took place at Montreal. W. G. Grace opened the tourists' batting and hit the bowling to all parts of the outfield and beyond. The home bowlers despaired of getting his wicket, but Mr Benjamin, a stout fielder with spectacles on his nose and a pipe in his mouth, suddenly received the ball in his abdomen, where it lodged, and the Champion of England was forced to retire caught. The batting of the Canadians was even poorer than their bowling and the match was won with an innings to spare. The second game took place in Ottawa and again W. G. Grace scored heavily and another innings victory resulted. It was here that the team were entertained to a vast

R. A. Fitzgerald's team to Canada in 1872. Back row: A. Lubbock, W. G. Grace, T. C. Patteson, C. J. Ottaway. Centre: E. Lubbock, R. A. Fitzgerald, A. Appleby. Front: F. P. U. Pickering, Hon G. Harris, A. N. Hornby, W. M. Rose, C. K. Francis.

1872: R. A. Fitzgerald's Team to North America

1st Match: v XXII of Montreal (Montreal)   Aug 22, 23, 24.
England 255 (W. G. Grace 81) beat Montreal 48 (W. M. Rose 15-22) & 67 (W. M. Rose 17 wkts) by an inns & 140 runs.

2nd Match: v XXII of Ottawa (Ottawa)   Aug 27, 28.
England 201 (W. G. Grace 73) beat Ottawa 43 (A. Appleby 12-3) & 49 (W. M. Rose 14-22) by an inns & 109 runs.

3rd Match: v XXII of Toronto (Toronto)   Sept 2, 3, 4.
England 319 (W. G. Grace 142, J. Wright 5-102) beat Toronto 97 (W. M. Rose 12-57) & 117 (A. Appleby 11-30) by an inns & 105 runs.

4th Match: W. G. Grace's XII v A. Appleby's XII. Exhibition Game. (Toronto)   Sept 6, 7.
W. G. Grace's XII 168 (Hon G. R. Harris 65) & 119 beat A. Appleby's XII 165 (C. K. Francis 45) & 63 by 59 runs.

5th Match: v XXII of London (or Canada) (London)   Sept 9, 10, 11.
England 89 (Gillean 6-38) & 161 (W. G. Grace 76) beat London 55 (W. M. Rose 12-33) & 65 (W. M. Rose 9-23) by 130 runs.

6th Match: v XXII of Hamilton (Hamilton)   Sept 12, 13.
England 181 (C. J. Ottaway 45) beat Hamilton 86 (W. M. Rose 11-37) & 79 (W. M. Rose 10-27, W. G. Grace 10-49) by an inns & 16 runs.

7th Match: v XXII of St George's C.C. (Hoboken, New York)   Sept 18, 19.
St George's 66 (A. Appleby 12-18) & 44 (W. G. Grace 11-27) lost to England 249 (W. G. Grace 68, A. Lubbock 51) by an inns & 139 runs.

8th Match: v XXII of Young America, Germantown & Philadelphia (Germantown) Sept 21, 23, 24
Young America etc 63 (W. G. Grace 9-22) & 74 (W. G. Grace 12-45) lost to England XII 105 (C. Newhall 6-45) & 34-7 by 4 wkts.

9th Match: v XXII of Boston (Boston)   Sept 26, 27.
Boston 51 (W. M. Rose 10-38) & 43 (W. G. Grace 13-35) drew with England 51 (G. Wright 5-24) & 22-6 (D. Eastwood 5-10).

banquet, the main meat dish being leg of bear, which none of them really relished. Toronto was the venue of the third match – another innings victory and century from W. G. Grace. Good crowds watched the Toronto match, about 5,000 attending each day's play: 'each Englishman was as narrowly scanned and felt as the prize beasts at an Agricultural Show. It was honestly meant and as honestly and kindly taken.' From Toronto the team went to a terrible hotel in London, where 'starvation and flies formed the menu', but another victory was attained. Hamilton was the next stop followed by a three-day excursion to the Niagara Falls and then the match in New York against the local Twenty-two – another innings victory. The great match was in Philadelphia, where about 12,000 spectators watched on the first day. Tremendous shouts greeted the dismissal of Grace for only 14 and the match throughout was punctuated with music from the band on the roof of the club house. The English team were surprised at the great interest shown by the ladies in the cricket – much more so than in England.

The final fixture was at Boston. The ground was terrible, resembling a building plot. The English team were dismissed for 51 and the local Twenty-two managed the same total. Everyone was pleased when 6 o'clock arrived and the stumps were drawn.

The party retraced its steps to Quebec and arrived back in Liverpool on 8 October.

It was hoped that the visit gave encouragement to cricket in North America, but the team found the Americans completely absorbed in the materialistic things of life and everything else was pushed aside in consequence.

1873-74: W. G. takes a party to Australia

In the summer of 1872, W. G. Grace was invited to take a team to Australia, but the offer failed to tempt him and plans were abandoned. The following year, however, the Melbourne Club approached Grace with a better offer and he set about trying to gather a team. Alfred Shaw, the leading slow bowler of the day, refused the terms, as did the best Yorkshire all-rounder, Tom Emmett. Of the wicket-keepers, Pooley of Surrey was in disgrace and Pinder of Yorkshire in domestic disarrangement. Several amateurs, including A. N. Hornby, promised and then withdrew.

The team was finally made up of four Gloucester amateurs, W. G. and his brother G. F. Grace, J. A. Bush, the wicket-keeper, and W. R. Gilbert; a young Surrey amateur, F. H. Boult; R. Humphrey and H. Jupp, the leading Surrey batsmen; James Southerton, who played for Surrey and Sussex as a slow bowler; James Lillywhite, the best Sussex bowler; William Oscroft and Martin McIntyre, both Notts professionals and the Yorkshire batsman, A. Greenwood.

The team left Southampton on 23 October, called at Malta, at Alexandria, where the British Consul asked the side to disembark for a day and play a match, the request being declined, and at Galle, where they changed ships. Melbourne was reached after 52 days – the ship broke the record for the journey between Galle and Australia. On arrival the team found that the organisers in Australia had booked rooms in one hotel for the amateurs and in another for the professionals and this arrangement did not do much to foster team spirit.

The first game commenced on Boxing Day against Eighteen of Victoria. B. B. Cooper, formerly of Middlesex and Kent, hit 84 for the home side, the highest individual innings made up to that time against an English side in Australia, then the tourists collapsed twice, only W. G. batting well, and an innings defeat was suffered. From the financial viewpoint the match was a great success, with 40,000 spectators paying half-a-crown each. There followed three games against local Twenty-twos, during the second of which Humphrey was thrown out of a trap and unable to play for some time due to his injuries. The second major game took place at Sydney against Eighteen of New South Wales. Once more the batting failed and the best innings of the match came from the home batsman Pocock, who was a cousin of the Graces. The tourists lost by 8 wickets.

It had been arranged to play the next game at Maitland, but the ground there was under water and the team went to Bathurst instead. The principal contest of the tour took place at Sydney against a Combined Fifteen of New South Wales and Victoria. Owing to some splendid bowling by Lillywhite, backed up by good fielding and wicket-keeping, a win by the large margin of 218 runs was obtained, making up for the previous defeats, at least to an extent.

The tourists sailed from Sydney back to Melbourne, where G. F. Grace owing to quinsy missed the up-country game at Sandhurst – he recovered for the next match, only to be hit on the head by the first ball he received – this was at Castlemaine, where a dreadful wicket had been 'prepared'. Martin McIntyre, the Notts fast bowler, took full advantage of the conditions, according to the report: 'he played merrily about the ribs of those Castlemaniacs and enjoyed himself in a pure and innocent fashion to the full'.

Since the English Team had been easily beaten in the first match against Eighteen of Victoria, in the return fixture the Victorians reduced the odds to Fifteen. The home side were however too optimistic and lost by 7 wickets – B. B. Cooper again made the best score for his side, but this time it was only 20.

From Melbourne the side sailed across to Tasmania – a large crowd gathered to greet the ship at Launceston, but the passage being rough the English cricketers were unable to return the welcome. The Tasmanians made a poor show with both bat and ball – the best of them being J. C. Lord, who was a useful cricketer in Hampshire at one time. From Launceston the team went by coach to Hobart and though the locals batted better, G. F. Grace hit a great innings of 154 and provided another easy victory. Back the team went to Victoria for a third match against that colony – the odds were increased to Eighteen and the game was fairly even on first innings, after which rain washed out any further play. The final fixture was Kadina in South Australia, where the wicket was pebbles and grit, but no grass – McIntyre chuckled distinctly as he inspected it and the locals were dismissed for 42 and 13 – McIntyre had seven wickets for one run in the second innings. Though the official programme of matches was now at an end, the team arranged an extra fixture at Adelaide – much to the annoyance of the promoters – and the Twenty-two of South Australia were beaten by 7 wickets.

Sailing from Glenelg, the cricketers had a pleasant voyage back to Galle, where they again changed ships. They ran aground twice in the Suez Canal, spent a day at the Races in Alexandria, stopped briefly at Malta and Gibraltar and arrived back in Southampton on 17 May.

There was little doubt that cricket in Australia had improved immensely since the previous visit and the Victorians – thanks to William Caffyn in a large part – were the best side met on the tour.

The professionals received £150 for the tour plus £20 in spending money. In addition, many of them took out cricketing equipment to sell and made money from this and from betting on the matches – for example the seven professionals put up £50 for a bet that the tourists would beat the Combined Fifteen of New South Wales and Victoria. Another feature of the tour was the side-betting among spectators – which batsman would score most runs, etc. On one occasion a complete stranger came up to Oscroft before he went in to bat and offered him £20 if he beat W. G. Grace's score.

1876-77: Pooley arrested and Australia win 'first Test Match'

The tour of 1873-74 had not been a success from the team viewpoint because of the division between the amateurs and the professionals. In 1876, therefore, it was decided to revert to an all-professional side and for the first time the tour was run as a speculation on the part of the English, rather than being promoted by the Australians.

James Lillywhite, the Sussex cricketer, arranged, managed and captained the tourists. He picked five Yorkshiremen, G. Ulyett, A. Hill, T. Emmett, Andrew Greenwood and T. Armitage; two from Notts, Alfred Shaw and John Selby; three from Surrey, H. Jupp, E. Pooley and James Southerton (vice-capt); and H. R. J. Charlwood from Sussex. In Shaw, Hill, Emmett and Southerton the side possessed arguably the best bowlers in England, Pooley was the best 'keeper, but without Daft, Lockwood and Shrewsbury the batting looked a little thin.

The ship left Southampton on 21 September and stopped at Gibraltar and Malta. A day was spent in Ceylon and although the locals tried to arrange a match it proved impractical. South Australia was reached on 6 November and nine days were spent in practice before the first match – in Adelaide against Twenty-two of South Australia. Southerton spent a week before the game preparing the wicket and in consequence run-getting was much easier than on the previous visit. About 14,000 watched the play and an innings victory plus a profit of £750 augured well for the tour. In the second game at Sydney, the New South Wales side fielded only Fifteen men and the play was fairly even throughout, so that on the fourth morning of the match New South Wales required 26 to win with three wickets in hand. A strong gale was blowing, which made bowling difficult, but one batsman was quickly run out and the English hopes were still high. The home side however knocked off the runs without further loss. Over 30,000 watched the match, which was regarded as the best of the tour, only marred by the way the spectators disagreed with unfavourable umpiring decisions – the twelfth man of the England party stood as umpire in most matches. Following two victories in up-country games, the side met Fifteen of Victoria. Lillywhite won the toss and put the Victorians in, but a terrific storm quickly flooded the ground and ruined this advantage. In another close finish the tourists again lost. There were two more up-country games, before the return match with New South Wales, in which Spofforth and Evans routed the English side, who lost by 13 wickets. New South Wales immediately challenged the team on even terms, but ended with very much the worse of a draw.

From Sydney the side sailed to New Zealand for a series of eight odds matches, five of which were won by an innings. It was whilst in Christchurch that the constant betting which was a feature of all the cricket resulted in most unfortunate consequences. Pooley found a local spectator who was unfamiliar with the dodge whereby the promoter bets that he can forecast correctly the individual scores of each of the Twenty-two batsmen opposed to the English team. Pooley took odds of £1 to 1s on each batsman's total and wrote down a duck for each. As there were a total of 11 ducks, Pooley demanded £11 less 33 shillings for the innings in which runs had been made. The punter refused to pay up, and after the resulting fight Pooley was charged with assault and maliciously damaging property. He was forced to remain behind in New Zealand awaiting trial, when the English team returned to Australia for the rest of the tour. The loss of Pooley – the team's wicket-keeper – was serious enough, but Jupp, who was a useful substitute behind the stumps, had a bout of insanity as well as suffering from inflammation of the eyes and missed several matches in consequence. Whilst in New Zealand the team suffered from some hair-raising journeys between matches – on the way to Christchurch their coach and horses attempted to cross a swollen river only to be stuck in the middle. The cricketers leapt out of the coach and up to their waists in water and somehow dragged the horses to the bank. They reached a roadman's shelter, which boasted the name of the Otira Hotel, and, having no change of clothes, lit a great fire and stood naked in front of it, whilst they dried out. They spent the night on the floor and when they tried to leave in the morning found that a landslide had cut off the road, so they spent another day at the 'Hotel' whilst the way was cleared – the journey took 80 hours with little oppor-

*The team to Australia of 1876-77, led by James Lillywhite and photographed in Melbourne. The players are, as numbered:
1 H. Jupp, 2 T. Emmett, 3 H. Charlwood, 4 J. Selby, 5 J. Lillywhite, 6 T. Armitage, 7 J. Southerton, 8 A. Greenwood, 9 G. Ulyett, 10 A. Hill, 11 A. Shaw, 12 E. Pooley. This team played the first official Test match, but E. Pooley, who looks something of a gambler, was absent, being held in New Zealand on an assault charge arising from his not being paid a gambling debt.*

tunity to sleep, and at its end the team had immediately to start another match.

The New Zealand part of the tour, owing to bad arrangements, was a financial failure. After a rough voyage back to Melbourne, the tourists began the first eleven-a-side match ever to take place between an England side and a Combined Australian team on the following day. This game is now regarded as 'The First Test Match'. Australia batted first and scored 245, with Charles Bannerman making the celebrated first 'Test' century—the fact of the matter was that the English team were so exhausted after their New Zealand experiences, that not one of them was fit to field. Bannerman was dropped by Armitage, the batsman hitting a simple catch which struck the fielder in the stomach, and the English bowling was poor in the extreme with several deliveries going high over the batsman's head, whilst others rolled along the ground! Needless to say Australia won by a fair margin.

Three up-country odds matches followed before a return game was played against the Australian Eleven. This time, in better fettle, the English team won by 4 wickets—immediately the cry came up from the betting fraternity that the first match had been 'fixed' in order to promote the gate for the return encounter.

Following the victory against Australia, the team travelled to Adelaide where the final match took place against the local

Twenty-two and then the party set sail for Galle, arriving there on 8 May. After sailing to Brindisi, the rest of the journey was by the overland route and London was reached on 2 June, but still the misguided Pooley was absent. In fact, after his trial the New Zealand public thought he had been hard done by and a subscription was raised for him.

Pooley was dogged by misfortune throughout his life, and 20 years later, when interviewed in retirement by a journalist, he stated 'It was the workhouse, sir, or the river'. In fact, he spent most of his declining years in the workhouse in Lambeth crippled with rheumatism.

The English team found that Australian cricket had again improved upon the standard of 1873 and they were most impressed by Spofforth, Bannerman and the wicket-keeper, Murdoch, as well as the other young stumper, Blackham.

Each of the English team was guaranteed £150 plus first-class passage, but they each returned with about £300. It was reported that the profits from the matches in Sydney were £3,000 and in Melbourne £2,500.

1876-77: J. Lillywhite's Team to Australia and New Zealand

1st Match: v XXII of South Australia (Adelaide)   Nov 16, 17, 18.
England 153 (J. Selby 59) beat S. Australia 54 (A. Shaw 14-12) & 53 by an inns & 46 runs.

2nd Match: v XV of New South Wales (Sydney)   Dec 7, 8, 9, 11.
England 122 & 106 (E. Evans 5-37) lost to N.S.W. 81 (A. Shaw 6-24) & 151-12 by 2 wkts.

3rd Match: v XXII of Newcastle (Newcastle)   Dec 12, 13, 14.
England 96 & 77 beat Newcastle 31 & 68 by 74 runs.

4th Match: v XXII of Gouldburn (Gouldburn)   Dec 20, 21.
England 125 & 81 beat Gouldburn 60 & 51 by 95 runs.

5th Match: v XV of Victoria (Melbourne)   Dec 26, 28, 29, 30.
Victoria 190 (A. Shaw 6-43) & 105 (T. Emmett 6-31) beat England 135 (F. E. Allan 5-44) & 129 (W. E. Midwinter 7-54) by 31 runs.

6th Match: v XXII of Ballarat (Ballarat)   Jan 1, 2, 3.
England 123 (E. Figgis 5-74) & 179 (H. R. J. Charlwood 66) drew with Ballarat 146.

7th Match: v XXII of Geelong (Geelong)   Jan 5, 6, 7.
England 264 (H. R. J. Charlwood 56, Kendall 7-92) beat Geelong 74 (A. Shaw 11-41) & 87 (J. Southerton 10-47) by an inns & 103 runs.

8th Match: v XV of New South Wales (Sydney)   Jan 12, 13, 15.
England 35 (F. R. Spofforth 5-20) & 104 (E. Evans 6-49) lost to N.S.W. 124 (A. Shaw 7-32) & 17-1 by 13 wkts.

9th Match: v New South Wales (Sydney)   Jan 15, 16.
England 270 (E. Evans 5-96) drew with N.S.W. 82 (A. Shaw 5-19) & 140-6.

10th Match: v XXII of Auckland (Auckland)   Jan 29, 30, 31, Feb 1.
England 225 (H. R. J. Charlwood 65, Bennett 6-45) beat Auckland 109 (A. Shaw 13-39) & 94 by an inns & 22 runs.

11th Match: v XXII of Wellington (Wellington)   Feb 5, 6, 7, 8.
Wellington 31 (A. Shaw 13-11) & 38 (J. Lillywhite 13-22) lost to England 190 (H. R. J. Charlwood 56, Cross 5-60) by an inns & 121 runs.

12th Match: v XXII of Taranaki (New Plymouth)   Feb 12, 13.
Taranaki 32 (J. Lillywhite 13-19) & 47 (J. Southerton 13-25) lost to England 80 (Fitzpatrick 6-41) by an inns & 1 run.

13th Match: v XXII of Nelson (Nelson)   Feb 15, 16.
England 258 (J. Selby 82) beat Nelson 56 (A. Shaw 13-24) & 39 (A. Shaw 13-19) by an inns & 163 runs.

14th Match: v XXII of Westland (Greymouth)   Feb 20, 21, 22.
England 119 & 99-4 drew with Westland 50 (J. Southerton 13-33).

15th Match: v XVIII of Canterbury (Christchurch)   Feb 26, 27, 28.
England 70 (C. Frith 6-23) & 102 beat Canterbury 65 & 84 (A. Hill 12-17) by 23 runs.

16th Match: v XVIII of Otago (Dunedin)   March 2, 3, 5.
Otago 76 & 106 (J. Lillywhite 12-45) drew with England 163 (Millington 6-54).

17th Match: v XXII of Southland (Invercargill)   March 6, 7.
England 158 (A. Greenwood 66) beat Southland 47 (A. Hill 12-17) & 46 (J. Southerton 11-24) by an inns & 65 runs.

18th Match: v Australia (Melbourne)   March 15, 16, 17, 19.
Australia 245 (C. Bannerman 165) & 104 (A. Shaw 5-38) beat England 196 (H. Jupp 63, W. E. Midwinter 5-78) & 108 (T. Kendall 7-55) by 45 runs.

19th Match: v XXII of Bendigo (Bendigo)   March 20, 21, 22.
Bendigo 138 (J. Lillywhite 12-68) & 117 drew with England 99 & 67-3.

20th Match: v XXII of Ballarat (Ballarat)   March 23, 24.
England 159 (E. Morey 5-72) drew with Ballarat 67 (A. Shaw 12-23) & 73-13.

21st Match: v XXII of Ararat (Ararat)   March 26, 27.
England 204 (A. Shaw 86) drew with Ararat 38 & 21-8.

22nd Match: v Australia (Melbourne)   March 31, April 2, 3, 4.
England 261 (G. Ulyett 52) & 122-6 (G. Ulyett 63) by 4 wkts.

23rd Match: v XXII of South Australia (Adelaide)   April 14, 16, 17.
England 75 & 138 (G. Ulyett 58) drew with S. Australia 71 (A. Hill 10-9).

1878-79: betting troubles in Australia, and Lord Harris assaulted

In the spring of 1878, the Melbourne Cricket Club asked I. D. Walker, the Middlesex amateur, to collect a team of twelve amateur cricketers for a tour of Australia the following winter. It was found impossible to gather an amateur side of sufficient strength, and in consequence, two Yorkshire professionals, G. Ulyett and T. Emmett, were chosen to complete the side. I. D. Walker was unable to make the trip and Lord Harris was given the captaincy. The other members of the party were F. A. Mackinnon, F. Penn and C. A. Absolom of Kent, A. N. Hornby, V. P. F. A. Royle and S. S. Schultz of Lancashire, A. J. Webbe of Middlesex, A. P. Lucas of Surrey, H. C. Maul and L. Hone – neither of the last two named appeared in County Championship cricket, though the former played for Warwickshire in the county's second-class days and the latter for Ireland.

The team had a fair batting strength, but the bowling relied heavily on Emmett and no specialist wicket-keeper was taken. The tourists were not representative in any way of either England or even the amateur strength of the country, lacking as they did any member of the Gloucester side.

Going on the overland route to Italy and thence through the Suez Canal, the side reached Adelaide on 22 December. In the opening game, the English team fielded twelve men against the Eighteen of South Australia and won by 3 wickets. The second match commenced at Melbourne on Boxing Day with about 10,000 spectators and an even draw was played against Fifteen of Victoria, for whom the old Oxford Blue, Donald Campbell, hit 128. On the same ground a few days later, the first eleven-a-side match was played against a representative Australian team. Excellent bowling by Spofforth was too much for the visitors who suffered defeat by 9 wickets. This match is now designated an official 'Test Match' – but as pointed out previously the tourists at no time claimed to be repr-sentative of English cricket. Lord Harris ascribed the defeat to bad fielding and dreadful light.

The team sailed from Melbourne to Tasmania aboard a very crowded ship. The first match on the island was played at Hobart on a ground shaped like a hog's back – a very tall long-leg might just be able to see a gigantic deep mid-off! Following two matches of little consequence in Tasmania, the party made its way, via Melbourne back to Sydney, where they met the New South Wales side – again bad fielding lost the tourists the match. The return with New South Wales took place with a minor match at

Bathurst intervening. On the first day against N.S.W., the tourists hit an excellent 267, with Hornby, Lucas and Ulyett all making fifties; by stumps N.S.W. were 53 for 2. Murdoch carried his bat through the completed innings on the second day and in the afternoon, being 90 behind, N.S.W. followed on. Murdoch therefore went in again, and had made 10 when the umpire adjudged him run out. At this point the crowd, disagreeing with the decision, rushed on to the field and surrounded the English fielders, Lord Harris was struck across the body with a whip or stick and though the two ringleaders were arrested, the crowd occupied the ground so that no further play took place that day. Rumours were rife that the umpire had laid a large bet on an English victory – there was no foundation for this charge, but it incensed the mob still further. Gregory, the home captain, asked Lord Harris to change the umpire, but his Lordship refused to do so and Gregory therefore refused to let his batsmen continue. Eventually the matter was settled and play continued on Monday, when New South Wales collapsed on a sticky wicket, leaving the tourists victors by an innings.

In the next game against a local amateur club, Penn dislocated his knee and could not play again on the tour, whilst Lucas split his hand fielding a hard return. Victoria beat the visitors by 2 wickets, and once more bad fielding was the reason. There were two up-country matches before the last serious match – an eleven-a-side against Victoria – which provided Lord Harris with a victory by 6 wickets.

The party went home via New Zealand, where they played one match, and the United States, where a match was played in New York. Neither of these games were of any significance.

The failure of the side was due mainly to bad fielding and the lack of a wicket-keeper. Lord Harris criticised the amateur um-

---

1878-79: Lord Harris's Team to Australia, New Zealand and U.S.A.

Batting Averages

	M	I	NO	R	HS	Avge	100	c/s
G. Ulyett (Yorks)	5	9	0	306	71	34.00	0	3
Lord Harris (Kent)	5	9	0	289	67	32.11	0	2
F. Penn (Kent)	2	3	0	87	56	29.00	0	2
V. P. F. A. Royle (Lancs)	5	8	0	214	75	26.75	0	11
A. P. Lucas (Surrey)	5	9	1	158	51	19.75	0	3
A. N. Hornby (Lancs)	5	9	0	167	67	18.55	0	2
T. Emmett (Yorks)	5	8	2	110	41	18.33	0	2
C. A. Absolom (Kent)	5	8	0	128	52	16.00	0	3
A. J. Webbe (Middx)	5	9	1	101	27	12.62	0	7
F. A. Mackinnon (Kent)	3	6	3	37	15*	12.33	0	0
L. Hone	5	8	1	58	22	8.28	0	6/2
S. S. Schultz (Lancs)	5	8	2	46	20	7.66	0	1

Bowling Averages

	O	M	R	W	Avge	BB	5i
T. Emmett	482.1	255	512	44	11.61	8-47	6
A. N. Hornby	79	48	79	4	19.75	2-9	0
A. P. Lucas	239.1	105	347	14	24.78	3-32	0
C. A. Absolom	71	30	98	3	32.66	2-37	0
G. Ulyett	230	104	367	11	33.36	4-13	0
S. S. Schultz	80.3	27	174	4	43.50	2-8	0

Also bowled: V. P. F. A. Royle 4-1-6-0; Lord Harris 3-0-14-0; F. Penn 3-1-3-0.
Played in non-first-class matches only: H. C. Maul (Warwicks).

1878-79: Lord Harris's Team to Australia, New Zealand and U.S.A.

1st Match: v XVIII of South Australia (Adelaide) Dec 12, 13, 14.
South Australia 110 (T. Emmett 9-45) & 137 (G. Ulyett 9-43) lost to England XII 185 (A. N. Hornby 78) & 63-7 by 3 wkts.

2nd Match: v XV of Victoria (Melbourne) Dec 26, 27, 28.
Victoria 313 (D. Campbell 128) & 214 (G. Ulyett 8-78) drew with England 331 (A. P. Lucas 90, V. P. F. A. Royle 78).

3rd Match: v Australia (East Melbourne) Jan 2, 3, 4.
England 113 (C. A. Absolom 52, F. R. Spofforth 6-48) & 160 (F. R. Spofforth 7-62) lost to Australia 256 (A. C. Bannerman 73, T. Emmett 7-68) & 19-0 by 10 wkts.

4th Match: v XVIII of South Tasmania (Hobart) Jan 9, 10, 11.
Tasmania 82 (T. Emmett 9-33) & 144 (G. Ulyett 9-20) lost to England 133 (A. N. Hornby 61*) & 94-4 by 6 wkts.

5th Match: v XVIII of North Tasmania (Launceston) Jan 13.
North Tasmania 49 (T. Emmett 12-20) & 38-7 drew with England 212 (F. Penn 53).

6th Match: v New South Wales (Sydney) Jan 24, 25, 27, 28.
England 248 (F. Penn 56, G. Ulyett 51, E. Tindall 6-89) & 217 (E. Evans 5-82) lost to New South Wales 240 (W. L. Murdoch 70, N. Thompson 50) & 226-5 (H. H. Massie 78, C. Bannerman 60*) by 5 wkts.

7th Match: v XVIII of Bathurst (Bathurst) Jan 31, Feb 1.
Bathurst 47 drew with England 229.

8th Match: v New South Wales (Sydney) Feb 7, 8, 10.
England 267 (A. N. Hornby 67, G. Ulyett 55, A. P. Lucas 51, F. R. Spofforth 5-93, E. Evans 5-62) beat New South Wales 177 (W. L. Murdoch 82*, T. Emmett 8-47) & 49 (T. Emmett 5-21) by an inns & 41 runs.

9th Match: v XV of the Bohemian Club (Yarra Bend) Feb 17, 18.
Bohemian Club 228 (G. P. Robertson 78) & 262-12 drew with England 255 (A. J. Webbe 62, S. S. Schultz 53).

10th Match: v Victoria (Melbourne) Feb 21, 22, 24, 25
England 325 (G. Ulyett 71, V. P. F. A. Royle 57, A. N. Hornby 50, W. H. Cooper 5-79) & 171 lost to Victoria 261 (D. Campbell 51, T. Emmett 5-93) & 236-8 (T. P. Horan 69) by 2 wkts.

11th Match: v XXII of Bendigo (Sandhurst) Feb 26, 27.
Bendigo 141 & 161-20 drew with England 304 (A. N. Hornby 104).

12th Match: v XXII of Ballarat (Ballarat) March 1, 3.
England 311 (Lord Harris 89, A. N. Hornby 86, A. J. Webbe 53) beat Ballarat 140 (T. Emmett 11-54) & 123 by an inns & 48 runs.

13th Match: v Victoria (Melbourne) March 7, 8, 10.
England 248 (V. P. F. A. Royle 75, Lord Harris 67, G. E. Palmer 6-64) & 54-4 beat Victoria 146 (T. Emmett 6-41) & 155 (T. Emmett 5-68) by 6 wkts.

14th Match: v Canterbury (Christchurch).
Match drawn.

15th Match: v U.S.A. (Hoboken).
England beat U.S.A. by inns & 114 runs.

pires in Australia and would have nothing to do with the Australian theory that amateur umpires were more honest than their professional counterparts. He felt that the Australian bowlers were now better than their English rivals and that in a few years the Australian team would be the equal of a representative English one. His final point was that the professional betting element should be removed from Australian cricket.

The tour was financed by the Melbourne Club who paid all the expenses of the English amateurs and each of the professionals received about £200.

1879: Daft's professionals play cricket – and baseball – in America

J. P. Ford, a member of the Nottingham Town Council, who had interests in North America, asked Richard Daft, the Notts captain to select and lead a side of professionals on a tour of North America in the autumn of 1879. Daft picked six other Notts players: Alfred Shaw, John Selby, Arthur Shrewsbury, William Oscroft, William Barnes and Frederick Morley, plus five Yorkshiremen: Tom Emmett, George Ulyett, Ephraim Lockwood, William Bates and George Pinder, to accompany him. The team was very nearly representative of the full strength of English professional cricket, the strength of the Southern first-class counties being mainly amateur.

The Twelve left Liverpool on 28 August and after a rough seven days crossing reached Canada. The programme began with three matches at Toronto. The ground there was well looked after, but the home cricketers showed little skill and Shaw, Emmett and Morley were much too good for their batsmen. After two victories at Hamilton and London, the team moved to Detroit, where two Kentish cricketers, Littlejohn and Dale, tended the local ground. Rain caused the match here to be drawn, but, as in Canada, the home batsmen made a poor showing. From Detroit, the team moved, via the Niagara Falls, to New York for two matches, where the batsmen mainly went in for the cross-batted swipes of baseball players and Alfred Shaw had another field day. The most important fixture of the tour was in Philadelphia against the local Fifteen – about 25,000 attended the three-day game and due to this fixture the tour was a financial success. The strength of the home team lay in the four members of the Newhall family,

1879: R. Daft's Team to North America

1st Match: v XXII of Canada (Toronto)   Sept 10, 11.
Canada 31 (A. Shaw 11-17, F. Morley 10-12) & 72 (A. Shaw 11-17) lost to England 101 (D. J. Logan 7-35) & 3-0 by 19 wkts.

2nd Match: v XXII Anglo-Canadians (Toronto)   Sept 12, 13.
Anglo-Canadians 76 (F. Morley 12-24) & 69-14 drew with England 209 (A. Shrewsbury 66, W. Barnes 59, Simpson 6-100).

3rd Match: v XXII of Ontario (Toronto)   Sept 15, 16.
Ontario 65 (F. Morley 10-36) & 54 (T. Emmett 14-36) lost to England 122 (W. Bates 49*) by an inns & 3 runs.

4th Match: v XVII of Hamilton (Hamilton)   Sept 18, 19.
England 186 (D. J. Logan 6-39) beat Hamilton 48 (A. Shaw 13-37) & 35 by an inns & 103 runs.

5th Match: v XXII of Western Ontario (London)   Sept 22, 23.
England 71 (Kennedy 5-34) & 139 beat Western Ontario 37 (A. Shaw 13-12) & 38 (A. Shaw 14-24) by 135 runs.

6th Match: v XVIII of Detroit (Detroit)   Sept 25, 26, 27.
England 191 (W. Oscroft 52) drew with Detroit 59 & 5-1.

7th Match: v XXII of Central New York (Syracuse)   Sept 30, Oct 1.
England 163 (J. Selby 44) beat Central New York 43 (A. Shaw 11-15) & 50 (A. Shaw 13-28) by an inns & 70 runs.

8th Match: v XXII of United New York (States Island)   Oct 4, 5, 7.
United New York 67 (A. Shaw 10-29) & 94 (A. Shaw 11-27) lost to England 188 (G. Lane 5-57).

9th Match: v XV of Philadelphia (Nicetown)   Oct 10, 11, 13.
England 149 (W. Oscroft 62, C. Newhall 6-80) & 133 (E. W. Clarke 6-29) beat Philadelphia 70 (A. Shaw 9-18) & 67 (A. Shaw 7-19, F. Morley 7-32) by 145 runs.

10th Match: v XVIII Baseball Players (Brooklyn)   Oct 14, 15.
Baseball Players 62 & 27 lost to England 107 by an inns & 18 runs.

11th Match: v Young America (Germantown)   Oct 18, 20.
Young America 64 (F. Morley 6-30) & 47 (W. Bates 8-20) lost to England 171 (E. Lockwood 60, C. Newhall 8-62) by an inns & 60 runs.

12th Match: v XXII of Merion Club (Ardmore)   Oct 21, 22.
England 162 (E. Lockwood 88, Braithwaite 8-) drew with Merion 67 & 55-13.

13th Match: Notts v Yorkshire. Exhibition Game (Germantown)   Oct 23, 24.
Notts 148 (A. Shrewbury 51) & 22-0 beat Yorkshire 51 (A. Shaw 5-21) & 118 by 10 wkts.

but even they could not prevent an English victory. Back to New York went the team for two matches – one of cricket and the other baseball. The English players proved as inexpert at the latter as the New Yorkers were at the former.

The two remaining games were in Philadelphia. In the first the Young America Club actually challenged the tourists on equal terms, but suffered a great defeat as a result. In the second, rain caused a draw. An additional match was then arranged: Nottinghamshire v Yorkshire, the two elevens being made up mainly of English professionals engaged in America. Notts won by 10 wickets. On 25 October the side left by train for New York and the voyage home and on 4 November all were safe back in Liverpool. The tour was successful from all viewpoints and unlike most of its predecessors it was free from any minor disputes or disagreements.

Richard Daft's team which left for America in 1879. Back: G. Pinder, W. Barnes, E. Lockwood, J. P. Ford, R. Daft, Capt Holden, J. Selby. Centre: A. Shrewsbury, G. Ulyett, A. Shaw, W. Oscroft. Front: T. Emmett, W. Bates, F. Morley.

1881-82: England players try to throw a match against Victoria

James Lillywhite, together with the two Notts cricketers, Alfred Shaw (captain) and Arthur Shrewsbury, undertook the most ambitious tour made to date by English cricketers. They decided to go to Australia via America and New Zealand, playing matches in both countries on the way and thus making the trip more profitable. Apart from the three promoters, the party was made up of William Scotton and John Selby of Notts, William Bates, Tom Emmett, Edmund Peate and George Ulyett of Yorkshire, R. G. Barlow and R. Pilling of Lancashire and William Midwinter from Gloucestershire – an all-professional side.

Sailing from England on 17 September, the team (without Shrewsbury, who was ill) played its first match against Twelve of Philadelphia and won by an innings. Four other matches were played in America. All of them proved a financial loss. The train journey across America was painfully slow at times, with the team getting out and jogging alongside the train on some sections. The game in San Francisco was the low point of the tour – the venue resembled a stone quarry and the crowd was less than a hundred. The home team had little idea of the game and one of the few spectators who knew about cricket complained: 'This is a farce; it's like obtaining money by false pretences.' The lack of gate money in America meant that the team had very few dollars, and when they came to the shipping company for passage across the Pacific they found the Company would not accept Bank of England notes, so they had to cable to London for proof of their bona fides. The ship in which they left America also contained the King of the Sandwich Islands and his retinue. The King was impressed by the singing of some of the cricketers, especially Billy Bates. Tom Emmett was invited to sing, but replied: 'I beg your Majesty's pardon, but I make it a rule never to sing out of England.' When the ship reached Honolulu, the cricketers were invited to the King's palace. The fact that 'Thursday' was lost when the ship crossed the international date line, utterly confused most players.

Australia was reached on 16 November – it had been found impractical to play in New Zealand first – and the first five matches played were all against local Twenty-twos. In the last of these Pilling was unable to field due to sunstroke: some ungenerous things were insinuated about the nature of his illness, but they were untrue. The first serious match was against New South Wales – eleven-a-side – on 9 December etc. Despite two good innings by H. H. Massie, N.S.W. were beaten by 68 runs. About 40,000 spectators attended the game. The second eleven-a-side contest came in Melbourne against Victoria, where a brilliant second innings knock by Shrewsbury won the match after the visitors were forced to follow on. 20,000 attended the second day of this game – believed at the time to be a record.

The betting on cricket, which Lord Harris had deplored on his tour, was still very much in evidence during this match. On the final day, when Victoria needed 94 in their second innings, the odds were 30 to 1 against an English victory. Most of the English team wagered £1 and came away with £30. Another more unpleasant aspect of the game was the rumour that two of the English team had been paid £100 to throw the match. This rumour gained credence when the two players involved seemed to be fielding poorly, including the dropping of an easy catch. The press got hold of the story. It came out that the two players had tried to persuade a third – Midwinter – to come in with them, but Midwinter reported the matter to Alfred Shaw and was afterwards beaten up by the two conspirators.

After a match in Adelaide, the tourists returned to Melbourne to face a Combined Australian Eleven. High scoring necessitated the game going into the fourth day and the steamer which was to take the English side to New Zealand delayed its departure, but the match was still drawn.

1881-82: Lillywhite, Shaw and Shrewsbury's Team to America, New Zealand and Australia

1st Match: v XII of Philadelphia (Philadelphia)   Oct 1, 2, 3.
England 277 (W. E. Midwinter 73, G. Ulyett 71) beat Philadelphia 126 & 47 by an inns & 104 runs.

2nd Match: v XVIII of St George's Club (New York)   Oct 5, 6, 7.
England 254 (G. Ulyett 86, W. Bates 63) drew with St George's Club 65 & 46-13.

3rd Match: v XVIII of America (Miltown)   Oct 7, 8, 10.
England 114 & 166 (R. G. Barlow 59) beat America 71 & 77 by 132 runs.

4th Match: v XXII of St Louis (St Louis)   Oct 12, 13.
England 144-5 (G. Ulyett 55) rain ended play.

5th Match: v XXII of San Francisco (San Francisco)   Oct 20, 21.
England 93 & 313-2 (G. Ulyett 167*) drew with San Francisco 44.

6th Match: v XXII of Northern District (Maitland, N.S.W.)   Nov 25, 26.
Northern District 113 & 128 drew with England 157 (G. Ulyett 58) & 14-1.

7th Match: v XXII of Newcastle (Newcastle)   Nov 25, 26.
England 118 & 75 drew with Newcastle 79 & 70-9.

8th Match: v XXII of Orange (Orange)   Nov 29, 30.
England 199 (R. G. Barlow 60*) beat Orange 64 & 37 by an inns & 88 runs.

9th Match: v XXII of Bathurst (Bathurst)   Dec 2, 3.
England 115 & 73 beat Bathurst 44 & 68 by 76 runs.

10th Match: v XXII of Cumberland (Paramatta)   Dec 7, 8.
England 61 & 64 lost to Cumberland 78 & 48-16 by 5 wkts.

11th Match: v New South Wales (Sydney)   Dec 9, 10, 12, 13.
England 272 (R. G. Barlow 75, J. Selby 56) & 162 (E. Evans 6-60) beat N.S.W. 210 (W. L. Murdoch 76, H. H. Massie) & 156 (H. H. Massie 76) by 68 runs.

12th Match: v XVI of Cootamundra (Cootamundra) (One Day)   Dec 14.
England 185 beat Cootamundra 110 by 75 runs.

13th Match: v Victoria (Melbourne)   Dec 16, 17, 19, 20.
England 146 & 198 (A. Shrewsbury 80, G. E. Palmer 7-46) beat Victoria 251 (J. McC. Blackham 66, J. D. Edwards 65, P. S. McDonnell 51) & 75 (E. Peate 6-30) by 18 runs.

14th Match: v XV of South Australia (Adelaide)   Dec 23, 24, 26.
S. Australia 244 (G. Giffen 95) & 28-2 drew with England 293 (W. Bates 71, R. G. Barlow 62, J. Selby 51).

15th Match: v Australia (Melbourne)   Dec 31, Jan 2, 3, 4.
England 294 (G. Ulyett 87, W. Bates 58, J. Selby 55) & 308 (J. Selby 70, W. H. Scotton 50*, W. H. Cooper 6-120) drew with Australia 320 (T. P. Horan 124) & 127-3.

16th Match: v XVIII of Otago (Dunedin)   Jan 12, 13, 14.
Otago 84 & 74 lost to England 156 (W. Bates 66) & 4-0 by 10 wkts.

17th Match: v XXII of Oamaru (Oamaru)   Jan 16, 17.
England 146 beat Oamaru 60 & 57 by an inns & 29 runs.

18th Match: v XXII of Timaru (Timaru) (One Day)   Jan 18.
Timaru 111 lost to England 119-4 (J. Selby 57) by 6 wkts.

19th Match: v XVIII of Canterbury (Christchurch)   Jan 23, 24.
Canterbury 100 & 15-6 drew with England 230 (R. G. Barlow 77, G. Ulyett 59).

20th Match: v XXII of Wellington (Wellington)   Jan 25, 26.
Wellington 80 & 54-10 drew with England 222 (A. Shrewsbury 70).

21st Match: v XXII of Waikato (Waikato) (One Day)   Jan 31.
Waikato 44 & 53 lost to England 84 on first innings by 40 runs.

22nd Match: v XXII of Auckland (Auckland)   Feb 2, 3, 4.
Auckland 122 & 94 lost to England 214 (A. Shrewsbury 77) & 3-0 by 10 wkts.

23rd Match: v XVIII of Stanmore (Stanmore, N.S.W.)   Feb 14, 15.
England 119 & 153 (W. Bates 80) drew with Stanmore 83.

24th Match: v Australia (Sydney)   Feb 17, 19, 20, 21.
England 133 (G. E. Palmer 7-68) & 232 (G. Ulyett 67, R. C. Barlow 62) lost to Australia 197 & 169-5 by 5 wkts.

25th Match: v XXII of Hawkesbury (Windsor) (One Day)   Feb 22.
Hawkesbury 61 lost to England 135-4 (R. G. Barlow 50*) on first innings.

26th Match: v Victoria (Melbourne)   Feb 24, 25, 27, 28.
Victoria 249 & 92 (W. Bates 5-17) lost to England 285 (W. Bates 84, A. Shrewsbury 72*) & 57-2 by 8 wkts.

27th Match: v Australia (Sydney)   March 3, 4, 6, 7.
England 188 (A. Shrewsbury 82, G. E. Palmer 5-46) & 134 (T. W. Garrett 6-78) lost to Australia 260 (P. S. McDonnell 147, A. C. Bannerman 70, E. Peate 5-43) & 66-4 by 6 wkts.

28th Match: v Australia (Melbourne)   March 10, 12, 13, 14.
England 309 (G. Ulyett 149, T. W. Garrett 5-80) & 234-2 (G. Ulyett 64, R. G. Barlow 56, W. Bates 52*) drew with Australia 300 (W. L. Murdoch 85, P. S. McDonnell 52).

29th Match: v XXII of Dunolly (Dunolly)   March 15, 16.
Dunolly 79 & 49 lost to England 141 by an inns & 13 runs.

30th Match: v XX of Ballarat (Ballarat)   March 17, 18.
Ballarat 141 & 54-2 drew with England 327 (G. Ulyett 77, W. E. Midwinter 77, A. Shrewsbury 75).

Seven matches – all against odds – were played in New Zealand. The two matches from which a reasonable financial return was expected proved otherwise. The game at Christchurch was ruined by rain and at Auckland the promoters discovered that the match was arranged on the Domain, which the public could enter free.

1881-82: Lillywhite, Shaw and Shrewsbury's Team to America, New Zealand and Australia

Batting Averages

	M	I	NO	R	HS	Avge	100	c/s
G. Ulyett (Yorks)	7	14	0	549	149	39.21	1	5
A. Shrewsbury (Notts)	7	12	2	382	82	38.20	0	8
R. G. Barlow (Lancs)	7	14	1	391	75	30.07	0	3
W. Bates (Yorks)	7	13	1	349	84	29.08	0	3
J. Selby (Notts)	7	13	1	312	70	26.00	0	1
W. H. Scotton (Notts)	7	12	1	228	50*	20.72	0	3
E. Peate (Yorks)	7	13	7	104	33*	17.33	0	1
W. Midwinter (Glos)	7	12	0	166	48	13.83	0	8
A. Shaw (Notts)	7	12	0	137	40	11.41	0	5
T. Emmett (Yorks)	7	12	0	109	27	9.08	0	9
R. Pilling (Lancs)	7	13	3	87	23	8.70	0	12/6

Bowling Averages

	O	M	R	W	Avge	BB	5i
W. Bates	402.2	205	520	30	17.33	5-17	1
E. Peate	484.3	234	552	30	18.40	6-30	2
A. Shaw	196	120	171	8	21.37	3-5	0
G. Ulyett	138.1	45	257	10	25.70	2-11	0
T. Emmett	180	74	274	10	27.40	3-27	0
W. Midwinter	301	128	435	13	33.46	4-81	0
R. G. Barlow	94.2	36	147	3	49.00	1-4	0

Played in non-first-class matches only: Jas Lillywhite (Sussex).

The tourists returned to Australia for a second game against Australia, this time at Sydney, and lost by 5 wickets, because Shaw, who won the toss, elected to bat on a sticky wicket. As usual a fresh wicket was cut for the Australian innings.

Two other matches were played against Australia, one of which was lost and the other drawn. By way of consolation, the tourists beat Victoria by 8 wickets.

After a final odds match at Ballarat, the side set sail for England on 22 March from Melbourne and arrived in Naples on 2 May, where half the party took the overland route and most of the remainder went by steamer to Plymouth.

It was remarkable that not a single player was injured on the tour; Ulyett was the most successful batsman—his two innings of 149 and 64 in the final game against Australia being outstanding. Shrewsbury also had an excellent tour. Peate and Midwinter did most of the bowling, the former taking over 200 wickets in all.

The tourists found the Australian wickets much improved and the run-getting was therefore that much higher compared with previous visits.

Each player received £300 and the promoters made a considerable profit, despite the problems in America and the United States.

1882-83: England bring back the Ashes

The Melbourne Cricket Club agreed to organise and manage a tour by a mixed side of amateurs and professionals under the captaincy of the Hon Ivo Bligh, the Kent batsman. The composition of the side was as follows: four professionals, F. Morley and W. Barnes of Notts, and W. Bates of Yorkshire and R. G. Barlow of Lancashire; eight amateurs, the captain (Bligh), A. G. Steel of Lancashire, four Middlesex men in C. T. Studd, G. B. Studd, G. F. Vernon and C. F. H. Leslie plus E. F. S. Tylecote of Kent and W. W. Read of Surrey.

The historic significance of the tour was the pledge by the captain to bring back 'The Ashes' of English cricket, following the obituary which had been published when Australia defeated England at the Oval during the 1882 English season. The tour programme included three matches against the returning victorious Australian side of 1882.

The English team set out from home in two groups, meeting up at Suez and from there sailed to Ceylon, where they played a match—the first of its kind—against a local side. Continuing the voyage, the ship was 360 miles out from Colombo when it collided with a sailing vessel. The two ships then limped back to Colombo for repairs and eventually the team arrived ten days late in Adelaide. The most serious result of the accident was the injury to Fred Morley, the team's only fast bowler, who broke a rib. He carried on through the tour very gamely, but was almost useless.

The delay on the journey meant that the team had to play the first match immediately, with no opportunity for practice and without Ivo Bligh, who had injured his hand on the voyage. Rain happily cut short the first day's play and the match was drawn without even the first two innings being completed. The side then returned to the water for the voyage to Melbourne. The first eleven-a-side game v Victoria was an easy win, because the principal Australian players were absent. After two up-country matches, the side went to Sydney, where they beat the New South Wales eleven by an innings—again the principal players were absent from the home side. Three more odds matches came and went before the tourists met the Australian side which had been

A. Shaw's All-England Eleven, which toured America, Australia and New Zealand. Back: G. Ulyett, R. Pilling, J. Lillywhite (umpire), J. Conway (manager), W. Midwinter, W. Bates. Centre: A. Shrewsbury, A. Shaw, T. Emmett, E. Peate. Front: R. G. Barlow, W. H. Scotton, J. Selby.

in England in 1882. This meeting at Melbourne commenced on 30 December and though the captain was well enough to play, poor Morley was confined to bed. The public excitement concerning the match built up to fever pitch and some 54,000

attended the three-day game. Brilliant hitting by Bonnor, who made 85, won the match for the Australians and the tourists paid dearly for dropped catches. Two matches were played in Tasmania before the second meeting with the 1882 Australians.

Bligh won the toss for this crucial match and, batting first, the tourists put together a fair total of 294. From then on the match belonged to Bates who took no less than 15 wickets, including the hat-trick, and the game was won by an innings. The third and deciding match followed immediately, with both sides travelling to Sydney. Bligh again won the toss and over 20,000 watched the English team commence batting. Five wickets went for 76, before Read and Tylecote came together and added 115. The total reached 247. Australia replied with 133 for 1 by the end of the second day, but collapsed to 218 all out. The tourists made only 123 in their second innings, leaving the home side 153 to win. Barlow was equal to the task and in taking 7 wickets bowled them out for 83. During the game there was some unpleasantness when the Australians accused Barlow of running on to the wicket, and cutting up the surface with his spikes; the English captain replied that Spofforth did the same when he bowled.

After the tourists had won this game and thus the series of three by two to one, some ladies burnt the bails used in the match, placed the 'Ashes' in a small urn and presented it to Ivo Bligh – he had won back the ashes of English cricket.

Two other eleven-a-side matches were played on the tour, the

1882-83: the Hon Ivo Bligh's Team to Ceylon and Australia

1st Match: v XVIII of Colombo (Colombo) Oct 13, 14.
Colombo 92 & 16-7 drew with England 155.

2nd Match: v XV of South Australia (Adelaide) Nov 10, 11.
England 153 (E. F. S. Tylecote 59) drew with S. Australia 128-7.

3rd Match: v Victoria (Melbourne) Nov 17, 18, 20.
England 273 (C. T. Studd 57, C.F.H. Leslie 51, W. H. Cooper 5-89) & 1-0 beat Victoria 104 & 169 by 10 wkts.

4th Match: v XXII of Sandhurst (Sandhurst) Nov 22, 23.
Sandhurst 100 & 119 (A. G. Steel 10-35) drew with England 117 & 28-0.

5th Match: v XXII of Castlemaine (Castlemaine) Nov 24, 25.
Castlemaine 136 & 22-8 drew with England 238 (C. T. Studd 52).

6th Match: v New South Wales (Sydney) Dec 1, 2, 4.
N.S.W. 152 (A. G. Steel 5-32) & 165 (J. Davis 85) lost to England 461 (C. F. H. Leslie 144, R. G. Barlow 80, A. G. Steel 52, E. Evans 6-146) by an inns & 144 runs.

7th Match: v XVIII of Maitland (Maitland) Dec 6, 7.
England 155 beat Maitland 49 & 91 by an inns & 15 runs.

8th Match: v XVIII of Newcastle (Newcastle) Dec 8, 9.
Newcastle 67 & 54-15 (A. G. Steel 10-29) drew with England 339 (W. W. Read 64, C. F. H. Leslie 51).

9th Match: v XVIII of Ballarat (Ballarat) Dec 26, 27, 28.
Ballarat 226 (P. McGregor 53, J. Worrall 52) & 176-14 drew with England 272 (W. W. Read 55).

10th Match: v Australia (Melbourne) Dec 30, Jan 1, 2.
Australia 291 (G. J. Bonnor 85) & 58-1 beat England 177 (G. E. Palmer 7-65) & 169 by 9 wkts.

11th Match: v XVIII of Northern Tasmania (Launceston) Jan 8, 9.
N. Tasmania 114 & 81 (A. G. Steel 10-33) lost to England 270 (C. T. Studd 99) by an inns & 75 runs.

12th Match: v XVIII of Southern Tasmania (Hobart) Jan 12, 13.
S. Tasmania 82 & 95 lost to England 110 & 68-3 by 7 wkts.

13th Match: v Australia (Melbourne) Jan 19, 20, 22.
England 294 (W. W. Read 75, W. Bates 55, C. F. H. Leslie 54, G. E. Palmer 5-103) beat Australia 114 (W. Bates 7-28) & 153 (W. Bates 7-74) by an inns & 27 runs.

14th Match: v Australia (Sydney) Jan 26, 27, 29, 30.
England 247 (W. W. Read 66, E. F. S. Tylecote 66) & 123 (F. R. Spofforth 7-44) beat Australia 218 (A. C. Bannerman 94) & 83 (R. G. Barlow 7-40) by 69 runs.

15th Match: v XVIII of Queensland (Brisbane) Feb 2, 3.
England 265 (W. W. Read 84) beat Queensland 62 (A. G. Steel 10-28) & 49 by an inns & 154 runs.

16th Match: v XVIII of Maryborough (Maryborough) Feb 8, 9.
Maryborough 42 & 79 lost to England 179 (W. W. Read 66) by an inns & 58 runs.

17th Match: v Australia (Sydney) Feb 17, 19, 20, 21.
England 263 (A. G. Steel 135) & 197 lost to Australia 262 (G. J. Bonnor 87, J. McC. Blackham 57) & 199-6 (A. C. Bannerman 63, J. McC. Blackham 58*) by 4 wkts.

18th Match: v Victoria (Melbourne) March 9, 10, 12.
Victoria 284 (W. E. Midwinter 92*, G. J. Bonnor 54, W. Barnes 6-70) beat England 55 & 156 (A. G. Steel, G. E. Palmer 7-65) by an inns & 73 runs.

1882-83: the Hon Ivo Bligh's Team to Ceylon and Australia

Batting Averages

	M	I	NO	R	HS	Avge	100	c/s
A. G. Steel (Lancs)	7	11	1	415	135	41.50	1	7
C. F. H. Leslie (Middx)	7	11	1	310	144	31.00	1	2
R. G. Barlow (Lancs)	7	12	2	281	80	28.10	0	6
W. Bates (Yorks)	7	11	1	271	55	27.10	0	6
W. W. Read (Surrey)	7	11	0	291	75	26.45	0	1
C. T. Studd (Middx)	7	11	0	253	56	23.00	0	4
E. F. S. Tylecote (Kent)	7	11	0	209	66	19.00	0	11/5
G. F. Vernon (Middx)	4	6	1	60	24	12.00	0	1
W. Barnes (Notts)	7	11	1	113	32	11.30	0	5
Hon I. F. W. Bligh (Kent)	5	9	1	64	19	8.00	0	7
G. B. Studd (Middx)	7	12	2	40	9	4.00	0	10
F. Morley (Notts)	5	7	3	9	3	2.25	0	2

Bowling Averages

	O	M	R	W	Avge	BB	5i
C. F. H. Leslie	43	19	61	4	15.25	3-31	0
A. G. Steel	283	113	401	24	16.70	5-32	1
W. Bates	312	150	429	24	17.81	7-28	2
W. W. Read	53	18	92	5	18.40	4-28	0
C. T. Studd	194.2	118	174	9	19.33	3-28	0
R. G. Barlow	376	203	473	23	20.56	7-40	1
W. Barnes	199.2	75	306	13	23.53	6-70	1
F. Morley	187	105	197	8	24.62	4-47	0

Played in non-first-class matches only: G. Alexander, M. Cobbett.

first against 'Combined Australia' was lost through bad catching and the second against Victoria was lost through bad batting, though the wicket was all against the visitors. The tour ended on 12 March and the team split into three groups for the journey home, the first group reaching England on 25 April.

The visit was a financial success – each professional received £220 and the amateurs their expenses. Without W. G. Grace, Ulyett, Lucas and Hornby the side was perhaps not the full strength of England, and considering the fact that it never fielded its best eleven fully fit – owing to Morley's injury and various mishaps to Bligh, Steel, Leslie and Barnes – the results were better than expected.

One point which surprised the English visitors was the total absence in Australia of bowlers with doubtful actions, this being a problem which was plaguing English County cricket at the time.

1884-85 : dust storms and financial squabbles in Australia

James Lillywhite, Alfred Shaw and Arthur Shrewsbury arranged and managed their second speculative venture to Australia in the winter of 1884-85. This time Lillywhite acted purely as an umpire, whilst Alfred Shaw did not play in any major matches and took over the job as manager. Arthur Shrewsbury was chosen as captain. The other ten tourists were William Barnes, W. H. Scotton, William Attewell, and Wilfred Flowers of Notts; J. Hunter, R. Peel, W. Bates and G. Ulyett of Yorkshire, Johnny Briggs of Lancashire and J. Maurice Read of Surrey. The party contained no amateurs and in the estimation of Shaw was the strongest team ever to represent England in Australia. Writing in 1902, Shaw noted: 'A better side than this, alike for defence and attack, could not then, and I am certain cannot now, be chosen from the ranks of English cricketers.' The comment is of interest, since present-day historians tend to claim that the period commencing 1902 was The Golden Age of English Cricket! Shaw obviously was not of that opinion.

The side sailed from Plymouth on 19 September and after an unusually calm run through the Bay of Biscay arrived at Port Said in eleven days – the stop at Naples was omitted owing to an outbreak of cholera in that city. A match was played in Suez against a combined Army and Navy side on a matting wicket. Several members of the side went on a sight-seeing tour of the Pyramids and Cairo, in the company of Thomas Cook, who had come to Egypt to see the Khedive and arrange for tours up the Nile by his travel firm. On returning to the ship after the sight-seeing, Shaw and Ulyett engaged two Arabs to row them across to the anchorage. The Arabs rowed half the distance and then refused to go further without extra payment. Ulyett grabbed one oarsman by the collar and threw him in the sea, then proceeded to row to the ship, whilst the man swam alongside to the accompaniment of some decorated Yorkshire lingo from George.

The tourists arrived at Adelaide on 29 October, only to be greeted by the news that poor Fred Morley – who had never recovered from the injuries he received on the outward voyage of the last tour – had died. This caused depression among the players, all of whom were friends of Fred.

There were only two days practice before the first game against Fifteen of South Australia and after a close struggle the English side won by 3 wickets – the attendance however was very poor. The cricketing knowledge of the Australians though had increased beyond all recognition compared with a few years back – the English wicket-keeper, for example, was criticised for standing too far from the wicket. Not only was the criticism justified, but such a fine point would never have occurred to the spectators in Australia in the mid-70s.

Following a second odds match, the journey was made by sea

The team Shaw and Shrewsbury took to Australia in 1884-85, photographed in Sydney. The players are as numbered: 1 M. Read, 2 G. Ulyett, 3 W. H. Scotton, 4 R. Peel, 5 Joe Hunter, 6 W. Attewell, 7 A. Shrewsbury, 8 A. Shaw, 9 W. Barnes, 10 J. Lillywhite, 11 W. Flowers, 12 J. Briggs, 13 W. Bates. Notice the blazers and caps compared to the similar picture of 1876–77.

to Melbourne where the first eleven-a-side game was played against Victoria. The members of the 1884 Australian team in England however refused to play for Victoria and the visitors won easily. Without any up-country matches, the side went straight to Sydney to play New South Wales and the 1884 Australians once more refused to participate in the match, which provided another win for the English Eleven. The attendance was some 30,000 which was an improvement on the previous matches. Three odds matches followed, the first of which was played on matting laid on concrete, thus providing a much better wicket than normally seen in these matches.

The South Australian Cricket Association arranged a match between the tourists and the 1884 Australians at Adelaide – the first match of such importance ever staged in the city. The locals agreed to pay each team £450 and were therefore taking a great financial risk in promoting the game. A general holiday was proclaimed for the opening day, but with the admission charge at 2 shillings, only 4,000 spectators turned up. On the second day admission was reduced to a shilling and about 10,000 watched the game. It was on this day that a violent dust-storm occurred and the fielders were forced to lie down flat to avoid being suffocated. The forecasters claimed the dust-storm heralded rain, and sure enough the next day – Sunday – the ground was flooded. The English side, despite having the worst of the pitch, won a decisive

1884-85: Lillywhite, Shaw and Shrewsbury's Team to Egypt and Australia

Batting Averages

	M	I	NO	R	HS	Avge	100	c/s
W. Barnes (Notts)	8	13	1	520	134	43.33	1	15
A. Shrewsbury (Notts)	8	14	3	440	105*	40.00	1	12
W. Bates (Yorks)	8	12	0	363	68	30.25	0	4
J. Briggs (Lancs)	8	12	1	216	121	19.63	1	5
W. H. Scotton (Notts)	8	14	1	224	82	17.23	0	4
J. M. Read (Surrey)	8	12	1	178	56	16.18	0	5
W. Flowers (Notts)	8	13	0	189	56	14.53	0	1
J. Hunter (Yorks)	8	11	4	97	39*	13.85	0	11/6
W. Attewell (Notts)	8	11	2	108	30	12.00	0	6
R. Peel (Yorks)	8	11	4	84	21*	12.00	0	8
G. Ulyett (Yorks)	8	12	0	136	68	11.33	0	4

Bowling Averages

	O	M	R	W	Avge	BB	5i
W. Barnes	282.1	149	344	26	13.23	6-31	1
W. Bates	126.1	96	206	14	14.71	5-24	2
W. Flowers	298.2	158	332	22	15.07	8-31	2
W. Attewell	527.1	332	428	28	15.28	5-19	1
G. Ulyett	249	126	361	20	18.05	4-52	0
R. Peel	663.2	346	673	35	19.22	7-27	2
J. Briggs	8	3	13	0			

Played in non-first-class matches only: A. Shaw (Notts), Jas Lillywhite (Sussex), G. F. Hearne, R. Henderson (Surrey).

the Australians were supposed to be amateurs. Murdoch however continued to demand half the profits of each match and though Shaw offered 30 per cent and then £20 per man, both these suggestions were declined. Most of the Australian press and public seemed to side with the English team in this financial squabble, as did the Australian Cricket Associations. The result was that the second match between 'England and Australia' at Melbourne was played without any of the 1884 Australians taking part and the tourists won by 10 wickets. Six up-country games preceded the match with New South Wales, where once again the 1884 Australians refused to play and the English team won easily.

In the third 'England v Australia' match, four of the 1884 Australians agreed to play, and the tourists were beaten by 7 runs. In this game, the most effective English bowler on the tour, William Barnes, did not bowl. According to the reports the captain, Shrewsbury, asked him to bowl, but he refused–there being some friction between the two–undoubtedly this refusal by Barnes lost the match for England.

Of the other two international matches, each side won one, and in spite of the problems with the 1884 Australians, the series proved a popular one with the paying public.

The most serious injuries received on the tour occurred not on the playing field, but on, or rather off, horseback to 'Boy' Briggs. On the first occasion, he dismounted on the wrong side, being left-handed, and the horse kicked him, almost sending the inexperienced rider over a precipice, and on the second occasion he tried to slow down his runaway mount and went flying over its head, falling flat on his face. Unfortunately he was smoking a pipe at the time and the stem was rammed into the roof of his mouth.

victory by 8 wickets. Murdoch, the Australian captain, refused to permit either Lillywhite or Shaw to umpire and the result was that a totally inexperienced local man was used–his decisions were quite hopeless, but seemed to be evenly distributed.

The fact that both teams were paid an equal amount for the match was a sore point with the English team. Shaw argued that when in England the Australians had made a handsome profit, whilst the English professionals had been paid £10 per man. Also

1884-85: Lillywhite, Shaw and Shrewsbury's Team to Egypt and Australia

1st Match: v XXII of Army & Navy (Suez) Oct 2.
England 117 drew with Army & Navy 40-11.

2nd Match: v XV of South Australia (Adelaide) Oct 31, Nov 1, 3, 4, 5.
England 239 (G. Ulyett 100, A. Shrewsbury 52) & 124-7 beat S. Australia 217 (W. Flowers 7-54) & 144 (W. Attewell 7-61, R. Peel 6-52) by 3 wkts.

3rd Match: v XVIII of South Australia (Norwood) Nov 6, 7, 8.
England 170 & 243-9 (W. H. Scotton 62, W. Barnes 60) drew with S. Australia 117 (R. Peel 5-28, W. Flowers 5-31).

4th Match: v Victoria (Melbourne) Nov 14, 15, 17, 18.
England 202 (A. Shrewsbury 80, W. Barnes 61) & 150 (W. R. Robertson 5-46) beat Victoria 146 & 88 (W. Flowers 8-31) by 118 runs.

5th Match: v New South Wales (Sydney) Nov 21, 22, 24.
N.S.W. 184 & 44 (W. Attewell 5-19) lost to England 110 & 119-6 by 4 wkts.

6th Match: v XXII of Hawkesbury (Windsor) Nov 26, 27.
England 273 (W. Flowers 74, W. H. Scotton 60, J. Briggs 57) drew with Hawkesbury 63 (R. Peel 13-32) & 51-6.

7th Match: v XVIII of Cumberland (Parramatta) Nov 28, 29.
Cumberland 85 (R. Peel 9-62) & 96 (R. Peel 9-37) lost to England 173 (G. Ulyett 57) & 9-1 by 9 wkts.

8th Match: v XXII of Clarence River (Grafton) Dec 1, 2.
Clarence River 87 (R. Peel 11-31) & 134 (W. Flowers 9-19) lost to England 121 & 100-2 (G. Ulyett 56*) by 8 wkts.

9th Match: v 1884 Australians (Adelaide) Dec 12, 13, 15, 16.
Australians 243 (P. S. McDonnell 124, J. McC. Blackham 66, W. Bates 5-31) & 191 (P. S. McDonnell 83, R. Peel 5-51) lost to England 369 (W. Barnes 134, W. H. Scotton 82, G. Ulyett 68, G. E. Palmer 5-81) & 67-2 by 8 wkts.

10th Match: v XXII of Maryborough (Maryborough) Dec 20, 22.
England 116 & 112 drew with Maryborough 72 (W. Attewell 14-25) & 79-17 (R. Peel 6-9).

11th Match: v XVIII of Bendigo (Sandhurst) Dec 23, 24.
Bendigo 82 (W. Barnes 9-15) drew with England 576-6 (W. Barnes 109, W. Bates 107, J. Briggs 98*, W. Flowers 92).

12th Match: v XXII of Ballarat (Ballarat) Dec 26, 27.
England 229 (W. Barnes 85*) drew with Ballarat 234-14 (H. Musgrove 109, J. Worrall 67)

13th Match: v XXII of Benalla (Benalla) Dec 29, 30.
Benalla 163 (W. Attewell 11-48) & 141 (W. Bates 8-46) drew with England 113 & 41-3.

14th Match: v Combined Australia (Melbourne) Jan 1, 2, 3, 5.
England 401 (J. Briggs 121, A. Shrewsbury 72, W. Barnes 58) & 7-0 beat Australia 279 (A. H. Jarvis 82, T. P. Horan 63, J. W. Trumble 59) & 126 (W. Barnes 6-31) by 10 wkts.

15th Match: v XXII of Wagga Wagga (Wagga Wagga) (One Day) Jan 7.
Wagga Wagga 126 (R. Peel 13-57) lost to England 130-8 (W. Barnes 55*) by 2 wkts.

16th Match: v XXII of Wollongong (Wollongong) Jan 9, 10.
England 171 beat Wollongong 40 (R. Peel 14-15) & 67 (W. Bates 11-34) by an inns & 62 runs.

17th Match: v XXII of Candelo (Candelo) Jan 12, 13.
Candelo 71 (R. Peel 13-36) & 80 (R. Peel 11-32, W. Attewell 10-37) lost to England 163 by an inns & 12 runs.

18th Match: v XXII of Shoalhaven (Nowra) Jan 16, 17.
England 181 (J. M. Read 59) drew with Shoalhaven 87 (R. Peel 13-49) & 32-10.

19th Match: v XXII of Yass (Yass) Jan 20.
England 103 drew with Yass 70-11.

20th Match: v XXII of Moss Vale (Moss Vale) Jan 21, 22.
England 432 (W. H. Scotton 123, W. Bates 111, G. Ulyett 56) drew with Moss Vale 14 (Peel 18-7) & 19-4.

21st Match: v New South Wales (Sydney) Jan 24, 26, 27.
England 205 (W. Bates 68, S. P. Jones 5-54) beat N.S.W. 60 (R. Peel 7-27) & 108.

22nd Match: v XXII of Brisbane (Brisbane) Jan 31, Feb 2, 3.
Brisbane 114 (R. Peel 11-41) & 45 (R. Peel 13-21) lost to England 128 (W. Barnes 60) & 33-1 by 9 wkts.

23rd Match: v XXII of Maryborough (Maryborough) Feb 5, 6.
England 131 (G. Ulyett 53) & 183 (G. Ulyett 106*) beat Maryborough 92 (R. Peel 11-29, W. Flowers 10-38) & 93 (R. Peel 12-42) by 129 runs.

24th Match: v XXII of Gympie (Gympie) Feb 7, 9.
Gympie 74 (W. Attewell 12-27) & 108 (W. Bates 13-40) lost to England 148 & 37-2 by 8 wkts.

25th Match: v XXII of Maitland (Maitland) Feb 14, 16.
Maitland 93 (W. Attewell 11-38, R. Peel 10-51) & 100-14 drew with England 67.

26th Match: v XXII of Singleton (Singleton) Feb 17, 18.
England 141 & 118-8 drew with Singleton 91 (W. Attewell 12-49).

27th Match: v Combined Australia (Sydney) Feb 20, 21, 23, 24.
Australia 181 (T. W. Garrett 51*, W. Flowers 5-46) & 165 (W. Bates 5-24) beat England 133 (T. P. Horan 6-40) & 207 (W. Flowers 56, J. M. Read 56, F. R. Spofforth 6-90) by 7 runs.

28th Match: v XXII of Narrabri (Narrabri) Feb 27, 28.
England 187 beat Narrabri 74 (R. Peel 12-41) & 69 (W. Flowers 14-27).

29th Match: v XXII of Armidale (Armidale) March 2, 3.
Armidale 91 (R. Peel 12-47) & 138-17 drew with England 183 (W. Bates 50).

30th Match: v XVIII of Junior Cricket Assoc. (Ashfield) March 5, 6, 7.
Juniors 100 (R. Peel 11-51) & 184-12 drew with England 188 (J. M. Read 52*).

31st Match: v XXII of Wellington (Wellington) March 9, 10.
Wellington 70 (R. Peel 11-40) drew with England 198 (W. Bates 50).

32nd Match: v Australia (Sydney) March 14, 16, 17
England 269 (W. Bates 64, W. Barnes 50, G. Giffen 7-117) & 77 (F. R. Spofforth 5-30) lost to Australia 309 (G. J. Bonnor 128, A. C. Bannerman 51) & 38-2 by 8 wkts.

33rd Match: v Australia (Melbourne) March 21, 23, 24, 25.
Australia 163 (F. R. Spofforth 50) & 125 lost to England 386 (A. Shrewsbury 105*, W. Barnes 74, W. Bates 61) by an inns & 98 runs.

34th Match: v XV of South Australia (Adelaide) April 2, 4, 6.
England 367 (J. Briggs 81, W. Barnes 76, W. Bates 58) drew with S. Australia 141.

Briggs was unconscious for about four hours and in fact it was reported that he had been killed; luckily he survived, but with a face so bruised that on inspecting it in the mirror, he did not recognise the reflection.

The team returned to Adelaide for the last match of the tour, which was marred by another dust-storm and torrential rain. The side left Australia on 4 April and split up in the Mediterranean, half taking the overland route and the rest sailing to Plymouth.

Financially the promoters were well-rewarded and the players, as well as their £300, received numerous prizes for best performances in the up-country matches – in two games some of the players won shares in gold-mines, which they auctioned off at a handsome profit.

1885: Philadelphia beat North American tourists

E. J. Sanders arranged a short tour of North America for September 1885 and gathered a reasonably strong team of amateurs for the trip. The players involved were Rev R. T. Thornton, A. J. Thornton and T. R. Hine-Haycock of Kent, W. E. Roller and C. E. Horner of Surrey, A. E. Newton of Somerset, H. O. Whitby of Warwickshire, J. A. Turner of Leicestershire, A. R. Cobb of Oxford University, H. Bruen of Ireland and W. E. T. Bolitho of Devon. The team left Liverpool on 20 August and on the return left New York for home on 1 October. The most important fixtures were those against Philadelphia, of which one was won and the other lost – unfortunately W. E. Roller injured his arm during the third game of the tour and could not bowl in either of the Philadelphian games. The attendance in Philadelphia was high, with 8,000 or 9,000 present on some days, and the tourists were surprised to see that nearly half the crowd were women. Rev R. T. Thornton captained the side and the leading batsman was W. E. Roller, whilst Bruen and Horner took most wickets.

The victory by Philadelphia in the first match was a significant milestone for cricket in the United States, being the first time that an English team had tasted defeat. On the afternoon of the third day it appeared that the tourists would save the game – only $1\frac{3}{4}$ hours remained and the brothers A. J. and R. T. Thornton seemed well set. Their partnership realised 47 runs when C. Newhall bowled R. T. Thornton. The other four wickets then fell for 28 runs, Dan Newhall capturing the final wicket with a lob.

1885: E. J. Sanders' Team to United States and Canada

1st Match: v XII of Staten Island (Staten Is)   Sept 1, 2.
Sanders' XII 91 (J. L. Pool 7-43) & 244 (J. A. Turner 52) drew with Staten Island XII 62 (H. Bruen 8-27) & 72-3.

2nd Match: v XV of Peninsular Club (Detroit)   Sept 5, 7.
Sanders' XI 283 beat Peninsular Club 69 (C. E. Horner 8-29) & 49 (H. O. Whitby 5-11) by an inns & 165 runs.

3rd Match: v Canada (Toronto)   Sept 10, 11.
Canada 76 (W. E. Roller 6-32) & 38 lost to Sanders' XI 133 (E. R. Ogden 5-59) by an inns & 20 runs.

4th Match: v XV of Montreal (Montreal)   Sept 14.
Sanders' XI 110 beat XV of Montreal 28 (H. Bruen 9-14) & 42 (A. J. Thornton 11-27) by an inns & 40 runs.

5th Match: v Philadelphia (Nicetown)   Sept 17, 18, 19.
Philadelphia 200 (C. E. Horner 6-61) & 178 beat Sanders' XI 147 (A. J. Thornton 55, W. C. Lowry 5-55) & 122 by 109 runs.

6th Match: v New York (Staten Island)   Sept 21, 22.
New York 66 (H. Bruen 7-25) & 76 lost to Sanders' XI 267 (A. E. Newton 129, J. L. Pool 6-53) by an inns & 125 runs.

7th Match: v Philadelphia (Nicetown)   Sept 24, 25, 26.
Sanders' XI 193 (W. E. Roller 64) & 317 (R. T. Thornton 107, T. R. Hine-Haycock 85, H. McNutt 6-82) beat Philadelphia 147 (J. A. Scott 56*) & 120 (H. Bruen 6-54) by 243 runs.

8th Match: v XV of New England (Longwood)   Sept 28, 29.
Sanders' XI 59 (Chambers 6-34) & 53 (G. Wright 6-25) beat New England 66 & 30 by 16 runs.

1886: revenge against Philadelphia

E. J. Sanders repeated his tour of the previous year. T. R. Hine-Haycock, J. A. Turner, A. R. Cobb, W. E. Roller of 1885 again went with Sanders, together with H. W. Bainbridge (Warwickshire), K. J. Key (Surrey), Rev A. T. Fortescue (Oxford U), E. H. Buckland (Middx), C. E. Cottrell (Middx), H. Rotherham (Warwicks) and F. T. Welman (Middx). Roller captained the side, which left Liverpool on 19 August and arrived in New York on 29 August, after a rough passage. As previously the two major matches were against Philadelphia, this time however the tourists being victorious in both.

The team was perhaps stronger than in 1885, the leading batsman being K. J. Key, whilst Roller and Cottrell both took 50 wickets at a low cost and were the principal bowlers. The final match ended on 4 October.

Soon after the team returned to England A. R. Cobb died of typhoid – a tragic loss to cricket, since he had been in the Winchester side of 1883 and in 1886 hit 50 for Oxford v Cambridge at Lord's.

1886: E. J. Sanders' Team to America

1st Match: v Staten Island (New York)   Sept 1, 2.
Sanders' XII 203 beat Staten Island 74 (C. E. Cottrell 7-17) & 80 (H. Rotherham 7-25) by an inns & 49 runs.

2nd Match: v Ontario (Toronto)   Sept 7, 8.
Sanders' XI 169 (A. T. Fortescue 58*, E. H. Buckland 54) & 15-2 beat Ontario 72 (C. E. Cottrell 6-31) & 111 by 8 wkts.

3rd Match: v XVI of Montreal (Montreal)   Sept 11, 13, 14.
Sanders' XII 257 (J. A. Turner 57, K. J. Key 52) beat Montreal 85 & 55 by an inns & 117 runs.

4th Match: v XV of Longwood Club (Boston)   Sept 15, 16, 17.
Longwood 96 (W. E. Roller 11-44) & 43 lost to Sanders' XI 77 & 64-7 by 3 wkts.

5th Match: v XV of New England (Boston)   Sept 17, 18.
Sanders' XI 116 (Dutton 5-41) & 136-6 (A. R. Cobb 52) drew with New England 109 (C. E. Cottrell 6-45).

6th Match: v XVIII of Baltimore (Baltimore)   Sept 21, 22.
Sanders' XI 257 (K. J. Key 96) beat Baltimore 82 & 117 by an inns & 58 runs.

7th Match: v Philadelphia (Philadelphia)   Sept 23, 24, 25.
Philadelphia 168 (E. H. Buckland 6-53) & 139 (E. H. Buckland 6-52) lost to Sanders' XI 323 (K. J. Key 109, W. E. Roller 75, H. I. Brown 5-113) by an inns & 16 runs.

8th Match: v All New York (New York)   Sept 27, 28, 29.
New York 143 (W. E. Roller 5-56) & 41 (C. E. Cottrell 8-21) lost to Sanders' XI 75 & 113-1 (W. E. Roller 55*) by 9 wkts.

9th Match: v Philadelphia (Philadelphia)   Oct 1, 2, 4.
Philadelphia 128 (C. E. Cottrell 5-55) & 146 (E. H. Buckland 7-63) lost to Sanders' XI 235 (E. H. Buckland 82, A. R. Cobb 51) & 40-4 by 6 wkts.

1886-87: the 'strongest all-round team yet' go to Australia

The combination of Lillywhite, Shaw and Shrewsbury took a third side to Australia in the winter of 1886-87. As on the previous trip, Lillywhite acted as umpire, Shaw as manager and Shrewsbury as captain. In addition there were five Notts cricketers, W. Barnes, W. Gunn, W. H. Scotton, W. Flowers and M. Sherwin; G. A. Lohmann and J. M. Read from Surrey; W. Bates from Yorkshire and J. Briggs and R. G. Barlow of Lancashire – so discounting Shaw there were only eleven players, a fact that caused problems later.

The side left Plymouth on 18 September and the only break in the voyage occurred in Aden, where the ship stopped for ten hours. The Indian Ocean was distinctly choppy, Gunn, Bates and Briggs being the worst sufferers. Adelaide was reached on 29 October and the first game – against the local Fifteen – began the following day. A perfect wicket had been produced and Shrewsbury, despite having no practice, had little difficulty in hitting a hundred, and Barnes also scored well. The attendance however was poor, only 1,000 being present on the opening day, which was a half-holiday. The match was drawn, as was the second game against Victoria – here again there was a perfect wicket and the bowlers were ineffective. For the first time the journey between Adelaide and Melbourne was made by train, rather than sea, though the time taken was 28½ hours, including a break of six hours at Border Town – the through trains with sleeping cars which did the journey in 18 hours were introduced the following year. A magnificent new grandstand had been erected on the Melbourne Ground since the previous English visit and this, combined with the scoreboard which showed the batsmen's names, made the facilities at Melbourne unequalled.

The rain which was to dog the party for most of the tour arrived at Parramatta, where in a low scoring affair on a sticky wicket, the first up-country game was staged. Going on to Sydney, Shrewsbury won the toss and decided to bat on a wicket which turned out to be slow and treacherous. Turner and Ferris, the two New South Wales bowlers, completely baffled the Englishmen and the home side won in two days by 6 wickets. Four odds matches in the N.S.W. country districts produced four victories, the most amazing being at Lithgow, where the Twenty-two were dismissed for 18 and 27, which is possibly a record – Briggs took 27 wickets in the match for 20 runs. To be fair however it must be mentioned that it had rained non-stop for four days prior to the match and the square was under water. A strip of matting was laid on some higher ground which made a very short boundary, counting two, on one side, whilst on the other the fielders had to wade through water to retrieve the ball. The report of the match contains the following description of Barnes' innings: 'Barnes only just managed to crack his egg when a noise behind warned him to depart.'

The return game against New South Wales produced revenge for the visitors. This time, on winning the toss, Shrewsbury put the home side in and they were quickly dismissed by Briggs and Barlow. Turner and Ferris were defied by Shrewsbury and although the Australian pair took all the English wickets, sufficient lead was gained on the first innings to enable a nine wickets victory to be obtained.

The team returned to Melbourne where they played the first of three matches against the Australian side which toured England

in 1886 – the weather was poor, both rain and dust-storms marring the play and reducing the attendance to little more than 2,000 each day. Being 93 behind on first innings the tourists were forced to follow on, but, led by Shrewsbury, so well did they play in the latter half of the match that victory was achieved by 57 runs – Briggs' bowling and the English field in the final innings was quite excellent.

The tourists drew their game at Geelong, where everyone was football mad, the local side being the Champions of Victoria, and then won at Ballarat, before their second encounter with the 1886 Australians. Three or four dropped catches in the Australian second innings meant that the English side needed 220 to win in 210 minutes, but the loss of three quick wickets caused the game to be drawn. The two teams immediately left the ground for the express train to Sydney, where the third match was arranged to be played. Here Shrewsbury was lucky to win the toss and bat first, for the wicket got progressively worse and the tourists were able to enforce the follow on and won by 9 wickets. On the Saturday – the second day – about 10,000 watched the game, the best attendance so far.

The party which visited Australia in 1886-87, photographed in Melbourne. This was the team led by Shaw, Shrewsbury and Lillywhite. Back: W. Flowers, A. Shrewsbury, G. A. Lohmann, W. Gunn, W. Barnes, J. M. Read. Seated: W. Bates, A. Shaw, J. Lillywhite (umpire), M. Sherwin, W. H. Scotton, R. G. Barlow. Front: J. Briggs.

1886-87: Lillywhite, Shaw and Shrewsbury's Team to Australia

1st Match: v XV of South Australia (Adelaide)   Oct 30, 31, Nov 1.
England 329 (A. Shrewsbury 100, W. Barnes 84) drew with S. Australia 132 (R. G. Barlow 6-30) & 127-8.

2nd Match: v Victoria (Melbourne)   Nov 6, 8, 9, 10.
Victoria 329 (T. P. Horan 117*, R. S. Houston 68, P. G. McShane 65, G. A. Lohmann 6-115) & 207 (S. Morris 54*) drew with England 352 (W. Barnes 109, R. G. Barlow 86, W. Flowers 52).

3rd Match: v XVIII of Parramatta (Parramatta)   Nov 12, 13.
England 67 (Cleeve 7-20) & 78 beat Parramatta 73 (J. Briggs 8-31) & 49 (G. A. Lohmann 12-21) by 23 runs.

4th Match: v New South Wales (Sydney)   Nov 19, 20.
England 74 (C. T. B. Turner 6-20) & 98 (C. T. B. Turner 7-34) lost to N.S.W. 111 & 62-4 by 6 wkts.

5th Match: v XVIII of Goulburn (Goulburn)   Nov 26, 27.
Goulburn 83 (J. Briggs 9-26) & 70 (R. G. Barlow 10-30) lost to England 212 (Dennis 5-74) by an inns & 59 runs.

6th Match: v XXII of Cootamundra (Cootamundra)   Nov 29, 30.
England 154 & 29-0 beat Cootamundra 67 (W. Flowers 12-21) & 113 by 10 wkts.

7th Match: v XVIII Sydney Juniors (Sydney)   Dec 3, 4.
Juniors 76 (G. A. Lohmann 10-36) & 107 (J. Briggs 8-24) lost to England 312 (A. Shrewsbury 92, W. Bates 82) by an inns & 130 runs.

8th Match: v XXII of Lithgow (Lithgow)   Dec 8, 9.
England 80 & 42 beat Lithgow 18 (J. Briggs 10-7) & 27 (J. Briggs 17-13) by 77 runs.

9th Match: v N.S.W. (Sydney)   Dec 10, 11, 13.
N.S.W. 117 (J. Briggs 5-45) & 107 (W. Flowers 5-21, G. A. Lohmann 5-47) lost to England 220 (A. Shrewsbury 64, C. T. B. Turner 7-77) & 5-1 by 9 wkts.

10th Match: v 1886 Australians (Melbourne)   Dec 17, 18, 20, 21, 22.
Australia 294 & 114 (J. Briggs 5-42) lost to England 201 & 264 (A. Shrewsbury 62) by 57 runs.

11th Match: v XVIII of Geelong (Geelong)   Dec 23, 24.
England 324 (R. G. Barlow 104, A. Shrewsbury 70, P. G. McShane 5-102) drew with Geelong 110 (W. Bates 11-69) & 85-5.

12th Match: v XX of Ballarat (Ballarat)   Dec 27, 28, 29.
England 292 (J. M. Read 121, J. Worrall 6-97) beat Ballarat 188 & 91 (W. Bates 9-43) by an inns & 13 runs.

13th Match: v 1886 Australians (Melbourne)   Jan 1, 3, 4, 5.
Australia 246 (J. McC. Blackham 63, W. Bates 5-72) & 249 drew with England 276 (W. Barnes 93, W. Bruce 5-56) & 125-4 (W. Gunn 61*).

14th Match: v 1886 Australians (Sydney)   Jan 7, 8, 10, 11.
Australia 132 (W. Barnes 7-51) & 203 (J. W. Trumble 60) lost to England 280 (J. Briggs 69, J. M. Read 53, T. W. Garrett 6-53) & 57-1 by 9 wkts.

15th Match: v XVIII of Bathurst (Bathurst)   Jan 14, 15.
Bathurst 131 & 72-4 drew with England 294 (W. Barnes 84, W. Bates 67, J. M. Read 52).

16th Match: v XXII of Orange (Orange)   Jan 17, 18.
England 131 (W. Marsh 8-58) & 224-7 (J. M. Read 88, J. Briggs 60*) drew with Orange 64 (J. Briggs 12-17).

17th Match: v XXII of Bowral (Bowral)   Jan 23, 24.
Bowral 124 drew with England 25-1.

18th Match: v XXII of Camden (Camden)   Jan 25, 26.
Camden 133 (W. Bates 8-58) drew with England 129-4 (W. Gunn 68*).

19th Match: v Combined Australia (Sydney)   Jan 28, 29, 31.
England 45 (C. T. B. Turner 6-15) & 184 (J. J. Ferris 5-76) beat Australia 119 & 97 (W. Barnes 6-28) by 13 runs.

20th Match: v XXII of Narrabri (Narrabri)   Feb 4, 5.
England 305 (W. Flowers 62, A. Shrewsbury 53) drew with Narrabri 59-13.

21st Match: v XXII of Armidale (Armidale)   Feb 7, 8.
Armidale 111 (G. A. Lohmann 9-50) & 33-8 drew with England 225 (W. Flowers 54).

22nd Match: v XVIII of Newcastle (Newcastle)   Feb 10, 11, 12.
England 236 (J. M. Read 72) drew with Newcastle 135 & 109-13.

23rd Match: v XVIII of Singleton (Singleton)   Feb 15, 16.
England 95 & 102 drew with Singleton 54 (J. Briggs 11-26) & 87-12.

24th Match: v New South Wales (Sydney)   Feb 18, 19, 21.
N.S.W. 141 (G. A. Lohmann 5-56) & 180 (H. Moses 73, G. A. Lohmann 6-41) beat England 99 (C. T. B. Turner 8-32) & 100 (C. T. B. Turner 6-27) by 122 runs.

25th Match: v Combined Australia (Sydney)   Feb 25, 26, 28, 29.
England 151 (C. T. B. Turner 5-41, J. J. Ferris 5-71) & 154 beat Australia 84 (G. A. Lohmann 8-35) & 150 by 71 runs.

26th Match: v Victoria (Melbourne)   March 4, 5, 7, 8.
Victoria 245 (J. McIlwraith 64, W. Bruce 62, W. Flowers 5-50) & 156 (G. A. Lohmann 5-44) lost to England 283 (A. Shrewsbury 144, W. Bruce 7-72) & 119-1 (W. Bates 86) by 9 wkts.

27th Match: v XV of East Melbourne (Melbourne)   March 11, 12, 14.
East Melbourne 130 & 208-9 drew with England 271 (G. A. Lohmann 100, W. H. Scotton 71).

28th Match: v XVIII of Sandhurst (Sandhurst)   March 15, 16.
Sandhurst 346 (H. F. Boyle 115) drew with England 283-6 (J. M. Read 140).

29th Match: v XV of South Australia (Adelaide)   March 24, 25, 26.
S. Australia 229 (A. H. Jarvis 77, J. M. Read 7-21) & 132-12 drew with England 279 (R. G. Barlow 53, J. Briggs 53).

Four up-country games were all drawn, three due to rain. At Orange, the English batting order was decided by taking names out of a hat, whilst at Bowral, deep puddles were a feature of the outfield – the weather however was so hot after some torrential rain that the fielders found it quite pleasant running through the water. At Bathurst, the gate had been sold to a local publican for £90 and he even tried to force the players to pay an entrance fee.

Following these country diversions, the tourists went to Sydney where a team representing 'Combined Australia' was met. The first day was disastrous: the Sydney morning papers stated that the game had been postponed and therefore few spectators turned up and the English side, batting first, collapsed before Turner and Ferris for a mere 45. Brilliant English fielding plus a stubborn second innings however pulled the game round and victory – the best of the tour – was obtained by 13 runs. The success was marred to some extent by the bitter argument between Barnes and the Australian batsman, Percy McDonnell. The two came to blows and Barnes took a tremendous swipe at his adversary's face, missed and smashed his fist against a wall. The Notts all-rounder missed almost all the remaining matches as a result.

Lillywhite and Shaw took Barnes' place in the next series of up-country matches, nearly all of which suffered from torrential rain, but in the eleven-a-side games, R. Wood, a Lancastrian, engaged on the Melbourne Ground was co-opted. Turner bowled in great form in the first of these – for New South Wales – and provided the home side with an easy win. Shrewsbury was bowled Turner 0 in both his innings and was presented with a small pair of gold spectacles as a result. A second game against 'Combined Australia' came directly after the defeat by New South Wales – Turner and Ferris again were most effective, but Lohmann was even more so and the English team won by 71 runs.

Moving to Melbourne for the final leg of the tour, the tourists found the game against Victoria clashed with an important race meeting, which ruined the attendance. It had been intended to play a third match against 'Combined Australia' at Melbourne, but the best N.S.W. players couldn't come and the curious Smokers v Non-Smokers match was substituted, the English team being divided with the Victorians. The Non-Smokers hit 803, the runs coming at about 100 an hour. Few members of the public however were attracted to the game, only 500 coming on the Saturday and scarcely 100 on the last day, when at the end of play Scotton, who was batting, picked up the ball as a souvenir and was given out 'handled ball'.

Before catching the boat in Adelaide a final odds match was played against the local Fifteen, but again few spectators turned out. The tourists boarded the *Massilia* for home on 26 March. A stoppage was made at Colombo and also at Aden, where Gunn took part in an athletics match and won four events – Briggs, the ship's champion at the potato race, was however disqualified, through failing to pick up a potato.

According to the Australian newspapes the side was ranked as the finest all-round team ever to visit the Southern Hemisphere. The fielding was generally excellent, the side batted right down the order and it had six good bowlers in Barnes, Flowers, Lohmann, Bates, Briggs and Barlow.

The tourists arrived back in England on 8 May. As a footnote it should be pointed out that the English team was invited to go to New Zealand, but apart from the offer from Auckland, the financial terms were so poor that the invitation was declined.

1887-88: a rival tour goes to Australia and New Zealand

Major Wardill, who managed the 1886 Australian team to England, stated before leaving England that the Melbourne Club intended to invite a mixed team of amateurs and professionals to tour Australia in the winter of 1887-88, and that several prominent amateurs had provisionally agreed to go. In January of 1887—six months after the announcement of the tour sponsored by the Melbourne Club—it was stated that Lillywhite, Shaw and Shrewsbury intended to manage an English team to Australia in conjunction with the New South Wales Association.

Though the professional trio were asked to reconsider their plans, they refused to do so, and both tours went ahead with the inevitably disastrous financial consequences. Alfred Shaw in his reminiscences states: 'The responsibility for the clashing of interests certainly did not rest with us.' It is however difficult to justify this claim.

Both teams travelled on the Orient steamer *Iberia*, the Melbourne side under the Hon M. B. Hawke went on board at Tilbury on 15 September, whereas the other side joined the boat at Plymouth, and the cricketers all landed at Adelaide on 25 October.

The side for the tour arranged by the Melbourne Club consisted of the Hon M. B. Hawke (Yorkshire) (capt), G. F. Vernon, A. E. Stoddart and T. C. O'Brien, all Middlesex, A. E. Newton (Somerset), W. W. Read and M. P. Bowden (Surrey) and the professionals R. Abel and J. Beaumont (Surrey), J. T. Rawlin, W. Bates and R. Peel (Yorkshire) and W. Attewell (Notts).

The first match took place in Adelaide, where, for the first time,

1887-88: G. F. Vernon's Team to Australia

Batting Averages

	M	I	NO	R	HS	Avge	100	c/s
W. W. Read (Surrey)	8	13	2	610	183	55.45	3	13
R. Peel (Yorks)	9	15	2	449	55	34.53	0	11
A. E. Stoddart (Middx)	9	15	0	450	94	30.00	0	8
R. Abel (Surrey)	8	14	1	320	95	24.61	0	8
A. E. Newton (Somerset)	8	12	1	264	77	24.00	0	7/2
W. Attewell (Notts)	9	14	3	212	43	19.27	0	9
T. C. O'Brien (Middx)	7	10	0	186	45	18.60	0	7
J. T. Rawlin (Yorks)	8	12	1	193	78*	17.54	0	5
G. F. Vernon (Middx)	6	9	0	155	50	17.22	0	3
Lord Hawke (Yorks)	3	5	0	76	48	15.20	0	1
M. P. Bowden (Surrey)	6	10	3	99	35	14.14	0	6/5
W. Bates (Yorks)	3	5	0	59	28	11.80	0	2
J. Beaumont (Surrey)	8	12	5	40	16	5.71	0	3

Bowling Averages

	O	M	R	W	Avge	BB	5i
W. Attewell	746.2	404	590	54	10.92	7-15	4
R. Peel	747.2	371	822	50	16.44	5-18	3
W. Bates	136.1	55	194	9	21.55	3-36	0
W. W. Read	19	5	52	2	26.00	1-16	0
A. E. Stoddart	113.3	45	187	7	26.71	2-31	0
J. Beaumont	480	248	668	22	30.36	3-34	0
J. T. Rawlin	234.1	134	221	5	44.20	2-87	0
R. Abel	29	9	46	1	46.00	1-23	0

Played in non-first-class matches only: F. H. Walters, F. Williams, J. Phillips, . McArthur. Note: Records in Test Match by 'Combined' Team included.

1887-88: G. F. Vernon's Team to Australia

1st Match: v South Australia (Adelaide)   Oct 28, 29, 31, Nov 1.
G. F. Vernon's XI 104 (G. Giffen 5-32) & 291 (R. Abel 95, A. E. Stoddart 64, J. J. Lyons 5-75) beat S. Australia 118 (R. Peel 5-31) & 206 (G. Giffen 81) by 71 runs.

2nd Match: v Victoria (Melbourne)   Nov 9, 10, 11.
Victoria 152 (J. McIlwraith 60) & 126 (J. McC. Blackham 68) lost to G. F. Vernon's XI 296 (A. E. Stoddart 94, R. Peel 55) by an inns & 18 runs.

3rd Match: v XXII of Castlemaine (Castlemaine)   Nov 14, 15.
Castlemaine 109 & 134 (A. E. Stoddart 8-27) drew with G. F. Vernon's XI 181 (R. Peel 63).

4th Match: v XVIII of Sandhurst (Sandhurst)   Nov 16, 17.
G. F. Vernon's XI 417 (R. Peel 67, W. Attewell 59*, R. Abel 57, W. W. Read 52, A. E. Newton 51) drew with Sandhurst 135-11.

5th Match: v XVIII of Ballarat (Ballarat)   Nov 18, 19.
G. F. Vernon's XI 477 (A. E. Stoddart 95, Hon M. B. Hawke 70, W. W. Read 65, R. Peel 65, W. Attewell 50) drew with Ballarat 67 and 51-2.

6th Match: v New South Wales (Sydney)   Nov 25, 26, 28, 29, 30.
G. F. Vernon's XI 340 (R. Abel 88, A. E. Stoddart 55, R. Peel 54, C. T. B. Turner 7-106) & 106 (J. J. Ferris 7-49) lost to N.S.W. 408 (P. S. McDonnell 112, H. Moses 77, S. P. Jones 60) & 40-1 by 9 wkts.

7th Match: v XVIII of Parramatta (Parramatta)   Dec 2, 3.
Parramatta 144 (W. Attewell 7-55) & 166-6 drew with G. F. Vernon's XI 116 (Thorpe 7-41).

8th Match: v XXII of Hawkesbury (Richmond)   Dec 5, 6.
G. F. Vernon's XI 84 & 108 drew with Hawkesbury 52 (W. Attewell 11-25) & 49-15 (W. Attewell 9-17).

9th Match: v XVIII of Manly (Manly) (One Day)   Dec 7.
Manly 148 (A. E. Stoddart 7-34) drew with G. F. Vernon's XI 126-5 (W. Bates 54).

10th Match: v XVIII Melbourne Juniors (Melbourne)   Dec 10, 12.
G. F. Vernon's XI 556 (A. E. Stoddart 285, R. Peel 95) drew with Juniors 70-15.

11th Match: v XXII of Maryborough (Maryborough)   Dec 14, 15.
G. F. Vernon's XI 258 (A. E. Stoddart 81, T. C. O'Brien 75) drew with Maryborough 98 (R. Peel 10-40) & 55-14.

12th Match: v XXII of Gippsland (Sale)   Dec 19, 20.
Gippsland 51 (R. Peel 14-16) & 98 (R. Peel 10-36) lost to G. F. Vernon's XI 152 by an inns & 3 runs.

13th Match: v South Australia (Adelaide)   Dec 24, 26, 27, 28.
G. F. Vernon's XI 382 (W. W. Read 183, G. Giffen 5-163) & 59-0 drew with S. Australia 143 (A. H. Jarvis 75) & 493 (G. Giffen 203, W. Godfrey 119).

14th Match: v Combined Australia (Melbourne)   Dec 31, Jan 2, 3.
G. F. Vernon's XI 292 (J. T. Rawlin 78*, A. E. Newton 77, G. F. Vernon 50) beat Australia 136 & 78 by an inns & 78 runs.

15th Match: v XV of Yarra Bend (Yarra Bend) (One Day)   Jan 5.
G. F. Vernon's XI 186 (T. C. O'Brien 66) beat Yarra Bend 57 (A. E. Stoddart 8-36) by 129 runs.

16th Match: v XVIII of Northern Tasmania (Launceston)   Jan 13, 14.
G. F. Vernon's XI 195 (A. E. Stoddart 91) & 27-3 drew with N. Tasmania 162.

17th Match: v XXII of North West Coast (Latrobe)   Jan 17, 18.
G. F. Vernon's XI 271 (W. Attewell 122) beat North West Coast 66 (J. Beaumont 9-12) & 97 (R. Peel 13-54) by an inns & 108 runs.

18th Match: v XVIII of South Tasmania (Hobart)   Jan 20, 21.
S. Tasmania 59 (R. Peel 11-21) & 91-7 drew with G. F. Vernon's XI 146 (R. Peel 51).

19th Match: v XV of Tasmania (Hobart)   Jan 26, 27, 28.
G. F. Vernon's XI 297 (R. Peel 119) drew with Tasmania 405 (K. Burn 99, MacLeod 50, R. Peel 6-89).

20th Match: v XVIII of Benalla (Benalla)   Feb 2, 3.
G. F. Vernon's XI 271 beat Benalla 126 & 92 by an inns & 53 runs.

21st Match: v XXII of Cootamundra (Cootamundra)   Feb 7, 8.
Cootamundra 105 (R. Peel 13-61) & 20-2 drew with G. F. Vernon's XI 243 (R. Abel 92*).

22nd Match: v New South Wales (Sydney)   Feb 17, 18, 20, 21.
G. F. Vernon's XI 337 (W. W. Read 119, C. T. B. Turner 5-128) & 109-2 (W. W. Read 53*, R. Peel 52*) beat N.S.W. 193 & 252 (P. S. McDonnell 56) by 8 wkts.

23rd Match: v XXII of Goulburn (Goulburn)   Feb 24, 25.
Goulburn 124 (R. Peel 13-43) drew with G. F. Vernon's XI 31 (Knopp 5-12) & 157.

24th Match: v XVIII of Wagga Wagga (Wagga Wagga)   Feb 28, 29.
Wagga Wagga 62 & 106 lost to G. F. Vernon's XI 173 by an inns & 5 runs.

25th Match: v 1888 Australians (Melbourne)   March 2, 3, 5.
G. F. Vernon's XI 221 (A. E. Newton 54) & 117 (C. T. B. Turner 7-48) beat Australians 219 (T. P. Horan 67, W. Attewell 5-33) & 32 (W. Attewell 7-15) by 87 runs.

26th Match: v Victoria (Melbourne)   March 9, 10, 12.
G. F. Vernon's XI 130 & 368 (W. W. Read 142, A. E. Stoddart 75, J. Worrall 5-33) beat Victoria 81 (W. Attewell 6-30) & 135 (W. Attewell 5-28) by 282 runs.

Match by Combined English Teams: v Australia (Sydney)   Feb 10, 11, 13, 14, 15.
England 113 (C. T. B. Turner 5-44) & 137 (C. T. B. Turner 7-43) beat Australia 42 (G. A. Lohmann 5-17, R. Peel 5-18) & 82 (R. Peel 5-40) by 126 runs.

G. F. Vernon's party to Australia in 1887-88, photographed in Melbourne. Back: J. T. Rawlin, M. P. Bowden, G. F. Vernon, Sir T. C. O'Brien, J. Beaumont. Centre: A. E. Newton, W. Bates, the Hon M. B. Hawke (captain), W. Attewell, R. Peel. Front: R. Abel, W. W. Read, A. E. Stoddart.

the South Australians met an England touring party on even terms. Unfortunately several of the best locals could not play, but as matters turned out the English side did not have the walk-over they expected, winning by only 71 runs. Neither W. W. Read (sprained ankle) or G. F. Vernon (badly cut ear) could turn out in this game. Poor weather and a poor attendance matched each other for the second game – against Victoria at Melbourne – which resulted in an innings victory for the tourists. Three up-country matches were contested before the side went to Sydney to play New South Wales. After a fairly even first innings, the visitors collapsed against Turner and Ferris and N.S.W. knocked off the runs required for the loss of one wicket. The Saturday was almost rained off, but a crowd of about 5,000 was present on each of two of the other days. Six odd matches were played in succession – in the second of these at Hawkesbury the captain, the Hon M. B. Hawke, learnt of the death of his father, and immediately left the team in order to travel back to England. G. F. Vernon was appointed captain in his place.

The next eleven-a-side match was the return with South Australia. The high scoring match – W. W. Read made 183 and George Giffen 203 – went into the fifth day, and despite an agreement that it would be played out was left drawn so that the team could travel to Melbourne for the scheduled match against 'Combined Australia'. The effort to get the best Australian eleven failed, only five of the side being worthy of a place in such a team. The Englishmen had no difficulty in winning by an innings.

A match at Yarra Bend was followed by a trip to Tasmania, where four matches against odds were played. Of these the best was at Hobart against Eighteen of Combined Tasmania. The locals hit 405 of which J. Burn made 99 – according to some sources he actually reached 100. At any rate a collection was made for him on the ground.

Getting back to the mainland, the side played at Cootamundra and then the two English touring sides selected the best eleven from among themselves and met Australia in what should have been the best match ever played between the two countries. Six of the leading Australians however could not or would not play, and in rotten weather with few spectators, the England side won with ease, aided by the fact that the Australian captain, McDonnell, put them in to bat on a dead wicket. Walter Read led the Combined England Team.

New South Wales were handicapped by the absence of Ferris for their return game with the tourists. A splendid century by Walter Read gave his team a good lead on first innings and the match was won by 8 wkts – the match was played in pleasant weather, but did not attract the crowds.

Of the two remaining eleven-a-side matches one was against the Australian Team due to tour England in 1888, in which match rain caused the wicket to become very nasty in the final innings, and although needing just 120, the Australians were all out for 32,

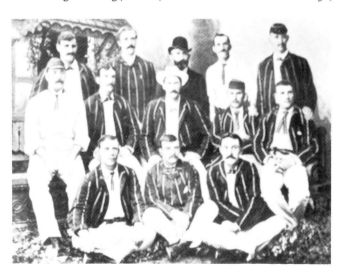

1887-88: Lillywhite, Shaw and Shrewsbury's Team to Australia and New Zealand

1st Match: v XVIII of Parramatta (Parramatta) Nov 4, 5.
Parramatta 72 (J. Briggs 9-33) & 241-16 drew with A. Shrewsbury's XI 272 (G. Ulyett 73).

2nd Match: v New South Wales (Sydney) Nov 11, 12.
A. Shrewsbury's XI 49 (J. J. Ferris 6-24) & 66 (C. T. B. Turner 6-23) lost to N.S.W. 94 (G. A. Lohmann 5-26) & 25-0 by 10 wkts.

3rd Match: v XVIII of Queensland (Brisbane) Nov 18, 19, 21.
Queensland 79 & 59 (C. A. Smith 10-28) lost to A. Shrewsbury's XI 138 & 2-0 by 10 wkts.

4th Match: v XXII of Maryborough (Maryborough) Nov 23, 24.
A. Shrewsbury's XI 166 beat Maryborough 41 (J. Briggs 14-25) & 104 (C. A. Smith 11-11, G. A. Lohmann 10-51) by an inns & 21 runs.

5th Match: v XXII of Gympie (Gympie) Nov 25-26.
Gympie 45 (J. Briggs 13-24) & 79 lost to A. Shrewsbury's XI 269 (L. C. Docker 58) by an inns & 145 runs.

6th Match: v XVIII of Queensland (Brisbane) Dec 2, 3, 5.
A. Shrewsbury's XI 133 (A. Coningham 5-73) & 185 (G. A. Lohmann 53) beat Queensland 93 (G. A. Lohmann 7-30) & 116 (J. Briggs 12-47) by 114 runs.

7th Match: v New South Wales (Sydney) Dec 9, 10, 12.
N.S.W. 149 (H. Moses 68*) & 165 lost to A. Shrewsbury's XI 279 (C. A. Smith 68, C. T. B. Turner 7-117) & 39-0 by 10 wkts.

8th Match: v Victoria (Melbourne) Dec 16, 17, 19.
Victoria 68 & 100 lost to A. Shrewsbury's XI 624 (A. Shrewsbury 232, G. Brann 118, J. Briggs 75) by an inns & 456 runs.

9th Match: v XXII of Ballarat (Ballarat) Dec 24, 26, 27.
Ballarat 102 & 127 lost to A. Shrewsbury's XI 152 (L. C. Docker 50, J. Duffy 5-37) & 83-2 (J. M. Read 51*) by 8 wkts.

10th Match: v XVIII of Bendigo (Sandhurst) Dec 31, Jan 2.
A. Shrewsbury's XI 389 (J. M. Preston 78, R. Pilling 67, G. Ulyett 64, G. Brann 56*) drew with Bendigo 165 & 61-6.

11th Match: v XVIII Melbourne Juniors (North Fitzroy) Jan 6, 7.
A. Shrewsbury's XI 124 (A. Shrewsbury 51) & 131 drew with Juniors 158 (G. A. Lohmann 8-52).

12th Match: v XXII of Bowral (Bowral) Jan 10, 11.
A. Shrewsbury's XI 126 beat Bowral 42 (J. Briggs 14-20) & 57 (C. A. Smith 9-15) by an inns & 27 runs.

13th Match: v New South Wales (Sydney) Jan 13, 14, 16, 17.
N.S.W. 153 (H. Moses 58, G. A. Lohmann 7-68) & 216 (H. Moses 109, G. A. Lohmann 7-97) beat A. Shrewsbury's XI 87 (C. T. B. Turner 8-39) & 129 (A. Shrewsbury 56, C. T. B. Turner 8-40) by 153 runs.

14th Match: v XXII of Bourke (Bourke) Jan 20, 21.
A. Shrewsbury's XI 69 & 157-6 drew with Bourke 104 (J. M. Preston 8-44).

15th Match: v XXII of Orange (Orange) Jan 27, 28.
Orange 76 (J. Briggs 12-37) & 52 lost to A. Shrewsbury's XI 208 (J. M. Read 55) by an inns & 80 runs.

16th Match: v Combined Australia (Sydney) Feb 3, 4, 6, 7.
Australia 262 (P. S. McDonnell 54, G. A. Lohmann 5-83) & 83 (G. A. Lohmann 7-43) lost to A. Shrewsbury's XI 295 (G. Ulyett 72, W. Newham 53, P. G. McShane 5-103) & 51-5 by 5 wkts.

17th Match: v XVIII of Newcastle (Newcastle) Feb 16, 17, 18.
A. Shrewsbury's XI 226 (J. Briggs 80) & 42-1 drew with Newcastle 107 (G. A. Lohmann 7-37) & 222 (Wooden 51, C. A. Smith 6-13).

18th Match: v XXII of Tamworth (Tamworth) Feb 21, 22.
Tamworth 104 (J. Briggs 11-45) & 98 (G. A. Lohmann 7-12) lost to A. Shrewsbury's XI 183 & 20-1 by 9 wkts.

19th Match: v 1888 Australians (Sydney) Feb 24, 25.
A. Shrewsbury's XI 173 (A. Shrewsbury 51, C. T. B. Turner 5-64) beat Australians 75 (J. Briggs 6-40) & 56 (J. Briggs 5-18, G. A. Lohmann 5-37) by an inns & 42 runs.

20th Match: v XVIII Sydney Juniors (Sydney) March 2, 3, 5.
Juniors 181 (McDowall 58, J. M. Preston 8-45) & 153 drew with A. Shrewsbury's XI 175 & 5-1.

21st Match: v XVIII of Bathurst (Bathurst) March 6, 7.
Bathurst 57 & 129 lost to A. Shrewsbury's XI 180 & 7-2 by 8 wkts.

22nd Match: v 1888 Australians (Sydney) March 9, 10, 12, 13.
A. Shrewsbury's XI 212 (C. A. Smith 59, C. T. B. Turner 7-72) & 402 (A. Shrewsbury 206, J. Briggs 54) beat Australians 190 (J. McC. Blackham 97) & 266 (S. P. Jones 134) by 158 runs.

23rd Match: v XVIII of Wellington (Wellington) March 23, 24.
A. Shrewsbury's XI 207 (J. M. Read 70) & 21-1 drew with Wellington 86 (G. A. Lohmann 13-37) & 222 (Werry 53*).

24th Match: v XVIII of Canterbury (Christchurch) March 26, 27, 28, 29.
Canterbury 145 & 80 (J. Briggs 9-43) drew with A. Shrewsbury's XI 78 & 31-0.

25th Match: v XVIII of Canterbury (Christchurch) March 30, 31.
A. Shrewsbury's XI 140 (R. Halley 6-50) & 100 (H. R. Mathias 6-36) drew with Canterbury 64 (J. Briggs 9-26) & 37-9.

The team taken by Shaw and Shrewsbury to Australia in 1887-88. Back: G. Brann, L. C. Docker, J. Lillywhite, J. M. Read, A. D. Pougher. Centre: G. Ulyett, R. Pilling, C. A. Smith (capt), A. Shrewsbury, G. A. Lohmann. Front: J. M. Preston, J. Briggs, W. Newham. The captain, 'Round-the-Corner' Smith, later became the famous film actor, C. Aubrey Smith.

1887-88: Lillywhite, Shaw and Shrewsbury's Team to Australia

Batting Averages

	M	I	NO	R	HS	Avge	'100	c/s
A. Shrewsbury (Notts)	8	14	1	766	232	58.92	2	14
G. Brann (Sussex)	5	8	2	158	118	26.33	1	3
C. A. Smith (Sussex)	6	8	0	197	69	24.62	0	4
G. Ulyett (Yorks)	6	10	1	201	72	22.33	0	3
J. Briggs (Lancs)	8	13	1	229	75	19.08	0	7
J. M. Read (Surrey)	8	13	0	218	39	16.76	0	3
A. D. Pougher (Leics)	6	9	2	107	25*	15.28	0	5
L. C. Docker (Derbys)	7	11	1	138	48	13.80	0	6
G. A. Lohmann (Surrey)	8	13	0	173	39	13.30	0	10
W. Newham (Sussex)	7	12	0	146	53	12.16	0	6
J. M. Preston (Yorks)	7	10	1	81	27	9.00	0	3
R. Pilling (Lancs)	8	12	5	48	10	6.85	0	16/6

Bowling Averages

	O	M	R	W	Avge	BB	5i
G. A. Lohmann	659.1	354	755	63	11.98	7-43	7
J. Briggs	371.1	215	436	30	14.53	6-40	2
A. D. Pougher	156	79	189	12	15.75	4-40	0
J. M. Preston	216.2	102	307	17	18.05	4-16	0
C. A. Smith	121	57	153	7	21.85	3-11	0
G. Ulyett	22	5	49	1	49.00	1-32	0

Played in non-first-class matches only: McCormick and Charleston (or Clarkson).
Note: Records in Test Match by 'Combined' Team included.

Attewell taking 7 for 15, and the other was against Victoria, when after a low scoring first innings by each team, Walter Read hit 142 not out and victory was obtained by 282 runs.

After this game a One-day match was organised for the benefit of William Bates, who had been hit in the eye whilst at net practice in Melbourne and had missed most of the fixtures as a result. Considering the loss of both Bates and Lord Hawke for most of the tour, the team had an excellent record – it was a pity that attendances were poor and the visit clashed with the rival venture. It was reported that the Melbourne Club lost £2,000 on the speculation. The team arrived back at Plymouth on 28 April, but without Stoddart who remained in Australia.

Turning to the travels of the party under Lillywhite, Shaw and Shrewsbury, the team, which played its first match at Parramatta on 4 November, consisted of C. A. Smith (capt), W. Newham and G. Brann of Sussex; L. C. Docker of Warwickshire and the following professionals: A. Shrewsbury (Notts); G. Ulyett and J. M. Preston (Yorkshire); A. D. Pougher (Leics); J. Briggs and R. Pilling (Lancashire); G. A. Lohmann and J. M. Read (Surrey). Alfred Shaw did not make the trip.

In their second game the side were caught on a sticky wicket at Sydney and Turner and Ferris bowled them out twice for 115, the match – against New South Wales – being lost by 10 wickets. From Sydney, the team went by steamer to Brisbane, where they played Eighteen of Queensland on the new Exhibition Ground. A fair crowd watched the game and saw the visitors win a low-scoring contest.

At Maryborough, the experiment was made of laying the matting wicket on a thick spread of sawdust. This resulted in a very slow pitch, but with the ball doing the unexpected, it was not a success. An eleven-a-side exhibition game preceded the return with Queensland, which was poorly attended – on the Saturday, a beautiful day, only 1,200 turned up and the last day only 50. Crowds were much improved at Sydney for the second game against New South Wales and for once the English batsmen mastered Turner and Ferris to win the match by 10 wickets.

Victoria put out a very poor side against the tourists and suffered mightily; Shrewsbury took the opportunity to make 232 and the total rose to 624 – victory was achieved by an innings and 456 runs. In reporting the game, one journalist noted: 'Cricket in Melbourne is now very dull, in fact, more so than in any other Australian metropolis. The leading cricketers themselves are stupidly lukewarm, and, seeing that that is the case, the apathy of the public is not surprising.' Shrewsbury's score, the team total and the margin of the win were all records for matches between English teams and the colonies.

Four up-country games came after the success at Melbourne and then the side again pitted its strength against Turner and Ferris – Turner took 16 wickets for 79 and only a splendid fifty

by Shrewsbury prevented complete humiliation. As it was the defeat was by a margin of 153 runs – the second and happily last loss of the tour.

The next major fixture was against 'Combined Australia' and the home side was fairly strong, though Ferris (injured) had to stand down. On the first two days some good cricket was seen, then rain ruined the wicket and gave the bowlers an easy time. The tourists however achieved a deserved victory by 5 wickets. The next eleven-a-side match was also against an Australian team. Shrewsbury hit a workmanlike fifty and then Lohmann and Briggs bowled the tourists to an innings victory. Rain kept the attendance down. The return match against the same Australian combination took place a fortnight later on a hard and true wicket. The first two innings were very even, but Shrewsbury then proceeded to hit another double century and the side just topped 400. S. P. Jones went in at the fall of the second wicket for Australia and carried out his bat for an excellent 134, but the English side won by 158 runs. This was the final match in Australia – the tourists travelled to New Zealand, but without L. C. Docker, arriving on 22 March. The programme in New Zealand consisted of three matches only – one at Wellington and two at Christchurch, all against odds. The side returned to England in the *Coptic*, which reached Plymouth on 12 May.

The tour was a success from the playing angle, but financially Shaw and Shrewsbury lost £2,400 – Lillywhite was unable to meet his share of the loss. It was the last speculative venture by the professional trio.

1888-89: C. Aubrey Smith captains the first tour to South Africa

Major R. Gardner Warton, who served in South Africa for five years on the General Staff, retired at the beginning of 1888 and determined to take a party of English cricketers to Southern Africa in the winter of 1888-89. Major Warton had a difficult task when selecting the team, since the strength of cricket in South Africa compared to that in England was an unknown quantity. The team he chose contained seven men who appeared regularly in first-class County cricket in 1888: C. A. Smith (Sussex) (capt), M. P. Bowden (Surrey) and professionals R. Abel (Surrey), J. M. Read (Surrey), H. Wood (Surrey), J. Briggs (Lancs), F. Hearne (Kent). There was one other professional, A. J. Fothergill (Somerset) and five amateurs of good club standard: Hon C. J. Coventry, J. E. P. McMaster, J. H. Roberts, B. A. F. Grieve and A. C. Skinner.

The side left England on 21 November aboard the *Garth Castle*, calling at Lisbon and Madeira before landing at Cape Town on 14 December. The first match was played on the Newlands Ground against Twenty-two of Western Province and after a close finish was lost by 17 runs. After six games had been completed, four of which were lost, the press were critical of the strength of the English side, but this was of course comment made with hindsight. About Christmas time the side lost J. H. Roberts, who was called back to England on account of the death of his mother. Major Warton then decided to acquire the services of George Ulyett, the Yorkshire batsman, but he did not join the team until 6 February. Away from the Cape, the team encountered cricket fields with not a single blade of grass on them. The grounds, being brick coloured clay, were sprinkled with sand to absorb the moisture. The surface of the wicket had been rolled until it was as hard as asphalt and as level as a billiard table. The ball came off the pitch much faster than in England and rose about six inches higher.

Following the poor start the side improved. Twenty-two of

The play however was not very noteworthy, the English team winning by 8 wickets.

C. A. Smith went down with an attack of fever shortly after the match and for the final fixtures, M. P. Bowden took on the role of captain. A return match against South Africa terminated the visit – Abel hit another chanceless hundred and Briggs took 15 wickets for 28 runs to give 'England' victory by an innings.

The side sailed back to England in the *Garth Castle* arriving on 16 April. C. A. Smith and M. P. Bowden remained behind in South Africa.

From the playing viewpoint the visit, after a deceptive start, was a great success, but despite quite good attendances, the receipts did not cover Major Warton's expenses.

1889-90: one defeat for the first tourists to India

In the autumn of 1889 a team of amateurs under the captaincy and management of G. F. Vernon left England for the Indian sub-continent. Although this was the first English tour to that part of the world, two Indian sides had already visited England and demonstrated that the standard of cricket in India was rapidly improving, both in regard to the native Indian sides and to the cricket played by the Europeans in India. The quality of cricket in Ceylon was not so high, but English teams calling there on the way to Australia could be in no doubt as to the enthusiasm of the population for the game.

The main body of the touring party was G. F. Vernon, J. G. Walker and H. Philipson (Middx), E. M. Lawson-Smith, A. E. Leatham, J. H. J. Hornsby, A. E. Gibson, T. K. Tapling and G. H. Goldney, who left Tilbury on 31 October. Lord Hawke, the Yorkshire cricketer, had gone on ahead, and E. R. de Little

Johannesburg were beaten by 10 wickets, thanks to some extent to the insistence of C. A. Smith that a green matting wicket be used, thus cutting down the glare. Abel hit a chanceless hundred in the next game and Fifteen of Transvaal were beaten by an innings – to the surprise of the tourists no Dutchmen appeared in the opposition team. Several gold mines were visited during the stay in Johannesburg, and on the final day there the public banquet for the team went on so long that no sleep at all was obtained. Two games were played at Pietersmaritzburg, both providing innings victories with Briggs taking most wickets. Travelling to Durban, the side returned to a grass outfield with a matting wicket. The steamy hot weather worried most of the tourists and a very even draw against the local Eighteen resulted. The journey from Durban to East London was made by boat and three successive wins by innings were obtained – two at Kingwilliamstown and one at Grahamstown, all against Twenty-twos.

The most important match of the tour and the first eleven-a-side fixture was staged at Port Elizabeth on a green matting wicket. The opposing team was a representative South African eleven, which except for the absence of Theunissen of Cape Town, was quite the strongest team that could be formed. About 3,000 people were present to witness the start of this game, which is now regarded as the first Test Match between the two countries.

and F. L. Shand were to join the side in Colombo. It was hoped that C. I. Thornton would play in some matches, since he was also visiting India – in fact he did not. As the side contained only three cricketers who appeared regularly in county matches in 1889 – Vernon, Walker and Lord Hawke – it would be generous to say that as a whole the party was 'first-class' by English standards.

Arriving in Colombo on 26 November, the cricketers found that the Colombo Cricket Club had arranged a large programme of entertainments in honour of the visit, including various balls, dinners and theatricals.

As T. K. Tapling had had to stop over in Naples and neither Shand (playing in Ceylon) or de Little were available, the first match was played with three substitutes, but the tourists still won with an innings to spare. The second – and only other game in Ceylon – was also won by an innings.

From Ceylon the side went to Calcutta and opposed the local Club. Calcutta batted first and C. E. Greenway carried his bat right through the innings for a faultless 130. A. E. Gibson hit a century for the tourists and the game appeared very even. The Calcutta Club however collapsed in its second innings and the tourists won by nine wickets. After five further matches, the team met the Parsis Eleven in Bombay for the most important fixture of the visit. About 10,000 spectators attended on the first day of the three-day game and saw the tourists dismissed for 97. The Parsis in their turn went for only 82 but some excellent bowling by M. E. Pavri put them back in the game – he took 7 for 34 – and the Parsis required only 77 to win the final innings. M. E. Pavri scored a vital 21 and the tourists suffered their only defeat by 4 wickets. The four remaining matches were rather an anti-climax, three being won by large margins and the fourth drawn.

The tour helped to stimulate interest in the game in India and was generally regarded as a success; unfortunately Lord Hawke was taken ill and could play in only four matches, the Hon A. M. Curzon being co-opted into the team. No less than 14 players were included in the team during the tour in emergency!

United States where cricket took pride of place over baseball and this was reflected in the other matches of the tour. In these engagements the opposition was poor and, though enjoyable from the social viewpoint, the matches were almost non-contests. In Boston there were two good bowlers, Chambers and Wright, in Chicago a good all-rounder, Dr Ogden, and Boyd in Toronto and Bristow in Ottawa showed themselves useful batsmen, but the rest were enthusiastic club cricketers.

The only casualty of the tour was G. W. Hillyard who suffered from sunstroke and came home early. The programme of matches ended on 24 October and the team were back in England on 5 November.

1891: Lord Hawke takes a side to the United States and Canada

G. F. Vernon had intended to take a second team to India in the autumn of 1891, but this having been abandoned, C. W. Alcock, the Surrey secretary, began to organise an amateur tour to North America. Alcock, for business reasons, could not complete the arrangements and Lord Hawke, the Yorkshire captain, took over the managing and selecting of the side. The team contained only five who appeared regularly in first-class games in 1891: the captain, H. T. Hewett (Somerset), S. M. J. Woods (Cambridge U and Somerset), K. J. Key (Surrey) and C. W. Wright (Notts). The remainder of the party consisted of Lord Throwley, the Hon H. A. Milles, G. W. Ricketts, C. Wreford-Brown, K. McAlpine, J. H. J. Hornsby and G. W. Hillyard.

The side was a little stronger than Vernon's Team of 1889-90 and might be described as a moderate first-class combination.

Leaving England on 16 September, the team suffered a rough sea passage, and landing in New York went straight to Philadelphia to play the two most important fixtures of the programme. The initial match was on the ground of the Germantown Club, which the visitors regarded as the equal of any in the world, a splendid pavilion having been recently erected. The Philadelphians, though losing the toss, played well, with G. S. Patterson their best bat making 68 and 43 not out, and the visitors were defeated by 8 wickets. In the return fixture S. M. J. Woods, helped by an over-watered wicket, bowled out the Philadelphians cheaply and avenged the defeat. Philadelphia was the only city in the

1891-92: Lord Sheffield's speculative tour to revive Australian interest

Since the disastrous dual tours of 1887-88, cricket in Australia had been falling in popularity. The Australian side which visited England in 1890 had been beaten in both Tests and its predecessor of 1888 had lost the Test series 2 matches to 1. The internal squabbles between Melbourne and Sydney had done nothing to improve the standing of the game. The press were of the opinion that an English tour was required to stimulate the game in Australia, but as no one in Australia cared to finance such a venture, Lord Sheffield, the great patron of Sussex cricket, decided to try and organise a tour. He first stated that he would not finance the side unless W. G. Grace would agree to captain it and when the Grand Old Man assented, this virtually insured the success of the scheme. Both Shrewsbury and Gunn, the Notts batsmen, refused the terms offered, but Lord Sheffield met with no other refusals of consequence and the side was composed of W. G. Grace and O. G. Radcliffe (Gloucestershire), A. E. Stoddart (Middlesex), G. MacGregor (Cambridge U) and H. Philipson (Northumberland) and the professionals G. A. Lohmann, R. Abel, J. M. Read and J. W. Sharpe (Surrey), W. Attewell (Notts), R. Peel (Yorks), J. Briggs (Lancs) and G. Bean (Sussex). Alfred Shaw, who was employed by Lord Sheffield, went as manager.

The team played matches at Malta and Colombo on the outward journey and began the tour proper at Adelaide on 20 November. The team were confident of victory in the three Tests and wins by an innings at Adelaide and then at Melbourne against Victoria seemed to justify this confidence. Peel missed the Victorian match due to an attack of pleurisy, which happily was of brief duration. W. G. Grace carried his bat through the visitors' innings and appropriately the band struck up 'See the Conquering Hero Comes', as the famous old cricketer went to the wicket.

The third game – against New South Wales – had its start delayed by an hour, when the home captain objected to D. Cotter standing as umpire and W. G. Grace refused to replace him; eventually Alfred Shaw agreed to stand to the satisfaction of both parties. The English win in this game was only by 4 wickets, due to their old adversary Turner, who took 11 wickets.

Six up-country matches were played in succession before the tourists met Australia in the First Test at Melbourne. A crowd of 20,110 came to watch the first day's play and the same number on the second, whilst over 10,000 came on both the third and fourth days. England seemed to have the match in hand, but collapsed against Turner in the final innings after 60 runs were on the board with one wicket down. The better side won and both elevens suffered equally from injury – Briggs and Bean had cut hands, Moses strained his leg and Turner was ill in bed on the first day.

Another six up-country fixtures went by before the Second Test at Sydney. The betting opened at 3 to 1 on England – the bookmakers being as common as on previous English visits. Excellent bowling by Lohmann, after Australia won the toss and elected to bat, reduced the home side to 145 all out. Moses, who was injured in the previous Test, again strained his leg, but the request for a substitute fielder when England batted was at first refused by Grace, who then relented, but refused to permit Syd Gregory to act in that capacity – Gregory being a much better fielder than Moses. A determined innings by Abel, who carried out his bat, gave England a lead of 162 and England looked set for an innings victory. Lyons, Bannerman and Giffen however put Australia back in the game and then rain made the wicket difficult. Dropped catches aided Australia's cause still further, so that England needed 230 to win. Abel, Bean and Grace were all out for 11 and good bowling by Turner and Giffen ran through the remainder. The report of the game ends: 'The enthusiasm at the finish was something to remember. The crowd howled and yelled, and cheered themselves hoarse and it was sometime before they left the ground.'

The next eleven-a-side game was the return with New South Wales. Centuries from Maurice Read and Lohmann, the latter rather lucky, took the score to 414 and from then the result of the game was hardly in doubt. One of the umpires took objection to a remark made by W. G. Grace concerning a decision and the official refused to stand in the remainder of the match. The match against Victoria provided another win for the English team and came directly before the final fixture, the third Test at Adelaide.

1891-92: Lord Sheffield's Team to Australia

Batting Averages

	M	I	NO	R	HS	Avge	100	c/s
W. G. Grace (Gloucs)	8	11	1	448	159*	44.80	1	17
R. Abel (Surrey)	8	12	2	388	132*	38.80	1	10
A. E. Stoddart (Middx)	8	12	0	450	134	37.50	1	5
J. M. Read (Surrey)	8	11	0	328	106	29.81	1	3
R. Peel (Yorks)	7	11	2	229	83	25.44	0	8
G. A. Lohmann (Surrey)	8	11	1	222	102	22.20	1	9
J. Briggs (Lancs)	8	13	0	262	91	20.15	0	8
G. Bean (Sussex)	7	11	1	178	50	17.80	0	5
H. Philipson (Middx)	2	2	1	16	15*	16.00	0	2/3
W. Attewell (Notts)	8	11	3	126	43*	15.75	0	7
G. MacGregor (Middx)	7	9	2	101	31	14.42	0	10/2
J. W. Sharpe (Surrey)	7	9	3	63	26	10.50	0	5
O. G. Radcliffe (Gloucs)	2	3	0	31	18	10.33	0	0

Bowling Averages

	O	M	R	W	Avge	BB	5i
W. Attewell	497.5	241	573	44	13.02	6-34	4
J. Briggs	212.4	71	420	32	13.12	6-49	4
G. A. Lohmann	416.3	178	640	40	16.00	8-58	2
R. Peel	192.3	83	283	15	18.13	4-50	0
W. G. Grace	73.1	21	134	5	26.80	3-64	0
J. W. Sharpe	287	113	508	17	29.88	6-40	2

Also bowled: A. E. Stoddart 9-3-22-0.
Played in non-first-class matches only: K. McArthur.

Lord Sheffield's team to Australia in 1891-92, photographed in the Botanical Gardens in Adelaide. Back: A. Shaw, A. E. Stoddart, J. M. Read, H. Phillipson, O. G. Radcliffe. Front: R. Abel, G. A. Lohmann, G. MacGregor, J. Briggs, R. Peel, Dr W. G. Grace (captain), W. Attewell, G. Bean, J. Sharpe.

1891-92: Lord Sheffield's Team to Malta, Ceylon and Australia

1st Match: v Malta (Naval Ground) (One Day)   Oct 9.
Lord Sheffield's XII 200-9 dec drew with Malta XVIII 88-13.

2nd Match: v XXII of Ceylon (Colombo) (One Day)   Oct 27.
Lord Sheffield's XI 143 (A. E. Stoddart 70) drew with Ceylon 70-10 (J. Briggs 6-31).

3rd Match: v South Australia (Adelaide)   Nov 20, 21, 22.
S. Australia 163 (W. Attewell 5-47) & 98 (W. Attewell 6-34) lost to Lord Sheffield's XI 323 (J. Briggs 91, A. E. Stoddart 78, J. M. Read 60, G. Giffen 7-152) by an inns & 62.

4th Match: v Victoria (Melbourne)   Nov 27, 28.
Victoria 73 (J. W. Sharpe 6-40) & 104 (W. Attewell 5-41, G. A. Lohmann 5-41) lost to Lord Sheffield's XI 284 (W. G. Grace 159) by an inns & 107 runs.*

5th Match: v New South Wales (Sydney)   Dec 4, 5, 7.
N.S.W. 74 (J. Briggs 5-10) & 172 (H. Moses 55, W. Attewell 6-49) lost to Lord Sheffield's XI 94 (C. T. B. Turner 6-45) & 155-6 (C. T. B. Turner 5-77) by 4 wkts.

6th Match: v XX of Cumberland (Parramatta)   Dec 9, 10.
Cumberland 67 (J. Briggs 12-38) & 141 drew with Lord Sheffield's XII 113 & 29-2.

7th Match: v XXII of Camden (Camden)   Dec 11, 12.
Lord Sheffield's XII 184 (H. Philipson 50) beat Camden 54 (G. A. Lohmann 12-17) & 87 (J. Briggs 13-29) by an inns & 43 runs.

8th Match: v XXIV of Bowral (Bowral)   Dec 15, 16.
Lord Sheffield's XII 156 & 64-7 dec beat Bowral 77 (J. Briggs 12-46) & 76 (J. Briggs 12-41) by 67 runs.

9th Match: v XXII of Goulburn (Goulburn)   Dec 18, 19.
Goulburn 57 (R. Peel 15-27) & 114 lost to Lord Sheffield's XII 187-5 dec (J. M. Read 53) by an inns & 16 runs.*

10th Match: v XVI of Melbourne Club (Melbourne)   Dec 22, 23.
Melbourne 156 & 88-2 drew with Lord Sheffield's XII 175 (G. Bean 57).

11th Match: v XX of Ballarat (Ballarat)   Dec 26, 28, 29.
Lord Sheffield's XII 424 (G. A. Lohmann 106, W. G. Grace 62) beat Ballarat 139 & 151 (J. Williams 53) by an inns & 134 runs.

12th Match: v Combined Australia (Melbourne)   Jan 1, 3, 4, 5, 6.
Australia 240 (W. Bruce 57, J. W. Sharpe 6-84) & 236 (J. J. Lyons 51) beat England 264 (W. G. Grace 50, G. Bean 50, R. W. McLeod 5-55) & 158 (C. T. B. Turner 5-51) by 54 runs.

13th Match: v XVI of East Melbourne (East Melbourne)   Jan 7, 8.
E. Melbourne 177 (A. S. Carter 55) & 35-2 drew with Lord Sheffield's XII 201 (R. Abel 50, C. Letcher 5-63).

14th Match: v XVI of South Melbourne (Melbourne)   Jan 9, 11.
Lord Sheffield's XII 438 (W. G. Grace 69, G. McGregor 61, J. M. Read 60) drew with S. Melbourne 102-8.

15th Match: v XXII of Williamstown (Williamstown)   Jan 13.
Williamstown 154 (W. G. Grace 11-53) drew with Lord Sheffield's XII 43-1.

16th Match: v XXII of Bairnsdale (Bairnsdale)   Jan 15, 16.
Lord Sheffield's XII 269 (G. A. Lohmann 86) beat Bairnsdale 41 (J. Briggs 13-29) & 130 (R. Abel 11-61) by an inns & 98 runs.

17th Match: v XXII of Malvern (Malvern)   Jan 21, 22.
Malvern 191 (A. Haddrick 59, G. A. Lohmann 12-40) & 23-2 drew with Lord Sheffield's XII 143.

18th Match: v XX Melbourne Juniors (Melbourne)   Jan 23, 25, 26.
Lord Sheffield's XII 116 (A. E. Stoddart 52, P. O'Shannassy 5-26) & 155 drew with Juniors 131 (G. A. Lohmann 13-57) & 105-16.

19th Match: v Combined Australia (Sydney)   Jan 29, 30, Feb 1, 2, 3.
Australia 145 (G. A. Lohmann 8-58) & 391 (J. J. Lyons 134, A. C. Bannerman 91, W. Bruce 72) beat England 307 (R. Abel 132*) & 157 (A. E. Stoddart 69, G. Giffen 6-72) by 72 runs.

20th Match: v XX of Newcastle (Newcastle)   Feb 5, 6.
Lord Sheffield's XII 269 (J. M. Read 85, R. Peel 68, W. G. Grace 54, Creswick 6-51) drew with Newcastle 42-6.

21st Match: v XXII of Manly (Manly)   Feb 11, 12.
Lord Sheffield's XII 136 (S. Ridge 5-65) & 282 (G. Bean 84, R. Peel 71, W. Fraser 5-83, S. Ridge 5-109) drew with Manly 98.*

22nd Match: v XXII Sydney Juniors (Sydney)   Feb 12, 13, 15.
Juniors 318 (W. Camphin 71, R. Driver 71) drew with Lord Sheffield's XII 162 (Morgan 5-59) & 33-2.

23rd Match: v XXIII of Nepean (Penrith)   Feb 16, 17.
Nepean 112 (W. G. Grace 10-39) & 71-12 drew with Lord Sheffield's XII 162.

24th Match: v New South Wales (Sydney)   Feb 19, 20, 22, 23.
Lord Sheffield's XII 414 (J. M. Read 94, G. A. Lohmann 102) & 42-3 beat N.S.W. 244 (C. T. B. Turner 66) & 210 (S. E. Gregory 93) by 7 wkts.*

25th Match: v XXII of Illawara (Wollongong)   Feb 26, 27.
Lord Sheffield's XII 144-8 (R. Abel 50) rain ended play.

26th Match: v XV of Southern Tasmania (Hobart)   March 4, 5, 7.
Lord Sheffield's XII 243 (A. E. Stoddart 84, Kendall 7-79) beat S. Tasmania 66 (G. A. Lohmann 12-50) & 138 (G. A. Lohmann 13-53) by an inns & 39 runs.

27th Match: v XVIII of N. Tasmania (Launceston)   March 10, 11, 12.
Lord Sheffield's XII 400 (J. M. Read 95, J. Briggs 74) drew with N. Tasmania 130 & 135-6.

28th Match: v Victoria (Melbourne)   March 17, 18, 19.
Victoria 137 (W. Bruce 54) & 100 (W. Bruce 50, J. Briggs 5-33) lost to Lord Sheffield's XI 184 (J. Worrall 5-34) & 57-1 by 9 wkts.

29th Match: v Combined Australia (Adelaide)   March 24, 25, 26, 28.
England 499 (A. E. Stoddart 134, R. Peel 83, W. G. Grace 58, J. M. Read 57) beat Australia 100 (J. Briggs 6-49) & 169 (J. Briggs 6-87) by an inns & 230 runs.

On a splendid wicket, England batted first and with Stoddart hitting a well-judged 134 and Peel making 82, the total realised 499, but Australia must take some 'credit' for this as their fielding was decidedly poor. Rain on the second afternoon transformed the wicket and with Briggs taking full advantage of the conditions, England ended their tour with an innings victory.

The fielding and bowling of the side was fully up to expectations, but the team lacked steady batsmen of the calibre of Gunn and Shrewsbury, and this resulted in the loss of two Tests. Although the attendances were good in the three main centres, the tour lost money, Lord Sheffield being out of pocket to the tune of £2,000 – the total cost of the visit having been £16,000.

1891-92: bowlers too good for South Africans

It was thought that the idea of an English cricket tour to South Africa in the winter of 1891-92 would not be judicious, at least from the financial aspect, as a team of Rugby footballers had been touring South Africa during the summer. This indeed proved the case and the up-country matches were poorly attended. The cricketers were led by W. W. Read of Surrey and the party consisted of W. Brockwell, H. Wood, G. W. Ayres (Surrey), W. L. Murdoch and G. Brann (Sussex), J. J. Ferris (Gloucester), J. T. Hearne (Middx), A. D. Pougher (Leics), A. Hearne, G. G. Hearne, F. Martin and E. Leaney (Kent), W. Chatterton (Derby) and V. A. Barton (Hants). Much stronger than Major Warton's Team, the side had five good bowlers in J. T. Hearne, Alec Hearne, Martin, Pougher and Ferris, the last named being the old Australian Test player.

Sailing in the *Dunottar Castle*, the tourists arrived at Cape Town on 8 December and had 12 days practice before the first match against Eighteen of Western Province; both this and the following game were draws, but the third match provided an easy win. The features of the three games were the bowling of Ferris and the batting of Chatterton and Alec Hearne. Two matches against Fifteen of Cape Colony – at Port Elizabeth and Kimberley – provided two victories by an innings and neither game went into the third day. The point that the tourists were equipped with bowlers who were much too good for the home batsmen was now obvious to all and this fact further reduced public enthusiasm for the visit.

Fifteen of Transvaal were beaten by nine wickets and in their return game fielded Eighteen men and managed to draw.

The principal match of the tour and the only eleven-a-side fixture was also the final official match, being played at Cape Town on 19, 21 and 22 March. This match is now regarded as a 'Test', but at the time 'Wisden' thought so little of it that no details at all were given of the two South African innings. As in so many other games on the tour, Ferris proved too good for the South African batsmen, taking 13 for 91 in all. In their turn the English batsmen hit the bowling all over the field and Wood scored 134 not out – the only century he ever made in a first-class career which encompassed 316 matches. England won the Test by an innings and 189 runs, though it should be stated that the home side were without A. B. Tancred. F. Hearne, the brother of G. G. and Alec, who played for England, played for South Africa, having emigrated there after the previous tour.

The tour closed with an extra game for the benefit of the professionals. Ferris was the outstanding figure for the visitors, his wicket total being 234, whilst both J. T. Hearne and Martin captured over 100 wickets each.

Apart from an unfortunate incident when the team left Cape Town, no unpleasantness marred the tour, which, socially, was a success, but financially not so. The team arrived back in England in mid-April.

1891-92: W. W. Read's Team to South Africa

1st Match: v XVIII of Western Province (Cape Town)   Dec 19, 21, 22.
English XI 200 (W. Chatterton 83) & 146-5 dec drew with W. Province 145 (J. J. Ferris 6-19) & 127-6.

2nd Match: v XV of Cape Colony (Cape Town)   Dec 23, 26, 27.
English XI 180 (A. Hearne 64, I. Grimmer 6-58) & 218-2 dec (A. Hearne 91) drew with Cape Colony 197 & 142-10.

3rd Match: v XXII of Port Elizabeth (Port Elizabeth)   Jan 1, 2, 3.
English XI 74 (E. Crage 6-41) & 205 (W. Chatterton 72) beat Port Elizabeth 78 (J. J. Ferris 9-43) & 92 (J. J. Ferris 8-13) by 109 runs.

4th Match: v XV of Cape Colony (Port Elizabeth)   Jan 5, 6, 7.
English XI 246 (W. W. Read 67) beat Cape Colony 97 (F. Martin 8-54) & 110 (J. T. Hearne 8-23) by an inns & 39 runs.

5th Match: v XV of Griqualand West (Kimberley)   Jan 11, 12, 13.
Griqualand West 124 (F. Martin 8-60) & 74 (F. Martin 9-41) lost to English XI 218 (W. Chatterton 80, W. L. Murdoch 64) by an inns & 20 runs.

6th Match: v XV of Cape Colony (Kimberley)   Jan 14, 15, 16.
Cape Colony 142 & 77 lost to English XI 236 (W. L. Murdoch 77) by an inns & 17 runs.

7th Match: v XVIII of Johannesburg (Johannesburg)   Jan 21, 22, 23.
Johannesburg 156 (J. J. Ferris 12-44) & 161 (J. J. Ferris 8-53) lost to English XI 189 (G. G. Hearne 56) & 129-3 (A. D. Pougher 52) by 7 wkts.*

8th Match: v XV of Transvaal (Johannesburg)   Jan 25, 26, 27.
Transvaal 159 (J. T. Hearne 7-43) & 145 (J. T. Hearne 10-60) lost to English XI 283 (G. Brann 142) & 23-1 by 9 wkts.

9th Match: v XXII of Pretoria (Pretoria)   Jan 29, 30.
Pretoria 41 (J. T. Hearne 10-6, J. J. Ferris 10-31) & 126 (A. D. Pougher 14-59) lost to English XI 196 (E. Leaney 54) by an inns & 29 runs.

10th Match: v XVIII of Transvaal (Johannesburg)   Feb 1, 2, 3.
English XI 179 (W. L. Murdoch 63, P. H. de Villiers 5-56) & 153-2 dec (W. L. Murdoch 62) drew with Transvaal 132 (J. J. Ferris 9-83) & 62-3.

11th Match: v XVIII of Pietermaritzburg (Pietermaritzburg)   Feb 8, 9, 10.
Pietermaritzburg 116 (F. Martin 8-39) & 141 lost to English XI 251 (H. Wood 61, A. Hearne 56, A. D. Maul 5-89) & 7-0 by 10 wkts.

12th Match: v XVIII of Durban (Durban)   Feb 11, 12, 13.
Durban 90 (J. J. Ferris 10-41) & 73 (F. Martin 10-37) lost to English XI 134 (G. Brann 70, P. F. Madden 8-39) & 34-2 by 8 wkts.

13th Match: v XXII of Border (Kingwilliamstown)   Feb 18, 19, 20.
Border 59 (J. J. Ferris 16-23) & 155 (J. J. Ferris 9-46) drew with English XI 109 (W. H. Ashley 5-30) & 48-2.

14th Match: v XXII of Albany (Grahamstown)   Feb 22, 23, 24.
Albany 69 (J. T. Hearne 11-35, J. J. Ferris 10-28) & 77 (J. T. Hearne 11-15) drew with English XI 78 & 27-0.

15th Match: v XVIII of Eastern Province (Port Elizabeth)   Feb 26, 27, 29.
English XI 77 (D. Parkin 5-27, E. Crage 5-43) & 113 beat E. Province 50 (J. J. Ferris 12-24) & 74 (J. T. Hearne 9-24) by 66 runs.

16th Match: v XXII of Orange Free State (Bloemfontein)   March 3, 4, 5.
O.F.S. 142 (J. J. Ferris 13-31) & 130-9 dec drew with English XI 162 & 14-2.

17th Match: v XXII of Griqualand West (Kimberley)   March 7, 8, 9.
Griqualand West 135 (J. J. Ferris 9-72) & 136-14 dec (J. J. Ferris 9-61) drew with English XI 113 & 96-3.

18th Match: v XV of Western Province (Cape Town)   March 13, 14, 15, 16.
W. Province 144 & 107 (A. D. Pougher 8-21) lost to English XI 204 (W. Chatterton 77, C. Mills 6-60) & 48-1 by 9 wkts.

19th Match: v XXII of Country Clubs (Cape Town)   March 17, 18.
English XI 201-2 dec (W. Chatterton 105, A. Hearne 53) beat Country Clubs 72 (J. T. Hearne 12-44) & 27 (A. D. Pougher 11-8) by an inns & 102 runs.*

20th Match: v South Africa (Cape Town)   March 19, 21, 22.
South Africa 97 (J. J. Ferris 6-54) & 83 (J. J. Ferris 7-37) lost to England 369 (H. Wood 134) by an inns & 189 runs.*

21st Match: v Malay XVIII (Cape Town) (Extra Match)   March 22, 23.
Malay XVIII 113 (L. Samoodien 55) & 70 (A. D. Pougher 11-24) lost to English XI 176 (J. T. Hearne 67) & 8-0 by 10 wkts.

1892-93: another successful tour to Ceylon and India

Lord Hawke captained the second team of amateurs to the Indian sub-continent. The side, which contained three of the 1889-90 team, was somewhat stronger than that combination and the equal of the weakest of the first-class county sides. The full team consisted of Lord Hawke (Yorks) (capt), A. J. L. Hill and F. S. Jackson (Cambridge U), C. W. Wright and J. S. Robinson (Notts), M. F. Maclean, J. H. J. Hornsby, G. F. Vernon, H. F. Wright, A. E. Gibson, A. E. Leatham, G. A. Foljambe, C. Heseltine and J. A. Gibbs, most of whom made an odd appearance in English first-class matches in 1892 for M.C.C. or similar elevens.

The side left Tilbury on 14 October, except for J. H. J. Hornsby who was travelling overland to Naples and Lord Hawke who was indisposed. Arriving at Colombo, the team had two days to get rid of their sea-legs before the first fixture. J. H. J. Hornsby showed excellent form with bat and ball in this game (against Colombo) and the tourists were well placed when rain ended the match. In the second game Hornsby hit 41 out of an all out total of 81 to save the side from disaster, but the opposition made only 24 and 44 to give the Englishmen their first win. The final game in Ceylon was also won, after which the team sailed to Madras. Lord Hawke had now joined the side and the three fixtures in Madras were two against European sides, which were even draws,

1892-93: Lord Hawke's Team to Ceylon and India

1st Match: v Colombo (Colombo)   Nov 11, 12.
Lord Hawke's XI 252 (J. H. J. Hornsby 72, M. F. Maclean 69) drew with Colombo 106 & 34-0.*

2nd Match: v Colts of Colombo (Colombo)   Nov 14, 15.
Lord Hawke's XI 81 & 107 beat Colts 24 & 44 by 120 runs.

3rd Match: v Up-Country Clubs (Radella)   Nov 18, 19.
Lord Hawke's XI 237 (F. S. Jackson 109, C. W. Wright 53) beat Up-Country XI 82 & 62 by an inns & 93 runs.

4th Match: v Madras C.C. (Madras)   Nov 28, 29.
Madras 184 & 170-6 (H. Reynolds 61) drew with Lord Hawke's XI 138 (F. S. Jackson 50, H. Reynolds 7-58).

5th Match: v Native XI (Madras)   Nov 30.
Native XI 29 (C. Heseltine 8-10) & 46 (C. Heseltine 5-16, J. H. J. Hornsby 5-29) lost to Lord Hawke's XI 137-5 dec by an inns & 62 runs.

6th Match: v Madras Presidency (Madras)   Dec 2, 3.
Lord Hawke's XI 126 & 112 drew with Madras Presidency 123 & 15-2.

7th Match: v Madras Presidency (Bangalore)   Dec 6, 7.
Madras 203 (E. H. D. Sewell 70, J. Reeves 52) & 112 (A. J. L. Hill 5-25) lost to Lord Hawke's XI 280 (Lord Hawke 69, A. J. L. Hill 59, C. W. Wright 52) & 36-1 by 9 wkts.*

8th Match: v Bangalore & District (Bangalore)   Dec 9, 10.
Bangalore 51 (J. H. J. Hornsby 8-27) & 132 lost to Lord Hawke's XI 272 (H. F. Wright 68, Lord Hawke 56) by an inns & 89 runs.

9th Match: v Poona Gymkhana (Poona)   Dec 16, 17.
Poona 84 & 207 drew with Lord Hawke's XI 185 (Lord Hawke 62) & 58-5.

10th Match: v Parsis (Bombay)   Dec 22, 23, 24.
Parsis 93 (A. J. L. Hill 5-7) & 182 (N. C. Bapasola 52) beat Lord Hawke's XI 73 & 93 (M. E. Pavri 6-36) by 109 runs.

11th Match: v Bombay Presidency (Bombay)   Dec 26, 27, 28.
Lord Hawke's XI 263 (Lord Hawke 79, Capt Newnham 6-70) & 35-2 beat Bombay 157 & 140 by 8 wkts.

12th Match: v Parsis (Bombay)   Dec 29, 30, 31.
Lord Hawke's XI 139 & 85 (D. N. Writer 8-35) beat Parsis 127 (J. H. J. Hornsby 7-46) & 90 (J. H. J. Hornsby 8-40) by 7 runs.

13th Match: v Calcutta Club (Calcutta)   Jan 5, 6.
Lord Hawke's XI 291 (J. H. J. Hornsby 86, R. K. Hair 6-92) beat Calcutta 116 & 92 by an inns & 83 runs.

14th Match: v Bengal Presidency (Calcutta)   Jan 13, 16.
Lord Hawke's XI 158 & 83-6 drew with Bengal 72 (J. H. J. Hornsby 6-35) & 268.

15th Match: v Behar Wanderers (Mozufferpore)   Jan 18, 19, 20.
Behar Wanderers 169 (F. S. Jackson 5-37) & 116 (A. E. Gibson 55, G. A. Foljambe 5-17) beat Lord Hawke's XI 90 (A. J. Pilcher 5-31) & 127 (J. S. Robinson 53, A. E. Gibson 7-43) by 69 runs.

16th Match: v Upper India (Allahabad)   Jan 23, 24.
Upper India 140 (F. S. Jackson 5-35) & 92 (J. H. J. Hornsby 6-49) lost to Lord Hawke's XI 225 (A. J. L. Hill 62, E. O. Elliott 5-51) & 10-0 by 10 wkts.*

17th Match: v All India (Allahabad)   Jan 23, 24.
India 139 & 199 (N. C. Bapasola 65) lost to Lord Hawke's XI 343 (A. J. L. Hill 132, A. E. Gibson 58, G. F. Vernon 50) by an inns & 5 runs.

18th Match: v Oudh (Oudh)   Jan 31, Feb 1.
Lord Hawke's XI 315 (M. F. Maclean 99, A. J. L. Hill 51, I. Malling 5-62) beat Oudh 79 & 92 (F. S. Jackson 5-19) by an inns & 144 runs.

19th Match: v Agra (Agra)   Feb 6, 7.
Agra 108 (F. S. Jackson 7-52) & 77 (J. H. J. Hornsby 5-26) lost to Lord Hawke's XI 61 (Murphy 6-27) & 115-6 by 4 wkts.

20th Match: v Umballa (Umballa)   Feb 16, 17, 18.
Lord Hawke's XI 182 (H. Reynolds 6-40) & 146 drew with Umballa 145 (Major Wintour 78).

21st Match: v Punjab (Lahore)   Feb 20, 21.
Punjab 128 & 111 lost to Lord Hawke's XI 243 (F. S. Jackson 95) by an inns & 4 runs.

22nd Match: v Sindh (Lahore)   Feb 23, 24, 25.
Lord Hawke's XI 138 (F. S. Jackson 62, R. Jones 6-71) & 26-3 beat Sindh 50 (J. H. J. Hornsby 5-28) & 112 by 7 wkts.*

23rd Match: v Peshawur (Peshawur)   Feb 28, Mar 1, 2.
Peshawur 68 (J. H. J. Hornsby 6-36) & 112 lost to Lord Hawke's XI 483 (A. J. L. Hill 85, G. F. Vernon 59, C. W. Wright 59, F. S. Jackson 59) by an inns & 303 runs.

and a win against a native eleven. The two fixtures in Bangalore, the next stopping place, were both victories. Trask and Troup, the former county cricketers, were in the opposition team in Poona and their batting made the game very finely balanced when stumps were drawn. The three major games took place at Bombay, the first being against the Parsis. J. S. Robinson could not play for the tourists, but Hill bowled to excellent effect in the first innings: 5-2-7-5 and the Parsis were all out for 93. Lord Hawke's side could only manage 73 however and the Parsis won by a large margin due to M. E. Pavri's bowling backed up by good field. Lord Harris, the Governor of Bombay and former England cricketer, watched the match. The tourists had their revenge in the return fixture, winning by the narrow margin of 7 runs, with Hornsby taking 15 wickets. The tedious journey was made from Bombay to Calcutta where the local club was beaten by an innings, but the Bengal Presidency, after following on, obtained a well-deserved draw.

The second defeat of the tour was at the hands of the Behar Wanderers. A. E. Gibson, playing against the tourists, was mainly responsible for this, but Lord Hawke and J. S. Robinson could not play and A. E. Leatham had his first game.

In Allahabad the team met 'All India' – the title however was a little misleading and the Englishmen won by an innings. In the last match of the tour, the visitors hit 483, with seven of the side hitting over 40 and a victory by a margin of an innings and 303 runs was obtained at the expense of Peshawar. The tour finished with a visit to the Khyber Pass under an escort of the Bengal Cavalry. The party then split up, Lord Hawke and three others going off to Nepal for some shooting whilst the rest made their various ways home.

Everyone agreed it was a most successful tour both socially and from the cricketing viewpoint.

1894: Philadelphia invites an amateur team to North America

Under the auspices of the two major Philadelphian Cricket Clubs – Merion and Germantown – an amateur team under Lord Hawke made a short tour of North America in the autumn of 1894. The side, which was undoubtedly a first-class one by English standards, consisted of Lord Hawke (Yorks), L. C. V. Bathurst, G. J. Mordaunt and G. R. Bardswell (Oxford U), A. J. L. Hill (Hants), C. E. de Trafford (Leics), R. S. Lucas (Middx), G. W. Hillyard (Leics), J. S. Robinson and C. W. Wright (Notts), W. F. Whitwell (Durham) and K. McAlpine.

The team left Southampton on 8 September in the S.S. *New York* and arrived in New York on 14 September, the boat creating a new record for the crossing. The first match – on the Staten Island Ground – was ruined by rain, though A. J. L. Hill took the opportunity of hitting a faultless 99 before the weather ended the proceedings.

1894: Lord Hawke's Team to North America

1st Match: v New York (Staten Island C.C.)   Sept 17, 18.
Lord Hawke's XII 289 (A. J. L. Hill 99, L. C. V. Bathurst 53, Kelly 5-84) drew with New York XII – did not bat rain.

2nd Match: v Philadelphia (Merion C.C.)   Sept 21, 23.
Lord Hawke's XI 187 (Lord Hawke 78, H. P. Baily 7-65) & 235 (G. J. Mordaunt 62) beat Philadelphia 169 (F. H. Bohen 79) & 122 (L. C. V. Bathurst 8-44) by 131 runs.

3rd Match: v Philadelphia (Germantown C.C.)   Sept 28, 29.
Lord Hawke's XI 211 beat Philadelphia 107 & 64 (W. F. Whitwell 5-25) by an inns & 40 runs.

4th Match: v Gents of Canada (Toronto)   Oct 3, 4.
Lord Hawke's XI 147 drew with Canada 55 (L. C. V. Bathurst 5-22, A. J. L. Hill 5-33) & 125-5.

5th Match: v XV of Massachusetts (Lowell)   Oct 6, 8.
Lord Hawke's XII 176 (C. E. de Trafford 75, J. Chambers 9-77) beat Massachusetts 53 (G. W. Hillyard 9-15) & 104 by an inns & 19 runs.

The two principal fixtures of the tour were against the Gentlemen of Philadelphia. In the first of these, poor fielding by Philadelphia gave the tourists the match; Lord Hawke made a very lucky 78, which was the highest individual innings. In the second match, the home side batted half-heartedly and lost by an innings – the loss of their best player, G. S. Patterson, due to an injured finger did not help their cause.

The fourth game was at Toronto against Canada. The home side were outplayed and again the fielding was poor. In the final match the tourists had no difficulty in beating Fifteen of Massachusetts.

The team were back in Southampton on 14 October – the reason for the short duration of the tour being that the Oxford men had to be back for the new term.

1894-95: the growing importance of Test Matches in Australia

For the first time the authorities in Melbourne and Sydney joined forces to promote an English team to Australia. A. E. Stoddart, the Middlesex batsman, was invited to captain the team and arrangements to select a side were well in hand even before the English season of 1894 was half over. The full team consisted of A. C. MacLaren (Lancashire), F. G. J. Ford (Middlesex), H. Philipson (Middlesex), L. H. Gay (Somerset) and the professionals T. Richardson, W. Brockwell and W. H. Lockwood (Surrey), Albert Ward and J. Briggs (Lancashire), R. Peel and J. T. Brown (Yorkshire) and Walter A. Humphreys (Sussex). In that the side did not contain W. G. Grace, F. S. Jackson, R. Abel, and W. Gunn the batting was not representative of England, but it is believed that the only bowler who declined terms was William Attewell, so the attack was well chosen.

The side left Tilbury on board the *Ophir* on 21 September, except for H. Philipson, who took the overland route to Naples. A match was played at Colombo on 16 October and though the opening game of the Australian visit commenced at Gawler on 3 November, the first serious match was the eleven-a-side at Adelaide. South Australia were much improved compared to previous tours and the English team were happy to see virtually all their batsmen succeed and the first innings total reach 476. Some slovenly fielding allowed the home side to make 383. George Giffen then routed the tourists for 130 and followed this up with some good batting to inflict a decisive defeat on Stoddart's hopefuls. MacLaren hit 228 in the third match – against Victoria – providing his side with a win, and more good batting, this time by Stoddart, Brown and Brockwell, took the visitors to victory over New South Wales. The only other eleven-a-side match prior to the first Test was against Queensland, the first time that side had attempted to meet an English Team even-handed. It provided an easy win for the tourists. The wicket at Sydney looked plumb and when Australia, winning the toss, hit 586, including 200 by Gregory, then England made 325 and were forced to follow on, the game looked over. Some very stout batting in the second innings set Australia needing 177 to win. At the end of the fifth day, the home side were 113 for 2. Rain came and the character of the wicket changed out of all recognition, Peel bowling England to an unexpected win. Interest in the match was tremendous, the receipts of £2,945 indicated that financially the tour would be a success. A bad wicket was met in the second Test, but at the beginning. England were skittled out for 75 and Australia for 123. The ground recovered, Stoddart batted over 5 hours for 173 and Australia needed 428 in the last innings. They made an excellent start – 190 for 1 – but Brockwell broke through and England won by 94 runs. Australia had to win the third Test to save the rubber

1st Match: v XIII of Colombo (Colombo) (One Day)   Oct 16.
English XI 76 (A. Raffel 9-48) & 88-8 beat Colombo 58 (J. Briggs 6-6) by 18 runs.

2nd Match: v XVIII of Gawler (Gawler)   Nov 3, 5.
English XI 368 (A. Ward 118, J. T. Brown 56) drew with Gawler 153 (J. Briggs 10-94) & 22-5.

3rd Match: v South Australia (Adelaide)   Nov 9, 10, 12, 13, 14.
English XI 476 (J. T. Brown 115, A. E. Stoddart 66, F. G. J. Ford 66, G. Giffen 5-174) & 130 (G. Giffen 6-49) lost to S. Australia 383 (J. Darling 117, G. Giffen 64, R. Peel 5-69) & 226-4 (J. Reedman 83, G. Giffen 58*) by 6 wkts.

4th Match: v Victoria (Melbourne)   Nov 16, 17, 19, 20.
English XI 416 (A. C. MacLaren 228, A. E. Stoddart 77, A. E. Trott 6-103) & 288 (A. E. Stoddart 78, R. Peel 65) beat Victoria 306 (J. Harry 70, J. Briggs 5-97) & 253 (G. H. S. Trott 63, R. McLeod 62, R. Peel 5-73) by 145 runs.

5th Match: v New South Wales (Sydney)   Nov 23, 24, 26, 27.
N.S.W. 293 (F. A. Iredale 133) & 180 (S. E. Gregory 87, R. Peel 5-64) lost to English XI 394 (J. T. Brown 117, A. E. Stoddart 79, W. Brockwell 81, W. P. Howell 5-44) & 81-2 by 8 wkts.

6th Match: v XXII of New England (Armidale)   Nov 30, Dec 1.
English XI 67 & 197 (Cooper 5-52) drew with New England 147 (W. A. Humphreys 10-52) & 11-1.

7th Match: v XVIII of Toowoomba (Toowoomba)   Dec 5, 6.
Toowoomba 113 (W. A. Humphreys 9-48) & 105 (J. Briggs 9-52) drew with English XI 216.

8th Match: v Queensland (Brisbane)   Dec 7, 8, 10.
English XI 494 (A. E. Stoddart 149, A. Ward 107, A. C. MacLaren 74*, H. Philipson 59, A. Coningham 5-152) beat Queensland 121 (T. Richardson 8-52) & 99 by an inns & 274 runs.

9th Match: v Australia (Sydney)   Dec 14, 15, 17, 18, 19, 20.
Australia 586 (S. E. Gregory 201, G. Giffen 161, F. A. Iredale 81, T. Richardson 5-181) & 166 (J. Darling 53, R. Peel 6-67) lost to England 325 (A. Ward 75, J. Briggs 57) & 437 (A. Ward 117, J. T. Brown 53) by 10 runs.

10th Match: v XVIII Sydney Juniors (Sydney)   Dec 21, 23.
Juniors 442-9 dec (M. A. Noble 152*, V. T. Trumper 67) drew with English XI 151-6.

11th Match: v Australia (Melbourne)   Dec 29, 31, Jan 1, 2, 3.
England 75 (C. T. B. Turner 5-32) & 475 (A. E. Stoddart 173, R. Peel 53, G. Giffen 6-155) beat Australia 123 (T. Richardson 5-57) & 333 (G. H. S. Trott 95, F. A. Iredale 68, W. Bruce 54) by 94 runs.

12th Match: v XVIII of Ballarat (Ballarat)   Jan 5, 7.
English XI 187 (J. T. Brown 64, Pearce 7-95) & 149-7 drew with Ballarat 103 (W. A. Humphreys 10-51).

13th Match: v Australia (Adelaide)   Jan 11, 12, 14, 15.
Australia 238 (G. Giffen 58, T. Richardson 5-75) & 411 (F. A. Iredale 140, W. Bruce 80, A. E. Trott 72*) beat England 124 (G. Giffen 5-76, S. T. Callaway 5-37) & 143 (A. E. Trott 8-43) by 382 runs.

14th Match: v XVIII of Broken Hill (Broken Hill)   Jan 18, 19.
Broken Hill 68 (W. A. Humphreys 10-36) & 102 lost to English XI 178 (A. C. MacLaren 56, A. E. Stoddart 55, Ross 5-60) by an inns & 8 runs.

15th Match: v XVIII of Dandenong (Dandenong)   Jan 25, 26.
English XI 193 (A. E. Stoddart 81) & 45-2 drew with Dandenong 224 (W. Wauchope 66).

16th Match: v Australia (Sydney)   Feb 1, 2, 4.
Australia 284 (H. Graham 105, A. E. Trott 85*) beat England 65 & 72 (G. Giffen 5-26) by an inns & 147 runs.

17th Match: v XVIII of New England (Armidale)   Feb 9, 11.
English XI 187 (A. E. Stoddart 88, Mereweather 5-48) & 112-7 drew with New England 111 (R. Peel 11-45).

18th Match: v Combined N.S.W. & Queensland (Brisbane)   Feb 15, 16, 18, 19.
English XI 192 (A. C. MacLaren 107, T. R. McKibbin 5-98) beat Combined XI 107 (T. Richardson 5-42) & 86 by 278 runs.

19th Match: v XVIII of Newcastle (Newcastle)   Feb 22, 23.
Newcastle 189 (Giles 58) & 87-5 drew with English XI 241 (W. Brockwell 73, A. Ward 63).

20th Match: v Australia (Melbourne)   March 1, 2, 4, 5, 6.
Australia 414 (J. Darling 74, S. E. Gregory 70, G. Giffen 57, J. J. Lyons 55) & 267 (G. Giffen 51, J. Darling 50, T. Richardson 6-104) lost to England 385 (A. C. MacLaren 120, R. Peel 73, A. E. Stoddart 68) & 298-4 (J. T. Brown 140, A. Ward 93) by 6 wkts.

21st Match: v XVIII of N. Tasmania (Launceston)   March 9, 11, 12.
N. Tasmania 178 (N. R. Westbrook 51, W. A. Humphreys 10-98) & 219-13 drew with English XI 291 (A. E. Stoddart 73*, W. Brockwell 69, E. A. Windsor 5-117).

22nd Match: v XV of S. Tasmania (Hobart)   March 14, 15, 16.
English XI 91 (C. J. Eady 5-60) drew with S. Tasmania 189-13 (J. S. Howe 51*, F. G. J. Ford 9-56).

23rd Match: v Victoria (Melbourne)   March 21, 22, 23, 25.
English XI 131 (H. Trott 8-63) & 270 (F. G. J. Ford 85) lost to Victoria 269 (C. L. McLeod 52) & 136-3 (W. Bruce 72*) by 7 wkts.

24th Match: v South Australia (Adelaide)   March 28, 29, 30, April 1, 2.
S. Australia 397 (C. Hill 150*, W. F. Giffen 81, T. Richardson 5-148) & 255 (C. Hill 56) lost to English XI 609 (A. Ward 219, F. G. J. Ford 106, J. T. Brown 101, R. Peel 57, G. Giffen 5-309) & 45-0 by 10 wkts.

Batting Averages

	M	I	NO	R	HS	Avge	100	c/s
A. E. Stoddart (Middx)	10	18	1	870	173	51.17	2	7
A. C. MacLaren (Lancs)	11	20	3	804	228	47.29	3	4
J. T. Brown (Yorks)	12	21	2	825	140	43.42	4	10
A. Ward (Lancs)	12	22	0	916	219	41.63	3	6
L. H. Gay (Som)	6	11	5	186	39*	31.00	0	9/5
F. G. J. Ford (Middx)	11	20	1	508	106	26.73	1	6
W. Brockwell (Surrey)	12	22	1	504	81	24.00	0	11
R. Peel (Yorks)	12	21	1	421	73	21.05	0	10
J. Briggs (Lancs)	12	20	1	360	57	18.93	0	6
W. Lockwood (Surrey)	10	14	2	224	39	18.66	0	5
H. Phillipson (Middx)	9	15	1	187	59	13.35	0	15/3
W. A. Humphreys (Sussex)	4	7	3	42	18*	10.50	0	4
T. Richardson (Surrey)	11	19	5	114	20	8.14	0	1

Bowling Averages

	O	M	R	W	Avge	BB	5i
T. Richardson	592.2	148	1616	68	23.76	8-52	7
J. Briggs	376.1	71	1057	44	24.02	5-97	1
R. Peel	641.2	176	1441	57	25.28	6-67	3
A. E. Stoddart	3	0	31	1	31.00	1-31	0
W. Lockwood	284.4	69	791	18	43.94	4-54	0
W. Brockwell	120	38	336	7	48.00	3-33	0
W. A. Humphreys	112	12	314	6	52.33	2-62	0
F. G. J. Ford	44	8	159	1	159.00	1-47	0

and so determined were they, despite the two losses, that the betting started at evens. This time the rain did not affect the wicket, Australia batted with authority, but the English side fell apart – the highest scorer in either innings was Brown with 39 – and Albert Trott, making his debut, took 8 for 43 in England's second innings. England lost by 382 runs. In mitigation, it should perhaps be noted that the game was played in intense heat which upset the tourists much more than the Australians. There were two up-country games prior to the fourth Test which was staged at Sydney. Lockwood was injured, but Stoddart still preferred him to Humphreys, the lob bowler, who had failed to find any form in the serious matches. The wicket at the start was described as 'sticky as glue' and England put Australia in. Six wickets went down for 51, then Graham played an excellent innings of 105 – though he was dropped three times – and Trott hit 86 unbeaten. The catching and ground fielding of the English team was shocking, and this decided the game, since the wicket remained bad and England's batsmen were all at sea. The series was now level at two each.

The final Test at Melbourne was the vital game and public interest could hardly have been higher. Thankfully the pitch was perfect throughout, so neither side had an unfair advantage. Both first innings saw high scoring and only 29 runs separated the sides when Australia began their second knock. Splendid bowling by Richardson aided by good fielding dismissed Australia for 267 and the betting was even as England began the fifth day at 28 for 1 – about 14,000 people came to watch the crucial last innings. A second England wicket – that of Stoddart – fell quickly, but Brown and Ward, particularly the former, batted in great style. Brown reached 140 in 145 minutes and when he was out the match and series were as good as won.

Four matches were played after the fifth Test, and the fitting climax came at Adelaide, where the team had been defeated at the tour's outset. This time they hit 609 and won by 10 wickets.

The tour made a profit of some £7,000 from total receipts of over £18,000. The tourists arrived back in Plymouth on 8 May.

The interest shown in England in the Test Match series was greater than for any other tour, and finally established the domination of the 'Tests' in the programme of English teams in Australia.

Of those who toured Australia, Humphreys was completely ineffective with his underarm lobs and Gay kept wicket so poorly in the early games that Philipson was soon established as the principal keeper. Lockwood for some reason failed both with bat and ball and his county colleague, Brockwell, did not live up to his reputation. The batting of MacLaren, Stoddart, Brown and Ward however was excellent, whilst Richardson, Peel and Briggs formed a good bowling trio.

1894-95: the first England tour to the West Indies

English cricketers broke fresh ground in the winter of 1894-95 when the first tour to the West Indies was undertaken. Lord Stamford, together with N. Lubbock, Dr R. B. Anderson and Lord Hawke, organised the arrangements and selected the team. It was hoped that Lord Hawke would tour as captain, but in his absence, R. S. Lucas the Middlesex amateur led the party, the remainder of whom were R. Leigh-Barratt (Norfolk), R. Berens, F. W. Bush (Ex-Surrey), H. R. Bromley-Davenport (Cambridge U), J. M. Dawson (Cambridge U), A. Priestley (M.C.C.), R. P. Sewell (Essex), H. S. Smith-Turbeville (M.C.C.), W. H. Wakefield (Oxford U), J. H. Weatherby (M.C.C.), M. M. Barker (M.C.C.) and R. L. Marshall. The all-amateur side was by no stretch of the imagination first-class by English standards. The trip was mainly a social one and the cricket was not taken too seriously. The team left Southampton on 16 January in the *Medway* and arrived in Bridgetown on 28 January.

There was much interest in the opening match against Barbados and about 6,000 turned up to watch the play. A right-arm medium bowler, C. Goodman, bowled most effectively for the home side, who won the game by 5 wickets. The return against Barbados lasted five days and scoring was very high. The tourists were no less than 214 behind on first innings, but a century from Dawson and 91 from Bromley-Davenport meant that Barbados required 185 in their last innings, when they collapsed for 157, giving the visitors a well-earned victory. Travelling round the islands the team had easy wins over Antigua, St Kitts and St Lucia, but were beaten in a One-day fixture at Vincent on a pitch totally devoid of grass.

In Trinidad large crowds watched both matches, which were low scoring affairs. Trinidad won the second game, due to an innings of 77 by A. Warner, by 8 wickets. Two games were played against Demerara in Georgetown and again fair crowds watched the games, though the home side did not look as good as the Trinidad Eleven. The visit to Demerera was cut by three days when the boat was delayed and the team went on to Jamaica via Barbados. The passage from Barbados to Jamaica took four days.

1894-95 to West Indies

1st Match: v Barbados (Pickwick C.C.)   Jan 29, 30.
R. S. Lucas' XI 48 (C. Goodman 6-14) & 168 (R. S. Lucas 64, R. P. Sewell 51, C. Goodman 8-71) lost to Barbados 100 (F. W. Bush 6-38) & 118-5 by 5 wkts.

2nd Match: v United Services (Pickwick C.C.) (13-a-side)   Jan 31, Feb 1.
R. S. Lucas's XIII 247 (R. Leigh-Barratt 56, Hughes 6-84) drew with United Services XIII 124 (F. W. Bush 6-50) & 148-5 (Hughes 70).

3rd Match: v Barbados (Pickwick C.C.)   Feb 5, 6, 7, 8, 9.
Barbados 517 (G. Learmond 86, W. Alleyne 82, G. Cox 68, H. Cole 67, C. Browne 74, A. Somers-Cocks 62*) & 157 (H. R. B-Davenport 5-42) lost to R. S. Lucas's XI 303 (F. W. Bush 105, C. Goodman 6-104) & 396 (J. M. Dawson 138, H. R. B-Davenport 91, R. Berens 50, A. Somers-Cocks 8-99) by 25 runs.

4th Match: v Antigua (St John's)   Feb 14, 15, 16.
Antigua 107 (H. R. B-Davenport 5-43, F. W. Bush 5-44) & 99 lost to R. S. Lucas' XI 275 (J. M. Dawson 54, H. Smith-Turberville 50, E. Samuel 5-74) by an inns & 69 runs.

5th Match: v St Kitts-Nevis (Springfield)   Feb 18, 19.
St Kitts 41 (H. R. Bromley-Davenport 6-3) & 93 lost to R. S. Lucas' XI 169 by an inns & 35 runs.

6th Match: v St Lucia (Castries) (12-a-side)   Feb 22, 23.
St Lucia 94 (F. W. Bush 7-34) & 94 (H. R. Bromley-Davenport 9-11) lost to R. S. Lucas' XII 148 (A. Burcher 5-43) & 41-1 by 10 wkts.

7th Match: v St Vincent (Kingston) (One Day)   Feb 25.
R. S. Lucas' XII 63 (T. Osment 5-26) lost to St Vincent 138-9. (In another account this was a draw.)

8th Match: v Queen's Park C.C. (Queen's Park)   Feb 28, Mar 1.
Queen's Park XII 71 (F. W. Bush 9-22) & 181 (H. R. B-Davenport 6-80) lost to R. S. Lucas' XII 164 (A. Tqitt 5-62) & 89-8 by 3 wkts.

9th Match: v All Trinidad (Queen's Park)   March 4, 5.
Trinidad 180 (A. Warner 77) & 78-2 beat R. S. Lucas' XI 94 (J. Woods 6-39) & 162 (R. P. Sewell 66, J. H. Weatherby 56) by 8 wkts.

10th Match: v Demerera (Bourda)   March 16, 18.
R. S. Lucas' XI 119 (E. F. Wright 5-34) & 1-0 beat Demerera 73 (H. R. B-Davenport 6-22) & 46 (H. R. B-Davenport 7-17) by 10 wkts.

11th Match: v Demerera (Bourda)   March 19, 20.
Demerera 184 (E. F. Wright 54) drew with R. S. Lucas' XI 67-4.

12th Match: v All Jamaica (Kingston) (12-a-side)   March 30, April 1.
Jamaica 72 (F. W. Bush 7-46) & 47 (F. W. Bush 7-15) lost to R. S. Lucas' XII 215 by an inns & 96 runs.

13th Match: v Jamaica Born (Kingston)   April 2, 3.
R. S. Lucas' XI 285 (R. P. Sewell 77) beat Jamaica Born 58 (F. W. Bush 6-24) & 133 H. R. B-Davenport 5-45, F. W. Bush 5-67) by an inns & 94 runs.

14th Match: v Western Jamaica (Montego Bay)   April 5, 6.
R. S. Lucas' XI 181 (F. W. Bush 63) beat W. Jamaica 42 (H. R. B-Davenport 6-13) & 77 (R. S. Lucas 7-40) by an inns & 62 runs.

15th Match: v North Jamaica (St Ann's Bay)   April 8, 9.
N. Jamaica XII 61 (H. R. Bromley-Davenport 6-13) & 58 (H. R. B-Davenport 5-25) lost to R. S. Lucas' XI 81 & 39-3 by 7 wkts.

16th Match: v All Jamaica (Sabina Park)   April 11, 12.
R. S. Lucas' XI 83 (J. W. Toone 6-29) & 114 (J. W. Toone 6-51) lost to Jamaica 171 (H. R. B-Davenport 7-68) & 28-2 by 8 wkts.

R. S. Lucas's team for one of the matches on the first tour to the West Indies in 1894-95. Back: Mr Barney (umpire), R. Leigh-Barratt, A. Priestley. Centre: R. Berens, R. L. Marshall, F. W. Bush, R. S. Lucas, R. P. Sewell, J. H. Weatherby, M. M. Barker. Front: J. M. Dawson, H. R. Bromley-Davenport.

1894-95: R. S. Lucas's Team to the West Indies

Batting Averages

	M	I	NO	R	HS	Avge	100	c/s
J. M. Dawson (Cambr U)	5	7	0	184	138	26.28	1	4
R. P. Sewell (Essex)	8	12	1	269	77	24.45	0	9
F. W. Bush (Surrey)	7	10	0	242	101	24.20	1	3
J. H. Weatherby	8	11	0	248	56	22.54	0	4
H. Smith-Turbeville	1	2	1	20	14	20.00	0	0
H. R. Bromley-Davenport (Cambr U)	8	11	0	212	91	19.27	0	11
R. S. Lucas (Middx)	8	13	1	209	64	17.41	0	6
A. Priestley	8	11	1	144	36	14.40	0	6
R. Berens	8	12	1	136	50	12.36	0	3
R. Leigh-Barratt (Norfolk)	6	9	1	82	19	10.25	0	5
M. M. Barker	8	11	1	94	30	9.40	0	9
R. L. Marshall	8	11	5	55	19*	9.16	0	0
W. H. Wakefield (Oxford U)	6	9	2	30	16	4.28	0	11/4

Bowling Averages

	O	M	R	W	Avge	BB	5i
H. R. Bromley Davenport	317.2	95	561	56	10.01	7-17	5
F. W. Bush	284.4	90	610	51	11.96	7-25	5
R. P. Sewell	62.3	15	189	11	17.18	4-29	0
H. Smith-Turbeville	8	0	28	1	28.00	1-28	0
R. Leigh-Barratt	33	8	89	3	29.66	3-75	0
R. L. Marshall	46	6	163	5	32.60	3-71	0
R. S. Lucas	28.4	0	153	3	51.00	2-111	0

Also bowled: M. M. Barker 1-0-7-0.

In the game against All-Jamaica at Kingston, F. W. Bush came into his own, capturing 14 wickets as the tourists won by an innings. Altogether five games were played in Jamaica of which four were won and the final one lost by 8 wickets. The team sailed back to Barbados and left there on 25 April aboard R.M.S. *Atrato*, arriving back in England on 1 May.

H. R. Bromley-Davenport and F. W. Bush were the mainstay of the tourists' bowling and both took over 100 wickets. There was not much to choose between the principal batsmen, though F. W. Bush scored the most runs.

1895: university men tour North America

Frank Mitchell, the Hon Sec of Cambridge University Cricket Club in 1895, led an amateur side to North America in late summer, 1895. The team consisted of nine Cambridge men: F. Mitchell, N. F. Druce, C. D. Robinson, W. McG. Hemingway, R. A. Studd, C. E. M. Wilson, W. W. Lowe, W. Mortimer and H. H. Marriott; three from Oxford: F. A. Phillips, H. A. Arkwright and J. C. Hartley; and two current county amateurs: V. T. Hill (Somerset) and F. W. Milligan (Yorkshire).

The team, which was quite first-class, sailed from Southampton on 24 August in the *St Louis* and played their first match against New York on 3 and 4 September and their second game against Canada in Toronto. Neither of these opponents caused the young team any problems, but they found sterner stuff in Philadelphia. The first of the three matches played there was against Pennsyl-

1895 to United States and Canada

1st Match: v New York (Staten Island) Sept 3, 4.
New York XII 112 & 268 (W. R. Cobb 73, Rokeby 66) lost to F. Mitchell's XII 323 (N. F. Druce 121, F. A. Phillips 88) & 58-3 by 8 wkts.

2nd Match: v All Canada (Toronto) Sept 6, 7.
Canada 137 & 86 drew with F. Mitchell's XII 188 (F. A. Phillips 51) & 15-1.

3rd Match: v Pennsylvania University (Past & Present) (Haverford) Sept 13, 14, 16.
F. Mitchell's XI 284 (F. Mitchell 58, G. S. Patterson 5-95) & 61 (G. S. Patterson 5-22) lost to Pennsylvania Univ 138 & 307 (G. S. Patterson 63, C. Coates 63, W. W. Noble 62) by 100 runs.

4th Match: v Philadelphia (Germantown C.C.) Sept 20, 21, 23.
Philadelphia 234 (G. S. Patterson 109*, F. W. Ralston 53, F. W. Milligan 6-71) & 138 (G. S. Patterson 67, W. W. Lowe 6-15) lost to F. Millingan's XI 156 (J. B. King 7-55) & 220-8 (N. F. Druce 57) by 2 wkts.

5th Match: v Philadelphia (Merion C.C.) Sept 24, 25, 27.
F. Mitchell's XI 198 (J. B. King 5-47) & 167 (J. B. King 6-61) lost to Philadelphia 404 (F. H. Bohlen 115, W. W. Noble 57, G. S. Patterson 74) by an inns & 29 runs.

vania University (Past and Present), where, after the tourists gained a good first innings lead, they collapsed against Patterson and Clark to lose the match by 100 runs. The final two games were against the formidable Philadelphian side. The first was won, due to some stout batting from Wilson, who carried out his bat for 20 after a two-hour stay. The Philadelphians more than had their revenge in the return match. The Englishmen were dismissed for 198 and the home side replied by adding 200 before the first wicket fell – Patterson and Bohlen being the batsmen. Philadelphia from that moment kept their grip on the match and some good bowling by J. B. King brought victory by an innings.

The tour was regarded as a great success and gave a tremendous boost to American cricket. The tourists arrived back in Southampton on 15 October.

Before the tour began, K. McAlpine was also in the process of arranging an English team to visit America, but as soon as it was realised that two separate sides were being raised, the Philadelphian authorities took steps to cancel Mr McAlpine's tentative plans before they got too far.

1895-96: a strong side do well in South Africa

For reasons both political and accidental, the tour to South Africa under the leadership of Lord Hawke and the management of George Lohmann suffered more than its fair share of disruptions. Lord Hawke, Sir T. C. O'Brien and H. T. Hewett, all of whom travelled separately from the main party, were delayed due to an accident to their steamer and missed the first match. The Jameson Raid caused the postponement of the third fixture and seriously affected the gates at some subsequent ones. H. T. Hewett was summoned back to England by important business after only three matches. S. M. J. Woods began the tour with a strained shoulder which prevented him bowling and then suffered a strained leg, whilst Tyler missed several games through ill-health and C. B. Fry strained his ankle late on, missing the last two fixtures. Added to this catalogue of disasters was a fearful explosion in Johannesburg, which caused the abandonment of one game. The miracle was that the tour itself was not a financial failure and in fact a small profit was reported.

The side consisted of Lord Hawke (Yorks) (capt), T. W. Hayward and G. A. Lohmann (Surrey), C. B. Fry and H. R. Butt (Sussex), S. M. J. Woods, H. T. Hewett and E. J. Tyler (Somerset), A. J. L. Hill and C. Heseltine (Hants), Sir T. C. O'Brien and H. R. Bromley-Davenport (Middx), C. W. Wright (Notts) and A. M. Miller (Wilts). With most members playing regular first-class cricket and two or three players worth their place in the England side, the team was the strongest to visit South Africa up to that date and despite the problems only two games were lost.

The main party landed in Cape Town on 22 December and the first game commenced at Newlands on Boxing Day before a crowd of some 6,000. Batting very poorly the tourists lost by 77 runs against Fifteen of Western Province. The Province then challenged the visitors to a One Day match on even terms and won again – by a single wicket. In the third match the visitors found their feet, hit up 405, with Fry 148 and Woods 89, and won by an innings. There was a nine-day break due to the political situation, but a series of seven odds matches were played with one defeat before the team met the South African Eleven at Port Elizabeth. Unfortunately four of the best home players – Innes, Rowe, A. B. Tancred and A. Richards – could not come, and the English players had the advantage of a turf wicket, most South Africans being used to matting. In fact the English batting was moderate enough, but the South Africans were humiliated by Lohmann, who took 15 for 45. In the second 'Test' at Johannesburg, Lohmann again routed the opposition and with the visitors

1895-96 to South Africa

1st Match: v XV of Western Province (Cape Town)   Dec 26, 27.
W. Province 115 (G. A. Lohmann 7-50) & 130 (G. A. Lohmann 7-43) beat Lord Hawke's XI 79 (J. Middleton 7-50) & 92 (J. Willoughby 6-15) by 77 runs.

2nd Match: v Western Province (Cape Town) (One Day)   Dec 28.
Lord Hawke's XI 148 (Smith 6-53) lost to W. Province 151-9 by 1 wkt.

3rd Match: v XIII of Cape Colony (Cape Town)   Jan 1, 2, 3.
Lord Hawke's XI 405 (C. B. Fry 148, S. M. J. Woods 89, T. W. Hayward 73) beat Cape Colony 118 (A. J. L. Hill 5-3) & 162 (F. Hearne 94, G. A. Lohmann 8-40) by an inns & 125 runs.

4th Match: v XV of Johannesburg (Johannesburg)   Jan 13, 14, 15.
Lord Hawke's XII 178 (H. T. Hewett 57, J. H. Sinclair 7-60) & 268-8 dec (A. J. L. Hill 58) drew with Johannesburg 193 (J. H. Sinclair 75) & 195-8 (T. A. Routledge 86).

5th Match: v XV of Pietermaritzburg (Pietermaritzburg)   Jan 18, 20, 21.
Lord Hawke's XII 229 (W. M. Henderson 5-62) & 433-9 (C. B. Fry 153, T. C. O'Brien 118) drew with Pietermaritzburg 310 (R. M. Poore 112, C. F. Hime 62).

6th Match: v XV of Natal (Durban)   Jan 23, 24, 25.
Lord Hawke's XII 154 (P. F. Madden 7-88) & 173 lost to Natal 100 (G. A. Lohmann 9-42) & 228-5 (R. M. Poore 107*) by 9 wkts.

7th Match: v XXII of Kingwilliamstown (Kingwilliamstown)   Jan 27, 28.
Kingwilliamstown 200 (W. S. Taberer 51, E. J. Tyler 8-72) drew with Lord Hawke's XII 109 (T. W. Hayward 84*, B. E. Gordon 7-55) & 155 (C. B. Fry 50).

8th Match: v XXII of Albany (Grahamstown)   Feb 1, 3.
Albany 89 & 161 (G. A. Lohmann 11-64) drew with Lord Hawke's XI 110 (C. B. Fry 51*) & 74-7.

9th Match: v XXII of Midlands (Cradock)   Feb 5, 6.
Lord Hawke's XI 392 (A. J. L. Hill 102, T. C. O'Brien 88, H. R. B-Davenport 68*, Lord Hawke 59, E. H. Gedye 8-143) drew with Midlands 170 (G. A. Lohmann 9-55) & 84-14.

10th Match: v XVIII of Port Elizabeth (Port Elizabeth)   Feb 8, 10.
Port Elizabeth 93 (G. A. Lohmann 15-38) & 108 (G. A. Lohmann 11-44) lost to Lord Hawke's XII 162 & 42-3 by 8 wkts.

11th Match: v South Africa (Port Elizabeth)   Feb 13, 14, 15.
England 185 (J. Middleton 5-64) & 226 (S. M. J. Woods 53) beat South Africa 93 (G. A. Lohmann 7-38) & 30 (G. A. Lohmann 8-7) by 288 runs.

12th Match: v XVI of Orange Free State (Bloemfontein)   Feb 18, 19.
Lord Hawke's XI 192 (C. G. Fichardt 6-93) & 269-7 (T. W. Hayward 95) drew with O.F.S. 165.

13th Match: v XV of Pretoria (Pretoria)   Feb 26, 28.
Pretoria 167 (P. J. Korsten 59) & 87 (C. Heseltine 6-13) lost to Lord Hawke's XI 160 (G. A. Lohmann 50*, G. O. McArthur 5-46) & 98-5 by 5 wkts.

14th Match: v South Africa (Johannesburg)   March 2, 3, 4.
England 482 (T. W. Hayward 122, C. W. Wright 71, A. J. L. Hill 65, C. B. Fry 64, G. A. Rowe 5-115) beat South Africa 151 (G. A. Lohmann 9-28) & 134 (C. Heseltine 5-38) by an inns & 197 runs.

15th Match: v XV of Griqualand West (Kimberley)   March 7, 9, 10.
Lord Hawke's XI 95 (T. A. Samuels 7-42) & 231 (A. J. L. Hill 89, M. J. Woods 63, G. Glover 6-75) beat Griqualand West 144 & 169 by 13 runs.

16th Match: v XX of J. D. Logan's Team (Matjiesfontein)   March 16.
J. D. Logan's XX 277 (G. A. Lohmann 64, Lt. Armstrong 54) drew with Lord Hawke's XI 183-9 (S. M. J. Woods 66).

17th Match: v Western Province (Cape Town)   March 17, 18, 19.
Lord Hawke's XI 224 (T. W. Hayward 83, C. W. Wright 68, J. Middleton 7-85) & 168-9 drew with W. Province 122 (G. A. Lohmann 6-48).

18th Match: v South Africa (Cape Town)   March 21, 23.
South Africa 115 (G. A. Lohmann 7-42) & 117 lost to England 265 (A. J. L. Hill 124) by an inns & 33 runs.

Lord Hawke's team to South Africa in 1895-96. Back: E. J. Tyler, Sir T. C. O'Brien, A. M. Miller, T. W. Hayward, G. A. Lohmann. Centre: C. B. Fry, J. D. Logan, Lord Hawke, C. W. Wright, C. Heseltine, A. J. L. Hill. Front: S. M. J. Woods, H. R. Bromley-Davenport, H. R. Butt.

hitting 482, victory was by an innings and 197 runs.

The following match against Fifteen at Griqualand West proved a much closer contest. A local bowler, T. B. Samuels, took 7 for 42 and dismissed the tourists for 95. Helped by some dropped catches Hill and Woods put the Eleven back in the match with a second innings of 231, but some stout batting in the final innings meant that the English side won by the fine margin of 13 runs. Rain caused a draw in the match against Western Province and little interest was shown by the public in either this or the third and final 'Test' which followed. South Africa managed to gather a reasonably representative eleven, but once more Lord Hawke's combination proved far too strong, and, apart from an innings of 30 by Frank Hearne, the South African batting collapsed twice for little over a hundred.

In the evening after this match, Lord Hawke announced that the cup which had been presented by the Union Steamship Company to be awarded to the team which gave the best display against the tourists should go to Kimberley.

The outstanding success of the tour was Lohmann, who took three times as many wickets as the next man. Of the batsmen, the three who stood out from the rest were C. B. Fry, A. J. L. Hill and T. W. Hayward.

The main body of the side arrived back in England in the second week of April.

1896-97: Lord Hawke's team to the West Indies

Lord Hawke had been invited to take the 1894-95 team out to the West Indies, but had had to withdraw. It was understood however that he would try to take a side out in 1896-97 and following an invitation from the Governor of British Guiana and from Trinidad, Barbados and Jamaica, Lord Hawke determined to organise a West Indian Tour. Unfortunately his telegram accepting the islands' invitations was never received and another English party under A. Priestley was being arranged, having accepted an invitation from Jamaica. Lord Hawke met Mr Priestley, but the two could not come to an amicable settlement and both decided to go independently to the West Indies. Fortunately both teams were composed of amateurs and therefore the financial considerations were not of paramount importance, thus the disastrous losses of the twin tours to Australia in 1887-88 were not repeated.

Lord Hawke's team, which sailed from Southampton on 13 January, consisted of Lord Hawke (Yorks) (capt), H. D. G. Leveson-Gower (Oxford U and Surrey), P. F. Warner (Oxford U and Middx), G. R. Bardswell (Oxford U), H. R. Bromley-Davenport (Middx), C. Heseltine (Hants), A. E. Leatham (Gloucs), W. H. Wakefield and R. Berens (Oxford U Authentics), J. M. Dawson and R. W. Wickham (Yorks Gents) and A. D. Whatman (Eton Ramblers), with Kirk the Trent Bridge dressing room attendant. The team was just about first-class by English standards.

Barbados was reached on 25 January and the side were met by Priestley's Team, who had already played three matches. Without playing any fixtures in Barbados, Lord Hawke's Team sailed to

The team which toured the West Indies in 1896-97. Back row: an unnamed umpire, R. W. Wickham, G. R. Bardswell, A. E. Leatham, C. Heseltine, J. M. Dawson. Centre: W. H. Wakefield, A. D. Whatman. Front: P. F. Warner, H. D. G. Leveson-Gower, Lord Hawke (captain), H. R. Bromley-Davenport, R. Berens.

Trinidad and the first game was played there on 29-30 January. This proved to be a draw, but in the second game against All Trinidad the side met with defeat, the home bowlers Cumberbatch and Woods soon removing all except P. F. Warner with little difficulty. The same bowlers inflicted a second defeat on the tourists in the return fixture. There were three easy victories in Grenada and St Vincent before the next serious matches – against Barbados. In the first of these the tourists obtained a good first innings lead, but, following on, Barbados hit 319 and the match was drawn. The return game was won by P. F. Warner, who hit an undefeated 113 in the second innings, for a 4-wicket win.

The other important matches were against British Guiana at the end of the tour. Three games had been arranged at Georgetown. The tourists won the first two, after which they had a week's holiday from cricket when they sailed up the Demerera River. The final game was unfortunately rained off after the first day. About 5,000 spectators had watched each of the first two fixtures, but only 1,000 turned up for the first day of the final match.

The side sailed back to Barbados and there boarded the *Medway* for the voyage to England. P. F. Warner was the success of the tour and hit four centuries. Bromley-Davenport returned the best bowling figures, but missed some matches in the middle of the tour, due to a broken finger.

1896-97: A. Priestley also takes a team to the West Indies

The team invited to the West Indies by Jamaica and under the leadership of Arthur Priestley left Southampton on 30 December. The members of the side were A. E. Stoddart, C. A. Beldam and W. Williams (Middx), S. M. J. Woods, R. C. N. Palairet and H. T. Stanley (Somerset), R. P. Lewis (Oxford U), C. C. Stone (Leics), F. W. Bush, R. Leigh Barratt, J. Leigh, Dr G. Elliott and A. Priestley (capt).

Arriving in Barbados, the team commenced their first game with almost no practice and were soundly beaten by an innings, Clifford Goodman taking 12 wickets for the home side. The tourists won their second game by an innings, but the opposition

1896-97: A. Priestley's Team to the West Indies

1st Match: v All Barbados (Bridgetown)   Jan 13, 14.
A. Priestley's XI 106 (C. Goodman 7-59) & 126 (C. Goodman 5-45) lost to Barbados 273 (G. B. Y. Cox 67, H. B. G. Austin 63) by an inns & 41 runs.

2nd Match: v St Vincent (Bridgetown)   Jan 15, 16.
St Vincent 51 (W. Williams 8-20) & 86 (A. E. Stoddart 6-29) lost to A. Priestley's XI 276-5 dec (A. E. Stoddart 153*) by an inns & 139 runs.

3rd Match: v All Barbados (Bridgetown)   Jan 18, 19.
Barbados 172 & 52 (A. E. Stoddart 6-11) lost to A. Priestley's XI 143 (C. Goodman 5-60) & 82-7 by 3 wkts.

4th Match: v Barbados (Bridgetown)   Jan 21, 22, 23.
Barbados 130 & 177 (H. B. G. Austin 54, S. M. J. Woods 6-60) beat A. Priestley's XI 77 (C. Goodman 8-40) & 94 (C. Goodman 6-50) by 136 runs.

5th Match: v Antigua (St John's)   Jan 28, 29, 30.
A. Priestley's XI 272 (A. E. Stoddart 107, R. Leigh Barratt 96) beat Antigua 101 & 75 by an inns & 96 runs.

6th Match: v St Kitts (Springfield)   Feb 1, 2, 3.
A. Priestley's XI 269 (A. E. Stoddart 133) beat St Kitts 48 & 29 by an inns & 192 runs.

7th Match: v United Services (Bridgetown)   Feb 6, 8.
United Services 135 & 106 (A. E. Stoddart 5-32) lost to A. Priestley's XI 252 (C. A. Beldam 98, A. E. Stoddart 59) by an inns & 11 runs.

8th Match: v Queens Park (Port of Spain)   Feb 12, 13.
Queens Park 222 drew with A. Priestley's XI 191-1 (A. E. Stoddart 108*, H. T. Stanley 63*).

9th Match: v All West Indies (Port of Spain)   Feb 15, 16, 18.
A. Priestley's XI 179 (C. Goodman 5-72) & 176 (B. Cumberbatch 5-67) lost to West Indies (H. B. G. Austin 75*) & 142-7 (A. E. Stoddart 5-49) by 3 wkts.

10th Match: v Trinidad (Port of Spain)   Feb 19, 20, 22.
Trinidad 174 & 1-0 beat A. Priestley's XI 33 (B. Cumberbatch 6-11) & 141 (B, Cumberbatch 5-48) by 10 wkts.

11th Match: v Trinidad (Port of Spain)   Feb 25, 26, 27.
Trinidad 284 (L. S. D'Ade 140*, S. Rudder 53, A. E. Stoddart 5-71) & 94-2 beat A. Priestley's XI 162 (R. C. N. Palariet 65*, J. Woods 5-51) & 212 (J. Woods 6-64) by 8 wkts.

12th Match: v Jamaica (Kingston)   March 13, 15.
Jamaica 58 (S. M. J. Woods 5-23) & 68 (A. E. Stoddart 5-29) lost to A. Priestley's XI by an inns & 3 runs.

13th Match: v Jamaica (Kingston)   March 16, 17.
A. Priestley's XI 200 (A. E. Stoddart 100, G. V. Livingstone 7-49) & 32-0 beat Jamaica 68 & 163 (R. D. Richmond 60, W. Williams 7-47) by 10 wkts.

14th Match: v Black River XII (Black River)   March 19, 20.
Black River 122 (A. E. Stoddart 7-47) & 64 (A. E. Stoddart 5-28) lost to A. Priestley's XI 83 (W. Williams 6-34) & 105-3 by 7 wkts.

15th Match: v North Side XII (St Ann's Bay)   March 24, 25.
A. Priestley's XII 221 (A. E. Stoddart 52) beat North Side XII 60 (A. E. Stoddart 6-31) & 36 (A. E. Stoddart 5-17) by an inns & 125 runs.

16th Match: v Jamaica (Kingston)   March 27, 29.
A. Priestley's XII 237 (A. E. Stoddart 143, G. V. Livingstone 6-62) beat Jamaica 143 (B. H. Drury 65, A. E. Stoddart 7-67) & 79 (W. Williams 7-38) by an inns & 15 runs.

Mr Priestley's team in the West Indies in 1896-97, photographed in Barbados, before the Pavilion.

1896-97: A. Priestley's Team to the West Indies

Batting Averages

	M	I	NO	R	HS	Avge	100	c/s
A. E. Stoddart (Middx)	9	15	0	416	143	27.73	2	10
R. C. N. Palairet (Som)	8	14	1	336	65*	25.84	0	8
F. W. Bush	8	13	1	169	45*	14.08	0	6
S. M. J. Woods (Som)	9	14	0	193	28	13.78	0	8
G. Elliott	5	8	2	78	36*	13.00	0	3
C. A. Beldam (Middx)	7	11	2	115	24*	12.77	0	3
J. Leigh	8	13	0	150	26	11.53	0	4
R. Leigh-Barratt	9	15	0	171	38	11.40	0	7
H. T. Stanley (Som)	9	15	0	151	38	10.06	0	6
W. Williams (Middx)	9	15	3	98	40	8.16	0	6
C. C. Stone (Leics)	3	6	1	38	16*	7.60	0	0
R. P. Lewis (Oxford U)	8	12	7	16	7	3.20	0	7/6
A. Priestley	9	15	1	37	9	2.64	0	5

Bowling Averages

	O	M	R	W	Avge	BB	5i
A. E. Stoddart	303.4	128	520	53	9.81	7-67	5
W. Williams	202.3	55	464	43	10.79	7-38	3
S. M. J. Woods	230.2	75	501	35	14.31	6-60	2
H. T. Stanley	9	2	39	2	19.50	2-20	0
G. Elliott	12	3	29	1	29.00	1-13	0
F. W. Bush	102.4	19	245	8	30.62	2-15	0
R. Leigh-Barratt	113	41	225	6	37.50	3-40	0
C. A. Beldam	11	1	54	1	54.00	1-30	0

Also bowled: J. Leigh 3.2-0-14-0; C. C. Stone 4-2-8-0.
Played in non-first-class matches only: G. A. Maclean.

was the less formidable St Vincent XI. There were two other matches against Barbados, and each side won one.

Stoddart began his great run of success in the next game, hitting 107 v Antigua, 133 v St Kitts, 59 v United Services and 108 v Queens Park. The first three of these games were all innings victories, but the fourth was rained off.

The ninth fixture of the tour, at Port of Spain, was the most important game played up to that date in the West Indies, for it was the first time a representative West Indian Eleven had opposed an English touring team. The West Indian team was captained by Aucher Warner, brother of P. F. Warner, and contained players from Trinidad, British Guiana and Barbados. The match proved to be a fitting one for the occasion. The West Indies went in for the final innings requiring 141 to win, but six wickets fell for 41 and the Englishmen seemed sure of victory. Clarke and Constantine then added 75 and turned the tables on the visitors, the home side winning a great contest amid enormous excitement.

Following the defeat at the hands of the West Indies XI, the tourists played Trinidad twice and lost both encounters due to poor batting. The final fixtures of the tour were all in Jamaica, where all five games were won. In these matches the dominant feature was the all-round performances of Stoddart, who hit two more hundreds and on three occasions took 10 wickets in a match.

The team, except for C. C. Stone who was laid low with typhoid in Antigua, arrived back in England on 14 April. The results achieved by the touring team were disappointing, with five out of nine major fixtures ending in defeat. Stoddart did wonders, being easily top of both batting and bowling tables and without him, things would have been serious indeed.

In the issue of *Cricket* for 8 April 1897 was published the correspondence between Mr Priestley and Lord Hawke, and it would appear from the details set out that Lord Hawke treated Mr Priestley in a rather high-handed manner.

1897: tourists 0 for 4 against Philadelphia

In the summer of 1897, the associated cricket clubs of Philadelphia invited P. F. Warner to take a side out to the United States. According to Warner he had precisely a fortnight to find a suitable team and put them on the boat. The side was composed of P. F. Warner (Middx) (capt), G. L. Jessop (Gloucs), H. D. G. Leveson-Gower and H. B. Chinnery (Surrey), H. H. Marriott and F. W. Stocks (Leics), J. N. Tonge (Kent), F. G. Bull (Essex), R. A. Bennett (Hants), J. R. Head (Middx), W. M. Hemingway (Gloucs) and A. D. Whatman (Eton Ramblers).

As nearly all the team appeared in county cricket in 1897 and several indeed achieved quite distinguished records, this team was probably stronger than the preceding combination under F. Mitchell.

The team left Southampton on the *St Louis* on 4 September and arrived in America on the evening of 10 September. The first game against New York at Staten Island was a convincing win, but the standard of the New York side was much improved on some of the earlier efforts against English touring parties. Two odds matches of not much importance followed and then the tourists took on Philadelphia. The feature of the match was the

P. F. Warner's team to the U.S.A. in 1897. Back : G. L. Jessop, F. W. Stocks, A. D. Whatman, R. A. Bennett, J. R. Head. Centre : W. McG. Hemingway, J. N. Tonge, P. F. Warner, H. D. G. Leveson-Gower, H. B. Chinnery. Front : F. G. Bull, H. H. Marriott.

1897: P. F. Warner's Team to United States

1st Match: v New York (Staten Island)   Sept 13, 14.
P. F. Warner's XI 196 (M. R. Cobb 5-83) & 249 (J. R. Head 86, R. A. Bennett 53*, M. R. Cobb 7-125) beat New York 78 (F. G. Bull 6-41) & 123 (F. G. Bull 6-56) by 244 runs.

2nd Match: v New York (Staten Island) (One Day)   Sept 15.
New York 182-7 dec drew with P. F. Warner's XI 129-8.

3rd Match: v XXII Colts of Philadelphia (Manheim)   Sept 17, 18, 20.
Colts 148 (G. L. Jessop 11-53) & 240-13 dec (N. Z. Graves 57) drew with P. F. Warner's XI 159 (J. R. Head 51, S. G. Climenson 5-41) & 134-5 (P. F. Warner 56*).

4th Match: v XVI of Baltimore (Baltimore)   Sept 22, 23.
P. F. Warner's XII 252 (R. A. Bennett 64, W. M. Hemingway 61, K. Mallinckrodt 9-103) drew with Baltimore 147 & 41-4.

5th Match: v Philadelphia (Belmont C.C.)   Sept 24, 25, 27.
Philadelphia 242 (J. A. Lester 73, F. G. Bull 6-95) & 194-6 beat P. F. Warner's XI 63 (J. B. King 9-25) & 372 (J. R. Head 101, H. D. G. L-Gower 63, W. M. Hemingway 56, P. F. Warner 51, P. H. Clark 5-60) by 4 wkts.

6th Match: v Philadelphia (Merion C.C.)   Oct 1, 2, 4.
P. F. Warner's XI 322 (H. D. G. L-Gower 85, G. L. Jessop 66, H. B. Chinnery 63, P. H. Clark 5-78) & 70-3 beat Philadelphia 132 (G. L. Jessop 5-55, F. G. Bull 5-64) & 256 (J. B. King 68, W. W. Noble 64, F. G. Bull 5-98) by 7 wkts.

bowling of J. B. King. On the first evening he reduced the tourists to 4 wickets down without a run on the board, though it must be admitted that the light was poor. The next morning he ended with 9 for 25. Despite a much better second innings the English team could not recover lost ground and were defeated by 4 wickets. Before the return match, the side visited Niagara Falls, but they did not play any matches in Canada. The home team were without J. A. Lester, their highest scorer in the first game, for the return and Warner's XI managed to cope with J. B. King, going on to win by 7 wickets.

The side sailed for Southampton on 6 October, though Jessop and Marriott stayed behind in New York.

1897-98: Clem Hill's great innings for Australia

Following the success which attended A. E. Stoddart and his team in Australia in 1894-95, the authorities in Sydney and Melbourne invited the Middlesex cricketer to take a second side out in 1897-98. He selected the following 12 to accompany him: A. C. MacLaren (Lancs), J. R. Mason (Kent), N. F. Druce (Surrey), K. S. Ranjitsinhji (Sussex) and the professionals T. Richardson and T. W. Hayward (Surrey), J. T. Hearne (Middx), J. Briggs (Lancs), J. H. Board (Gloucs), W. Storer (Derbys), E. Wainwright (Yorks) and G. H. Hirst (Yorks). E. G. Wynyard (Hants) was selected but had to withdraw, whilst F. S. Jackson and W. Attewell declined. Two criticisms were levelled at the side prior to its voyage, the first being that 13 players were not enough and the second that the bowling was weak. The critics however were a little vague as to the cricketers who might strengthen the bowling.

The team sailed from Tilbury on 17 September, except for Ranjitsinhji, who joined the side later. Although the team stopped at Port Said and Colombo no cricket was played at either. They arrived at their destination on 25 October, the first game commencing three days later against South Australia. Clem Hill played a brilliant innings of 200 for the home team to which Ranjitsinhji replied with a lucky 189 and the match was drawn. Owing to 'flu, Stoddart could not bat for the tourists. The second match against Victoria, a side which was not very strong, was won by 2 wickets. The team went straight to Sydney and playing on the easiest wicket so far they relied heavily on two centuries from MacLaren for victory by 8 wickets. A series of odds matches then came to precede the first Test. This initial game between England and Australia began with some controversy. The Sydney ground authorities decided on the eve of the match that play should not commence on the scheduled first day. This decision was taken without consulting either captain and Stoddart made a formal protest, though in fact the postponement (due to the state of the pitch) helped England, since Ranjitsinhji was unwell. Stoddart did not play owing to a family bereavement, but even in his absence England won by the large margin of nine wickets. A fortnight later Australia redressed the balance with an even bigger victory at Melbourne, though England had the worse of the wicket. Only two odds matches separated this defeat from the third Test. Here again the best English bowler–Richardson– failed and the remainder of the attack seemed to lose heart. Joe Darling batted superbly but when England went to the wicket their leading batsmen were soon dismissed. Following on, MacLaren and Ranji looked as if they might save the game, but when Ranji went the batting collapsed to present Australia with

A. E. Stoddart's team in Australia playing the first Test match at Sydney, which the tourists won by 9 wickets.

a second innings victory. This time England could not blame the wicket.

For England the fourth Test was crucial since the rubber depended upon it. The visitors were without Hirst who had been injured at Adelaide and Wainwright played. About 18,000 people watched the start of the game and saw Australia tumble to six for 58. Clem Hill, the 20-year-old Australian, then played what has

1897-98: A. E. Stoddart's Team to Australia

1st Match: v South Australia (Adelaide)   Oct 28, 29, 31, Nov 1.
S. Australia 409 (C. Hill 200, F. Jarvis 79, T. Richardson 5-117) & 187-5 (J. J. Lyons 56) drew with English XI 475 (K. S. Ranjitsinhji 189, W. Storer 84, J. R. Mason 79, E. Jones 7-189).

2nd Match: v Victoria (Melbourne)   Nov 6, 8, 9, 10.
Victoria 306 (W. Bruce 88, C. E. McLeod 63, J. T. Hearne 5-61) & 247 (J. Worrall 83, J. Harry 50, T. W. Hayward 5-66) lost to English XI 250 (W. Storer 71*) & 305-8 (J. R. Mason 128*, K. S. Ranjitsinhji 64) by 2 wkts.

3rd Match: v New South Wales (Sydney)   Nov 12, 13, 15, 16.
N.S.W. 311 (H. Donnan 104, F. A. Iredale 89, A. C. Mackenzie 80) & 260 (A. C. Mackenzie 59, T. Richardson 5-80) lost to English XI 335 (A. C. MacLaren 142, W. Storer 81, M. A. Noble 5-111, T. R. McKibbin 5-139) & 237-2 (A. C. MacLaren 100, K. S. Ranjitsinhji 112*) by 8 wkts.

4th Match: v XVIII of Newcastle (Newcastle)   Nov 19, 20.
Newcastle 189 & 211-9 drew with English XI 429 (G. H. Hirst 139, A. E. Stoddart 116).

5th Match: v XXII of Glen Innes (Glen Innes)   Nov 22, 23.
Glen Innes 120 & 149 (A. E. Stoddart 10-49) lost to English XI 386-8 dec (T. W. Hayward 107*, N. F. Druce 56, J. R. Mason 53*) by an inns & 117 runs.

6th Match: v XIII of Queensland & N.S.W. (Brisbane)   Nov 26, 27, 29.
English XI 636 (A. C. MacLaren 181, N. F. Druce 126, G. H. Hirst 75*, J. R. Mason 74, K. S. Ranjitsinhji 67, T. R. McKibbin 5-158) drew with Queensland & N.S.W. 316-8 (S. E. Gregory 77, S. P. Jones 69, L. W. Pye 55).

7th Match: v XVIII of Toowoomba (Toowoomba)   Nov 30, Dec 1.
English XI 197 (T. W. Hayward 68) & 115-4 drew with Toowoomba 243-13 dec (P. Thomas 85).

8th Match: v XXII of New England (Armidale)   Dec 3, 4.
English XI 141 drew with New England 8-1 – rain.

9th Match: v Australia (Sydney)   Dec 13, 14, 15, 16, 17.
England 551 (K. S. Ranjitsinhji 175, A. C. MacLaren 109, T. W. Hayward 72, G. H. Hirst 62) & 96-1 (A. C. MacLaren 50*) beat Australia 237 (H. Trumble 70, C. E. McLeod 50*, J. T. Hearne 5-42) & 408 (J. Darling 101, C. Hill 96) by 9 wkts.

10th Match: v XVIII of Bendigo (Bendigo)   Dec 27, 28, 29.
Bendigo 150 & 212 (J. Briggs 9-84) lost to English XI 286 (J. R. Mason 128) & 79-0 by 10 wkts.

11th Match: v Australia (Melbourne)   Jan 1, 2, 4, 5.
Australia 520 (C. E. McLeod 112, F. A. Iredale 89, G. H. S. Trott 79, S. E. Gregory 71, C. Hill 58) beat England 315 (K. S. Ranjitsinhji 71, W. Storer 51) & 150 (M. A. Noble 6-49) by an inns & 55 runs.

12th Match: v XVIII of Ballarat (Ballarat)   Jan 7, 8.
Ballarat 283 (E. Wanliss 80) & 10-3 drew with English XI 342 (A. E. Stoddart 111, G. H. Hirst 59, J. R. Mason 58).

13th Match: v XXII of Stawell (Stawell)   Jan 10, 11.
English XI 214 drew with Stawell 233-16.

14th Match: v Australia (Adelaide)   Jan 14, 15, 17, 18, 19.
Australia 573 (J. Darling 178, F. A. Iredale 84, C. Hill 81, S. E. Gregory 52) beat England 278 (G. H. Hirst 85, T. W. Hayward 70) & 282 (A. C. MacLaren 124, K. S. Ranjitsinhji 77, C. E. McLeod 5-65, M. A. Noble 5-84) by an inns & 13 runs.

15th Match: v XXII of Western District (Hamilton)   Jan 21, 22.
Western District 168 & 119-5 drew with English XI 179.

16th Match: v Australia (Melbourne)   Jan 29, 31, Feb 1, 2.
Australia 323 (C. Hill 188, J. T. Hearne 6-98) & 115-2 (C. E. McLeod 64*) beat England 174 & 263 (K. S. Ranjitsinhji 55) by 8 wkts.

17th Match: v New South Wales (Sydney)   Feb 5, 7, 9, 10, 11.
New South Wales 415 (A. C. Mackenzie 130, L. W. Pye 80*) & 574 (S. E. Gregory 171, A. L. Newell 68*, W. P. Howell 95, H. Donnan 59, A. C. Mackenzie 52, J. T. Hearne 6-126) beat English XI 387 (N. F. Druce 109, T. W. Hayward 63, A. C. MacLaren 61, E. Wainwright 50, M. A. Noble 6-131) & 363 (A. C. MacLaren 140, E. Wainwright 68, T. W. Hayward 64*, M. A. Noble 6-117) by 239 runs.

18th Match: v XIII of Sydney & Melbourne Univ (Sydney)   Feb 12, 14.
English XI 333-7 dec (W. Storer 92, K. S. Ranjitsinji 60, N. F. Druce 54*, G. H. Hirst 56) drew with Universities 76-6.

19th Match: v Queensland & Victoria (Brisbane)   Feb 19, 21, 22.
English XI 133-5 rain stopped play.

20th Match: v Australia (Sydney)   Feb 26, 28, March 1, 2.
England 335 (A. C. MacLaren 65, N. F. Druce 64, E. Jones 6-82) & 178 lost to Australia 239 (C. E. McLeod 64, T. Richardson 8-94) & 276-4 (J. Darling 160, J. Worrall 62) by 6 wkts.

21st Match: v Victoria (Melbourne)   March 11, 12, 14, 15.
Victoria 328 (H. Trumble 107, J. H. Stuckey 59) & 132 (T. Richardson 5-35) lost to English XI 278 (T. W. Hayward 96, K. S. Ranjitsinhji 61, W. Roche 5-77) & 183-3 (K. S. Ranjitsinhji 61*) by 7 wkts.

22nd Match: v South Australia (Adelaide)   March 19, 21, 22, 23.
English XI 222 (J. H. Board 59, E. Jones 7-80) & 399 (E. Wainwright 105, J. R. Mason 84, E. Jones 7-157) drew with S. Australia 287 (J. Darling 88, J. J. Lyons 79, J. R. Mason 5-41) & 267-2 (C. Hill 124*, J. Darling 96).

1897-98: A. E. Stoddart's Team to Australia

Batting Averages

	M	I	NO	R	HS	Avge	100	c/s
K. S. Ranjitsinhji (Sussex)	12	22	3	1157	189	60.89	3	8
A. C. MacLaren (Lancs)	11	20	1	1037	142	54.57	5	4
T. W. Hayward (Surrey)	12	21	3	695	96	38.61	0	4
W. Storer (Derbys)	11	17	1	604	84	37.75	0	22
N. F. Druce (Surrey)	11	18	1	474	109	27.88	1	8
E. Wainwright (Yorks)	10	17	0	460	105	27.05	1	5
J. R. Mason (Kent)	12	21	1	514	128*	25.70	1	12
J. H. Board (Gloucs)	4	6	0	140	59	23.33	0	5/2
G. H. Hirst (Yorks)	11	17	1	338	85	21.12	0	10
A. E. Stoddart (Middx)	7	11	0	205	40	18.63	0	3
J. Briggs (Lancs)	8	12	3	165	46*	18.33	0	1
J. T. Hearne (Middx)	12	18	10	87	31*	10.87	0	5
T. Richardson (Surrey)	11	15	3	105	25*	8.42	0	6

Bowling Averages

	O	M	R	W	Avge	BB	5i
J. R. Mason	181.1	48	502	20	25.10	5-41	1
T. Richardson	518.2	107	1594	54	29.51	8-94	4
J. T. Hearne	559.2	188	1307	44	29.70	6-98	4
A. E. Stoddart	31	7	104	3	34.66	2-50	0
T. W. Hayward	184	40	645	15	43.00	5-66	1
W. Storer	73.3	8	284	6	47.33	4-79	0
J. Briggs	282	79	779	12	64.91	3-96	0
G. H. Hirst	232.2	62	682	9	75.77	4-66	0
E. Wainwright	72	14	249	1	249.00	1-32	0

Also bowled: K. S. Ranjitsinhji 19.4-5-58-0; J. H. Board 1-1-0-0; N. F. Druce 1-0-1-0.
Played in non-first-class matches only: A. Priestley.

been described as one of the greatest innings ever witnessed. Hill relished the fast bowling of Richardson and found little difficulty with the remainder of the attack. In contrast the English batting was wretched and once more the tourists followed on. Stouter resistance was displayed in the second innings – even Storer with a fractured finger played his part – and Australia needed 115 to win in their second innings. They had little difficulty in reaching their goal.

The English side suffered a further defeat at the hands of New South Wales, before meeting Australia in the final Test, at Sydney. For this game Stoddart stood down – he had totally failed with the bat in eleven-a-side matches and indeed had not even hit a fifty. MacLaren led England, as he had in the other Tests when Stoddart was absent. England batted well in their first innings and Richardson, bowling faster than any previous time on the tour, took 8 wickets in the Australian first innings to give his side a substantial lead. The match was then thrown away by careless batting which Trumble exploited and in the final innings Australia required 275 to win. Three catches were dropped and the home side won, taking the rubber by 4 matches to 1.

The two remaining games of the tour were the returns against Victoria and South Australia. The team left Adelaide on 24 March and the professionals arrived back in England by the overland route through France on 23 April. The amateurs chose to continue by sea, arriving a few days later, except for Ranji who left the team at Colombo.

The English public were most disappointed by the lack of success of the team and only MacLaren and Ranjitsinhji among the batsmen really came up to the mark. Of the bowlers, Hearne was the steadiest and Richardson came off a few times, but the rest found the Australian wickets too good for them.

For Australia the two left-handers Darling and Hill were the successes of the Test series; the former averaged 67.12 and the latter 56.50, both having eight completed innings – needless to say both were well ahead of the best English batsman. Noble was decidedly the most outstanding home bowler, his flighting of the ball being too subtle for the touring batsmen; Jones and Tumble were also most effective. In comparison it was surprising how poorly several of the visiting bowlers performed in the Tests – the great Yorkshireman Hirst took only two wickets for 304 runs.

The barracking of the Australian crowds came in for some criticism from the England captain, but apart from this the social aspect of the tour was unclouded.

The problem of 'throwing', which at one time seemed to be absent from Australian cricket, raised its head, and James Phillips, who umpired for the tourists, no-balled E. Jones twice.

1898: Pelham Warner returns to Canada and the United States

The Associated Cricket Clubs of Philadelphia issued a second invitation to P. F. Warner in 1898 to bring out a team of English Amateurs. This second side was in fact stronger than the first and the members were P. F. Warner (Middx) (capt), E. H. Bray (Middx), C. J. Burnup (Kent), C. O. H. Sewell (Gloucs), R. S. A. Warner, G. E. Winter (Cambridge U), F. Mitchell (Yorks), V. T. Hill (Som), E. C. Lee (Hants), B. J. T. Bosanquet (Middx), R. Berens (Oxford Authentics), J. L. Ainsworth (Liverpool) and E. F. Penn (Eton Ramblers). The team set sail from Liverpool on 27 August. Penn missed the boat and sailed in another which was fortunate for him, since the boat carrying the team broke down three times, the third time being in mid-Atlantic in a considerable gale, which resulted in numerous accidents to passengers and crew.

The first match was on a terrible wicket in Montreal and shooters were the order of the day. W. R. Gilbert and F. W. Terry were two old county cricketers among the opposing Fourteen, but neither achieved much. Before the second match began, two of the tourists, Penn and Lee, went down with scarlet fever. Ontario however were rather foolish to attempt an eleven-a-side match and the English team had an easy win.

Travelling to Philadelphia the side played the first game against the Philadelphians. The match was a very low scoring affair, none of the three completed innings reaching 100 and the visitors, due to Ainsworth's bowling, won by 8 wickets.

New York were quickly disposed of in the next match and after two odds matches, the team played the return against Philadelphia. About 9,000 turned out on the first day of this match, which was by far the best of the tour. The batsmen once more had a poor time, Ainsworth and the Philadelphian, J. B. King, taking the honours with their bowling.

The final fixture was in Chicago. The locals were no match for the visitors on even terms and when a thunderstorm ended the match, Chicago were very near defeat.

After a pretty dreadful series of train journeys between Chicago and New York, the team boarded the liner *Majestic* which docked in Liverpool on 19 October. Penn and Lee recovered from their illness and returned to England in mid-November.

1898: P. F. Warner's Team to North America

1st Match: v XIV of Eastern Canada (Montreal)   Sept 8, 9.
P. F. Warner's XII 130 (C. B. Godwin 6-33) & 105 beat E. Canada 82 (B. J. T. Bosanquet 5-9) & 65 by 88 runs.

2nd Match: v Ontario (Toronto)   Sept 12, 13, 14.
P. F. Warner's XI 437 (F. Mitchell 128, C. O. H. Sewell 122) beat Ontario 133 (J. L. Ainsworth 7-39) & 164 by an inns & 140 runs.

3rd Match: v Philadelphia (Wissahickon)   Sept 16, 17.
Philadelphia 94 (J. L. Ainsworth 6-54) & 59 (J. L. Ainsworth 5-14) lost to P. F. Warner's XI 84 & 70-2 by 8 wkts.

4th Match: v New York (Livingston)   Sept 21, 22.
New York 49 (B. J. T. Bosanquet 5-22, J. L. Ainsworth 5-25) & 123 lost to P. F. Warner's XI 419 (V. T. Hill 84, E. H. Bray 83, F. Mitchell 66, C. J. Burnup 61) by an inns & 247 runs.

5th Match: v XVIII Colts of Philadelphia (Haverford)   Sept 23, 24, 26.
Colts 77 (J. L. Ainsworth 8-31) & 159 (B. J. T. Bosanquet 8-43) drew with P. F. Warner's XI 133 (D. H. Adams 6-27) & 30-1.

6th Match: v XV of Baltimore (Catonsville)   Sept 28, 29.
Baltimore 126 (J. L. Ainsworth 7-35) & 30 (B. J. T. Bosanquet 8-13) lost to P. F. Warner's XI 150 & 8-1 by 9 wkts.

7th Match: v Philadelphia (Manheim)   Sept 30, Oct 1, 3.
Philadelphia 143 (J. L. Ainsworth 7-61) & 127 (A. M. Wood 53, J. L. Ainsworth 6-55) lost to P. F. Warner's XI 133 (J. B. King 6-32) & 161-6 by 4 wkts.

8th Match: v Chicago (Chicago) (12 a-side)   Oct 8, 10.
Chicago 74 & 83-7 (V. T. Hill 5-21) drew with P. F. Warner's XII 298 (B. J. T. Bosanquet 94, V. T. Hill 60).

1898-99: a train crash and a plague of locusts in South Africa

The fourth Tour to South Africa and the second under Lord Hawke was promoted by the Hon J. D. Logan of Matjesfontein. The side was composed of Lord Hawke (Yorks) (capt), A. G. Archer (Shropshire), H. R. Bromley-Davenport (Middx), F. Mitchell (Yorks), F. W. Milligan (Yorks), P. F. Warner (Middx), C. E. M. Wilson (Yorks) and the professionals J. H. Board (Gloucs), W. R. Cuttell (Lancs), S. Haigh (Yorks), A. E. Trott (Middx), J. T. Tyldesley (Lancs). The old Surrey cricketer G. A. Lohmann, who now resided in South Africa, acted as manager, A. A. White came as umpire and H. Kirk, the Trent Bridge dressing room attendant, was general dogsbody.

The team was by no means representative of England, but merely of good county standard. The inclusion of Haigh and Trott however meant that the bowling was in excellent hands.

Sailing from Southampton in the *Scot* on 3 December, the only break in the journey was for coaling at Madeira, and after a good voyage the team landed at Cape Town on 20 December. Following a knock-up match on 22 December, the first serious game was against Thirteen of Western Province, and a crowd of some 8,000 attended on the second day (Boxing Day). The batsmen found it difficult to get used to the matting wicket and only some good bowling by Haigh won the match. The second game was supposed to be against Western Province, with the home team including Brown, Tate, Guttridge and Barnes (four English coaches in South Africa) but there were objections to this arrangement and it was dropped. It was not until the fifth match of the tour that the team were met on even terms. The game should have been against South Africa, but some unpleasantness between Transvaal and Port Elizabeth prevented this, and the opponents were the Cape Colony XI, except that Bisset and Rowe were absent. The game was finely balanced after the first innings, but Mitchell then hit 81 and again Trott and Haigh won the match. A plague of locusts visited the ground on the last afternoon. At Grahamstown, White no-balled a local – Madden – for throwing, but the tourists were not unduly troubled, winning by 10 wickets.

In Johannesburg the second eleven-a-side game was staged, but the opponents, Transvaal, were completely outclassed and the tourists' score of 539 for 6 declared, containing hundreds by Mitchell, Tyldesley and Trott, broke several records. In Pretoria, the locals included Braund, the Surrey professional, who hit the highest score and returned the best bowling figures. Whilst in Pretoria, two of the team visited President Kruger and unsuccessfully tried to persuade him to come to the match.

The first game against South Africa took place at Johannesburg and large crowds turned out to see the match. At the close of play on the second day, the tourists having been 106 behind on first innings were 173 for 7 and South Africa seemed certain to win. Warner however carried out his bat for 132, then Trott, Haigh and Cuttell bowled out the home side for 99. On South Africa's part however the result was a vast improvement compared to the drubbing in the previous 'Tests'.

The team broke fresh ground by travelling to Bulawayo, where two matches were played. The ground there was laid out in three weeks after the rebellion had been quelled, and looked likely to develop into one of the best in Southern Africa. The wicket was matting and the outfield was bare of grass. Best feature of the first game was the left hand bowling of J. Bissett, who took 9 for 59. Lord Hawke could not play in the second match – against Fifteen of Rhodesia – but the home team's batting was very poor, except for Hallward, the old Lancing captain, who made 52.

The proposed match at Mafeking was abandoned as the local club could not raise a team and the tourists went on to Kimberley.

Lord Hawke's team to South Africa in 1898-99. Back: F. Hearne (umpire), A. G. Archer, W. R. Cuttell, F. Mitchell, C. E. M. Wilson, A. A. White (umpire). Centre: H. R. Bromley-Davenport, F. W. Milligan, S. Haigh, Lord Hawke, J. H. Board, A. E. Trott. Front: J. T. Tyldesley, P. F. Warner.

1898-99: Lord Hawke's Team to South Africa

1st Match: v XIII of Western Province (Cape Town) Dec 24, 26, 27.
English XI 141 (J. Middleton 7-54) & 140 (G. A. Rowe 5-54) beat W. Province 149 (A. E. Trott 7-68) & 107 by 25 runs.

2nd Match: v XIII of Western Province (Cape Town) Jan 2, 3.
English XI 186 (J. Middleton 5-70, G. A. Rowe 5-74) & 149 (G. A. Rowe 6-55) beat W. Province 104 (A. E. Trott 7-52) & 125 by 106 runs.

3rd Match: v XXII of Midlands (Graaf Reinet) Jan 6, 7.
English XI 191 (P. Gardiner 5-71, W. Greybe 5-118) & 63-2 beat Midlands 99 (A. E. Trott 12-38) & 154 by 8 wkts.

4th Match: v XV of Port Elizabeth (Port Elizabeth) Jan 10, 11, 12.
English XI 166 (O'Halloran 5-68) & 187 (A. E. Trott 84, O'Halloran 5-72) beat Port Elizabeth 173 & 80 (A. E. Trott 10-45) by 100 runs.

5th Match: v Cape Colony (Port Elizabeth) Jan 14, 16, 17.
English XI 134 (W. R. Cuttell 53, R. Graham 5-54) & 228 (F. Mitchell 81) beat Cape Colony 112 & 149 by 101 runs.

6th Match: v XV of Eastern Province (Grahamstown) Jan 20, 21.
English XI 210 (A. E. Trott 69, J. Martin 6-160) & 11-0 beat E. Province 88 (A. E. Trott 9-19) & 131 (F. W. Milligan 8-17) by 10 wkts.

7th Match: v XV of Border (Kingwilliamstown) Jan 25, 26.
Border 84 (A. E. Trott 8-41) & 147 (N. H. Giddy 66) lost to English XI 294 (S. Haigh 74) by an inns & 63 runs.

8th Match: v XV of Johannesburg (Johannesburg) Feb 1, 2, 3.
Johannesburg 136 (W. R. Solomon 64, F. W. Milligan 10-64) & 221-8 (J. H. Sinclair 56) drew with English XI 309 (J. H. Sinclair 5-81).

9th Match: v Transvaal (Johannesburg) Feb 4, 6, 7.
Transvaal 211 (A. E. Trott 7-74) & 123 lost to English XI 537-6 dec (F. Mitchell 162, J. T. Tyldesley 114, A. E. Trott 101*) by an inns & 203 runs.

10th Match: v XV of Transvaal (Pretoria) Feb 9, 10, 11.
English XI 230 (P. F. Warner 92, W. R. Cuttell 62, L. C. Braund 5-72) & 64-1 beat Transvaal 207 & 85 (A. E. Trott 10-29) by 9 wkts.

11th Match: v South Africa (Johannesburg) Feb 14, 15, 16.
England 145 & 237 (P. F. Warner 132*, J. Middleton 5-51) beat South Africa 251 (J. H. Sinclair 86) & 99 (A. E. Trott 5-49) by 32 runs.

12th Match: v XV of Griqualand West (Kimberley) Feb 20, 21.
Griqualand West 236 (W. A. Shalders 76) & 106 lost to English XI 367 (F. Mitchell 82, P. F. Warner 75, W. R. Cuttell 65, C. E. M. Wilson 51, J. Backmann 5-40) by an inns & 25 runs.

13th Match: v XVIII of Bulawayo (Bulawayo) March 1, 2, 3.
Bulawayo 123 & 180 (S. Haigh 11-44) lost to English XII 172 (S. Haigh 52, J. T. Tyldesley 51, J. Bissett 9-59) & 135-1 (P. F. Warner 54*) by 10 wkts.

14th Match: v XV of Rhodesia (Bulawayo) March 4, 6, 7.
English XI 275 (P. F. Warner 80, J. T. Tyldesley 71, H. M. Taberer 5-62) beat Rhodesia 121 (H. Hallward 52, S. Haigh 9-36) & 89 by an inns & 65 runs.

15th Match: v XV of Griqualand West (Kimberley) March 11, 12.
English XI 126 & 16-1 drew with Griqualand West (A. W. Powell 72, S. Haigh 9-44).

16th Match: v Cape Colony (Cape Town) March 25, 27, 28.
Cape Colony 110 (S. Haigh 8-34) & 138 (A. E. Trott 6-73) lost to English XI 277 (W. R. Cuttell 98, C. E. M. Wilson 69, R. Graham 6-97) by an inns & 29 runs.

17th Match: v South Africa (Cape Town) April 1, 3, 4.
England 92 (J. H. Sinclair 6-26) & 330 (J. T. Tyldesley 112) beat South Africa 177 (J. H. Sinclair 106) & 35 (S. Haigh 6-11).

Batting first, 9 wickets went down for 54, then Milligan and Archer added 72 for the last wicket. The local Fifteen, thanks to a brilliant innings by Powell, gained a lead on first innings, but a heavy thunderstorm abruptly ended the game as the Englishmen stood at 16 for 1 in their second innings. Haigh performed the hat-trick in this game. On the journey from Kimberley the train in which the team were travelling was involved in a collision. The train slid backwards when negotiating an incline and the brakes failed, allowing it to crash into the train behind. Milligan cut his nose and had his eye blacked, whilst Trott's thumb was put out of joint. Many of the windows were smashed, but the journey resumed and the next stop—Matjesfontein—was reached with no further mishap. The two remaining eleven-a-side fixtures were against Cape Colony (an easy win) and the return against South Africa at Newlands. For some inexplicable reason the South African side included two wicket-keepers in Halliwell and Prince and this strange selection was much criticised. There was a record gate for Newlands on the second day (Easter Monday) and excellent all-round cricket by Sinclair gave the home eleven a lead on first innings of 85. The tourists made 330 in their second attempt with Tyldesley hitting 112, but South Africa collapsed when going for the runs and were all out in 45 minutes, Haigh and Trott making the ball fizz off the matting.

1898-99: Lord Hawke's Team to South Africa

Batting Averages

	M	I	NO	R	HS	Avge	100	c/s
F. Mitchell (Yorks)	5	8	0	372	162	46.50	1	4
J. T. Tyldesley (Lancs)	5	8	0	299	114	37.37	2	4
W. R. Cuttell (Lancs)	5	8	0	271	98	33.87	0	4
A. G. Archer	1	2	1	31	24*	31.00	0	0
P. F. Warner (Middx)	5	8	1	214	132*	30.57	1	1
C. E. M. Wilson (Yorks)	5	8	1	178	69	25.42	0	2
A. E. Trott (Middx)	5	8	1	153	101*	21.85	1	6
F. W. Milligan (Yorks)	5	8	0	120	38	15.00	0	3
J. H. Board (Gloucs)	5	7	2	70	29	14.00	0	6/2
Lord Hawke (Yorks)	5	8	2	69	31*	11.50	0	4
S. Haigh (Yorks)	5	7	1	55	25	9.16	0	4
H. R. Bromley-Davenport (Middx)	4	5	0	7	4	1.40	0	1

Bowling Averages

	O	M	R	W	Avge	BB	5i
W. R. Cuttell	108.3	47	174	16	10.87	4-18	0
S. Haigh	199.3	77	419	33	12.69	8-34	2
A. E. Trott	254.1	84	546	42	13.00	7-74	3
F. W. Milligan	60	23	134	4	33.50	2-13	0

Also bowled: H. R. Bromley-Davenport 8-3-17-0; C. E. M. Wilson 5-0-15-0.
Played in non-first-class matches only: Hon E. Fiennes.

Milligan stayed behind when the Englishmen boarded the *Norman* at Cape Town–he was soon embroiled in the South African war. Southampton was reached on 21 April.

The tour was a great success and there was much surprise at the improvement in South African cricket since the initial tour, only ten years before.

1899: K. S. Ranjitsinhji's team in the United States and Canada

The team which sailed from Liverpool bound for New York on 16 September 1899 consisted of K. S. Ranjitsinhji (Sussex) (capt), G. Brann (Sussex), G. L. Jessop and C. L. Townsend (Gloucs), C. Robson and C. B. Llewellyn (Hants), S. M. J. Woods (Somerset), A. C. MacLaren (Lancs), A. E. Stoddart (Middx), B. J. T. Bosanquet (Oxford U), W. P. Robertson (Cambridge U) and A. Priestley (M.C.C.). In addition V. Barton, the Hampshire professional, travelled as baggage man.

It was obvious from the outset that the team was much too strong, despite being composed purely of amateurs, and it was rather foolish of the organiser to take a sledgehammer to a walnut.

Arriving on 20 September, the team went straight to Philadelphia to play a Colts Twenty-two, but rain and cold marred the drawn match. The first match, which was described as a 'Test Match' in some quarters, against Philadelphia, was most one sided. MacLaren hit 149 in 200 minutes and Jessop 64 in 35 minutes. Apart from Wood and Graves the home batsmen could do little.

In the New York game, the first pair of home batsmen added 109 before a wicket fell, but the tourists had it all their own way for the remainder of the game. The return against Philadelphia was very much a repeat of the first match, except that the English fielding was terrible.

As might be expected, Canada could do no better than Philadelphia in the last match of the tour and the team recorded another innings victory. The tour ended on 13 October and it is believed that the Philadelphian clubs were out of pocket on the venture.

1899: K. S. Ranjitsinhji's Team to North America

1st Match: v XXII Colts of Philadelphia (Elmwood) Sept 25, 26, 27.
Colts 205 (C. B. Llewellyn 7-55) & 95-9 drew with K. S. Ranjitsinhji's XII 185 (B. J. T. Bosanquet 56, W. P. O'Neill 6-70).

2nd Match: v Philadelphia (Haverford) Sept 29, 30, Oct 2.
Philadelphia 156 (G. L. Jessop 6-52) & 106 lost to K. S. Ranjitsinhji's XI 435 (A. C. MacLaren 149, G. L. Jessop 64, K. S. Ranjitsinhji 57, A. E. Stoddart 56) by an inns & 173 runs.

3rd Match: v XIV of New York (Staten Island) Oct 4, 5.
New York 149 (M. R. Cobb 77, G. L. Jessop 9-17) & 132-11 drew with K. S. Ranjitsinhji's XI 330-8 dec (G. Brann 137*, G. L. Jessop 51, M. R. Cobb 5-93).

4th Match: v Philadelphia (Germantown C.C.) Oct 7, 9, 10.
K. S. Ranjitsinhji's XI 363 (A. E. Stoddart 74, K. S. Ranjitsinhji 68, A. C. MacLaren 52, P. H. Clark 5-77) beat Philadelphia 85 & 147 by an inns & 131 runs.

5th Match: v Canada (Toronto) Oct 12, 13.
Canada 87 (C. L. Townsend 6-33) & 174 lost to K. S. Ranjitsinhji's XI 267-7 dec (G. L. Jessop 66, A. E. Stoddart 63*) by an inns & 6 runs.

1901: Philadelphia still a force in cricket

The team which accompanied B. J. T. Bosanquet to North America in 1901 was a much more realistic one than had been Ranjitsinhji's side of 1899. The 1901 team was still a first-class one in English terms and the equal of one of the lesser County Championship sides. Arriving in New York from Liverpool on 16 September, the full complement was B. J. T. Bosanquet (Middx) (capt), F. Mitchell (Yorks), E. M. Dowson (Surrey), V. F. S. Crawford (Surrey), E. R. Wilson (Cambridge U), R. E. More (Middx), A. M. Hollins (Oxford U), P. R. Johnson (Cambridge U), R. O. Schwarz (Middx), W. E. Harrison, I. U. Parkin and A. Priestley.

In the first match against the Colts, the tourists were tied up by W. G. Graham, a slow left-armer, and lost by 186 runs–all nineteen of the opposition fielded which made matters more difficult. In the first of the two Philadelphian matches, J. A. Lester batted finely, but no one supported him and the Englishmen won by a good match. Breaking new ground the team then went to Bayonne and needed 55 to win in an hour on the last afternoon, and they scored the runs in 45 minutes with 7 wickets in hand. Philadelphia played better than for some years in the return match. Brown hit the first hundred against a touring side since 1892 and the Philadelphians achieved a commanding first innings lead. Clark took the last five wickets in the English second innings in 7 balls and the tourists lost by 229 runs. The final game was against Canada. The tourists had little difficulty in winning, despite missing Mitchell, who had to return home, and More who was ill.

The tour was a success and gave a boost to North American cricket.

1901: B. J. T. Bosanquet's Team to North America

1st Match: v XVIII Colts & Captain (Wissahickon) Sept 20, 21, 23.
Colts 173 & 242 (R. E. More 7-88) beat B. J. T. Bosanquet's XII 131 (W. G. Graham 6-37) & 98 (W. G. Graham 6-26) by 186 runs.

2nd Match: v Philadelphia (Philadelphia) Sept 27, 28, 30.
B. J. T. Bosanquet's XI 198 (J. B. King 8-78) & 143 (J. B. King 6-57) beat Philadelphia 103 (R. E. More 6-28) & 177 (J. A. Lester 73*, R. E. More 6-73) by 61 runs.

3rd Match: v Knickerbocker A.C. (Bayonne, N.J.) Oct 2, 3.
Knickerbocker XII 143 (R. E. More 7-44) & 79 (B. J. T. Bosanquet 7-22) lost to B. J. T. Bosanquet's XII 168 (F. F. Kelly 8-56) & 58-4 by 7 wkts.

4th Match: v Philadelphia (Manheim) Oct 4, 5, 7.
Philadelphia 312 (R. D. Brown 103, F. H. Bohlen 60, C. C. Morris 55, E. R. Wilson 5-100) & 186 (J. A. Lester 69, R. E. More 6-62) beat B. J. T. Bosanquet's XI 166 (J. B. King 6-74) & 103 (P. H. Clark 7-22) by 229 runs.

5th Match: v Canada (Toronto) Oct 11, 12.
Canada 97 (E. M. Dowson 7-51) & 114 lost to B. J. T. Bosanquet's XI 218 (B. J. T. Bosanquet 97) by an inns & 7 runs.

1901-02: a poor side do badly in Australia

The 1901-02 visit to Australia was possibly as ill-advised as the twin tours of 1887-88. The M.C.C. agreed in the spring of 1901 to make the necessary arrangements in England and select the team for the tour, but on 13 May, the Committee at Lord's announced that it was impossible to recruit a representative English team and withdrew from the venture. A. C. MacLaren, the Lancashire captain, was then persuaded to attempt the task and eventually gathered the following cricketers to his banner: G. L. Jessop (Gloucs), A. O. Jones (Notts), H. G. Garnett (Lancs), C. P. McGahey (Essex), C. Robson (Hants), T. W. Hayward (Surrey), J. T. Tyldesley (Lancs), William Quaife (Warwicks), A. F. A. Lilley (Warwicks), L. C. Braund (Somerset), C. Blythe (Kent), S. F. Barnes (Lancs) and J. R. Gunn (Notts). The Yorkshire Committee refused to allow W. Rhodes and G. H. Hirst–the two outstanding bowlers of the 1901 season–to go. It was then reported that the 1902 Australians would refuse to play Yorkshire, but this proved to be a false rumour. Several well-known amateurs, including the top three in the 1901 averages, Fry, Ranjitsinhji and Palairet, were also absent. The surprise selection of the side was S. F. Barnes, who was totally unknown to the cricket public at large. Most of Barnes' cricket had been in the Lancashire League, for Rishton and latterly for Burnley, though he had played the odd games for Warwickshire and Lancashire.

The team left Tilbury on board the *Omrah* on 27 September, except for Jessop, who took the overland route to Marseilles. The first match of the tour began in Adelaide five days after landing. Clem Hill hit 107 and 80 and George Giffen picked up 13 wickets to provide an easy win for South Australia. Going on to Melbourne, Barnes was too much for the Victorian team and gave the tourists their first victory in a low scoring match. Runs came much more freely at Sydney in the third match. MacLaren hit a century but when the visitors appeared to have the match in hand the late order N.S.W. batsmen completely altered matters and a finely fought game was lost by 53 runs. There were four odds matches before the first Test at Sydney. MacLaren won the toss and batted. He and Hayward put on 154, there was a middle-order collapse, but all the later men played well and the total realised was 464. The expected large reply from Australia never materialised. Barnes, Braund and Blythe ran through the home batting twice and England attained victory by an innings. Another four odds matches came and went before the second Test at Melbourne. MacLaren won the toss and put Australia in on a sticky wicket. Barnes and Blythe had them all out for 112, but England gave a dreadful display against Noble and Trumble to fall for 61. Australia then slid to 48 for 5 by the close of play. On the next day Hill hit a magnificent 99 and then Duff scored a century, which left England needing 405 to win. Only Tyldesley of the English batsmen looked at home and Australia went on to win by 229 runs. The batsmen partially redeemed themselves in the next two odds matches with Braund, McGahey, Hayward and MacLaren scoring centuries.

Injuries to Barnes and Blythe during the match were the reasons for Australia winning the third Test at Adelaide. The home side required 315 for victory when starting the fourth innings of the game, but with Barnes in bed with an injured knee and Blythe useless through an injured finger, the England attack was too weak to control Clem Hill or indeed any of his colleagues.

The tourists were without Barnes and Blythe for the return with New South Wales, but some extraordinary batting by MacLaren, Hayward and Tyldesley produced a total of 769 and with New South Wales getting the worse of the wicket in their second innings, the English team had a massive win. Barnes could still not play in the fourth Test and though MacLaren won the toss for the fourth time and went on to hit a brilliant 92, the batting in the England second innings was appalling and Australia had no difficulty in winning the rubber. Victoria were beaten in the return game and in the final Test it appeared as if England

1901-02: A. C. MacLaren's Team to Australia

Batting Averages

		M	I	NO	R	HS	Avge	100	c/s
A. C. MacLaren	(Lancs)	10	16	0	929	167	58.06	4	19
T. W. Hayward	(Surrey)	11	19	1	701	174	38.94	1	5
J. T. Tyldesley	(Lancs)	11	19	0	696	142	36.63	2	5
L. C. Braund	(Som)	11	19	5	404	103*	28.85	1	24
Wm. Quaife	(Warks)	11	19	1	440	68	24.44	0	6
C. Robson	(Hants)	1	2	1	24	17*	24.00	0	0/3
A. F. A. Lilley	(Warks)	11	18	0	406	84	22.55	0	20/6
C. P. McGahey	(Essex)	7	12	2	210	57	21.00	0	3
G. L. Jessop	(Gloucs)	10	18	0	359	87	19.94	0	5
A. O. Jones	(Notts)	11	19	1	229	44	12.72	0	13
S. F. Barnes	(Lancs)	6	10	2	90	26*	11.25	0	5
J. R. Gunn	(Notts)	9	16	2	154	30	11.00	0	6
H. G. Garnett	(Lancs)	4	6	1	41	17	8.20	0	3/1
C. Blythe	(Kent)	8	14	6	62	20	7.75	0	3

Bowling Averages

	O	M	R	W	Avge	BB	5i
S. F. Barnes	285.4	51	676	41	16.48	7-38	5
T. W. Hayward	71	28	208	10	20.80	4-22	0
C. Blythe	298.5	51	711	34	20.91	5-45	1
C. P. McGahey	61.4	12	165	7	23.57	3-58	0
J. R. Gunn	307.1	94	769	29	26.51	5-73	2
L. C. Braund	623.5	147	1779	62	28.69	6-90	7
G. L. Jessop	129	30	397	12	33.08	4-68	5
A. O. Jones	49	8	161	3	53.66	1-24	0

Also bowled: Wm. Quaife 5-0-18-0.
Played in non-first-class matches only: S. V. Green, S. M. J. Woods.

1901-02: A. C. MacLaren's Team to Australia

1st Match: v South Australia (Adelaide) Nov 9, 11, 12, 13.
S. Australia 230 (C. Hill 107) & 207 (C. Hill 80, C. Blythe 5-45) beat English XI 118 (G. Giffen 7-46) & 86 (G. Giffen 6-47) by 233 runs.

2nd Match: v Victoria (Melbourne) Nov 15, 16, 17, 18.
English XI 166 (C. E. McLeod 5-75) & 174 (C. P. McGahey 57, C. E. McLeod 5-57) beat Victoria 133 (S. F. Barnes 5-61) & 89 (S. F. Barnes 7-38) by 118 runs.

3rd Match: v New South Wales (Sydney) Nov 22, 23, 25, 26, 27.
N.S.W. 288 (V. T. Trumper 67, L. C. Braund 6-109) & 422 (L. O. S. Poidevin 151*, M. A. Noble 74, F. A. Iredale 67, L. C. Braund 6-130) beat English XI 332 (A. C. MacLaren 145) & 325 (A. F. A. Lilley 80, A. C. MacLaren 73, J. T. Tyldesley 57, T. W. Hayward 53, G. C. Clarke 6-133) by 53 runs.

4th Match: v XVIII of West Maitland (West Maitland) Nov 29, 30.
West Maitland 558-15 dec (E. Capp 117, N. Lindsay 104, McGlinchy 92) drew with English XI 221-5 (T. W. Hayward 66, Wm Quaife 55*).

5th Match: v XVIII of Glen Innes (Glen Innes) Dec 2, 3.
Glen Innes 141 (C. Blythe 10-61) & 79 (J. R. Gunn 9-37) lost to English XI 309-7 dec (T. W. Hayward 100, J. R. Gunn 97) by an inns & 89 runs.

6th Match: v XVIII of Armidale (Armidale) Dec 4, 5.
English XI 254 (J. R. Gunn 119*) & 204-7 (L. C. Braund 72) drew with Armidale 111.

7th Match: v XV of Newcastle (Newcastle) Dec 7, 9.
English XI 315 (C. P. McGahey 52) & 216 (G. L. Jessop 85) drew with Newcastle 241 (Mackay 68) & 73-0.

8th Match: v Australia (Sydney) Dec 13, 14, 16.
England 464 (A. C. MacLaren 116, A. F. A. Lilley 84, T. W. Hayward 69, L. C. Braund 58) beat Australia 168 (S. F. Barnes 5-65) & 172 (L. C. Braund 5-61) by an inns & 124 runs.

9th Match: v XVIII of Goulburn (Goulburn) Dec 20, 21.
Goulburn 190 (A. O. Jones 10-49) & 165-16 dec (Newton 52) lost to English XI 192 (C. P. McGahey 55) & 164-4 (H. G. Garnett 54) by 6 wkts.

10th Match: v XVIII of Bendigo (Bendigo) Dec 26, 27, 28.
English XI 341 (T. W. Hayward 100, Wm Quaife 83, A. O. Jones 66) & 204-5 (J. T. Tyldesley 73) drew with Bendigo 295 (C. Eeles 78).

11th Match: v Australia (Melbourne) Jan 1, 2, 3, 4.
Australia 112 (S. F. Barnes 6-42) & 353 (R. A. Duff 104, C. Hill 99, S. F. Barnes 7-121) beat England 61 (M. A. Noble 7-17) & 175 (J. T. Tyldesley 66, M. A. Noble 6-60) by 229 runs.

12th Match: v XVIII of Stawell (Stawell) Jan 8, 9.
English XI 626 (L. C. Braund 127, C. P. McGahey 101, A. O. Jones 95, G. L. Jessop 68, A. C. MacLaren 56) & 164-3 (C. Robson 74, J. R. Gunn 59) drew with Stawell 130 (L. C. Braund 7-42).

13th Match: v XVIII of Ballarat (Ballarat) Jan 10, 11.
English XI 469 (T. W. Hayward 197, A. C. MacLaren 138) drew with Ballarat 235-10.

14th Match: v Australia (Adelaide) Jan 17, 18, 20, 21, 22, 23.
England 388 (L. C. Braund 103*, T. W. Hayward 90, Wm Quaife 68, A. C. MacLaren 67) & 247 (H. Trumble 6-74) lost to Australia 321 (C. Hill 98, V. T. Trumper 65, S. E. Gregory 55, J. R. Gunn 5-76) & 315-6 (C. Hill 97, J. Darling 69, H. Trumble 62*) by 4 wkts.

15th Match: v XVI of Country (Melbourne) Jan 25, 27, 28.
English XI 377-6 dec (Wm Quaife 91, C. P. McGahey 79, T. W. Hayward 57) & 2-0 beat Country XVI 111 & 267 (J. Harry 64) by 10 wkts.

16th Match: v New South Wales (Sydney) Jan 31, Feb 1, 3, 4, 5.
N.S.W. 432 (S. E. Gregory 147, M. A. Noble 56, R. A. Duff 50) & 209 (S. E. Gregory 75, L. C. Braund 6-90) lost to English XI 769 (T. W. Hayward 174, A. C. MacLaren 167, J. T. Tyldesley 142, G. L. Jessop 87, Wm Quaife 62) by an inns & 128 runs.

17th Match: v XVIII of Western District (Bathurst) Feb 7, 8.
English XI 505 (Wm Quaife 159*, H. G. Garnett 89, A. C. MacLaren 79, C. P. McGahey 71) drew with Western District 177 (L. C. Braund 12-48).

18th Match: v Australia (Sydney) Feb 14, 15, 17, 18.
England 317 (A. C. MacLaren 92, J. T. Tyldesley 79) & 99 (J. V. Saunders 5-43, M. A. Noble 5-54) lost to Australia 299 (M. A. Noble 56, W. W. Armstrong 55) & 121-3 (R. A. Duff 51*) by 7 wkts.

19th Match: v Victoria (Melbourne) Feb 22, 24, 25.
Victoria 129 (T. Warne 61*, L. C. Braund 5-67) & 182 (H. Stuckey 54) lost to English XI 298 (A. C. MacLaren 100, F. Collins 5-52) & 14-2 by 8 wkts.

20th Match: v Australia (Melbourne) Feb 28, March 1, 3, 4.
Australia 144 & 255 (C. Hill 87, L. C. Braund 5-95) beat England 189 (H. Trumble 5-62) & 178 (M. A. Noble 6-98) by 32 runs.

21st Match: v XVIII of Broken Hill (Broken Hill) March 11, 12.
English XI 173 & 190-7 (J. T. Tyldesley 69, Wm Quaife 50) drew with Broken Hill 221 (Caust 90*).

22nd Match: v South Australia (Adelaide) March 14, 15, 17, 18.
S. Australia 207 (N. Claxton 61, J. R. Gunn 5-73, L. C. Braund 5-116) & 306 (N. Claxton 83, C. Hill 61) lost to English XI 318 (J. T. Tyldesley 126, T. W. Hayward 57) & 196-4 by 6 wkts.

might find further consolation. A first innings lead of 45 was achieved and though Clem Hill managed 87 in his second innings, England needed only 211 for victory and were 87 for 3 at the close of the third day. Unfortunately the wicket got more difficult overnight and against Noble the rest of the side disintegrated.

The tour ended at Adelaide with the return against South Australia, which provided a win for the departing team.

The main party of the touring side arrived back in England on 27 April. The side won bouquets for its fielding, Jessop, Braund, MacLaren and Jones being outstanding. Only MacLaren and Hayward of the batsmen came off and Jessop, Jones and Gunn were complete failures. The bowling, which was weak to begin with, could not stand the absence of Barnes. Australia were not regarded as outstanding and the critics were of the opinion that Stoddart's 1897-98 side would have brought home the 'Ashes'.

1901-02: an amateur team tour the West Indies

H. D. G. Leveson-Gower selected the following team of English amateurs to tour the West Indies in 1901-02: R. A. Bennett (capt), R. N. R. Blaker (Kent), B. J. T. Bosanquet (Middx), T. H. K. Dashwood (Herts), E. W. Dillon (Kent), E. M. Dowson (Surrey), F. L. Fane (Essex), F. H. Hollins (Oxford U), E. C. Lee (Hants), A. D. Whatman (Eton Ramblers) and E. R. Wilson (Cambridge U). The all-amateur side, which contained three of the team that had recently returned from the tour to North America, was about the same strength as that combination. Leaving Southampton on 8 January aboard s.s. *Atrato*, the party arrived in Barbados on 20 January and commenced their first match two days later against Barbados. E. R. Wilson, owing to the death of his mother, and E. M. Dowson, who was ill, could not play and the tourists enrolled L. Arbuthnot and J. A. Davenport to make up the side. The ground was under water when play was scheduled to start, but it quickly dried out and on an easy wicket Barbados ran up a large total. Fast bowling by M. L. Horne then skittled the tourists out and Barbados won by an innings. Wilson and Dowson played in the return game and this made all the difference, the tourists winning by 8 wickets. The third game was against a Combined team of Trinidad, British Guiana and Barbados. Although the Combined side had a lead of 89 on the first innings, their eventual victory was due to the rain-affected wicket on which the tourists played their second innings.

From Barbados the Englishmen went to Jamaica where they took the island by storm. Six matches were played and all were victories, five of them by an innings. The standard of cricket in Jamaica was not up to that of Barbados.

The Combined team of Grenada and St Vincent was beaten twice and the tourists travelled on to Trinidad, where they were

1901-02: R. A. Bennett's Team to the West Indies

1st Match: v Barbados (Wanderers C.C.)   Jan 22, 23, 24.
Barbados 317 (V. Challenor 67, G. Cox 58, F. Hinds 55, B. J. T. Bosanquet 6-89) beat R. A. Bennett's XI 97 (M. L. Horne 8-39) & 149 (F. L. Fane 50, Shepherd 5-53, Layne 5-54) by an inns & 71 runs.

2nd Match: v Barbados (Bridgetown)   Jan 27, 28.
Barbados 193 (E. M. Dowson 5-89) & 141 lost to R. A. Bennett's XI 236 (F. H. Hollins 58) & 99-2 by 8 wkts.

3rd Match: v West Indies (Bridgetown)   Jan 29, 30.
R. A. Bennett's XI 147 (Burton 7-54) & 85 (Woods 7-38) lost to West Indies 236 (H. B. G. Austin 68, G. C. Learmond 54) by an inns & 4 runs.

4th Match: v Jamaica (Sabina Park)   Feb 8, 10.
R. A. Bennett's XI 326 (E. R. Wilson 81, F. H. Hollins 54*) beat Jamaica 33 (E. M. Dowson 8-21) & 154 (E. M. Dowson 8-37) by an inns & 139 runs.

5th Match: v XVI Colts (Sabina Park) (One Day)   Feb 11.
R. A. Bennett's XI 227 beat Colts 78 (E. M. Dowson 10-38) & 43-4 by 149 runs.

6th Match: v Jamaica Born (Sabina Park)   Feb 12, 13.
R. A. Bennett's XI 298 (B. J. T. Bosanquet 58*, E. C. Lee 53, F. A. Foster 6-128) & 134-3 dec (F. L. Fane 56*, R. N. R. Blaker 55) beat Jamaica Born 172 (G. C. Linton 60) & 121 (E. M. Dowson 5-48) by 139 runs.

7th Match: v Jamaica (Sabina Park)   Feb 14, 15.
R. A. Bennett's XI 362 (F. H. Hollins 74, F. A. Foster 6-147) beat Jamaica 117 & 177 (S. Snow 54, B. J. T. Bosanquet 5-29) by an inns & 68 runs.

8th Match: v St Elizabeth XII (Black River)   Feb 18, 19.
St Elizabeth XII 92 (B. J. T. Bosanquet 5-78) & 117 (E. M. Dowson 6-26) lost to R. A. Bennett's XII 330 (T. H. K. Dashwood 120*, E. M. Dowson 80, Gooden 5-78) by an inns & 121 runs.

9th Match: v Combined XI (Sabina Park)   Feb 21, 22.
Combined XI 139 (E. R. Wilson 6-39) & 72 (B. J. T. Bosanquet 8-30) lost to R. A. Bennett's XI 293 (E. R. Wilson 71, B. J. T. Bosanquet 63, E. W. Dillon 50, G. H. Withers 5-77) by an inns & 82 runs.

10th Match: v Grenada & St Vincent (Grenada)   March 5, 6.
Grenada & St Vincent 87 (B. J. T. Bosanquet 5-15) & 108 (B. J. T. Bosanquet 5-35) lost to R. A. Bennett's XI 214 (W. H. Mignon 5-70, R. Olliviere 5-37) by an inns & 19 runs.

11th Match: v Grenada & St Vincent (Grenada)   March 6, 7.
R. A. Bennett's XI 140 (R. Olliviere 9-79) & 109 (A. H. Hughes 5-25) beat Grenada & St Vincent 64 (E. M. Dowson 6-33) & 120 (B. J. T. Bosanquet 5-41) by 65 runs.

12th Match: v Trinidad (Oval, Trinidad) (12-a-side)   March 10, 11, 12.
Trinidad 322 (E. R. Wilson 5-64) & 116 lost to R. A. Bennett's XII 178 (B. J. T. Bosanquet 73, S. Smith 8-88) & 127-6 by 5 wkts.

13th Match: v Trinidad (Queen's Park)   March 14, 15.
Trinidad 114 (B. J. T. Bosanquet 5-72) & 104 (E. M. Dowson 7-30) lost to R. A. Bennett's XII 122 (S. Smith 6-56) & 97-2 by 9 wkts.

14th Match: v West Indies (Queen's Park)   March 20, 21.
West Indies 200 (L. S. Constantine 84, W. Weber 59) & 79 (B. J. T. Bosanquet 5-33) beat R. A. Bennett's XI 71 (S. Smith 9-34) & 97 (S. Smith 7-51) by 111 runs.

15th Match: v British Guiana (Georgetown)   March 31, April 1, 2.
R. A. Bennett's XI 131 (Burton 5-30, Woods 5-81) & 89 (Burton 6-37) lost to British Guiana 154 (E. R. D. Moulder 64, E. R. Wilson 6-30) & 69-6 by 4 wkts.

16th Match: v West Indies (Georgetown)   April 4, 5, 7.
West Indies 92 (E. R. Wilson 7-46) & 33 (E. R. Wilson 7-16) lost to R. A. Bennett's XI 455 (E. M. Dowson 112, B. J. T. Bosanquet 69, A. D. Whatman 60) by an inns & 330 runs.

17th Match: v British Guiana (Georgetown)   April 7, 8, 9, 10.
R. A. Bennett's XI 90 (Burton 6-39) & 277 (B. J. T. Bosanquet 57) lost to British Guiana 206 (E. R. D. Moulder 64) & 163-6 (E. R. D. Moulder 94*) by 4 wkts.
Two other matches were played as 'fill-in' games.

18th Match: v United Services (Bridgetown) (One Day)   Jan 25.
R. A. Bennett's XI 162 (E. W. Dillon 71, Whapham 6-27) beat United Services 152 by 10 runs.

19th Match: v W. Bowring's XI (Barbados)   Jan 31, Feb 1.
R. A. Bennett's XI 384-6 dec (R. N. R. Blaker 100, B. J. T. Bosanquet 97, W. Hoad 5-91) drew with W. Bowring's XI 187 & 175-4 (W. Bowring 55).

headed on first innings, due to some excellent bowling by the left-handed S. Smith, but the combination of Bosanquet, Wilson and Dowson proved too much for Trinidad in their second innings and the tourists won by 5 wickets. Two very bad wickets at Queen's Park provided a second win for the tourists over Trinidad, but a loss against All West Indies, when S. Smith took 9 for 34 and 7 for 51.

The three last matches of the tour were in British Guiana, where, curiously, British Guiana beat the tourists twice, but the visitors managed to defeat the All West Indies Eleven by the large margin of an innings and 330 runs. Wilson took 14 wickets in this match and Dowson hit a century.

The tour was a most pleasant one and Wilson, Dowson and Bosanquet were very successful with the ball. The poor wickets told against the batsmen, only Bosanquet being consistently among the runs.

1901-02: R. A. Bennett's Team to the West Indies

Batting Averages

	M	I	NO	R	HS	Avge	100	c/s
B. J. T. Bosanquet (Middx)	13	22	4	623	69	34.61	0	13
E. R. Wilson (Cambr U)	12	17	1	402	81	26.80	0	12
F. H. Hollins (Oxford U)	12	20	4	382	74	23.87	0	19
F. L. Fane (Essex)	13	22	2	456	56*	22.80	0	7
E. M. Dowson (Surrey)	12	17	1	342	112	21.37	1	8
E. W. Dillon (Kent)	13	21	0	417	54	19.85	0	6
A. D. Whatman	13	18	4	200	60	14.28	0	11/4
R. N. R. Blaker (Kent)	12	19	0	256	55	13.47	0	12
R. A. Bennett	10	13	2	141	32*	12.81	0	14/17
E. C. Lee (Hants)	12	18	0	224	53	12.44	0	13
T. H. K. Dashwood (Herts)	13	19	1	200	32	11.11	0	10
L. Arbuthnot	7	11	6	44	17*	8.80	0	2
J. A. Davenport	1	2	0	0	0	0.00	0	0

Bowling Averages

	O	M	R	W	Avge	BB	5i
E. R. Wilson	414.1	144	767	67	11.44	7-16	5
E. M. Dowson	404.5	121	997	80	12.46	8-21	5
R. N. R. Blaker	30	9	74	5	14.80	2-1	0
E. W. Dillon	122.1	24	325	20	16.25	3-18	0
B. J. T. Bosanquet	338.3	92	906	55	16.47	8-30	5
F. H. Hollins	3	0	20	1	20.00	1-20	0
E. C. Lee	17	5	56	1	56.00	1-41	0

Also bowled: A. D. Whatman 9-3-23-0.
Played in non-first-class matches only: A. G. Robinson.

1902-03: the first full tour of New Zealand

The 1902-03 tour of Lord Hawke's team was a new departure for English cricket, since, for the first time, the principal object of the venture was to visit New Zealand, the American and Australian sections being appendages to the main programme.

The tour was undertaken at the request of the New Zealand Cricket Council, who asked Lord Hawke to select and lead the team. Owing to his mother's illness, Lord Hawke was unable to travel with the side and the duties of captaincy devolved on P. F. Warner (Middx). He was accompanied by C. J. Burnup (Kent), T. L. Taylor (Yorks), F. L. Fane (Essex), B. J. T. Bosanquet (Middx), P. R. Johnson (Somerset), E. M. Dowson (Surrey), J. Stanning (Lancs), A. E. Leatham (Gloucs), A. D. Whatman (Eton Ramblers) and two professionals, G. J. Thompson (Northants) and S. Hargreave (Warwicks). The side, except for Taylor, left Liverpool in the s.s. *Majestic* on 12 November. Arriving at New York, they stayed there overnight and then travelled to San Francisco via Chicago. In San Francisco a single innings match was played on a ground totally unsuitable for cricket – the umpires carried brooms and swept the wicket after each over! Having crossed the Pacific, calling at Honolulu, the tourists arrived in New Zealand and commenced their opening match, against Auckland. Bad fielding by the home side, who then had to bat on a difficult wicket, enabled the visitors to claim an innings victory. In the second game neither Whatman or Stanning could play, so an old Etonian, J. W. Williams, was co-opted – that and the next three odds games were won with ease. The second eleven-a-side contest occurred at Wellington, where about 7,000 spectators attended the first day. Wellington played well for the first two innings, but their batting collapsed in their second attempt and Burnup and Warner hit off the runs for victory without loss. Four more odds matches were played prior to meeting Canterbury. Here the left-handed home batsman, Reese, hit a brilliant hundred, and the Australian, Callaway, bowled well, but the tourists won by 128 runs. Otago did not fare as well as Canterbury. Warner hit 211 in 270 minutes and the home side could only manage 243 in their second innings. The two principal tour games – the final two played – were against Combined New Zealand. Neither match really extended Lord Hawke's team. Having ended the tour of New Zealand the team travelled to Australia, where three first-class matches were played.

The difference in the team's results in New Zealand and

1902-03: Lord Hawke's Team to North America, New Zealand and Australia

Batting Averages

	M	I	NO	R	HS	Avge	100	c/s
P. F. Warner (Middx)	10	16	2	771	211	55.07	2	7
F. L. Fane (Essex)	10	14	1	552	124	42.46	1	4
C. J. Burnup (Kent)	10	16	2	562	103	40.14	1	4
P. R. Johnson (Som)	9	12	4	301	88	37.62	0	9
G. J. Thompson (Northts)	10	13	4	305	80*	33.88	0	3
T. L. Taylor (Yorks)	10	14	0	468	105	33.42	2	8/1
E. M. Dowson (Surrey)	9	12	0	383	86	31.91	0	6
J. Stanning (Lancs)	9	12	3	241	38	26.77	0	7
B. J. T. Bosanquet (Middx)	10	14	1	316	82	24.30	0	8
A. E. Leatham (Gloucs)	5	5	1	45	13	11.25	0	3
A. E. Trott (Middx)	3	5	0	34	17	6.80	0	2
A. D. Whatman	6	6	1	29	13	5.80	0	7/5
S. Hargreave (Warks)	9	11	1	43	14	4.30	0	8

Bowling Averages

	O	M	R	W	Avge	BB	5i
G. J. Thompson	439.2	130	1074	76	14.13	9-85	7
C. J. Burnup	143.5	35	412	28	14.71	6-36	3
E. M. Dowson	129.1	22	353	23	15.34	5-19	1
S. Hargreave	312.1	100	641	23	27.86	6-12	1
B. J. T. Bosanquet	190.1	12	749	26	28.80	6-153	1
A. E. Trott	114.5	15	482	12	40.16	6-88	1

Also bowled: P. F. Warner 1-1-0-0.
Played in non-first-class matches only: J. N. Williams, R. H. Raphael, R. A. Williams.

1902-03: Lord Hawke's Team to the United States, Australia and New Zealand

1st Match: v XVIII of California (San Francisco) Nov 26.
California 125 (B. J. T. Bosanquet 11-37) lost to Lord Hawke's XII 155-8 (P. F. Warner 52) by 3 wkts and 30 runs.

2nd Match: v Auckland (Auckland) Dec 19, 20, 22.
Lord Hawke's XI 321 (F. L. Fane 82, W. Stemson 5-111) beat Auckland 120 & 72 (E. M. Dowson 5-19) by an inns & 129 runs.

3rd Match: v XVIII of Taranaki (Hawera) Dec 30, 31.
Taranaki 146 (F. H. Robertson 52) & 38 (S. Hargreave 9-10, G. J. Thompson 8-19) lost to Lord Hawke's XI 157 (Gudgeon 5-36) & 28-1 by 9 wkts.

4th Match: v XVIII of North Taranaki (New Plymouth) Jan 1, 2.
Lord Hawke's XI 320 (B. J. T. Bosanquet 66, T. L. Taylor 62) beat North Taranaki 86 & 131 by an inns & 103 runs.

5th Match: v XV of Wanganui (Wanganui) Jan 3, 5.
Wanganui 120 & 77 lost to Lord Hawke's XII 140 (Howden 5-40) & 59-3 by 8 wkts.

6th Match: v XVIII of Manawatu (Palmerston) Jan 7, 8.
Lord Hawke's XI 307-8 dec (F. L. Fane 76*, P. F. Warner 69) beat Manawatu 105 & 72 by an inns & 130 runs.

7th Match: v XV of Hawke's Bay (Napier) Jan 10, 12, 13.
Lord Hawke's XII 461 (B. J. T. Bosanquet 136, C. J. Burnup 82, G. J. Thompson 67, A. E. Trott 6-225) beat Hawke's Bay 106 (Lusk 56, S. Hargreave 5-31) & 157 (S. Hargreave 6-34) by an inns & 198 runs.

8th Match: v Wellington (Wellington) Jan 15, 16, 17.
Wellington 243 (Tucker 86, C. Hickson 73) & 140 (G. J. Thompson 7-51) lost to Lord Hawke's XI 289 (C. J. Burnup 69) & 97-0 (C. J. Burnup 50*) by 10 wkts.

9th Match: v XXII of Wairarapa (Greytown) Jan 20, 21.
Lord Hawke's XI 405-7 dec (E. M. Dowson 218*) beat Wairarapa 205 (S. Hargreave 12-51) & 119 (G. J. Thompson 9-27) by an inns & 80 runs.

10th Match: v XXII of Marlborough (Blenheim) Jan 23, 24.
Lord Hawke XI 204 (E. M. Dowson 94) & 18-1 beat Marlborough 59 (G. J. Thompson 15-11) & 162 by 9 wkts.

11th Match: v XVIII of Nelson (Nelson) Jan 27, 28.
Lord Hawke's XI 185 (A. D. Whatman 56) beat Nelson 29 (G. J. Thompson 9-7) & 77 (C. J. Burnup 10-14) by an inns & 79 runs.

12th Match: v XXII of Westland (Greymouth) Jan 30, 31, Feb 2.
Westland 111 (S. Hargreave 10-38) & 64 (S. Hargreave 10-28, G. J. Thompson 10-28) lost to Lord Hawke's XI 69 (Ongley 8-36) & 106-5 (C. J. Burnup 53*) by 5 wkts.

13th Match: v Canterbury (Christchurch) Feb 6, 7, 9.
Lord Hawke's XI 352 (G. J. Thompson 80*, C. J. Burnup 65, P. F. Warner 57, T. L. Taylor 54, S. T. Callaway 5-93, F. S. Frankish 5-124) & 159-7 dec (P. F. Warner 52, F. S. Frankish 5-70) beat Canterbury 224 (D. Reese 111, G. J. Thompson 6-76) & 154 (G. J. Thompson 5-54) by 128 runs.

14th Match: v Otago (Dunedin) Feb 13, 14.
Lord Hawke's XI 473 (P. F. Warner 211, F. L. Fane 85, A. Downes 5-161) beat Otago 124 (C. J. Burnup 5-50) & 119 (H. G. Siedeberg 52, G. J. Thompson 5-35) by an inns & 230 runs.

15th Match: v XV of Southland (Invercargill) Feb 18, 19.
Southland 87 & 104 lost to Lord Hawke's XI 107 (Taylor 5-59) & 87-3 by 7 wkts.

16th Match: v South Island (Dunedin) Feb 21, 23.
Lord Hawke's XI 314 (T. L. Taylor 105, B. J. T. Bosanquet 82) beat South Island 51 (S. Hargreave 6-12) & 133 (C. J. Burnup 6-36) by an inns & 130 runs.

17th Match: v XVIII of South Canterbury (Timaru) Feb 25, 26.
Lord Hawke's XI 172 & 121-7 dec (T. L. Taylor 63*) beat South Canterbury 81 (G. J. Thompson 10-23) & 88 by 124 runs.

18th Match: v New Zealand (Christchurch) Feb 27, 28, March 2.
New Zealand 164 (K. Tucker 50, G. J. Thompson 6-38) & 214 (K. Tucker 67) lost to Lord Hawke's XI 304 (F. L. Fane 124, T. L. Taylor 54) & 75-3 by 7 wkts.

19th Match: v New Zealand (Wellington) March 4, 5, 6.
New Zealand 274 (D. Reese 148, G. J. Thompson 8-124) & 84 (C. J. Burnup 5-8) lost to Lord Hawke's XI 380 (P. F. Warner 125, P. R. Johnson 88) by an inns & 22 runs.

20th Match: v Victoria (Melbourne) March 13, 14, 16.
Lord Hawke's XI 350 (E. M. Dowson 51, B. J. T. Bosanquet 51, J. V. Saunders 6-118) & 134 (F. Collins 7-61) lost to Victoria 271 & 217-3 (H. Graham 92) by 7 wkts.

21st Match: v New South Wales (Sydney) March 20, 21, 23, 24.
New South Wales 144 (A. E. Trott 6-88) & 463 (A. Duff 194, A. J. Hopkins 133, B. J. T. Bosanquet 6-153) drew with Lord Hawke's XI 282 (E. M. Dowson 86, B. J. T. Bosanquet 52, M. A. Noble 5-78) & 32-0.

22nd Match: v South Australia (Unley Oval) March 27, 28, 30, 31.
Lord Hawke's XI 553 (T. L. Taylor 105, C. J. Burnup 103, E. M. Dowson 66, B. J. T. Bosanquet 57, P. R. Johnson 54) & 108 (H. Hay 9-67) lost to S. Australia 304 (N. Claxton 88, C. Hill 58, C. B. Jennings 52, G. J. Thompson 9-85) & 454 (D. R. A. Gehrs 100, F. T. Hack 90, C. Hill 73) by 97 runs.

Australia clearly illustrated the difference in standard between the two countries and Lord Hawke's team proved that even the full strength of New Zealand was not yet up to the average first-class county standard in England. The tour however gave a great boost to New Zealand cricket and it was pleasing that financially it paid its way.

The team travelled back to England via the Suez Canal in the s.s. *Oroya*. Dowson, Bosanquet, Thompson and Hargreave took the overland route and got back to England on 4 May and the remainder of the side landed a few days later.

1902-03: Oxford University Authentics in India

The first major tour by an English team to India for 10 years was the joint venture of E. Britten-Holmes and F. H. Stewart, respectively secretaries of the Oxford University Authentics and the Calcutta Cricket Club. Led by K. J. Key (Surrey), the remainder of the team were G. H. Simpson-Hayward, F. G. H. Clayton, J. N. Ridley, C. Headlam, J. E. Tomkinson, F. Kershaw, R. H. Raphael, A. H. Hornby, F. H. Hollins, H. B. Chinnery, J. B. Aspinall, R. A. Williams and H. J. Powys-Keck. The side contained five or six first-class county amateurs and in English terms might be described as just about first-class. The team left

---

1902-03: Oxford Authentics to India

1st Match: v Bombay Presidency (Gymkhana Maidan)   Nov 17, 18, 19.
Bombay 204 (Capt Lowis 72, F. G. H. Clayton 7-70) & 412 (J. G. Greig 204, R. A. Williams 5-94) beat Authentics 313 (R. A. Williams 105, J. S. Milne 5-61) & 257 (F. G. H. Clayton 59, H. C. John 5-53) by 46 runs.

2nd Match: v Hindus (Bombay)   Nov 21, 22.
Authentics 356 (F. H. Hollins 141, Balu 5-131) drew with Hindus 158 & 227.

3rd Match: v Parsis (Bombay)   Nov 24, 25.
Authentics 311 (R. H. Raphael 111, A. H. Mehta 6-97) & 124 lost to Parsis 406 (D. D. Kanga 116, K. R. Driver 66, H. D. Kanga 66) & 30-2 by 8 wkts.

4th Match: v Secunderabad (Secunderabad)   Nov 28, 29.
Authentics 249 (F. H. Hollins 121, G. H. Simpson-Hayward 53, Milman 6-80) & 79-4 drew with Secunderabad 106 (G. H. Simpson-Hayward 7-39) & 289-9 dec (Capt McEwan 119*, Milman 78).

5th Match: v Mysore State (Bangalore)   Dec 4, 5, 6.
Mysore 105 (R. A. Williams 9-58) & 248 (B. Jayaram 97) lost to Authentics 209 (H. B. Chinnery 88, Kanaakarathnam 5-43) & 146-4 (R. H. Raphael 62) by 6 wkts.

6th Match: v Madras Presidency (Madras)   Dec 8, 9, 10.
Authentics 85 (J. F. Tweedie 8-30) & 373 (F. H. Hollins 185*) beat Madras 149 & 200 (E. E. L. Challenor 62, C. T. Studd 56, R. A. Williams 5-59) by 109 runs.

7th Match: v South India (Trichinopoly)   Dec 12, 13.
Authentics 215 (A. H. Hornby 67, E. Narayan Rao 7-66) beat South India 89 & 31 (R. A. Williams 6-12) by an inns & 95 runs.

8th Match: v Bengal Presidency (Calcutta)   Dec 22, 23, 24.
Authentics 106 & 275-5 dec (F. H. Hollins 62, H. B. Chinnery 57, A. H. Hornby 52) drew with Bengal 85 (H. J. Powys-Keck 5-33) & 139-5 (S. R. Hignell 51).

9th Match: v Calcutta (Calcutta)   Dec 25, 26, 27.
Authentics 352 (A. H. Hornby 111, K. J. Key 95, F. H. Hollins 90) beat Calcutta 66 (R. A. Williams 6-34) & 95 by an inns & 333 runs.

10th Match: v Gents of India (Bombay)   Jan 5, 6, 7.
Gentlemen 118 (R. A. Williams 5-38) & 143 (W. Marsham 68, H. J. Powys-Keck 5-27) lost to Authentics 135 (A. H. Hornby 54, H. G. Hoare 5-51) & 128-4 (A. H. Hornby 70*) by 6 wkts.

11th Match: v Peshawar (Peshawar)   Jan 12, 13, 14.
Authentics 696 (G. H. Simpson-Hayward 203*, F. H. Hollins 120, A. H. Hornby 72, R. H. Raphael 65) beat Peshawar 168 (M. Lannowe 64, G. H. Neale 55) & 202 (G. H. Neale 124*, G. H. Simpson-Hayward 7-31) by an inns & 330 runs.

12th Match: v Northern Punjab (Rawalpindi)   Jan 15, 16.
Authentics 360 (A. H. Hornby 143, K. J. Key 63) beat N. Punjab 49 (R. A. Williams 7-25) & 106 (H. J. Powys-Keck 9-21) by an inns & 205 runs.

13th Match: v Punjab (Lahore)   Jan 19, 20, 21.
Authentics 150 (K. J. Key 52, S. M. Robinson 7-65) & 145 beat Punjab 101 & 94 (G. H. Simpson-Hayward 5-20) by 100 runs.

14th Match: v Aligarh College (Past & Present) (Aligarh)   Jan 23, 24.
Authentics 97 (Ali Hasan 5-43, Shafkat 5-49) & 141 drew with Aligarh College 57 (G. H. Simpson-Hayward 7-34).

15th Match: v Bundelkhand (Jhansi)   Jan 29, 30.
Bundelkhand 154 (Whatford 82, H. J. Powys-Keck 8-58) & 153 (Whatford 55) lost to Authentics 316-8 dec (R. A. Williams 54, R. H. Raphael 53, Fateh Mahomed 5-110) by an inns & 9 runs.

16th Match: v United Provinces (Allahabad)   Jan 31, Feb 2.
Authentics 265 (G. H. Simpson-Hayward 100, H. B. Chinnery 60) beat United Provinces 68 & 157 by an inns & 42 runs.

17th Match: v Behar Wanderers (Mozufferpore)   Feb 5, 6, 7.
Authentics 246 (H. B. Chinnery 89, F. H. Hollins 65*, P. B. Hudson 6-61) & 273-9 dec (H. B. Chinnery 69, S. Lang 7-116) beat Behar Wanderers 128 (G. H. Simpson-Hayward 7-22) & 47 by 345 runs.

18th Match: v Oudh (Lucknow)   Feb 12, 13, 14.
Authentics 390 (F. G. H. Clayton 85, F. H. Hollins 74, A. H. Hornby 70, G. H. Simpson-Hayward 50, McPherson 6-152) beat Oudh 56 (G. H. Simpson-Hayward 8-19) & 107 by an inns & 227 runs.

19th Match: v Northern India (Cawnpore)   Feb 16, 17.
Authentics 482 (K. J. Key 116, G. H. Simpson-Hayward 88, Robinson 7-146) drew with N. India 176 (K. O. Goldie 57, R. A. Williams 5-40) & 223-7 (Beasley 86).

Tilbury in the s.s. *Caledonia* on 24 October and played its first match against the Bombay Presidency on 17 November. Captain Greig, the Hampshire cricketer, hit a splendid 204 for the home team in his second innings and completely altered the complexion of the game, for the tourists had a first innings lead of 109. The Presidency won by 46 runs, but probably because Chinnery was absent ill in the Authentics' second innings. The second game in Bombay was a draw, much in favour of the visitors, against the Hindus, but the Parsis beat the tourists by 8 wickets and the team felt quite shattered after these three very hard opening matches.

In the fourth match at Secunderabad, the tourists were set 146 in 40 minutes and made a fair attempt before the wickets began to fall. Three successive victories followed, then only an earlier drawing of stumps prevented another win at Calcutta against the Bengal Presidency. A weak Calcutta Club however were easily overcome as were the Gentlemen of India, who lacked M. R. Jardine, C. T. Studd, J. G. Greig and H. F. Bateman-Champain. In Peshawar Simpson-Hayward hit 203 not out and the Authentics' total reached 696. Simpson-Hayward was again in form against United Provinces, his century coming in 100 minutes. The team were not troubled in the remaining matches.

It was generally thought that the tour gave an impetus to cricket in India, but due to the Durbar many of the best English cricketers were unable to appear against the Authentics, which made the local teams much weaker than usual. The worst part of the tour was the long distances between many matches – the journey between Trichinopoly and Calcutta by train actually took five days due to floods washing away the line. Considering the problems faced by cricketers in India, the tourists were surprised at the enthusiasm and relatively high standard of play. Except at Delhi, the matches were not played on matting, but the grounds generally were not well equipped.

1903: the first county tour

For the first time, a county side undertook a major overseas tour when Kent travelled to the United States in 1903. The team was J. R. Mason (capt), C. J. Burnup, E. W. Dillon, J. Seymour, W. M. Bradley, H. Z. Baker, A. Hearne, H. C. Stewart, K. L. Hutchings, C. Blythe, F. H. Huish, and G. J. V. Weigall with T. Pawley as manager. The side was the full 1903 Kent team minus S. H. Day, whose scholastic duties prevented his going.

Sailing from Liverpool in the s.s. *Oceanic* on 9 September, the team played its first match in Philadelphia against Nineteen Colts and on a rain-affected wicket won with ease. The game against Philadelphia was very even on first innings, but as on previous occasions, when the home side batted a second time only J. A. Lester played the bowling with confidence and Kent went on to a 7 wickets victory. The tourists then journeyed to New York, where they had no difficulty in beating the local side, and their final game was the return with Philadelphia which provided another win, on a fiery wicket. The team arrived back in Liverpool on 17 October, but without Burnup, who went to Mexico.

The complete success of the tour came as a surprise, since the Philadelphians had toured England in 1903 and defeated Kent.

1903: Kent to the United States

1st Match: v XIX Colts (Manheim)   Sept 18, 19.
Colts 79 (C. Blythe 6-29) & 114 (A. Hearne 8-25) lost to Kent XII 169 (D. Graham 7-32) & 25-3 by 8 wkts.

2nd Match: v Philadelphia (Wissahickon)   Sept 25, 26, 27.
Philadelphia 128 (W. M. Bradley 5-58) & 194 (J. A. Lester 93*) lost to Kent 132 (J. B. King 7-39) & 192-3 (C. J. Burnup 94*) by 7 wkts.

3rd Match: v New York (Livingston)   Sept 30, Oct 1.
Kent 202 (H. Z. Baker 55) & 76-4 dec beat New York 100 & 54 by 124 runs.

4th Match: v Philadelphia (Merion C.C.)   Oct 2, 3, 5.
Philadelphia 66 (C. Blythe 5-30) & 177 lost to Kent 180 (E. W. Dillon 64, E. M. Cregar 6-53) & 64-3 by 7 wkts.

1903-04: R. E. Foster hits 287 on first M.C.C. tour of Australia

For the first time, an English side went to Australia under the auspices of the M.C.C. in 1903-04. Originally A. C. MacLaren was asked by the Australians to take out a side, but when S. F. Barnes and W. H. Lockwood refused to accompany him, he declined the invitation. It was not until late June 1903, that the M.C.C. announced that they would be responsible for the English team, and at the same time they announced that P. F. Warner (Middx) would lead the team. At the end of July the party was announced as P. F. Warner (Middx) (capt), R. E. Foster (Worcs), B. J. T. Bosanquet (Middx), and the following professionals: G. H. Hirst (Yorks), W. Rhodes (Yorks), T. W. Hayward (Surrey), H. Strudwick (Surrey), E. G. Arnold (Worcs), L. C. Braund (Somerset), A. F. A. Lilley (Warwicks), A. Fielder (Kent), A. E. Relf (Sussex) and J. T. Tyldesley (Lancs). The final place was later given to A. E. Knight (Leics). The following, all amateurs, declined the invitation: C. B. Fry (Sussex), Hon F. S. Jackson (Yorks), A. C. MacLaren (Lancs), G. L. Jessop (Gloucs), L. C. H. Palairet (Somerset), E. M. Dowson (Surrey) and H. Martyn (Somerset). The terms accepted by the tourists were, for the amateurs, all expenses, for the professionals, all expenses plus £300 and a bonus if the tour were financially successful. It is interesting that no mention in the M.C.C. announcements was made of either Barnes or Lockwood.

Three weeks before the team sailed R. H. Spooner (Lancs) was invited to join the tour, but refused, and the tourists left Tilbury on the s.s. *Orontes* on 25 September. J. A. Murdoch, assistant secretary of M.C.C., accompanied the side. Arriving at Fremantle on 29 October, the tourists opened their programme at Adelaide on 7 November with some excellent batting and would have won the match had time permitted. This encouraging start was maintained in Melbourne, where Victoria collapsed twice against Rhodes and provided the M.C.C. with an innings victory. Going on to Sydney to meet the most powerful state, Rhodes again caused the downfall of the home batsmen and another innings victory was achieved. Queensland did much better than expected in the fourth match, but still lost by 6 wickets and after

two odds matches, the tourists arrived at Sydney for the first Test. The game belonged to R. E. Foster, who created a new Test record by hitting 287 – he batted nearly seven hours and played a splendid innings, which gave England a lead of nearly 300 on first innings. Trumper played brilliant cricket for his side, but his innings of 185 not out could not save Australia, who lost by 5 wickets.

In the second Test, Foster had to retire with a severe chill and could not bat in the second innings, but rain on the first evening made the 221 runs England scored on the first day priceless and Australia were utterly destroyed by Rhodes and England won by 185 runs. The fielding on both sides was described as quite dreadful. Only one up-country game separated the second Test from the third, which was played on a hard fast wicket, unlike the first two games. Here Trumper, Hill and Gregory mastered the English attack and then the visiting batsmen found the pace of the ball off the wicket too much for them. Warner and Hirst

1903-04: M.C.C. to Australia								
Batting Averages								
	M	I	NO	R	HS	Avge	100	c/s
T. W. Hayward (Surrey)	11	17	0	785	157	46.17	2	4
R. E. Foster (Worcs)	13	22	4	821	287	45.61	1	14
B. J. T. Bosanquet (Middx)	12	19	3	587	124*	36.81	2	12
J. T. Tyldesley (Lancs)	13	22	2	670	97	33.50	0	7
G. H. Hirst (Yorks)	12	18	1	569	92	33.47	0	7
A. E. Knight (Leics)	10	16	2	444	104	31.71	1	2
P. F. Warner (Middx)	14	24	1	694	79	30.17	0	5
L. C. Braund (Som)	11	17	0	395	102	23.23	1	17
W. Rhodes (Yorks)	14	18	7	239	49*	21.72	0	14
A. F. A. Lilley (Warks)	11	16	3	226	91*	17.38	0	16/13
A. E. Relf (Sussex)	9	12	2	167	31	16.70	0	13
E. G. Arnold (Worcs)	10	15	3	167	34	13.91	0	13
A. Fielder (Kent)	7	8	3	59	23	11.80	0	3
H. Strudwick (Surrey)	6	5	0	53	21	10.60	0	11/9
G. H. Drummond	1	1	0	1	1	1.00	0	0
Bowling Averages								
	O	M	R	W	Avge	BB	5i	
W. Rhodes	423.3	112	1055	65	16.23	8-68	7	
E. G. Arnold	381.1	102	884	46	19.22	4-8	0	
L. C. Braund	279	58	729	37	19.70	8-43	3	
A. E. Knight	14	2	43	2	21.50	2-34	0	
A. Fielder	139.1	42	323	14	23.07	3-35	0	
G. H. Hirst	359.5	87	881	36	24.47	5-37	2	
B. J. T. Bosanquet	273.4	23	1011	37	27.32	6-45	2	
A. E. Relf	129.4	44	302	10	30.20	3-48	0	
R. E. Foster	7	2	34	1	34.00	1-34	0	

Also bowled: T. W. Hayward 14-5-27-0; P. F. Warner 10-3-28-0; A. F. A. Lilley 8-2-23-0; G. H. Drummond 5-0-21-0; J. T. Tyldesley 8-1-28-0; H. Strudwick 5-2-6-0.
Played in non-first-class matches only: G. S. Whitfield.

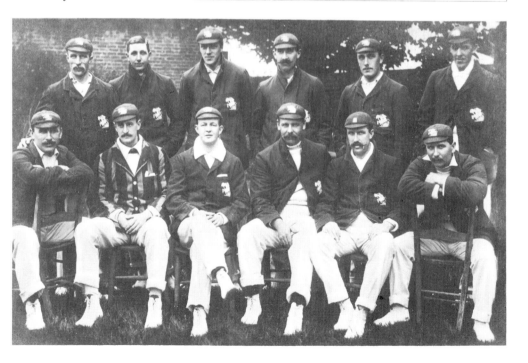

The first M.C.C. team to Australia. Led by Pelham Warner, it brought back the Ashes. Back: A. E. Knight, L. C. Braund, B. J. T. Bosanquet, A. E. Relf, W. Rhodes, E. G. Arnold. Front: G. H. Hirst, R. E. Foster, P. F. Warner, T. W. Hayward, A. F. A. Lilley, J. T. Tyldesley. Foster scored a record 287 in the first Test.

1903-04: M.C.C. to Australia

1st Match: v South Australia (Adelaide)   Nov 7, 9, 10, 11.
M.C.C. 483-8 dec (T. W. Hayward 157, A. F. A. Lilley 91*, P. F. Warner 65, L. C. Braund 58) drew with S. Australia 172 & 343-7 (C. Hill 116, C. B. Jennings 77*, F. T. Hack 54).

2nd Match: v Victoria (Melbourne)   Nov 13, 14, 16.
Victoria 162 (W. Rhodes 5-26) & 210 (W. Bruce 51) lost to M.C.C. 443-8 dec (G. H. Hirst 92, J. T. Tyldesley 90, B. J. T. Bosanquet 79, R. E. Foster 71) by an inns & 71 runs.

3rd Match: v New South Wales (Sydney)   Nov 20, 21, 23.
N.S.W. 108 (W. Rhodes 6-55) & 201 lost to M.C.C. 319 (J. T. Tyldesley 80, G. H. Hirst 66) by an inns & 10 runs.

4th Match: v Queensland (Brisbane)   Nov 27, 28, 30.
Queensland 242 (R. Macdonald 59, W. T. Evans 72) & 91 (L. C. Braund 5-50) lost to M.C.C. 215 (T. J. Byrnes 5-74) & 119-4 by 6 wkts.

5th Match: v XVIII of Northern District (West Maitland)   Dec 2, 3.
N. District 284 (P. S. Waddy 93, L. C. Braund 8-73) & 241-6 (P. S. Waddy 102, Lindsay 61*) drew with M.C.C. 453 (A. F. A. Lilley 102*, J. T. Tyldesley 101, B. J. T. Bosanquet 99, T. W. Hayward 59).

6th Match: v XV of Newcastle (Newcastle)   Dec 4, 5.
M.C.C. 306 (R. E. Foster 105, T. W. Hayward 87) & 381-8 (J. T. Tyldesley 127, L. C. Braund 64*, G. H. Hirst 51) drew with Newcastle 203.

7th Match: v Austrlia (Sydney)   Dec 11, 12, 14, 15, 16, 17.
Australia 285 (M. A. Noble 133) & 485 (V. T. Trumper 185*, R. A. Duff 84, C. Hill 51, W. Rhodes 5-94) lost to England 577 (R. E. Foster 287, L. C. Braund 102, J. T. Tyldesley 53) & 194-5 (T. W. Hayward 91, G. H. Hirst 60*) by 5 wkts.

8th Match: v XVIII Juniors of Melbourne (Melbourne)   Dec 19, 21, 22.
M.C.C. 416 (G. H. Hirst 87, P. F. Warner 76, A. E. Knight 50) beat Juniors 124 & 193 (Delves 52, L. C. Braund 8-48) by an inns & 99 runs.

9th Match: v XVIII of Bendigo (Bendigo)   Dec 26, 28.
Bendigo 94 (A. Fielder 11-32) & 64-7 drew with M.C.C. 273-5 dec (T. W. Hayward 115, A. E. Knight 78).

10th Match: v England (Melbourne)   Jan 1, 2, 4, 5.
England 315 (J. T. Tyldesley 97, P. F. Warner 68, T. W. Hayward 58) & 103 (J. T. Tyldesley 62, H. Trumble 5-34) beat Australia 122 (V. T. Trumper 74, W. Rhodes 7-56) & 111 (W. Rhodes 8-68) by 185 runs.

11th Match: v XVIII of Ballarat (Ballarat)   Jan 8, 9.
M.C.C. XII 326 (A. E. Knight 109, A. F. A. Lilley 59) & 226 (Stevens 6-55) drew with Ballarat 197 (C. Baker 61, L. C. Braund 10-87).

12th Match: v Australia (Adelaide)   Jan 15, 16, 18, 19, 20.
Australia 388 (V. T. Trumper 113, C. Hill 88, R. A. Duff 79, M. A. Noble 59) & 351 (S. E. Gregory 112, M. A. Noble 65, V. T. Trumper 59) beat England 245 (G. H. Hirst 58) & 278 (P. F. Warner 79, T. W. Hayward 67) by 216 runs.

13th Match: v Tasmania (Hobart)   Jan 25, 26.
M.C.C. 185 & 354-4 dec (B. J. T. Bosanquet 124*, J. T. Tyldesley 85, P. F. Warner 64) drew with Tasmania 191 & 63-1.

14th Match: v Tasmania (Launceston)   Jan 29, 30.
Tasmania 141 (G. H. Hirst 5-37) & 259-3 (J. H. Savigny 164*, O. H. Douglas 59) drew with M.C.C. 353 (T. W. Hayward 134, G. H. Hirst 51).

15th Match: v Victoria (Melbourne)   Feb 5, 7, 8, 9.
Victoria 299 (P. A. McAlister 139, W. Rhodes 6-62) & 15 (W. Rhodes 5-6) lost to M.C.C. 248 (T. W. Hayward 77) & 68-2 by 8 wkts.

16th Match: v New South Wales (Sydney)   Feb 12, 13, 15.
M.C.C. 190 (B. J. T. Bosanquet 54, A. Cotter 5-44) & 461 (B. J. T. Bosanquet 114, A. E. Knight 104) beat N.S.W. 232 (A. J. Hopkins 52) & 141 (A. J. Hopkins 56, B. J. T. Bosanquet 6-45) by 278 runs.

17th Match: v XV of Bathurst (Bathurst)   Feb 19, 20.
Bathurst 249 (C. W. Gregory 139*) & 151-3 dec (R. N. Hickson 82) drew with M.C.C. XII 176 (T. W. Hayward 59, J. Marsh 5-55) & 115-5.

18th Match: v Australia   Feb 26, 27, 28, Mar 1, 2, 3.
England 249 (A. E. Knight 70*, M. A. Noble 7-100) & 210 (T. W. Hayward 52) beat Australia 131 & 171 (M. A. Noble 53*, B. J. T. Bosanquet 6-51) by 157 runs.

19th Match: v Australia (Melbourne)   March 5, 7, 8.
Australia 247 (V. T. Trumper 88, L. C. Braund 8-81) & 133 (G. H. Hirst 5-48) beat England 61 (A. Cotter 6-40) & 101 (H. Trumble 7-28) by 218 runs.

20th Match: v South Australia (Adelaide)   March 12, 14, 15.
S. Australia 259 (D. R. A. Gehrs 63, P. M. Newland 50) & 77 (L. C. Braund 8-43) lost to M.C.C. 154 (P. F. Warner 50, N. H. Claxton 5-56) & 184-1 (R. E. Foster 73*, P. F. Warner 54, J. T. Tyldesley 50*) by 9 wkts.

batted well, but the rest were all at sea and Australia saved the rubber.

Both Victoria and New South Wales were beaten in the return fixtures and these matches as well as a visit to Tasmania came before the fourth Test. About 30,000 turned up to watch the second day, which was marred by rain—the crowd became restless at the delay in re-starting after the rain and the bottle-throwing and barracking became pretty intense. Rhodes again caused an Australian collapse and though the English batting was none too robust, Australia required 329 to win in the final innings. Bosanquet took 6 for 51 giving England the Ashes. The fifth Test began only two days after the end of the fourth. Trumper batted in splendid form to hit 88 out of 142 and rain then ruined the wicket

—England were shot out for 61, with Cotter picking up 6 wickets. Australia made 133 in their second innings and with Hayward in bed with tonsilitis, the English position was hopeless. Trumble did the hat-trick and took 7 for 28 as England plunged to defeat.

The last game was the return with South Australia which gave the M.C.C. a farewell victory, Warner, Tyldesley and Foster hitting off 184 for the loss of one wicket in the final innings. In terms of matches the tour was the shortest to Australia since 1882-83.

The success of the English team was due to the variety of the attack—on the batting side, in Trumper, Duff, Noble and Hill, Australia had a better quartet than the best four English batsmen, but the Australian bowling was all right-arm medium, or nearly so, until Cotter was introduced. Lilley kept wicket much better than Kelly, and Warner's captaincy was a large factor in the English victory. In fact the tour was a most satisfactory venture, except from the financial angle, the M.C.C. losing £1,500.

The team arrived back in England on 17 April, taking the overland route from Marseilles.

1904-05: Lord Brackley's team find West Indies improving

Lord Brackley captained his own side to the West Indies in the winter of 1904-05. The team, which left England on 31 December, consisted of Lord Brackley, C. P. Foley (Middx), E. G. Wynyard (Hants), T. G. O. Cole (Lancs), R. C. W. Burn (Oxford U), G. H. T. Simpson-Hayward (Worcs), H. V. Hesketh-Prichard (Hants), H. J. Powys-Keck (Worcs), A. W. F. Somerset (Sussex), C. H. M. Ebden (Sussex), G. H. Drummond (M.C.C.), and two professionals, E. G. Hayes (Surrey) and G. J. Thompson (Northants), together with J. Moss as umpire. The Lancashire batsman Hallows was invited but had to withdraw on medical advice.

The team began their tour in Jamaica and were lucky to draw their first fixture against the island side. In the return, however, Wynyard hit 157 and the tourists had an innings victory. Barbados and a weak West Indian team were also beaten, but the tourists lacked Hayes in their return with Barbados and, collapsing for 95 in their second innings, suffered their first defeat.

1904-05: Lord Brackley's Team to the West Indies

Batting Averages

	M	I	NO	R	HS	Avge	100	c/s
E. G. Wynyard (Hants)	8	14	0	562	157	40.14	2	8/1
A. W. F. Somerset (Sussex)	9	15	5	326	68*	32.60	0	10/3
E. G. Hayes (Surrey)	9	16	1	425	100*	28.33	2	8
C. H. M. Ebden (Sussex)	10	18	0	384	78	21.33	0	7
T. G. O. Cole (Lancs)	10	17	2	295	68	19.66	0	5
G. H. T. Simpson-Hayward (Worcs)	8	16	0	312	67	19.50	0	11
G. J. Thompson (Northts)	10	17	1	274	37	17.12	0	3
Lord Brackley	9	16	3	191	34	14.69	0	5/1
C. P. Foley (Middx)	10	17	0	239	58	14.05	0	1
G. H. Drummond	6	11	0	110	34	10.00	0	1
R. C. W. Burn (Oxford U)	9	15	3	107	23	8.91	0	6
H. V. Hesketh-Prichard (Hants)	5	9	1	65	37	8.12	0	0
H. J. Powys-Keck (Worcs)	5	8	3	37	25*	7.40	0	0
Bellamy	1	1	1	0	0*	—	0	1

Bowling Averages

	O	M	R	W	Avge	BB	5i
E. G. Hayes	121.4	23	325	26	12.50	3-19	0
G. J. Thompson	353.5	81	1048	75	13.97	7-65	10
G. H. T. Simpson-Hayward	177.5	25	564	32	17.62	5-29	1
H. J. Powys-Keck	67.2	11	233	12	19.41	4-24	0
H. V. Hesketh-Prichard	101.4	17	311	14	22.21	5-49	1
R. C. W. Burn	144.5	37	349	14	24.92	4-1	0

Also bowled: E. G. Wynyard 5-0-28-0; Bellamy 2-0-20-0.
Played in non-first-class matches only: J. Moss, S. Beton.

Three matches in St Lucia all proved easy victories and the Englishmen then moved on to British Guiana, where they achieved two victories over the colony, though the second proved quite a close encounter. In Trinidad, however, the tourists met their match in Cumberbatch who bowled his team to two victories. In between these two games was the return with the West Indies. The visitors were without Wynyard, who injured his leg, and in a very exciting finish won by 4 runs. The batting of Constantine was perhaps the feature of the match.

The outstanding quality of the tourists was their fielding and very few catches were dropped throughout the tour. Hayes proved himself to be undoubtedly the best all-rounder, while Thompson took over a hundred wickets.

Apart from some unpleasantness concerning the umpiring in St Vincent, the tour was most enjoyable and showed that the standard of West Indian cricket was still improving.

1905: M.C.C. make summer tour of the United States and Canada

Departing from the usual arrangements for tours to North America, the team which went in 1905 left England in July and completed its programme by mid-August. The team, under the auspices of the M.C.C., went at the invitation of the cricket clubs in both the United States and Canada.

The team was almost entirely composed of University players. From Cambridge came E. W. Mann (capt), M. W. Payne, G. G. Napier, C. H. Eyre, H. C. McDonell, F. J. V. Hopley, R. T. Godsell and L. J. Moon; and from Oxford F. A. H. Henley, R. C. W. Burn, H. J. Wyld and V. A. S. Stow; K. O. Hunter completed the party.

Arriving in New York, the tourists began the fixtures with the major one against Philadelphia and had the satisfaction of winning by 7 wickets. The home team however got their revenge in the return, when J. A. Lester put in a splendid all-round performance, hitting a century in the second innings and capping this with 7 wickets for 33. The game against New York was much closer than is usual with these encounters and it is reported that the crowd was a record for a cricket match in that city. The tourists proceeded to Canada for a programme of four matches, but the Canadians proved much too weak and rather foolishly met the English team on even terms in three of the fixtures.

The final game ended on 17 August and the tour could be regarded as successful from every standpoint.

1905-06: one-wicket Test win for South Africa

The first M.C.C. tour to South Africa went out under a guarantee against financial loss given by the South African authorities. Sailing in the *Kinfauns Castle*, the tourists arrived in Cape Town on 28 November. The voyage had been a particularly rough one – windows in the smoking room and cabins had been smashed and at times the waves swept right over the boat.

The team consisted of P. F. Warner (Middx) (capt), F. L. Fane

(Essex), J. N. Crawford (Surrey), E. G. Wynyard (Hants), L. J. Moon (Middx), J. C. Hartley (Sussex), H. D. G. Leveson-Gower (Surrey) and the professionals D. Denton (Yorks), S. Haigh (Yorks), E. G. Hayes (Surrey), W. S. Lees (Surrey), C. Blythe (Kent), A. E. Relf (Sussex) and J. H. Board (Gloucs). The team was in no way representative of England's full strength and was regarded when it set out as the equal of the middle range of the first-class counties.

After some net practice and a scratch game, the programme opened with the game against Western Province. A good all-round performance by the visitors allied to some weak, nervous batting on the part of the home team, gave M.C.C. an easy first win. This was followed by a win in an odds match and another win in the return against Western Province. The fourth match at Kimberley provided yet another victory. At Johannesburg, M.C.C. met Transvaal and gained a substantial first innings lead due to a good knock by Denton. Faulkner batted well for the home side and though M.C.C. required less than 200 in their final innings, they never looked like making the runs. Schwarz spun the ball off the mat at a great pace and no one could master him.

Following an odds match at Potchefstroom, the team returned to Johannesburg for the first Test. This game went all in favour of England until the final day. South Africa, who made only 91 in their first innings, required 284 for victory in their second. The score fell to 105 for 6 and an English win looked assured. Nourse and White then added 121. Further wickets fell to take the total to 239 for 9. Nourse, now partnered by Sherwell, went on to take South Africa to an historic victory by a single wicket. As the final runs were made the crowd rushed onto the ground and carried the two batsmen into the pavilion. It should be mentioned that Haigh, the best English bowler, was absent ill on the final day. Three minor games followed the Test and provided three wins by an innings. Natal were then met and beaten twice, though Nourse again proved a problem, hitting a magnificent 100, and a collection on the ground realised £46 for him.

The second and third Tests were played as consecutive fixtures and both were disasters for England. In the second Test the England batting was quite deplorable and good all-round play by the home side gave them a nine-wicket victory. The third Test was a much higher scoring match, but the home side managed matters rather better than the tourists and won by 243 runs; England left out Wynyard and Board due to illness and injury, but the absence of these two did not materially alter the strength

1905-06: M.C.C. to South Africa

Batting Averages

	M	I	NO	R	HS	Avge	100	c/s
F. L. Fane (Essex)	12	19	3	607	143	37.93	1	3
D. Denton (Yorks)	12	20	1	613	132*	32.26	2	9
J. N. Crawford (Surrey)	11	18	1	531	74	31.23	0	13
A. E. Relf (Sussex)	9	16	1	404	61*	26.93	0	8
L. J. Moon (Middx)	9	15	0	373	80	24.86	0	5/5
Sir G. Lagden	1	1	0	21	21	21.00	0	0
H. D. G. Leveson-Gower (Surrey)	5	6	1	99	67*	19.80	0	2
E. G. Wynyard (Hants)	6	10	2	156	54*	19.50	0	1
P. F. Warner (Middx)	12	22	3	314	56	16.52	0	3
J. H. Board (Gloucs)	8	14	4	145	39	14.50	0	9/5
E. G. Hayes (Surrey)	8	14	1	186	35	14.30	0	8
S. Haigh (Yorks)	12	19	2	212	61	12.47	0	9
W. S. Lees (Surrey)	10	16	5	127	25*	11.54	0	2
C. Blythe (Kent)	11	15	4	94	27	8.54	0	8
J. C. Hartley (Sussex)	6	8	0	49	29	6.12	0	7

Bowling Averages

	O	M	R	W	Avge	BB	5i
F. L. Fane	2.4	0	17	2	8.50	2-17	0
S. Haigh	241.2	63	625	39	16.02	7-58	2
J. C. Hartley	108	16	333	19	17.52	6-32	1
C. Blythe	480.2	168	1046	57	18.33	6-68	4
W. S. Lees	366.3	132	771	42	18.35	6-78	3
J. N. Crawford	230.3	58	627	34	18.44	6-79	2
A. E. Relf	133.1	32	342	12	28.50	3-40	0
P. F. Warner	8	1	36	1	36.00	1-17	0
E. G. Hayes	32	5	123	2	61.50	1-18	0

Also bowled: Sir G. Lagden 1-0-4-0; H. D. G. Leveson-Gower 6-1-26-0; L. J. Moon 1-1-0-0; E. G. Wynyard 4-0-17-0.
Played in non-first-class matches only: I. D. Difford.

1905-06: M.C.C. to South Africa

1st Match: v Western Province (Cape Town) Dec 2, 4, 5.
M.C.C. 365 (D. Denton 78, A. E. Relf 61*, F. L. Fane 60, P. F. Warner 56, Whitehead 6-100) beat W. Province 96 (S. Haigh 5-29) & 142 (J. N. Crawford 5-41) by an inns & 127 runs.

2nd Match: v XVIII of Worcester (Worcester) Dec 6, 7.
Worcester 107 (J. C. Hartley 9-26) & 203 lost to M.C.C. XII 362 (H. D. G. Leveson-Gower 82, D. Denton 68, P. de Villiers 6-76) by an inns & 52 runs.

3rd Match: v Western Province (Cape Town) Dec 9, 11, 12.
W. Province 81 & 233 (S. J. Snooke 80, S. E. Horwood 74, J. N. Crawford 6-79) lost to M.C.C. 272 (S. Haigh 61, A. E. Relf 60, L. J. Moon 57) & 43-0 by 10 wkts.

4th Match: v XV of Griqualand West (Kimberley) Dec 15, 16.
M.C.C. XII 374 (E. G. Hayes 125, E. G. Wynyard 82, G. A. Verheyen 5-82) & 9-0 beat Griqualand West 174 (A. E. Relf 8-36) & 207 by 11 wkts.

5th Match: v XV of Griqualand West (Kimberley) Dec 19, 20, 21.
Griqualand West 233 (J. F. Mitchell 51) & 187 lost to M.C.C. 432-8 dec (J. N. Crawford 98, D. Denton 64, F. L. Fane 62, E. G. Wynyard 62*, A. E. Relf 51) by an inns & 12 runs.

6th Match: v Transvaal (Johannesburg) Dec 26, 27, 28.
Transvaal 135 (W. S. Lees 5-34) & 305 (W. A. Shalders 66, G. A. Faulkner 63*) beat M.C.C. 265 (D. Denton 132*) & 115 (R. O. Schwarz 5-34) by 60 runs.

7th Match: v XVIII of Western Transvaal (Potchefstroom) Dec 29, 30.
W. Transvaal 92 & 115 lost to M.C.C. 317-6 dec (P. F. Warner 125, F. L. Fane 63) by an inns & 110 runs.

8th Match: v South Africa (Johannesburg) Jan 2, 3, 4.
England 184 & 190 (P. F. Warner 51) lost to South Africa 91 (W. S. Lees 5-34) & 287-9 (A. W. Nourse 93*, G. C. White 81) by 1 wkt.

9th Match: v Pretoria (Pretoria) Jan 6, 8.
M.C.C. 338 (J. C. Hartley 77) beat Pretoria 87 (J. N. Crawford 5-6) & 171 (J. N. Crawford 6-54) by an inns & 70 runs.

10th Match: v Middelburg & District XVIII (Middelburg) Jan 10, 11.
M.C.C. 392 (P. F. Warner 128, F. L. Fane 68, J. N. Crawford 56, Barnes 6-121) beat Middelburg 86 & 187 by an inns & 119 runs.

11th Match: v The Army (Roberts' Heights) Jan 12, 13.
M.C.C. 480-7 dec (D. Denton 130, L. J. Moon 80, H. D. G. Leveson-Gower 67*, J. N. Crawford 54) beat The Army 97 (Mitford 65*) & 165 (McFarlane 68) by an inns & 218 runs.

12th Match: v Natal (Durban) Jan 16, 17, 18.
Natal 191 (A. W. Nourse 119) & 113 (C. Blythe 5-41) lost to M.C.C. 175 (D. Denton 53, A. W. Nourse 5-52) & 176-6 (F. L. Fane 77*) by 4 wkts.

13th Match: v Natal (Pietermaritzburg) Jan 20, 22, 23.
Natal 117 & 173 (S. Haigh 7-58) lost to M.C.C. 191 (F. L. Fane 59, C. F. Hime 5-18) & 100-6 by 4 wkts.

14th Match: v XV of East London (East London) Jan 27, 29.
East London 120 & 73 lost to M.C.C. 206 (J. H. Board 57) by an inns & 13 runs.

15th Match: v XV of Kingwilliamstown (Kingwilliamstown) Feb 3, 5.
M.C.C. XII 415-8 dec (D. Denton 147, F. L. Fane 111) beat Kingwilliamstown 75 & 44 (A. E. Relf 8-12) by an inns & 296 runs.

16th Match: v XVIII of Queenstown (Queenstown) Feb 6, 7.
M.C.C. XII 400-8 dec (J. N. Crawford 212*, A. E. Relf 61) beat Queenstown 111 (C. Blythe 9-16) & 113 by an inns & 176 runs.

17th Match: v XXII of Midlands (Cradock) Feb 12, 13.
Midlands 256 (W. Solomon 54, A. E. Relf 8-58) drew with M.C.C. 413-8 (F. L. Fane 67, P. F. Warner 65, J. C. Hartley 58*).

18th Match: v XVIII of Albany (Grahamstown) Feb 14, 15.
Albany 129 (E. Fock 51) & 51-4 drew with M.C.C. XII 241 (J. C. Hartley 59, F. Bayes 5-45).

19th Match: v XV of Port Elizabeth (Port Elizabeth) Feb 16, 17, 19.
Port Elizabeth 72 (S. Haigh 8-14) & 106 lost to M.C.C. 255 (L. J. Moon 98, A. G. Lyons 7-66) by an inns & 77 runs.

20th Match: v Eastern Province (Port Elizabeth) Feb 20, 21, 22.
E. Province 132 (J. C. Hartley 6-32) & 92 (C. Blythe 5-30) lost to M.C.C. 201 (J. N. Crawford 64, E. G. Wynyard 54*, A. E. E. Vogler 6-56) & 24-0 by 10 wkts.

21st Match: v South-Western Districts XXII (Oudtshoorn) Feb 24, 26.
M.C.C. 60 (G. Rogers 5-24) & 152-6 dec drew with S-W Districts 77 (J. N. Crawford 13-33) & 97-9.

22nd Match: v South Africa (Johannesburg) March 6, 7, 8.
England 148 & 160 (F. L. Fane 65) lost to South Africa 277 (J. H. Sinclair 66) & 33-1 by 9 wkts.

23rd Match: v South Africa (Johannesburg) March 10, 12, 13, 14.
South Africa 385 (C. M. H. Hathorn 102, A. W. Nourse 61, W. S. Lees 6-78) & 349-5 dec (G. C. White 147, L. J. Tancred 73, A. W. Nourse 55) beat England 295 (F. L. Fane 143) & 196 (D. Denton 61, S. J. Snooke 8-70) by 243 runs.

24th Match: v XV of Orange River Colony (Bloemfontein) March 17, 19, 20, 21.
Orange River 279 (Weir 76) & 123 drew with M.C.C. 203 (E. G. Hayes 66) & 169-4.

25th Match: v South Africa (Cape Town) March 24, 26, 27.
South Africa 218 (C. Blythe 6-68) & 138 (G. C. White 73, C. Blythe 5-50) lost to England 198 & 160-6 (F. L. Fane 66*) by 4 wkts.

26th Match: v South Africa (Cape Town) March 30, 31, April 2.
England 187 (J. N. Crawford 74) & 130 lost to South Africa 333 (A. E. E. Vogler 62*, S. J. Snooke 60) by an inns & 16 runs.

of the eleven. Nourse had two good innings and such an advantage did the South Africans gain that they were able to declare with 5 wickets down in their second innings and leave the English team needing 440 to win. The fast right-arm bowling of Snooke finished off the tourists.

Only one game–another odds match–was played prior to the fourth Test, which was staged at Newlands. It was assumed that since South Africa had won the rubber, there would be little interest in the fourth match, but in fact a large crowd watched the contest. This time Blythe bowled splendidly, keeping an accurate length, and only White batted well against him. England needed 159 in the final innings and due to Fane won by 4 wickets. The fifth and final Test followed straight on from the fourth. Once more the English batting let the side down and this time the bowlers did not come to the rescue, the tourists having to suffer a last wicket stand of 94 between Sherwell and Vogler–the latter made some tremendous drives and the crowd of some 10,000 made a collection for him. The South Africans won the match with an innings to spare.

The team arrived back in England on 21 April. Wynyard had come home early due to illness and Leveson-Gower and Moon remained behind in South Africa.

The failure of the English team was due to the poor batting on matting wickets against an attack which was largely made up of leg-break bowlers. The lack of form of several Englishmen–Warner, Denton and Hayes for example–in the Tests was inexplicable, though Hayes did suffer from ill-health on part of the tour.

1906-07: M.C.C. tour New Zealand after internal Australian squabbles

Throughout the English summer of 1906, the public were bombarded with reports of the M.C.C. taking a team to Australia. Originally the difficulties concerning such a tour lay in the squabbles between the Australian authorities, but when these had been ironed out, the M.C.C. stated it was too late to raise a team. Influential figures then stepped in to try to change the M.C.C.'s decision and it was not until the second week of September that, at a special Committee Meeting, the M.C.C. decided the tour was

1906-07: M.C.C. to South Africa and New Zealand

1st Match: v Western Province (Newlands) (One Day) Dec 10.
W. Province 129-6 dec lost to M.C.C. XII 133-10 (J. J. Kotze 5-52) by 1 wkt.

2nd Match: v Auckland (Auckland) Dec 14, 15, 17.
M.C.C. 172 (P. R. Johnson 64, P. White 6-21) & 241 (G. T. Branston 73) drew with Auckland 195 (A. Haddon 56*, G. H. Simpson-Hayward 6-39) & 131-5 (L. G. Hemus 80).

3rd Match: v XV of Wanganui (Wanganui) Dec 21, 22.
M.C.C. 453-9 dec (W. P. Harrison 103, C. C. Page 68, W. B. Burns 55) beat Wanganui 124 & 95 (J. W. H. T. Douglas 10-23) by an inns & 234 runs.

4th Match: v Wellington (Wellington) Dec 25, 26, 27.
M.C.C. 204 (W. B. Burns 51, H. W. Monaghan 7-50) & 259 (C. C. Page 61, W. B. Burns 59, E. F. Upham 6-78) drew with Wellington 211 (A. B. Williams 100) & 148-5 (K. H. Tucker 50*).

5th Match: v Canterbury (Christchurch) Dec 29, 31, Jan 1.
M.C.C. 202 (W. J. H. Curwen 76, J. H. Bennett 5-80) & 156 (S. T. Callaway 7-75) lost to Canterbury 241 (K. M. Ollivier 78, J. D. Lawrence 61, G. T. Branston 5-54) & 120-3 by 7 wkts.

6th Match: v Otago (Dunedin) Jan 4, 5, 7.
M.C.C. 224 (C. C. Page 66, A. Downes 5-82) & 278 (A. Downes 5-85) beat Otago 176 (P. R. May 5-53) & 94 (P. R. May 5-37) by 232 runs.

7th Match: v XVIII of West Coast (Greymouth) Jan 11, 12, 14.
West Coast 132 & 200 lost to M.C.C. XII 252 (C. E. de Trafford 85, W. P. Harrison 72) & 81-5 by 6 wkts.

8th Match: v XV of Nelson & Marlborough (Nelson) Jan 18, 19.
Nelson & Marlborough 98 & 121 drew with M.C.C. XII 149 (G. T. Branston 55, Knapp 5-46) & 29-3.

9th Match: v XIII of Manawatu (Palmerston) Jan 22, 23.
Manawatu 123 (G. H. Simpson-Hayward 7-38) & 95 lost to M.C.C. 253 (G. T. Branston 120, W. H. Bartlett 6-64) by an inns & 35 runs.

10th Match: v Auckland (Auckland) Jan 26, 28, 29.
Auckland 127 & 241 (C. E. MacCormick 77, W. Brook-Smith 70*, J. W. H. T. Douglas 6-73) lost to M.C.C. 214 & 156-8 (J. W. H. T. Douglas 64*) by 2 wkts.

11th Match: v Canterbury (Christchurch) Feb 2, 4, 5.
M.C.C. 305 (G. T. Branston 119, W. P. Harrison 62) & 260-9 dec (C. C. Page 78, J. Bennett 5-82) beat Canterbury 221 (S. Orchard 68) & 108 by 236 runs.

12th Match: v Otago (Dunedin) Feb 8, 9, 11.
M.C.C. 496 (W. P. Harrison 105, P. R. Johnson 87, G. H. Simpson-Hayward 71, J. W. H. T. Douglas 67, C. C. Page 55, R. H. Fox 54, C. G. Austin 5-156) beat Otago 257 & 144 by an inns & 95 runs.

13th Match: v Wellington (Wellington) Feb 15, 16, 18.
M.C.C. 201 (P. R. Johnson 50, E. F. Upham 7-78) & 48-5 drew with Wellington 191.

14th Match: v XV of Wairarapa (Masterton) Feb 19, 20.
Wairarapa 120 & 65 (A. A. Torrens 8-36) lost to M.C.C. 272-7 dec (P. R. Johnson 72, W. B. Burns 64*) by an inns & 87 runs.

15th Match: v Hawke's Bay (Napier) Feb 22, 23, 25.
M.C.C. 394 (A. A. Torrens 87, N. C. Tufnell 85, W. B. Burns 52) beat Hawke's Bay 151 (Fulton 60, J. W. H. T. Douglas 5-41) & 163 (Lusk 65*) by an inns & 80 runs.

16th Match: v New Zealand (Christchurch) Feb 28, Mar 1, 2, 4.
New Zealand 207 (J. J. Mahoney 71*, J. W. H. T. Douglas 5-56) & 187 (E. V. Sale 66) lost to M.C.C. 257 (P. R. Johnson 99) & 140-1 (P. R. Johnson 76*) by 9 wkts.

17th Match: v New Zealand (Wellington) March 8, 9, 11.
New Zealand 165 (J. W. H. T. Douglas 7-49) & 249 (A. B. Williams 72, A. Haddon 71, J. W. H. T. Douglas 5-75) beat M.C.C. 160 (E. F. Upham 6-84) & 198 (A. H. Fisher 5-61) by 56 runs.

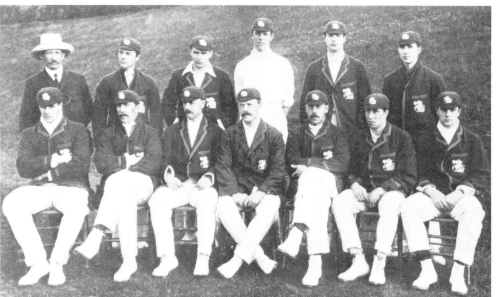

The M.C.C. team photographed in New Zealand in 1906-07. This was an all-amateur side. Back: J. Moss (umpire), W. P. Harrison, P. R. May, W. J. H. Curwen, C. C. Page, N. C. Tufnell. Front: G. T. Branston, A. A. Torrens, C. E. de Trafford, E. G. Wynyard (captain), G. H. Simpson-Hayward, J. W. H. T. Douglas, W. B. Burns.

1906-07: M.C.C. to South Africa and New Zealand								
Batting Averages								
	M	I	NO	R	HS	Avge	100	c/s
J. W. H. T. Douglas (Essex)	9	14	3	398	67	36.18	0	7
P. R. Johnson (Som)	10	18	1	546	99	32.11	0	7
W. B. Burns (Worcs)	11	20	2	499	59	27.72	0	7
N. C. Tufnell	7	12	4	203	85	25.37	0	5
G. T. Branston (Notts)	10	17	0	424	119	24.94	1	11
W. P. Harrison (Middx)	9	15	0	371	105	24.73	1	3
G. H. T. Simpson-Hayward (Worcs)	9	15	0	369	71	24.60	0	10
C. C. Page (Middx)	11	18	0	439	78	24.38	0	2
R. H. Fox	10	17	3	307	54	21.92	0	12/8
P. R. May (Surrey)	9	16	5	176	32*	16.00	0	3
W. J. H. Curwen (Surrey)	8	14	1	203	76	15.53	0	4
A. A. Torrens	6	9	0	135	87	15.00	0	1
C. E. de Trafford (Leics)	9	16	1	156	28*	10.40	0	4
P. F. C. Williams	1	1	0	3	3	3.00	0	0
E. G. Wynyard (Hants)	3	3	3	86	48*	—	0	1
Bowling Averages								
	O	M	R	W	Avge	BB	5i	
J. W. H. T. Douglas	239.1	51	663	50	13.26	7-49	5	
P. R. May	248.4	46	719	45	15.97	5-37	3	
G. H. T. Simpson-Hayward	218.4	31	591	35	16.89	6-39	1	
G. T. Branston	250	70	673	36	18.69	5-54	1	
W. P. Harrison	26	3	124	6	20.66	4-61	3	
R. H. Fox	15	1	51	2	25.50	1-17	0	
W. J. H. Curwen	74	23	178	5	35.60	3-47	0	
W. B. Burns	18	1	78	2	39.00	1-8	0	
A. A. Torrens	99.2	21	250	6	41.66	3-44	0	

Also bowled: C. C. Page 3-0-14-0.

definitely off, but would probably go ahead in 1907-08.

This wrangling quite overshadowed the preparations for the M.C.C. tour of New Zealand. The New Zealand Cricket Council invited the M.C.C. to send a team and guaranteed the visit, each major Association contributing £500 and the minor Associations £100 each. The all-amateur team consisted of: E. G. Wynyard (Hants) (capt), C. E. de Trafford (Leics), G. H. T. Simpson-Hayward (Worcs), P. R. Johnson (Somerset), G. T. Branston (Notts), W. J. H. Curwen (Surrey), P. R. May (Surrey), W. B. Burns (Worcs), W. P. Harrison (Middx), R. H. Fox (M.C.C.), C. C. Page (Middx), A. A. Torrens (Kent), N. C. Tufnell, J. W. H. T. Douglas (Essex) and the old Notts player J. Moss as umpire. The New Zealand authorities complained to no avail about the team bringing its own umpire. Sailing from Tilbury in the s.s. *Corinthie*, except for Johnson, who went via Suez, the team travelled to South Africa, where the tour opened with a match against Western Province at Newlands – the one-day game

was won by one wicket.

Before discussing the New Zealand matches, it should be noted that the side contained only five regular 1906 County cricketers plus four 1906 university players, so the team could be described as weak first-class in English terms.

The party reached Wellington on 5 December and travelled straight from there to Auckland for the first match. The home side looked like winning until Branston and Wynyard, in M.C.C.'s second innings, added 119 for the 8th wicket, which forced a draw. The second eleven-a-side game – against Wellington – was also drawn, but was the scene of three injuries – Wynyard broke a tendon in his right leg and missed the rest of the tour, Torrens strained his left leg and Douglas strained his side. It was not surprising therefore that the match against Canterbury, which began only three hours after a rough sea voyage, was lost by 7 wickets. Better fortune awaited the team in Dunedin, where good batting by Page and Simpson-Hayward produced a win. Three odds matches caused the tourists little anxiety, but the return against Auckland was a close thing, two excellent innings by Douglas tipping the balance. The returns against Canterbury and Otago provided the tourists with large victories, though the match at Wellington had to be drawn due to rain.

The most important games of the visit were those against the full strength New Zealand eleven. The first, at Christchurch, was dominated by Johnson who hit 99 and an unbeaten 76, the M.C.C. winning by 9 wickets. For the second game, the tourists were without Simpson-Hayward, the lob bowler having a damaged hand. On a fiery wicket, Douglas took 7 wickets, but Upham retaliated for New Zealand and the home side gained a first innings lead of 5. In the end M.C.C. required 255 to win, but never looked like reaching the target and New Zealand won by 56 runs.

Judged by the results, the M.C.C.'s choice of a suitable team for New Zealand proved entirely satisfactory. The only gap in the side was the lack of a good slow bowler. The batting happily did not rely on one or two men, but had plenty of depth, even without Wynyard – in his absence, de Trafford led the side. The only unfortunate side of the tour was financial. The players did not attract large crowds and the New Zealand Cricket Council lost a considerable sum on the venture.

The team travelled to Sydney after their last match and stayed long enough for some practice with V. T. Trumper at the Cricket Ground, before boarding the s.s. *Ophir* for the voyage home.

1907: South Africans join M.C.C. tour to the United States and Canada

The M.C.C. side which visited North America in the autumn of 1907 differed in one important particular compared with previous English touring sides. The party included the leading two cricketers of the South African tourists to England in the same year. The full side was H. V. Hesketh-Prichard (Hants) (capt), G. T. Branston (Notts), F. H. Browning, L. G. A. Collins (Berks), L. P. Collins (Berks), G. H. Simpson-Hayward (Worcs), G. MacGregor (Middx), E. G. Wynyard (Hants), J. W. H. T. Douglas (Essex), K. O. Goldie (Sussex), R. O. Schwarz (South Africa) and S. J. Snooke (South Africa).

The majority of the team sailed on the *Lucania* from Liverpool on 7 September, but the two South Africans travelled later. The tour opened in New York on 17 September, and as Snooke and Schwarz had not yet arrived, F. H. Bohlen and R. E. Bonner took their places. About 3,000 watched the first day's play, but rain curtailed the remainder of the fixture. Rain then ruined the first match with Philadelphia, which was confined to not much more than one innings each – remarkably 10,000 turned up on the second day, believed to be a record for a match in the United States. The tourists easily beat the Colts, but the return with Philadelphia was most exciting, only five runs separating the teams on first innings and in the final stages the last two home batsmen survived for 13 minutes to save the game.

The last match was against Canada; both teams found batting hard work on a tricky pitch but Canada forced a draw, being 8 wickets down and still 66 in arrears when stumps were drawn.

The only thing that marred the tour was the poor weather, rain interfering with three of the five matches. L. G. A. Collins had the misfortune to crack a rib prior to the first match and appeared just once – in the final game.

```
1907: M.C.C. to North America

1st Match: v New York (Staten Island)   Sept 17, 18.
M.C.C. 338-4 dec (E. G. Wynyard 145, L. P. Collins 102, J. W. H. T. Douglas 63) drew
with New York 66-3.

2nd Match: v Philadelphia (Manheim)   Sept 21, 22, 23.
M.C.C. 162 (G. T. Branston 63, H. V. Hordern 5-41) & 64-3 drew with Philadelphia 157
(R. O. Schwarz 8-55).

3rd Match: v XVII Colts & Captain (St Martin's)   Sept 24, 25.
M.C.C. 329 (K. O. Goldie 147) beat Colts 86 & 70 (G. H. Simpson-Hayward 13-33) by
an inns & 173 runs.

4th Match: v Philadelphia (Haverford)   Sept 27, 28, 29, Oct 1.
M.C.C. 222 & 124 (H. V. Hordern 5-38, J. B. King 5-39) drew with Philadelphia 227 &
60-9 (H. V. Hesketh-Prichard 7-20).

5th Match: v Canada (Ottawa)   Oct 2, 3.
M.C.C. 113 & 115-5 dec (R. O. Schwarz 51*) drew with Canada 94 (G. H. Simpson-
Hayward 5-25) & 74-8.
```

1907-08: last wicket stand of 39 wins Test, but Australia retain Ashes

As announced when the M.C.C. declined to tour Australia in 1906-07, the tour was postponed and took place the following winter. The team sailed from Tilbury on 20 October, except for Young, who joined the boat at Plymouth and Hutchings, Fane and Rhodes, who chose the overland route to Marseilles.

The full side was A. O. Jones (Notts) (capt), F. L. Fane (Essex), K. L. Hutchings (Kent), J. N. Crawford (Surrey), R. A. Young (Sussex) and the professionals W. Rhodes (Yorks), L. C. Braund (Somerset), E. G. Hayes (Surrey), J. B. Hobbs (Surrey), C. Blythe (Kent), A. Fielder (Kent), J. Hardstaff (Notts), J. Humphries (Derbys), S. F. Barnes (Staffs). Also on board were George Gunn (Notts), who was going to Australia for his health, but would be available to play if required, and Tarrant of Middlesex. The professionals were paid £300 plus the first-class sea passage, hotel expenses in Australia, travelling expenses etc, and £2 per week for out of pocket expenses. As a matter of interest, the Australian players were each to be paid £25 as an 'honorarium' for each Test.

The M.C.C. team was in no way representative of the full

```
1907-08: M.C.C. to Australia

1st Match: v Western Australia (Perth)   Oct 26, 28, 29.
M.C.C. 402 (F. L. Fane 133, L. C. Braund 59, A. Christian 5-132) beat W. Australia 152
(T. H. Hogue 60*) & 116 by an inns & 134 runs.

2nd Match: v South Australia (Adelaide)   Nov 9, 11, 12, 13.
S. Australia 343 (C. Hill 104, C. B. Jennings 79, N. H. Claxton 57) & 134 (C. Hill 61,
J. N. Crawford 5-40) lost to M.C.C. 660-8 dec (L. C. Braund 160, J. Hardstaff 135,
A. O. Jones 119, J. N. Crawford 114) by an inns & 183 runs.

3rd Match: v Victoria (Melbourne)   Nov 15, 16, 18, 19, 20.
Victoria 233 (F. A. Tarrant 65, V. S. Ransford 51, A. Fielder 5-71) & 463 (V. S. Ransford
102, F. A. Tarrant 81, L. P. Vernon 62, C. McKenzie 54, A. Fielder 5-98) drew with
M.C.C. 198 (L. C. Braund 62) & 422-9 (J. Hardstaff 95*, A. O. Jones 82, K. L. Hutchings
91).

4th Match: v New South Wales (Sydney)   Nov 22, 23. 25.
M.C.C. 304 (J. Hardstaff 53) & 301 (J. Hardstaff 71, W. Rhodes 50) beat N.S.W. 101
(S. F. Barnes 6-24) & 96 (A. Fielder 6-27) by 408 runs.

5th Match: v Queensland (Brisbane)   Nov 30, Dec 2.
Queensland 78 (C. Blythe 5-35) & 186 (R. J. Hartigan 59, C. Blythe 6-48) lost to M.C.C.
308 (W. Rhodes 70*, A. O. Jones 69, K. L. Hutchings 67, J. W. MacLaren 5-104) by an
inns & 44 runs.

6th Match: v An Australian XI (Brisbane)   Dec 6, 7, 9.
An Australian XI 299 (S. J. Redgrave 66, P. A. McAlister 57, L. C. Braund 7-117) &
110-2 (R. J. Hartigan 55*, P. A. McAlister 51*) drew with M.C.C. 223 (K. L. Hutchings 72).

7th Match: v Australia (Sydney)   Dec 13, 14, 16, 17, 18, 19.
England 273 (G. Gunn 119, A. Cotter 6-101) & 300 (G. Gunn 74, J. Hardstaff 63)
lost to Australia 300 (C. Hill 87, A. Fielder 6-82) & 275-8 (H. Carter 61) by 2 wkts.

8th Match: v A Victorian XI (South Melbourne)   Dec 21, 23, 24.
M.C.C. 503-9 dec (W. Rhodes 105*, E. G. Hayes 98, J. B. Hobbs 77, A. Fielder 50*)
drew with A Victorian XI 488-9 (F. A. Tarrant 159, W. W. Armstrong 117, J. F. Horan 75).

9th Match: v XVIII of Bendigo (Bendigo)   Dec 26, 27, 28.
M.C.C. 213 (J. B. Hobbs 58, E. G. Hayes 53, Anderson 6-26) drew with Bendigo 55.

10th Match: v Australia (Melbourne)   Jan 1, 2, 3, 4, 6, 7.
Australia 266 (M. A. Noble 61, J. N. Crawford 5-79) & 397 (W. W. Armstrong 77,
M. A. Noble 64, V. T. Trumper 63, C. G. Macartney 54, H. Carter 53, S. F. Barnes
5-72) lost to England 382 (K. L. Hutchings 126, J. B. Hobbs 83, A. Cotter 5-142)
& 282-9 (F. L. Fane 50) by 1 wkt.

11th Match: v Australia (Adelaide)   Jan 10, 11, 13, 14, 15, 16.
Australia 285 (C. G. Macartney 75) & 506 (C. Hill 160, R. J. Hartigan 116,
M. A. Noble 65) beat England 363 (G. Gunn 65, J. N. Crawford 62, J. Hardstaff
61) & 183 (J. Hardstaff 72, J. A. O'Connor 5-40, J. V. Saunders 5-65) by 245 runs.

12th Match: v Tasmnia (Launceston)   Jan 18, 20, 21.
M.C.C. 321 (J. B. Hobbs 104, J. Hardstaff 66, W. Richardson 5-87) & 249 (J. Hardstaff
85, J. B. Hobbs 65, E. A. Windsor 5-85) beat Tasmania 276 (T. A. Tabart 57, E. W.
Harrison 54) & 174 (E. A. Windsor 75) by 120 runs.

13th Match: v Tasmania (Hobart)   Jan 24, 25, 27.
M.C.C. 455 (W. Rhodes 119, J. Hardstaff 106, F. L. Fane 62, J. B. Hobbs 58, K. L.
Hutchings 51) drew with Tasmania 113 (L. C. Braund 5-55) & 317-8 (K. E. Burn 112,
C. J. Eady 66, T. A. Tabart 55).

14th Match: v Victoria (Melbourne)   Feb 1, 3, 4.
M.C.C. 338 (J. Hardstaff 122, J. N. Crawford 69, G. H.S. Trott 5-116) & 241-4 dec
(J. B. Hobbs 115, K. L. Hutchings 51) beat Victoria 77 (S. F. Barnes 5-32) & 172 (E. V.
Carroll 61, S. F. Barnes 5-35) by 330 runs.

15th Match: v Australia (Melbourne)   Feb 7, 8, 10, 11.
Australia 214 (V. S. Ransford 51, J. N. Crawford 5-48) & 385 (W. W. Armstrong
133*, H. Carter 66, V. S. Ransford 54) beat England 105 (J. B. Hobbs 57, J. V.
Saunders 5-28) & 186 by 308 runs.

16th Match: v New South Wales (Sydney)   Feb 14, 15, 17, 18, 19, 20.
M.C.C. 298 (K. L. Hutchings 73, R. A. Young 59, A. O. Jones 57*, L. A. Minnett 7-131) &
456 (L. C. Braund 132*, F. L. Fane 101, J. Hardstaff 73, W. Rhodes 58) drew with
N.S.W. 368 (E. F. Waddy 107*, C. G. Macartney 96, A. J. Bowden 87, C. Blythe 5-93) &
375-9 (W. Bardsley 108, V. T. Trumper 74, E. F. Waddy 57, W. Rhodes 5-73).

17th Match: v Australia (Sydney)   Feb 21, 22, 24, 25, 26, 27.
Australia 137 (S. F. Barnes 7-60) & 422 (V. T. Trumper 166, S. E. Gregory 56,
J. N. Crawford 5-141) beat England 281 (G. Gunn 122*, J. B. Hobbs 72) & 229
(W. Rhodes 69, J. V. Saunders 5-82) by 49 runs.

18th Match: v South Australia (Adelaide)   March 2, 3, 4.
M.C.C. 404 (G. Gunn 102, W. Rhodes 78*, F. L. Fane 59, J. N. Crawford 54, W. A. Hewer
5-149) & 134-4 (J. Hardstaff 63) drew with S. Australia 445 (C. E. Dolling 140, E. R.
Mayne 74, L. C. Braund 6-149).

19th Match: v Western Australia (Perth)   March 13, 14, 16.
W. Australia 256 (C. Howard 69) & 265-7 (H. Rowe 105) drew with M.C.C. 362-7 dec
(G. Gunn 122*, S. F. Barnes 93).
```

England strength, Foster, Hayward, Hirst, Tyldesley and Lilley were all asked but refused. For some reason C. B. Fry was not invited.

The *Ophir* arrived in Fremantle on 24 October and the first match took place in Perth, commencing 26 October – there had been a scratch game in Colombo, but since the touring side was composed of only five M.C.C. men, the other seven being passengers from the boat, it is not included as a tour match.

A record attendance welcomed the tourists on the inaugural match against Western Australia, and despite leaving the boat only 48 hours before the start, the M.C.C. found no difficulty in obtaining an innings victory. In Adelaide a second innings victory was achieved, though Rhodes' bowling was affected by an attack of tonsilitis. In the third game, against Victoria, the tourists were lucky to escape defeat, the last man going in with 10 minutes playing time remaining – at the other end Hardstaff batted in great form to carry out his bat for 95. New South Wales were convincingly beaten in the fourth game, the bowling of Barnes and Fielder removing the best state side for 101 and 96. 42,000 watched the

1907-08: M.C.C. to Ceylon and Australia

Batting Averages

	M	I	NO	R	HS	Avge	100	c/s
G. Gunn (Notts)	11	18	3	817	122*	54.46	4	11
J. Hardstaff (Notts)	17	28	2	1360	135	52.30	3	5
W. Rhodes (Yorks)	17	27	8	929	119	48.89	2	8
J. B. Hobbs (Surrey)	13	22	1	876	115	41.71	2	8
A. O. Jones (Notts)	11	15	1	518	119	37.00	1	18
L. C. Braund (Som)	16	25	3	783	160	35.59	2	25
K. L. Hutchings (Kent)	17	28	0	953	126	34.03	1	23
F. L. Fane (Essex)	16	24	1	774	133	33.65	2	6
J. N. Crawford (Surrey)	16	24	1	610	114	26.52	1	15
S. F. Barnes (Staffs)	12	19	4	342	93	22.80	0	3
R. A. Young (Sussex)	10	15	0	260	59	17.33	0	15/7
A. Fielder (Kent)	10	16	8	134	50*	16.75	0	4
E. G. Hayes (Surrey)	11	14	0	230	98	16.42	0	9/1
C. Blythe (Kent)	11	14	1	145	27*	11.15	0	6
J. Humphries (Derbys)	10	13	1	92	16	7.66	0	18/4

Bowling Averages

	O	M	R	W	Avge	BB	5i
S. F. Barnes	534	145	1185	54	21.95	7-60	5
C. Blythe	393.2	97	935	41	22.80	6-48	3
A. Fielder	418.5	73	1208	50	24.16	6-27	4
J. N. Crawford	566	115	1663	66	25.19	5-40	4
J. B. Hobbs	39	8	128	4	32.00	2-14	8
L. C. Braund	434.5	63	1644	50	32.88	7-117	3
W. Rhodes	427.4	106	1069	31	34.48	5-73	1
E. G. Hayes	46	1	193	5	38.60	2-35	0
J. Hardstaff	29	7	86	2	43.00	1-12	0
G. Gunn	16	5	43	1	43.00	1-16	0
K. L. Hutchings	63.5	11	279	3	93.00	1-3	0

three days' play, 24,000 being present on the second. Queensland proved no match for the M.C.C., Blythe removing them cheaply and M.C.C. having another easy win. After this game A. O. Jones was taken ill and forced to miss the next eight matches, including three Tests. F. L. Fane took over the leadership, but Jones' illness was a bitter blow to the tourists. Rain ruined the match against An Australian Eleven and the side went on to Sydney for the first Test. A very close game was won by Australia by 2 wickets –

George Gunn was co-opted into the England team and hit the highest score in each England innings: 119 and 74. England were condemned for playing a batsman-wicketkeeper, Young, instead of Humphries, and indeed this made the difference between success and failure since Young made numerous wicket-keeping errors and scored only 13 and 3.

The second Test proved even more exciting than the first. England required 73 to win with two wickets remaining. Humphries and Barnes added 34 for the 9th wicket and against all the odds Fielder and Barnes made the other 39 – Hazlitt should have run out Fielder as the tail-enders scrambled the winning run. The third Test at Adelaide followed directly on top of the second. England gained a substantial first innings lead, Australian wickets fell quickly in their second innings, but Hartigan and Hill joined forces in a splendid partnership of 243 which altered the whole match – unfortunately for England both batsmen were dropped early in their innings. Set 429 to win, the visitors never looked like making the runs, especially when Hobbs had to retire injured after scoring a single. Hardstaff with 72 put on a brave fight but in vain.

The team went to Tasmania and played two relaxing games on that island. The return against Victoria, which followed, was none too serious and won by 330 runs – the state fielded its second team. The fourth Test was vital for England, who made one change in their eleven; Jones came in as captain. Australia went in to bat on an easy wicket, but were bundled out by Crawford, whose variations of pace were too subtle for the Australian batsmen. Rain however then completely altered the nature of the wicket and England collapsed. When the home team went in a second time, the English bowlers however did not use the pitch to its full advantage and allowed the Australians to survive to continue their innings as the wicket eased. Armstrong hit a well-judged 100 and England required 495 to win – the tourists' batting simply fell apart and Australia won the rubber.

England won the toss in the fifth Test and Jones put Australia in. The decision seemed to pay off as the home side were shot out by Barnes and a first innings lead of 144 attained. Trumper played his best knock of the series in Australia's second innings and England were left requiring 279. The wicket however was not good and although it improved, by that time England's best batsmen had come and gone.

Drawn games with South Australia and Western Australia closed the tour. From England's viewpoint, the tour was a failure, but the difference between the two sides was not very great and one or two blunders by the English side made all the difference. The scoring was very slow and adversely commented upon by many critics, runs coming at only about 50 per hour.

The first of the tourists, Hobbs, Hardstaff and Gunn, arrived back in England on 13 April and most of the remainder the following day.

1909: the first tour to Egypt

The M.C.C. broke fresh ground when they organised a tour to Egypt in the spring of 1909. The main party left Tilbury aboard the R.M.S. *Omrah* on 19 February, whilst the remainder of the side joined the boat at Marseilles. The team, which played its first game on 4 March, consisted of: G. H. Simpson-Hayward (Worcs) (capt), G. T. Branston (Notts), C. H. M. Ebden (Middx); E. G. Wynyard (Hants), E. J. Metcalfe (Herts), R. M. Bell, K. L. Gibson (Essex), A. C. G. Luther (Sussex), Viscount Brackley, B. P. Dobson, A. V. Drummond and H. C. Moorhouse. The all-amateur team was not far below English first-class standard.

Eight matches were played, five of which were one-day games, but the three others against Egypt produced some good cricket, with the tourists winning the series by two to one. Luther was the team's best batsman, whilst Branston was the most effective bowler.

1909-10: Faulkner's performances win Test rubber for South Africa

After the failure of the M.C.C. tour to South Africa in 1905-06, the side chosen to tour in 1909-10 was stronger, but by no means up to the full England team – of the batsmen only Hobbs was worth his place in the best eleven. Several notable amateurs were asked to go but declined, including K. L. Hutchings, A. P. Day and C. B. Fry. The full team was H. D. G. Leveson-Gower (Surrey) (capt), F. L. Fane (Essex), G. H. T. Simpson-Hayward (Worcs), E. G. Wynyard (Hants), M. C. Bird (Surrey), N. C. Tufnell (Cambridge U), and the professionals J. B. Hobbs (Surrey), H. Strudwick (Surrey), F. E. Woolley (Kent), G. J. Thompson (Northants), D. Denton (Yorks), W. Rhodes (Yorks), C. Blythe (Kent) and C. P. Buckenham (Essex). The party left Southampton on R.M.S. *Saxon* on 6 November and arrived in Cape Town on 23 November.

Following a match against Sixteen Colts, the tourists met the current Currie Cup holders, Western Province, and overwhelmed them, Hobbs hitting 114 in 115 minutes and Thompson picking up 7 for 26 in the first innings – he did not bowl in the second. The tour progressed without a hitch until the fifth match at Johannesburg, where over 10,000 watched the first day and where Faulkner's splendid all-round cricket gave Transvaal victory by 308 runs.

This defeat was followed by another brilliant all-round performance by Faulkner to give South Africa victory in the first Test. In the two games Faulkner had innings of 46, 148*, 78 and 123 and bowling figures of 4-49, 5-34, 5-120, 3-40. At the end of the Test, Faulkner was carried shoulder high round the ground. The total attendance was 29,600. The next two games were both against Natal. In the first the home side had to thank two good innings by Nourse for saving the game. In the second Blythe took 7 for 20 to dismiss Natal in the opening innings for 50 and they never recovered.

The second Test provided a second win for the home country. England were set 348 to make in the final innings. Hobbs batted in excellent form, but Faulkner in the end was too good for both the Surrey maestro and most of the other Englishmen and the margin of the victory was 95 runs.

The M.C.C. had three easy games prior to meeting Transvaal. In the first of two matches, Denton hit a century in each innings

1st Match: v XVI Colts (Cape Town)   Dec 1, 2.
M.C.C. XII 320-7 dec (J. B. Hobbs 110, M. C. Bird 67) & 49-3 drew with Colts 223 (F. J. V. Hopley 96).

2nd Match: v Western Province (Cape Town)   Dec 4, 6.
M.C.C. 351 (J. B. Hobbs 114, M. C. Bird 76) beat W. Province 67 (G. J. Thompson 7-26) & 151 by an inns & 133 runs.

3rd Match: v XV of Griqualand West (Kimberley)   Dec 10, 11, 13.
M.C.C. XI 190 (E. G. Wynard 58, A. Penny 6-65) & 251-6 dec (F. L. Fane 62*) beat Griqualand West 116 & 125 by 200 runs.

4th Match: v XV of Orange Free State (Bloemfontein)   Dec 15, 16, 17.
M.C.C. 231 (M. C. Bird 115, F. J. Wyatt 7-81) & 216-8 dec (J. B. Hobbs 55, F. E. Woolley 50) beat O.F.S. 112 & 135 by 200 runs.

5th Match: v The Reef (Vogelfontein)   Dec 21, 22, 23, 24.
M.C.C. 157 (A. E. Vogler 6-58) & 160-3 (W. Rhodes 56*) drew with The Reef 160 (S. J. Snooke 72).

6th Match: v Transvaal (Johannesburg)   Dec 27, 28, 29, 30.
Transvaal 260 (S. J. Snooke 59, R. O. Schwarz 50, G. J. Thompson 5-85) & 421-9 dec (G. A. Faulkner 148*, S. J. Snooke 64, J. W. Zulch 50) beat M.C.C. 196 (M. C. Bird 56) & 177 (D. Denton 63, G. A. Faulkner 5-34) by 308 runs.

7th Match: v South Africa (Johannesburg)   Jan 1, 3, 4, 5.
South Africa 208 (G. A. Faulkner 78, A. W. Nourse 53, G. H. Simpson-Hayward 6-43) & 345 (G. A. Faulkner 123) beat England 310 (J. B. Hobbs 89, W. Rhodes 66, A. E. E Vogler 5-87, G. A. Faulkner 5-120) & 224 (G. J. Thompson 63, A. E. E. Vogler 7-94) by 19 runs.

8th Match: v Natal (Durban)   Jan 8, 10, 11.
Natal 250 (A. W. Nourse 129, H. W. Taylor 55, W. Rhodes 5-43) & 162-8 (A. W. Nourse 54*) drew with M.C.C. 331 (J. B. Hobbs 163, W. Rhodes 64, L. R. Tuckett 7-77).

9th Match: v Natal (Pietermaritzburg)   Jan 14, 15, 17, 18.
Natal 160 (C. Blythe 7-20) & 203 lost to M.C.C. 229 (F. L. Fane 70, H. D. G. Leveson-Gower 56, S. V. Samuelson 5-90) & 26-1 by 9 wkts.

10th Match: v South Africa (Durban)   Jan 21, 22, 24, 25, 26.
South Africa 199 & 347 (G. C. White 118, A. W. Nourse 69, S. J. Snooke 53) beat England 199 (J. B. Hobbs 53, A. E. E. Vogler 5-83) & 252 (J. B. Hobbs 70, G. A. Faulkner 6-87) by 95 runs.

11th Match: v Border (East London)   Jan 29, 31, Feb 1.
Border 144 & 151 lost to M.C.C. 137 & 159-6 (J. B. Hobbs 70) by 4 wkts.

12th Match: v XV of North-Eastern District (Queenstown)   Feb 4, 5.
N-E District 81 & 95 lost to M.C.C. 239 (H. O. Yates 6-75) by an inns & 63 runs.

13th Match: v Eastern Province (Port Elizabeth)   Feb 11, 12.
E. Province 45 (C. Blythe 5-21) & 79 (G. H. Simpson-Hayward 5-14) lost to M.C.C. 263 (J. B. Hobbs 79) by an inns & 139 runs.

14th Match: v Transvaal (Johannesburg)   Feb 18, 19, 21.
M.C.C. 291 (D. Denton 139, G. C. White 5-42) & 271 (D. Denton 138, J. B. Hobbs 55) beat Transvaal 270 (G. C. White 71, J. W. Zulch 53) & 242 (F. le Roux 51*, C. P. Buckenham 6-92) by 50 runs.

15th Match: v Transvaal (Pretoria)   Feb 22, 23, 24.
Transvaal 371-3 (J. W. Zulch 176*, L. Stricker 101, F. le Roux 68*) – rain.

16th Match: v South Africa (Johannesburg)   Feb 26, 28, Mar 1, 2.
South Africa 305 (G. A. Faulkner 76, G. C. White 72, A. E. E. Vogler 65, C. P. Buckenham 5-115) & 237 (S. J. Snooke 52, G. H. Simpson-Hayward 5-69) lost to England 322 (D. Denton 104, F. E. Woolley 58*) & 221-7 (J. B. Hobbs 93*) by 3 wkts.

17th Match: v South Africa (Cape Town)   March 7, 8, 9.
England 203 (F. E. Woolley 69, M. C. Bird 57) & 178 (F. E. Woolley 64, A. E. E. Vogler 5-72) lost to South Africa 207 & 175-6 by 4 wkts.

18th Match: v South Africa (Cape Town)   March 11, 12, 14, 15.
England 417 (J. B. Hobbs 187, W. Rhodes 77, G. J. Thompson 51) & 16-1 beat South Africa 103 (C. Blythe 7-46) & 327 (G. A. Faulkner 99) by 9 wkts.

Batting Averages

	M	I	NO	R	HS	Avge	100	c/s
J. B. Hobbs (Surrey)	11	18	1	1124	187	66.17	3	4
D. Denton (Yorks)	12	19	1	650	139	36.11	3	8
W. Rhodes (Yorks)	13	20	1	499	77	26.26	0	12
H. D. G. Leveson-Gower (Surrey)	10	13	2	259	56	23.54	0	4
G. J. Thompson (Northts)	12	18	2	342	63	21.37	0	5
F. L. Fane (Essex)	12	17	0	346	70	20.35	0	5
M. C. Bird (Surrey)	13	21	1	390	76	19.50	0	7
F. E. Woolley (Kent)	12	19	1	343	69	19.05	0	24
G. H. T. Simpson-Hayward (Worcs)	9	14	2	205	37*	17.08	0	4
C. Blythe (Kent)	10	12	8	60	14*	15.00	0	3
C. P. Buckenham (Essex)	8	13	2	75	22	6.81	0	5
E. G. Wynyard (Hants)	4	5	1	25	10*	6.25	0	7
N. C. Tufnell (Cambr U)	6	6	0	37	16	6.16	0	3/3
H. Strudwick (Surrey)	10	14	2	72	15	6.00	0	15/7
Hon R. Ponsonby	1	1	1	3	3*	—	0	0

Bowling Averages

	O	M	R	W	Avge	BB	5i
C. Blythe	382.3	120	783	50	15.66	7-20	3
G. H. T. Simpson-Hayward	262.2	39	714	40	17.85	6-43	2
M. C. Bird	76	16	217	10	21.70	3-11	0
C. P. Buckenham	301	49	839	37	22.67	6-92	2
G. J. Thompson	416	115	1093	48	22.77	7-26	2
W. Rhodes	192.5	47	535	21	25.47	5-43	1
F. E. Woolley	197.2	44	458	15	30.53	3-47	0
J. B. Hobbs	80.2	16	233	7	33.28	2-31	0
E. G. Wynyard	25	1	102	1	102.00	1-93	0

Also bowled: D. Denton 2-1-1-0; H. D. G. Leveson-Gower 4-0-16-0; N. C. Tufnell 3-0-19-0.

The failure to win the rubber was attributed to the batsmen being unaccustomed to matting wickets and the googly bowling with which most of the South Africans exploited these wickets.

The tour was financially a great success and the only problem which caused any headaches was the fact that certain of the tourists were employed as newspaper correspondents and the comments printed under their names during and directly after matches were not always as tactful as they might have been.

When the tour was officially ended Leveson-Gower with Fane, Bird and Simpson-Hayward went with seven South Africans to Rhodesia and played three matches, in Bulawayo, Gwelo and Salisbury.

1910-11: M.C.C. recover from bad start in the West Indies

The team that sailed in the R.M.S.P. *Clyde* on 18 January for the West Indies was a decidedly weak combination. A. C. Johnston, L. H. W. Troughton and G. J. Thompson had all withdrawn from the published side and only eleven players journeyed across the Atlantic in the name of the M.C.C. The press were extremely dubious about the party and a dispute between the shipping company and the Government nearly caused the tour to be abandoned. The team was A. W. F. Somerset (Sussex) (capt), A. P. F. C. Somerset (Sussex), T. A. L. Whittington (Glamorgan), S. G. Smith (Northants), B. H. Holloway (Sussex), D. C. F. Burton (Yorks), H. L. Gaussen and D. S. G. Burton, with the three professionals G. Brown (Hants), J. W. Hearne (Middx) and H. I. Young (Essex). Containing only three regular first-class county men, the team could barely be described as first-class by English standards.

The first three matches of the tour were played in Barbados, two against an island eleven and the third a 'Test Match' against West Indies. The first game, which was delayed by rain, was lost very easily, the tourists falling for 93 and 91. The second match was another massacre and the eleven tourists were reduced to ten by an injury to Holloway–Simpson of Demerera substituted. Owing to quarantine restrictions no Trinidad players could appear in the West Indies team for the 'First Test', but the M.C.C. were

to give M.C.C. a 50-run win. In the second Transvaal made 371 for 3 when rain prevented any further play. England had to win the third Test to save the rubber. The match was evenly balanced throughout, but Hobbs batted soundly after an uncertain start and carrying his bat for 93 not out took England to their first win of the series by 3 wickets.

The fourth Test at Newlands commenced four days after the end of the third. The pattern of the match was similar to its predecessor, but this time South Africa batted last and the irresistible Faulkner took his team to victory in Test and rubber with an undefeated 49–the touring captain, Leveson-Gower, stood down for both this Test and the next, the team being led by Fane.

Unusually the fifth Test followed straight on after the fourth and on the same ground. On a perfect wicket Hobbs and Rhodes gave England a marvellous start with 221 in 157 minutes for the first wicket and from then England remained in charge, though Faulkner hit 99 in the South Africa's second innings.

The last Test was the final match of the tour and the team sailed home on s.s. *Armadale Castle*, landing in Southampton on 2 April.

1910-11: M.C.C. to West Indies

1st Match: v Barbados (Kensington Oval)   Feb 8, 9.
M.C.C. 93 & 91 (S. Worme 5-40) lost to Barbados 287 (H. B. G. Austin 85, C. A. Browne 66, A. P. F. C. Somerset 5-62) by an inns & 103 runs.

2nd Match: v Barbados (Kensington Oval)   Feb 10, 11.
M.C.C. 139 (C. R. Browne 6-60) & 191 (J. W. Hearne 50) lost to Barbados 352 (L. Archer 63, W. O. Gibbs 56, C. A. Browne 57) by an inns & 22 runs.

3rd Match: v West Indies (Kensington Oval)   Feb 15, 16, 17.
West Indies 271 (G. Challenor 75, H. I. Young 5-61) & 165 lost to M.C.C. 288 (B. H. Holloway 71) & 149-5 (S. G. Smith 54*) by 5 wkts.

4th Match: v British Guiana (Georgetown)   Feb 23, 24, 25.
M.C.C. 225 (T. A. L. Whittington 86) & 333-6 dec (T. A. L. Whittington 154, B. H. Holloway 100) beat British Guiana 190 (J. W. Hearne 5-100) & 133 (S. G. Smith 6-42) by 235 runs.

5th Match: v West Indies (Georgetown)   Feb 27, 28, Mar 1.
West Indies 172 (J. W. Hearne 6-91) & 272 (H. C. Bayley 59, O. Layne 59) lost to M.C.C. 301 (H. I. Young 73, S. G. Smith 59) & 144-6 by 4 wkts.

6th Match: v West Indian XI (Georgetown)   March 2, 3, 4.
West Indian XI 203 (C. V. Hunter 66, J. W. Hearne 6-76) & 224 (C. V. Hunter 58) drew with M.C.C. 332 (H. L. Gaussen 77, A. W. F. Somerset 60, T. A. L. Whittington 58, G. John 5-106, O. Layne 5-104) & 72-5.

7th Match: v Trinidad (St Clair)   March 7, 8, 9.
M.C.C. 90 (J. C. Rogers 5-18) & 127 lost to Trinidad 294 (A. Cipriani 135, J. C. Rogers 67) by an inns & 77 runs.

8th Match: v Trinidad (St Clair)   March 10, 11, 12.
M.C.C. 177 (D. C. F. Burton 57) & 162 (S. G. Smith 52, G. John 5-35) lost to Trinidad 216 (J. C. Rogers 74*, L. S. Constantine 53, J. W. Hearne 7-68) & 126-3 (A. Cipriani 65) by 7 wkts.

9th Match: v Jamaica (Kingston)   March 24, 25, 27.
Jamaica 263 (J. K. Holt 72, J. W. Hearne 6-89) & 310 (F. A. Foster 56, H. C. Duncker 55, J. W. Hearne 5-122) drew with M.C.C. 318 (T. A. L. Whittington 115*, D. C. F. Burton 51) & 51-1.

10th Match: v Jamaica (Kingston)   March 28, 29.
M.C.C. 103 (H. Kennedy 6-47) & 231 (J. W. Hearne 56) drew with Jamaica 153 (S. G. Smith 6-45) & 109-8.

11th Match: v Port Antonio (Port Antonio)   March 31, April 1.
M.C.C. 206 (H. I. Young 54) & 154-5 dec (S. G. Smith 56*) beat Port Antonio 124 & 92 (J. W. Hearne 8-32) by 144 runs.

12th Match: v Jamaica (Kingston)   April 3, 4, 5.
M.C.C. 269 (S. G. Smith 81, B. H. Holloway 59, O. Scott 6-77) & 131 (O. Scott 5-61) tied with Jamaica 173 (S. G. Smith 5-35) & 227.

now without D. C. F. Burton, and a local player substituted for him – happily Holloway had recovered, and in fact a good innings from him probably won the match, though Worme, the best West Indies bowler, had to retire with a broken finger, which aided the visitors' cause.

Moving on to British Guiana, the first match there began after three days of continuous rain. Brilliant batting by Whittington and Holloway however placed the tourists in an invincible position. The pair added 230 for the 1st wicket, a new record for the colony, and the game was won by 235 runs. Smith bowled quite splendidly in this match.

The 'Second Test' provided another victory for the M.C.C., Smith and Hearne bowling out the home side on a perfect wicket for 172, and with Young hitting 73 a substantial first innings lead

1910-11: M.C.C. to West Indies

Batting Averages

	M	I	NO	R	HS	Avge	100	c/s
T. A. L. Whittington (Glam)	11	20	2	678	154	37.66	2	7
S. G. Smith (Northts)	11	21	3	547	81	30.38	0	6
B. H. Holloway (Sussex)	10	17	0	416	100	24.47	1	7
D. C. F. Burton (Yorks)	10	17	0	334	57	19.64	0	3
J. W. Hearne (Middx)	11	21	2	344	50	18.10	0	11
A. W. F. Somerset (Sussex)	11	17	5	214	60	17.83	0	6/2
G. Brown (Hants)	11	21	1	298	35	14.90	0	9/2
H. L. Gaussen	10	18	0	260	77	14.44	0	5
H. I. Young (Essex)	11	19	2	225	73	13.23	0	5
D. S. G. Burton	10	17	5	138	38*	11.50	0	2
A. P. F. C. Somerset	11	19	5	120	33	8.57	0	5

Also played in one match: L. Heath 15 & 12* (ct 2); C. Simpson 27 & 0 (ct 1); G. Liddlelow 13 & 5; E. L. G. N. Grell 25 & 17 (ct 1).

Bowling Averages

	O	M	R	W	Avge	BB	5i
S. G. Smith	300.2	57	845	47	17.97	6-42	3
H. I. Young	204	41	517	25	20.68	5-61	1
J. W. Hearne	398.4	62	1450	67	21.64	7-68	6
A. P. F. C. Somerset	144.3	15	558	24	23.35	5-62	1
G. Brown	106	15	409	9	45.44	3-26	0

was gained which led to a four-wicket win. Another match against West Indies was arranged in place of the return against British Guiana, but when Archer was dropped from the West Indies team, the two other Barbados players in the squad refused to play. The match was in fact drawn, very much in favour of the tourists.

Travelling to Trinidad, the tourists found themselves coming straight off the boat and on to the cricket field. In these circumstances, it is hardly surprising that they lost the match against Trinidad by an innings. The M.C.C. also lost the return, but having two men injured were forced to recruit two locals as substitutes. The remaining four games were in Jamaica. Rain was the cause for two drawn matches, but the final game ended in a tie.

Considering the difficulties faced by the tourists, the visit could be regarded as a limited success.

1911-12: Hobbs and Rhodes make 323 for first wicket against Australia

The leading question of 1911 was, would C. B. Fry captain the M.C.C. team to Australia? The fact that Fry did not make up his mind whether he could go until the middle of August put the selectors in some difficulty and it was not until 18 August that it was announced that P. F. Warner (Middx) would lead the tourists. The remainder of the team was: J. W. H. T. Douglas (Essex), F. R. Foster (Warwicks) and the professionals J. B. Hobbs (Surrey), W. Rhodes (Yorks), F. E. Woolley (Kent), S. F. Barnes (Staffs), J. W. Hearne (Middx), G. Gunn (Notts), E. J. Smith (Warwicks), C. P. Mead (Hants), J. W. Hitch (Surrey), H. Strudwick (Surrey), S. Kinneir (Warwicks), J. Vine (Sussex), J. Iremonger (Notts) and T. Pawley (manager). Apart from Fry, only R. H. Spooner and G. L. Jessop declined the M.C.C.'s invitation. The team chosen was as strong as it was possible to obtain and there was little criticism, except perhaps at the absence of Hayward.

The side sailed from Tilbury on the s.s. *Orvieto* on 24 September. A match was played in Colombo and the Australian tour reverted to Adelaide for its opening, rather than Perth. The South Australians were completely outplayed, Warner, Gunn and Foster making hundreds, whilst Foster, Barnes and Douglas swept through the home batting. The match against Victoria was not so easy, but was eventually won by a narrow margin. The most disturbing news on the tour so far however was the illness that kept Warner out of the team. Rain ruined the third match – against New South Wales – and though Queensland did well in the first half of their match, they collapsed to Barnes and Foster in the second innings to provide M.C.C. with another win. The invalid list was however growing. It was stated that Warner could not play for some time, Gunn had a damaged hand and Hitch a strained groin. In the match between the M.C.C. and 'An Australian Eleven', the visitors' batting just folded up and was saved only by a splendid hundred from Douglas. The match, limited to three days was drawn, so that the M.C.C. came to the first Test unbeaten. In a high, but slow, scoring match England were outmanoeuvred from the time they lost the toss – Douglas, who led England in Warner's absence, was taken to task for not giving Barnes the first use of the ball in either innings. The best bat in England's second innings was Gunn, who played with his damaged hand bandaged. For Australia the feature of the play was Trumper's 113, made without a chance.

The second Test was played over the New Year. Barnes this time opened the English bowling and after 5 overs had four wickets for one run. The home team never recovered from this initial shock and though the English batting was a trifle shaky and Australia did much better the second time around, Hobbs played a masterly innings to take England to an unexpected victory. Australia had almost the same unfortunate start to the third Test, but this time the bowler was Foster, and on a perfect wicket only 133 were scored. Hobbs made another excellent hundred in England's first innings and he received support from nearly everyone, so that England built up a lead of colossal proportions. Australia batted very well in their second innings, but Trumper, being injured, could only make a token appearance and this told against the Australians, although England's advantage was so

Below *The M.C.C. party for Australia, 1911-12. Back: E. J. Smith, F. E. Woolley, S. F. Barnes, J. Iremonger, C. P. Mead, J. Vine, H. Strudwick. Centre: W. Rhodes, J. W. H. T. Douglas, P. F. Warner (captain), F. R. Foster, T. Pawley (manager), J. B. Hobbs, G. Gunn. Front: J. W. Hitch, J. W. Hearne. S. Kinneir was in the picture until the glass negative was broken.* Bottom *Action from the second Test Match in Melbourne, 1911-12. This is Hordern pushing the bowling of England captain J. W. H. T. Douglas into the covers.*

1st Match: v Ceylon (Colombo) (One Day)   October 21.
M.C.C. 213 beat Ceylon 59 by 154 runs.

2nd Match: v South Australia (Adelaide)   Nov 10, 11, 13, 14.
M.C.C. 563 (F. R. Foster 158, P. F. Warner 151, G. Gunn 106) beat S. Australia 141 (C. Hill 51) & 228 (E. R. Mayne 84, J. N. Crawford 63, J. W. H. T. Douglas 5-65) by an inns & 194 runs.

3rd Match: v Victoria (Melbourne)   Nov 17, 18, 20, 21.
M.C.C. 318 (F. R. Foster 101) & 234 (J. B. Hobbs 88, W. Rhodes 66) beat Victoria 274 (H. H. L. Kortlang 74, D. B. M. Smith 68) & 229 (D. B. M. Smith 84) by 49 runs.

4th Match: v New South Wales (Sydney)   Nov 24, 25, 27, 28.
M.C.C. 238 (G. Gunn 50) drew with N.S.W. 198-8 (S. E. Gregory 66, R. B. Minnett 52*).

5th Match: v Queensland (Brisbane)   Dec 1, 2, 4.
Queensland 290 (C. B. Jennings 91, R. J. Hartigan 59) & 124 (F. R. Foster 6-31) lost to M.C.C. 275 (C. P. Mead 79, W. Rhodes 64*, J. W. Hearne 53) & 140-3 (C. P. Mead 54) by 7 wkts.

6th Match: v Toowoomba (Toowoomba)   Dec 6, 7.
M.C.C. 340-6 dec (F. E. Woolley 99, S. Kinneir 80, J. Iremonger 50*) beat Toowoomba 96 (J. W. H. T. Douglas 5-30) & 110 (A. H. Jones 54) by an inns & 134 runs.

7th Match: v An Australian XI (Brisbane)   Dec 8, 9, 11.
M.C.C. 267 (J. W. H. T. Douglas 101*, S. Kinneir 63) & 279-4 (J. W. Hearne 89*, C. P. Mead 50) drew with Australian XI 347 (J. N. Crawford 110, R. B. Minnett 69, C. Kelleway 66, S. F. Barnes 5-89).

8th Match: v Australia (Sydney)   Dec 15, 16, 18, 19, 20, 21.
Australia 447 (V. T. Trumper 113, R. B. Minnett 90, W. W. Armstrong 60) & 308 (C. Kelleway 70, C. Hill 65, F. R. Foster 5-92) beat England 318 (J. W. Hearne 76, J. B. Hobbs 63, F. R. Foster 56, H. V. Hordern 5-85) & 291 (G. Gunn 62, H. V. Hordern 7-90) by 146 runs.

9th Match: v XV of Bendigo (Bendigo)   Dec 26, 27.
M.C.C. 176 (J. B. Hobbs 67) & 188 (F. E. Woolley 64, W. Rhodes 50) drew with Bendigo 164 (J. W. Hitch 7-47).

10th Match: v Australia (Melbourne)   Dec 30, Jan 1, 2, 3.
Australia 184 (S. F. Barnes 5-44) & 299 (W. W. Armstrong 90, F. R. Foster 6-91) lost to England 265 (J. W. Hearne 114, W. Rhodes 61) & 219-2 (J. B. Hobbs 126*) by 8 wkts.

11th Match: v XV of Geelong (Geelong)   Jan 5, 6.
M.C.C. 285-8 dec (C. P. Mead 65, G. Gunn 51) & 118-4 drew with Geelong 277 (A. E. Liddicut 129).

12th Match: v Australia (Adelaide)   Jan 12, 13, 15, 16, 17.
Australia 133 (F. R. Foster 5-36) & 476 (C. Hill 98, H. Carter 72, W. Bardsley 63, T. J. Matthews 53, S. F. Barnes 5-105) lost to England 501 (J. B. Hobbs 187, F. R. Foster 71, W. Rhodes 59) & 112-3 (W. Rhodes 57*) by 7 wkts.

13th Match: v XV of Ballarat (Ballarat)   Jan 19, 20.
Ballarat 318 (M. Herring 129, E. Herring 62, J. Iremonger 7-66) drew with M.C.C. 349-2 (S. Kinneir 114, J. Vine 112*, J. B. Hobbs 74).

14th Match: v Tasmania (Launceston)   Jan 23, 24, 25.
Tasmania 217 (S. M. McKenzie 59, L. R. Tumilty 56, J. Iremonger 5-52) & 165 lost to M.C.C. 332 (C. P. Mead 98) & 56-2 by 8 wkts.

15th Match: v Tasmania (Hobart)   Jan 26, 27, 29.
Tasmania 124 & 355 (G. D. Paton 112, C. Martin 54, E. T. Boddam 52, J. F. Hudson 51) lost to M.C.C. 574-4 dec (F. E. Woolley 305*, W. Rhodes 102, J. W. Hearne 97) by an inns & 95 runs.

16th Match: v Victoria (Melbourne)   Feb 2, 3, 5, 6.
M.C.C. 467 (J. W. Hearne 143, J. W. H. T. Douglas 140) & 43-2 beat Victoria 195 (W. W. Armstrong 51*) & 314 (W. W. Armstrong 120*, C. McKenzie 78) by 8 wkts.

17th Match: v Australia (Melbourne)   Feb 9, 10, 12, 13.
Australia 191 (R. B. Minnett 56, S. F. Barnes 5-74) & 173 (J. W. H. T. Douglas 5-46) lost to England 589 (W. Rhodes 179, J. B. Hobbs 178, G. Gunn 75, F. E. Woolley 56, F. R. Foster 50) by an inns & 225 runs.

18th Match: v New South Wales (Sydney)   Feb 16, 17, 19, 20.
N.S.W. 106 (F. R. Foster 7-36) & 403 (S. E. Gregory 186*, S. H. Emery 65, V. T. Trumper 53) lost to M.C.C. 315 (W. Rhodes 119, G. R. Hazlitt 7-95) & 195-2 (W. Rhodes 109, G. Gunn 56*) by 8 wkts.

19th Match: v Australia (Sydney)   Feb 23, 24, 26, 27, 28, March 1.
England 324 (F. E. Woolley 133*, G. Gunn 52, H. V. Hordern 5-95) & 214 (G. Gunn 61, H. V. Hordern 5-66) beat Australia 176 & 292 (R. B. Minnett 61, V. T. Trumper 50) by 70 runs.

Batting Averages

	M	I	NO	R	HS	Avge	100	c/s
P. F. Warner (Middx)	1	1	0	151	151	151.00	1	0
F. E. Woolley (Kent)	14	18	4	781	305*	55.78	2	14
J. B. Hobbs (Surrey)	11	18	1	943	187	55.47	3	8
W. Rhodes (Yorks)	14	24	4	1098	179	54.90	4	11
G. Gunn (Notts)	9	15	2	665	106	51.15	1	8
J. W. Hearne (Middx)	13	22	4	808	143	44.88	2	5
F. R. Foster (Warks)	13	19	1	641	158	35.61	2	7
J. W. H. T. Douglas (Essex)	12	15	3	416	140	34.66	2	5
C. P. Mead (Hants)	13	18	2	531	98	33.18	0	4
S. Kinneir (Warks)	5	8	0	219	63	27.42	0	1
H. Strudwick (Surrey)	7	7	3	68	28	17.00	0	13/4
E. J. Smith (Warks)	7	9	0	124	47	13.77	0	16/2
S. F. Barnes (Staffs)	13	14	3	126	35	11.45	0	7
J. W. Hitch (Surrey)	8	9	2	79	33*	11.28	0	3
J. Vine (Sussex)	8	9	2	78	36	11.14	0	3
J. Iremonger (Notts)	6	7	0	57	31	8.14	0	4

Bowling Averages

	O	M	R	W	Avge	BB	5i
J. B. Hobbs	18.1	3	62	5	12.40	4-25	0
F. R. Foster	485.1	110	1252	62	20.19	7-36	5
J. W. Hitch	169.4	23	548	27	20.29	4-41	0
S. F. Barnes	472.2	118	1231	59	20.86	5-44	4
J. W. H. T. Douglas	316.5	74	803	37	21.70	5-46	2
F. E. Woolley	156.1	27	503	17	29.58	3-71	0
J. Iremonger	159.5	45	397	12	33.08	5-52	1
J. Vine	38.1	5	182	4	45.50	2-36	0
J. W. Hearne	168.3	12	701	14	50.07	4-66	0

Also bowled: W. Rhodes 62-9-234-0.
Played in non-first-class matches only: W. J. H. Curwen.

crowd had gathered at the railway station to welcome them.

In explaining the success of the England side, P. F. Warner attributed it in some part to internal strife and bitterness in Australian cricket. On the field however the bowling of Barnes and Foster was undoubtedly the great match winner. Douglas gave the leading pair excellent support, but the other bowlers were of little account. Hitch suffered from injury and Hearne could not keep a length, whilst Vine's leg-breaks were easy meat and Iremonger was only of use as a defensive bowler. The fielding was good – Hobbs superb in the covers, Gunn and Woolley safe in the slips, Rhodes useful anywhere and Barnes not as absent-minded as he sometimes looked. Hobbs and Rhodes were the principal batsmen, but Gunn was very sound in his individual manner. The way in which Smith read the bowling of Foster meant that the Warwickshire stumper was preferred to Strudwick.

The Test series was the last in which the great Victor Trumper played, for he refused to tour England with the 1912 Australian team. The season was not a success for him, save for the century in the first Test, and in fact none of the Australian batsmen had much of a record in 1911-12. The best home bowler by a mile was Hordern, who was the only man to average less than 30 runs per wicket.

large that even Trumper could not have altered the result.

The tourists went off to Tasmania leading two to one in the rubber and they came back to clinch the series at Melbourne. Australia were put in on a soft wicket and fell cheaply to Barnes and Foster. Hobbs made yet another hundred and with Rhodes added 323 for the first English wicket. The Australian batting broke down in the second innings, leaving the tourists victors by an innings and 225 runs.

The final Test went into the seventh day due to rain and Australia made some drastic changes in their eleven, but the English team was always in control and thus won the series by four matches to one. There were no other fixtures after the last Test. The team returned home, and taking the overland route from Toulon arrived at Charing Cross on 7 April, where a big

1911-12: M.C.C. play three 'Tests' in the Argentine

At the invitation of the Argentine, the M.C.C. sent over a fairly strong amateur team in the winter of 1911-12. The large English community in the Argentine had developed a good standard of club cricket during the closing years of the 19th century and a body to control cricket in the country was set up. Several cricketers living in the Argentine had had some experience of county cricket in England and the feature of the tour was the series of 'Tests'.

The touring party comprised Lord Hawke (Yorks) (capt), A. C. MacLaren (Lancs), C. E. de Trafford (Leics), A. J. L. Hill (Hants), M. C. Bird (Surrey), W. Findlay (Surrey secretary), E. R. Wilson (Yorks), N. C. Tufnell (Cambridge U), C. E. Hatfeild (Kent), L. H. W. Troughton (Kent), E. J. Fulcher (Norfolk) and Capt H. H. C. Baird (Army). Sailing on the s.s.

A strong amateur side under Lord Hawke went to Argentina in 1912. This team was, back: J. O. Anderson (umpire), Capt H. H. C. Baird, N. C. Tufnell, E. R. Wilson, C. E. Hatfeild, W. Findlay. Front: L. H. W. Troughton, M. C. Bird, C. E. de Trafford, Lord Hawke, A. C. MacLaren, A. J. L. Hill.

Asturias from Southampton on 26 January, the side played its first match on 13 and 14 February. Both this and the second game were drawn due to high scoring, but in the 'First Test', M.C.C. fared badly against Dorning and Foy and some consistent batting by the home team led to an Argentine win by 4 wickets.

The tourists had their revenge in the 'Second Test'. Hill and Bird hit up 106 for the second wicket in the first innings and Bird was again in form in the second innings, and needing 310 to win in the final innings, Argentine collapsed before the bowling of Wilson and were all out for 100.

In the 'Third Test', MacLaren led the M.C.C., due to Lord Hawke being injured. The match was very even throughout, and although M.C.C. only needed 102 to win in the last innings, a determined knock by MacLaren was required to save the day and M.C.C. won by just two wickets.

The nine-match tour, though it created little interest in England, did a great deal to encourage cricket in the Argentine – it was regretted that the tourists did not have time for a brief visit to Chile.

The side arrived back in England on 6 April, except for Lord Hawke, who remained in South America, C. E. de Trafford, who went on to the West Indies and W. Findlay, who had travelled by an earlier boat.

1912-13: Barbados, but not the West Indies, beat M.C.C.

For a second winter A. W. F. Somerset (Sussex) captained the M.C.C. team to West Indies and was accompanied by four of the previous side – his son, A. P. F. C. Somerset (Sussex), S. G. Smith (Northants), T. A. L. Whittington (Glamorgan) and D. C. F. Burton (Yorks). The other members of the side were three professionals, E. Humphreys (Kent), A. E. Relf (Sussex) and W. C. Smith (Surrey), and the amateurs G. A. M. Docker, M. H. C. Doll (Middx), B. P. Dobson, A. Jaques (Hants), S. G. Fairbairn (Bucks). The side was a little stronger than its predecessor, and sailing in the R.M.S. *Magdalena* it reached Barbados on 27 January. The first game, against the island team, commenced three days later. Barbados were without P. A. Goodman, injured, and H. B. G. Austin but still thrashed the tourists, whose bowling was torn apart. The medicine was repeated in the return game – another innings defeat. As however had happened on a previous visit to the West Indies as a whole proved weaker than in part, and the M.C.C. won the 'First Test' by 9 wickets. The representative eleven did not include any Jamaican players, but five from Barbados, three from Trinidad and one each from British Guiana, St Vincent and Grenada. The English side owed their victory to some capital bowling by Humphreys, who took 13 wickets.

Voyaging to Trinidad, the tourists beat the local side by 8 wickets, but were lucky to draw the return, after being dismissed for 87 in their first innings and being forced to follow on 247 in arrears. Many fielding errors led to an English defeat in the

1911-12: M.C.C. to the Argentine

1st Match: v Southern Suburbs (Los Talleres)   Feb 13, 14.
M.C.C. 439 (C. E. de Trafford 116, L. H. W. Troughton 71) drew with Southern Suburbs 202 (C. P. Russ 54) & 274-8 (S. A. Cowper 182).

2nd Match: v Combined Camps (Hurlingham)   Feb 15, 16.
M.C.C. 109 (C. M. Horsfall 5-21) & 489-7 (L. H. W. Troughton 112*, J. O. Anderson 89, W. Findley 69, Lord Hawke 54) drew with Combined Camps 162 (J. R. Garrod 88).

3rd Match: v Argentine (Hurlingham)   Feb 18, 19, 20.
M.C.C. 186 (E. R. Wilson 67*, H. Dorning 6-65) & 157 (L. H. W. Troughton 59*, P. A. Foy 5-49) lost to Argent:ne 209 & 136-6 by 4 wkts.

4th Match: v Northern Suburbs (Belgrano)   Feb 22, 23.
M.C.C. 181 & 300-6 dec (A. J. L. Hill 60, E. R. Wilson 52) beat Northern Suburbs 204 (C. E. Hatfeild 5-42) & 129 (H. H. C. Baird 6-50) by 148 runs.

5th Match: v Argentine (Palermo)   Feb 24, 25, 26.
M.C.C. 266 (M. C. Bird 74, E. J. Fulcher 51) & 250 (M. C. Bird 61) beat Argentine 206 & 100 (E. R. Wilson 6-36) by 210 runs.

6th Match: v South (Buenos Aires)   Feb 28, 29.
South 137 (N. W. Jackson 51, E. R. Wilson 5-45) & 192 (N. W. Jackson 79, C. E. Hatfeild 5-47) lost to M.C.C. 409-9 dec (E. R. Wilson 105, C. E. Hatfeild 90, C. E. de Trafford 51) by an inns & 80 runs.

7th Match: v Argentine (Lomas)   March 2, 3.
Argentine 171 (H. G. Garnett 51*) & 98 lost to M.C.C. 169 (P. A. Foy 7-84) & 102-8 (P. A. Foy 5-42) by 2 wkts.

8th Match: v Argentine-born (Hurlingham)   March 6, 7.
Argentine-born 123 (C. E. Hatfeild 7-46) & 167 (C. E. Hatfeild 6-75) lost to M.C.C. 387-4 dec (A. C. MacLaren 172, N. C. Tufnell 163*) by an inns & 97 runs.

9th Match: v North (Rosario)   March 9, 10.
North 226 (H. A. Cowes 56, E. R. Wilson 6-66) & 41 (E. R. Wilson 8-10) lost to M.C.C. 209 (A. C. MacLaren 64, P. A. Foy 5-68) & 60-4 by 6 wkts.

'Second Test'. The M.C.C. captain very sportingly allowed Cumberbatch to continue his innings after he had been clean bowled – the batsman's attention had been distracted by leaves blowing across the ground.

A tricky wicket greeted the team in Georgetown, but they won a very low scoring game by 66 runs. In the 'Third Test', the home team was not fully represented and on a docile wicket, the West Indies bowling, which was virtually all fast, suffered greatly. The M.C.C. therefore won the three-match series and the local journalists rather amusingly wrote of 'the Ashes going home'. The tourists ended the tour in splendid style with an innings victory against British Guiana, Humphreys bowling well on an easy pitch. Indeed the all-round performances of Humphreys were the feature of the tour, though Relf ran him a close second.

The captain regretted that the team did not visit Jamaica, but he pointed out that it was a nine-day voyage to that island from the rest of the British West Indies and such a break in the tour programme was impractical.

1913: Incogniti tour the United States

Under the leadership of Col C. E. Greenway, the Incogniti C.C. toured the United States in September 1913. Virtually all the side had experience in first-class county cricket and the team might be regarded as just about 'first-class' by English standards. The full party was Col C. E. Greenway, W. G. M. Sarel (Surrey), the Hon H. G. H. Mulholland (Cambridge U), G. R. R. Colman (Oxford U), M. Falcon (Cambridge U), C. L. St J. Tudor (Sussex), C. E. Hatfeild (Kent), B. G. von B. Melle (Hants), E. J. Metcalfe, D. M. P. Whitcombe, P. Collins and B. P. Dobson.

The tour opened in Philadelphia, where the English team declared in their second innings against Germantown C.C., setting the home side 241 in 120 minutes – the match ended with the total 168 for 5. The second game was against another club side, Merion, who were beaten by an innings, Falcon giving a great all-round display. New York were also defeated by an innings and then came the first of the two important matches of the tour, against Philadelphia. Despite lacking J. B. King and P. H. Clark, the Philadelphians won by 3 wickets. For some reason the Philadelphians made eight changes in the return match, though King and Clark still could not play, and this weakened side lost by 8 wickets. Hatfeild bowled well for the tourists.

The visit ended with a club game against Philadelphia C.C. J. B. King played for the locals and bowled brilliantly taking 12 for 95 in the match. Falcon however improved even on this by skittling out Philadelphia in their second innings for 61 and returning figures of 8 for 14, thus bringing victory by 77 runs.

1913-14: Barnes' haul of wickets in South Africa

The South African authorities raised guarantees worth over £5,000 to enable the M.C.C. tourists to visit them in 1913-14, but, prior to the visit, the home press felt that the South African players would not prove a match for the Englishmen. Rhodesia was again not on the itinerary because the clubs there could not raise the funds to finance the matches.

The M.C.C., after the failure of the team sent in 1909-10, made a great effort to secure the strongest possible side and, apart from refusals by Jessop and P. R. Johnson, the team was as selected. The party was made up of J. W. H. T. Douglas (Essex) (capt), M. C. Bird (Surrey), the Hon L. H. Tennyson (Hants), D. C. Robinson (Gloucs) and the professionals J. B. Hobbs (Surrey), C. P. Mead (Hants), J. W. Hearne (Middx), F. E. Woolley (Kent),

W. Rhodes (Yorks), M. W. Booth (Yorks), H. Strudwick (Surrey), A. E. Relf (Sussex) and S. F. Barnes (Staffs).

On arrival in South Africa, the team suffered a blow when D. C. Robinson, the reserve wicket-keeper fell ill, and as it was unlikely that he would recover in time to play any matches, E. J. Smith (Warwicks) was sent for and arrived in time to appear in the eighth match.

The opening game against Western Province at Newlands saw the tourists still recovering from their voyage. P. T. Lewis hit 151

in 185 minutes for the home side, his innings being the feature of a drawn game. The most important match prior to the first Test was the meeting with Natal. H. W. Taylor played a splendid innings for the Province, carrying out his bat for 83 out of 124. Hobbs also batted in good form, but rain cut the playing time by half and the match was drawn. In the first Test, Taylor repeated his Natal innings, hitting 109 for South Africa out of a total of 182 – no one else could master Barnes. England, aided by several dropped catches, hit 450 and went on to an innings victory. The match against Transvaal followed the same pattern and so did the second Test, though here Barnes' figures created a new record, as he dismissed no less than 17 batsmen – the report of the game noted he bowled with 'great devil'. The English batting collapsed after an excellent start, but this made little difference to the outcome of the match. The third Test began with just a single day separating it from the second, and both were staged at Johannesburg. England won the toss and Hobbs and Rhodes got the visitors off to a fine start, but the later batting failed again, with Blanckenberg bowling very effectively. South Africa's batsmen managed to contain Barnes only to fall to Hearne, who took 5 for 49. England scored more consistently in their second innings and South Africa required 396 in the final innings. Taylor and Zulch made an excellent stand for the first wicket to take the total to 153, but the middle order failed and England won by 91 runs – for South Africa the match was a vast improvement.

A general strike caused problems during the next two games in Transvaal and there was little public interest. Both Griqualand West and Orange Free State were too weak to worry the M.C.C. Transvaal, however, in their return did much better and Barnes, for once, suffered, with Beaumont batting particularly well. The game was drawn. For the local sides, matters improved when Natal, in their return game, beat the M.C.C. by 4 wickets. The defeat was due to two splendid innings from H. W. Taylor – 91 out of 153 and 100 out of 216-6 – and a lack-lustre batting performance by M.C.C., who, without Hobbs, looked rather poor.

Although England had won the rubber, Natal's victory gave South Africa some confidence for the fourth Test, which followed. South Africa went in first and once more collapsed to Barnes, but the South African left-arm bowler, Carter, going round the wicket against a strong wind, completely baffled the English batting, and the home country obtained a first innings lead. A masterly innings by H. W. Taylor then increased the South African advantage and England were set to make 313. Hobbs and Rhodes put on 133

1913-14: M.C.C. to South Africa

1st Match: v Western Province (Cape Town)   Nov 8, 9, 11.
W. Province 376 (P. T. Lewis 151, F. D. Conry 53, A. E. Relf 5-67) drew with M.C.C. 199 (J. B. Hobbs 72) & 330 (J. W. Hearne 83, J. B. Hobbs 80, J. W. H. T. Douglas 61, J. M. Blanckenberg 5-91).

2nd Match: v XV of South-Western Districts (Robertson)   Nov 14, 15.
M.C.C. 382-7 dec (J. B. Hobbs 107, C. P. Mead 78, M. C. Bird 61) beat S-W Districts 158 (A. de Villiers 74*, F. E. Woolley 5-62) & 136 (W. Rhodes 6-44) by an inns & 88 runs.

3rd Match: v XV of South-Western Districts (Oudtshoorn)   Nov 17, 18.
S-W Districts 104 & 93 (S. F. Barnes 7-11) lost to M.C.C. 257 (W. Rhodes 70) by an inns & 60 runs.

4th Match: v Cape Province (Port Elizabeth)   Nov 21, 22.
M.C.C. 385 (J. B. Hobbs 170) beat Cape Province 158 & 60 (S. F. Barnes 7-25) by an inns & 167 runs.

5th Match: v XV of Grahamstown & Colleges (Grahamstown)   Nov 26, 27.
M.C.C. 321-5 dec (C. P. Mead 84, W. Rhodes 64, A. E. Relf 64*) beat Grahamstown & Colleges 112 & 176 (S. F. Barnes 8-35).

6th Match: v Border (East London)   Nov 29, Dec 1, 2.
M.C.C. 356-8 dec (J. W. H. T. Douglas 102*, J. B. Hobbs 57, M. W. Booth 57) beat Border 121 (C. Johnson 51) & 103 (M. W. Booth 5-24) by an inns & 132 runs.

7th Match: v Border (Kingwilliamstown)   Dec 3, 4.
M.C.C. 204 (L. H. Tennyson 66) & 163-4 dec (F. E. Woolley 55) drew with Border 126 & 159-6 (S. G. Fuller 72, R. H. Randall 71).

8th Match: v Natal (Pietermaritzburg)   Dec 8, 9, 10.
Natal 124 (H. W. Taylor 83*, F. E. Woolley 6-41) & 69-0 drew with M.C.C. 219-7 dec (J. W. H. T. Douglas 70*, J. B. Hobbs 66, J. L. Cox 6-41).

9th Match: v South Africa (Durban)   Dec 13, 15, 16, 17.
South Africa 182 (H. W. Taylor 109, S. F. Barnes 5-57) & 111 (S. F. Barnes 5-48) lost to England 450 (J. W. H. T. Douglas 119, J. B. Hobbs 82, M. C. Bird 61, L. H. Tennyson 52) by an inns & 157 runs.

10th Match: v Transvaal (Johannesburg)   Dec 20, 22, 23.
Transvaal 202 (R. Beaumont 62) & 196 (R. Beaumont 52) lost to M.C.C. 427-8 dec (J. B. Hobbs 102, F. E. Woolley 116, M. C. Bird 67) by an inns & 29 runs.

11th Match: v South Africa (Johannesburg)   Dec 26, 27, 29, 30.
South Africa 160 (G. P. D. Hartigan 51, S. F. Barnes 8-56) & 231 (A. W. Nourse 56, S. F. Barnes 9-103) lost to England 403 (W. Rhodes 152, C. P. Mead 102, A. E. Relf 63, J. M. Blanckenberg 5-83) by an inns & 12 runs.

12th Match: v South Africa (Johannesburg)   Jan 1, 2, 3, 5.
England 238 (J. B. Hobbs 92) & 308 (C. P. Mead 86, J. W. H. T. Douglas 77) beat South Africa 151 (J. W. Hearne 5-49) & 304 (J. W. Zulch 82, H. W. Taylor 70, J. M. Blanckenberg 59, S. F. Barnes 5-102) by 91 runs.

13th Match: v Transvaal (Pretoria)   Jan 9, 10, 12.
Transvaal 245 (D. J. Meintjes 87, F. le Roux 69) & 21-2 drew with M.C.C. 330 (C. P. Mead 145, J. W. H. T. Douglas 73, F. le Roux 6-64).

14th Match: v A Transvaal XI (Vogelfontein)   Jan 14, 15.
Transvaal XI 170 (L. J. Tancred 68) drew with M.C.C. 350-4 dec. (J. B. Hobbs 137, J. W. Hearne 96, A. E. Relf 55*).

15th Match: v Griqualand West (Kimberley)   Jan 17, 19.
M.C.C. 346 (J. B. Hobbs 141, J. W. Hearne 81) beat Griqualand West 75 (S. F. Barnes 5-22, A. E. Relf 5-24) & 170 (W. V. Ling 63, S. F. Barnes 5-22) by an inns & 101 runs.

16th Match: v Orange Free State (Bloemfontein)   Jan 23, 24, 25.
M.C.C. 565-8 dec (M. C. Bird 200, J. W. Hearne 108, W. Rhodes 68, J. W. H. T. Douglas 51) beat O.F.S. 117 (S. F. Barnes 7-41) & 74 (S. F. Barnes 6-38) by an inns & 374 runs.

17th Match: v Transvaal (Johannesburg)   Jan 30, 31, Feb 1.
M.C.C. 386 (J. W. Hearne 136, W. Rhodes 62) & 211-0 dec (J. B. Hobbs 131*, W. Rhodes 76*) drew with Transvaal 347 (F. le Roux 66, R. Beaumont 65, J. W. Zulch 62, L. J. Tancred 54) & 145-6.

18th Match: v XV of Northern Natal (Ladysmith)   Feb 4, 5.
Northern Natal 94 & 141-8 (D. Taylor jun 81) drew with M.C.C. 289-4 dec (A. E. Relf 106, L. H. Tennyson 105).

19th Match: v Natal (Durban)   Feb 7, 9, 10.
M.C.C. 132 & 235 (C. P. Carter 6-58) lost to Natal 153 (H. W. Taylor 91, S. F. Barnes 5-44) & 216-6 (H. W. Taylor 100, A. W. Nourse 59) by 4 wkts.

20th Match: v South Africa (Durban)   Feb 14, 16, 17, 18.
South Africa 170 (P. A. M. Hands 51, S. F. Barnes 7-56) & 305-9 dec (H. W. Taylor 93, S. F. Barnes 7-88) drew with England 163 (J. B. Hobbs 64, C. P. Carter 6-50) & 154-5 (J. B. Hobbs 97).

21st Match: v South Africa (Port Elizabeth)   Feb 27, 28, March 2, 3.
South Africa 193 (P. A. M. Hands 83) & 228 (H. W. Taylor 87, J. W. Zulch 60) lost to England 411 (C. P. Mead 117, F. E. Woolley 54) & 11-0 by 10 wkts.

22nd Match: v Western Province (Cape Town)   March 7, 9, 10.
M.C.C. 322 (J. W. H. T. Douglas 93) & 177-4 dec drew with W. Province 210 (M. Commaille 52, J. W. Hearne 7-78) & 178-9 (P. T. Lewis 59).

1913-14: M.C.C. to South Africa

Batting Averages

	M	I	NO	R	HS	Avge	100	c/s
J. B. Hobbs (Surrey)	16	22	2	1489	170	74.75	5	13
J. W. H. T. Douglas (Essex)	18	21	5	827	119	51.68	2	12
J. W. Hearne (Middx)	12	16	1	695	136	46.33	2	9
C. P. Mead (Hants)	16	20	0	745	145	39.21	3	5
W. Rhodes (Yorks)	17	24	3	731	152	34.80	1	29
M. W. Booth (Yorks)	12	14	4	291	57	29.10	0	1
M. C. Bird (Surrey)	17	21	2	551	200	29.00	1	15
F. E. Woolley (Kent)	18	23	1	595	116	27.04	1	29
E. J. Smith (Warks)	8	8	2	146	36	24.33	0	6/1
Hon L. H. Tennyson (Hants)	18	24	0	498	66	20.75	0	10
A. E. Relf (Sussex)	18	21	2	310	55*	16.31	0	22
H. Strudwick (Surrey)	14	13	4	86	26	9.55	0	23/7
S. F. Barnes (Staffs)	12	14	7	49	20*	7.00	0	7
W. H. Crease	1	1	0	2	2	2.00	0	0
R. R. Relf (Sussex)	1	1	1	14	14*	—	0	2

Bowling Averages

	O	M	R	W	Avge	BB	5i
S. F. Barnes	460.2	129	1117	104	10.74	9-103	13
C. P. Mead	8	1	35	2	17.50	2-35	0
J. W. H. T. Douglas	181	31	531	30	17.70	4-14	0
M. C. Bird	53	10	171	9	19.00	3-20	0
M. W. Booth	188	31	530	26	20.38	5-24	1
W. Rhodes	235.1	53	662	31	21.35	4-27	0
A. E. Relf	380.2	109	856	40	21.40	5-24	2
F. E. Woolley	258.3	61	717	33	21.72	6-41	1
J. W. Hearne	209.5	32	724	27	26.81	7-78	2
Hon L. H. Tennyson	14	1	76	1	76.00	1-2	0

Also bowled: J. B. Hobbs 1-0-4-0; E. J. Smith 3-0-21-0; H. Strudwick 3-0-27-0. Played in non-first-class matches only: I. D. Difford, G. P. Harrison.

before the first English wicket fell and the match faded to a draw. The teams went straight from the fourth Test to Port Elizabeth for the fifth. Barnes was too ill to play and thus South Africa were in a strong position to win this last game. The wicket at Port Elizabeth proved much faster than those for the previous matches and this seemed to upset the South African batsmen, whilst suiting the Englishmen. England won by 10 wickets.

The last match of the tour took place at Cape Town, being the return with Western Province. The home team just managed to bat out time to save the game.

The two outstanding figures of the tour were Hobbs and Barnes. Hobbs was perhaps not as brilliant as on his previous tour to South Africa, but his wicket was probably harder to take, whilst Barnes exploited his wonderful length and variation of spin to its full and it needed exceptional footwork on the part of the batsman to score from him. Rhodes, Relf and Douglas were the other successes of the tour, but Mead, Hearne and Woolley never really lived up to their English reputations. Booth suffered in a motor accident just prior to the first Test and never recovered his form, whilst Bird had few opportunities. The fielding was generally of a high standard, with Hobbs and Tennyson, who disappointed with the bat, brilliant in the out-field.

South Africa missed the great quartette of Schwarz, Vogler, Faulkner and Pegler, all of whom had moved to England. Young Blanckenberg could not make up for the loss of these, but he tried very hard and had some success. The bouquet for batting went to Taylor, whose footwork against Barnes was a revelation. Of the others Zulch and later, P. A. M. Hands, did useful work.

1920: Incogniti unbeaten in the United States and Canada

The following side toured North America in 1920: E. J. Metcalfe (Herts) (capt), T. A. L. Brocklebank, R. C. Brooks, G. H. M. Cartwright, R. St L. Fowler (Hants), D. R. Jardine (Surrey), E. C. Lee (Hants), T. C. Lowry (Cambridge U), J. S. F. Morrison (Somerset), D. Roberts, G. O. Shelmerdine (Cambridge U), E. G. Wynyard (Hants) and M. B. Burrows (Surrey).

Playing nine matches in all, the Incogniti won seven and drew the other two. The two principal matches were against All Philadelphia, over three days each. Both were won.

Fowler was the outstanding player, taking 44 wickets at 10.70 each and scoring 294 runs at an average of 42.00. Jardine hit two centuries, both in New York.

The team sailed to America on the *Mauretania* on 21 August and returned on the same boat on 30 September.

1920: Incogniti to United States and Canada

1st Match: v Frankford (St Martin's)   Aug 31, Sept 1.
Incogniti 282 beat Frankford 147 & 114 by an inns & 21 runs.

2nd Match: v Philadelphia C.C. (St Martin's)   Sept 3, 4.
Philadelphia 255 & 120 lost to Incogniti 406-7 dec (G. O. Shermadine 143) by inns & 31 runs.

3rd Match: v Merion (Haverford)   Sept 6, 7.
Merion 192 & 93-5 drew with Incogniti 317-6 dec.

4th Match: v New York XI (Haverford)   Sept 8, 9.
Incogniti 375-6 dec (D. R. Jardine 157) beat New York XI 150 & 89 by an inns & 136 runs.

5th Match: v All Philadelphia (Haverford)   Sept 10, 11, 13.
Incogniti 326 (R. St. L. Fowler 142) & 259-9 dec beat All Philadelphia 308 & 135 by 142 runs.

6th Match: v Germantown (Manheim)   Sept 14, 15.
Germantown 124 & 151 lost to Incogniti 245 & 32-1 by 9 wkts.

7th Match: v All Philadelphia (Manheim)   Sept 17, 18, 20.
Incogniti 219 & 93-5 beat All Philadelphia 86 & 225 by 5 wkts.

8th Match: v All New York (Staten Island)   Sept 22, 23.
Incogniti 377 (D. R. Jardine 133) beat All New York 147 & 89 by an inns & 141 runs.

9th Match: v All Toronto (Toronto) (12 a-side)   Sept 25, 27.
All Toronto 126 & 213 drew with Incogniti 281 & 53-5.

1920-21: Australia win all five Test Matches

The First World War caused a break both in English first-class cricket and in English teams travelling overseas, but within a few months of hostilities ending, the Australian authorities invited the M.C.C. to send out a team. This invitation was declined, but it was impossible to refuse a second for the following winter and, despite some misgivings, the M.C.C. set about organising a party for 1920-21. R. H. Spooner was asked to lead the side, but, having accepted, had to ask to be released for domestic reasons. Jupp also was forced to stand down, but otherwise the selectors met with no major refusals and the team which left Tilbury aboard R.M.S. *Osterley* was: J. W. H. T. Douglas (Essex) (capt), P. G. H. Fender (Surrey), E. R. Wilson (Yorks) and the professionals J. W. Hearne (Middx), E. H. Hendren (Middx), F. E. Woolley (Kent), J. W. H. Makepeace (Lancs), W. Rhodes (Yorks), A. Dolphin (Yorks), A. Waddington (Yorks), H. Howell (Warwicks) and C. A. G. Russell (Essex), with F. C. Toone, Yorkshire's secretary, as manager. J. W. Hitch (Surrey) travelled on a later boat, whilst J. B. Hobbs (Surrey), H. Strudwick (Surrey) and C. H. Parkin (Lancs) joined the boat to Toulon.

Leaving on 18 September, the boat called at Toulon on 25 September, and then continued to Naples, where the team went to view Pompeii. The only other stop was at Port Said before Colombo was reached on 11 October and a one-day game played.

During the run from Colombo to Fremantle, a case of typhoid was reported on the boat and this resulted in the team spending a week in quarantine in Fremantle, and the cancellation of the four-day match in Perth. A one-day match was all that could be managed. The first serious game therefore took place at Adelaide. Parkin bowled splendidly in the first innings and as the M.C.C. found no terrors with the home attack, the game was won by an innings. The second match was a repetition of the first, Victoria also being beaten with an innings to spare. Travelling on from Melbourne to Sydney, the tourists met the strongest state side. The first innings belonged to M.C.C., with Hobbs hitting 112 in 168 minutes and the bowlers dismissing New South Wales cheaply. The home side required 334 to win, which seemed a tall order, but Macartney and Collins tore the M.C.C. bowling to shreds, with an opening stand of 244 in 186 minutes, and Macartney's batting was quite remarkable as New South Wales went to a 6-wicket victory.

After this upset, the visitors played four matches, none of which caused them any sleepless nights, before the first Test in Sydney. To everyone's surprise, Australia won the toss, batted and were dismissed for 267. On the second day, however, before a crowd of some 40,000, England collapsed. Australia seized the initiative and with Collins and Armstrong hitting hundreds in the second innings, they scored 581 in 540 minutes to leave England an impossible fourth innings target.

For the second Test, Australia were without Macartney, but for England worse was in store when Hearne was taken ill so seriously with lumbago on the first day that he could not play again on the tour. Australia again batted first, but this time hit up 499, then rain ruined the wicket and England, apart from Hobbs, who played his best innings of the tour, just folded up, losing by an innings. Only an odds match at Ballarat separated the second and third Tests. The latter was vital for England if the rubber was to be saved. England dismissed Australia for 354 and then, due to Russell, obtained a first innings lead of nearly a hundred. Australia lost 3 second innings wickets for 71 and England appeared on top, but centuries for Kelleway, Armstrong and Pellew quickly reversed the situation. The England fielding left something to be desired, but there were some odd umpiring decisions, which rather depressed the bowlers. Left to make 490, England still looked hopeful – Hobbs played another great innings, but the

1920-21: M.C.C. to Ceylon and Australia

1st Match: v Ceylon (Colombo) (One Day) Oct 11.
Ceylon 122 drew with M.C.C. 108-9.

2nd Match: v Western Australia (Perth) (One Day) Oct 30.
M.C.C. 276-8 dec (J. W. H. Makepeace 117, J. B. Hobbs 63, E. H. Hendren 60) drew with W. Australia 119-7.

3rd Match: v South Australia (Adelaide) Nov 5, 6, 8, 9.
S. Australia 118 (C. H. Parkin 8-55) & 339 (A. Richardson 111, P. D. Rundell 75, C. E. Pellew 64) lost to M.C.C. 512-5 dec (J. W. Hearne 182, C. A. G. Russell 156, E. H. Hendren 79, A. Smith 5-120) by an inns & 55 runs.

4th Match: v Victoria (Melbourne) Nov 12, 13, 15, 16.
Victoria 274 (A. W. Lampard 111) & 85 (W. Rhodes 6-39) lost to M.C.C. 418-3 dec (J. B. Hobbs 131, E. H. Hendren 106*, J. W. Hearne 87) by an inns & 59 runs.

5th Match: v New South Wales (Sydney) Nov 19, 20, 22.
M.C.C. 236 (J. B. Hobbs 112, E. H. Hendren 67) & 250 (J. W. Hearne 81, P. G. H. Fender 54, J. M. Gregory 5-67) lost to N.S.W. 153 & 335-4 (C. G. Macartney 161, H. L. Collins 106) by 6 wkts.

6th Match: v Queensland (Brisbane) Nov 27, 29, 30.
Queensland 186 (G. S. Moore 85) & 192 lost to M.C.C. 419 (W. Rhodes 162, J. W. H. Douglas 84, C. A. G. Russell 73, S. W. Ayres 5-112) by an inns & 41 runs.

7th Match: v An Australian XI (Brisbane) Dec 3, 4, 6.
Australian XI 255 (C. G. Macartney 96, J. W. Hearne 53, C. J. Tozer 51, J. W. H. Douglas 5-45) & 182-5 (C. J. Tozer 53, H. Carter 50) drew with M.C.C. 357 (E. H. Hendren 96, C. A. G. Russell 72, E. R. Wilson 56).

8th Match: v Toowoomba (Toowoomba) Dec 8, 9.
M.C.C. 208 dec (W. Rhodes 100, J. W. H. Makepeace 50) beat Toowoomba 62 (A. Waddington 7-29) & 27 (C. H. Parkin 5-5) by an inns & 119 runs.

9th Match: v N.S.W. Colts XII (Sydney) Dec 14, 15.
Colts XII 84 (A. Waddington 8-33) & 148-4 drew with M.C.C. 702 (E. H. Hendren 211, J. W. Hearne 144, J. B. Hobbs 64, F. E. Woolley 64).

10th Match: v Australia (Sydney) Dec 17, 18, 20, 21, 22.
Australia 267 (H. L. Collins 70) & 581 (W. W. Armstrong 158, H. L. Collins 104, C. Kelleway 78, C. G. Macartney 69, W. Bardsley 57, J. M. Taylor 51) beat England 190 (F. E. Woolley 52) & 281 (J. B. Hobbs 59, J. W. Hearne 57, E. H. Hendren 56) by 377 runs.

11th Match: v XV of Bendigo (Bendigo) Dec 27, 28.
M.C.C. 371 (J. W. H. Douglas 119, J. W. H. Makepeace 58, J. B. Hobbs 52) beat Bendigo 65 & 42 by an inns & 264 runs.

12th Match: v Australia (Melbourne) Dec 31, Jan 1, 3, 4.
Australia 499 (C. E. Pellew 116, J. M. Gregory 100, J. M. Taylor 68, H. L. Collins 64, W. Bardsley 51) beat England 251 (J. B. Hobbs 122, E. H. Hendren 67, J. M. Gregory 7-69) & 157 (F. E. Woolley 50) by an inns & 91 runs.

13th Match: v XV of Ballarat (Ballarat) Jan 7, 8.
Ballarat 211 (N. Philip 53, W. M. Woodfull 50) & 30 (A. Waddington 8-15) lost to M.C.C. 384-9 dec (F. E. Woolley 159*, P. G. H. Fender 106, C. A. G. Russell 50) by an inns & 143 runs.

14th Match: v Australia (Adelaide) Jan 14, 15, 17, 18, 19, 20.
Australia 354 (H. L. Collins 162, W. A. S. Oldfield 50, C. H. Parkin 5-60) & 582 (C. Kelleway 147, W. W. Armstrong 121, C. E. Pellew 104, J. M. Gregory 78*) beat England 447 (C. A. G. Russell 135*, F. E. Woolley 79, J. W. H. Makepeace 60, J. W. H. Douglas 60, A. A. Mailey 5-160) & 370 (J. B. Hobbs 123, C. A. G. Russell 59, E. H. Hendren 51, A. A. Mailey 5-142) by 119 runs.

15th Match: v XVI of Hamilton (Hamilton) Jan 25, 26.
M.C.C. 320 (F. E. Woolley 87, J. B. Hobbs 74) drew with Hamilton 98 & 169-13.

16th Match: v XV of Geelong (Geelong) Jan 28, 29.
M.C.C. 457 (J. B. Hobbs 138, J. W. H. Makepeace 98, W. Rhodes 68, A. Waddington 53) drew with Geelong 261-10 (W. Sharland 102).

17th Match: v Victoria (Melbourne) Feb 4, 5, 7, 8.
Victoria 268 (G. A. Davies 61, J. Ryder 54) & 295 (J. Ryder 108, H. C. A. Sandford 72) lost to M.C.C. 486 (E. H. Hendren 271, J. W. H. Douglas 133*, E. A. McDonald 6-145) & 78-3 by 7 wkts.

18th Match: v Australia (Melbourne) Feb 11, 12, 14, 15, 16.
England 284 (J. W. H. Makepeace 117, J. W. H. Douglas 50) & 315 (W. Rhodes 73, J. W. H. Douglas 60, P. G. H. Fender 59, J. W. H. Makepeace 54, A. A. Mailey 9-121) lost to Australia 389 (W. W. Armstrong 123*, J. M. Gregory 77, H. L. Collins 59, W. Bardsley 56, P. G. H. Fender 5-122) & 211-2 (J. M. Gregory 76*, J. Ryder 52*) by 8 wkts.

19th Match: v New South Wales (Sydney) Feb 18, 19, 21, 22.
M.C.C. 427 (E. H. Hendren 102, J. W. H. Makepeace 73, P. G. H. Fender 60, W. Rhodes 50, A. A. Mailey 7-172) & 381 (F. E. Woolley 138, J. W. H. Douglas 82, E. H. Hendren 66) drew with N.S.W. 447 (C. G. Macartney 130, J. M. Taylor 107*, A. Punch 59, T. J. E. Andrews 54, J. M. Gregory 52, J. W. H. Douglas 7-98) & 151-2 (H. S. T. L. Hendry 66*, A. Punch 63*).

20th Match: v Australia (Sydney) Feb 25, 26, 28, Mar 1.
England 204 (F. E. Woolley 53) & 280 (J. W. H. Douglas 68, A. A. Mailey 5-119) lost to Australia 392 (C. G. Macartney 170, J. M. Gregory 93, P. G. H. Fender 5-90) & 93-1 (W. Bardsley 50*) by 9 wkts.

21st Match: v XV of Albury (Albury) March 4, 5.
Albury 146 & 101-10 drew with M.C.C. 326-6 dec (C. A. G. Russell 146, E. R. Wilson 62).

22nd Match: v XVII of Benalla (Benalla) March 7, 8.
M.C.C. 348-6 dec (P. G. H. Fender 83*, W. Rhodes 71, E. H. Hendren 69, A. Dolphin 58) beat Benalla 69 (A. Waddington 10-31) & 178 by an inns & 101 runs.

23rd Match: v South Australia (Adelaide) March 11, 12, 14, 15.
S. Australia 195 (P. G. H. Fender 7-75) & 369 (P. D. Rundell 121, G. W. Harris 84, P. G. H. Fender 5-109) lost to M.C.C. 627 (W. Rhodes 210, C. A. G. Russell 201, J. W. H. Douglas 106*) by an inns & 63 runs.

1920-21: M.C.C. to Ceylon and Australia

Batting Averages

	M	I	NO	R	HS	Avge	100	c/s
J. W. Hearne (Middx)	6	7	0	434	182	62.00	1	3
E. H. Hendren (Middx)	12	20	1	1178	271	62.00	3	10
C. A. G. Russell (Essex)	10	15	1	818	201	58.44	3	7
J. W. H. T. Douglas (Essex)	13	18	4	816	133*	58.28	2	5
J. B. Hobbs (Surrey)	12	19	1	924	131	51.33	4	6
W. Rhodes (Yorks)	12	19	0	730	210	38.42	2	6
F. E. Woolley (Kent)	13	20	2	619	138	34.38	1	13
J. W. H. Makepeace (Lancs)	9	16	1	449	117	29.93	1	0
P. G. H. Fender (Surrey)	9	13	1	325	60	27.08	0	7
E. R. Wilson (Yorks)	7	8	0	124	56	15.50	0	2
A. Waddington (Yorks)	5	8	2	82	51*	13.66	0	2
J. W. Hitch (Surrey)	3	3	0	24	19	8.00	0	1
H. Strudwick (Surrey)	8	13	3	80	24	8.00	0	18/2
C. H. Parkin (Lancs)	11	16	1	134	36	7.88	0	3
H. Howell (Warks)	8	10	5	22	6	4.40	0	1
A. Dolphin (Yorks)	5	5	1	9	6*	2.25	0	8/8

Bowling Averages

	O	M	R	W	Avge	BB	5i
W. Rhodes	183.4	36	479	18	26.61	6-39	1
P. G. H. Fender	233	17	983	32	30.71	7-75	4
C. H. Parkin	404.4	62	1344	43	31.25	8-55	2
F. E. Woolley	424.2	106	1051	31	33.90	4-27	0
J. W. H. T. Douglas	269.2	33	918	27	34.00	7-98	2
J. W. Hitch	47	5	176	5	35.20	4-28	0
E. R. Wilson	135	39	290	8	36.25	2-18	0
J. W. Hearne	147.5	29	407	11	37.00	3-63	0
A. Waddington	122	25	327	7	46.71	3-63	0
H. Howell	248	31	856	17	50.35	4-81	0

Also bowled: J. B. Hobbs 14-3-35-0; E. H. Hendren 3-1-15-0.

other batsmen failed, though they couldn't blame the wicket.

A shipping strike prevented the team going to Tasmania and two odds matches were substituted into the fixture list. M.C.C. then beat Victoria in the return, though the state side were without Armstrong, who had a disagreement with the officials.

In the fourth Test, Russell could not play, but his absence was more than outweighed by the illness of Macartney. Armstrong, though suffering from malaria, hit a century to give Australia a good first innings lead and from then the game ran Australia's way. The margin of victory was 8 wickets. There was a high-scoring draw against New South Wales prior to the fifth Test. Hobbs was lame and should not have played for England, but it was very doubtful if his injury affected the match, since Australia strolled to an easy victory by 9 wickets and thus won all five Tests – the first time this had been achieved.

Three other matches completed the tour, which ended at Adelaide on 15 March. The team returned on the *Osterley* to Toulon, where the journey was continued by train, and Victoria station was reached at 10 p.m. on 17 April.

Of the touring batsmen, only Hobbs and Douglas maintained their reputations. Hendren and Woolley were most disappointing and Russell and Makepeace owed their averages to a few high scores. The less said about the bowling the better. The English fielding also did not bear comparison with the Australian.

The Australians' outstanding bowler was Gregory, but Mailey was very persistent and usually removed the later English batsmen with ease. The home batting was sound throughout, with Macartney, Taylor and Gregory being brilliant.

1922-23: M.C.C. win narrowly in South Africa

The side selected to go to South Africa, though believed to be strong enough to beat the opposition, was not representative of England's full might, since Hobbs, Sutcliffe, Hearne and Parkin all declined invitations. The team which landed at Cape Town on 9 November was: F. T. Mann (Middx) (capt), A. E. R. Gilligan (Sussex), P. G. H. Fender (Surrey), A. W. Carr (Notts), G. T. S. Stevens (Oxford U), V. W. C. Jupp (Sussex) and the following

Some of the M.C.C. team arriving back home at Waterloo from South Africa in March 1923. From left: A. W. Carr, P. G. H. Fender, F. T. Mann, A. E. R. Gilligan and G. T. S. Stevens. The first four all captained England during their careers.

professionals: C. A. G. Russell (Essex), A. Sandham (Surrey), C. P. Mead (Hants), F. E. Woolley (Kent), G. G. Macaulay (Yorks), G. Brown (Hants), A. S. Kennedy (Hants), and W. H. Livsey (Hants).

Despite the fact that the first match began the day after the team's arrival, the M.C.C. found little difficulty in disposing of Western Province and indeed the opposition in the fixtures that followed was scarcely more taxing, until Transvaal were met at Johannesburg and some 14,000 spectators turned up to see the first day's play. Apart from Sandham and Woolley, the M.C.C. batting failed against Nupen and Transvaal gained a first innings

lead—rain however ended the game prematurely.

England were without Russell, injured, for the first Test but looked to have the game well in hand when Kennedy and Jupp dismissed South Africa for 148; Blanckenberg struck back and the English batting crumbled, only the tailenders taking the side into a modest lead. H. W. Taylor then hit a superb 176 and the home team reached 420 in their second innings. Nupen and Blanckenberg made certain that England had no hope of reaching the 387 needed to win and South Africa obtained victory by 168 runs. The second Test followed straight on after this defeat, but the teams travelled to Cape Town. Russell was able to play, but it was a

---

1922-23: M.C.C. to South Africa

1st Match: v Western Province (Cape Town)   Nov 10, 11, 13.
W. Province 145 & 205 lost to M.C.C. 331 (C. P. Mead 97, P. G. H. Fender 96, I. D. Buys 5-121) & 40-4 by 6 wkts.

2nd Match: v South-Western Districts (Oudtshoorn)   Nov 15, 16.
S-W Districts 124 (V. W. C. Jupp 6-23) & 96 (V. W. C. Jupp 6-24) lost to M.C.C. 284 (A. Sandham 75, C. P. Mead 73) by an inns & 64 runs.

3rd Match: v Eastern Province (Port Elizabeth)   Nov 18, 20, 21.
M.C.C. 336-9 dec (P. G. H. Fender 89, F. T. Mann 52, A. W. Carr 50, C. Munro 5-67) beat E. Province 127 (A. E. R. Gilligan 7-75) & 200 (J. Dold 55, W. Brann 52, A. S. Kennedy 5-83) by an inns & 9 runs.

4th Match: v Grahamstown XV (Grahamstown)   Nov 22, 23.
Grahamstown XV 132-9 dec drew with M.C.C. 350-5 (A. Sandham 124, C. P. Mead 93*, P. G. H. Fender 60).

5th Match: v Border (East London)   Nov 25, 27.
Border 70 (A. S. Kennedy 5-7) & 120 (A. L. Wainwright 61, F. E. Woolley 6-43) lost to M.C.C. 271-8 dec (A. Sandham 102) by an inns & 81 runs.

6th Match: v North-Eastern Districts (Queenstown)   Nov 29, 30.
N-E Districts 53 (A. S. Kennedy 6-8) & 44 lost to M.C.C. 242 (V. W. C. Jupp 89) by an inns & 145 runs.

7th Match: v Griqualand West (Kimberley)   Dec 2, 4.
Griqualand West 198 (N. V. Tapscott 57) & 196 lost to M.C.C. 353 (F. E. Woolley 83, C. P. Mead 68, A. Sandham 68, C. M. Francois 7-114) & 42-2 by 8 wkts.

8th Match: v East Rand (Benoni)   Dec 9, 11.
East Rand 196 (S. J. Snooke 76, G. G. Macaulay 5-40) & 46-4 drew with M.C.C. 284 (A. Sandham 128).

9th Match: v Pretoria (Pretoria)   Dec 13, 14.
Pretoria 137 (A. S. Kennedy 6-19) & 116 (G. G. Macaulay 6-18) lost to M.C.C. 300-7 dec (C. A. G. Russell 77, A. W. Carr 63) by an inns & 47 runs.

10th Match: v Transvaal (Johannesburg)   Dec 16, 18, 19.
M.C.C. 240 (F. E. Woolley 76, A. Sandham 75, E. P. Nupen 5-76) & 119-0 (C. A. G. Russell 77*) drew with Transvaal 291 (R. H. Catterall 128).

11th Match: v South Africa (Johannesburg)   Dec 23, 26, 27, 28.
South Africa 148 & 420 (H. W. Taylor 176, W. H. Brann 50) beat England 182 (J. M. Blanckenberg 6-76) & 218 (E. P. Nupen 5-53) by 168 runs.

12th Match: v South Africa (Cape Town)   Jan 1, 2, 3, 4.
South Africa 113 & 242 (R. H. Catterall 76, H. W. Taylor 68, G. G. Macaulay 5-64) lost to England 183 (J. M. Blanckenberg 5-61) & 173-9 (A. E. Hall 7-63) by 1 wkt.

13th Match: v Orange Free State (Bethlehem)   Jan 9, 10.
Northern O.F.S. XV 170 (S. W. Smart 58, V. W. C. Jupp 6-30) & 120 (B. Bourke 52) lost to M.C.C. 325 (C. A. G. Russell 110, A. Sandham 57) by an inns & 35 runs.

14th Match: v Natal (Pietermaritzburg)   Jan 12, 13, 15.
M.C.C. 248 (M. E. Billing 7-95) & 242-6 dec (C. A. G. Russell 86, A. Sandham 76) beat Natal 124 (F. E. Woolley 5-24) & 130 (P. G. H. Fender 5-36) by 236 runs.

15th Match: v South Africa (Durban)   Jan 18, 19, 20, 22.
England 428 (C. P. Mead 181, F. T. Mann 84, P. G. H. Fender 60) & 11-1 drew with South Africa 368 (H. W. Taylor 91, C. M. Francois 72, R. H. Catterall 52, A. W. Nourse 52, A. S. Kennedy 5-88).

16th Match: v Zululand (Eshowe)   Jan 26, 27.
Zululand 105 (G. G. Macaulay 6-19) & 79-3 drew with M.C.C. 206-3 dec (G. Brown 64, A. W. Carr 62*).

17th Match: v Northern Districts (Newcastle)   Jan 30, 31.
N. Districts 137 (A. E. R. Gilligan 5-34) & 67-8 drew with M.C.C. 284-8 dec (F. T. Mann 79, F. E. Woolley 58).

18th Match: v Transvaal (Johannesburg)   Feb 3, 5, 6.
M.C.C. 262 (C. A. G. Russell 81, F. E. Woolley 62, E. P. Nupen 5-48) & 288-4 dec (A. Sandham 114, C. A. G. Russell 58, F. E. Woolley 52) beat Transvaal 171 (R. H. Catterall 68) & 180 by 199 runs.

19th Match: v South Africa (Johannesburg)   Feb 9, 10, 12, 13.
England 244 (A. W. Carr 63, A. E. Hall 6-82) & 376-6 dec (F. E. Woolley 115*, C. A. G. Russell 96, F. T. Mann 59, A. Sandham 58) drew with South Africa 295 (T. A. Ward 64, A. W. Nourse 51, L. E. Tapscott 50) & 247-4 (H. W. Taylor 101, A. W. Nourse 63).

20th Match: v South Africa (Durban)   Feb 16, 17, 19, 20, 21, 22.
England 281 (C. A. G. Russell 140, C. P. Mead 66) & 241 (C. A. G. Russell 111) beat South Africa 179 & 234 (H. W. Taylor 102, A. S. Kennedy 5-76) by 109 runs.

21st Match: v Orange Free State (Bloemfontein)   Feb 24, 26, 27.
M.C.C. 265 (A. Sandham 122, V. W. C. Jupp 55) & 282 (G. B. Street 88, V. W. C. Jupp 55) beat O.F.S. 163 (D. J. de Villiers 59) & 128 (P. G. H. Fender 7-55) by 256 runs.

22nd Match: v Western Province (Cape Town)   March 3, 5, 6.
W. Province 118 & 181 (P. A. M. Hands 94, A. S. Kennedy 5-35) lost to M.C.C. 236 & 64-0 by 10 wkts.

Batting Averages

	M	I	NO	R	HS	Avge	100	c/s
C. A. G. Russell (Essex)	11	18	2	901	140	56.31	2	12
A. Sandham (Surrey)	14	24	2	985	122	44.77	3	1
G. B. Street (Sussex)	4	7	3	155	88	38.75	0	2/5
C. P. Mead (Hants)	14	21	2	695	181	36.58	1	7
F. E. Woolley (Kent)	12	19	1	551	115*	30.61	1	14
F. T. Mann (Middx)	14	23	4	504	84	26.52	0	5
P. G. H. Fender (Surrey)	14	21	1	459	96	22.95	0	21
V. W. C. Jupp (Sussex)	12	18	3	294	55	19.60	0	4
A. W. Carr (Notts)	14	24	2	428	63	19.45	0	2
G. G. Macaulay (Yorks)	8	12	7	96	29*	19.20	0	9
A. E. R. Gilligan (Sussex)	9	12	4	143	39*	17.87	0	5
A. S. Kennedy (Hants)	12	16	4	187	41*	15.58	0	10
G. Brown (Hants)	11	15	2	155	26	11.92	0	18/2
G. T. S. Stevens (Middx)	5	7	1	66	20	11.00	0	1

Bowling Averages

	O	M	R	W	Avge	BB	5i
F. T. Mann	1	0	7	1	7.00	1-7	0
G. Brown	19	7	42	3	14.00	2-23	0
G. T. S. Stevens	57	7	169	11	15.36	4-30	0
G. G. Macaulay	243	68	475	29	16.37	5-64	1
A. S. Kennedy	469.4	169	1024	61	16.79	5-7	4
F. E. Woolley	194.5	69	448	23	19.47	6-43	2
P. G. H. Fender	380.1	81	1136	58	19.57	7-55	3
V. W. C. Jupp	258.5	60	686	34	20.17	4-31	0
A. E. R. Gilligan	206	42	573	26	22.07	7-75	1

Played in non-first-class matches only: W. H. Livsey (Hants).

bowler's match. England again began by dismissing South Africa cheaply, but Blanckenberg and a new cap, Hall, kept South Africa in the game and another good innings by Taylor set England 173 to make to win. Hall bowled brilliantly and but for dropped catches would have won the match for South Africa; as it was England scraped home by 1 wicket in a tense finish. Hall was carried shoulder high off the field.

The third Test, which was awaited with great interest, was unfortunately ruined by rain shortly after each side had had an innings. In the fourth Test more good bowling by Hall gave South Africa a first innings lead of 51, but, batting again, England, through Russell and Woolley gained an impregnable position. Mann declared in the hope of bowling South Africa out, but Taylor hit a well-judged century and the match was drawn.

As each team had won one game, it was announced that the fifth Test would be played to a finish. For some unknown reason, South Africa dropped their most formidable bowler, Nupen, replacing him by Conyngham, and this was perhaps the decisive move in the game. Two great innings by Russell, who hit two hundreds in the match, despite feeling unwell, were the backbone of the English batting and indeed the saving of both English innings.

Most unusually for a visiting player, a collection was taken on the ground for Russell, who benefitted by over £90. South Africa required 344 in the final innings and reached 111 for 3 when bad light stopped play at the end of the fourth day. Rain did not allow very much play on the fifth day, but three more wickets went down, while the score rose to 203. Taylor was 76 not out, but on the sixth day even he could not save the match and fell just after reaching his hundred. England thus won the rubber by two to one.

Two more matches—against the Free State and Western Province—brought the tour to a close. The outstanding English batsman was Russell, who adapted himself well to matting wickets. His strength lay in his great defensive powers. The best bowler was Kennedy, though at times Macaulay proved very dangerous. For the South Africans, Taylor remained head and shoulders above the rest, but all the bowlers did good work.

It should be mentioned that Livsey, the reserve wicket-keeper, broke a finger in the sixth match and Street of Sussex was cabled for and appeared in a few games in the latter half of the programme.

When the English side left England it was thought that they would have no difficulty in beating South Africa, so the results, though favourable to England, did nothing to indicate that English cricket was really on the mend after the defeats in 1920-21 and in 1921, at home, against Australia.

1922-23: MacLaren takes an M.C.C. 'A' side to New Zealand

Having selected the leading English team for South Africa, the M.C.C. undertook the arrangements for a second tour to New Zealand. The team chosen was: A. C. MacLaren (Lancs) (capt), A. P. F. Chapman (Berkshire), G. Wilson (Yorks), Hon F. S. Gough-Calthorpe (Warwicks), T. C. Lowry (Cambridge U), C. H. Gibson (Cambridge U), W. W. H. Hill-Wood (Derbys), C. H. Titchmarsh (Herts), J. F. MacLean (Worcs), J. C. Hartley, W. A. C. Wilkinson (Army), Hon D. F. Brand and two professionals, A. P. Freeman (Kent) and H. Tyldesley (Lancs). H. D. Swan was appointed manager. R. St L. Fowler, the Army cricketer, was to have gone, but could not obtain leave.

The standard of the team was perhaps that of one of the weaker county sides and the party sailed from England on 30 September, travelling via the Suez Canal. Over 10,000 came to watch the one-day game in Colombo, despite rain which prevented a start before 1.15. From Colombo the voyage continued on the s.s. *Orvieto* to Australia, where a two-day game was played at Perth, before the first serious match at Adelaide. Here South Australia proved too strong for the visitors. Two good innings from Chapman at Melbourne meant that Victoria only beat the tourists by two wickets and at Sydney Chapman scored a splendid hundred, whilst the veteran captain, MacLaren, hit a fifty and the visitors actually gained a first innings lead over the formidable New South Wales eleven, though later the state side took control and won by five wickets. All in all the weak M.C.C. side had acquitted itself well on the Australian leg of its programme and the team moved from Sydney to New Zealand.

After two two-day matches, the first major game in New Zealand was at Christchurch. Chapman hit a brilliant 183, whilst Gibson took 12 wickets to provide a victory by 8 wickets. Blunt scored a hundred for the home side, but was dropped three times. The M.C.C. were seen to even greater advantage in the 'First Test'. MacLaren hit a double century in 270 minutes, whilst Gibson and Freeman bowled out New Zealand with little difficulty. About 6,500 people watched the first day's play. The

Batting Averages

	M	I	NO	R	HS	Avge	100	c/s
A. C. MacLaren (Lancs)	6	8	2	398	200*	66.33	1	8
A. P. F. Chapman (Berks)	15	24	1	1315	183	57.17	4	25
C. H. Titchmarsh (Herts)	15	25	3	887	154	40.31	1	9
W. A. C. Wilkinson (Army)	11	19	2	530	102	31.76	1	6
J. C. Hartley (Sussex)	11	12	5	203	60*	29.00	0	1
W. W. H. Hill-Wood (Derbys)	10	18	2	455	122*	28.43	1	5
G. Wilson (Yorks)	13	21	3	508	142*	28.22	1	5
Hon F. S. Gough-Calthorpe (Warks)	14	22	1	570	110	27.14	1	7
T. C. Lowry (Cambr U)	13	19	0	473	130	24.89	1	9/2
J. F. Maclean (Worcs)	11	16	3	320	84	24.61	0	15/11
Hon D. F. Brand (Cambr U)	13	17	2	244	60	16.26	0	4
A. P. Freeman (Kent)	13	17	7	144	57	14.40	0	12
C. H. Gibson (Cambr U)	14	16	5	133	30*	12.09	0	8
H. Tyldesley (Lancs)	5	8	0	39	15	4.87	0	6
H. D. Swan	1	1	0	0	0	0.00	0	0

Bowling Averages

	O	M	R	W	Avge	BB	5i
J. C. Hartley	48.1	6	164	9	18.22	4-55	0
A. P. Freeman	462.2	97	1654	69	23.97	7-87	5
H. Tyldesley	107	13	399	15	26.60	5-100	1
Hon D. F. Brand	166.5	27	702	26	27.00	4-31	0
C. H. Gibson	548.2	118	1687	62	27.20	8-57	4
F. S. Gough-Calthorpe	310	75	1062	36	29.50	6-53	1
A. P. F. Chapman	27.7	10	124	3	41.33	1-10	0
G. Wilson	7	0	44	1	44.00	1-44	0

Also bowled: W. W. H. Hill-Wood 28-2-165-0.

Played in non-first-class matches only: P. H. Slater, B. S. H. Hill-Wood.

'Second Test' followed directly after the first. The New Zealanders showed much better form and set the M.C.C. 262 to make in 120 minutes – the tourists did not attempt the task. In the 'Third Test', which came six matches later, the M.C.C. were without MacLaren,

who had injured his knee, but Lowry hit a century and Chapman 71, whilst most of the New Zealanders struggled, Gough-Calthorpe bowling well, and the visitors went to an innings victory. The match was followed by two minor games and then the return with Auckland, which resulted in another innings victory. Going back to Australia, the M.C.C. played four drawn games to conclude the tour – all were high scoring, except one disastrous first innings against Victoria, when the side collapsed for 71, but made an amazing recovery in their second innings to reach 282 for 0, Hill-Wood and Wilson making hundreds.

Without a doubt the star of the team was Chapman, both his batting and fielding being quite exceptional. C. H. Gibson bowled well. The former was to go on to captain England, but the latter's cricket was mainly to be confined to South America. Brand was another who looked most promising, but was not to be seen in first-class county cricket. After MacLaren's injury, the side was led by J. C. Hartley, who also batted well.

W. Ferguson, the Australian scorer, joined the side in Fremantle and acted as scorer and baggage master through the tour. The only black spot of the visit was on the financial side. The attendances in New Zealand were good on Saturdays, but otherwise poor, with all the up-country games losing money. A strike meant the cancellation of the match with Queensland, which might have improved the situation, and the total loss was £1,929, of which half was borne by the M.C.C.

1923: Free Foresters invited to Canada

Sailing on the s.s. *Montlaurier* from Liverpool on 24 August, the tourists landed at Quebec on 1 September and played their first game at Montreal beginning two days later.

The team consisted of E. G. Wynyard (capt), J. C. Hartley, R. St L. Fowler, F. H. Hollins, O. W. Cornwallis, A. E. L. Hill, J. E. Frazer, D. M. Ritchie, Lord Romilly, J. S. Hughes, J. C. Masterman, M. Patten, G. le Roy Burnham, C. E. Thompson.

The outstanding player of the eight-match tour was R. St L. Fowler, who not only headed the batting averages, but also took 57 wickets at a cost of 7.71 each. The two major matches were against Toronto C.C., in both of which Fowler's bowling proved too much for the opposition, though the tourists' batting did not produce many more runs than Toronto's.

The English side were invited over by the Canadian Cricket Clubs and the leading light in organising the tour was Norman Seagram of Toronto.

1922-23: M.C.C. to Ceylon, Australia and New Zealand

1st Match: v Ceylon (Colombo) Oct 23.
Ceylon 147-5 dec (E. Kelaart 59*) drew with M.C.C. 100-4.

2nd Match: v Western Australia (Perth) Nov 3, 4.
M.C.C. 190 (A. P. F. Chapman 75) & 132-3 (A. P. F. Chapman 58, C. H. Titchmarsh 50*) drew with W. Australia 234 (A. Heindricks 91*, A. Evans 53).

3rd Match: v South Australia (Adelaide) Nov 10, 11. 13.
S. Australia 442 (A. J. Richardson 150, V. Y. Richardson 118, H. Tyldesley 5-100) & 60-4 beat M.C.C. 205 (W. A. C. Wilkinson 64) & 294 (G. Wilson 61, A. P. F. Chapman 53) by 6 wkts.

4th Match: v Victoria (Melbourne) Nov 17, 18, 20.
M.C.C. 210 (A.P.F. Chapman 73, W. A. C. Wilkinson 62, A. E. V. Hartkopf 5-23) & 231 (C. H. Titchmarsh 82, A. P. F. Chapman 69, A. E. V. Hartkopf 8-105) lost to Victoria 278 (A. E. V. Hartkopf 86, W. M. Woodfull 74) & 164-8 (C. B. Willis 60) by 2 wkts.

5th Match: v New South Wales (Sydney) Nov 24, 25, 27.
M.C.C. 360 (A. P. F. Chapman 100, C. H. Titchmarsh 79, A. C. MacLaren 54) & 121 lost to N.S.W. (C. G. Macartney 63) & 283-5 (C. G. Macartney 84, T. J. E. Andrews 74) by 5 wkts.

6th Match: v Auckland (Auckland) Dec 15, 16.
M.C.C. 350 (C. H. Titchmarsh 154, A. C. MacLaren 58, W. A. C. Wilkinson 50, A. Anthony 6-43) drew with Auckland 107-5.

7th Match: v Wanganui (Wanganui) Dec 19, 20.
Wanganui 129 (H. Lambert 66) & 200 (H. Lambert 63, C. H. Gibson 5-72) lost to M.C.C. 296 (F. S. Gough-Calthorpe 117) & 56-0 by 10 wkts.

8th Match: v Canterbury (Christchurch) Dec 23, 25, 26.
M.C.C. 454-6 dec (A. P. F. Chapman 183, W. A. C. Wilkinson 102, F. S. Gough-Calthorpe 60) & 23-2 beat Canterbury 181 & 295 (R. C. Blunt 174, R. D. Worker 65, C. H. Gibson 8-57) by 8 wkts.

9th Match: v New Zealand (Wellington) Dec 30, Jan 1, 2.
M.C.C. 505-8 dec (A. C. MacLaren 200*, J. F. Maclean 72, F. S. Gough-Calthorpe 63) beat New Zealand 222 (A. P. Freeman 5-114) & 127 (C. H. Gibson 5-42, A. P. Freeman 5-72) by an inns & 156 runs.

10th Match: v New Zealand (Christchurch) Jan 5, 6, 8.
New Zealand 375 (D. C. Collins 102, J. S. Shepherd 66) & 270-8 dec (N. C. Snedden 58, C. C. R. Dacre 58) drew with M.C.C. 384 (A. P. F. Chapman 77, T. C. Lowry 61, J. C. Hartley 60*, W. A. C. Wilkinson 59) & 145-5.

11th Match: v Minor Associations (Temuka) Jan 9, 10.
Minor Associations 52 (H. Tyldesley 5-19) & 151 lost to M.C.C. 407 (D. F. Brand 85, A. P. F. Chapman 84*, F. S. Gough-Calthorpe 50, G. McWhirter 6-153) by an inns & 204.

12th Match: v Otago (Dunedin) Jan 12, 13, 15.
Otago 202 (J. Shepherd 52) & 129 (J. McMullan 69) lost to M.C.C. 222 (C. H. Titchmarsh 73, A. P. F. Chapman 53) & 112-4 by 6 wkts.

13th Match: v Southland (Invercargill) Jan 20, 22.
M.C.C. 319 (F. S. Gough-Calthorpe 77) & 101-5 dec beat Southland 153 & 71 (F. S. Gough-Calthorpe 5-17) by 196 runs.

14th Match: v Wellington (Wellington) Jan 26, 27, 29.
Wellington 104 & 133 lost to M.C.C. 107 (W. S. Brice 5-52) & 131-6 (W. S. Brice 5-45) by 4 wkts.

15th Match: v Minor Associations (Nelson) Jan 30, 31.
Minor Associations 119 (K. Saxon 51, A. P. Freeman 6-27) lost to M.C.C. 249 (A. P. F. Chapman 71*, W. A. C. Wilkinson 52, J. Newman 5-93) by an inns & 75 runs.

16th Match: v New Zealand (Wellington) Feb 2, 3, 5.
New Zealand 166 (E. H. Bernan 61, F. S. Gough-Calthorpe 6-53) & 215 (D. C. Collins 69, R. C. Blunt 68, C. H. Gibson 5-65) lost to M.C.C. 401 (T. C. Lowry 130, A. P. F. Chapman 71, J. F. Maclean 53) by an inns & 20 runs.

17th Match: v Minor Associations (Palmerston North) Feb 6, 7.
M.C.C. 306-8 dec (F. S. Gough-Calthorpe 136, C. H. Gibson 58) & 53-6 dec beat Minor Associations 123 & 96 by 140 runs.

18th Match: v East Coast Associations (Napier) Feb 9, 10.
M.C.C. 140 (Temperton 5-48) & 163-4 dec (C. H. Titchmarsh 63*) drew with East Coast 68 (C. H. Gibson 6-28) & 137-4 (Ellis 54).

19th Match: v Auckland (Auckland) Feb 17, 19.
M.C.C. 365 (A. P. F. Chapman 108, F. S. Gough-Calthorpe 78, C. H. Titchmarsh 53, W. W. Hill-Wood 52, C. Allcott 6-86) beat Auckland 178 (A. P. Freeman 7-87) & 183 (E. McLeod 50, A. P. Freeman 5-71) by an inns & 4 runs.

20th Match: v New South Wales (Sydney) March 2, 3, 5.
M.C.C. 275 (A. P. F. Chapman 91, D. F. Brand 60) & 296 (F. S. Gough-Calthorpe 110, H. S. T. L. Hendry 5-118) drew with N.S.W. 314 (W. Bardsley 90, J. M. Taylor 73, A. F. Kippax 59, C. H. Gibson 6-140) & 102-5 (J. M. Taylor 52).

21st Match: v Combined Universities (Melbourne) March 7, 8.
M.C.C. 258 (W. W. Hill-Wood 84, H. W. Fisher 6-68) & 135-5 drew with Combined Universities 332 (L. F. Freemantle 59, O. E. Nothling 56, W. H. Bailey 51).

22nd Match: v Victoria (Melbourne) March 9, 10, 12.
M.C.C. 71 (P. Wallace 6-50) & 282-0 (G. Wilson 142*, W. W. Hill-Wood 122*) drew with Victoria 617-6 dec (H. S. Love 192, V. S. Ransford 118*, A. E. Liddicut 102, R. L. Park 101, W. H. Ponsford 62).

23rd Match: v South Australia (Adelaide) March 15, 16, 17.
S. Australia 495 (A. J. Richardson 280, L. Bowley 76, J. W. Rymill 50, A. P. Freeman 6-176) & 204-4 dec (C. E. Pellew 69) drew with M.C.C. 372 (F. S. Gough-Calthorpe 96, G. Wilson 78, A. P. Freeman 57, H. M. Fisher 5-96) & 248-4 (A. P. F. Chapman 134*).

1923: Free Foresters to Canada

1st Match: v All Montreal (Montreal) Sept 3, 4.
Montreal 139 (R. St L. Fowler 7-46) & 98 lost to Free Foresters 128 (J. E. Frazer 82) & 110-6 (R. St L. Fowler 53*) by 4 wkts.

2nd Match: v McGill C.C. (Montreal) Sept 5, 6.
McGill 76 & 212 lost to Free Foresters 276 (R. St L. Fowler 126) & 14-0 by 10 wkts.

3rd Match: v Toronto C.C. (Toronto) (12 a-side) Sept 8, 10.
Toronto 92 (R. St L. Fowler 7-21) & 183 (R. St L. Fowler 5-27) lost to Free Foresters 139 (F. H. Hollins 53, H. G. Wookey 5-45) & 78-6 by 5 wkts.

4th Match: v XVIII of Public Schools (Toronto) Sept 12, 13.
Public Schools 146 (J. S. Hughes 10-38) & 109 drew with Free Foresters 136 (F. Lyon 6-57) & 63-4.

5th Match: v Toronto (Toronto) (12 a-side) Sept 15, 17.
Toronto 146 & 123 lost to Free Foresters 195 & 78-1 by 10 wkts.

6th Match: v XV of Hamilton (Hamilton) Sept 17, 18.
Hamilton 124 & 123 lost to Free Foresters 265 (R. St L. Fowler 52, F. H. Hollins 52, D. M. Ritchie 51, D. Verrier 6-69) by an inns & 18 runs.

7th Match: v Western Ontario (Gault) Sept 21, 22.
Abandoned.

8th Match: v Ottawa Valley C.C. (Ottawa) Sept 25, 26.
Ottawa Valley 183 (R. St L. Fowler 6-62) & 61 (D. M. Ritchie 5-17) lost to Free Foresters 437 (C. E. Thompson 85, J. C. Masterman 59, J. S. Hughes 56, O. W. Cornwallis 55) by an inns & 193 runs.

1924: Incogniti tour the United States

Arriving in New York on 8 September, the Incogniti played their first match on matting in Brooklyn, rather than on the grass wicket at Staten Island, as previous teams had done. The Incogs declared in this game to set New York 93 in an hour, but the home side were too surprised by this tactic to take full advantage and the game was drawn. The best match was the first against All Philadelphia. The tourists required 221 to win in their second innings and reached 215 for 8 – some brilliant fielding by the Philadelphians was the feature of the game. Unfortunately the return match was ruined by rain, as were several other of the fixtures.

The touring party were: E. J. Metcalfe (capt), G. F. Earle, T. C. Lowry, T. Arnott, J. J. Thorley, G. B. Cuthbertson, A. H. White, A. H. H. Gilligan, P. H. Irwin, T. A. L. Brocklebank, H. Hargreaves, G. A. S. Hickton, F. B. Landale.

Although the strength of cricket in Philadelphia was still fairly good, there was an almost complete lack of young players and this did not augur well for the future.

1924: Incogniti to United States

1st Match: v New York (Brooklyn)   Sept 12, 13.
Incogniti 234 & 153-6 dec (T. Arnott 50) drew with New York 295 (J. L. Poyer 101) & 63-5.

2nd Match: v Merion C.C. (Philadelphia)   Sept 15, 16.
Merion 204 (J. M. Crosman 50) & 132 (C. C. Morris 52) lost to Incogniti 310-9 dec (T. C. Lowry 105, P. H. Irwin 78) & 33-0.

3rd Match: v All Philadelphia (Philadelphia)   Sept 18, 19, 20.
Philadelphia 315 (J. M. Crosman 91, G. Bottomley 58) & 141 drew with Incogniti 236 & 215-8.

4th Match: v Philadelphia C.C. (St Martin's)   Sept 22, 23.
Philadelphia 192 (E. Hopkinson 58. J. H. Mason 53) drew with Incogniti 279-6 (A. H. White 101, G. B. Cuthbertson 66*).

5th Match: v Frankford (St Martin's)   Sept 25, 26.
Frankford 138 & 119 lost to Incogniti 317 (A. H. H. Gilligan 117, T. C. Lowry 56*) by an inns & 60 runs.

6th Match: v All Philadelphia (Manheim)   Sept 27, 28, 29.
Incogniti 275 (T. Arnott 54) drew with Philadelphia 30-2.

7th Match: v Germantown (Manheim)   Oct 1, 2.
Incogniti 243 drew with Germantown 125 & 75-6.

1924-25: Hobbs and Sutcliffe brilliant, but Australia win

Seven members of the disastrous M.C.C. side of 1920-21, returned to Australia with the 1924-25 side. The full team read: A. E. R. Gilligan (Sussex) (capt), J. L. Bryan (Kent), A. P. F. Chapman (Kent), J. W. H. T. Douglas (Essex) and the professionals J. B. Hobbs (Surrey), H. Sutcliffe (Yorks), E. H. Hendren (Middx), A. Sandham (Surrey), F. E. Woolley (Kent), J. W. Hearne (Middx), W. W. Whysall (Notts), R. Kilner (Yorks), M. W. Tate (Sussex), R. K. Tyldesley (Lancs), A. P. Freeman (Kent), H. Strudwick (Surrey), H. Howell (Warwicks), and as manager F. C. Toone (Yorks secretary).

The only major player to decline an invitation was C. H. Gibson, but his choice raised a storm of controversy, since he did not play in English first-class cricket, so perhaps his withdrawal for business reasons was allied with tact. Originally Hobbs also refused, but changed his mind. It was thought also by the critics that the inclusion of three leg-break bowlers – Tyldesley, Hearne and Freeman – was rather optimistic and that Geary should have travelled instead of Freeman.

The team played the now traditional one-day match in Colombo on the voyage out and landed in Western Australia on 14 October. There were four not very energetic matches, including two against Western Australia, before the side moved to Adelaide for the first important game, which was marked by an uncharacteristic declaration on the part of the home side in their first innings at 346 for 4. This led eventually to an easy M.C.C. win, when South Australia collapsed completely in the second innings to the bowling of Hearne. Against the rather moderate Victorian attack however, the tourists suffered their first defeat, though Hearne with an injured knee could not bat in the second innings. It was a surprise therefore that the visitors went straight from defeat at Melbourne to victory over the much vaunted New South Wales team at Sydney. Tate exploited the damp wicket splendidly and only Bardsley defied him in the first innings, but in the second innings Tyldesley took control. The game was won by 3 wickets. The two games at Brisbane were both drawn and then followed two minor matches, before the first Test at Sydney. Public interest in the game was enormous and about 163,500 people attended the match. Hobbs and Sutcliffe gave England two great starts with partnerships of 157 and 110, and both batsmen made a hundred and a fifty, but the rest of the English batting was nothing like as consistent as Australia's, and though England created a record by making 411 in the final innings, the game was still lost by 195 runs.

The second Test followed the pattern set by its predecessor. Hobbs and Sutcliffe put on 283 for the first wicket and the Yorkshire opener went on to hit a century in each innings, but once more the remaining English batsmen failed. Tate bowled quite splendidly, but he couldn't make up for England's lack of runs, and Australia won by 81 runs. The two major Australian batsmen were Ponsford, who made a century in both Tests and V. Y. Richardson, but A. J. Richardson and Taylor also made

The most famous opening pair in Test history, who performed great deeds, particularly against Australia. Jack Hobbs (left) and Herbert Sutcliffe (right) going out to bat in the second Test match at Melbourne in 1925.

The M.C.C. party which toured Australia in 1924-25. Back: J. L. Bryan, R. K. Tyldesley, M. W. Tate, F. C. Toone (manager), W. W. Whysall, A. P. F. Chapman, A. Sandham. Centre: J. W. Hearne, H. Strudwick, J. W. H. T. Douglas, A. E. R. Gilligan (captain), J. B. Hobbs, F. E. Woolley. Front: R. Kilner, E. H. Hendren, A. P. Freeman, H. Sutcliffe, H. Howell.

notable contributions. No less than 180,605 people watched the game and the receipts were £22,628.

England had to win the third Test to save the rubber. The visitors made a great start by reducing Australia to 22 for 3, but then both Tate and Gilligan had to retire with injuries—in fact Gilligan retired from the match, apart from batting briefly, and Chapman took over the direction. Ryder hit a very sound double century to put Australia back on an even keel and though England's batting was more consistent, the home side obtained a first innings lead of 124. Rain helped England dismiss Australia a second time, which left 375 required. The tourists made a

tremendous fight of it and nearly all the batsmen came off—in the end the margin between the sides was a mere 11 runs.

The team went off to Tasmania for two holiday matches and came back to slaughter Victoria; Hearne and Kilner, making the most of a drying wicket, bowled the State out for 50 in their second innings to bring victory by an innings and 271 runs.

Everything went right for England in the fourth Test—Gilligan at last won the toss; Hobbs and Sutcliffe added 126 and the remaining batsmen all played a part in reaching a total of 548. When Australia batted showers affected the pitch, as did an impatient crowd, and England bowled the home country out

---

1924-25: M.C.C. to Ceylon and Australia

1st Match: v Ceylon (Colombo)   Oct 4.
M.C.C. 73 (W. T. Greswell 8-38) & 119-4 (A. P. F. Chapman 70*) drew with Ceylon 58.

2nd Match: v Western Australia (Perth)   Oct 17, 18, 20.
M.C.C. 330-7 dec (R. Kilner 103, J. W. H. T. Douglas 62) drew with W. Australia 57 & 157-7 (F. Taafe 71).

3rd Match: v Western Australian Colts (Perth)   Oct 22, 23.
W.A. Colts XV 195 (H. Cantwell 66) drew with M.C.C. 405-7 (W. W. Whysall 90, A. Sandham 79, J. B. Hobbs 74, F. E. Woolley 52).

4th Match: v Western Australia (Perth)   Oct 24, 25, 27, 28.
M.C.C. 397 (A. E. R. Gilligan 138, J. W. Hearne 54, R. Blundell 5-59) beat W. Australia 138 (A. P. Freeman 6-47) & 69 by an inns & 190 runs.

5th Match: v Goldfields Association XV (Kalgoorlie)   Oct 31, Nov 1.
M.C.C. 346-9 dec (F. E. Woolley 67, R. Kilner 63, C. Taylor 5-70) & 111-3 dec drew with Goldfields XV 42 & 52-7.

6th Match: v South Australia (Adelaide)   Nov 7, 8, 10, 11.
S. Australia 346-4 dec (A. J. Richardson 200*, V. Y. Richardson 87) & 103 (J. W. Hearne 5-17) lost to M.C.C. 406 (F. E. Woolley 90, J. W. Hearne 78, H. Sutcliffe 75, J. B. Hobbs 50) & 44-1 by 9 wkts.

7th Match: v Victoria (Melbourne)   Nov 14, 15, 17, 18, 19.
M.C.C. 240 (J. W. H. T. Douglas 59*) & 241 (A. Sandham 66, E. H. Hendren 54) lost to Victoria 229 (H. S. T. L. Hendry 63) & 253-4 (E. R. Mayne 87, W. M. Woodfull 61, A. E. V. Hartkopf 56*) by 6 wkts.

8th Match: v New South Wales (Sydney)   Nov 21, 22, 24, 25.
N.S.W. 271 (W. Bardsley 160, J. M. Taylor 51, M. W. Tate 7-74) & 221 (T. J. E. Andrews 86*, R. K. Tyldesley 6-83) lost to M.C.C. 193 (E. H. Hendren 75*) & 301-7 (J. B. Hobbs 81, A. P. F. Chapman 72) by 3 wkts.

9th Match: v Queensland (Brisbane)   Nov 29, Dec 1, 2.
M.C.C. 522 (E. H. Hendren 168, A. P. F. Chapman 80, A. Sandham 64, J. B. Hobbs 51, P. M. Hornibrook 5-210) drew with Queensland 275 & 131-3 (L. P. D. O'Connor 66*).

10th Match: v An Australian XI (Brisbane)   Dec 4, 5, 6, 8.
Australian XI 526 (F. C. Thompson 114, F. Taafe 86*, W. H. Ponsford 81, L. P. D. O'Connor 50, H. S. T. L. Hendry 68, A. P. Freeman 6-160) & 257 (A. J. Richardson 83, A. F. Kippax 82*) drew with M.C.C. 421 (E. H. Hendren 100, A. P. F. Chapman 92, J. W. H. T. Douglas 54, R. Kilner 52).

11th Match: v Toowoomba (Toowoomba)   Dec 9, 10.
M.C.C. 394-3 dec (J. W. Hearne 174*, M. W. Tate 94, H. Sutcliffe 90) beat Toowoomba XIII 181 (F. Drews 52, A. P. Freeman 6-48) & 87 (R. Kilner 7-36) by an inns & 126 runs.

12th Match: v Australian Juniors XII (Sydney)   Dec 13, 15, 16.
Juniors XII 169 & 93-7 drew with M.C.C. 319-5 dec (J. B. Hobbs 114, H. Sutcliffe 68, E. H. Hendren 54).

13th Match: v Australia (Sydney)   Dec 19, 20, 22, 23, 24, 26, 27.
Australia 450 (H. L. Collins 114, W. H. Ponsford 110, M. W. Tate 6-130) & 452 (J. M. Taylor 108, A. J. Richardson 98, H. L. Collins 60, M. W. Tate 5-98) beat

England 298 (J. B. Hobbs 115, E. H. Hendren 74*, H. Sutcliffe 59, J. M. Gregory 5-111) & 411 (F. E. Woolley 123, H. Sutcliffe 115, J. B. Hobbs 57, A. P. Freeman 50*) by 195 runs.

14th Match: v Australia (Melbourne)   Jan 1, 2, 3, 5, 6, 7, 8.
Australia 600 (V. Y. Richardson 138, W. H. Ponsford 128, A. E. V. Hartkopf 80, J. M. Taylor 72) & 250 (J. M. Taylor 90, M. W. Tate 6-99) beat England 479 (H. Sutcliffe 176, J. B. Hobbs 154) & 290 (H. Sutcliffe 127, F. E. Woolley 50, A. A. Mailey 5-92) by 81 runs.

15th Match: v Ballarat XV (Ballarat)   Jan 10, 12.
Ballarat XV 185 (R. Kilner 6-27) & 154 (H. Austin 64, R. K. Tyldesley 6-37) drew with M.C.C. 299 (J. L. Bryan 83, R. Kilner 64, J. W. Hearne 50).

16th Match: v Australia (Adelaide)   Jan 16, 17, 19, 20, 21, 22, 23.
Australia 489 (J. Ryder 201*, T. J. E. Andrews 72, A. J. Richardson 69) & 250 (J. Ryder 88) beat England 365 (J. B. Hobbs 119, E. H. Hendren 92) & 363 (W. W. Whysall 75, H. Sutcliffe 59, A. P. F. Chapman 58) by 11 runs.

17th Match: v Tasmania (Launceston)   Jan 27, 28, 29.
M.C.C. 218 (A. Sandham 116) & 331-7 dec (E. H. Hendren 101*, A. E. R. Gilligan 60, A. Sandham 51) beat Tasmania 166 (R. Kilner 5-35) & 264 (G. W. Martin 121) by 119 runs.

18th Match: v Tasmania (Hobart)   Jan 30, 31, Feb 2.
Tasmania 89 (M. W. Tate 6-26) & 224 (H. Howell 6-96) lost to M.C.C. 449 (H. Sutcliffe 188, A. Sandham 92, E. H. Hendren 50) by an inns & 136 runs.

19th Match: v Victoria (Melbourne)   Feb 6, 7, 9, 10.
M.C.C. 500 (J. W. Hearne 193, W. W. Whysall 89, H. Sutcliffe 88, J. L. Bryan 59, H. Ironmonger 5-93) beat Victoria 179 (V. S. Ransford 62, W. M. Woodfull 60, R. Kilner 5-48) & 50 (R. Kilner 5-18, J. W. Hearne 5-30) by an inns & 271 runs.

20th Match: v Australia (Melbourne)   Feb 13, 14, 16, 17, 18.
England 548 (H. Sutcliffe 143, W. W. Whysall 76, R. Kilner 74, J. B. Hobbs 66, E. H. Hendren 65) beat Australia 269 (J. M. Taylor 86) & 250 (J. M. Taylor 68, M. W. Tate 5-75) by an inns & 29 runs.

21st Match: v New South Wales (Sydney)   Feb 21, 23, 24, 25.
M.C.C. 626 (E. H. Hendren 165, F. E. Woolley 149, A. Sandham 137, J. L. Bryan 72) & 296-8 (A. Sandham 104, F. E. Woolley 80) drew with N.S.W. 619 (T. J. E. Andrews 224, H. L. Collins 173, R. Kilner 6-145).

22nd Match: v Australia (Sydney)   Feb 27, 28, March 2, 3, 4.
Australia 295 (W. H. Ponsford 80) & 325 (T. J. E. Andrews 80, C. Kelleway 73, W. A. S. Oldfield 65*, M. W. Tate 5-115) beat England 167 (C. V. Grimmett 5-45) & 146 (C. V. Grimmett 6-37) by 307 runs.

23rd Match: v Northern Districts (West Maitland)   March 6, 7.
N. Districts XV 157 (J. W. Hearne 8-18) & 153-2 (G. Bell 68) drew with M.C.C. 337-7 dec (H. Sutcliffe 136*, R. Kilner 66).

24th Match: v South Australia (Adelaide)   March 13, 14, 15.
M.C.C. 179 (A. Sandham 59, A. J. Richardson 5-52) & 264 (W. W. Whysall 101, A. Sandham 64, E. H. Hendren 59, C. V. Grimmett 7-85) lost to S. Australia 443 (J. W. Rymill 146, P. D. Rundell 90, D. E. Pritchard 87) & 1-0 by 10 wkts.

twice for under 300 to produce an innings victory – the first by England against Australia since 1912.

This success was however short-lived for in the fifth and final Test, the English batting once more collapsed – even Hobbs and Sutcliffe made a duck each and Australia won by 307 runs. The slow right-arm bowler, Grimmett, on his Test debut, was the cause of England's downfall, taking 11 for 82 in the match.

The last match of the tour was another defeat – at the hands of South Australia by 10 wickets – but the M.C.C. were without Hobbs and Sutcliffe. Those two batsmen were without doubt the outstanding players of the tour and their batting quite outshone that of their colleagues. Woolley and Hendren certainly improved on their efforts of 1920-21 but not to any marked extent. Chapman's impetuosity was his undoing, though he did play some useful innings. Whysall and Kilner also made runs, but Hearne and Sandham had a lean time. The bowling relied too heavily on Tate; Gilligan and Douglas proved of little account and as forecast Freeman was superfluous. It must however be noted that generally England out-fielded Australia, except perhaps in their returns to the wicket.

For Australia Taylor was the principal batsman and a much safer player than hitherto, but Ponsford was only a fraction behind him. Ryder unfortunately missed two Tests due to a bad back but headed the averages with some good innings. In the bowling Grimmett was the discovery of the season, whilst Gregory still remained a powerful force.

Financially the tour was most successful and socially no major upset marred its progress.

1924-25: England 'second team' draw series

Under the auspices of S. B. Joel, a strong English team went out to South Africa in the winter of 1924-25. The side was: the Hon L. H. Tennyson (Hants) (capt), T. O. Jameson (Hants), J. C. W. MacBryan (Somerset), F. W. H. Nicholas (Essex), A. H. H. Gilligan (Sussex), E. L. D. Bartley (Navy), C. S. Marriott (Kent) and the professionals G. E. Tyldesley (Lancs), E. H. Bowley

(Sussex), P. Holmes (Yorks), C. A. G. Russell (Essex), A. S. Kennedy (Hants), C. W. L. Parker (Gloucs), G. Geary (Leics) and W. E. Astill (Leics). F. W. Gilligan of Essex was invited but had to decline.

The fact that South Africa had done so well against the M.C.C. side in 1922-23 caused the critics to wonder if the present team were not attempting too much – with the leading English players being in Australia, this was of necessity the England second team. In view of what happened a few years later, it is interesting to note that there was considerable debate on the subject of the 'Test Matches' which were to be played on the tour. In the end it was generally agreed that these could not be official 'Tests' since

1924-25: S. B. Joel's Team to South Africa

Batting Averages

	M	I	NO	R	HS	Avge	100	c/s
G. E. Tyldesley (Lancs)	11	19	2	965	174	56.76	2	3
T. O. Jameson (Hants)	10	15	4	430	133	39.09	1	4
E. H. Bowley (Sussex)	14	22	1	732	131	34.85	2	18
P. Holmes (Yorks)	13	20	1	536	81	28.21	0	7
C. A. G. Russell (Essex)	12	19	2	469	80	27.58	0	4
J. C. W. MacBryan (Som)	10	16	0	426	120	26.62	2	8
A. S. Kennedy (Hants)	14	20	2	391	67*	21.72	0	4
Hon L. H. Tennyson (Hants)	14	23	2	342	57	16.28	0	5
F. W. H. Nicholas (Essex)	5	8	2	91	78	15.16	0	0
C. W. L. Parker (Gloucs)	13	18	5	191	51*	14.69	0	2
A. H. H. Gilligan (Sussex)	5	7	1	85	19	14.16	0	2
E. L. D. Bartley (Navy)	12	19	8	117	24	10.63	0	24/8
G. Geary (Leics)	11	16	1	143	37	9.40	0	7
W. E. Astill (Leics)	2	3	0	27	16	9.00	0	2
C. S. Marriott (Kent)	8	9	2	14	4	2.00	0	2

Bowling Averages

	O	M	R	W	Avge	BB	5i
G. Geary	407.5	104	955	59	16.18	6-37	3
C. W. L. Parker	284.1	77	721	44	16.38	5-39	1
A. S. Kennedy	478.5	119	1287	65	19.81	6-27	5
C. A. G. Russell	9	1	21	1	21.00	1-8	0
E. H. Bowley	29	3	112	5	22.40	3-18	0
C. S. Marriott	209	48	563	24	23.45	6-45	1
T. O. Jameson	113	21	343	14	24.50	3-13	0
W. E. Astill	117	40	223	8	27.87	5-82	1

Also bowled: Hon L. H. Tennyson 10-0-56-0.
Played in non-first-class matches only: A. S. Frames.

1925-26: M.C.C. to West Indies

1st Match: v Barbados Colts XV (Bridgetown) Jan 1, 2.
M.C.C. 310-8 dec (F. B. Watson 97, E. J. Smith 59) drew with Colts XV 96 (R. Kilner 7-24) & 116-7.

2nd Match: v Barbados (Bridgetown) Jan 4, 5, 6.
M.C.C. 151 (H. C. Griffith 5-54) & 65 (G. N. Francis 6-21) lost to Barbados 289-7 dec (G. Challenor 124) by an inns & 73 runs.

3rd Match: v West Indies (Bridgetown) Jan 8, 9, 11, 12.
M.C.C. 597-8 dec (W. R. Hammond 238*, T. O. Jameson 98, E. J. Smith 73, W. E. Astill 66, P. Holmes 63) drew with West Indies 147 (G. Challenor 63, P. H. Tarilton 50) & 21-6.

4th Match: v Barbados (Bridgetown) Jan 14, 15, 16.
Barbados 401-5 dec (P. H. Tarilton 178, E. L. G. Hoad 71, L. S. Birkett 62*) drew with M.C.C. 110 (G. N. Francis 7-50) & 184-8.

5th Match: v Trinidad (Port of Spain) Jan 21, 22, 23.
M.C.C. 272 (W. R. Hammond 56, H. L. Dales 50, G. John 5-54) & 198-6 (W. E. Astill 61, W. R. Hammond 52) drew with Trinidad 259 (A. Cipriani 103, W. R. Hammond 6-89).

6th Match: v Trinidad (Port of Spain) Jan 26, 27, 28.
Trinidad 173 (J. A. Small 57, W. H. Hammond 5-39) & 270-7 dec (W. H. St Hill 105, G. Dewhurst 56, R. Kilner 6-83) drew with M.C.C. 143 & 177-3 (P. Holmes 56).

7th Match: v West Indies (Port of Spain) Jan 30, Feb 1, 2, 3.
West Indies 275 (C. R. Browne 74, G. Dewhurst 55) & 281 (C. A. Wiles 75, H. B. G. Austin 69, W. E. Astill 6-67) lost to M.C.C. 319 (F. B. Watson 79, P. Holmes 65) & 240-5 by 5 wkts.

8th Match: v British Guiana (Georgetown) Feb 9, 10, 11.
M.C.C. 350 (F. B. Watson 73, W. E. Astill 69, T. O. Jameson 57) & 46-0 drew with British Guiana 373 (E. A. Phillips 92).

9th Match: v West Indies (Georgetown) Feb 13, 15, 16, 17.
West Indies 462 (C. R. Browne 102*, C. V. Wight 90, G. Challenor 82, W. H. St Hill 72, G. Dewhurst 54) drew with M.C.C. 264 (F. B. Watson 59, P. Holmes 53) & 243-8 (L. H. Tennyson 57*, W. E. Astill 51).

10th Match: v British Guiana (Georgetown) Feb 19, 20, 22.
M.C.C. 385 (W. R. Hammond 111, F. B. Watson 64, F. S. Gough-Calthorpe 64) & 124-2 drew with British Guiana 348 (M. P. Fernandes 120).

11th Match: v Jamaica (Kingston) March 10, 11, 12.
Jamaica 334 (E. A. Rae 75, C. M. Morales 74, F. R. Martin 66) & 128 (O. C. Scott 54, R. Kilner 7-50) lost to M.C.C. 238 (P. Holmes 62) & 227-5 (P. Holmes 62) by 5 wkts.

12th Match: v Jamaica (Kingston) March 13, 15, 16.
Jamaica 255 (O. C. Scott 58) & 277-5 (R. K. Nunes 140*, O. C. Scott 72) drew with M.C.C. 476-9 dec (T. O. Jameson 110, F. B. Watson 103*, L. G. Crawley 85, R. Kilner 54, E. J. Smith 50).

13th Match: v Jamaica (Kingston) March 18, 19, 20.
Jamaica 445-9 dec (R. K. Nunes 83, F. R. Martin 80, O. C. Scott 62, J. K. Holt 57) drew with M.C.C. 510-6 (P. Holmes 244, W. E. Astill 156, E. J. Smith 65).

England could not have a representative eleven in two countries at the same time.

The team left England aboard the *Edinburgh Castle* on 24 October and opened its campaign with a one-day match at Newlands on 13 November. The side more than held its own in the early matches and gained a creditable win over Transvaal, due to two good innings by Tyldesley and Kennedy's bowling. In the 'First Test', the tourists' batting failed badly, though they were without Holmes, who was ill. Nupen bowled well on the matting wicket, but the English bowlers could not use it to the same advantage. Holmes came into the team for the 'Second Test', as did Astill, who was coaching in South Africa. The latter played for Marriott, who was unwell. The addition of these two cricketers made all the difference – Holmes scored 101 runs and Astill took 6 wickets – and victory was obtained by 48 runs.

South Africa were without four of her leading players for the 'Third Test' and most importantly without Nupen. Geary found the wicket – matting over coarse grass – just to his liking, and as Tyldesley and Russell came off with the bat the visitors won the game at a canter. The home side were back at full strength for the 'Fourth Test', but a very even match had to be drawn because of rain on the final day.

The bowling of Nupen and Hall won South Africa the last 'Test', though the tourists fought back splendidly in the final innings and the difference between the sides was only 21 runs.

The tour was felt to be a success. The English side's tail was rather too pronounced. Tyldesley was the best bat, whilst Geary stole the bowling honours. Two of the features of the tour were the wicket-keeping of Bartley and Bowley's efforts at first slip. On the financial side, the venture lost about £4,000.

1925-26: Barbados again beat M.C.C., but 'Test' series won

In the previous winter, the M.C.C. had promised to send a team out to the West Indies and indeed had appointed R. St L. Fowler as captain and obtained promises from several other players. It was not until September that the tour was cancelled, but the M.C.C. then stated that if invited by the West Indian authorities, they would send a team in 1925-26. Unfortunately Fowler died in June 1925, at the early age of 34, and the team which travelled to the West Indies was: F. S. Gough-Calthorpe (Warwicks) (capt), the Hon L. H. Tennyson (Hants), T. O. Jameson (Hants), C. T. Bennett (Cambridge U), L. G. Crawley (Cambridge U), H. L. Dales (Middx) and the professionals W. E. Astill (Leics), G. C. Collins (Kent), W. R. Hammond (Gloucs), C. F. Root (Worcs), P. Holmes (Yorks), R. Kilner (Yorks), F. B. Watson (Lancs) and E. J. Smith (Warwicks). Capt C. Levick acted as manager and Collins was baggage-master.

The team might be described as of strong county standard, though there was only one fast bowler – Collins – which seemed a little odd, when it is recalled that fast bowlers are the life-blood of West Indian cricket.

The tour opened in Barbados at the beginning of January and, after a loosener against a Colts team, the tourists were totally outplayed by Barbados, the fast bowling of Francis and Griffith being altogether too much for them. In the 'First Test', which came immediately afterwards, the M.C.C. had their team picked for them owing to the indisposition of Watson and Bennett. Hammond and Jameson however batted quite brilliantly, the Gloucester man being in for 5 hours without giving a chance. Then the West Indies had to bat on a sticky wicket and only further rain saved them from a heavy defeat. Positions were reversed for the return against Barbados and time now saved M.C.C. from an innings defeat. Moving on to Trinidad, the tourists played two even draws against the island, before meeting West Indies. In this 'Second Test', the visitors won a match through all-round ability, no one player taking a decisive role.

The three games in British Guiana were all drawn. All were high scoring and with matches restricted to three days each, only in the 'Third Test' did a definite result look a possibility, but here rain flooded the ground on the last afternoon. The last leg of the tour began after the long voyage to Jamaica. The weakest of the four colonies, Jamaica were always behind in the three matches

1925-26: M.C.C. to West Indies

Batting Averages

	M	I	NO	R	HS	Avge	100	c/s
W. R. Hammond (Glos)	10	18	3	732	238*	48.80	2	15
P. Holmes (Yorks)	10	17	0	797	244	46.88	1	2
T. O. Jameson (Hants)	11	17	4	536	110*	41.23	1	9
F. B. Watson (Lancs)	10	18	2	651	103*	40.68	1	3
W. E. Astill (Leics)	12	17	1	579	156	36.19	1	6
L. G. Crawley (Worcs)	8	10	3	209	85	29.85	0	3
E. J. Smith (Warks)	11	17	0	489	73	28.76	0	8/4
R. Kilner (Yorks)	12	15	4	249	54	22.64	0	16
L. H. Tennyson (Hants)	11	16	4	268	57*	22.33	0	2
C. T. Bennett (Surrey)	4	5	1	72	32*	18.00	0	1
F. S. Gough-Calthorpe (Warks)	11	15	5	173	64	17.30	0	5
H. L. Dales (Middx)	6	10	1	149	50	16.55	0	1
G. C. Collins (Kent)	5	4	0	41	28	10.25	0	2
C. F. Root (Worcs)	11	11	2	92	25	10.22	0	2

Bowling Averages

	O	M	R	W	Avge	BB	5i
C. F. Root	287	97	654	25	26.16	4-9	0
W. R. Hammond	198	42	573	20	28.65	6-89	2
W. E. Astill	379	94	952	33	28.85	6-67	1
R. Kilner	425.2	128	1003	34	29.50	7-50	2
T. O. Jameson	152	23	366	11	33.27	3-58	0
F. S. Gough-Calthorpe	165	38	557	16	34.81	3-11	0
F. B. Watson	63	7	219	5	43.80	2-38	0
G. C. Collins	22	2	82	1	82.00	1-15	0

Also bowled: L. H. Tennyson 12-0-62-0; L. G. Crawley 4-1-16-0; P. Holmes 3-2-8-0; E. J. Smith 1-1-0-1.

played – even in the final one when they hit 445, the M.C.C. went to 510 for 6 before time ran out.

The best bat on the tour was Holmes and he would have had even better figures but for his sea-sickness. Hammond also batted in good style and was a wonderful fielder. Fourth in the batting was Watson, a difficult man to dislodge. The best bowler was Astill who turned the ball both ways and was effective on matting wickets. The only problem on the tour was in fact the umpiring, which except in British Guiana left much to be desired.

1926-27: first M.C.C. tourists unbeaten in India, Burma and Ceylon

This first M.C.C. tour to India, and indeed the first English tour of the sub-continent since 1902-03, was a much too ambitious venture. To fit in all 34 fixtures and the travelling entailed, many of the games were reduced to two-day matches and thus had little prospect of definite finishes. It was all done with the best of intentions, but to the players it seemed at times like a gruelling marathon that would never end.

The team was A. E. R. Gilligan (Sussex) (capt), P. T. Eckersley (Lancs), M. Ll. Hill (Somerset), G. F. Earle (Somerset), Major R. C. J. Chichester-Constable (Yorks 2nd), R. E. S. Wyatt (Warwicks) and the professionals W. E. Astill (Leics), G. S. Boyes (Hants), G. Brown (Hants), J. H. Parsons (Warwicks), A. Sandham (Surrey), G. Geary (Leics), M. W. Tate (Sussex) and J. Mercer (Glamorgan). Root had been invited but Worcester refused to release him.

Sailing from Tilbury on 24 September in the s.s. *Narcunda*, the team called at Marseilles and Port Said before reaching Bombay, where they stopped for a few hours and then voyaged on to Karachi, where the first four matches were played.

The first three games being only two days each were drawn, though the tourists were well placed in them all. In the three-day match against All Karachi, some hard-hitting batting by Parsons and the all-round cricket of Tate gave the tourists victory by an innings. Both matches at Rawalpindi were drawn, the most noteworthy feature being Tate's century in 120 minutes in the second.

Next stop on the tour was Lahore where four matches were contested and only the one of three-days duration provided the

tourists with another innings victory. Wyatt hit a careful hundred, whilst Geary took 11 wickets. By some misfortune both the tourists' wicket-keepers were injured prior to this game, Hill having a poisoned foot and Brown a hand injury. The team therefore called on A. Dolphin, the Yorkshire stumper, who was in India coaching. After two matches in Ajmere, the side arrived in Bombay for a series of five matches. In the first – against Hindus – some 45,000 attended on the two days and watched Nayudu hit 153 in 100 minutes off the visitors' attack. Victory by an innings was gained over Bombay Presidency, with Sandham and Wyatt giving the team a grand start by reaching 224 before a wicket fell. The 'First Test' followed this game. The Indians proved as good as the tourists and only the first innings of each team were completed. The other 'Test' was played at the team's next venue – Calcutta. Owing to injury and illness, the side were down to ten men and the Maharajah of Patiala made up the team in the two first-class matches in Calcutta, both of which ended in victory – in the second game, which was the 'Test', Wyatt played a brilliant undefeated innings of 97 on a worn pitch to take the M.C.C. to a hard-fought win.

Going on from Calcutta to Burma, the team played two games in Rangoon. Here the wicket was a matting one and the locals were saved in the first game by the old Essex cricketer Hubert Ashton, who scored 48 and an undefeated 60. In the second match, Boyes removed him cheaply twice and the M.C.C. won just in time by 10 wickets. From Rangoon and on to Madras, where three games took place – Wyatt, for a bet, drove round the ground on a motor-cycle with a woman's hat on his head, much to the amusement of the crowd.

In the first game in Ceylon, Tate completed the double of 1,000 runs and 100 wickets for the tour. The matches in Ceylon proved easy ones for the tourists and in the second Wyatt performed the unusual feat of scoring a century and taking a hat-trick.

The team returned to India and the last match was played in Patiala against the Maharajah's side, where the old Australian cricketer who used to play for Middlesex, Tarrant, scored a hard hit 68. The team returned to England in mid-March, having been undefeated in 34 matches. It is not strictly correct to state that the team were undefeated, since they were beaten in a one-day unofficial match against Delhi Ladies! Sandham and Wyatt were the leading run-getters, Tate and Geary shared bowling honours.

1926-27: M.C.C. to India, Burma and Ceylon

Batting Averages

	M	I	NO	R	HS	Avge	100	c/s
A. Sandham (Surrey)	27	30	2	1756	150	62.71	7	3
R. E. S. Wyatt (Warks)	29	37	4	1747	138	52.93	5	19
J. H. Parsons (Warks)	24	28	2	1289	160	49.57	2	30
M. W. Tate (Sussex)	28	33	0	1193	133	36.15	3	12
G. Geary (Leics)	22	24	7	609	75*	35.82	0	23
M. Leyland (Yorks)	2	2	0	71	51	35.50	0	3
G. F. Earle (Som)	23	27	2	808	130	32.32	1	13
P. T. Eckersley (Lancs)	26	32	5	791	86	29.29	0	4
G. Brown (Hants)	18	24	0	670	84	27.91	0	18/8
W. E. Astill (Leics)	24	25	2	642	66	27.91	0	18
M. Ll. Hill (Som)	13	13	7	164	34*	27.33	0	11/2
G. S. Boyes (Hants)	27	29	10	459	49	24.15	0	21
A. E. R. Gilligan (Sussex)	22	22	2	453	73	22.65	0	12
Maharajah of Patiala	5	6	0	75	23	12.50	0	1
Major R. C. J. Chichester-Constable	19	14	2	139	47*	11.58	0	5
J. Mercer (Glam)	14	12	5	76	31*	10.85	0	8
A. Dolphin (Yorks)	6	3	3	21	20*	—	0	7/1
Lieut. R. E. S. Yeldham	1	did not bat						0

Bowling Averages

	O	M	R	W	Avge	BB	5i
M. W. Tate	727.1	211	1599	116	13.78	6-34	10
G. Geary	528.1	154	1162	81	14.34	8-56	4
G. S. Boyes	457.3	127	1047	56	18.69	7-52	3
J. Mercer	301.1	65	904	42	21.52	6-39	2
W. E. Astill	547.5	147	1556	71	21.91	7-18	4
A. E. R. Gilligan	88	24	234	10	23.40	3-25	0
R. E. S. Wyatt	324.4	81	911	32	28.46	6-33	2
P. T. Eckersley	40.2	2	203	6	33.83	2-21	0
J. H. Parsons	31	2	90	2	45.00	2-27	0
G. Brown	33	1	143	2	71.50	1-16	0
G. F. Earle	47	7	196	2	98.00	1-18	0
R. C. J. Chichester-Constable	30.2	5	105	1	105.00	1-6	0

Also bowled: A. Sandham 13-0-74-0.

The M.C.C. depart from Tilbury on board the s.s. Narcunda *for the first tour of India since 1902-03 on 24 September 1926. On the steps wearing a pullover is R. E. S. Wyatt, later to lead M.C.C. in the West Indies.*

1926-27: M.C.C. to India, Burma and Ceylon

1st Match: v Parsis & Moslems (Karachi)   Oct 19, 20.
M.C.C. 339 (R. E. S. Wyatt 63, A. Sandham 57, M. W. Tate 57, A. E. R. Gilligan 57, Ghulam Mahomed 5-114) & 77-4 drew with Parsis & Moslems 187 (M. J. Mobed 54) & 138-3 dec.

2nd Match: v Hindus & Rest (Karachi)   Oct 23, 24.
Hindus & Rest 335 (D. Jagannath 73, L. Semper 64*, M. A. Gopaldas 62, M. W. Tate 5-61) drew with M.C.C. 249-5 (A. Sandham 129, J. H. Parsons 58).

3rd Match: v Europeans (Karachi)   Oct 26, 27.
M.C.C. 377 (A. Sandham 67, G. Geary 52) & 139-3 drew with Europeans 151.

4th Match: v Karachi (Karachi)   Oct 29, 30, 31.
Karachi 129 & 240 (J. Naomal 83, M. P. Dastur 61, M. W. Tate 5-35) lost to M.C.C. 517 (J. H. Parsons 139, M. W. Tate 77, A. E. R. Gilligan 73, G. F. Earle 51, N. J. O. Carbutt 5-135) by an inns & 148 runs.

5th Match: v Europeans (Rawalpindi)   Nov 3, 4.
M.C.C. 431-8 dec (A. Sandham 150, P. T. Eckersley 86, M. W. Tate 66, G. F. Earle 59, C. B. Barlow 5-93) & 185-5 dec (A. E. R. Gilligan 68) drew with Europeans 145 (F. J. Matthews 57) & 85-1.

6th Match: v Rawalpindi (Rawalpindi)   Nov 5, 6.
Rawalpindi 195 (Feroze Khan 83, G. S. Boyes 6-37) & 108-3 drew with M.C.C. 330-4 dec (R. E. S. Wyatt 125*, M. W. Tate 103).

7th Match: v The Army (Lahore)   Nov 10, 11.
The Army 73 (R. E. S. Wyatt 6-33) & 212-5 (R. E. H. Hudson 94, E. H. P. Mallinson 75) drew with M.C.C. 252-6 dec (A. Sandham 141*).

8th Match: v Southern Punjab (Lahore)   Nov 13, 14.
M.C.C. 285 (P. T. Eckersley 65, Nazir Ali 7-114) drew with S. Punjab 89 (M. W. Tate 5-39) & 148-9.

9th Match: v Northern Punjab (Lahore)   Nov 15, 16.
N. Punjab 169 (S. E. West 73, G. S. Boyes 5-28) drew with M.C.C. 373-8 (M. W. Tate 95, G. F. Earle 82, R. E. S. Wyatt 65, G. Geary 51).

10th Match: v Northern India (Lahore)   Nov 18, 19, 20.
N. India 100 (M. W. Tate 5-48) & 101 (G. Geary 7-34) lost to M.C.C. 333-6 dec (R. E. S. Wyatt 130*, A. Sandham 72) by an inns & 132 runs.

11th Match: v Rajputana & BBCI Railway (Ajmere)   Nov 23, 24.
Rajputana 155 (G. Geary 8-56) & 126-3 drew with M.C.C. 287 (A. Sandham 103).

12th Match: v Rajputana & Central India (Ajmere)   Nov 26, 27.
Rajputana & Central India 123 & 47 (G. Geary 5-14) lost to M.C.C. 337-9 dec (A. Sandham 81, J. H. Parsons 59*, M. Leyland 51) by an inns & 167 runs.

13th Match: v Hindus (Bombay)   Nov 30, Dec 1.
M.C.C. 363 (G. F. Earle 130, A. Sandham 52, M. W. Tate 50) & 74-1 drew with Hindus 356 (C. K. Nayudu 153, S. R. Godambe 58, L. P. Jai 53, W. E. Astill 5-75).

14th Match: v Parsis & Europeans (Bombay)   Dec 4, 5.
M.C.C. 334 (M. W. Tate 133, J. H. Parsons 73, R. J. Jamshedji 6-104) & 135 (R. J. Jamshedji 5-43) drew with Parsis & Europeans 252 (D. K. Kapadia 55, S. H. Colah 51).

15th Match: v Hindu-Mahommadan XI (Bombay)   Dec 7, 8.
Hindu-Mahommadan XI 167 (L. P. Jai 63) & 148-4 (Wazir Ali 67*) drew with M.C.C. 324 (G. Brown 84, A. Sandham 52) (Nazir Ali 6-128).

16th Match: v Bombay Presidency (Bombay)   Dec 10, 12, 13.
M.C.C. 435 (R. E. S. Wyatt 138, A. Sandham 124, W. E. Astill 53) beat Bombay Presidency 115 (G. Geary 5-28) & 203 (B. K. Kalapsi 77) by an inns & 117 runs.

17th Match: v All India (Bombay)   Dec 16, 17, 18.
M.C.C. 362 (R. E. S. Wyatt 83, J. H. Parsons 58) & 97-5 drew with All India 437 (D. B. Deodhar 148, J. G. Navie 74, K. M. Mistri 51).

18th Match: v Anglo-Indians in Bengal (Calcutta) (One Day)   Dec 22.
M.C.C. 222-2 dec (A. Sandham 112*, G. Brown 67) beat Anglo-Indians 103 (M. W. Tate 5-46).

19th Match: v British in Bengal (Calcutta) (One Day)   Dec 24.
British 152-7 dec drew with M.C.C. 102-5 (A. Sandham 53*).

20th Match: v Europeans in the East (Calcutta)   Dec 26, 28, 29.
Europeans 146 & 125 (G. S. Boyes 7-52) lost to M.C.C. 326 (A. Sandham 112, F. A. Tarrant 6-75) by an inns & 55 runs.

21st Match: v All India (Calcutta)   Dec 31, Jan 2, 3.
All India 146 (M. W. Tate 6-42) & 269 (J. L. Guise 91, F. R. R. Brooke 72) lost to M.C.C. 233 (W. E. Astill 66, M. W. Tate 58) & 185-6 (R. E. S. Wyatt 97*) by 4 wkts.

22nd Match: v Rangoon Gymkhana (Rangoon)   Jan 9, 10.
M.C.C. 381-6 dec (J. H. Parsons 160, G. Geary 75*) drew with Rangoon 173 (J. Mercer 6-39) & 211-5 (H. Ashton 60*, W. B. Giles 55).

23rd Match: v All Burma (Rangoon)   Jan 12, 13.
All Burma 144 (M. W. Tate 5-37) & 137 (M. W. Tate 5-35) lost to M.C.C. 276 (R. E. S. Wyatt 78, J. H. Parsons 64, G. Smith 5-94) & 7-0 by 10 wkts.

24th Match: v An Indian XI (Madras)   Jan 18, 19.
An Indian XI 238 (S. Mahomed Hussain 90, C. Ramaswamy 60) drew with M.C.C. 344 (R. E. S. Wyatt 55, W. E. Astill 54*).

25th Match: v Madras Europeans (Madras) (One Day)   Jan 21.
Europeans 201-9 dec drew with M.C.C. 155-8 (M. W. Tate 53).

26th Match: v All Madras (Madras)   Jan 23, 24, 25.
M.C.C. 361 (G. Brown 84, P. T. Eckersley 69*, J. H. Parsons 62, G. P. Ganapathy 5-72) & 233-7 dec (A. Sandham 82, G. Brown 56) beat Madras 256 (C. K. Nayudu 59, R. Nailer 54, C. P. Johnstone 51) & 127 by 211 runs.

27th Match: v Europeans in Ceylon (Colombo)   Jan 28, 29.
Europeans 154 (G. R. Neale 76, W. E. Astill 5-52) & 194-4 (A. E. Blair 95*) drew with M.C.C. 419 (R. E. S. Wyatt 76, J. H. Parsons 67, W. E. Astill 66, A. Sandham 51, E. P. Wedlake-Lewis 5-87).

28th Match: v Ceylonese (Colombo)   Jan 31, Feb 1.
Ceylonese 165 (S. Perinpanayagam 56) & 190-8 (C. T. van Geyzel 66, F. C. W. van Geyzel 59, R. E. S. Wyatt 5-39) drew with M.C.C. 483-8 dec (R. E. S. Wyatt 124, M. W. Tate 121, G. Geary 61*, G. Brown 51).

29th Match: v Up-Country XI (Daruwella)   Feb 3, 4.
M.C.C. 223 (A. Sandham 108, R. L. Kannangara 5-60) & 74-1 drew with Up-Country XI 166 (A. E. Blair 51, M. W. Tate 6-34).

30th Match: v All Ceylon (Colombo)   Feb 5, 7, 8.
M.C.C. 431-8 dec (R. E. S. Wyatt 101, W. E. Astill 65, J. H. Parsons 64, A. Sandham 57) beat Ceylon 105 (M. K. Albert 51, W. E. Astill 7-18) & 235 (F. A. Waldock 61, M. W. Tate 5-23) by an inns & 91 runs.

31st Match: v Aligarh University (Aligarh)   Feb 18, 19.
Aligarh Univ 86 (M. W. Tate 5-31, J. Mercer 5-52) lost to M.C.C. 197 (A. Sandham 52) by an inns & 14 runs.

32nd Match: v Delhi & District (Delhi) (One Day)   Feb 20.
M.C.C. 232-4 dec (G. Brown 98, A. Sandham 56) drew with Delhi 92-9.

33rd Match: v Northern India (Delhi)   Feb 22, 23, 24.
M.C.C. 369-9 dec (R. E. S. Wyatt 96, A. Sandham 74, J. H. Parsons 61, G. F. Earle 58, Nazir Ali 5-80) drew with N. India 185 (R. E. H. Hudson 61, W. E. Astill 5-45) & 260-1 (Wazir Ali 113*, Dilawar Hussain 85).

34th Match: v Patiala (Patiala)   Feb 26, 27.
Patiala 303-4 dec (Wazir Ali 149, F. A. Tarrant 68) drew with M.C.C. 252 (R. E. S. Wyatt 67, M. W. Tate 65).

1926-27: first English tourists to Uruguay, Chile and Peru

It was originally intended that the M.C.C. should send a team of amateurs to Argentine, but the programme was expanded until additional matches had been arranged in Uruguay, Chile and Peru—it was the first time an English side had been seen in any of those three countries.

The party consisted of: P. F. Warner (Middx) (capt), T. O. Jameson (Hants), G. O. B. Allen (Middx), G. R. Jackson (Derbys), G. J. V. Weigall (Kent), L. C. R. Isherwood (Sussex), J. C. White (Som), R. T. Stanyforth (Army), Lord Dunglass (Middx), M. F. S. Jewell (Worcs), H. P. Miles (M.C.C.), T. A. Pilkington.

Sailing on the s.s. *Andes*, the team played their first match in a suburb of Montevideo, before going on to the Argentine. The three major games of the tour were the 'Tests' against Argentina, who were captained by C. H. Gibson. In the 'First Test', Marshal hit a century for the home side, but rain forced a draw. At Belgrano in the 'Second Test', some good bowling by Jameson and White brought victory for M.C.C., but in the 'Third' a thunderstorm caused the wicket to be quite treacherous and Dorning quite unplayable, so that Argentina squared the series. It was then agreed to arrange a fourth and deciding 'Test' at Belgrano and the M.C.C. abandoned their proposed trip to Mar del Plata. Argentina scored 271 in their first innings, but some lively batting by the M.C.C. tail took the visitors' total to 384, at which point Warner declared, leaving just two hours playing time. J. C. White then bowled out the opposition with five minutes to spare and M.C.C. won by an innings.

The tourists crossed the Andes and played both Chile and Peru, before returning to England.

On a political note, it should be mentioned that one of the

'Tests' was watched by the President of the Argentine, whilst Lord Dunglass, who played, became better known as Sir Alec Douglas Home, who was Prime Minister in 1963-64.

The M.C.C. team of amateurs under P. F. Warner leaving London for the tour of Argentina, Uruguay, Chile and Peru in 1926-27. Warner is third from right. On the left is G. O. B. Allen and next to him Lord Dunglass.

1926-27: M.C.C. to South America

1st Match: v Montevideo (Blanqueado) Dec 24, 25.
M.C.C. 366-7 dec (T. O. Jameson 100, P. F. Warner 81, G. R. Jackson 61) beat Montevideo 64 (J. C. White 7-27) & 98 (T. O. Jameson 5-21) by an inns & 204 runs.

2nd Match: v Northern Suburbs (Saenz Pena) Dec 28, 29.
M.C.C. 459 (T. O. Jameson 120*, M. F. S. Jewell 88, G. O. B. Allen 87) drew with N. Suburbs 189 (R. A. de C. Lyons 71, G. O. B. Allen 6-29) & 174-6 (W. A. Cowes 67*).

3rd Match: v Argentine (Hurlingham) Dec 31, Jan 1, 2.
Argentine 327 (H. W. Marshal 105, K. Henderson 70, G. O. B. Allen 5-115) drew with M.C.C. 90-4.

4th Match: v Concordia (Concordia) Jan 4, 5.
Concordia 78 (H. P. Miles 6-29) & 173 (H. P. Miles 6-60) lost to M.C.C. 365 (L. C. R. Isherwood 101, G. J. V. Weigall 73, J. C. White 73*) by an inns & 114 runs.

5th Match: v Argentine (Belgrano) Jan 8, 9, 10.
M.C.C. 249 (R. T. Stanyforth 56, F. A. Bryans 5-67) & 193-8 dec beat Argentine 153 (T. O. Jameson 5-27) & 162 (T. O. Jameson 5-29) by 127 runs.

6th Match: v Rosario (Rosario) Jan 12, 13.
M.C.C. 112-6 dec & 54-5 drew with Rosario 76.

7th Match: v Argentine (Palermo) Jan 15, 16, 17.
Argentine 134 (J. C. White 5-65) & 63 beat M.C.C. 89 (H. Dorning 7-38) & 79 (D. Ayling 6-32) by 29 runs.

8th Match: v Argentine (Belgrano) Jan 20, 21, 22.
Argentine 271 (J. Knox 75) & 101 (J. C. White 5-25) lost to M.C.C. 384-9 dec (R. T. Stanyforth 91, G. R. Jackson 73) by an inns & 12 runs.

9th Match: v Chile (Valparaiso) Jan 26, 27.
Chile 158 (O. H. Bonham-Carter 62) & 149 lost to M.C.C. 221 (G. R. Jackson 52) & 87-3 by 7 wkts.

10th Match: v Lima (Lima) Feb 6.
Lima 28 (G. O. B. Allen 6-7) & 56 (G. O. B. Allen 6-15) lost to M.C.C. 173 (R. G. Brown 5-50) by an inns & 89 runs.

1926-27: draws for Tennyson in Jamaica

In the spring of 1927, the Hampshire captain, the Hon L. H. Tennyson, took a team on a month's tour of Jamaica. The side was the Hon L. H. Tennyson (Hants) (capt), T. Arnott (Glamorgan), L. Green (Lancs), H. M. Morris (Essex), A. L. Hilder (Kent), P. G. H. Fender (Surrey), Rev F. H. Gillingham (Essex), E. R. T. Holmes (Surrey), J. P. Parker (Hants) and four professionals G. E. Tyldesley (Lancs), J. O'Connor (Essex), D. Sullivan (Glamorgan) and H. C. Lock (Surrey).

Although the team was up to first-class county standard, it was very weak on bowlers and this was reflected in the results – six of the seven matches being drawn, including the three important fixtures against Jamaica. The four professionals were involved in a motor accident after the third match of the tour – Tyldesley was unable to play again on the tour and O'Connor and Sullivan missed the next two matches.

1926-27: Hon L. H. Tennyson's Team to Jamaica

1st Match: v XVI Colts (Melbourne Park) Feb 17, 18.
Tennyson's XI 440 (G. E. Tyldesley 106, J. O'Connor 103) drew with XVI Colts 366-10 (H. F. Bicknell 76*, J. O'Connor 6-100).

2nd Match: v Jamaica (Sabina Park) Feb 19, 21, 22.
Jamaica 419-9 dec (R. K. Nunes 200*, E. A. Rae 98) & 77-3 drew with Tennyson's XI 449 (G. E. Tyldesley 101, P. G. H. Fender 68).

3rd Match: v Jamaica (Melbourne Park) Feb 24, 25, 26.
Jamaica 304-5 dec (R. K. Nunes 108) drew with Tennyson's XI 146 (L. G. Hylton 5-34) & 367-9 (G. E. Tyldesley 118, T. Arnott 84).

4th Match: v XV of Cornwall (Montego Bay) March 1, 2.
Cornwall XV 315 drew with Tennyson's XI 389-9 (L. Green 105, E. R. T. Holmes 105).

5th Match: v Middlesex (Port Maria) March 5, 6.
Tennyson's XI 366-9 dec (L. Green 101, A. L. Hilder 92) beat Middlesex 126 (P. G. H. Fender 7-40) & 211 (L. E. Saunders 65) by an inns & 29 runs.

6th Match: v Portland Combination XV (Port Antonio) March 7, 8.
Combination XV 300 (S. Lynch 85) & 41-1 drew with Tennyson's XI 368 (J. O'Connor 147).

7th Match: v Jamaica (Sabina Park) March 9, 10, 11, 12.
Tennyson's XI 443 (J. O'Connor 154, L. H. Tennyson 90) & 280 (T. Arnott 71) drew with Jamaica 519 (F. R. Martin 204*, E. A. Rae 84) & 59-0.

1927-28: South Africa draw with weak M.C.C. side

The team which sailed from Southampton on the liner *Kenilworth Castle* on 21 October bound for Cape Town was as follows: Capt R. T. Stanyforth (Army) (capt), G. T. S. Stevens (Middx), E. W. Dawson (Leics), R. E. S. Wyatt (Warwicks), G. B. Legge (Kent), I. A. R. Peebles, and the professionals W. E. Astill (Leics), G. Geary (Leics), W. R. Hammond (Gloucs), H. Sutcliffe (Yorks), G. E. Tyldesley (Lancs), P. Holmes (Yorks), H. Elliott (Derbys), A. P. Freeman (Kent), S. J. Staples (Notts).

The press were quite critical of the party, stating that the M.C.C. seemed to underestimate the strength of South Africa, as indeed had been the case in the past. The major criticism was levelled at the appointment of Stanyforth, who had never played in county cricket, as captain, though he was only given the leadership after G. R. Jackson, the Derbyshire cricketer, who was originally chosen, had to decline through ill health. Certainly the team was not representative of England's full strength, being without Hobbs, Hendren, Tate, Larwood, Jardine and Chapman.

Arriving in Cape Town on 7 November, the team played their first game at Newlands. This was ruined by rain, though no less than 50 bags of sawdust were scattered on the pitch in a vain attempt to continue the match.

As on previous tours, the M.C.C. did not find the opposition

---

very taxing until they played Transvaal, and the only two points arising from these early games were the injury to Freeman at Kimberley and the consequent opportunity then afforded to young Peebles in the next game – the unknown bowler took 10 wickets in the match against the Free State. In both the first and second matches against Transvaal, the home side obtained a first innings lead, but stout batting in M.C.C.'s second innings saved the side each time. Holmes hit a century in the first match and Hammond in the second.

The first Test was staged in Johannesburg, and after Geary's spin diddled out the South Africans in the first innings, England remained in charge, though the batting presented a very odd picture – Holmes, Wyatt, Stevens and Legge all failed to score and centuries by Sutcliffe and Tyldesley were responsible for England's lead on first innings. The visitors won the game by 10 wickets. The second Test at Cape Town was played straight after the first. England, batting first, collapsed to Bissett, and South Africa gained a lead on first innings of 117. The English batting

---

1927-28: M.C.C. to South Africa

1st Match: v Western Province (Cape Town) Nov 13, 14, 15.
M.C.C. 138 drew with W. Province 67-6 (A. P. Freeman 5-15).

2nd Match: v Griqualand West (Kimberley) Nov 19, 21, 22.
M.C.C. 366-8 dec (G. E. Tyldesley 143, H. Sutcliffe 100) beat Griqualand West 118 (S. J. Staples 5-25) & 173 (N. V. Tapscott 75) by an inns & 75 runs.

3rd Match: v Orange Free State (Bloemfontein) Nov 25, 26, 28.
O.F.S. 192 (J. M. M. Commaille 77, I. A. R. Peebles 7-54) & 236 (T. E. Holmes 61, J. M. M. Commaille 54) lost to M.C.C. 592-7 dec (P. Holmes 279*, G. B. Legge 120, H. Sutcliffe 73, G. T. S. Stevens 51) by an inns & 164 runs.

4th Match: v Natal (Pietermaritzburg) Nov 30, Dec 1, 2.
Natal 171 (W. E. Astill 5-38) drew with M.C.C. 333 (G. E. Tyldesley 161).

5th Match: v Natal (Durban) Dec 3, 5, 6.
M.C.C. 354-6 dec (H. Sutcliffe 93, G. E. Tyldesley 76, R. E. S. Wyatt 56*, G. B. Legge 50*) drew with Natal 192 (I. J. Siedle 80, W. E. Astill 5-42) & 167-6 (R. H. Catterall 63).

6th Match: v Transvaal (Pretoria) Dec 9, 10, 11.
M.C.C. 205 (H. Sutcliffe 57, C. L. Vincent 6-59) & 328-3 (P. Holmes 184*) drew with Transvaal 382-7 dec (J. P. Duminy 95, A. H. C. Cooper 86).

7th Match: v XV of Transvaal & Natal Schoolboys (Witwatersrand) Dec 13, 14.
M.C.C. 312 (R. E. S. Wyatt 136*, G. T. S. Stevens 70) & 206-4 (W. R. Hammond 65*) drew with XV Schoolboys 199 (G. Geary 7-58).

8th Match: v Transvaal (Johannesburg) Dec 16, 17, 19.
M.C.C. 129 (H. Sutcliffe 59, E. P. Nupen 5-68) & 360-9 dec (W. R. Hammond 132, W. E. Astill 66, H. Sutcliffe 57, C. L. Vincent 5-78) drew with Transvaal 199 (H. G. Deane 65*, J. P. Duminy 55, G. Geary 6-75) & 183-3 (J. P. Duminy 74*).

9th Match: v A South African XI (Benoni) Dec 20, 21.
A South African XI 86 (W. R. Hammond 6-32) & 305-9 (L. T. H. Trotter 76) drew with M.C.C. 323 (P. Holmes 128, W. R. Hammond 61).

10th Match: v South Africa (Johannesburg) Dec 24, 26, 27.
South Africa 196 (R. H. Catterall 86, G. Geary 7-70) & 170 (C. L. Vintcent 53*, W. R. Hammond 5-36, G. Geary 5-60) lost to England 313 (G. E. Tyldesley 122, H. Sutcliffe 102, W. R. Hammond 51, H. L. E. Promnitz 5-58) & 57-0 by 10 wkts.

11th Match: v South Africa (Cape Town) Dec 31, Jan 2, 3, 4.
England 133 (G. F. Bissett 5-37) & 428 (H. Sutcliffe 99, R. E. S. Wyatt 91, P. Holmes 88, G. E. Tyldesley 87) beat South Africa 250 (H. W. Taylor 68) & 224 (H. W. Taylor 71) by 87 runs.

12th Match: v Eastern Province (Port Elizabeth) Jan 7, 9.
E. Province 136 (S. J. Staples 7-38) & 98 lost to M.C.C. 49 (A. L. Ochse 5-31) & 187-0 (R. E. S. Wyatt 101*, H. Sutcliffe 79*) by 10 wkts.

13th Match: v Border (East London) Jan 13, 14.
Border 146 (A. P. Freeman 8-48) & 107 (W. E. Astill 6-23) lost to M.C.C. 362-5 dec (W. R. Hammond 166*, E. W. Dawson 59) by an inns & 109 runs.

14th Match: v South Africa (Durban) Jan 21, 23, 24, 25.
South Africa 246 (H. G. Deane 77, E. P. Nupen 51) & 464-8 dec (J. F. W. Nicolson 78, R. H. Catterall 76, H. G. Deane 73, E. P. Nupen 69, H. W. Taylor 60) drew with England 430 (W. R. Hammond 90, G. E. Tyldesley 78, P. Holmes 70, G. T. S. Stevens 69, C. L. Vintcent 6-131) & 132-2 (G. E. Tyldesley 62*, P. Holmes 56).

15th Match: v South Africa (Johannesburg) Jan 28, 30, 31, Feb 1.
England 265 (R. E. S. Wyatt 58, A. E. Hall 6-100) & 215 (P. Holmes 63) lost to South Africa 328 (H. W. Taylor, H. B. Cameron 64) & 156-6 by 4 wkts.

16th Match: v South Africa (Durban) Feb 4, 6, 7, 8.
England 282 (G. E. Tyldesley 100, W. R. Hammond 66, H. Sutcliffe 51, E. P. Nupen 5-83) & 118 (G. F. Bissett 7-29) lost to South Africa 332-7 dec (R. H. Catterall 119, H. B. Cameron 53) & 69-2 by 8 wkts.

17th Match: v Combined South African Schools (Grahamstown) Feb 13, 14.
M.C.C. 222-5 dec (H. Sutcliffe 80, P. Holmes 68) & 204-5 (R. E. S. Wyatt 61*, G. B. Legge 50) drew with S.A. Schools 291 (R. Byron 101, H. Rees 60, H. G. O. Owen-Smith 55, A. P. Freeman 6-53).

18th Match: v Western Province (Cape Town) Feb 18, 20, 21.
M.C.C. 415-8 dec (R. E. S. Wyatt 73, R. T. Stanyforth 71*, W. E. Astill 66, H. Sutcliffe 62) & 87-2 beat W. Province 162 (L. Serrurier 74*, A. P. Freeman 5-49) & 339 (A. W. Palm 71, S. Steyn 51, A. P. Freeman 5-102) by 8 wkts.

1927-28: M.C.C. to South Africa

Batting Averages

	M	I	NO	R	HS	Avge	100	c/s
G. E. Tyldesley (Lancs)	14	21	2	1130	161	59.47	4	1
P. Holmes (Yorks)	14	22	3	1112	279*	58.52	3	3
H. Sutcliffe (Yorks)	14	23	3	1030	102	51.50	2	4
W. R. Hammond (Glos)	14	21	2	908	166*	47.78	2	13
R. E. S. Wyatt (Warks)	15	19	5	592	101*	42.28	1	7
G. B. Legge (Kent)	8	9	1	259	120	32.37	1	5
G. T. S. Stevens (Middx)	13	17	2	335	69	22.33	0	13
W. E. Astill (Leics)	13	15	0	331	66	22.07	0	11
E. W. Dawson (Leics)	8	9	1	129	59	16.12	0	1
S. J. Staples (Notts)	11	12	2	141	39	14.10	0	7
R. T. Stanyforth (Army)	14	14	2	120	71*	10.00	0	19/6
I. A. R. Peebles (Middx)	11	14	7	69	26*	9.85	0	3
A. P. Freeman (Kent)	12	11	3	39	9*	4.87	0	3
G. Geary (Leics)	10	10	1	33	24*	3.66	0	6
H. Elliott (Derbys)	3	3	0	4	3	1.33	0	4/2

Played in one match: J. C. Hubble (Kent) 10 (ct 5); S. K. Coen (Orange Free State) 3.

Bowling Averages

	O	M	R	W	Avge	BB	5i
G. Geary	224.3	61	489	28	17.46	7-70	3
A. P. Freeman	325.3	73	965	50	19.30	8-48	4
I. A. R. Peebles	179.1	37	588	28	21.00	7-54	1
S. J. Staples	413.5	108	842	40	21.05	7-38	2
W. E. Astill	279.2	68	782	35	22.34	6-23	3
W. R. Hammond	250	58	644	27	23.85	6-32	2
R. E. S. Wyatt	197	53	561	19	29.52	3-60	0
G. T. S. Stevens	163.4	22	559	17	32.88	3-31	0

Also bowled: G. B. Legge 3-0-23-3; G. E. Tyldesley 0.3-0-2-0; P. Holmes 2-0-13-0; H. Sutcliffe 1-0-10-0.

1927-28: The Hon L. H. Tennyson's Team to Jamaica

1st Match: v All Jamaica (Sabina Park) Feb 9, 10, 11, 13.
Jamaica 429 (C. M. Morales 143, N. N. Nethersole 71, F. R. Martin 65*, J. J. Cameron 52) & 253-6 dec (J. K. Holt 74, G. A. Headley 71) beat Tennyson's XI 227 (C. P. Mead 103*) & 237 (T. Arnott 60, O. C. Scott 6-75) by 218 runs.

2nd Match: v Middlesex XV (Port Maria) Feb 15, 16.
Tennyson's XI 240 (C. P. Mead 107) & 36-0 drew with Middlesex XV 226 (A. L. Hilder 9-49).

3rd Match: v All Jamaica (Melbourne Park) Feb 18, 20, 21, 22.
Tennyson's XI 252 (C. P. Mead 117) & 259 (G. M. Lee 97, F. J. Seabrook 59, O. C. Scott 8-67) lost to Jamaica 609 (G. A. Headley 211, J. K. Holt 100, C. M. Morales 84, R. K. Nunes 53) by an inns & 98 runs.

4th Match: v Cornwall XV (Montego Bay) Feb 24, 25.
Cornwall XV 125 & 249 (A. V. Lee 70) lost to Tennyson's XI 347-7 dec (L. H. Tennyson 125, T. Arnott 71, G. D. Kemp-Welch 63) & 29-1 by 9 wkts.

5th Match: v All Jamaica (Sabina Park) Feb 28, 29, March 1, 2, 3.
Jamaica 438 (J. K. Holt 142, F. R. Martin 63, L. G. Hylton 55, R. K. Nunes 53) & 338-6 dec (F. R. Martin 141*, L. G. Hylton 60, G. A. Headley 71) drew with Tennyson's XI 327 (A. K. Judd 75, L. H. Tennyson 70, M. J. C. Allom 62, T. Arnott 58) & 288-7 (C. P. Mead 151, P. T. Eckersley 50).

in the second innings however redressed the balance and Astill and Freeman took their side to victory. In this game Geary injured his elbow and was not able to play in the remaining Tests, which proved unfortunate for England. The success in the two Tests was quickly countered by Eastern Province who dismissed M.C.C. for 49—the lowest innings ever made by the M.C.C. in South Africa until then. Staples and Peebles, however, struck back and sparkling batting from Wyatt won the game.

South Africa, with the rubber at stake, fought hard in the third Test and consistent batting by the home side produced a draw. The two other Tests were played consecutively, with no minor matche intervening. Hall and Bissett—the contrast of a slow left-armer and fast right-arm—dismissed England twice in the fourth Test and without Geary the South African batting flourished to bring England its first defeat. In the last innings, the visitors were handicapped by an injury to Stanyforth and Freeman kept wicket for part of the time.

The fifth Test again showed South Africa to advantage. Once more Bissett and Hall kept the English batsmen within bounds, Bissett being absolutely deadly in the second innings; his pace was assisted by a strong wind and he found the knack of making the ball rear up in an alarming manner. South Africa won by eight wickets and deservedly squared the series.

The Union Castle liner *Saxon* brought the tourists back to Southampton, but without Dawson, who stayed behind, having become engaged to be married whilst on tour, and Tyldesley and Sutcliffe, who left the boat in Madeira for a brief holiday.

The failure of the English side to win the rubber was in part due to Geary's injury but also to the weakness of the later batting. Both the all-rounders, Astill and Stevens, failed to make runs in the Tests and since the tail of Stanyforth, Peebles and Freeman could not be relied upon, it made England very vulnerable should any of the leading batsmen fail. South Africa's batting had much more depth and in Bissett they possessed the bowler of the series.

1927-28: by banana boat to Jamaica

The Hon L. H. Tennyson repeated his venture of 1926-27, by taking a team to Jamaica in the spring of 1928. The team travelled in the banana boat *Changuinola* and had a very rough outward

journey. It was therefore not too surprising that Jamaica won the first match, which began on the second day after the tourists' arrival. The team was: Hon L. H. Tennyson (Hants) (capt), T. Arnott (Glamorgan), A. L. Hilder (Kent), M. J. C. Allom (Surrey), Col D. C. Robinson (Gloucs), G. D. Kemp-Welch (Warwicks), F. J. Seabrook (Gloucs), G. J. V. Weigall (Kent), P. T. Eckersley (Lancs), A. K. Judd (Hants) and the professionals C. P. Mead (Hants), G. M. Lee (Derbys), D. Sullivan (Glamorgan) and E. W. Clark (Northants).

The immediate effect of playing the first game so soon after arrival was not only defeat, but also strains to Allom and Clark, which rendered them useless for the rest of the tour. With these two bowlers out of action, the team were in the same state as the previous year—strong batting but no bowlers—and of the two other meetings with All Jamaica, one was lost and the other drawn.

The feature of the cricket was Mead's batting, but Kemp-Welch also played several good innings. Hilder proved to be the best bowler—a lot was expected of Lee, but he was too slow off the pitch. The fielding in general was good, especially Seabrook in the deep and the stumper, Sullivan.

1928-29: great batting by Hobbs, Sutcliffe and Hammond beats Australia

In choosing the side to visit Australia in 1928-29, the M.C.C. departed from its usual custom and instead of the M.C.C. Committee selecting the players, a team of selectors was appointed for the task—Lord Harris, J. W. H. T. Douglas, P. F. Warner, A. E. R. Gilligan, F. T. Mann and H. D. G. Leveson-Gower. The side they picked came in for considerable press criticism, mainly because only one all-rounder—Tate—was chosen, though the absence of Woolley, Hallows and Holmes was also noted.

The party selected was: A. P. F. Chapman (Kent) (capt), J. C. White (Somerset), D. R. Jardine (Surrey) and the professionals J. B. Hobbs (Surrey), G. E. Tyldesley (Lancs), H. Sutcliffe (Yorks), E. H. Hendren (Middx), C. P. Mead (Hants), M. W. Tate (Sussex), M. Leyland (Lancs), H. Larwood (Notts), S. J. Staples (Notts), G. Duckworth (Lancs), L. E. G. Ames (Kent), G. Geary (Leics), W. R. Hammond (Gloucs) and A. P. Freeman (Kent). F. C. Toone was again the manager.

The side left England in two groups, and joined up at Toulon for the voyage on the s.s. *Otranto*. The now traditional one-day game was played in Colombo and the team arrived at Fremantle two days prior to the match against Western Australia. The tourists gave a satisfactory account of themselves in this game,

The M.C.C. party which toured Australia in 1928-29. Back: G. Duckworth, L. E. G. Ames, C. P. Mead, M. W. Tate, E. H. Hendren. Centre: M. Leyland, S. J. Staples, W. R. Hammond, F. C. Toone (manager), H. Sutcliffe, H. Larwood, A. P. Freeman. Front: G. E. Tyldesley, J. C. White, A. P. F. Chapman (captain), D. R. Jardine, J. B. Hobbs. G. Geary is not in the picture.

Below England's two fast bowlers, Harold Larwood and Maurice Tate, on the cross-channel ferry Invicta on 20 April 1929 after the successful tour of Australia.

Sydney the scoring reached new heights. M.C.C. hit 734 for 7 declared, with Hammond, Hendren and Jardin all in three figures, but a young unknown by the name of Bradman scored 87 and 132 not out and with Kippax also making a hundred the fourth draw was recorded.

Victory came at last against An Australian Eleven, when Larwood, Tate and White managed to dismiss this experimental side for under 300 twice – though Bradman carried out his bat for 58. A second win came against the modest Queensland team, before the first Test at Brisbane. Winning the toss, England hit over 500, with a century by Hendren. Larwood then broke the back of the Australian innings and the home team were all out for 122 – Chapman had a lead of 399, but mindful of the runs still in the pitch, he did not enforce the follow-on, and when eventually Australia began their second innings, they faced a target of 742. Larwood took two quick wickets and then overnight rain did the rest, White picking up 4 wickets for 7 runs on the last day. England therefore won the first Test by 675 runs.

Following a country game, the second Test began at Sydney – by this time it had been decided that Staples was not fit enough to continue the tour and he returned home. Australia won the toss and batted. Some good bowling by Geary and Larwood dismissed the home side for 253, though Australia were most unlucky to lose

but press reports of the mounting casualty list were quite frightening. Geary broke his nose in the match, Staples was struck down with rheumatism, Freeman suffered a stiff neck and Tate a strained arm. Freeman was well enough however to appear in the second game, at Adelaide, where very high scoring was the order of the day, nearly 1,400 runs coming for the loss of 24 wickets. Hammond, Chapman and Leyland all made hundreds for the tourists, whilst V. Y. Richardson replied with a double century.

Larwood showed himself in fine form at Melbourne, taking 7 for 51 and dismissing Victoria for 164. Rain and more high scoring then arrived to produce a third drawn match. Tate made his first appearance in this game, but Staples was still too unwell. In

1928-29: M.C.C. to Ceylon and Australia

Batting Averages

		M	I	NO	R	HS	Avge	100	c/s
W. R. Hammond	(Glos)	13	18	1	1553	251	91.35	7	10/3
D. R. Jardine	(Surrey)	12	19	1	1168	214	64.88	6	5
E. H. Hendren	(Middx)	12	17	1	1033	169	64.56	3	8
L. E. G. Ames	(Kent)	8	8	3	295	100*	59.00	1	8/10
J. B. Hobbs	(Surrey)	11	18	1	962	142	56.58	2	2
H. Sutcliffe	(Yorks)	11	16	0	852	135	53.25	2	4
M. Leyland	(Yorks)	12	17	3	614	137	43.85	3	7
C. P. Mead	(Hants)	10	14	3	460	106	41.81	1	2
G. E. Tyldesley	(Lancs)	12	16	2	509	81	36.35	0	4
A. P. F. Chapman	(Kent)	14	17	1	533	145	33.31	1	23
H. Larwood	(Notts)	13	14	0	367	79	26.21	0	8
M. W. Tate	(Sussex)	13	17	1	322	59	20.12	0	8
G. Geary	(Leics)	12	16	3	215	66	16.53	0	7
J. C. White	(Som)	15	18	7	137	30	12.45	0	7
G. Duckworth	(Lancs)	9	13	6	84	39*	12.00	0	17/4
A. P. Freeman	(Kent)	10	7	3	42	11	10.50	0	1

Bowling Averages

	Balls	M	R	W	Avge	BB	5i
J. C. White	5213	223	1471	65	22.63	8-126	5
G. Geary	2757	104	956	37	25.83	5-35	3
M. W. Tate	4072	174	1329	44	30.11	5-35	1
H. Larwood	2726	61	1254	40	31.35	7-51	2
A. P. Freeman	2323	32	1136	35	32.45	5-51	3
W. R. Hammond	1594	50	661	11	60.09	3-53	0
M. Leyland	742	12	357	4	89.25	2-37	0

Also bowled: D. R. Jardine 112-3-67-2; G. Duckworth 8-0-7-0; E. H. Hendren 120-2-57-0; C. P. Mead 8-0-11-0; H. Sutcliffe 32-1-18-0.
S. J. Staples (Notts) was selected for the tour and travelled to Australia, but was taken ill before he played in a match and was sent home.

Some of the 1928-29 touring party to Australia photographed at the Scarborough festival in 1928. Left to right: Macaulay (who did not tour), M. Leyland, G. Geary, A. P. F. Chapman, W. R. Hammond, G. Duckworth, G. E. Tyldesley, H. Sutcliffe, J. B. Hobbs, E. H. Hendren, M. W. Tate.

Ponsford with a broken wrist. On the second day, the crowd numbered 58,456—a new record—and England through Hammond gradually built a commanding lead. Australia did better in their second innings, Woodfull and Hendry making hundreds, but they still lost by 8 wickets.

1928-29: M.C.C. to Ceylon and Australia

1st Match: v Ceylon (Colombo) (One Day)   Oct 6.
Ceylon 96-7 dec lost to M.C.C. 150-6 (A. P. F. Chapman 60, J. B. Hobbs 54) by 10 wkts.

2nd Match: v Western Australia (Perth)   Oct 18, 19, 20.
M.C.C. 406 (D. R. Jardine 109, E. H. Hendren 90, G. E. Tyldesley 66) & 26-0 drew with W. Australia 257 (W. Horrocks 75*, F. Bryant 61).

3rd Match: v South Australia (Adelaide)   Oct 26, 27, 29, 30.
M.C.C. 528 (W. R. Hammond 145, A. P. F. Chapman 145, H. Sutcliffe 76, C. P. Mead 58, C. V. Grimmett 6-109) & 341-4 (M. Leyland 114, H. Sutcliffe 70, J. B. Hobbs 64, C. P. Mead 58*) drew with S. Australia 524 (V. Y. Richardson 231, D. E. Pritchard 119, A. P. Freeman 5-180).

4th Match: v Victoria (Melbourne)   Nov 1, 2, 3, 5.
Victoria 164 (W. M. Woodfull 67*, H. Larwood 7-51) & 135-0 (H. S. T. L. Hendry 74*, W. H. Ponsford 60*) drew with M.C.C. 486 (D. R. Jardine 104, E. H. Hendren 100, H. Larwood 79, A. P. F. Chapman 71, J. B. Hobbs 51).

5th Match: v New South Wales (Sydney)   Nov 9, 10, 12, 13.
M.C.C. 734-7 dec (W. R. Hammond 225, E. H. Hendren 167, D. R. Jardine 140) drew with N.S.W. 349 (C. Kelleway 93*, D. G. Bradman 87, A. F. Kippax 64, A. P. Freeman 5-136) & 364-3 (A. F. Kippax 136*, D. G. Bradman 132*).

6th Match: v An Australian XI (Sydney)   Nov 16, 17, 19, 20.
Australian XI 231 (D. G. Bradman 58*) & 243 (A. Jackson 61, G. W. Harris 56) lost to M.C.C. 357 (G. E. Tyldesley 69, M. W. Tate 59, C. P. Mead 58, J. B. Hobbs 58) & 118-2 (J. B. Hobbs 67*) by 8 wkts.

7th Match: v Queensland (Brisbane)   Nov 24, 26, 27.
Queensland 116 (A. P. Freeman 5-51) & 160 (J. L. Litster 59, G. Geary 5-47) lost to M.C.C. 293 (M. Leyland 114, O. E. Nothling 5-78) by an inns & 17 runs.

8th Match: v Australia (Brisbane)   Nov 30, Dec 1, 3, 4, 5.
England 521 (E. H. Hendren 169, H. Larwood 70, A. P. F. Chapman 50) & 342-8 dec (C. P. Mead 73, D. R. Jardine 65*, C. V. Grimmett 6-131) beat Australia 122 (H. Larwood 6-32) & 66 by 675 runs.

9th Match: v Combined Country XI (Warwick)   Dec 8, 10.
Country XI 128 (A. P. Freeman 8-32) & 213 (A. P. Freeman 7-74) lost to M.C.C. 510 (G. E. Tyldesley 115, W. R. Hammond 110, H. Sutcliffe 77, M. Leyland 67*) by an inns & 169 runs.

10th Match: v Australia (Sydney)   Dec 14, 15, 17, 18, 19, 20.
Australia 253 (W. M. Woodfull 68, G. Geary 5-35) & 397 (H. S. T. L. Hendry 112, W. M. Woodfull 111, J. Ryder 79) lost to England 636 (W. R. Hammond 251, E. H. Hendren 74, G. Geary 66) & 16-2 by 8 wkts.

11th Match: v Newcastle & Hunter District XI (Newcastle)   Dec 21, 22.
District XI 350-9 dec (O. Osland 78, F. Henderson 60, R. H. B. Bettington 53) drew with M.C.C. 281 (H. Larwood 92).

12th Match: v Australia (Melbourne)   Dec 29, 31, Jan 1, 2, 3, 4, 5.
Australia 397 (J. Ryder 112, A. F. Kippax 100, D. G. Bradman 79) & 351 (D. G. Bradman 112, W. M. Woodfull 107, J. C. White 5-107) lost to England 417 (W. R. Hammond 200, D. R. Jardine 62, H. Sutcliffe 58, D. D. Blackie 6-94) & 332-7 (H. Sutcliffe 135) by 3 wkts.

13th Match: v XII of Geelong (Geelong) (One Day)   Jan 7.
M.C.C. 289-7 dec (H. Sutcliffe 56, J. B. Hobbs 50) drew with Geelong 124-6 (A. W. H. Urbahns 51).

14th Match: v XIII of Bendigo (Bendigo)   Jan 9, 10.
M.C.C. 305 (E. H. Hendren 73, G. E. Tyldesley 52) & 255 (D. R. Jardine 83*, W. R. Hammond 73) drew with Bendigo 168 (J. Thomas 63*, H. Larwood 6-20).

15th Match: v Tasmania (Launceston)   Jan 12, 14, 15.
Tasmania 229 (G. F. Martin 92) & 137 (M. W. Tate 5-35) lost to M.C.C. 482-8 dec (D. R. Jardine 214, C. P. Mead 106) by an inns & 116 runs.

16th Match: v Tasmania (Hobart)   Jan 18, 19.
Tasmania 66 & 93 lost to M.C.C. 223 (L. E. G. Ames 100*) by an inns & 64 runs.

17th Match: v South Australia (Adelaide)   Jan 25, 26, 28, 29.
M.C.C. 392 (H. Sutcliffe 122, E. H. Hendren 90, J. B. Hobbs 75, T. A. Carlton 5-64) & 307-5 dec (D. R. Jardine 114, J. B. Hobbs 101, L. E. G. Ames 51*) drew with S. Australia 178 (V. Y. Richardson 82, J. C. White 7-66) & 75-1.

18th Match: v Australia (Adelaide)   Feb 1, 2, 4, 5, 6, 7, 8.
England 334 (W. R. Hammond 119*, J. B. Hobbs 74, H. Sutcliffe 64, C. V. Grimmett 5-102) & 383 (W. R. Hammond 177, D. R. Jardine 98) beat Australia 369 (A. Jackson 164, J. Ryder 63, J. C. White 5-130) & 336 (J. Ryder 87, D. G. Bradman 58, A. F. Kippax 51, J. C. White 8-126) by 12 runs.

19th Match: v XIII of Ballarat (Ballarat)   Feb 9, 11.
M.C.C. 493-9 dec (L. E. G. Ames 127, J. B. Hobbs 82*, M. Leyland 75, G. E. Tyldesley 65, E. H. Hendren 61, G. Bennetts 7-127) drew with Ballarat 77 (A. P. Freeman 7-26) & 176-7.

20th Match: v New South Wales (Sydney)   Feb 15, 16, 18, 19.
N.S.W. 128 (J. C. White 5-48) drew with M.C.C. 144-4 (G. E. Tyldesley 68).

21st Match: v Western Districts (Bathurst)   Feb 21, 22.
M.C.C. 319 (L. E. G. Ames 123, G. E. Tyldesley 50) beat Western Districts 127 (H. Larwood 5-17) & 81 (A. P. Freeman 8-31).

22nd Match: v XIII of Southern Districts (Goulburn)   Feb 25, 26.
M.C.C. 250 (L. E. G. Ames 94, J. B. Hobbs 54, W. Lampe 5-46) & 226-5 dec (D. R. Jardine 85*) drew with Southern Districts 135 (A. P. Freeman 8-66) & 135-4 (A. Allsopp 79*).

23rd Match: v Victoria (Melbourne)   March 1, 2, 4, 5.
Victoria 572-9 dec (W. M. Woodfull 275*, L. S. Darling 87, J. Ryder 60) drew with M.C.C. 303 (W. R. Hammond 114, G. E. Tyldesley 81) & 308-3 (D. R. Jardine 115, G. E. Tyldesley 68*, M. Leyland 54).

24th Match: v Australia (Melbourne)   March 8, 9, 11, 12, 13, 14, 15, 16.
England 519 (J. B. Hobbs 142, M. Leyland 137, E. H. Hendren 95) & 257 (J. B. Hobbs 65, M. W. Tate 54, M. Leyland 53*, T. W. Wall 5-66) lost to Australia 491 (D. G. Bradman 123, W. M. Woodfull 102, A. G. Fairfax 65, G. Geary 5-105) & 287-5 (J. Ryder 57*) by 5 wkts.

25th Match: v An Australian XI (Perth)   March 21, 22, 23.
An Australian XI 310 (A. J. Richardson 101*, H. Rowe 73) & 186-3 (J. Ryder 81*, W. Horrocks 76) drew with M.C.C. 241 (W. R. Hammond 80).

Just over a week later, the third Test began—it was vital for Australia to win. Ryder certainly won the toss and batted, and he and Kippax both hit hundreds, but Hammond replied with a double century, so that the game remained level at the half-way mark. Bradman hit his first Test century in the second innings, leaving England with 332 to get on a wicket damaged by rain—most of the press appeared to believe that the visitors would be lucky to reach 100. Hobbs and Sutcliffe opened the batting and played a dead bat at everything that needed playing, whilst ignoring virtually all the other deliveries. The opening partnership of 105 was in the opinion of many the best piece of batting ever seen in a Test Match—Hobbs was out on 49, Sutcliffe, with the wicket easing all the time went on to 135, and England won the match by 3 wickets and with it the series. The total attendance was 262,467 and the receipts £22,561 18s.

The tourists then played four minor matches and a game against South Australia, before coming to the fourth Test at Adelaide. As can be seen from the four innings totals—334, 369, 383 and 336—the game was very finely balanced. England relied heavily on Hammond in their batting, and the Gloucester player hit two hundreds, whilst Australia owed most to Jackson who signalled his debut with a marvellous innings of 164. In the end England won a great match by 12 runs.

In the final Test Australia received some consolation—the scoring was generally very slow and the match dragged on for eight days, but Australia broke down the English batting in the second innings and had little difficulty in winning by 5 wickets. A concluding game was played at Perth and the team sailed home on the *Ormonde*, arriving in Toulon on 20 April and in England the following day.

Although Hammond was perhaps the success of the tour, the innings of Hobbs and Sutcliffe were also of great importance, as were those of Jardine. The surprise of the visit was possibly White, who bowled uncommonly well, his slow left-arm spin keeping all the batsmen quiet. Tate also did magnificent work throughout. Larwood bowled well at the start of the tour, but tired later and Geary also bowled well. Chapman led the side with flair, but his batting was not very sound. The public interest in the Tests was enormous and so were the profits—£17,968. There was a lot of adverse comment on the barracking, but apart from in one Victorian match, it was not exceptional.

1928-29: Julien Cahn's trip to Jamaica

For the third time in as many years, a privately organised tour went out to Jamaica. On this occasion, the team was that of Julien Cahn, the well-known Nottingham patron of the game.

The team was Lord Tennyson (Hants), E. W. Dawson (Leics), F. W. H. Nicholas (Essex), A. L. Hilder (Kent), F. C. W. Newman (Surrey) and W. H. Vaulkhard and the professionals A. Sandham (Surrey), J. Iddon (Lancs), W. E. Astill (Leics), H. A. Peach (Surrey), W. W. Whysall (Notts), J. O'Connor (Essex), M. S. Nichols (Essex), B. Lilley (Notts), J. Mercer (Glamorgan), F. J. Durston (Middx) and G. Shaw (Trent Bridge pavilion attendant).

The professionals travelled from Avonmouth on the *Comito* sailing direct to Kingston, whilst the amateurs sailed on the *Mauretania* from Southampton to New York, and the two parties joined forces in Jamaica on 14 February.

Julien Cahn, with his wife, as well as Mrs F. W. H. Nicholas also accompanied the tourists.

After an opening odds match, the first game against All Jamaica began on 21 February. In a very high-scoring game, the home

Julien Cahn's privately organised party which toured Jamaica in 1928-29. Back: G. Shaw, W. W. Whysall, J. Iddon, A. L. Hilder, F. J. Durston, M. S. Nichols, J. Mercer, W. E. Astill, H. A. Peach. Front: Unknown, A. Sandham, Lord Tennyson, J. Cahn, E. W. Dawson, F. W. H. Nicholas, B. Lilley, J. O'Connor.

side won by 7 wickets; unfortunately Cahn was injured and unable to play in the remaining matches. The second match against Jamaica was drawn, but in the third the tourists met with another defeat, though Sandham batted splendidly in both innings. The third game was in fact against a West Indies team, since Constantine, Small and Francis reinforced the local side. Judging by the strength of Cahn's team there was little doubt that cricket in Jamaica was making considerable progress. The tourists were most impressed by the batting of George Headley.

The team returned to England on 2 April.

1928-29: Julien Cahn's Team to Jamaica

1st Match: v Jamaica Next XV (Melbourne Pk)   Feb 18, 19.
Next XV 342-8 dec (F. C. Isaacs 71, A. L. Silvera 51) drew with Cahn's XI 290 (J. O'Connor 114, W. E. Astill 53).*

2nd Match: v Jamaica (Melbourne Pk)   Feb 21, 22, 25.
Cahn's XI 217 (J. Iddon 72, L. G. Hylton 5-24) & 336 (H. A. Peach 75, F. W. H. Nicholas 63, J. O'Connor 63) lost to Jamaica 503 (J. K. Holt 128, R. K. Nunes 112, I. Barrow 61, G. A. Headley 57, J. O'Connor 5-96) & 51-3 by 7 wkts.*

3rd Match: v Garrison XIII (Camp St Andrew)   Feb 26.
Garrison XIII 121 (J. Mercer 7-23) lost to Cahn's XI 196-9 (A. L. Hilder 63).

4th Match: v Jamaica (Sabina Pk)   Feb 27, 28, March 1.
Jamaica 462 (E. R. Rae 121, W. Beckford 74, F. R. Martin 64) & 211-9 dec (W. E. Astill 7-60) drew with Cahn's XI 343 (W. W. Whysall 80, Lord Tennyson 78, F. W. H. Nicholas 64, O. C. Scott 6-135) & 226-5 (Lord Tennyson 105).*

5th Match: v M.C.C. XV (Port Maria)   March 5, 6.
Cahn's XI 415 (W. W. Whysall 105, A. Sandham 66, J. O'Connor 56, B. Lilley 54) drew with M.C.C. XV 215-5 (H. B. Young 82, Lee Carr 72).*

6th Match: v West Indian XI (Sabina Park)   March 12, 13, 14, 15, 16.
West Indian XI 317 (J. K. Holt 128, E. A. Rae 64) & 447 (G. A. Headley 143, J. K. Holt 56) beat Cahn's XI 271 (A. Sandham 159, J. A. Small 7-77) & 349 (W. E. Astill 83, A. Sandham 62, J. Iddon 62) by 144 runs.*

1929: Martineau takes a team to Egypt

H. M. Martineau, who was a great supporter of cricket and ran a team based at his country house near Maidenhead, undertook the first of eleven tours to Egypt in the spring of 1929. His team contained a number of well-known amateur cricketers and though perhaps not as strong as the sides fielded by Julien Cahn was certainly on the borderline of 'first-class' by English standards. The touring party was: H. M. Martineau (capt), A. C. Johnston (Hants), L. C. R. Isherwood (Sussex), S. A. Block (Surrey), R. W. Skene (Oxford U), R. S. G. Scott (Oxford U), F. O. G. Lloyd, I. S. Akers-Douglas, C. H. Knott (Kent), C. K. Hill-Wood (Derbys) and G. E. C. Wood (Kent).

The tour consisted of five matches, played during the first two weeks in April, and the two most important fixtures were both three-day games against All Egypt. The first was a draw, but in the second Egypt seemed certain to win, setting the tourists 286 to make in their last innings. Akers-Douglas and Block however added 159 for the second wicket and the tourists won by 4 wickets.

1929: H. M. Martineau's Team to Egypt

1st Match: v Alexandria (Alexandria)   April 2, 3.
Martineau's XI 457-6 dec (C. H. Knott 151, R. W. Skeyne 116, A. C. Johnston 68) drew with Alexandria 231 (H. W. Grant 66) & 300-3 (M. C. O'Brian 118*, C. I. Thomas 68, J. de V. Biss 67*).*

2nd Match: v Gezira Sporting Club (Cairo)   April 5, 6.
Gezira Sporting Club 104 & 319 (J. H. de la Mare 102, H. S. Mitchell 99) drew with Martineau's XI 189 (R. W. Skene 50) & 145-8.

3rd Match: v All Egypt (Cairo)   April 8, 9.
Martineau's XI 310-8 dec (S. A. Block 93, C. H. Knott 90 & 170-5 dec (I. S. Akers-Douglas 67*) drew with All Egypt 194 (J. C. de V. Biss 74) & 151-7 (H. S. Mitchell 50).*

4th Match: v The Army (Cairo)   April 11, 12.
Army 283 (Rusbridge 54, Pope 53) & 223-5 dec (H. S. Mitchell 76, R. C. G. Joy 53*) drew with Martineau's XI 299 (L. C. R. Isherwood 98) & 96-5.*

5th Match: v All Egypt (Alexandria)   April 15, 16, 17.
All Egypt 217 (A. R. I. Mellor 75, R. C. G. Joy 53) & 327 (H. S. Mitchell 68, R. A. Rusbridge 69, G. S. Duckworth 51) lost to Martineau's XI 261 (C. H. Knott 88) & 286-6 (I. S. Akers-Douglas 142, S. A. Block 67) by 4 wkts.*

1929-30: Duleepsinhji wins praise in New Zealand

The M.C.C. took the unique step of organising two Test-playing tours in the winter of 1929–30, this one and that which follows, to West Indies. Obviously both teams could not be representative of England's full strength and in fact neither were. Not because the talents were evenly distributed between the two, but because many of the leading English players of 1929 remained aloof from both. The side which travelled to New Zealand was to be led by A. E. R. Gilligan, but because of ill-health he had to stand down and his brother took over the leadership. The party which sailed on 28 September aboard the R.M.S. *Orford* was A. H. H. Gilligan (Sussex) (capt), K. S. Duleepsinhji (Sussex), E. W. Dawson (Leics), G. B. Legge (Kent), M. J. L. Turnbull (Glamorgan), M. J. C. Allom (Surrey), G. F. Earle (Somerset), E. T. Benson (Oxford U), and the professionals F. E. Woolley (Kent), E. H. Bowley (Sussex), M. S. Nichols (Essex), T. S. Worthington (Derbys), F. Barratt (Notts) and W. L. Cornford (Sussex).

After the one-day game in Colombo, the side commenced the first-class section of the tour at Perth on 31 October. In this match and in the following one against South Australia the tourists won with ease, due to some effective bowling. Against the stronger Victorian team, things went well initially, but in the end Woodfull hit a good hundred to provide the state with a win by 7 wickets. As might have been expected the New South Wales side toyed with the tourists' attack, hundreds coming from Bradman, Kippax, Allsopp and Jackson, plus 90 from McCabe, but the M.C.C. were undaunted, Woolley made a double century, and the match was drawn. The visitors suffered a crop of injuries: Barratt had to stop bowling due to a strained arm, Bowley aggravated an old leg injury and also had to retire from bowling, whilst Nichols, suffering from tonsilitis, could not play. Cornford had received a bad cut over the eye in the previous game, but came on the field as a substitute, as indeed did Nichols. In the match against Queensland, Ducat, who was coaching in Australia, was co-opted into the side. There was a twelve-day break in the programme whilst the team made their way to New Zealand and this helped some of the injured to recover, though Bowley was out of action with sciatica until the end of January. The first six matches in New Zealand however caused the tourists few problems. The

---

1929-30: M.C.C. to Ceylon, Australia and New Zealand

Batting Averages

	M	I	NO	R	HS	Avge	100	c/s
K. S. Duleepsinhji (Sussex)	13	22	4	890	117	49.44	1	17
F. E. Woolley (Kent)	12	18	1	780	219	45.88	3	12
E. H. Bowley (Sussex)	6	7	1	256	109	42.66	1	3
M. S. Nichols (Essex)	11	17	5	482	82	40.16	0	11
G. B. Legge (Kent)	9	14	2	453	196	37.75	1	1
A. H. H. Gilligan (Sussex)	13	18	0	523	70	29.05	0	1
E. W. Dawson (Leics)	13	22	1	548	83*	26.09	0	2
T. S. Worthington (Derbys)	13	15	0	370	125	24.66	1	7
M. J. L. Turnbull (Glam)	8	13	2	232	100	21.09	1	6
G. F. Earle (Som)	7	10	0	191	49	19.10	0	4
M. J. C. Allom (Surrey)	12	15	10	82	18*	16.40	0	5
F. Barratt (Notts)	11	14	2	173	46	14.41	0	2
A. Ducat (Surrey)	1	2	0	23	13	11.50	0	0
E. T. Benson (Oxford U)	4	5	0	48	29	9.60	0	4/1
W. L. Cornford (Sussex)	10	13	2	104	29	9.45	0	18/8

Bowling Averages

	Balls	M	R	W	Avge	BB	5i
M. S. Nichols	1871	43	791	43	18.39	8-65	2
G. F. Earle	30	1	20	1	20.00	1-20	0
F. E. Woolley	1863	69	850	36	23.61	7-76	2
M. J. C. Allom	2384	67	961	39	24.64	5-26	2
G. B. Legge	84	0	78	3	26.00	3-24	0
T. S. Worthington	1782	56	806	30	26.86	3-16	0
K. S. Duleepsinhji	158	0	135	5	27.00	4-49	0
E. H. Bowley	626	13	353	12	29.41	5-30	1
F. Barratt	2260	55	887	27	32.85	5-32	2

Also bowled: E. W. Dawson 24-0-30-0; W. L. Cornford 42-3-20-0.

first Test took place at Christchurch. Allom and Nichols proved too much for the home batsmen and any chances New Zealand had of winning the match were thrown away by poor fielding.

The second Test produced much higher scoring. New Zealand began with an opening partnership worth 276 by Mills and Dempster though Woolley tricked out nearly all the others cheaply and England were never in danger of defeat, the match,

restricted to three days, petering out in a draw.

In the match against Auckland, Benson was adjudged out 'handled ball', though the Auckland wicket-keeper declared that the batsman did not even touch the ball!

Rain washed out the third Test, but not before Bowley and Duleepsinhji had hit centuries, Duleepsinhji's innings was described as the best seen in New Zealand in recent years. Because of the waterlogged third Test, an extra Test was staged, but this was just a high-scoring draw and the tour ended with a win at New Plymouth over Taranaki.

The team travelled home via the Panama Canal in the *Rangitane* and landed back in England on 2 April. The success of the tour was Duleepsinhji, whose batting won great praise. Both the veteran Woolley and young Nichols performed good work as all-rounders. Allom bowled well, his fast deliveries having plenty of life. Turnbull however was a disappointment, as was Barratt, who did well only in Australia. The fielding was very variable, so was Cornford's wicket-keeping.

The New Zealanders had good batsmen, but the bowling was weak and the fielding generally poor. The umpiring, especially in the minor matches, was very moderate.

1929-30: Sandham's 325 in the West Indies

The second major touring party of 1929-30 set off for the West Indies on 14 December aboard the *Carare* from Avonmouth. The team was the Hon F. S. Gough-Calthorpe (Warwicks) (capt), R. T. Stanyforth (Army), N. E. Haig (Middx), G. T. S. Stevens (Middx), R. E. S. Wyatt (Warwicks) and the professionals W. Rhodes (Yorks), G. Gunn (Notts), E. H. Hendren (Middx), W. E. Astill (Leics), A. Sandham (Surrey), L. E. G. Ames (Kent), J. O'Connor (Essex), L. F. Townsend (Derbys), W. Voce (Notts) and, on the advice of previous tourists, J. Hardstaff (Notts) as umpire. R. H. Mallett also accompanied the team as honorary manager. Although the team was by no means representative of England's full strength, it was probably the best side England had ever sent to the West Indies.

Arriving in Bridgetown on 27 December, the tourists played their first match against Barbados commencing on New Year's Day. Barbados batted and hit 345, with a 17-year-old—J. E. D.

Left *Bill Voce (below signature) and George Gunn (holding pipe and raincoat) being seen off on 14 December 1929 for the tour of the West Indies. Among those wishing them well are fellow Nottinghamshire players S. J. Staples (below signature) and Harold Larwood (to Gunn's left).*

Below *The party for the tour of the West Indies in 1929-30. With the captain, the Hon F. S. Gough-Calthorpe in the centre, the remaining players, clockwise from manager R. H. Mallett on the left are: N. E. Haig, G. Gunn, E. H. Hendren, R. E. S. Wyatt, A. Sandham, L. F. Townsend, G. T. S. Stevens, Capt R. T. Stanyforth, W. Rhodes, W. Voce, J. Hardstaff (umpire), L. E. G. Ames, J. O'Connor, W. E. Astill.*

Sealy—scoring exactly 100. The M.C.C. however were not over-awed by the infant prodigy and Hendren hit 223 not out in 330 minutes as the total reached 513. Rain interfered with play and the match was drawn. Hendren went on to hit another double century in the second match—the return against Barbados—and M.C.C. again exceeded 500 in another drawn match.

The third game played in Bridgetown was the first Test. Wyatt, who injured his foot was not available, but he was hardly required. The match was another high-scoring draw, though England would probably have won if time had allowed. Headley and Roach hit hundreds for the home team, whilst Sandham did likewise for England. Hendren contented himself with 80 and 36 not out. It was Hendren's flair for the hook shot that brought him so many runs. The West Indian fast bowling was just his cup of tea.

Going on to Trinidad, the tourists met matting wickets for the first time and the scoring dropped considerably. In the first game against the Colony, the team met its first defeat, but in the return, again with low scores, they had their revenge. Voce bowled exceptionally well and took 12 wickets, his medium-pace deliveries gathering speed off the wicket.

In the second Test, West Indies gained a first innings lead of 46, but Hendren immediately put the deficit to rights with yet another double century and enabled England to declare, setting West Indies 380 to win. Voce had all the home batsmen in trouble and taking 7 for 70 took England to a fine victory. It was during this Test and the preceding one that 'bodyline' bowling was experienced by the English batsmen, the leading exponent being Constantine, who kept up a continual barrage of bouncers round the batsman's head. The tactics of the England opener, Gunn, were of course designed to infuriate the fast West Indian bowlers. Gunn would start walking down the wicket before the ball was delivered and could play a dead bat shot which left the ball just a few feet in front of him. The West Indian press described Gunn as 'The man who walks about the pitch and tickles the ball where he likes'.

During one of Hendren's innings, when two unsuccessful appeals had been made, a wag in the crowd shouted, 'How much Patsy gib you, Mr Hardstaff?'

After the relatively low scores of Trinidad, the party sailed on to British Guiana—Hendren made another double century in the opening match there and M.C.C. won by an innings. Wyatt had recovered from his injured foot, but Stanyforth was injured and the manager cabled to England for another wicket-keeper. Price of Middlesex was sent out. British Guiana were also beaten by an innings in the return match, though Hendren managed only 171. In the third Test, England's fielding was very poor, numerous catches going down, and as the tourists' batting also failed in the

first innings, West Indies won with ease. Headley hit a century in each innings.

The final leg of the tour was in Jamaica. The first game against the Colony was drawn, with Gunn and Sandham creating a new record by adding 322 for the first wicket in M.C.C.'s second innings. The return was also a high-scoring draw, but when it came to the fourth Test, it was agreed, since each team had won one match so far, the game should be played to a finish. England hit 849 in the opening innings, with Sandham making 325 in ten hours batting. The West Indies scored only 286, but Gough-Calthorpe did not enforce the follow on, a tactic which brought him much criticism at the time. When England declared in their second innings, West Indies required 836 to win. Rain prevented any play for two days and when West Indies were 408 for 5, the match had to end to enable the English team to catch the boat home.

The tourists arrived back in England on 27 April. The matches had been well attended throughout the tour, which had been most successful. The outstanding cricketer was undoubtedly Hendren, but Sandham, Ames and Gunn also could point to good returns. The bowlers had to work hard for their wickets, with Rhodes, Stevens, Voce and Astill the best of the bunch.

1929-30: Sir Julien Cahn's team in the Argentine

For the second successive winter, Sir Julien Cahn took a side across the Atlantic, this time to visit the Argentine. The team sailed from Tilbury on the *Avelona Star* on 20 February, bound for Buenos Aires. The full party was Sir Julien Cahn (capt), F. W. H. Nicholas (Essex), F. C. W. Newman (Surrey), T. Arnott (Glamorgan), L. Green (Lancs), P. T. Eckersley (Lancs), H. R. Munt (Middx), R. W. V. Robins (Middx), H. R. S. Critchley-Salmonson (Somerset), G. F. H. Heane (Notts), S. D. Rhodes (Notts), C. W. Flood, C. A. Rowland and the two old Notts professionals J. R. Gunn and T. L. Richmond. H. D. Swan of Essex also accompanied the team.

Six matches were played in all, but the ones of importance were the three 'Tests' against Argentina. Some good bowling by Robins provided the tourists with victory in the 'First Test'. In the 'Second' they were lucky to scrape a draw and the 'Third' was also drawn, but in favour of the visitors. Owing to a split finger whilst practising before the first match of the tour, Rowland was unable to appear in any of the matches. The tourists found the standard of cricket fairly high in the Argentine and the cricket grounds excellent.

The side returned to England on the *Avila Star*, disembarking at Plymouth on 23 April.

1930: Egypt win a 'Test'

Mr Martineau took his second team to Egypt in April 1930 and again the programme was one of five matches, with two 'Tests' against All Egypt. In the 'First' Lloyd and Peebles dismissed Egypt for 77 whilst the tourists hit 400 and went on to win by an innings. The Egyptians however played much better in the return at Alexandria and though Peebles took ten wickets, including a hat-trick, and C. H. Knott hit 123 in a defiant second innings, the tourists were beaten by 62 runs.

The touring team was H. M. Martineau (capt), F. O. G. Lloyd, R. S. G. Scott (Sussex), C. H. Knott (Kent), C. K. Hill-Wood (Derbys), A. C. Johnston (Hants), I. A. R. Peebles (Middx), J. F. N. Mayhew (Oxford U), R. M. Handfield-Jones, W. G. L. F. Lowndes (Hants) and J. C. Masterman.

Knott was the outstanding bat of the tour, whilst Peebles took the bowling honours.

1930: H. M. Martineau's Team to Egypt

1st Match: v Alexandria (Alexandria)   April 1, 2.
Martineau's XI 355 (H. M. Martineau 104, C. K. Hill Wood 58) & 300-3 dec (A. C. Johnston 125*, W. G. Lowndes 74, C. H. Knott 70*) drew with Alexandria 326 (M. E. O'Brian 134, G. S. Duckworth 68*) & 183-5 (M. E. O'Brian 89).

2nd Match: v The Army (Cairo)   April 4, 5.
The Army 275 (R. A. Rusbridge 56, J. D. Radford 50) & 190 (E. S. Cole 57) drew with Martineau's XI 247 & 184-7 (C. H. Knott 62).

3rd Match: v Gezira Sporting Club (Cairo)   April 7, 8.
Gezira Sporting Club 228 (E. S. Cole 95*) & 245 (H. R. Holme 68, E. T. Castagli 57) lost to Martineau's XI 405-7 dec (W. G. Lowndes 180, C. H. Knott 130) & 70-7 by 3 wkts.

4th Match: v All Egypt (Cairo)   April 11, 12, 13.
All Egypt 77 & 183-5 drew with Martineau's XI 400 (R. S. Scott 96, C. K. Hill Wood 91, A. C. Johnston 68).

5th Match: All Egypt (Alexandria)   April 14, 15, 16.
All Egypt 297 (M. E. O'Brian 121, E. S. Cole 59) & 226 (K. F. Miles 54) beat Martineau's XI 182 & 279 (C. H. Knott 123) by 62 runs.

1930-31: South Africa win Test series

The team which went out on the *Edinburgh Castle* on 17 October to tour South Africa had two notable omissions in Sutcliffe and Larwood, and the fact that the Yorkshire batsman was not selected came in for a great deal of criticism, which by the end of the visit was proved justified.

Of those who were originally chosen in mid-July, only Ames was forced to stand down and his place was taken by Farrimond. The full party was: A. P. F. Chapman (Kent) (capt), J. C. White (Somerset), R. E. S. Wyatt (Warwicks), M. J. L. Turnbull (Glamorgan), I. A. R. Peebles (Middx), M. J. C. Allom (Surrey) and the professionals W. R. Hammond (Gloucs), E. H. Hendren (Middx), M. Leyland (Yorks), M. W. Tate (Sussex), T. W. J. Goddard (Gloucs), W. Voce (Notts), G. Duckworth (Lancs), W. Farrimond (Lancs) and A. Sandham (Surrey). The manager who joined the team in South Africa was W. Sewell – apparently the sole applicant for the job!

The arrival in Cape Town was followed by a warm-up game against a Colts Fifteen, before the initial first-class match against Western Province. This game and the two that came after it proved easy ones for the tourists, but at this point Sandham was injured in a motor accident and was unable to play again on the tour.

Meeting the strongest Province, Transvaal, at Johannesburg without Sandham and with Allom developing a chill and unable to bowl in the second innings, M.C.C. were lucky to get away with a draw. Travelling on to Rhodesia, the injury list lengthened. Hendren, Duckworth and Goddard all went down with 'flu, so

---

1930-31: M.C.C. to South Africa

1st Match: v Western Province Schools XV (Cape Town)   Nov 6.
W.P. Schools XV 115 (M. Leyland 7-7) lost to M.C.C. 294-6 (E. H. Hendren 100, R. E. S. Wyatt 58, A. Sandham 53) by 8 wkts.

2nd Match: v Western Province (Cape Town)   Nov 8, 10, 11.
W. Province 113 (M. W. Tate 5-18) & 122 lost to M.C.C. 412-7 dec (R. E. S. Wyatt 138, W. R. Hammond 100, A. Sandham 72, E. H. Hendren 58*) by an inns & 177 runs.

3rd Match: v Griqualand West (Kimberley)   Nov 15, 17, 18.
Griqualand West 310 (X. C. Balaskas 83, F. Nicholson 57) & 156-2 dec drew with M.C.C. 232 (W. Voce 57, W. R. Hammond 53, N. A. Quinn 5-56).

4th Match: v Natal (Durban)   Nov 21, 22, 23.
Natal 288 (J. Easterbrook 64, T. Woods 55, M. W. Tate 5-64) & 114-2 drew with M.C.C. 402 (A. P. F. Chapman 80, W. R. Hammond 75, R. E. S. Wyatt 63, E. H. Hendren 51).

5th Match: v Transvaal (Johannesburg)   Nov 29, Dec 1, 2.
M.C.C. 238 (W. R. Hammond 70, R. E. S. Wyatt 58) & 195 drew with Transvaal 176 (I. A. R. Peebles 5-45) & 206-4 (S. H. Curnow 83*, H. W. Taylor 56).

6th Match: v Rhodesia (Bulawayo)   Dec 6, 8, 9.
M.C.C. 278 (R. E. S. Wyatt 78, D. S. Tomlinson 5-106) & 322 (M. Leyland 169) drew with Rhodesia 248 (Hayward 95, Symington 60, I. A. R. Peebles 6-57).

7th Match: v Northern Rhodesia (Livingstone) (One Day)   Dec 11.
N. Rhodesia 73 lost to M.C.C. 234-9 (M. Leyland 65, M. J. L. Turnbull 63) by 9 wkts.

8th Match: v Transvaal (Johannesburg)   Dec 16, 17, 18.
M.C.C. 317 (A. P. F. Chapman 87, E. H. Hendren 75, C. L. Vincent 6-54) drew with Transvaal 279 (B. Mitchell 56, H. W. Taylor 54, M. W. Tate 5-55).

9th Match: v Transvaal Cricket Union (Berea Pk) (One Day)   Dec 19.
M.C.C. 39-0: rain.

10th Match: v South Africa (Johannesburg)   Dec 24, 25, 26.
South Africa 126 & 306 (B. Mitchell 72, R. H. Catterall 54, H. B. Cameron 51) beat England 193 (E. P. Nupen 5-63) & 211 (W. R. Hammond 63, M. J. L. Turnbull 61, E. P. Nupen 6-87) by 218 runs.

11th Match: v South Africa (Cape Town)   Jan 1, 2, 3, 5.
South Africa 513-8 dec (I. J. Siedle 141, B. Mitchell 123, H. W. Taylor 117, R. H. Catterall 56) drew with England 350 (E. H. Hendren 93, W. R. Hammond 57, M. Leyland 52) & 252 (E. H. Hendren 86, W. R. Hammond 65).

12th Match: v Natal (Durban)   Jan 10, 12.
Natal 107 & 107 (W. Voce 5-31) lost to M.C.C. 284 (E. H. Hendren 79, M. J. L. Turnbull 55, A. Woods 6-83) by an inns & 70 runs.

13th Match: v South Africa (Durban)   Jan 16, 17, 19, 20.
South Africa 177 (W. Voce 5-58) & 145-8 (H. W. Taylor 64*) drew with England 223-1 dec (W. R. Hammond 136*, R. E. S. Wyatt 54).

14th Match: v Cape Province (East London)   Jan 24, 26.
Cape Province 156 (K. G. Viljoen 86) & 131 lost to M.C.C. 336-8 dec (W. R. Hammond 126, M. W. Tate 72) by an inns & 49 runs.

15th Match: v Eastern Province (Port Elizabeth)   Jan 31, Feb 2, 3.
M.C.C. 272 (R. E. S. Wyatt 86, C. Maritz 5-53) & 199-6 dec (W. Farrimond 62) beat E. Province 140 & 105 (I. A. R. Peebles 6-51) by 226 runs.

16th Match: v Orange Free State (Bloemfontein)   Feb 7, 9, 10.
O.F.S. 148 (R. Fox 54) & 127 (I. A. R. Peebles 6-50) lost to M.C.C. 492 (E. H. Hendren 170, M. W. Tate 56, R. E. S. Wyatt 55, W. Farrimond 51*) by an inns & 217 runs.

17th Match: v South Africa (Johannesburg)   Feb 13, 14, 16, 17.
England 442 (M. Leyland 91, W. R. Hammond 75, E. H. Hendren 64) & 169-9 dec (E. P. Nupen 6-46) drew with South Africa 295 (H. W. Taylor 72, B. Mitchell 68, I. J. Siedle 62, I. A. R. Peebles 6-63) & 280-7 (B. Mitchell 74, H. B. Cameron 69*).

18th Match: v South Africa (Durban)   Feb 21, 23, 24, 25.
South Africa 252 (B. Mitchell 73, I. J. Siedle 57) & 219-7 dec drew with England 230 (M. W. Tate 50, C. L. Vincent 6-51) & 72-4.

19th Match: v South African Schools XV (Grahamstown)   March 2, 3.
M.C.C. 180 (E. H. Hendren 73*, Levick 5-43) & 305-9 (M. J. L. Turnbull 89, R. E. S. Wyatt 66) drew with Schools XV 130 (T. W. J. Goddard 5-31).

20th Match: v Western Province (Cape Town).
M.C.C. 254 (M. W. Tate 115*, E. H. Hendren 61) & 335-6 dec (M. J. L. Turnbull 139, M. Leyland 50, E. H. Hendren 50) drew with W. Province 316 (J. Goulden 75*, T. de Klerk 54, M. J. C. Allom 6-42) & 141-2 (G. F. Bond 77*, F. Martin 55).

---

there were only eleven fit players and in Northern Rhodesia, Crisp was co-opted into the team.

The first Test was staged at The Wanderers, Johannesburg, over the Christmas period. Peebles and Voce bowled out South Africa on the first day for 126 and by the close England had already gained a first innings lead and looked favourites to win the game. Over 20,000 came on the second day and saw the home team fight back – the English tail collapsed, then Mitchell and Cameron batted well, but England were without Peebles, who had strained a leg. On the third day the tourists were set 240 to win, but Nupen exploited his skill on the matting wicket to the full and South Africa took the game by 28 runs. Going straight on to Cape Town for the second Test, South Africa began in fine style, Mitchell and Siedle putting on 260 for the first wicket. Taylor also batted finely and England managed to draw the match only through some stubborn batting by Hendren. Again the tourists suffered through

injury, since Duckworth hurt his hand and Hammond took over behind the wicket.

For the next game, the M.C.C. co-opted H. W. Lee, the Middlesex cricketer, who was coaching in South Africa, and he appeared in four subsequent matches, including the fourth Test.

In the third Test at Durban, England were very much on top, but rain completely washed out the second day, making a draw inevitable. The three provincial matches that followed caused the tourists few worries and England went into the fourth Test with more confidence. The main problem was finding a good opening pair, but the partnership of Wyatt and Lee in this game did not solve it. There was however some very consistent batting in England's first innings and a total of 442 was reached. Peebles bowled out South Africa for 295 and on the final day England hit some quick runs to enable Chapman to declare, setting South Africa 316 to win. For a long time it was anybody's match, but in the end South Africa played out for a draw, with Cameron being unbeaten on 69.

In the fifth Test, Chapman won the toss and put South Africa in on a drying pitch, but when the home side had reached 32 without loss, rain ended play for the day. Slow batting by both sides on the second and third days made certain the game would be drawn and the final day's play was of no interest. The team, which had lost the Test series by one match to nil, played two other games before travelling back to England in the *Balmoral Castle*, reaching home on 30 March. Turnbull, Allom and Hammond travelled separately from the main party.

The most impressive bowlers on the tour were Peebles and Voce. The Notts player was distinctly effective on the matting wickets, his break off the wicket coming with a decided nip. Peebles on the other hand adjusted his bowling very well to suit both matting and turf and was much improved on his previous tour. Tate was a model of length and accuracy, as was White, but Goddard and Allom did not live up to their reputations.

Hammond and Hendren were the batsmen of the side, whilst Wyatt and Leyland were most consistent, but the lack of an opening batsman after Sandham's accident was very noticeable. On the South African side, Nupen remained the best bowler and Mitchell, Taylor and Siedle stood out in a good batting line-up.

1930-31 : M.C.C. to South Africa								
Batting Averages								
	M	I	NO	R	HS	Avge	100	c/s
W. R. Hammond (Glos)	13	19	2	1045	136*	61.47	3	18
E. H. Hendren (Middx)	14	18	1	914	170	53.76	1	12
W. Farrimond (Lancs)	9	13	5	297	62	37.12	0	6/6
M. Leyland (Yorks)	15	22	1	774	169	36.85	1	1
R. E. S. Wyatt (Warks)	15	23	1	768	138	34.90	1	3
M. W. Tate (Sussex)	12	17	2	516	115*	34.40	1	3
M. J. L. Turnbull (Glam)	14	21	2	541	139	28.47	1	3
A. P. F. Chapman (Kent)	14	17	0	471	87	27.70	0	12
H. W. Lee (Middx)	5	7	0	158	42	22.57	0	1
W. Voce (Notts)	13	18	3	296	57	19.73	0	3
J. C. White (Som)	13	18	2	256	36*	16.00	0	4
T. W. J. Goddard (Glos)	7	6	0	53	25	8.83	0	1
I. A. R. Peebles (Middx)	14	17	4	114	28	8.76	0	9
G. Duckworth (Lancs)	7	7	3	29	14*	7.25	0	11/5
M. J. C. Allom (Surrey)	9	9	2	50	19	7.14	0	1
Also played in two matches: A. Sandham 72, 6.								
Bowling Averages								
	O	M	R	W	Avge	BB	5i	
M. J. C. Allom	184	38	403	22	18.31	6-42	1	
M. W. Tate	347	106	621	33	18.81	5-18	3	
I. A. R. Peebles	444.4	80	1274	66	19.30	6-50	5	
W. Voce	479.5	139	1046	49	21.34	5-31	2	
J. C. White	348.4	107	698	29	24.06	3-13	0	
T. W. J. Goddard	160.2	40	380	13	29.23	4-43	0	
R. E. S. Wyatt	51	11	210	7	30.00	3-33	0	
M. Leyland	94	19	283	9	31.44	3-4	0	
W. R. Hammond	221.4	51	494	15	32.93	4-63	0	
Also bowled: A. P. F. Chapman 1-0-4-0; E. H. Hendren 3-1-7-0; H. W. Lee 7-1-26-1. R. J. Crisp played in one non-first-class match.								

1931: Martineau's third trip to Egypt

The following went to Egypt on the third tour arranged by H. M. Martineau: H. M. Martineau (capt), W. O'B. Lindsay (Oxford U), Col E. S. B. Williams (Army), G. D. Kemp-Welch (Warwicks), D. N. Moore (Gloucs), J. C. Masterman, W. G. L. F. Lowndes (Hants), C. H. Knott (Kent), Lord Dalmeny (Middx), H. W. F. Franklin (Essex) and J. H. Nevinson (Oxford U). The tour followed the same pattern as in the previous year, with five matches, of which two were against All Egypt. In the 'First Test' both sides collapsed, Cole taking 7 wickets for Egypt, but in the visitors' second innings Franklin and Williams batted well to set Egypt to make 410 in the final innings. Capt Rogers hit a fine 84 not out and consistent batting produced a score of 341, but it was not enough.

In the 'Second Test', the Egyptian fielding was very poor and allowed the tourists to reach the mammoth total of 531, with Knott hitting a double century and 256 being added in 110 minutes for the sixth wicket by Knott and Franklin. Egypt subsided to an innings defeat.

1931: H. M. Martineau's Team to Egypt

1st Match: v Alexandria (Alexandria)   March 31, April 1.
Martineau's XI 454-5 dec (D. N. Moore 115, C. H. Knott 93, W. O'B. Lindsay 76, S. B. Williams 56) beat Alexandria 253 (De Biss 85) & 168 (Bassett 51) by an inns & 33 runs.

2nd Match: v United Services (Cairo)   April 3, 4.
Martineau's XI 308 (G. D. Kemp-Welch 103, C. H. Knott 69) & 169 (C. H. Knott 57*) drew with United Services 270 (Cole 63, Radford 61) & 140-3.

3rd Match: v Gezira Sporting Club (Cairo)   April 6, 7.
Martineau's XI 334-9 dec (D. N. Moore 143, S. B. Williams 63, C. H. Knott 50) & 59-2 drew with Gezira Sporting Club 176 & 324-6 dec (Pank 114*, Dury 78*, Cole 61).

4th Match: v All Egypt (Cairo)   April 8, 9, 10.
Martineau's XI 195 (W. G. Lowndes 64) & 347 (H. W. F. Franklin 79, S. B. Williams 71) beat All Egypt 133 & 341 (Pank 95, Rogers 84*) by 68 runs.

5th Match: v All Egypt (Alexandria)   April 14, 15.
Martineau's XI 531 (C. H. Knott 227, H. W. F. Franklin 119, W. O'B. Lindsay 75) beat All Egypt 128 & 132 by an inns & 271 runs.

1931-32: Lord Tennyson in Jamaica

The winter of 1931-32 was a quiet one for English cricketers. The M.C.C. did not send a team abroad–the idea of a tour of India was mooted but nothing more was heard of it. In the spring Lord Tennyson took a party to Jamaica for a series of six matches.

The team was Lord Tennyson (Hants) (capt), A. P. F. Chapman (Kent), G. T. S. Stevens (Middx), B. H. Valentine (Kent), G. D. Kemp-Welch (Warwicks), C. F. Walters (Worcs), G. N. Scott-Chad (Norfolk), H. F. Bagnall (Northants) and the professionals G. Geary (Leics), W. E. Astill (Leics), G. Brown (Hants), E. H. Bowley (Sussex), M. S. Nichols (Essex) and C. C. R. Dacre (Gloucs).

The playing record of the side reflected the lack of bowling, which proved to be totally inadequate in the three matches against All Jamaica–there seemed no possibility of dismissing Headley, who hit 344 not out, 84 and 155 not out, and 140 in the three games. Kemp-Welch batted well for the tourists and most of the team made runs at various times on the tour, but the shadow of Headley loomed over all.

1931-32: Lord Tennyson's Team to Jamaica

1st Match: v Jamaica (Kingston)   Feb 18, 19.
Tennyson's XII 285 (B. H. Valentine 101, G. D. Kemp-Welch 75) & 88-3 drew with Jamaica XII 286-10 dec (J. Groves 89, G. T. S. Stevens 5-104).

2nd Match: v Jamaica (Kingston)   Feb 20, 22, 23, 24.
Jamaica 702-5 dec (G. A. Headley 344*, C. C. Passailaigue 261*) beat Tennyson's XI 354 (G. D. Kemp-Welch 105, A. P. F. Chapman 79, O. C. Scott 6-146) & 254 (B. H. Valentine 56) by an inns & 97 runs.

3rd Match: v Jamaica (Kingston)   Feb 27, 29, March 1, 2.
Tennyson's XI 402 (G. D. Kemp-Welch 186, C. C. R. Dacre 75, O. C. Scott 5-129) & 188 (O. C. Scott 6-91) lost to Jamaica 228 (G. A. Headley 84, G. T. S. Stevens 8-87) & 363-5 (G. A. Headley 155*, R. K. Nunes 125) by 5 wkts.

4th Match: v Cornwall XV (Kingston)   March 5, 6.
Cornwall XV 141 (M. S. Nichols 6-40) & 185-8 drew with Tennyson's XI 244 (E. H. Bowley 130, G. N. Scott-Chad 60).

5th Match: v Port Maria (Port Maria)   March 7, 8.
Tennyson's XI 139-5 dec (C. F. Walters 65) & 151 (Lord Tennyson 50) beat Port Maria 147-7 dec & 107 (M. S. Nichols 8-44) by 36 runs.

6th Match: v Jamaica (Kingston)   March 10, 11, 12, 14.
Tennyson's XI 333 (E. H. Bowley 69, C. F. Walters 50) & 359 (E. H. Bowley 115) lost to Jamaica 561 (I. Barrow 169, G. A. Headley 140, O. C. Da Costa 66) & 133-6 (I. Barrow 58*) by 4 wkts.

1932: Martineau's team lose both 'Tests' to Egypt

H. M. Martineau's team left England on 22 March on its now annual visit. The 1932 side was: H. M. Martineau (capt), E. W. Dawson (Leics), G. S. Wills, G. F. Earle (Somerset), J. V. Hermon, R. T. Stanyforth (Army), C. E. Awdry (Wilts), W. G. L. F. Lowndes (Hants), A. L. Hilder (Kent), I. A. R. Peebles (Middx) and A. E. L. Hill (Hants).

The tour was increased from five matches to seven and as usual the two major fixtures were the 'Tests' against Egypt. In the 'First Test', the tourists were set to make 340 in the last innings, but after 150 had been hit for the loss of only 3 wickets, the tail collapsed–unfortunately Earle was involved in a motor accident on the second day and could not bat. The 'Second Test' was altogether a remarkable game. Egypt were dismissed for 161 by Peebles in their first innings and were forced to follow on 175 in arrears. O'Brian then scored a century and took Egypt to 444. The tourists required only 270 to win, but never looked like making the runs and for the first time Egypt won both 'Tests'.

The tourists batting was inconsistent and the bowling relied heavily on Peebles, but the standard of cricket in Egypt was very high at this time.

1932: H. M. Martineau's Team to Egypt

1st Match: v Alexandria (Alexandria)   March 29, 30.
Martineau's XI 207 (A. L. Hilder 90) & 271 (R. T. Stanyforth 130*) beat Alexandria 139 (T. M. Sturgess 62) & 215 (J. C. de V. Biss 56) by 124 runs.

2nd Match: v United Services (Aboukir)   April 1, 2.
Martineau's XI 277 (A. L. Hilder 121) & 187-6 dec (E. W. Dawson 63, W. G. L. F. Lowndes 52) beat United Services 110 & 199 (Harston 53*, Peacock 52) by 155 runs.

3rd Match: v Gezira Sporting Club (Cairo)   April 4, 5, 6.
Martineau's XI 144 & 302 (A. L. Hilder 107, W. G. L. F. Lowndes 62) lost to Gezira Sporting Club 305 (E. S. Cole 145, H. R. Holme 68) & 142-4 (H. R. Holme 51*) by 6 wkts.

4th Match: v Maadi S.C. (Maadi)   April 8, 9.
Maadi 180 & 65 lost to Martineau's XI 286-7 dec (R. I. Campbell 111, R. T. Stanyforth 66*) by an inns & 61 runs.

5th Match: v United Services (Gezira)   April 11, 12, 13.
Martineau's XI 206 (E. W. Dawson 103*) & 222 (W. G. L. F. Lowndes 81, G. F. Earle 50) lost to United Services 190 (F. Ward 60) & 241-9 by 1 wkt.

6th Match: v All Egypt (Cairo)   April 15, 16, 18.
Egypt 259 (Rogers 79, R. G. W. Melsome 50) & 253 beat Martineau's XI 164 (E. W. Dawson 57) & 211 (E. W. Dawson 53) by 137 runs.

7th Match: v All Egypt (Alexandria)   April 21, 22, 23.
Martineau's XI 336 (W. G. L. F. Lowndes 95, I. A. R. Peebles 54, E. W. Dawson 50) & 140 lost to Egypt 161 & 444 (M. E. O'Brien 177, R. G. W. Melsome 74, F. Ward 64) by 129 runs.

1932-33: Jardine, Larwood and the 'bodyline' tour

Of all the pre-war English tours, the 1932-33 to Australia remains uppermost in the mind. The controversy regarding the policy of the English captain had long lasting repercussions on both Test and County cricket.

Preparations for the tour began in earnest in 1931, when the M.C.C. Committee decided on a selection Committee of three– P. F. Warner, P. A. Perrin and T. A. Higson–to act for two years, rather than the customary one, for the sole purpose of developing an England side to win back the Ashes, which Australia had gained during the 1930 series in England. The Tests in England in 1931 and 1932 against the weak New Zealand and Indian teams were to be used as experiments for the 1932-33 tour–there were no major tours in 1931-32. Prior to selecting the touring team, Lord Hawke was added to the selection committee as chairman. The

first move the committee made was on 4 July 1932, when it was announced that D. R. Jardine would lead the side – the only other candidate for the job was in reality Chapman, but there was no doubt that on his past record he was a liability as a batsman. A few days after Jardine's appointment, P. F. Warner and R. C. N. Palairet were appointed joint-managers. On 15 July the three principal batsmen and the two wicket-keepers for the tour were announced – Hammond, Sutcliffe, Duleepsinhji, Ames and Duckworth – no surprises here. The next group to be selected were G. O. B. Allen, Robins, F. R. Brown, Wyatt, Larwood, Voce and the Nawab of Pataudi – this was at the beginning of August. In mid-August Leyland, Verity and Tate were added to complete the team, but Robins decided to decline the invitation and his place finally went to T. B. Mitchell. At the last moment Duleepsinhji was compelled to stand down and his place went to Paynter, and finally Bowes was added to the side.

The team that sailed on the *Orontes* on 17 September was therefore: D. R. Jardine (Surrey) (capt), R. E. S. Wyatt (Warwicks) (vice-capt), G. O. B. Allen (Middx), F. R. Brown (Surrey), Nawab of Pataudi (Worcs), and the professionals W. R. Hammond (Gloucs), H. Sutcliffe (Yorks), M. Leyland (Yorks), H. Verity (Yorks), W. E. Bowes (Yorks), E. Paynter (Lancs), G. Duckworth (Lancs), L. E. G. Ames (Kent), T. B. Mitchell (Derbys), H. Larwood (Notts), W. Voce (Notts) and M. W. Tate (Sussex). By general consent it was the strongest available English combination, but was criticised for being too large. The fact that there were two managers – Warner and Palairet – was also thought a retrograde step.

Following the usual match in Colombo, the team started the tour in earnest at Perth on 21 October. Neither in this game nor the next three were the tourists greatly extended and indeed both South Australia and Victoria were overwhelmed. All the M.C.C. batsmen made runs in these games, centuries coming from the Nawab, Sutcliffe, Leyland, Jardine, Hammond and two fifties from Wyatt. All the bowlers took wickets, except Larwood, who bowled only 11 overs. The first serious problem occurred at

Above *The M.C.C. party for the famous tour of 1932-33 ready to sail from Tilbury on the Orient liner* Orontes *on 17 September 1932. Harold Larwood is being introduced to Captain O'Sullevan by M.C.C. captain Douglas Jardine. On the left are G. O. B. Allen and L. E. G. Ames. To the right are Duckworth and Hammond, with Leyland and Sutcliffe with their backs to the camera half hiding Mitchell, then Paynter, Verity, Voce and Wyatt.*

Below *The Yorkshiremen on the 1932-33 tour arrive at Kings Cross. From left: Leyland, Sutcliffe, Bowes and Verity.*

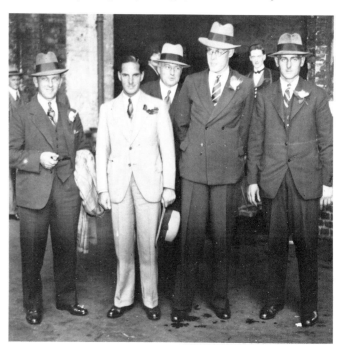

Melbourne in the fifth game against An Australian Eleven, when the tourists' batting folded up before the bowling of Nagel and on a reasonable wicket, the team was out for 60. The match was drawn due to rain, but the other interesting point was the cheap dismissal twice of Bradman by Larwood. In the next match, however, the M.C.C. batting recovered and the normally formidable New South Wales team was beaten by an innings.

The first Test commenced at Sydney directly after the victory over the State side. Australia won the toss and batted, but without Bradman, who was too ill to play. The opening day belonged to McCabe and Larwood. The Notts fast bowler quickly dismissed Ponsford, Fingleton and Kippax. Voce removed Woodfull, but McCabe played the innings of a lifetime and was 187 not out when the innings ended at 360. Sutcliffe, Hammond and the Nawab all made hundreds for England, then when Australia batted a second time the home side collapsed against Larwood, who took 5 for 28, and England won by 10 wickets. This was the first Test Match in which the English bowlers used leg-theory bowling, or 'bodyline' as the Australian press quickly tagged it. The idea was not a new one and in the recent past had been employed by certain West Indian fast bowlers, but unless a team possessed a bowler who was both exceptionally fast and at the same time accurate, the theory was more or less useless, and the batsmen would have a field day hooking the mediocre bowling to the boundary. England however had in Larwood a bowler who was both fast and accurate, so that the batsman faced with a fast short-pitched delivery on the leg stump had to attempt some sort of shot and any misjudgement would send the ball into the hands of a ring of short legs. This theory had been tried out to a limited extent in the two matches prior to the Test and had achieved the objective of dismissing Bradman, who had been so phenomenally successful during the 1930 Australian tour in England.

In the second Test, the usually fast Melbourne pitch, which ought to have been ideal for leg-theory bowling – and England included all four of their fast men, in Larwood, Voce, Bowes and Allen – was designed for the spinner. O'Reilly, the Australian leg-break and googly bowler, took ten wickets and England lost by 111 runs. Bradman played, scoring an unbeaten hundred in the second innings.

The great bodyline argument really exploded during the third Test at Adelaide. England, batting first, made a very poor start, but good innings by Leyland, Wyatt and Paynter took the total to

341. When Australia batted Larwood and Allen sent the first four batsmen back for 51 and in the course of this a ball from Larwood hit Woodfull severely on the chest. The crowd continuously barracked the English fast bowlers and the noise of 50,000 spectators roaring themselves hoarse with anger and fury was pretty intimidating – the fact that Jardine, the English captain, was the very personification of the aloof and austere Englishman further incensed the crowd. At close of play on the second day Australia had to some extent recovered to 109 for 4. When the game resumed on Monday, Jardine continued with his tactics of leg-theory, in spite of condemnation in the weekend press and the growing personal bitterness between the two opposing elevens – some remarks between the Australian captain, Woodfull and Pelham Warner had the effect of aggravating the situation still further. The situation became even worse when a ball from Larwood hit Oldfield on the head. The Australian batsman had to retire and was unable to take any further part in the match. From then on, for the remainder of the tour, the Australian players refused to attend any of the usual social functions given for the English team and two days later the Australian Board of Control sent a cable to M.C.C. which read:

'Body-line bowling has assumed such proportions as to menace the best interests of the game, making protection of the body by the batsman the main consideration. This is causing intensely bitter feeling between the players as well as injury. In our opinion it is unsportsmanlike. Unless stopped at once it is likely to upset the friendly relations existing between Australia and England.'

The M.C.C. reply deplored the statements in the cable and stated that the M.C.C. had the fullest confidence in the English captain and his team. It went on to say that the bowler was not to blame for the deliveries which hit Woodfull and Oldfield, but if the Australian authorities felt it wise to cancel the remainder of the tour they should do so.

England won the third Test by a large margin and in the interval of three weeks between the third and fourth Tests, tempers cooled and the Australian Board decided not to end the tour. In the meantime however questions were being asked at Government level, with the British Dominions Secretary involved, and judging by the rumpus in the press both in Australia and England, 'war' was about to be declared at any moment.

Happily there were no serious incidents in the fourth Test at Brisbane, and though Australia lost the match, it was due more to some plucky batting by Paynter, who had been hauled out of hospital by Jardine, than the bowlers. The first two innings of the fifth Test were very even, due to poor catching on both sides. It was estimated that England dropped no less than 14. Larwood hit 98 and was then caught in the deep by Ironmonger, the worst fieldsman on the home side. Australia collapsed, mainly to Verity, in their second innings and the tourists had no difficulty in winning the game by 8 wickets, thus ending a series which generated more ill-feeling between the two sets of players than any other. It also generated more books than any other, the rights and wrongs of bodyline bowling being furiously debated.

The tourists played two more State matches and then travelled to New Zealand where two Tests were played. Both these games were curtailed by rain and just the first innings of each side completed with England obtaining vast leads in each. In the second Hammond hit 336 not out which created a new record for Test cricket. He was at the wicket only 315 minutes. Jardine did not play in this game, England being led by Wyatt, and Larwood, who had injured his foot in the fifth Test against Australia, did not appear in any of the subsequent matches.

Hammond and Sutcliffe were the outstanding batsmen of the tour, but England's weak point was finding a replacement for Hobbs. Wyatt partnered Sutcliffe in the first two Australian Tests, Jardine for the other three. Neither was very successful. Lower down the order Leyland and Paynter both played useful innings. Pataudi however, after making a century in the first Test

1932-33 : M.C.C. to Ceylon, Australia and New Zealand								
Batting Averages								
	M	I	NO	R	HS	Avge	100	c/s
W. R. Hammond (Glos)	15	21	2	1569	336*	82.58	5	16
H. Sutcliffe (Yorks)	16	22	1	1345	194	64.05	5	4
Nawab of Pataudi (Worcs)	10	13	0	623	166	47.92	4	2
M. Leyland (Yorks)	13	21	1	880	152*	44.00	2	3
E. Paynter (Lancs)	14	19	3	626	102	39.12	1	5
R. E. S. Wyatt (Warks)	18	27	2	963	78	38.52	0	9
M. W. Tate (Sussex)	7	10	5	186	94*	37.20	0	2
D. R. Jardine (Surrey)	15	21	2	698	108*	36.74	1	15
L. E. G. Ames (Kent)	18	24	1	736	107	32.00	2	16/8
G. O. B. Allen (Middx)	14	17	0	409	66	24.06	0	14
H. Larwood (Notts)	10	13	2	258	98	23.45	0	3
F. R. Brown (Surrey)	11	15	1	301	74	21.50	0	8
W. Voce (Notts)	12	17	6	225	66	20.45	0	8
H. Verity (Yorks)	15	18	3	300	54*	20.00	0	16
G. Duckworth (Lancs)	9	11	5	108	27*	18.00	0	12/4
W. E. Bowes (Yorks)	12	11	6	49	20	9.80	0	1
T. B. Mitchell (Derbys)	11	8	1	28	10	4.00	0	7

Bowling Averages							
	Balls	M	R	W	Avge	BB	5i
E. Paynter	258	7	71	5	14.20	3-40	0
H. Larwood	2127	45	817	49	16.67	6-38	3
H. Verity	2818	128	809	45	17.98	7-37	3
T. B. Mitchell	1158	24	558	26	21.46	6-70	2
G. O. B. Allen	2206	51	965	41	23.54	5-69	1
W. E. Bowes	1864	29	900	37	24.32	6-34	1
W. Voce	2236	39	928	37	25.08	5-85	1
M. W. Tate	1093	38	379	15	25.27	4-53	0
F. R. Brown	1008	27	493	19	25.95	4-81	0
W. R. Hammond	1674	38	597	20	29.85	6-43	1

Also bowled: L. E. G. Ames 128-1-51-1; M. Leyland 101-1-55-1; R. E. S. Wyatt 144-2-74-1; D. R. Jardine 104-3-42-0; H. Sutcliffe 24-0-18-0.

Above *The Ashes-winning M.C.C. party of 1932-33, the 'bodyline' tour. Back: G. Duckworth, T. B. Mitchell, the Nawab of Pataudi, M. Leyland, H. Larwood, E. Paynter, W. Ferguson (scorer). Centre: P. F. Warner (manager), L. E. G. Ames, H. Verity, W. Voce, W. E. Bowes, F. R. Brown, M. W. Tate, R. C. N. Palairet (manager). Front: H. Sutcliffe, R. E. S. Wyatt, D. R. Jardine (capt), G. O. B. Allen, W. R. Hammond.*

Below *The Brisbane Test in 1932-33. Larwood is bowling to the Australian captain, Woodfull, and there is a semi-circle of six short legs waiting for a catch. The ball goes over Woodfull's head.*

1932-33: M.C.C. in Ceylon, Australia and New Zealand

1st Match: v Ceylon (Colombo) (One Day) Oct 8.
Ceylon 125-3 dec (W. T. Brindley 82*) drew with M.C.C. 186-7 (Nawab of Pataudi 62, R. E. S. Wyatt 54).

2nd Match: v Western Australia (Perth) Oct 21, 22, 23.
M.C.C. 334-8 dec (Nawab of Pataudi 166, H. Sutcliffe 54) & 152-5 (M. Leyland 69) drew with W. Australia 135.

3rd Match: v Combined Australian XI (Perth) Oct 27, 28, 29.
M.C.C. 583-7 dec (H. Sutcliffe 169, Nawab of Pataudi 129, D. R. Jardine 98, W. R. Hammond 77) drew with Combined XI 159 (H. Verity 7-37) & 139-4 (J. H. W. Fingleton 53*).

4th Match: v South Australia (Adelaide) Nov 4, 5, 7, 8.
M.C.C. 634-9 dec (H. Sutcliffe 154, M. Leyland 127, D. R. Jardine 108*, H. Larwood 81, R. E. S. Wyatt 61) beat S. Australia 290 (V. Y. Richardson 134, H. C. Nitschke 69) & 216 (W. E. Catchlove 65, H. Verity 5-42) by an inns & 128 runs.

5th Match: v Victoria (Melbourne) Nov 11, 12, 14, 15.
Victoria 231 (H. H. Oakley 83*) & 94 lost to M.C.C. 408-9 dec (W. R. Hammond 203, R. E. S. Wyatt 74) by an inns & 83 runs.

6th Match: v An Australian XI (Melbourne) Nov 18, 19, 21, 22.
M.C.C. 282 (H. Sutcliffe 87, R. K. Oxenham 5-53) & 60 (L. E. Nagel 8-32) drew with Australian XI 218 & 19-2.

7th Match: v New South Wales (Sydney) Nov 25, 26, 28, 29.
N.S.W. 273 (J. H. W. Fingleton 119*, S. J. McCabe 67, G. O. B. Allen 5-69) & 213 (F. S. Cummins 71, W. Voce 5-85) lost to M.C.C. 530 (H. Sutcliffe 182, L. E. G. Ames 90, R. E. S. Wyatt 72, Nawab of Pataudi 61, S. F. Hird 6-135) by an inns & 44 runs.

8th Match: v Australia (Sydney) Dec 2, 3, 5, 6, 7.
Australia 360 (S. J. McCabe 187*, H. Larwood 5-96) & 164 (H. Larwood 5-28) lost to England 524 (H. Sutcliffe 194, W. R. Hammond 112, Nawab of Pataudi 102) by 10 wkts.

9th Match: v Southern Districts (Wagga Wagga) Dec 10, 12.
S. Districts 226 (S. Sly 69*, L. Bennett 53, T. B. Mitchell 7-77) & 68-7 (T. B. Mitchell 5-26) drew with M.C.C. 313 (L. E. G. Ames 91, M. W. Tate 52*, F. R. Brown 51, M. Rumble 5-73).

10th Match: v Tasmania (Launceston) Dec 16, 17, 19.
M.C.C. 502 (Nawab of Pataudi 109, L. E. C. Ames 107, E. Paynter 102, H. Sutcliffe 101, G. J. James 6-96) beat Tasmania 229 (J. Badcock 57, S. Putman 56*, T. B. Mitchell 6-70) & 147 (T. B. Mitchell 5-74) by an inns & 126 runs.

11th Match: v Tasmania (Hobart) Dec 23, 24, 26.
Tasmania 103-5 dec & 89-4 drew with M.C.C. 330-7 dec (M. Leyland 65, H. Verity 54*, L. E. G. Ames 52, R. E. S. Wyatt 51).

12th Match: v Australia (Melbourne) Dec 30, 31, Jan 2, 3.
Australia 228 (J. H. W. Fingleton 83, D. G. Bradman 103*) beat England 169 (H. Sutcliffe 52, W. J. O'Reilly 5-63) & 139 (W. J. O'Reilly 5-66) by 111 runs.

13th Match: v Victorian Country XIII (Bendigo) Jan 7, 9.
Country XIII 215 (R. Porter 55) & 75 drew with M.C.C. 286 (H. Sutcliffe 91, W. R. Hammond 67).

14th Match: v Australia (Adelaide) Jan 13, 14, 16, 17, 18, 19.
England 341 (M. Leyland 83, R. E. S. Wyatt 78, E. Paynter 77, T. W. Wall 5-72) & 412 (W. R. Hammond 85, L. E. G. Ames 69, D. R. Jardine 56) beat Australia 222 (W. H. Ponsford 85) & 193 (W. M. Woodfull 73*, D. G. Bradman 66) by 338 runs.

15th Match: v Victorian Country XIII (Ballarat) Jan 21, 23.
M.C.C. 255 (Nawab of Pataudi 84, M. Leyland 62) drew with Country XIII 84-8.

16th Match: v New South Wales (Sydney) Jan 26, 27, 28.
N.S.W. 180 (R. C. Rowe 70, W. A. Brown 69) & 128 (D. G. Bradman 71, W. R. Hammond 6-43) lost to M.C.C. 199 (R. E. S. Wyatt 63, H. C. Chilvers 5-73) & 110-6 by 4 wkts.

17th Match: v Queensland Country XII (Toowoomba) Feb 1, 2.
M.C.C. 376 (L. E. G. Ames 121*, W. R. Hammond 101) & 187-3 (D. R. Jardine 77*) drew with Country XII 210 (L. Brittle 65*, R. C. Raymond 53, H. Larwood 8-28).

18th Match: v Queensland (Brisbane) Feb 4, 6, 7.
Queensland 201 (J. L. Litster 67, G. G. Cook 53) & 81 (H. Larwood 6-38) lost to M.C.C. 343 (L. E. G. Ames 80, G. O. B. Allen 66) by an inns & 61 runs.

19th Match: v Australia (Brisbane) Feb 10, 11, 13, 14, 15, 16.
Australia 340 (V. Y. Richardson 83, D. G. Bradman 76, W. M. Woodfull 67) & 175 lost to England 356 (H. Sutcliffe 86, E. Paynter 83) & 162-4 (M. Leyland 86) by 6 wkts.

20th Match: v Northern Districts (Newcastle) Feb 18, 20, 21.
N. Districts 322 (A. G. Chipperfield 82, R. G. Beattie 53) & 236 (R. C. J. Little 117, A. Baker 50) drew with M.C.C. 254 (Nawab of Pataudi 94*, V. Wright 6-79).

21st Match: v Australia (Sydney) Feb 23, 24, 25, 27, 28.
Australia 435 (L. S. Darling 85, S. J. McCabe 73, L. P. O'Brien 61, W. A. S. Oldfield 52) & 182 (D. G. Bradman 71, W. M. Woodfull 67, H. Verity 5-33) lost to England 454 (W. R. Hammond 101, M. Leyland 98, H. Sutcliffe 56, R. E. S. Wyatt 51) & 168-2 (W. R. Hammond 75*, R. E. S. Wyatt 61*) by 8 wkts.

22nd Match: v Victoria (Melbourne) March 3, 4, 6, 7.
M.C.C. 321 (M. W. Tate 94*, H. Sutcliffe 75, W. R. Hammond 59) & 183-9 dec (W. R. Hammond 64, H. Ironmonger 5-31) tied with Victoria 327 (L. S. Darling 103, H. I. Ebeling 68*, H. H. Oakley 50) & 177-3 (K. E. Rigg 88, E. H. Bromley 56*).

23rd Match: v South Australia (Adelaide) March 10, 11, 13, 14.
M.C.C. 298 (L. E. G. Ames 63, E. Paynter 62) & 371-8 dec (M. Leyland 152*, D. R. Jardine 65) drew with S. Australia 191 (A. J. Ryan 61) & 313-8 (H. C. Nitschke 87, B. J. Tobin 52*).

24th Match: v Wellington (Wellington) March 21, 22.
M.C.C. 223-8 dec (W. R. Hammond 58, E. Paynter 52) drew with Wellington 141-2: rain.

25th Match: v New Zealand (Christchurch) March 24, 25, 26.
England 560-8 dec (W. R. Hammond 227, L. E. G. Ames 103, F. R. Brown 74, W. Voce 66) drew with New Zealand 223 (G. L. Weir 66, J. L. Kerr 59) & 35-0.

26th Match: v New Zealand (Auckland) March 31, Apr 1, 2.
New Zealand 158 (C. S. Dempster 83*, W. E. Bowes 6-34) & 16-0 drew with England 548-7 dec (W. R. Hammond 336*, R. E. S. Wyatt 60).

---

was dropped—it was thought he made batting look more difficult than it really was.

Larwood was undoubtedly the man who won the Tests, none of the Australian batsmen, save for McCabe in the first Test, being happy against him and whatever the rights and wrongs of bodyline, Larwood was the ideal man to exploit it. Allen, who refused to use leg-theory, also bowled well and was perhaps the surprise of the tour. Bowes and Voce also bowled well at times, though the latter missed some matches due to illness.

The most disappointed tourist must have been Tate. On his two previous visits to Australia, he had been the backbone of the English attack: this time he was completely surplus to requirements.

The tourists travelled home via Fiji, Honolulu and Vancouver, and then across Canada, where they viewed the Niagara Falls. From the financial viewpoint, the tour was a success, but not on the scale of the 1928-29 tour.

1933: Martineau's team fight back

After the defeats of 1932, H. M. Martineau travelled to Egypt in 1933 with a stronger side: H. M. Martineau (capt), H. D. Read (Essex), G. N. B. Huskinson (Notts), A. W. Tyler (Army), B. H. Valentine (Kent), A. K. Judd (Hants), R. H. J. Brooke (Oxford U), C. E. Awdry (Wilts), E. W. Dawson (Leics), G. F. Earle (Somerset) and C. H. Knott (Kent).

Brooke, Knott and Valentine all returned batting averages over 50 and had a highly successful tour, whilst H. D. Read, the fast bowler who was to play for England a little later proved too good for many of the Egyptian batsmen. Both 'Tests' were won by large margins, but the tourists met with one defeat—against the United Services—when Cole took 8 wickets in 12 overs and bowled them out for 57. The innings of the tour was one of 191 by Knott, hit in about 85 minutes with 15 sixes and 17 fours.

1933: H. M. Martineau's Team to Egypt

1st Match: v United Services (Aboukir)
H. M. Martineau's XI 306-6 (C. H. Knott 86*, R. H. J. Brooke 60) drew with United Services 195-6 (A. Wilkinson 92, R. H. J. Brooke 5-65).

2nd Match: v Alexandria (Alexandria)
H. M. Martineau's XI 578-8 (C. H. Knott 191, G. F. Earle 118) drew with Alexandria 398 (R. D. Watt 115, R. S. Barcilon 77) and 186-3 (F. O. Thomas 80*).

3rd Match: v Gezira S.C. (Gezira)
H. M. Martineau's XI 368 (R. H. J. Brooke 136, E. W. Dawson 132) & 173 (T. Lyon Smith 6-68) beat Gezira 267 (A. C. Wilkinson 94) & 210 (J. D. G. Chaytor 121*) by 64 runs.

4th Match: v Maadi S.C. (Maadi)
Maadi S.C. 243 (R. Parkhouse 77) lost to H. M. Martineau's XI 252-5 (B. H. Valentine 80, C. H. Knott 83) by 5 wkts.

5th Match: v United Services (Gezira)
United Services 377 (A. J. H. Cassells 104) & 56-3 beat H. M. Martineau's XI 57 (E. S. Cole 8-11) & 375 (R. H. J. Brooke 194, B. H. Valentine 104).

6th Match: v All Egypt (Gezira) April 20, 21, 22.
Egypt 229 (G. A. Thomas 124, H. E. Russell 57) & 201 lost to H. M. Martineau's XI 286 (C. E. Awdry 73, E. W. Dawson 59, A. K. Judd 51*) & 145-2 (R. H. J. Brooke 65*) by 8 wkts.

7th Match: v All Egypt (Alexandria) April 24, 25, 26.
H. M. Martineau's XI 300 (A. K. Judd 97, G. F. Earle 73, A. Galloway 5-65) & 445 (B. H. Valentine 195, R. H. J. Brooke 122, A. J. H. Cassells 5-121) beat Egypt 248 (A. C. Wilkinson 104, W. Syfret 88, H. D. Read 6-53) & 200 (E. S. Cole 52) by 295 runs.

8th Match: v XV of Victoria College (Victoria College) April 27.
Drawn: Score not available.

1933: Sir Julien Cahn's team in North America and Bermuda

Sailing on the *Empress of Britain* from Southampton on 12 August, Sir Julien Cahn's team began its tour in Canada with two matches against Montreal, followed by two against Ottawa. There was a slight shock in the initial game, when the tourists were in difficulties on a matting wicket and won by a single wicket, but from then on most of the games provided easy wins for the visitors, until the team arrived in Bermuda and had two very good matches against Somerset C.C., winning one by three runs due to a magnificent catch on the boundary by Heane dismissing the last man. In the final game against Bermuda, an unbroken ninth wicket stand by Blunt and Maxwell saved the day and meant that the English side sailed for home unbeaten.

Cricket in North America remained at a low level and Cahn's team, which was of good first-class standard, found the opposition, with the exception of Bermuda, to be very mediocre in strength.

The tourists were: Sir Julien Cahn (capt), R. C. Blunt (New Zealand), P. A. Gibb (Cambridge U), S. D. Rhodes (Notts), D. P. B. Morkel (South Africa), G. F. H. Heane (Notts), G. F. Summers, E. W. Swanton, E. P. Solbe, F. C. W. Newman (Surrey), C. R. N. Maxwell, I. A. R. Peebles (Middx), R. W. V. Robins (Middx), T. B. Reddick (Middx) and H. R. Munt (Middx).

1933: Sir Julien Cahn's Team to North America and Bermuda

1st Match: v XV of Montreal (Montreal)   Aug 19.
Montreal 103 lost to Cahn's XI 122-9 by 1 wkt.

2nd Match: v XV of Montreal (Montreal)   Aug 21.
Cahn's XI 224 (D. P. B. Morkel 123) beat Montreal 66 by 158 runs.

3rd Match: v Ottawa XII (Ottawa)   Aug 22.
Cahn's XI 217-1 dec (P. A. Gibb 100*, G. F. Summers 72*) drew with Ottawa XII 121-9.

4th Match: v Ottawa XII (Ottawa)   Aug 23.
Ottawa XII 111 lost to Cahn's XI 225 (E. W. Swanton 57, I. A. R. Peebles 56) by 4 wkts.

5th Match: v Toronto Council (Toronto)   Aug 24.
Toronto Council 86 lost to Cahn's XI 252-7 (S. D. Rhodes 80, I. A. R. Peebles 57) by 7 wkts.

6th Match: v All Toronto (Armour Heights)   Aug 25.
Cahn's XI 304-8 dec (D. P. B. Morkel 64, R. C. Blunt 58, G. F. Parkinson 51) beat All Toronto 77 by 227 runs.

7th Match: v Toronto C.C. (Toronto)   Aug 26.
Toronto C.C. 142 lost to Cahn's XI 143-6 (G. F. H. Heane 67*) by 4 wkts.

8th Match: v Hamilton XV (Hamilton)   Aug 28.
Hamilton XV 72 lost to Cahn's XI 211 (P. A. Gibb 61, R. C. Blunt 53*) by 5 wkts.

9th Match: v Ridley College XV (St Catherine's)   Aug 29.
Ridley College XV 123 lost to Cahn's XI 127-5 by 5 wkts.

10th Match: v London XV (London)   Aug 30.
Cahn's XI 280-4 dec (G. F. Summers 80*, S. D. Rhodes 70) beat London XV 128 by 152 runs.

11th Match: XIV of Chicago (Chicago)   Sept 2.
Chicago XIV 62 lost to Cahn's XI 247 (E. W. Swanton 51, D. P. B. Morkel 51) by 10 wkts.

12th Match: v XV of Chicago (Chicago)   Sept 3.
Chicago XV 119 lost to Cahn's XI 133-5 (R. C. Blunt 74*) by 5 wkts.

13th Match: v New York XV (Livingstone)   Sept 6.
New York XV 136 lost to Cahn's XI 166-2 (R. C. Blunt 92*, S. D. Rhodes 62*) by 8 wkts.

14th Match: v New York XV (Staten Island)   Sept 7.
Cahn's XI 275-5 dec (D. P. B. Morkel 126, G. F. H. Heane 78) drew with New York XV 82-12.

15th Match: v Crescent Athletic Club XVI (Long Island)   Sept 8.
Crescent A.C. XVI 90 lost to Cahn's XI 200 by 4 wkts.

16th Match: v B.C.A. Colts XI (Prospect, Bermuda)   Sept 11.
Cahn's XI 196-4 dec (F. C. W. Newman 104) drew with Colts 71-7.

17th Match: v St Ged C.C. (Prospect)   Sept 12.
Cahn's XI 209 (G. F. Summers 82) beat St Ged C.C. 107 by 102 runs.

18th Match: v B.C.A. XI (Prospect)   Sept 13.
B.C.A. XI 134 (J. Benevides 51) lost to Cahn's XI 172-5 (S. D. Rhodes 90) by 8 wkts.

19th Match: v Somerset C.C. (Prospect)   Sept 14.
Cahn's XI 85 beat Somerset C.C. 82 by 3 runs.

20th Match: v All Bermuda (Prospect)   Sept 15.
All Bermuda 147 drew with Cahn's XI 91-8.

1933-34: strong England team beat India

The problems connected with bodyline bowling carried on through the 1933 English season and leg-theory was employed by the West Indian bowlers during the Tests of that summer. Jardine continued to lead England and in fact hit a century in the second Test against the leg-theory of Martindale and Constantine. Larwood missed almost the whole season through injury and did not appear in the Test series. The M.C.C. and the Australian Board of Control continued their discussions of the problem, which in reality boiled down to the question of whether leg-theory bowling was in the best interests of the game.

The original party chosen to tour India was Jardine, Walters, Valentine, Wyatt, Levett, Jas Langridge, Nichols, Verity, Townsend, Bakewell, E. W. Clark, Gregory, Paynter, Barnett, Ames and A. N. Other. Sutcliffe and Hammond both declined to go. Later Wyatt withdrew and so did Ames. The final team which sailed on 22 September was: D. R. Jardine (Surrey) (capt), C. F. Walters (Worcs), B. H. Valentine (Kent), C. S. Marriott (Kent), W. H. V. Levett (Kent), J. H. Human (Cambridge U), and the professionals A. Mitchell (Yorks), A. H. Bakewell (Northants), C. J. Barnett (Gloucs), R. J. Gregory (Surrey), Jas Langridge (Sussex), L. F. Townsend (Derbys), M. S. Nichols (Essex), H. Verity (Yorks), H. Elliott (Derbys) and E. W. Clark (Northants) with Major E. Ricketts as manager.

The tour opened in Karachi on 15 October, but it was not until the eighth match at Patiala that the tourists were seriously extended, Wazir Ali scoring a very sound 156 and giving a local side first innings lead for the first time on the tour – Tarrant, the old Middlesex all-rounder, also appeared in this match and his bowling worried several of the M.C.C. team.

The first Test was played in Bombay and a crowd of some 50,000 attended the first day's play – similar sized crowds also appeared on the other three days and the overall total was estimated at 250,000. Valentine hit a forceful hundred for England, though he was dropped twice, and good bowling by Nichols gave the visitors victory with 9 wickets in hand. India made five changes for the second Test, but only a splendid rearguard innings by C. K. Nayudu prevented a second England victory. The Test however was followed by the tourists' sole defeat of the programme. In a

---

1933-34: M.C.C. to India and Ceylon

Batting Averages

		M	I	NO	R	HS	Avge	100	c/s
D. R. Jardine	(Surrey)	14	19	3	835	102	52.18	2	20
C. F. Walters	(Worcs)	11	18	2	689	102	43.06	1	5
B. H. Valentine	(Kent)	14	22	1	834	145	39.71	2	10
C. J. Barnett	(Glos)	16	25	1	880	140	36.67	3	22
L. F. Townsend	(Derbys)	15	22	4	566	93*	31.44	0	8
Jas Langridge	(Sussex)	14	19	3	487	70	30.43	0	5
A. H. Bakewell	(Northts)	11	18	2	479	158	29.93	1	6
A. Mitchell	(Yorks)	13	21	0	616	161	29.33	1	18
H. Verity	(Yorks)	14	18	4	384	91*	27.42	0	e8
R. J. Gregory	(Surrey)	10	15	2	349	148	26.84	1	13
H. Elliott	(Derbys)	7	5	1	89	37*	22.25	0	9/6
M. S. Nichols	(Essex)	14	22	3	404	79	21.26	0	17
J. H. Human	(Cambr U)	10	14	2	186	48	15.50	0	4
W. H. V. Levett	(Kent)	12	18	6	144	25	12.00	0	18/9
E. W. Clark	(Northts)	14	14	8	62	11	10.33	0	0
C. S. Marriott	(Kent)	9	9	1	26	8	3.25	0	2

Bowling Averages

	O	M	R	W	Avge	BB	5i
L. F. Townsend	242.3	72	608	43	14.13	7-16	2
H. Verity	482.2	179	1180	78	15.12	7-37	5
E. W. Clark	381.1	111	890	56	15.89	6-24	2
M. S. Nichols	344.2	70	989	55	17.98	5-14	2
Jas Langridge	262.5	97	585	31	18.87	5-63	1
C. S. Marriott	288.4	103	669	32	20.90	6-35	2
J. H. Human	51.3	5	220	7	31.42	2-21	0
C. J. Barnett	80	20	211	3	70.33	1-22	0

Also bowled: R. J. Gregory 16-3-51-1; D. R. Jardine 2-0-6-0; A. Mitchell 9-1-32-2; B. H. Valentine 13-2-48-1; C. F. Walters 2-1-8-0.
The Maharajah of Patiala played in one non-first-class match.

After the controversy of the 'bodyline' tour of Australia, D. R. Jardine was also captain of the party to India in 1933-34. Here he is, with pipe, beginning the journey at St Pancras station on 22 September 1933, accompanied by some of his team.

1933-34: M.C.C. to India and Ceylon

1st Match: v C. B. Rubie's XI (Karachi)   Oct 15, 16.
M.C.C. 292 (C. F. Walters 71, C. J. Barnett 62, B. H. Valentine 59, J. Harris 5-89) & 70-4 dec drew with Rubie's XI 99 & 103-6.

2nd Match: v Karachi XI (Karachi)   Oct 18, 19.
M.C.C. 362-8 dec (C. F. Walters 101, A. H. Bakewell 96, B. H. Valentine 59, A. Mitchell 53) drew with Karachi XI 89 & 112-4.

3rd Match: v Sind (Karachi)   Oct 21, 22, 23.
M.C.C. 307-5 dec (C. J. Barnett 122, D. R. Jardine 101*) & 140-8 dec (C. J. Barnett 54) beat Sind 189 (H. Verity 6-46) & 167 (M. J. Mobed 60) by 91 runs.

4th Match: v N.W. Frontier Province (Peshawar)   Oct 28, 29.
N.W. Frontier 94 (M. S. Nichols 5-28) & 121 lost to M.C.C. 350-7 dec (L. F. Townsend 94, A. Mitchell 84, D. R. Jardine 67) by an inns & 135 runs.

5th Match: v Punjab Governor's XI (Lahore)   Nov 1, 2.
M.C.C. 402-7 dec (A. Mitchell 184, Jas Langridge 52, B. H. Valentine 51, L. F. Townsend 50) drew with Governor's XI 253-8 (C. K. Nayudu 116).

6th Match: v Northern India (Lahore)   Nov 4, 5.
N. India 53 & 58 lost to M.C.C. 246-7 dec (A. Mitchell 54, L. F. Townsend 50) by an inns & 135 runs.

7th Match: v Southern Punjab (Amritsar)   Nov 9, 10, 11.
S. Punjab 264 (N. B. Amarnath 109, Yuvaraj of Patiala 66) & 103-1 (S. Wazir Ali 63) drew with M.C.C. 450-7 dec (L. F. Townsend 93*, C. F. Walters 86, B. H. Valentine 75, M. S. Nichols 55).

8th Match: v Patiala (Patiala)   Nov 12, 13, 14, 15.
M.C.C. 330 (D. R. Jardine 80, A. Mitchell 59) drew with Patiala 335-6 (S. Wazir Ali 156, N. B. Amarnath 53).

9th Match: v Delhi & District (New Delhi)   Nov 18, 19.
Delhi 98 (H. Verity 5-40) & 102 lost to M.C.C. 333 (A. Mitchell 109, Maharajah of Patiala 54, C. J. Barnett 52) by an inns & 133 runs.

10th Match: v The Viceroy's XI (New Delhi)   Nov 21, 22, 23.
Viceroy's XI 160 (H. Verity 7-37) & 63 (M. S. Nichols 5-14) lost to M.C.C. 431-8 dec (B. H. Valentine 145, D. R. Jardine 93, C. F. Walters 65, A. Mitchell 59) by an inns & 208 runs.

11th Match: v Rajputana (Ajmer)   Nov 25. 26
M.C.C. 213 (C. J. Barnett 75) beat Rajputana 32 (E. W. Clark 5-10, L. F. Townsend 5-16) & 74 (L. F. Townsend 7-22) by an inns & 107 runs.

12th Match: v Western India States (Rajkot)   Nov 29, 30, Dec 1.
W. India States 64 (L. F. Townsend 7-16) & 249 (Dr. Gurtu 61, H. Verity 6-83) lost to M.C.C. 254-5 dec (C. J. Barnett 84, M. S. Nichols 52) & 60-6 by 4 wkts.

13th Match: v Jamnagar XI (Jamnagar)   Dec 3, 4.
Jamnagar 90 (Jas Langridge 5-18) & 45-6 drew with M.C.C. 151-8 dec (C. F. Walters 60).

14th Match: v Bombay Presidency (Bombay)   Dec 8, 9, 10.
Bombay 87 & 191-5 (V. M. Merchant 67*) drew with M.C.C. 481-8 dec (R. J. Gregory 148, D. R. Jardine 102, Jas Langridge 66, C. F. Walters 54).

15th Match: v Bombay City (Bombay)   Dec 12, 13.
Bombay 140 & 26-2 drew with M.C.C. 319-8 dec (A. H. Bakewell 107, R. J. Gregory 53*).

16th Match: v India (Bombay)   Dec 15, 16, 17, 18.
India 219 & 258 (N. B. Amarnath 118, C. K. Nayudu 67, M. S. Nichols 5-55) lost to England 438 (B. H. Valentine 136, C. F. Walters 78, D. R. Jardine 60, Mahomed Nissar 5-90) & 40-1 by 9 wkts.

17th Match: v Poona XI (Poona)   Dec 20, 21.
M.C.C. 161-5 dec (C. F. Walters 84) drew with Poona 83 (S. Nazir Ali 57, H. Verity 8-37) & 39-2.

18th Match: v British in Bengal (Calcutta) (One Day)   Dec 27.
M.C.C. 187-5 dec (C. J. Barnett 94) drew with British in Bengal 121-8.

19th Match: v Indians & Anglo-Indians (Calcutta) (One Day)   Dec 28.
Indians & Anglo-Indians 123 lost to M.C.C. 179-6 (A. H. Bakewell 54) by 8 wkts.

20th Match: v An Indian XI (Calcutta)   Dec 30, 31, Jan 1.
M.C.C. 331 (H. Verity 91*, L. F. Townsend 69, C. F. Walters 67) & 279-5 dec (M. S. Nichols 79, B. H. Valentine 74) drew with An Indian XI 168 & 152-1 (H. P. Ward 77*, C. P. Johnstone 69*).

21st Match: v India (Calcutta)   Jan 5, 6, 7, 8.
England 403 (Jas Langridge 70, D. R. Jardine 61, H. Verity 55*) & 7-2 drew with India 247 (M. Dilawar Hussain 59, V. M. Merchant 54) & 237 (M. Dilawar Hussain 57).

22nd Match: v Vizianagram's XI (Benares)   Jan 11, 12, 13.
Vizianagram's XI 124 & 140 (L. F. Townsend 5-30) beat M.C.C. 111 (B. H. Valentine 53, Mahomed Nissar 6-60) & 139 by 14 runs.

23rd Match: v Central India (Indore)   Jan 16, 17.
M.C.C. 157 (C. F. Walters 54, C. K. Nayudu 6-36) & 52-0 drew with Central India 157.

24th Match: v Central Provinces & Berar (Nagpur)   Jan 19, 20, 21.
Central Provinces 195 (C. K. Nayudu 107, C. S. Marriott 6-35) & 188 (C. S. Nayudu 61*) lost to M.C.C. 261 (C. J. Barnett 140, C. K. Nayudu 5-87) & 129-4 (B. H. Valentine 50*) by 6 wkts.

25th Match: v Moin-ud-Dowlah XI (Secunderabad)   Jan 23, 24, 25.
M.C.C. 112 (S. Mushtaq Ali 5-37) & 303 (M. S. Nichols 55, L. Amar Singh 5-82) drew with Moin-ud-Dowlah XI 194 (L. Amar Singh 58, H. Verity 5-63) & 188-9 (C. K. Nayudu 79).

26th Match: v Mysore (Mysore)   Jan 28, 29.
M.C.C. 451-7 dec (C. F. Walters 155, Jas Langridge 104, D. R. Jardine 66*) beat Mysore 107 (E. W. Clark 7-8) & 56 (E. W. Clark 5-19, C. J. Barnett 5-21) by an inns & 288 runs.

27th Match: v Madras (Madras)   Feb 3, 4, 5.
M.C.C. 603 (A. Mitchell 161, A. H. Bakewell 158, R. J. Gregory 66, L. F. Townsend 53*) beat Madras 106 & 145 (C. P. Johnstone 69, C. S. Marriott 5-43) by an inns & 352 runs.

28th Match: v Indian Cricket Federation (Madras) (One Day)   Feb 7.
M.C.C. 268-6 dec (M. S. Nichols 67, Jas Langridge 61, C. F. Walters 56) beat Indian Cricket Federation 81 by 187 runs.

29th Match: v India (Madras)   Feb 10, 11, 12, 13.
England 335 (A. H. Bakewell 85, D. R. Jardine 65, C. F. Walters 59, L. Amar Singh 7-86) & 261-7 dec (C. F. Walters 102) beat India 145 (H. Verity 7-49) & 249 (Yuvaraj of Patiala 60, Jas Langridge 5-63) by 202 runs.

30th Match: v All Ceylon (Colombo)   Feb 16, 17, 18.
All Ceylon 106 (E. W. Clark 6-24) & 189 (N. S. Joseph 78) lost to M.C.C. 272 (C. J. Barnett 116, W. T. Brindley 5-40) & 25-0 by 10 wkts.

31st Match: v Galle (Galle) (One Day)   Feb 20.
Galle 79-7 dec drew with M.C.C. 59-2.

32nd Match: v India & Ceylon (Colombo)   Feb 22, 23, 24.
M.C.C. 155 (L. F. Townsend 56, L. Amar Singh 6-62) & 78 (E. Kelaart 5-17) beat India & Ceylon 104 & 121 by 8 runs.

33rd Match: v Up Country XI (Darrawella)   Feb 26.
M.C.C. 228-2 dec (A. H. Bakewell 101*, A. Mitchell 66, C. J. Barnett 53) & 53-1 dec beat Up Country XI 72 & 100-2 on 1st inns by 156 runs.

34th Match: v An Indian XI (Bombay)   March 4, 5, 6.
M.C.C. 224 (A. Mitchell 91) & 215 (A. H. Bakewell 56, L. Amar Singh 5-109) drew with An Indian XI 238 (V. M. Merchant 89*) & 112-4.

low-scoring match at Benares, some fast bowling by Mohammad Nissar swept through the M.C.C. batting and the local side won by 14 runs, in spite of a gallant attempt by Jardine to save the game. It was most unfortunate for India that Nissar, through illness, could not play in the third and final Test at Madras. In addition Nazir Ali could not bowl in England's first innings and these two factors made all the difference, England winning by 202 runs. After the third Test, the team travelled to Ceylon, where two games were played, and then a final match took place at Bombay for the Indian Earthquake Fund. The Indian team might well have won this match, but, when set 202 to win, the batsmen went on the defensive, Jamshedji actually being at the wicket 150 minutes for 17 runs, and the stumps were drawn with the Indians 112 for 4. Spectators barracked their own players.

Compared with the previous M.C.C. tour of 1926-27, the Indian grounds had greatly improved, as had the accommodation for the players. The attendances at the matches were also much larger. The Indian fielding in the first half of the tour however was of a low standard and Jardine was very much the superior captain when it came to bowling and fielding changes.

Of the tourists, Jardine, Walters and Valentine were the best batsmen, whilst Verity was the most feared of the bowlers. Marriott did not come off and Human suffered from malaria.

1934: Martineau returns to Egypt

The programme of matches was increased to ten for Martineau's sixth tour of Egypt and the touring party was also increased in strength. The team was: H. M. Martineau (capt), D. F. Mendl, G. E. Livock (Middx), C. G. Ford, W. E. Harbord (Yorks), D. R. Wilcox (Essex), J. L. Guise (Middx), E. Cawston (Sussex), C. H. Knott (Kent), G. F. Earle (Somerset) and F. R. Brown (Surrey).

The two matches against Egypt were both won, but the second was very close and although Brown took 10 wickets for the tourists, Cole obtained some cheap wickets for the home side and Martineau's team won by just 2 wickets.

Brown was the all-rounder of the side, but J. L. Guise hit 661 runs in all with an average of 73.44, and Knott again did well.

1934: H. M. Martineau's Team to Egypt

1st Match: v Alexandria (Alexandria)
Alexandria 295 (F. R. Brown 6-72) & 151 (C. H. Knott 5-25) lost to H. M. Martineau's XI 442 (C. G. Ford 100, J. L. Guise 83, B. de Botton 6-102) & 5-0 by 10 wkts.

2nd Match: v R.A.F. Depot (Abukir)
H. M. Martineau's XI 316-6 dec (F. R. Brown 117, E. Cawston 65) beat R.A.F. Depot 104 (F. R. Brown 8-34) by 212 runs.*

3rd Match: v United Services (Gezira)
United Services 71 (J. L. Guise 5-26) & 217 (E. S. Cole 52, F. R. Brown 5-97) lost to H. M. Martineau's XI 271 (D. R. Wilcox 73, G. F. Earle 63) & 18-2 by 8 wkts.*

4th Match: v Gezira S.C. (Gezira)
H. M. Martineau's XI 352-7 dec (J. L. Guise 145) & 105-1 (D. F. Mendl 74) beat Gezira S.C. 245 & 211 by 9 wkts.

5th Match: v Other Ranks XII (Abbassia).
H. M. Martineau's XI 326-7 dec (C. H. Knott 129) beat Other Ranks XII 137 by 189 runs.*

6th Match: v Maadi S.C. (Maadi).
Maadi S.C. 217 beat H. M. Martineau's XI 127 (R. M. Bradley 5-33) by 90 runs.

7th Match: v Y.M.C.A. (Willcocks Recreation Grd).
H. M. Martineau's XI 297-7 dec (E. Cawston 82, J. L. Guise 76) beat Y.M.C.A. 127 (C. H. Knott 6-33) by 170 runs.

8th Match: v All Egypt (Gezira)   April 19, 20, 21.
Egypt 179 (I. J. Kilgour 74) & 282 (R. M. Bradley 69, Partridge 59) lost to H. M. Martineau's XI 588-5 dec (J. L. Guise 217, C. H. Knott 171, F. R. Brown 121) by an innings & 127 runs.

9th Match: v Victoria College XII (Victoria Coll).
H. M. Martineau's XI 261-8 dec (G. F. Earle 121) beat Victoria College 61 by 200 runs.

10th Match: v All Egypt (Alexandria)   April 25, 26, 27.
All Egypt 181 (F. R. Brown 5-58) & 146 (F. R. Brown 5-45) lost to H. M. Martineau's XI 218 (E. Cawston 113, E. S. Cole 6-46) & 110-8 by 2 wkts.

1934-35: England captain's jaw fractured in the West Indies

As was usual with tours other than those to Australia, the English team was in no way representative of the full strength of the country. On the batting side, Sutcliffe was absent, but on the bowling, Verity and Bowes–two of the three main bowlers of the 1934 series in England against Australia–were elsewhere. The team which sailed was: R. E. S. Wyatt (Warwicks) (capt), E. R. T. Holmes (Surrey) (vice-capt), D. C. H. Townsend (Oxford U), K. Farnes (Essex), W. E. Harbord (Yorks), W. R. Hammond (Gloucs), E. H. Hendren (Middx), M. Leyland (Yorks), L. E. G. Ames (Kent), J. Iddon (Lancs), G. A. E. Paine (Warwicks), C. I. J. Smith (Middx), W. E. Hollies (Warwicks), W. Farrimond (Lancs) and the manager T. H. Carlton Levick.

The party had a very rough crossing of the Atlantic, most of the side being very sea-sick and quite unfit for cricket when they arrived in Barbados. In the opening match against the colony, the home team had much the better of a drawn game, only Hendren with a defensive second innings fifty saving the team from defeat. Things went much better in the return fixture. Hammond hit a glorious double century and with Smith had a tenth wicket stand of 122–rain prevented M.C.C. from winning on the final day.

The first Test was quite sensational. Wyatt put the West Indies in on a damp wicket and Farnes' fast bowling dismissed the formidable West Indian batting for 102. England struggled to 81 for 7, but rain had made the wicket even worse and Wyatt declared at this modest total. The West Indies then collapsed to 51 for 6 and Grant had the audacity to declare also, though leaving England a day and a half to make just 73! Wyatt then reversed the England batting order in the hope that the tail might survive long enough to let the wicket improve. Six England wickets dis-

---

1934-35: M.C.C. to West Indies

1st Match: v Barbados (Bridgetown)   Dec 29, 31, Jan 1.
Barbados 382 (J. E. D. Sealey 87, E. L. G. Hoad 69, W. E. Hollies 5-81) & 149-7 dec drew with M.C.C. 170 & 221-5 (E. H. Hendren 54, R. E. S. Wyatt 51).

2nd Match: v Barbados (Bridgetown)   Jan 3, 4, 5.
M.C.C. 601 (W. R. Hammond 281, C. I. J. Smith 83, R. E. S. Wyatt 65) drew with Barbados 177 (G. M. Carew 68) & 8-1.

3rd Match: v West Indies (Bridgetown)   Jan 8, 9, 10.
West Indies 102 & 51-6 dec (C. I. J. Smith 5-15) lost to England 81-7 dec & 75-6 (E. A. Martindale 5-22) by 4 wkts.

4th Match: v Trinidad (Port of Spain)   Jan 15, 16, 17.
M.C.C. 348 (W. R. Hammond 116, L. E. G. Ames 69*, C. I. J. Smith 54) & 200-6 dec (M. Leyland 77*) drew with Trinidad 371-7 dec (A. Maynard 200*, G. A. E. Paine 5-68) & 159-8.

5th Match: v Trinidad (Port of Spain)   Jan 19, 21, 22.
M.C.C. 226 (L. E. G. Ames 67) & 103 (M. Leyland 59, B. J. Sealey 5-26) drew with Trinidad 230-9 dec (L. N. Constantine 68, R. E. S. Wyatt 5-10) & 86-6.

6th Match: v West Indies (Port of Spain)   Jan 24, 25, 26, 28.
West Indies 302 (J. E. D. Sealey 92, L. N. Constantine 90) & 280-6 dec (G. A. Headley 93) beat England 258 (E. R. T. Holmes 85*, J. Iddon 73) & 107 by 217 runs.

7th Match: v British Guiana (Georgetown)   Feb 5, 6, 7.
British Guiana 102 (W. E. Hollies 5-29) & 284-2 (F. I. de Caires 80*, C. Jones 72*, C. de Freitas 71) drew with M.C.C. 421 (E. H. Hendren 148, J. Iddon 68).

8th Match: v British Guiana (Georgetown)   Feb 10, 11, 12.
British Guiana 188-8 dec (K. L. Wishart 56, G. A. E. Paine 6-67) & 57 lost to M.C.C. 41-5 dec & 205-1 (W. R. Hammond 106*, D. C. H. Townsend 93*) by 9 wkts.

9th Match: v West Indies (Georgetown)   Feb 14, 15, 16, 18.
England 226 & 160-6 dec (R. E. S. Wyatt 71) drew with West Indies 184 (G. A. Headley 53, K. L. Wishart 52, W. E. Hollies 7-50) & 104-5.

10th Match: v Jamaica (Kingston)   March 5, 6, 7.
Jamaica 305 (I. Barrow 108, C. H. Moodie 94) & 146-3 dec drew with M.C.C. 289 (E. H. Hendren 118, E. R. T. Holmes 72) & 75-1.

11th Match: v Jamaica (Kingston)   March 9, 11, 12.
M.C.C. 321 (L. E. G. Ames 89, J. Iddon 58, E. H. Hendren 54, H. H. Johnson 5-71, D. P. Beckford 5-90) & 109-3 drew with Jamaica 452-6 dec (G. A. Headley 127, R. L. Fuller 113*, C. H. Moodie 60*, I. Barrow 59).

12th Match: v West Indies (Kingston)   March 14, 15, 16, 18.
West Indies 535-7 dec (G. A. Headley 270*, J. E. D. Sealey 91, R. S. Grant 77, G. A. E. Paine 5-168) beat England 271 (L. E. G. Ames 126, J. Iddon 54) & 103 by an inns & 161 runs.

appeared for 49 and it appeared as if Grant's bold move would pay off, but Wyatt then joined Hammond and the pair took England to a remarkable win. Hammond, who made 43 and 29, stated later that they were the hardest innings he had ever played.

Moving on to Trinidad, the island had the best of both matches against the tourists and then came the second Test. Wyatt gambled and put the West Indies in. The ploy didn't work. Constantine hit a brilliant 90 and Sealy 92. England failed to gain a first innings lead and were eventually left with 325 to get. Wyatt baffled everyone by reversing the batting order again and England staggered to 75 for 5 – his theory was that England couldn't win, but that West Indies only stood a chance if they dismissed the major batsmen with the new ball. At any rate the theory failed and so did England.

There was yet another odd match at Georgetown. British

The M.C.C. team to tour the West Indies at Paddington station on 15 December 1934. Left to right: D. C. H. Townsend, E. R. T. Holmes, Sir Stanley Jackson, Maurice Leyland, R. E. S. Wyatt (captain), K. Farnes, J. Iddon, W. Farrimond, C. I. J. Smith, W. E. Hollies.

Guiana declared when they had made 188 for 8, then M.C.C. declared at 41 for 5 and proceeded to dismiss the colony for 57 in their second innings. Hammond knocked up a century on an easy wicket on the third day and the match was won. The third Test proved a dull affair.

The final leg of the tour was in Jamaica, which was reached via Panama. In the first game against Jamaica both Hollies and Farrimond were injured – Wyatt acted as wicket-keeper – and in the second match the tourists co-opted T. Arnott (Glamorgan), who was in Kingston on holiday, into the side. Both matches were drawn. The result of the rubber depended on the fourth Test. Headley scored a marvellous double century, none of the English bowlers causing him the least worry, and West Indies declared at 535 for 7. When England batted, Wyatt was hit by a ball from Martindale which fractured his jaw and the England captain was out of the match – he was taken unconscious to hospital. Oddly enough, Grant, the West Indies captain was injured later in the game, so that the match ended with two new captains – Holmes and Constantine. The fast bowling of Martindale and Constantine proved too much for the England batsmen and West Indies won the match with an innings to spare.

During the tour the M.C.C. in England solved the bodyline problem by amicable means, though there were great upheavals at Trent Bridge.

Neither Martindale or Constantine used leg-theory on this tour and the only complaints came from some weird umpiring decisions. Leyland suffered from a very strange leg before wicket dismissal, and he came into the dressing room without a word, slowly sat down and glanced round, then muttered: 'I've never seen owt like it.'

England lacked fast bowlers on this tour, and an injury to Farnes which kept him out of several games was a serious blow. Headley was without a doubt the batsman of the series – none of the English players being very consistent. Once more England had underestimated the strength of the West Indians.

1934-35: M.C.C. to the West Indies

Batting Averages

		M	I	NO	*R	HS	Avge	100	c/s
W. R. Hammond	(Glos)	10	17	3	789	281*	56.35	3	15
L. E. G. Ames	(Kent)	11	18	5	566	126	43.53	1	12/3
E. H. Hendren	(Middx)	11	18	1	673	148	39.58	2	4
J. Iddon	(Lancs)	11	15	3	351	73	29.25	0	7
R. E. S. Wyatt	(Warks)	12	19	3	386	71	24.12	0	7/1
E. R. T. Holmes	(Surrey)	12	17	5	285	85*	23.75	0	9
D. C. H. Townsend	(Oxf U)	11	19	1	424	93*	23.55	0	2
M. Leyland	(Yorks)	11	18	2	347	77*	21.68	0	5
C. I. J. Smith	(Middx)	9	13	0	240	83	18.46	0	2
W. E. Harbord	(Yorks)	4	6	0	81	32	13.50	0	2
W. Farrimond	(Lancs)	4	5	1	52	24*	13.00	0	6/4
G. A. E. Paine	(Warks)	10	15	3	125	49	10.41	0	13
W. E. Hollies	(Warks)	8	8	3	49	20	9.80	0	1
K. Farnes	(Essex)	7	8	1	56	22	8.00	0	4

Also played in one match: T. Arnott (Glam) 1 (ct 1).

Bowling Averages

	O	M	R	W	Avge	BB	5i
R. E. S. Wyatt	96	25	307	18	17.05	5-10	1
W. E. Hollies	206.4	58	498	26	19.15	7-50	3
T. Arnott	29	4	88	4	22.00	4-88	0
G. A. E. Paine	369	103	957	40	23.92	6-67	3
J. Iddon	69.5	13	207	7	29.57	4-14	0
K. Farnes	184	34	550	18	30.55	4-40	0
C. I. J. Smith	238	48	705	21	33.57	5-15	1
M. Leyland	166.5	48	453	11	41.18	4-54	0
W. R. Hammond	57	11	161	2	80.50	1-10	0
E. R. T. Holmes	113	16	458	5	91.60	1-10	0

Also bowled: W. E. Harbord 1-0-1-0; E. H. Hendren 1-0-11-0; D. C. H. Townsend 5-1-22-0.

1935: Martineau's team to Egypt

Perhaps in view of the success attained in 1934, Martineau took a slightly weaker team out in 1935, but found he had underestimated the opposition and suffered no less than four defeats, including both 'Test Matches'.

The touring party were: H. M. Martineau (capt), D. R. Wilcox (Essex), A. W. G. Hadingham (Surrey), C. G. Ford, D. A. M. Rome, A. K. Judd (Hants), A. G. Hazlerigg (Leics), R. Page (Army), A. R. Legard (Oxford U), E. L. Armitage (Hants) and B. H. Valentine (Kent). In the 'First Test', running commentaries were broadcast by the Egyptian State Broadcasting Service and this must have inspired the home team who won by an innings. For the first time, the tourists met a team composed entirely of native-born Egyptians and only just won the single innings match. In the game against Other Ranks, the whole touring party fell ill with food poisoning – the doctor's remedy being half a tin of Eno's per man, which rather upset the batting order.

D. R. Wilcox and B. H. Valentine were the best batsmen, whilst Judd and Legard had almost identical bowling returns – averaging 19.90 and 19.91 respectively.

1935: H. M. Martineau's Team to Egypt

1st Match: v Alexandria (Alexandria).
Alexandria 341 & 144-2 drew with H. M. Martineau's XI 334-9 dec (E. L. Armitage 77, D. R. Wilcox 71) & 49-0.

2nd Match: v Quails (Alexandria).
Quails 170 (P. C. Organ 85, A. K. Judd 6-54) lost to H. M. Martineau's XI 174-4 (B. H. Valentine) by 6 wkts.

3rd Match: v Gezira (Gezira).
H. M. Martineau's XI 210 (D. R. Wilcox 78) & 217-6 dec (D. A. M. Rome 76) drew with Gezira S.C. 184 & 211-6 (Thomas 76).

4th Match: v United Services (Gezira).
H. M. Martineau's XI 275 (D. R. Wilcox 115*, A. W. G. Hadingham 72, Booker 8-68) & 97 (F. Rawson 5-45, Booker 5-50) lost to United Services 167 (Booker 50*) & 206-5 (M. J. Lindsay 80) by 5 wkts.

5th Match: v All Egypt (Gezira).
All Egypt 507 (Thomas 139, Musson 97, F. Rawson 81) beat H. M. Martineau's XI 141 (E. S. Cole 5-37) & 201 (A. W. G. Hadingham 70, C. G. Ford 51) by an inns & 165 runs.

6th Match: v Maadi S.C. (Maadi).
H. M. Martineau's XI 361-3 dec (D. R. Wilcox 154, A. G. Hazlerigg 79) beat Maadi S.C. 129 (A. K. Judd 5-38) by 232 runs.

7th Match: v Egyptian C.C. (Gezira).
H. M. Martineau's XI 141-8 dec (Abdou 8-51) beat Egyptian C.C. 122 (Z. Taker 72) by 19 runs.

8th Match: v Other Ranks (Abbassia).
H. M. Martineau's XI 187 (D. A. M. Rome 62) lost to Other Ranks 188-9 (Ward 78) by 1 wkt.

9th Match: v Victoria College (Victoria Coll).
H. M. Martineau's XI 256-6 dec (A. K. Judd 80, D. A. M. Rome 73) drew with Victoria College 142-7 (G. G. Edwards 81*).

10th Match: v All Egypt (Alexandria).
All Egypt 264 (B. de Botton 115, A. R. Legard 6-99) & 167 (R. G. Musson 55) beat H. M. Martineau's XI 196 (Booker 9-92) & 130 (Booker 7-43) by 105 runs.

1935-36: young M.C.C. party tour New Zealand

The team which represented M.C.C. on the tour of 1935-36 was essentially a side of up and coming young players – the eldest being 34 and no less than 10 of the 14 being under 30. Apart from giving New Zealand the chance of entertaining a full tour from England, rather than a brief visit after a major tour in Australia, the object of the venture was to give experience to the young players in the hope that several of them would be suitable for the tour to Australia in 1936-37.

The M.C.C. originally asked Wyatt to captain the side, but he

---

1935-36: M.C.C. to Ceylon, Australia and New Zealand

1st Match: v Ceylon (Colombo).
Ceylon 107 drew with M.C.C. 27-3.

2nd Match: v W. Australia (Perth)   Oct 31, Nov 1, 2.
M.C.C. 344 (D. Smith 83, Jas Langridge 59, N. S. Mitchell-Innes 58) & 266 J. Hardstaff jun 55, J. H. Parks 51, E. R. T. Holmes 51) drew with W. Australia 232 (F. A. Taafe 76, J. M. Sims 7-95) & 23-1.

3rd Match: v South Australia (Adelaide)   Nov 8, 9, 11, 12.
M.C.C. 371 (J. Hardstaff jun 90, J. H. Human 87, J. H. Parks 67, D. Smith 52, M. G. Waite 5-42) & 174 beat S. Australia 322 (C. W. Walker 65*, M. G. Waite 58) & 187 (D. G. Bradman 50) by 36 runs.

4th Match: v Victoria (Melbourne)   Nov 15, 16, 18, 19.
Victoria 332-9 dec (K. E. Rigg 112, H. J. Plant 64, J. W. Scaife 60) & 122-1 dec (K. E. Rigg 59*) drew with M.C.C. 252 (J. H. Parks 72, R. G. Gregory 5-69) & 46-3.

5th Match: v New South Wales (Sydney)   Nov 22, 23, 25.
M.C.C. 260 (J. Hardstaff jun 77, J. H. Parks 55) & 163 lost to N.S.W. 385 (A. E. Marks 88, F. A. Easton 77, A. D. McGilvray 66, J. M. Sims 6-125) & 39-0 by 10 wkts.

6th Match: v Queensland (Brisbane)   Nov 29, 30, Dec 2.
Queensland 203 (E. C. Bensted 64) & 249 (R. M. Levy 76, J. A. J. Christy 66*, A. D. Baxter 5-61) lost to M.C.C. 558 (J. H. Human 118, D. Smith 109, W. Barber 91, E. R. T. Holmes 80, T. Allen 5-108) by an inns & 106 runs.

7th Match: v An Australian XI (Sydney)   Dec 6, 7, 9, 10.
M.C.C. 411-9 dec (J. Hardstaff jun 230*, Jas Langridge 53, H. I. Ebeling 5-101) & 207-9 dec (J. Hardstaff jun 63, H. I. Ebeling 6-58) beat An Australian XI 227 (A. E. Marks 64) & 188 by 203 runs.

8th Match: v Wellington (Wellington)   Dec 20, 21, 23.
Wellington 164 (J. R. Lamason 62, J. M. Sims 8-53) & 146 (J. Ell 61) beat M.C.C. 166 & 130 (E. D. Blundell 5-50) by 14 runs.

9th Match: v Canterbury (Christchurch)   Dec 24, 25, 26.
Canterbury 243 (J. L. Kerr 146*) & 172 (J. L. Kerr 71, H. D. Read 6-61) lost to M.C.C. 364 (W. Barber 116, Hon. C. J. Lyttelton 80, N. S. Mitchell-Innes 50, I. B. Cromb 5-52) & 52-0 by 10 wkts.

10th Match: v South Canterbury (Timaru)   Dec 27, 28.
M.C.C. 182 (E. R. T. Holmes 61) & 278-6 (N. S. Mitchell-Innes 90*, J. H. Parks 58, W. Barber 50) drew with S. Canterbury 219 (C. Allcott 74).

11th Match: v Otago (Dunedin)   Dec 31, Jan 1, 2.
Otago 78 & 357 (V. G. Cavenagh 66, D. Smith 52) lost to M.C.C. 550 (D. Smith 165, J. H. Parks 103, N. S. Mitchell-Innes 87, J. Hardstaff jun 86, J. H. Human 57) by an inns & 115 runs).

12th Match: v Southland (Invercargill)   Jan 4, 6.
M.C.C. 489 (J. H. Parks 201, E. R. T. Holmes 100, Jas Langridge 118, N. McGowan 5-96) drew with Southland 53-4: rain.

13th Match: v New Zealand (Dunedin)   Jan 10, 11, 13.
New Zealand 81 (H. D. Read 6-26) & 205-7 (H. G. Vivian 87*, H. D. Read 5-74) drew with M.C.C. 653-5 dec (W. Barber 173, Jas Langridge 106*, J. H. Parks 100, J. H. Human 97, J. Hardstaff jun 76, E. R. T. Holmes 54*).

14th Match: v New Zealand (Wellington)   Jan 17, 18, 20.
New Zealand 242 (A. W. Roberts 75*) & 229-3 dec (J. L. Kerr 105*, H. G. Vivian 96) drew with M.C.C. 156 (N. S. Mitchell-Innes 57) & 130-7 (Jas Langridge 61*).

15th Match: v Wanganui (Wanganui)   Jan 24, 25.
M.C.C. 202-2 dec (J. H. Parks 113*) & 198-8 dec (J. Hardstaff jun 60, F. Warnes 5-71) beat Wanganui 130 & 75 (J. M. Sims 5-40) by 195 runs.

16th Match: v Taranaki (New Plymouth)   Jan 27, 29.
M.C.C. 221 (J. M. Sims 51) & 214-5 dec (J. Hardstaff jun 109*) drew with Taranaki 66 (J. M. Sims 5-19) & 138-9 (A. D. Baxter 5-34).

17th Match: v Rangitikei (Marton)   Jan 31, Feb 1.
M.C.C. 248 (Jas Langridge 77, H. Marshall 7-102) & 186-4 dec (N. S. Mitchell-Innes 104*) drew with Rangitikei 47 (A. D. Baxter 6-20) & 18-1.

18th Match: v Manawatu (Palmerston)   Feb 5, 6.
M.C.C. 176 (J. Hardstaff jun 75, J. Murchison 6-51) drew with Manawatu 85-7: rain.

19th Match: v Hawke's Bay (Napier)   Feb 7, 8.
Hawke's Bay 88 (Jas Langridge 8-25) & 97-6 drew with M.C.C. 171-8 dec.

20th Match: v Poverty Bay (Gisborne)   Feb 11, 12.
M.C.C. 296-5 dec (J. H. Human 50*) & 158-9 dec beat Poverty Bay 105 (S. D. Reeves 51) & 67 by 192 runs.

21st Match: v Bay of Plenty (Rotorua)   Feb 15.
Bay of Plenty 99 (J. M. Sims 5-26) lost to M.C.C. 291-6 (J. H. Human 107) by 9 wkts.

22nd Match: v Piako (Matamata)   Feb 18, 19.
Piako 140 drew with M.C.C. 100-4: rain.

23rd Match: v Auckland (Auckland)   Feb 21, 22, 24.
Auckland 306-6 dec (W. M. Wallace 113, P. E. Whitelaw 73, L. F. Townsend 53) drew with M.C.C. 329 (J. H. Parks 88, W. Barber 72, C. J. Lyttelton 60, J. M. Sims 52).

24th Match: v New Zealand (Auckland)   Feb 28, 29, March 2.
New Zealand 368 (C. J. Elmes 99, I. B. Cromb 74) &128-3 (A. M. Matheson 50*) drew with M.C.C. 435 (J. Hardstaff jun 147*, W. Barber 93, J. H. Parks 65).

25th Match: v New Zealand (Christchurch)   March 6, 7, 9.
M.C.C. 195 (W. Barber 60) & 142-2 drew with New Zealand 334 (J. L. Kerr 132, H. D. Read 5-72).

---

declined and the position was filled by Holmes. The full team was: E. R. T. Holmes (Surrey) (capt), J. H. Human (Middx), Hon C. J. Lyttelton (Worcs), N. S. Mitchell-Innes (Somerset), S. C. Griffith (Surrey), A. G. Powell (Essex), A. D. Baxter (Lancs), H. D. Read (Essex) and the professionals W. Barber (Yorks),

Above *An M.C.C. party with some young new faces for the tour of New Zealand in 1935-36. Back: J. H. Parks, S. C. Griffith, A. G. Powell, D. Smith, J. M. Sims, J. Hardstaff, jun, James Langridge. Front: W. Barber, H. D. Read, the Hon C. J. Lyttelton, E. R. T. Holmes, A. D. Baxter, N. S. Mitchell-Innes, J. H. Human.*

Right *One of the greatest foes England faced on the cricket field, either at home or on tour, was Australia's captain, Don Bradman. Here he is getting a ball away through the slips, watched by England's wicket-keeper batsman, Leslie Ames.*

J. Hardstaff jun (Notts), Jas Langridge (Sussex), J. H. Parks (Sussex), J. M. Sims (Middx) and D. Smith (Derbys).

The team played the usual one-day match in Colombo and then began the tour in earnest at Perth, where they had the best of a drawn game. At Adelaide, they met South Australia captained by Bradman and with a good team performance won by 36 runs. Rain spoilt the game at Melbourne, where the State had the better of a draw and then the tourists were defeated at Sydney due to poor batting. Queensland however lost by an innings, with Barber and Smith giving the M.C.C.'s innings a good start by adding 201 before being parted; Holmes and Human also batted in style.

The last match in Australia proved a triumph for Hardstaff, who hit an unbeaten 230 against An Australian XI.

In New Zealand the first match was lost by 14 runs, when the M.C.C. were caught on a tricky wicket, but after that the batsmen flourished and when it came to the first 'Unofficial Test', the visitors hit 653 for 5 declared in reply to New Zealand's 81 all out; Vivian batted stubbornly in the second innings to save the home side from defeat. The second 'Unofficial Test' was played directly after the first and in this the positions were reversed, with the M.C.C., through James Langridge struggling for a draw.

The other two 'Tests' were played at the end of the tour. In the match at Auckland, Hardstaff hit a good hundred, but high scoring throughout meant a drawn game, whilst at Christchurch rain washed out the final day.

The success of the tour was Hardstaff, who easily headed the batting averages and alone completed 1,000 in the first-class games. The Sussex pair of Parks and Langridge showed good all-round form, but a tendency to feel for deliveries outside the off-stump led to the downfall of Smith on too many occasions. Sims' slows proved most effective, but Read was a disappointment. Socially the tour was a success, but the New Zealand Cricket Council reported a financial loss of £3,400.

1935-36: M.C.C. to Ceylon, Australia and New Zealand

Batting Averages

	M	I	NO	R	HS	Avge	100	c/s
J. Hardstaff jun (Notts)	13	21	4	1044	230*	61.41	2	2
D. Smith (Derbys)	11	18	3	711	165	47.40	2	10
Jas Langridge (Sussex)	12	18	5	554	106*	42.61	1	6
W. Barber (Yorks)	13	19	0	797	173	41.94	2	12
J. H. Parks (Sussex)	13	21	1	808	103	40.40	2	9
J. H. Human (Middx)	12	17	0	519	118	30.52	1	5
Hon C. J. Lyttelton (Worcs)	9	15	0	371	80	24.73	0	2
J. M. Sims (Middx)	14	19	3	388	52	24.25	0	11
N. S. Mitchell-Innes (Som)	10	15	0	335	87	22.33	0	9
E. R. T. Holmes (Surrey)	12	17	1	333	80	20.81	0	3
S. C. Griffith (Cambr U)	11	13	4	152	35	16.88	0	11/2
A. G. Powell (Essex)	4	7	1	40	32	6.66	0	6/1
H. D. Read (Essex)	10	12	4	47	25*	5.87	0	3
A. D. Baxter (Lancs)	10	11	2	48	10*	5.33	0	1

Bowling Averages

	Balls	M	R	W	Avge	BB	5i
J. M. Sims	3144	59	1563	70	22.32	8-53	3
H. D. Read	1897	30	1053	44	23.93	6-26	4
A. D. Baxter	1941	47	864	31	27.87	5-61	1
Jas Langridge	1413	46	488	16	30.50	4-53	0
J. H. Parks	1964	81	751	24	31.29	4-46	0
J. H. Human	432	9	221	7	31.57	2-27	0
E. R. T. Holmes	558	13	253	7	36.14	1-2	0

Also bowled: Hon C. J. Lyttelton 104-1-49-0; J. Hardstaff jun 28-0-6-0; N. S. Mitchell-Innes 20-0-13-0; D. Smith 5-0-5-1.

1935-36: Yorkshire tour Jamaica

Following the precedent of Kent, who went to the U.S.A. some thirty years before, Yorkshire took their County side to Jamaica in the early months of 1936. The team sailed on the s.s. *Ariguani* on 30 January and played the first match against a team of Fifteen Schoolboys on 15 February.

The members of the touring party were: P. A. Gibb (capt), A. Mitchell, A. Wood, M. Leyland, H. Verity, E. P. Robinson, H. Fisher, L. Hutton, C. Turner, H. Sutcliffe, T. F. Smailes and W. E. Bowes. G. H. Hirst went as umpire. The County captain, A. B. Sellers, was unable to go.

The three important matches were against All Jamaica. In the first, Jamaica were dismissed relatively cheaply after winning the toss and batting. Yorkshire, through Mitchell, obtained a first innings lead and then managed to dismiss Jamaica a second time for under 300, Verity bowling very well. Mitchell hit an unbeaten hundred as Yorkshire obtained a 5-wicket win, with two minutes playing time in hand. The other two matches fell into the category of high-scoring draws, with neither side having an advantage, though Yorkshire enforced the follow on in the second match.

Mitchell was certainly the batsman of the tour, and the bowling honours were shared between Verity, Robinson and Bowes.

1935-36: Yorkshire to Jamaica

1st Match: v Schoolboys XV (Sabina Pk)   Feb 15, 17.
Schoolboys XV 194 (R. C. Humphries 57) & 61-5 drew with Yorkshire 222 (P. A. Gibb 50*).

2nd Match: v Jamaica Next XII (Sabina Pk)   Feb 19, 20.
Next XII 185 & 116-1 (V. A. Valentine 53*) drew with Yorkshire 214 (P. A. Gibb 74, V. A. Valentine 5-54).

3rd Match: v Jamaica (Melbourne Pk)   Feb 22, 24, 25, 26.
Jamaica 280 (W. G. Beckford 65, G. A. Headley 62, I. Barrow 59, L. G. Hylton 52, H. Verity 5-34) & 257 (G. A. Headley 74, W. G. Beckford 54, H. Verity 5-62) lost to Yorkshire 325 (E. P. Robinson 68, A. Mitchell 66) & 214-5 (A. Mitchell 101*, E. P. Robinson 63) by 5 wkts.

4th Match: v Cornwall (Montego Bay)   Feb 28, 29.
Yorkshire 295-6 dec (H. Sutcliffe 151, J. R. S. Raper 62) & 220-3 (L. Hutton 107*) drew with Cornwall 156 (Russell 55*).

5th Match: v Jamaica (Melbourne Pk)   March 4, 5, 6, 7, 9.
Yorkshire 465 (M. Leyland 115, A. Wood 94, P. A. Gibb 58) & 60-0 drew with Jamaica 314 (O. C. Stephenson 76) & 349-8 dec (D. P. Beckford 114, E. A. Rae 56).

6th Match: v Jamaica (Sabina Pk)   March 11, 12, 13, 14, 16.
Yorkshire 556-8 dec (H. Verity 101, A. Mitchell 77, A. Wood 77, M. Leyland 75, C. Turner 65, L. Hutton 59) & 68-1 drew with Jamaica 592 (C. Boy 139, G. A. Headley 118, C. C. Passailaigue 82, L. G. Hylton 80).

1936: F. R. Brown helps Martineau in Egypt

The annual April visit of H. M. Martineau's team to Egypt contained the same programme of fixtures as in the previous year, but the touring sides results were greatly improved, due in the main to some splendid bowling by F. R. Brown, who captured 64 wickets at 14 runs apiece. The touring party was H. M. Martineau (capt), D. R. Wilcox (Essex), C. H. Knott (Kent), F. R. Brown (Surrey), D. A. M. Rome, D. C. H. Townsend (Oxford U), R. E. S. Wyatt (Warwicks), K. A. Sellar (Sussex), A. W. Childs-Clarke (Middx), W. M. Welch, J. C. Atkinson-Clark (Middx) and F. S. Buckley (Berks).

Both the 'Tests' were won by Brown's bowling and in the second, Egypt had reached 119 for 3 – needing 151 to win – when the last 7 wickets went down for 20 runs. Wyatt was the outstanding bat of the tour and hit two centuries, but Sellar was unlucky in that he hit a beautiful hundred against the United Services and

then wrenched his knee. The fielding of Wyatt, Knott and Wilcox was superb.

The only defeat of the tour was against the Gezira Sporting Club and in this game the ninth tourists' wicket fell just five minutes from time – unfortunately Wilcox could not bat due to sunstroke.

1936: H. M. Martineau's Team to Egypt

1st Match: v Alexandria XII (Alexandria)   April 1, 2.
Alexandria XII 220 (A. J. Fletcher 113, F. R. Brown 6-31) & 89 (R. E. S. Wyatt 6-36) lost to Martineau's XII 239-8 dec (R. E. S. Wyatt 59, M. L. Eggar 6-80) & 72-1 by 10 wkts.

2nd Match: v Royal Navy (Alexandria)   April 3, 4.
Martineau's XI 276 (R. E. S. Wyatt 120*) beat Royal Navy 82 & 103 (Robson 51) by an inns & 93 runs.

3rd Match: v Gezira Sporting Club (Gezira)   April 6, 7.
Gezira 248 (R. G. Musson 113) & 222-9 dec (R. G. Musson 101) beat Martineau's XI 234 (D. C. H. Townsend 59) & 126 by 110 runs.

4th Match: v United Services (Gezira)   April 8, 9.
United Services 305 (R. G. Musson 50) & 144 (F. R. Brown 5-26) lost to Martineau's XI 371-9 dec (K. A. Sellar 108, D. A. M. Rome 69, F. R. Brown 61) & 79-6 by 4 wkts.

5th Match: v Army Other Ranks (Abbassia) (One Day)   April 11.
Martineau's XI 259-6 dec (W. M. Welch 67) drew with Army Other Ranks 191-7 (Hegele 71*, Moxley 51).

6th Match: v Egyptian C.C. (Gezira) (One Day)   April 13.
Martineau's XI 210-9 dec (K. A. Sellar 53) beat Egyptian C.C. 51 (J. C. Atkinson-Clark 5-24) by 159 runs.

7th Match: v R.A.F. (Gezira)   April 15, 16.
Martineau's XI 159 (R. E. S. Wyatt 51) & 358-8 dec (R. E. S. Wyatt 112, D. C. H. Townsend 79, C. H. Knott 65) beat R.A.F. 105 (F. R. Brown 8-33) & 219 (Cruikshanks 64) by 193 runs.

8th Match: v All Egypt (Gezira)   April 18, 20, 21.
All Egypt 166 (F. R. Brown 7-55) & 369 (Hegele 82*, Joy 84, Cruikshanks 59, F. R. Brown 8-126) lost to Martineau's XI 266 (D. R. Wilcox 135, R. E. S. Wyatt 56) & 271-2 (D. R. Wilcox 127, D. C. H. Townsend 119) by 8 wkts.

9th Match: v All Egypt (Alexandria)   April 23, 24, 25.
Martineau's XI 243 (C. H. Knott 79) & 246 (D. A. M. Rome 72, E. Cawston 6-67) beat All Egypt 339 (Halsey 107, Scott 62, Booker 56, Whitmarsh 51, R. E. S. Wyatt 7-78) & 139 (F. R. Brown 8-81) by 11 runs.

10th Match: v Victoria College XV (Victoria Coll) (One Day)   April 27.
Martineau's XI 251-5 dec (A. W. Childs-Clarke 108, F. R. Brown 68) beat Victoria Coll 103 (D. A. M. Rome 5-8) by 148 runs.

1936-37: Bradman brilliant in 3-2 Ashes victory for Australia

The bodyline controversy had been happily settled by the time the 1936-37 M.C.C. touring party left Southampton aboard the R.M.S. *Orion* on 12 September 1936. The team was G. O. B. Allen (Middx) (capt), R. W. V. Robins (Middx), R. E. S. Wyatt (Warwicks), K. Farnes (Essex), and the professionals W. R. Hammond (Gloucs), H. Verity (Yorks), M. Leyland (Yorks), L. E. G. Ames (Kent), W. Voce (Notts), C. J. Barnett (Gloucs), J. Hardstaff (Notts), T. S. Worthington (Derbys), W. H. Copson (Derbys), J. M. Sims (Middx), A. E. Fagg (Kent), L. B. Fishlock (Surrey), G. Duckworth (Lancs) and Capt R. Howard as the manager.

Only E. R. T. Holmes, who had been in the original party, had had to decline – his place was taken by Wyatt, who had been superseded as England captain by Allen in the 1936 series at home to India. Both Voce and Larwood had stated, after the bodyline controversy, that they did not wish to be picked for England, but in the summer of 1936, Voce had stated he would be available for selection if required. The surprise omission was Paynter, who had done so well in 1932-33.

The tourists played the usual one-day game in Colombo and arrived at Fremantle on 13 October, commencing their first match at Perth three days later. In this game an easy victory was obtained with centuries from Wyatt and Hammond. Unfortunately the injuries which were to dog the tourists also commenced. Duckworth fractured a finger and in practice after the game Robins also broke a finger. Before the second match, Ames had back

Right *The party for the full tour of Australia of 1936-37, the tour which followed the bodyline series. Back: W. Ferguson (scorer), L. B. Fishlock, T. S. Worthington, A. E. Fagg, J. Hardstaff, R. Howard (manager). Centre: T. H. Wade, H. Verity, C. J. Barnett, K. Farnes, W. H. Copson, J. M. Sims, W. Voce. Front: L. E. G. Ames, W. R. Hammond, R. W. V. Robins, G. O. B. Allen (captain), R. E. S. Wyatt, M. Leyland, G. Duckworth.*

Below *The captain, G. O. B. Allen, and R. E. S. Wyatt on the initial part of the journey to Australia in 1936, leaving Waterloo station.*

trouble, so that the team, after one first-class game, were without both wicket-keepers. The match was a high-scoring draw.

In the third Australian game – an up-country affair – Wyatt broke his wrist, and the M.C.C. therefore had to call on a substitute to complete the eleven for the match against South Australia. Two brilliant innings by Hammond saved the batting and Allen's bowling then won the game.

The team met its first defeat at the hands of New South Wales, when O'Reilly and Mudge took advantage of a wearing wicket and the middle batting as well as the tail just folded up.

A gallant hundred by Leyland aided by some poor catching saved the M.C.C. from defeat at the hands of An Australian Eleven and after a drawn game against Queensland, the first Test was staged at Brisbane. England went into the match very much as under-dogs. The batting up to now had been most unreliable, the fielding indifferent and the injury list appalling. On the day however, the home side were outplayed from start to finish – Voce, who had done nothing as yet on the tour, bowled splendidly and took 10 wickets for 57, Leyland saved the English batting in the

first innings, whilst in the second Allen made the highest score with 68. It is true that Australia were forced to bat in the final innings on a sticky wicket, but this did not affect the result, which went in England's favour to the tune of 322 runs. It was Bradman's first Test as Australia's captain.

An up-country game alone separated the first Test from the second. In this England were fortunate to win the toss. Batting first, the tourists reached 100 for 1 by lunch and 279 for 3 by the close of the first day – the total rose to 426 for 6 by the end of a rain interrupted second day, at which point Allen declared and put Australia in on another sticky wicket. They were all out for 80, Voce having 4 wickets for 10 runs. The pitch improved and Australia, following on, also improved, but still lost the match by an innings.

England had all the luck, but for a team that was written off in many quarters to win the first two Tests by vast margins required

1936-37: M.C.C. to Ceylon, Australia and New Zealand

Batting Averages

	M	I	NO	R	HS	Avge	100	c/s
W. R. Hammond (Glos)	14	23	2	1242	231*	59.14	5	11
C. J. Barnett (Glos)	15	25	0	1375	259	55.00	5	6
R. E. S. Wyatt (Warks)	12	18	1	785	144	46.17	3	4
M. Leyland (Yorks)	15	27	5	972	126	44.18	3	3
L. E. G. Ames (Kent)	14	23	0	811	109	35.26	1	25/4
J. Hardstaff jun (Notts)	18	31	3	929	110	33.17	1	7
G. O. B. Allen (Middx)	14	20	3	472	88	27.67	0	13
A. E. Fagg (Kent)	10	17	1	399	112	24.93	1	6
T. S. Worthington (Derby)	14	25	1	571	89	23.79	0	10
L. B. Fishlock (Surrey)	13	22	3	363	91	19.10	0	7
R. W. V. Robins (Middx)	12	16	0	297	61	18.56	0	4
W. H. Copson (Derby)	8	10	5	52	12	10.40	0	4
J. M. Sims (Middx)	13	16	1	147	43	9.80	0	12
W. Voce (Notts)	14	21	10	101	24*	9.18	0	8
H. Verity (Yorks)	13	22	2	180	31	9.00	0	10
G. Duckworth (Lancs)	7	8	2	46	15*	7.66	0	11/4
K. Farnes (Essex)	12	15	6	21	8*	2.33	0	7

Also played in two matches: T. H. Wade (Essex) 10,0, 0 (st 1).

Bowling Averages

	Balls	M	R	W	Avge	BB	5i
W. H. Copson	1253	23	535	27	19.81	4-32	0
K. Farnes	2033	30	928	44	21.09	6-96	1
W. R. Hammond	1507	27	577	27	21.37	5-39	2
J. M. Sims	2298	32	1125	47	23.93	5-37	2
G. O. B. Allen	2153	26	1085	43	25.23	6-53	2
W. Voce	2619	37	1164	43	27.06	6-41	1
H. Verity	3343	118	1043	38	27.44	5-42	2
R. W. V. Robins	1235	8	638	16	39.87	4-63	0
M. Leyland	211	1	130	2	65.00	1-1	0
T. S. Worthington	648	8	346	4	86.50	1-8	0

Also bowled: L. E. G. Ames 28-1-16-1; C. J. Barnett 80-1-24-2; L. B. Fishlock 6-0-8-0; J. Hardstaff jun 34-2-27-0; R. E. S. Wyatt 72-0-71-1.
Capt R. Howard (Lancs) played in 2 non-first-class matches.

1st Match: v All Ceylon (Colombo) (One Day)   Oct 3.
Ceylon 149-4 dec lost to M.C.C. 232-5 (G. O. B. Allen 82, J. Hardstaff jun 65*) by 5 wkts.*

2nd Match: v Western Australia (Perth)   Oct 16, 17, 18.
W. Australia 142 & 147 (J. M. Sims 5-79) lost to M.C.C. 469-4 dec (W. R. Hammond 141, R. E. S. Wyatt 106, J. Hardstaff jun 87*, C. J. Barnett 54) by an inns & 180 runs.

3rd Match: v Combined Western Australia XI (Perth)   Oct 22, 23, 24.
M.C.C. 497 (W. R. Hammond 107, L. B. Fishlock 91, T. S. Worthington 89, G. O. B. Allen 65) & 120-4 drew with Combined XI 436 (C. L. Badcock 167, W. Horrocks 140).

4th Match: v Clare County XI (Clare) (One Day)   Oct 28.
Clare County 62-4 dec lost to M.C.C. 141-6 by 9 wkts.

5th Match: v South Australia (Adelaide)   Oct 30, 31, Nov 2, 3.
M.C.C. 233 (W. R. Hammond 104, F. A. Ward 5-79) & 236 (W. R. Hammond 136, F. A. Ward 5-98) beat S. Australia 162 (G. O. B. Allen 6-53) & 202 (V. Y. Richardson 55) by 105 runs.

6th Match: v Victoria (Melbourne)   Nov 6, 7, 9, 10.
M.C.C. 344 (C. J. Barnett 131, J. Hardstaff jun 85, J. Frederick 6-65) & 36-3 drew with Victoria 384 (I. S. Lee 160, R. G. Gregory 128).

7th Match: v New South Wales (Sydney)   Nov 13, 14, 16, 17.
N.S.W. 273 (R. H. Robinson 91, S. J. McCabe 83, W. R. Hammond 5-39) & 326 (A. G. Chipperfield 97*) beat M.C.C. 153 (C. J. Barnett 70, H. Mudge 6-42) & 311 (W. R. Hammond 91, M. Leyland 79, W. J. O'Reilly 5-67) by 135 runs.

8th Match: v An Australian XI (Sydney)   Nov 20, 21, 23, 24.
M.C.C. 288 (M. Leyland 80, L. E. G. Ames 76, R. W. V. Robins 53, A. G. Chipperfield 8-66) & 245-8 (M. Leyland 118*) drew with An Australian XI 544-8 dec (C. L. Badcock 182, W. A. Brown 71, D. G. Bradman 63, J. H. W. Fingleton 56).

9th Match: v Queensland (Brisbane)   Nov 27, 28, 30, Dec 1.
M.C.C. 215 (M. Leyland 98) & 528-8 dec (C. J. Barnett 259, A. E. Fagg 112, L. E. G. Ames 60) drew with Queensland 243 (W. A. Brown 74, R. E. Rogers 62) & 227-9 (G. G. Baker 63).

10th Match: v Australia (Brisbane)   Dec 4, 5, 7, 8, 9.
England 358 (M. Leyland 126, C. J. Barnett 69, W. J. O'Reilly 5-102) & 256 (G. O. B. Allen 68, F. A. Ward 6-102) beat Australia 234 (J. H. W. Fingleton 100, S. J. McCabe 51, W. Voce 6-41) & 58 (G. O. B. Allen 5-46) by 322 runs.

11th Match: v Queensland Country XI (Ipswich)   Dec 12, 14.
Country XI 300 (T. Allen 118, J. G. Maddern 62) & 124 drew with M.C.C. 406 (W. R. Hammond 109, T. S. Worthington 72).

12th Match: v Australia (Sydney)   Dec 18, 19, 21, 22.
England 426-6 dec (W. R. Hammond 231*, C. J. Barnett 57) beat Australia 80 & 324 (S. J. McCabe 93, D. G. Bradman 82, J. H. W. Findleton 73) by an inns & 22 runs.

13th Match: v New South Wales Country XI (Newcastle)   Dec 26, 28.
Country XI 188-4 dec (R. G. Beattie 124*) drew with M.C.C. 178-4 (A. E. Fagg 67).

14th Match: v Australia (Melbourne)   Jan 1, 2, 4, 5, 6, 7.
Australia 200-9 dec (S. J. McCabe 63) & 564 (D. G. Bradman 270, J. H. W. Fingleton 136) beat England 76-9 dec (M. W. Sievers 5-21) & 323 (M. Leyland 111*, R. W. V. Robins 61, W. R. Hammond 51, L. O'B. Fleetwood-Smith 5-124) by 365 runs.

15th Match: v Tasmania (Launceston)   Jan 9, 11.
Tasmania 104 & 209 (S. W. L. Putman 77, J. M. Sims 5-39) lost to M.C.C. 317 (L. E. G. Ames 109, A. E. Fagg 60, J. Hardstaff jun 55, T. S. Worthington 50, S. W. L. Putman 5-87) by an inns & 4 runs.

16th Match: v Tasmania (Launceston) (One Day)   Jan 12.
M.C.C. 250 (D. Thollar 5-67) drew with Tasmania 145-5.

17th Match: v Tasmania Combined XI (Hobart)   Jan 15, 16, 18.
M.C.C. 418 (C. J. Barnett 110, J. Hardstaff jun 110, G. O. B. Allen 55) & 111-1 (R. E. S. Wyatt 68*) drew with Combined XI 134 (W. A. S. Oldfield 60*).

18th Match: v South Australia (Adelaide)   Jan 22, 23, 25, 26.
M.C.C. 301 (C. J. Barnett 78, G. O. B. Allen 60, R. E. S. Wyatt 53) drew with S. Australia 194-4 (A. J. Ryan 71): rain.

19th Match: v Australia (Adelaide)   Jan 29, 30, Feb 1, 2, 3, 4.
Australia 288 (S. J. McCabe 88) & 433 (D. G. Bradman 212, S. J. McCabe 55, R. G. Gregory 50, W. R. Hammond 5-57) beat England 330 (C. J. Barnett 129, L. E. G. Ames 52) & 243 (R. E. S. Wyatt 50, L. O'B. Fleetwood-Smith 6-110) by 148 runs.

20th Match: v Victorian Country XI (Geelong)   Feb 6, 8.
M.C.C. 282 (J. Hardstaff jun 94, L. E. G. Ames 51, J. Collins 5-48) & 251 (M. Leyland 53) drew with Country XI 161 (R. W. V. Robins 5-36).

21st Match: v Southern New South Wales (Canberra)   Feb 10, 11.
M.C.C. 380 (L. E. G. Ames 82, J. Hardstaff jun 67, M. Leyland 67, R. E. S. Wyatt 51, C. V. Jackson 5-143) beat Southern N.S.W. 162 & 78 (W. H. Copson 7-16) by an inns & 140 runs.

22nd Match: v New South Wales (Sydney)   Feb 13, 15, 16, 17.
N.S.W. 231 & 246 (S. J. McCabe 93, J. H. W. Fingleton 60) beat M.C.C. 73 (J. G. Lush 6-43) & 299 (C. J. Barnett 117, J. Hardstaff jun 64, L. E. G. Ames 60, J. G. Lush 7-72) by 105 runs.

23rd Match: v Victoria (Melbourne)   Feb 19, 20, 22, 23.
M.C.C. 187 (L. E. G. Ames 64) & 132-3 (J. Hardstaff jun 60*, W. R. Hammond 56) drew with Victoria 292 (R. G. Gregory 86, A. L. Hassett 54).

24th Match: v Australia (Melbourne)   Feb 26, 27, March 1, 2, 3.
Australia 604 (D. G. Bradman 169, C. L. Badcock 118, S. J. McCabe 112, K. Farnes 6-96) beat England 239 (J. Hardstaff jun 83, W. J. O'Reilly 5-51) & 165 (W. R. Hammond 56) by an inns & 200 runs.

25th Match: v Victorian Country XII (Benalla)   March 5, 6.
M.C.C. XII 344 (L. B. Fishlock 104, W. R. Hammond 53, W. Voce 53*) & 118-6 drew with Country XII 147-8 dec (A. Davidson 52).

26th Match: v Combined Universities (Sydney)   March 8, 9.
M.C.C. 212-9 dec (W. R. Hammond 103) drew with Universities XII 169-7 (A. Chapman 57).

27th Match: v Canterbury & Otago (Christchurch)   March 19, 20, 22.
M.C.C. 217 (R. E. S. Wyatt 63) & 250-8 (R. E. S. Wyatt 100, T. S. Worthington 79) drew with Canterbury & Otago 157.

28th Match: v A New Zealand XI (Wellington)   March 24, 25, 27.
M.C.C. 427 (R. E. S. Wyatt 144, L. E. G. Ames 97, G. O. B. Allen 88) drew with New Zealand XI 265 (H. G. Vivian 88, M. L. Page 50) & 163 (W. A. Hadlee 82).

29th Match: v Auckland & Wellington (Auckland)   April 1, 2, 3.
Auckland & Wellington 183 (P. E. Whitelaw 99*) & 123 (H. Verity 5-42) lost to M.C.C. 205 (R. E. S. Wyatt 56, J. Hardstaff jun 51) & 192-3 by 7 wkts.

a trifle more than luck, and the team played very well.

Again only an up-country game came before the third Test, which Australia had to win to save the rubber. Interest in the game was tremendous – 350,534 attended, a new record. Bradman won the toss, but Australia collapsed to 200 for 9. Due to rain however the wicket was getting progressively worse and Bradman declared. England wickets fell with alarming rapidity, so that Allen also declared at 76 for 9 – he was roundly criticised for this on the grounds that he ought to have closed the innings earlier. Australia, through a double hundred by Bradman and a century by Fingleton, went on to a total of 564 and England lost.

The trip to Tasmania and a rain-ruined fixture against South Australia preceded the fourth Test. Bradman hit a second double hundred and the England batting was very patchy on a plumb wicket. Australia levelled the series.

The deciding Test was held at Melbourne. Australia built up the huge total of 604 in the first innings, assisted by dropped catches and some indifferent ground fielding. The England batting however failed, apart from Hardstaff, who played his best innings of the tour, and following on the visitors faced a spinners' wicket. Australia won the 'Ashes' with little difficulty.

The tourists went on to New Zealand, playing three matches there, but no Test. From New Zealand the side sailed to Honolulu and Los Angeles, spending a few days in Hollywood, then across America to New York and home on the *Queen Mary*.

Financially the tour had been a great success, the total gross English share being £40,000. The professionals received a minimum £400 for the tour.

England's failure can be attributed to a combination of poor batting and brilliance on the part of Bradman. Of the England batsmen, only Hammond, Leyland and Barnett maintained their reputations. Fagg unfortunately contracted rheumatic fever and returned home early. Voce was the bowler of the tour, but was better in the first three Tests than the last two, which told against England, since Allen, with a strained leg muscle, was not really fit for the final Test.

1936-37: Cahn's team to Ceylon and Malaya

In the spring of 1937, Sir Julien Cahn took his team on a nine-match tour of Ceylon and Malaya. The side, which arrived in Colombo on 4 March, consisted of Sir Julien Cahn (capt), C. S. Dempster (Leics), R. J. Crisp (South Africa), I. A. R. Peebles (Middx), D. P. B. Morkel (South Africa), C. R. N. Maxwell (Notts), R. E. C. Butterworth (Middx), B. H. Lyon (Gloucs), S. D. Rhodes (Notts), T. B. Reddick (Middx), J. B. Hall (Notts), C. C. Goodway (Staffs), G. F. Summers and two New South Wales bowlers, who joined the team in Ceylon, H. Mudge and J. E. Walsh. E. G. Wolfe, Sir Julien's brother-in-law, acted as manager.

Of the five games played in Ceylon, the most important was

Sir Julien Cahn's party to Ceylon and Malaya in 1936-37.
Back : J. E. Walsh, H. Mudge, S. D. Rhodes, G. F. Summers,
T. B. Reddick, E. G. Wolfe, J. B. Hall, R. E. C. Butterworth.
Front : I. A. R. Peebles, B. H. Lyon, C. R. Maxwell, Sir Julien
Cahn, D. P. B. Morkel, C. S. Dempster.

that against All Ceylon, which was won by 6 wickets. Mudge and
Dempster hit hundreds; Crisp made 43 in 14 minutes. Peebles,
who suffered from shoulder trouble, had to drop out after the first
two matches.

In Malaya, a three-day game was played against All Malaya,
but was drawn due to rain. There were three country matches, in
which the local sides proved very inferior to the tourists, who were
well on top in every game, winning one by an innings. Cahn's
team however was an exceptionally strong one, well above average
first-class county standard.

1936-37 : Sir Julien Cahn's Team to Ceylon and Malaya

1st Match : v Ceylon Cricket Association (Colombo)
Ceylon C.A. 345 (J. Pulle 88, H. Roberts 85, M. Spittel 58, J. E. Walsh 5-89) drew with
Cahn's XI 190 (C. S. Dempster 58) & 190-6 (C. R. N. Maxwell 56).

2nd Match : v D. A. Wright's XI (Colombo).
Cahn's XI 288 (R. C. Butterworth 78, C. R. N. Maxwell 64, C. Allen 5-89) & 206-9 dec
(B. H. Lyon 52) drew with D. A. Wright's XI 189 & 244-5 (T. Kelaart 90*).

3rd Match : v Ceylonese XI (Colombo).
Cahn's XI 388 (C. S. Dempster 97, T. B. Reddick 92, C. R. N. Maxwell 81, H. Mudge 57)
drew with Ceylonese XI 362 (F. C. de Saram 102, A. Gooneratne 64*).

4th Match : v Combined Colleges (Colombo).
Combined Colleges 158 (R. J. Crisp 7-28) lost to Cahn's XI 203 (T. B. Reddick 57,
P. Pereira 6-33).

5th Match : v All Ceylon (Colombo)   March 18, 19, 20.
All Ceylon 207 (H. Roberts 70, G. S. Hubert 66) & 334 (F. C. Saram 66, M. Spittel 59,
J. E. Walsh 5-96) lost to Cahn's XI 478 (H. Mudge 118, C. S. Dempster 112, R. C.
Butterworth 76, C. R. N. Maxwell 58, G. Pereira 7-158) & 66-4 by 6 wkts.

6th Match : v All Malaya (Singapore)   March 27, 28, 29.
All Malaya 161 (J. E. Walsh 5-42) & 206-7 dec (H. O. Hopkins 78) drew with Cahn's XI
193 & 122-5 (C. S. Dempster 50*).

7th Match : v Selangor (Kuala Lumpur).
Selangor 81 & 56 (J. E. Walsh 5-21) lost to Cahn's XI 372 (H. Mudge 110, C. R. N.
Maxwell 86, B. Mayo 5-88) by an inns & 235 runs.

8th Match : v Perak (Ipoh).
Perak 63 & 81-6 drew with Cahn's XI 293 (R. C. Butterworth 70, C. S. Dempster 68).

9th Match : v Penang (Penang).
Penang 134 (J. E. Walsh 5-41) & 137-6 (H. O. Hopkins 50*) drew with Cahn's XI 281
(R. C. Butterworth 69, C. R. N. Maxwell 50).

1937 : Martineau continues Egyptian tours

The team which H. M. Martineau took to Egypt in the spring of
1937 was not as strong as the previous year. The side was H. M.
Martineau (capt), D. R. Wilcox (Essex), N. Vere-Hodge (Essex),

---

1937 : H. M. Martineau's Team to Egypt

1st Match : v Alexandria (Alexandria)   March 30, 31.
Martineau's XII 408-9 dec (A. G. Powell 115, N. Vere-Hodge 74, D. Roberts 59) beat
Alexandria XII 83 & 318 (R. H. Werner 109) by an inns & 7 runs.

2nd Match : v R.A.F. Depot (Abukir)   April 2, 3.
R.A.F. Depot 131 (Taylor 62*, J. H. Nevinson 5-45) & 223-9 (Taylor 57, A. W. Childs-
Clarke 7-112) drew with Martineau's XI 388-6 dec (D. R. Wilcox 179. J. Gillespie 94*).

3rd Match : v Gezira Sporting Club (Gezira)   April 5, 6.
Gezira 146 & 264-7 (G. A. Thomas 127*, I. J. Kilgour 56, S. Enderby 54) drew with
Martineau's XI 171-9 dec (R. M. Munro 5-39) & 119-7 (D. R. Wilcox 60*).

4th Match : v R.A.F. (Heliopolis)   April 7.
R.A.F. 249-9 dec (A. C. Howie 64, A. W. Childs-Clarke 5-52) drew with Martineau's XI
192-4 (J. Gillespie 71*).

5th Match : v United Services (Gezira)   April 9, 10, 13.
Martineau's XI 345 (N. Vere-Hodge 127) & 132-4 dec (D. R. Wilcox 91*) drew with
United Services 196 (I. J. Kilgour 54, Cruikshanks 52, N. Turner 5-74) & 158-7 (Lawson
62, A. C. Howie 58*).

6th Match : v Maadi Sporting Club (Maadi) (One Day)   April 12.
Martineau's XI 271-6 dec (D. R. Wilcox 102) beat Maadi 63 by 208 runs.

7th Match : v Army Other Ranks (Abbassie) (One Day)   April 14.
Martineau's XI 192 (J. A. Deed 56, J. Gillespie 53) beat Other Ranks 174 (Brown 57,
W. Isaacs 5-69) by 18 runs.

8th Match : v Egyptian C.C. (Cairo) (One Day)   April 15.
Martineau's XI 91 (Abdou 5-25) beat Egyptian C.C. 72 (J. H. Nevinson 5-24) by 19 runs.

9th Match : v All Egypt (Gezira)   April 17, 19, 20.
All Egypt 277 (I. J. Kilgour 86, G. A. Thomas 55) & 170 (J. H. Nevinson 5-44) beat
Martineau's XI 237 (D. R. Wilcox 70, N. Vere-Hodge 66, T. E. Clarke 5-16) & 136 (J.
Gillespie 72, Abdou 9-60) by 74 runs.

10th Match : v All Egypt (Alexandria)   April 22, 23
All Egypt 224 (R. H. Werner 85, Cruikshanks 62, J. H. Nevinson 5-69, N. Turner 5-76) &
122 (A. W. Childs-Clarke 5-48, J. H. Nevinson 5-58) lost to Martineau's XI 374 (D. R.
Wilcox 126, A. G. Powell 76, A. W. Childs-Clarke 59) by an inns & 28 runs.

11th Match : v Victoria College (Victoria Coll)   April 26.
Martineau's XI 271-9 dec (J. Gillespie 96, N. Vere-Hodge 57, L. Bolton 6-66) beat
Victoria College 147 by 124 runs.

J. V. Gillespie, W. J. H. Isaacs, J. A. Deed (Kent), N. F. Turner, D. Roberts, A. G. Powell (Essex), A. W. Childs-Clarke (Middx), D. A. M. Rome and J. H. Nevinson (Middx).

Despite the rather weak nature of the team, the 'Tests' with Egypt were drawn one each. In the first of these, the first native Egyptian to appear on the home side, Abdou, bowled splendidly and took 9 wickets for 60 in the first innings. In the second match good bowling by Nevinson won the game for the tourists. The native Egyptian team in their single innings game against the Englishmen lost a close contest by just 19 runs, Abdou again bowling well.

As expected, the results of the tour did not compare favourably with 1936.

(Essex), N. G. Wykes (Essex), K. A. Sellar (Sussex), A. P. Singleton (Worcs), J. M. Brocklebank (Cambridge U), N. M. Ford (Middx), D. F. Mendl, J. C. Masterman, C. H. Taylor (Leics), D. W. Forbes and J. T. Neve.

The team found the great heat and the vast distances to be travelled more formidable than the opposition and were described after the only defeat—against Hon R. C. Matthews' team—as in an advanced state of exhaustion and decrepitude. Nearly everywhere matches were played on matting wickets, which took the shine off the ball after about three overs and thus put the burden of the attack on the spinners, Brocklebank and Singleton. The former headed the averages with 52 wickets at 10 runs each. Wykes and Sellar were the leading batsmen.

1937: an exhausting M.C.C. tour of Canada

A tour of Canadian cricketers had taken place in England in the summer of 1936 and as it proved a successful venture, the Canadian cricket authorities invited M.C.C. to send an English team to Canada in 1937. The all-amateur side was composed of G. C. Newman (Middx) (capt), H. J. Enthoven (Middx), A. G. Powell

---

1937: M.C.C. to Canada

1st Match: v All Toronto (Toronto) Aug 2.
M.C.C. 251-4 dec (H. J. Enthoven 101*, K. A. Sellar 56) drew with All Toronto 189-7 (L. A. Percival 78).

2nd Match: v Toronto C.C. (Toronto) Aug 3.
Toronto C.C. 209 (P. F. Seagram 66, D. W. Forbes 6-54) drew with M.C.C. 119-9 (N. G. Wykes 56, E. Carlton 5-42).

3rd Match: v United Colleges (Ridley) Aug 4.
M.C.C. 238-6 dec (N. G. Wykes 89) drew with United Colleges 133-8 (L. C. Bell 56, J. T. Neve 5-37).

4th Match: v Waterloo C.C. (Waterloo) Aug 5.
Waterloo 145 lost to M.C.C. 192-7 (N. G. Wykes 72) by 4 wkts.

5th Match: v R. C. Matthews' XI (Toronto) Aug 6, 7
R. C. Matthews' XI 288 (L. C. Bell 93) & 7-0 beat M.C.C. 157 (E. Jemmott 6-39) & 137 (K. A. Sellar 111) by 10 wkts.

6th Match: v Royal Society of St George (Winnipeg) Aug 10
St George 81 (D. Forbes 6-31) & 17-7 (G. C. Newman 5-7) lost to M.C.C. 124 (C. Bligh 5-53) by 3 wkts.

7th Match: v Royal Society of St George (Winnipeg) Aug 11.
St George 46 & 39-3 lost to M.C.C. 139-9 dec (C. Bligh 5-71) by 9 wkts.

8th Match: v Regina (Regina) Aug 12.
M.C.C. 202 (R. H. Foster 5-88) & 116-3 beat Regina 50 (J. M. Brocklebank 5-22) by 152 runs.

9th Match: v Alberta (Calgary) Aug 13.
Alberta 129 (J. M. Brocklebank 6-30) lost to M.C.C. 185-6 (N. G. Wykes 58) by 7 wkts.

10th Match: v Alberta (Calgary) Aug 14.
Alberta 98 (J. M. Brocklebank 5-54) lost to M.C.C. 159 (G. Pain 5-32) by 4 wkts.

11th Match: v Mainland League (Brockton Point) Aug 17.
Mainland League 184 lost to M.C.C. 231-6 (K. A. Sellar 92*) by 5 wkts.

12th Match: v Victoria (Victoria) Aug 18.
Victoria 87 (J. M. Brocklebank 5-21, A. P. Singleton 5-12) & 94-5 dec lost to M.C.C. 97 (J. Payne 5-23) & 94-3 by 1 wkt.

13th Match: v Cowichan (Duncan) Aug 19.
Cowichan 61 (J. T. Neve 5-19) & 50-7 lost to M.C.C. 135 by 5 wkts.

14th Match: v Vancouver Colts XV (Brockton Point) Aug 20.
Colts XV 162 (A. P. Singleton 6-58) lost to M.C.C. 195-7 (K. A. Sellar 70, N. G. Wykes 52) by 8 wkts.

15th Match: v British Colombia (Brockton Point) Aug 21.
M.C.C. 119-1 (C. H. Taylor 62*): rain.

16th Match: v Eastern Canada XI (Westmount) Aug 28, 29.
M.C.C. 221 (A. G. Powell 68, E. F. Loney 5-63) & 274-6 dec (N. G. Wykes 83, A. G. Powell 59) drew with E. Canada 216 (K. Ross 85) & 154-5.

17th Match: v Ottawa Valley (Ottawa) Aug 31.
Ottawa Valley 199-6 dec (J. Seager 70, G. Dicker 60) drew with M.C.C. 141-3 (J. F. Mendl 50*).

18th Match: v Montreal XV (Montreal) Sept 1.
Montreal XV 121 (J. M. Brocklebank 10-27) lost to M.C.C. 161-1 (N. G. Wykes 74*) by 9 wkts.

19th Match: v All Montreal (Montreal) Sept 2.
M.C.C. 255-7 dec (C. H. Taylor 118) beat All Montreal 214 (M. Davies 118*) by 41 runs.

1937-38: Lord Tennyson wins rubber in India

Lord Tennyson was unable to obtain the best possible team for his tour of India. The side that left Victoria Station for the journey overland to Marseilles and thence on board the *Viceroy of India* to Bombay was Lord Tennyson (Hants) (capt), T. O. Jameson (Hants), I. A. R. Peebles (Middx), N. W. D. Yardley (Yorks), P. A. Gibb (Yorks), T. S. Worthington (Derbys), A. W. Wellard (Somerset), A. R. Gover (Surrey), J. H. Parks (Sussex), Jas Langridge (Sussex), J. Hardstaff (Notts), G. H. Pope (Derbys), W. J. Edrich (Middx), T. P. B. Smith (Essex) and N. McCorkell (Hants). A. P. F. Chapman, W. R. Hammond and T. W. J. Goddard declined invitations, whilst Yorkshire refused to allow Leyland to go.

The team arrived in Bombay on 25 October and went to Baroda for a two-day game before travelling by ship to Karachi for the first first-class match. This was a high scoring draw against Sind. There were two minor games before the 'First Test', which the tourists won, with Yardley making the highest score of the match, 96. A severe earthquake held up play on the second day. Switching from turf to matting the team then suffered its first defeat by 2 wickets against Rajputana. However the 'Second Test' brought another victory, with Gover taking ten wickets and Edrich

---

1937-38: Lord Tennyson's Team to India

Batting Averages

	M	I	NO	R	HS	Avge	100	c/s
W. J. Edrich (Middx)	14	24	5	876	140*	46.10	2	11
J. Hardstaff jun (Notts)	12	21	3	706	213	39.22	1	0
Jas Langridge (Sussex)	13	20	1	650	144	34.21	1	11
T. S. Worthington (Derby)	11	18	2	530	82	33.12	0	7
A. W. Wellard (Som)	10	16	1	433	90	28.86	0	16
N. W. D. Yardley (Yorks)	12	20	0	519	96	25.95	0	4
G. H. Pope (Derby)	13	20	2	441	89	24.50	0	15
J. H. Parks (Sussex)	12	20	0	480	89	24.00	0	9
P. A. Gibb (Yorks)	12	18	3	349	136*	23.26	1	21/1
I. A. R. Peebles (Middx)	8	9	4	93	37*	18.60	0	6
N. T. McCorkell (Hants)	10	16	3	241	58	18.53	0	16/5
Lord Tennyson (Hants)	12	18	2	263	118	16.43	1	6
Capt T. O. Jameson (Hants)	6	7	0	83	47	11.85	0	1
T. P. B. Smith (Essex)	10	15	5	83	25*	8.30	0	4
A. R. Gover (Surrey)	9	13	3	72	18*	7.20	0	2

Also played in one match: A. L. Hosie (Hants) 11.

Bowling Averages

	O	M	R	W	Avge	BB	5i
G. H. Pope	341.4	71	924	58	15.93	5-27	6
J. H. Parks	60.4	22	123	7	17.57	2-12	0
Jas Langridge	120.3	17	354	20	17.70	6-41	1
A. R. Gover	257.5	38	876	47	18.63	5-40	3
A. W. Wellard	321.2	40	1022	47	21.74	6-46	2
T. S. Worthington	140.1	20	426	18	23.67	4-46	0
W. J. Edrich	97.5	9	318	13	24.46	4-25	0
T. P. B. Smith	199	24	675	23	29.34	4-61	0
Capt T. O. Jameson	38	3	109	3	36.33	1-5	0
I. A. R. Peebles	104.5	7	404	6	67.33	2-72	0

Also bowled: J. Hardstaff jun 4-0-18-1; N. W. D. Yardley 10-1-40-1; Lord Tennyson 2-1-4-0.

batting well on a worn wicket to make the necessary runs in the final innings.

With Mushtaq Ali and Amarnath hitting hundreds in the 'Third Test', India won by 93 runs and the home country did even better in the 'Fourth', winning by an innings, the swing bowling of Amar Singh proving too good for the visitors after Mankad had hit an impressive hundred. The 'Fifth Test' followed directly after the 'Fourth' and on its result depended the rubber. Amar Singh again proved too much for the English batsmen who were dismissed for 130. Pope and Wellard struck back and removed India for 131. In the second innings the tourists did much better and since Wellard and Pope again destroyed India, Lord Tennyson's side won the rubber.

The players nearly all suffered ailments or injury at some time on the tour and rarely could Lord Tennyson put his best eleven into the field—even he went down with dysentery at Porbandar. Langridge strained his right thigh and Gover his right knee.

Wellard was probably the best bowler but he suffered a vast number of dropped catches. Pope also bowled well and hit many useful runs. The outfielding of Yardley, Edrich and Hardstaff was much applauded throughout the tour. The visit was socially a great success, but the cricketers discovered that the travelling was very arduous.

The great discovery in the opposition camp was Vinoo Mankad, whose all-round cricket impressed everybody.

1937-38: Sir T. E. W. Brinckman's tour to South America

The following team left Southampton aboard the s.s. *Arlanza* on 27 November 1937 bound for South America: Sir T. E. W. Brinckman (capt), R. E. S. Wyatt (Warwicks), A. Sandham (Surrey), L. C. Eastman (Essex), F. E. Covington (Middx), M. W. Tate (Sussex), W. F. F. Price (Middx), F. J. Durston (Middx), A. Wood (Yorks), W. R. Skinner (M.C.C.), F. R. Santall (Warwicks), E. A. Watts (Surrey), H. W. Dods (Lincs)

1937-38: Lord Tennyson's Team to India

1st Match: v Baroda (Baroda)   Oct 26, 27.
Tennyson's XI 399 (P. A. Gibb 105, W. J. Edrich 69, T. O. Jameson 57*, Y.E. Shaikh 5-61) & 51-1 drew with Baroda 177 (R. Nimbalkar 74).

2nd Match: v Sind (Karachi)   Oct 31, Nov 1, 2
Sind 348 (Qamar Din 90) & 83-5 dec drew with Tennyson's XI 303 (W. J. Edrich 140, Lord Tennyson 118, Khadim Hussain 5-81) & 58-0.

3rd Match: v North Western Frontier Province (Peshawar)   Nov 6, 7.
N W. Frontier 80 (A. R. Gover 5-15) & 167 (R. L. Holdsworth 80*, I. A. R. Peebles 7-38) lost to Tennyson's XI 225 (J. Hardstaff jun 80, Abdul Latif 7-77) & 23-2 by 8 wkts.

4th Match: v Universities of India (Lahore)   Nov 10, 11.
Tennyson's XI 376-8 dec (Jas Langridge 108, J. Hardstaff jun 100) & 108-4 (P. A. Gibb 50*) drew with Universities 139 (T. P. B. Smith 6-35).

5th Match: v India (Lahore)   Nov 13, 14, 15, 16.
India 121 (A. R. Gover 5-40) & 199 lost to Tennyson's XI 207 (N. W. D. Yardley 96, W. J. Edrich 54) & 114-1 (W. J. Edrich 50*) by 9 wkts.

6th Match: v Rajputana & District (Ajmer)   Nov 19, 20, 21.
Tennyson's XI 212 (G. H. Pope 52) & 112 (N. Kesari 7-41) lost to Rajputana 237 (S. Mushtaq Ali 82) & 89-8 (G. H. Pope 5-27) by 2 wkts.

7th Match: v W.I.S.C.A. & Gurjarat (Ahmedabad)   Nov 23, 24, 25
Tennyson's XI 420 (P. A. Gibb 136*, Jas Langridge 80, G. H. Pope 60) drew with W.I.S.C.A. & Gujarat 211 (Faiz Ahmad 53) & 228-9 (Seead Ahmad 86).

8th Match: v Jam Sahib of Jamnagar's XI (Jamnagar)   Nov 27, 28, 29
Jam Sahib's XI 206 (M. H. Mankad 62) & 223-7 dec (L. Amar Singh 81, M. H. Mankad 67*) beat Tennyson's XI 126 (L. Amar Singh 5-35) & 269 (A. W. Wellard 90, W. J. Edrich 53, L. Amar Singh 5-68) by 34 runs.

9th Match: v Maharashtra (Poona)   Dec 4, 5.
Tennyson's XI 319 (J. H. Parks 64, N. W. D. Yardley 50, M. K. Patwardhan 5-99) & 42-2 drew with Maharashtra 273 (D. B. Deodhar 118).

10th Match: v Cricket Club of India (Bombay)   Dec 7, 8, 9.
Tennyson's XI 367 (Jas Langridge 144, N. W. D. Yardley 87, S. N. Banerjee 6-89) drew with C.C. of India 189 (Mahomed Saeed 53) & 297-5 (N. B. Amarnath 64, V. M. Merchant 63, M. H. Mankad 50).

11th Match: v India (Bombay)   Dec 11, 12, 13, 14.
India 153 (A. R. Gover 5-46) & 208 (M. H. Mankad 88, A. R. Gover 5-88) lost to Tennyson's XI 191 & 171-4 (W. J. Edrich 86*) by 6 wkts.

12th Match: v United Provinces (Lucknow)   Dec 18, 19.
Tennyson's XI 145 (W. J. Edrich 52, Mahomed Nissar 7-58) & 201-7 dec (J. Hardstaff jun 50) drew with United Provinces 154 (T. P. B. Smith 6-54) & 67-1.

13th Match: v Central India (Indore)   Dec 21, 22, 23.
Central India 191 (J. N. Bhaya 78, G. H. Pope 5-51) & 182-9 dec drew with Tennyson's XI 192 (T. S. Worthington 62, V. S. Hazare 6-54) & 126-4 (W. J. Edrich 66*).

14th Match: v Bihar (Jamshedpur) (One Day)   Dec 29.
Bihar 84 lost to Tennyson's XI 211-6 (N. T. McCorkell 75, P. A. Gibb 59) by 10 wkts.

15th Match: v India (Calcutta)   Dec 31, Jan 1, 2, 3.
India 350 (L. Amarnath 123, S. Amarnath 101, M. H. Mankad 55, G. H. Pope 5-70) & 192 (D. D. Hindlekar 60, S. Mushtaq Ali 55, Jas Langridge 6-41) beat Tennyson's XI 257 (J. Hardstaff jun 59, Mahomed Nissar 5-79) & 192 by 93 runs.

16th Match: v Maharaja of Cooch Behar's XI (Calcutta)   Jan 6, 7, 8
Tennyson's XI 316 (J. H. Parks 89, Jas Langridge 83) & 121-1 dec (J. Hardstaff jun 64*) beat Cooch Behar's XI 167 & 83 (G. H. Pope 5-35) by 187 runs.

17th Match: v Maharaja of Patiala's XI (Patiala)   Jan 11, 12, 13.
Patiala's XI 142 (A. W. Wellard 6-46) & 264-5 (L. Amarnath 109, D. R. Havewalla 106) drew with Tennyson's XI 445-9 dec (A. W. Wellard 78, Jas Langridge 77, J. H. Parks 64).

18th Match: v Delhi & District (New Delhi)   Jan 15, 16.
Tennyson's XI 353-6 dec (P. A. Gibb 117, Jas Langridge 80, T. S. Worthington 62) drew with Delhi 305-8 (Freeland 74, Tamaj-ul-Hussain 73, Major Cassels 50).

19th Match: v Central Province & Berar (Nagpur)   Jan 19, 20.
Central Province 76 (G. H. Pope 5-21) & 112 lost to Tennyson's XI 151-9 dec (N. D. Sane 5-36) & 39-2 by 8 wkts.

20th Match: v Madras (Madras)   Jan 23, 24, 25.
Tennyson's XI 448-8 dec (J. Hardstaff jun 213, G. H. Pope 89, J. H. Parks 53) & 324-5 (W. J. Edrich 130*, N. W. D. Yardley 71) drew with Madras 305 (M. J. Gopalan 98, H. P. Ward 68).

21st Match: v Nawab of Moin-ud-Dowlah's XI (Secunderabad)   Jan 27, 28, 29
Tennyson's XI 148 (Mohammed Lateef 5-30) & 293 (T. S. Worthington 82, N. T. McCorkell 58) lost to Moin-ud-Dowlah's XI 317 (N. B. Amarnath 121, S. Mahomed Hussain 53) & 127-4 by 6 wkts.

22nd Match: v Mysore (Bangalore)   Feb 1, 2.
Mysore 83 & 141 (Safi Darasha 56, A. R. Gover 5-39) lost to Tennyson's XI 305-6 dec (W. J. Edrich 96, J. Hardstaff jun 83) by an inns & 81 runs.

23rd Match: v India (Madras)   Feb 5, 6, 7.
India 263 (M. H. Mankad 113*, G. H. Pope 5-51) beat Tennyson's XI 94 (L. Amar Singh 5-38) & 163 (L. Amar Singh 6-58) by an inns & 6 runs.

24th Match: v India (Bombay)   Feb 12, 13, 14
Tennyson's XI 130 (L. Amar Singh 5-47) & 288 (T. S. Worthington 68, W. J. Edrich 56) beat India 131 (G. H. Pope 5-49) & 131 (M. H. Mankad 57, A. W. Wellard 5-58) by 156 runs.

1937-38: Sir T. E. W. Brinckman's Team to South America

1st Match: v Southern Suburbs XII (Lomas)   Dec 20, 21.
Southern Suburbs XII 291 (K. S. Bush 73) drew with Brinckman's XII 155 (A. Sandham 54) & 195-4.

2nd Match: v Northern Suburbs XII (Saenz O Pena)   Dec 22, 23.
Northern Suburbs 307 (Eric Ayling 54, L. C. Eastman 5-81) drew with Brinckman's XII 148 & 186-4 (F. R. Santall 69*, L. C. Eastman 56*).

3rd Match: v All Argentine (Belgrano)   Dec 26, 27.
All Argentine 203 (K. S. Bush 63, J. M. Sims 5-66) & 239 (Cecil Ayling 75, G. W. Fergusson 68, J. M. Sims 7-108) lost to Brinckman's XI 298 (R. E. S. Wyatt 162) & 148-8 (A. Sandham 51, D. Ayling 5-50) by 2 wkts.

4th Match: v Venado Tuerto XV (Venado Tuerto)   Dec 28, 29.
Brinckman's XI 374-8 dec (A. Wood 104, F. R. Santall 100) & 135-1 dec (L. C. Eastman 67, W. R. Skinner 54*) beat Venado Tuerto XV 190 (F. J. Durston 5-34) & 110 (J. M. Sims 8-54) by 209 runs.

5th Match: v The Argentine (San Isidro)   Jan 1, 2.
Brinckman's XI 240 (E. A. Watts 76) & 51-0 dec drew with The Argentine 142 (K. S. Bush 77, L. C. Eastman 6-18) & 86-3.

6th Match: v Concordia XV (Concordia)   Jan 4, 5.
Concordia XV 66 (J. M. Sims 8-12) & 169 (F. M. Binder 76) lost to Brinckman's XI 358 (R. E. S. Wyatt 146, F. E. Covington 117, A. Sandham 50, J. MacLeod 5-97) by an inns & 123 runs.

7th Match: v All Argentine (Hurlingham)   Jan 8, 9, 10.
All Argentine 250 (K. S. Bush 54, A. L. S. Jackson 53) & 185 (R. E. S. Wyatt 6-39) beat Brinckman's XI 141 (W. F. F. Price 63, D. Ayling 5-67) & 72 (D. Ayling 6-10) by 222 runs.

8th Match: v Rosario XV (Plaza Jewell)   Jan 12, 13.
Brinckman's XI 313-5 dec (L. C. Eastman 111, R. E. S. Wyatt 106*) & 124-3 dec (A. Sandham 65*) drew with Rosario XV 116 (F. J. Durston 5-25) & 125-5 (P. E. Talbot 78*).

9th Match: v All Argentine (Belgrano)   Jan 15, 16, 17.
Brinckman's XI 417 (H. W. Dods 104, F. R. Santall 86) & 91-6 drew with All Argentine 164 & 384 (D. Ayling 88, Cecil Ayling 59, K. S. Bush 53, Cyril Ayling 50, J. M. Sims 6-164).

10th Match: v Argentine XIV (Palermo) (One Day)   Jan 19.
Argentine XIV 95 (F. J. Durston 5-24) & 140-4 (G. Pellens 68*) lost to Brinckman's XI 172-4 dec (R. E. S. Wyatt 67*).

11th Match: v Montevideo (Blangueada)   Jan 20, 21.
Brinckman's XI 268 (F. R. Santall 55, R. E. S. Wyatt 51, C. A. Lucas 5-83) & 411-6 dec (R. E. S. Wyatt 187, H. W. Dods 105) beat Montevideo 80 & 124 (J. M. Sims 7-27).

and W. R. Albertini (Berks), with E. W. S. Thompson as manager and F. Chester as umpire. In addition J. M. Sims, who was coaching in the Argentine, would join the party on arrival.

During a stop in Lisbon on the way out, Tate got a poisoned foot and as a result did not play in a single match. The boat was 30 hours late arriving in Montevideo, so the proposed match there was postponed and the tourists pressed onward to Buenos Aires. There were two two-day fixtures, both drawn in favour of the home teams before the 'First Test' at Belgrano. Wyatt hit a brilliant 162 out of a total of 298 and the tourists won by just 2 wickets. In the 'Second Test' however the English side were caught on a crumbling wicket and D. Ayling, bowling his off-spinners round the wicket, was quite unplayable. In the deciding 'Test', the tourists' batting proved more solid. Dods hit a hundred and a total of 417 was realised. Argentina then collapsed to Watts, but following on the home side made 384 and the tourists required 132 in 70 minutes to win—the score was 91 for 6 at stumps.

The team sailed for home on the *Highland Brigade* and reached England on 10 February. The tour was most successful, but the matches were not well attended, there being little interest in cricket outside the British community.

1938: Martineau's annual trip to Egypt

The team which H. M. Martineau took to Egypt in 1938 was back to the standard of 1936, if not higher. Ten matches were won and the only loss was against the Gezira Sporting Club, when Sumner played two good innings and Cripps bowled well. The tourists were however handicapped in their second innings since Powell was absent ill. In the 'First Test' a violent sandstorm prevented any play on the first day. Wilcox hit his hundred in 90 minutes

---

1938: H. M. Martineau's Team to Egypt

1st Match: v Alexandria C.C. (Alexandria)   March 29, 30.
Alexandria 158 (R. G. Dyson 54) & 231 (R. G. Dyson 58, L. G. Irvine 53) lost to Martineau's XI 427-3 dec (D. R. Wilcox 195, B. H. Valentine 119, R. E. Evans 78) by an inns & 38 runs.

2nd Match: v R.A.F. Depot (Abukir)   April 1, 2.
Martineau's XI 107 (Cook 6-14) & 401-6 dec (B. H. Valentine 194, F. St. G. Unwin 58) beat R.A.F. Depot 192 (H. F. Benka 5-67) & 143 (H. F. Benka 5-48) by 173 runs.*

3rd Match: v Army Other Ranks (Abbassia) (One Day)   April 4.
Martineau's XI 253 (A. P. F. Chapman 74) beat Army Other Ranks 129 (H. F. Benka 5-37) by 124 runs.

4th Match: v Gezira Sporting Club (Gezira)   April 5, 6.
Martineau's XI 146 & 217 (A. P. F. Chapman 68, V. Cripps 5-26) lost to Gezira 187 (W. A. R. Sumner 88, D. C. Rought-Rought 5-40, H. F. Benka 5-66) & 177-6 (W. A. R. Sumner 95) by 4 wkts.

5th Match: v R.A.F. (Heliopolis) (One Day)   April 8.
R.A.F. 236-7 dec (Cook 72) drew with Martineau's XI 182-6 (D. C. S. Ball 88*).*

6th Match: v Egyptian C.C. (Gezira) (One Day)   April 9.
Martineau's XI 189-0 dec (D. R. Wilcox 109, R. E. Evans 76*) beat Egyptian C.C. 97 (A. E. C. Smith 5-15) by 92 runs.*

7th Match: v United Services (Gezira)   April 11, 12, 13.
Martineau's XI 319 (H. F. Benka 75, A. P. F. Chapman 57, D. C. S. Ball 54) & 191 beat United Services 201 (S. Enderby 52, H. F. Benka 5-50) & 278 (W. A. R. Sumner 64, H. F. Benka 5-109) by 31 runs.

8th Match: v Willcocks S.C. (Gezira) (One Day)   April 14.
Willcocks S.C. 176 (J. S. Dawson 51, H. F. Benka 6-73) lost to Martineau's XI 178-8 by 2 wkts.

9th Match: v All Egypt (Gezira)   April 17, 18, 19, 20.
Martineau's XI 399 (D. R. Wilcox 180, H. F. Benka 58) & 248-8 dec (H. F. Benka 77) beat All Egypt 290 (C. P. Hamilton 51, R. E. S. Yeldham 55) & 268 (C. P. Hamilton 80, W. A. R. Sumner 57) by 89 runs.*

10th Match: v R.A.F. (Alexandria) (One Day)   April 21.
Martineau's XI 284-7 dec (A. E. C. Smith 74, Cook 5-56) beat R.A.F. 68 (H. F. Benka 5-22) by 216 runs.

11th Match: v All Egypt (Alexandria)   April 22, 23, 25.
All Egypt 208 (H. F. Benka 9-81) & 367 (C. P. Hamilton 130, A. Cook 98) lost to Martineau's XI 532 (D. C. S. Ball 196, A. P. F. Chapman 88, B. H. Valentine 72) & 45-1 by 9 wkts.

12th Match: v Victoria College (Victoria Coll) (One Day)   April 26.
Martineau's XI 373-4 dec (D. R. Wilcox 120, F. St. Unwin 82, A. W. Childs-Clarke 69) beat Victoria College 45 (Unwin 5-7) by 330 runs.

---

and on the last day Egypt were set to make 358 in under three hours. Hamilton and Sumner actually put on 138 for the first wicket in 52 minutes, and 268 were scored in 160 minutes, but Egypt lost with 15 minutes remaining.

Clever spin bowling by Benka dismissed Egypt for 208 in the first innings of the 'Second Test', and the tourists replied with 532, Ball making 196. Hamilton hit the only century of the tour against the tourists in Egypt's second innings, but it was a vain attempt and the home team only just avoided an innings defeat.

The side that toured was: H. M. Martineau (capt), A. P. F. Chapman (Kent), B. H. Valentine (Kent), D. R. Wilcox (Essex), A. G. Powell (Essex), A. W. Childs-Clarke (Middx), H. F. Benka (Middx), D. C. Rought-Rought (Cambridge U), F. St G. Unwin (Essex), R. E. Evans (Kent 2nd), D. C. S. Ball, A. E. C. Smith (Middx). R. E. S. Wyatt was forced to decline his invitation at the last moment due to a family bereavement.

1938-39: Combined Oxford and Cambridge tour of Jamaica

To celebrate the 75th anniversary of Kingston Cricket Club, the Club invited a team of University players to tour Jamaica in July and August 1938. The object of the tour was to play both cricket and football and to this end no less than 21 players went out. The members who played in the seven cricket matches were: E. J. H. Dixon (capt), R. C. M. Kimpton, W. Murray-Wood, M. M. Walford, G. R. J. de Soysa, R. E. Whetherly, B. H. Belle, M. D. P. Magill (all Oxford) and J. H. Cameron, A. H. Brodhurst, A. H. Fabian, R. G. Sturdy, N. W. Beeson, M. A. C. P. Kaye, D. C. Wilson (all Cambridge). The others, who confined their efforts to the football field, were J. W. Naylor, J. Allen, I. D. McIntosh, R. M. Hollis, E. Hirst, J. H. Binch and J. C. N. Burrowe. (J. H. Cameron did not travel with the tourists, but played in the two matches against All Jamaica.)

The feature of the tourists' cricket was their fielding, which, even on the rough outfields, was excellent. In the first important match against Jamaica, the island required 25 to win with two wickets in hand when the game ended and the Universities had misfortune to bat on wet wickets in both this game and the return, which was won by Jamaica. The wet weather also affected the attendances at these matches and the Kingston Club suffered a financial loss on the venture. The outstanding batsman of the tour was Kimpton, who hit the best hundred of his career against Jamaica. Murray-Wood did well in the club games, but failed in the two important ones. Walford batted consistently and discovered he could bowl. Wilson was the most effective bowler after the captain had worked out the best field placings for him.

1938-39: Combined Oxford and Cambridge Team to Jamaica

1st Match: v Kingston C.C. Minor XI (Dunoon Pk) (One Day)   July 31.
Oxf/Cambr XI 284 (W. Murray-Wood 128, M. M. Walford 56) drew with Kingston 81-3.

2nd Match: v Melbourne C.C. (Melbourne Pk) (One Day)   Aug 2.
Oxf/Cambr XI 180-7 dec (G. R. de Soysa 75) drew with Melbourne 159-2 (O. Stephenson 74, I. Barrow 51).*

3rd Match: v Kensington (Kensington Oval) (One Day)   Aug 4.
Oxf/Cambr XI 223-7 dec (W. Murray-Wood 55) drew with Kensington 131-9.

4th Match: v Kingston C.C. (Sabina Pk)   Aug 5, 6.
Kingston 250 (R. C. Marley 78) & 125 lost to Oxf/Cambr XI 273-5 dec (M. M. Walford 124, G. R. de Soysa 61) & 105-4 by 6 wkts.

5th Match: v Jamaica (Sabina Pk)   Aug 10, 11, 13.
Oxf/Cambr XI 355 (R. C. M. Kimpton 113, J. H. Cameron 62, M. M. Walford 51) & 99 (G. H. Moodie 5-32) drew with Jamaica 227 (O. C. Stephenson 76, M. M. Walford 6-49) & 204-8 (K. H. Weekes 106).

6th Match: v Lucas C.C. (Sabina Pk)   Aug 16, 18.
Lucas 255-6 dec (K. H. Weekes 126) lost to Oxf/Cambr XI 257-9 (W. Murray-Wood 66, R. C. M. Kimpton 65) by 2 wkts.*

7th Match: v Jamaica (Sabina Pk)   Aug 20, 22, 23, 24.
Oxf/Cambr XI 128 & 141 (G. H. Moodie 5-63) lost to Jamaica 343 (S. M. Abrahams 110, I. Barrow 65, K. H. Weekes 58, D. C. Wilson 5-81) by an inns & 74 runs.

1938-39: ten-day 'timeless' Test in South Africa

The tour to South Africa in 1938-39 will always be remembered for its last match – the timeless Test, which ended in a draw after ten days, only because the tourists had to catch the ship back to England. Many records were broken in this game, but the fact that no Test had ever lasted so long will be its lasting memorial.

Hammond, who had changed his status from professional to amateur, captained England in the 1938 Tests against Australia and was the automatic choice as captain of the touring team to South Africa. The full party, which sailed on the *Athlone Castle* on 21 October, was W. R. Hammond (Gloucs), (capt), H. T. Bartlett (Sussex), K. Farnes (Essex), P. A. Gibb (Yorks), B. H. Valentine (Kent), N. W. D. Yardley (Yorks) and the professionals L. E. G. Ames (Kent), W. J. Edrich (Middx), T. W. J. Goddard (Gloucs), L. Hutton (Yorks), E. Paynter (Lancs), R. T. D. Perks (Worcs), H. Verity (Yorks), L. L. Wilkinson (Lancs), D. V. P. Wright (Kent) and A. J. Holmes as manager. In the rough seas of the Bay of Biscay, Yardley fell, cracking a rib, and was unable to play in the first few matches. D. C. S. Compton had declined the invitation to tour due to his commitments to Arsenal Football Club.

The programme opened with a Country match on 8 November and as in previous visits to South Africa the M.C.C. had few problems in the initial matches, winning five of the first six. In Johannesburg however the Transvaal side found the English attack posed few problems. Mitchell and Viljoen both played excellent innings and the Provincial side declared at 428 for 8. The M.C.C. were unfortunate to have Hutton injured in the first over, struck on the head by a ball from Davies, and this prevented him playing in the first Test. Transvaal gained a large first innings lead, but rain marred the closing stages of the game, which was drawn.

The first Test began on the same ground six days later. Gibb was included in place of Hutton and had innings of 93 and 106 – even this great effort was surpassed by Paynter who hit a century in each innings. Goddard knocked out the middle of the home batting with a hat-trick, but Dalton, coming in at No. 8, hit a century and the match went on to a predictable draw. There was a record attendance of 22,000 on the second day (Boxing Day).

Travelling straight on to Cape Town for the second Test, the tourists found rain preventing a start before 3.30 on the first day, but the wicket had been covered and played easily. Hammond, Ames and Valentine hit hundreds for England, whilst Nourse, son of the old Test cricketer, hit a hundred for South Africa and another draw was completed.

When Hammond won the toss in the third Test and England strolled to 469 for 4, with Paynter making a double century and the captain 120, another draw looked likely, but Farnes somehow extracted a little life from the docile pitch and South Africa collapsed for 103. Following on, they recovered their poise; the deficit was however too great and England just won by an innings.

Both matches in Rhodesia were ruined by rain, though Goddard had time to perform a second hat-trick in the game at Salisbury.

Hammond won the toss again in the fourth Test – his eighth

1938-39: M.C.C. to South Africa

Batting Averages

		M	I	NO	R	HS	Avge	100	c/s
E. Paynter	(Lancs)	12	14	0	1072	243	76.57	5	5
L. Hutton	(Yorks)	14	19	1	1168	202	64.88	5	7
W. J. Edrich	(Middx)	15	20	5	914	219	60.93	4	12
W. R. Hammond	(Glos)	15	18	1	1025	181	60.29	4	15
N. W. D. Yardley	(Yorks)	11	12	2	577	182*	57.70	3	2
L. E. G. Ames	(Kent)	13	16	3	683	115	52.53	2	14/7
H. T. Bartlett	(Sussex)	10	10	3	358	100	51.14	1	5
B. H. Valentine	(Kent)	13	16	3	590	112	45.38	2	6
P. A. Gibb	(Yorks)	12	17	0	738	120	43.41	2	10/1
D. V. P. Wright	(Kent)	13	10	2	248	61	31.00	0	6
H. Verity	(Yorks)	12	12	2	245	39	24.50	0	7
K. Farnes	(Essex)	14	11	4	146	33*	20.85	0	5
R. T. D. Perks	(Worcs)	10	7	3	57	22	14.25	0	2
T. W. J. Goddard	(Glos)	10	8	2	76	33	12.66	0	2
L. L. Wilkinson	(Lancs)	12	6	2	25	13*	6.25	0	4

Also played in one match: Ft-Lieut A. J. Holmes (Sussex) 3*.

Bowling Averages

	O	M	R	W	Avge	BB	5i
L. L. Wilkinson	231.3	31	830	44	18.86	5-10	2
H. Verity	428	132	937	47	19.93	7-22	3
T. W. J. Goddard	311	72	817	31	26.35	6-38	1
K. Farnes	384.7	59	1207	44	27.43	7-38	2
D. V. P. Wright	343.4	35	1453	51	28.49	6-55	2
R. T. D. Perks	244.5	29	788	25	31.52	5-100	1
W. J. Edrich	143	16	458	13	35.23	4-10	0
W. R. Hammond	97	23	260	7	37.14	1-3	0
L. Hutton	24	1	108	2	54.00	1-20	0

Also bowled: B. H. Valentine 3-1-12-0; N. W. D. Yardley 3-0-15-0; E. Paynter 2-0-7-0.

1938-39: M.C.C. to South Africa

1st Match: v Western Province Country XI (Cape Town)   Nov 8, 9.
M.C.C. 589-8 dec (E. Paynter 193, W. R. Hammond 106, B. H. Valentine 69, L. Hutton 68, H. Verity 66*, P. Sleigh 5-161) beat Country XI 140 & 107 by an inns & 342 runs.

2nd Match: v Western Province (Cape Town)   Nov 12, 14, 15.
W. Province 174 & 169 (A. Ralph 61, K. Farnes 7-38) lost to M.C.C. 276 (H. T. Bartlett 91*) & 69-2 by 8 wkts.

3rd Match: v Griqualand West (Kimberley)   Nov 19, 21, 22.
M.C.C. 676 (E. Paynter 158, L. Hutton 149, N. W. D. Yardley 142, W. J. Edrich 109, J. P. McNally 5-154, E. V. Franz 5-105) beat Griqualand West 114 (H. Verity 7-22) & 273 (A. P. Steyn 65, F. Nicholson 61) by an inns & 289 runs.

4th Match: v Orange Free State (Bloemfontein)   Nov 26, 28.
O.F.S. 128 (L. L. Wilkinson 5-10, D. V. P. Wright 5-81) & 260 (S. K. Coen 61, H. Verity 7-75) lost to M.C.C. 412-6 dec (N. W. D. Yardley 182*, H. T. Bartlett 100) by an inns & 24 runs.

5th Match: v Natal (Durban)   Dec 3, 5, 6.
Natal 307 (R. L. Harvey 92, W. W. Wade 56) & 30-0 drew with M.C.C. 458 (W. R. Hammond 122, L. Hutton 108, W. J. Edrich 98, E. L. Dalton 6-116).

6th Match: v North-Eastern Transvaal (Pretoria)   Dec 10, 12, 13.
N-E Transvaal 161 (L. Brown 75, L. L. Wilkinson 5-24) & 142 lost to M.C.C. 379-6 dec (E. Paynter 102, B. H. Valentine 100, L. Hutton 66).

7th Match: v Transvaal (Johannesburg)   Dec 16, 18, 19.
Transvaal 428-8 dec (B. Mitchell 133, K. G. Viljoen 97, A. B. C. Langton 58) & 174-2 (S. H. Curnow 51) drew with M.C.C. 268 (L. E. G. Ames 109, E. Q. Davies 6-82).

8th Match: v South Africa (Johannesburg)   Dec 24, 26, 27, 28.
England 422 (E. Paynter 117, B. H. Valentine 97, P. A. Gibb 93, N. Gordon 5-103) & 291-4 dec (P. A. Gibb 106, E. Paynter 100, W. R. Hammond 58) drew with South Africa 390 (E. L. Dalton 102, B. Mitchell 73, A. D. Nourse 73, A. B. C. Langton 64*, K. G. Viljoen 50) & 108-1.

9th Match: v South Africa (Cape Town)   Dec 31, Jan 2, 3, 4.
England 559-9 dec (W. R. Hammond 181, L. E. G. Ames 115, B. H. Valentine 112, P. A. Gibb 58, N. Gordon 5-157) drew with South Africa 286 (A. D. Nourse 120, H. Verity 5-70) & 201-2 (E. A. B. Rowan 89*, P. G. V. van der Bijl 87).

10th Match: v Eastern Province (Port Elizabeth)   Jan 7, 9.
E. Province 172 (A. H. Coy 54*, K. Farnes 5-58) & 111 lost to M.C.C. 518-6 dec (L. Hutton 202, E. Paynter 99, W. R. Hammond 52, P. A. Gibb 51) by an inns & 235 runs.

11th Match: v Border (East London)   Jan 13, 14, 16.
Border 121 & 275 (R. J. Evans 88, D. Dowling 61) lost to M.C.C. 320 (N. W. D. Yardley 126, D. V. P. Wright 61) & 79-1 (W. J. Edrich 50*) by 9 wkts.

12th Match: v South Africa (Durban)   Jan 20, 21, 23.
England 469-4 dec (E. Paynter 243, W. R. Hammond 120) beat South Africa 103 & 353 (B. Mitchell 109, E. A. B. Rowan 67, K. G. Viljoen 61) by an inns & 13 runs.

13th Match: v Combined Transvaal XI (Johannesburg)   Jan 27, 28, 30.
Combined Transvaal 304 (B. Mitchell 83, K. G. Viljoen 76) & 220-2 (A. Melville 107, E. A. B. Rowan 67*) drew with M.C.C. 434 (L. Hutton 148, W. R. Hammond 79, B. H. Valentine 71, S. F. Viljoen 6-91).

14th Match: v Rhodesia (Bulawayo)   Feb 4, 6, 7.
M.C.C. 307-5 dec (L. Hutton 145, E. Paynter 53) drew with Rhodesia 242 (P. N. F. Mansell 62).

15th Match: v Rhodesia (Salisbury)   Feb 10, 11, 13.
M.C.C. 180 (J. H. Charsley 6-58) & 174-2 dec (W. J. Edrich 101*) drew with Rhodesia 96 (T. W. J. Goddard 6-38) & 95-6.

16th Match: v South Africa (Johannesburg)   Feb 18, 20, 21, 22.
England 215 (L. Hutton 92, A. B. C. Langton 5-58) & 203-4 (W. R. Hammond 61*) drew with South Africa 349-8 dec (E. A. B. Rowan 85, A. Melville 67, B. Mitchell 63).

17th Match: v Natal (Pietermaritzburg)   Feb 25, 27, 28.
Natal 295 (E. L. Dalton 110, A. D. Nourse 67) & 219 (D. V. P. Wright 6-55) lost to M.C.C. 407 (W. J. Edrich 150, L. E. G. Ames 62) & 110-1 (L. Hutton 53*) by 9 wkts.

18th Match: v South Africa (Durban)   March 3, 4, 6, 7, 8, 9, 10, 11, 13, 14
South Africa 530 (P. G. V. van der Bijl 125, A. D. Nourse 103, A. Melville 78, R. E. Grieveson 75, E. L. Dalton 57, R. T. D. Perks 5-100) & 481 (A. Melville 103, P. G. V. van der Bijl 97, B. Mitchell 89, K. G. Viljoen 74) drew with England 316 (L. E. G. Ames 84, E. Paynter 62) & 654-5 (W. J. Edrich 219, W. R. Hammond 140, P. A. Gibb 120, E. Paynter 75, L. Hutton 55).

Two members of the touring party to South Africa in 1938-39 return home in March 1939, Ken Farnes (left) and Hedley Verity (right). They are being greeted by Farnes' father (centre). This is a particularly poignant picture, as these two were the best-known English cricketers killed in the Second World War.

successive correct call in Test Matches—and England batted first, but showers soon came to assist the bowlers and for the only time in this Test series South Africa dismissed England cheaply. The home team went on to achieve a first innings lead of 134, but their slow scoring allied to more rain which washed out the third day produced a third drawn match.

The fifth Test followed a win over Natal. South Africa won the toss and batted for the first two and a half days to total 530. England fared poorly on the fourth day and were 268 by the close for the loss of 7 wickets. South Africa gained a lead of 214 on first innings, but did not enforce the follow on and when their second innings ended shortly before stumps on the sixth day, England required 696 to win. Hutton, Gibb and Edrich made a determined effort on the seventh day and by its close England had moved to 253 for 1, Gibb 78 not out, Edrich 107 not out. Rain prevented any play on the eighth day (Saturday) and on the Monday England went on to 496 for 3, needing only 200 more for victory. On the tenth day, South Africa bowled and fielded very tightly—only 39 runs came in the first hour—but then England, seeing rain in the air, began to hit out. The score reached 654 for 5, only 42 needed, when a thunderstorm just before 4 o'clock ended the game, the tourists having to travel back to Cape Town—a distance of about 1,000 miles—to catch the *Athlone Castle* for home. The match was therefore drawn and England won the series one match to nil.

Hammond was criticised for his over-cautious approach in the Test Matches, delaying declarations on several occasions until all hope of a win had gone. The batting was also very slow. The tourists' batsmen had a tremendous time, and scarcely anyone failed, but the bowlers struggled, the perfect pitches being the problem. Everywhere, except in Rhodesia, the matches were played on turf rather than matting, quite a change from the earlier tours, and the excessive care with which the groundsmen prepared these relatively new turf wickets can take the blame for the dullness of the big matches.

1938-39: Sir Julien Cahn's last tour to New Zealand

At the invitation of the New Zealand Cricket Council, Sir Julien Cahn took his team out there in the early months of 1939. The team, which left England on 6 January, was Sir Julien Cahn (capt), C. S. Dempster (Leics), A. H. Dyson (Glamorgan), C. C.

Goodway (Warwicks), J. Hardstaff (Notts), G. F. H. Heane (Notts), V. E. Jackson (Leics), J. G. Lush (New South Wales), C. R. N. Maxwell (Notts), H. Mudge (New South Wales), N. Oldfield (Lancs), W. E. Phillipson (Lancs), T. P. B. Smith (Essex), E. A. Watts (Surrey), J. E. Walsh (Leics) and W. E. Astill (Leics) acting as scorer.

After four minor games, the side met Canterbury at Lancaster Park, where a determined innings of 180 by Hardstaff prevented the tourists collapsing and the game was drawn. Large crowds watched the match, the receipts being £510. In the second important match, Otago were beaten by an innings. Dempster batted 337 minutes for his double century and Smith's spin dismissed Otago twice for under 200. The 'Test Match' was completely ruined by rain, but about 5,000 watched the only day's play. The last important game was staged in Auckland, where Cahn's side hit 456 and gained a large first innings lead but could not force a win when Auckland followed on.

The tour was a great success and despite some bad weather a profit of £155 was made, which Sir Julien gave to the New Zealand Cricket Council. Owing to a shipping strike, the return voyage to England was delayed and the county players only just arrived back for the start of the English season.

This was the last overseas tour undertaken by Sir Julien Cahn—he died on 26 September 1944.

1938-39: Sir Julien Cahn's Team to New Zealand

1st Match: v Secondary Schools (Auckland) (One Day) Feb 13.
Schools 85 (J. E. Walsh 7-24) lost to Cahn's XI 286-8 (J. Hardstaff jun 56).

2nd Match: v Waikato (Hamilton) Feb 15, 16.
Waikato 131 drew with Cahn's XI 304-8 (C. S. Dempster 64, W. E. Phillipson 52*).

3rd Match: v Wanganui (Wanganui) (One Day) Feb 18.
Wanganui 121 (H. Cuming 57, J. G. Lush 5-16) lost to Cahn's XI 291-3 (A. H. Dyson 103, H. Mudge 72*, C. S. Dempster 52).

4th Match: v Minor Associations (Palmerston North) Feb 21, 22.
Minor Associations XII 206 (Evans 72, J. E. Walsh 8-37) & 119-10 (E. A. Watts 5-37) drew with Cahn's XII 418 (J. Hardstaff jun 160, E. A. Watts 80*).

5th Match: v Canterbury (Christchurch) Feb 24, 25, 27.
Canterbury XII 464 (J. L. Kerr 124, R. E. J. Menzies 77, I. B. Cromb 66) & 233 (M. P. Donnelly 56) drew with Cahn's XII 410 (J. Hardstaff jun 180, G. F. H. Heane 67, A. W. Roberts 5-107).

6th Match: v Secondary Schools (Oamaru) March 1, 2.
Cahn's XI 380-6 dec (V. E. Jackson 135, N. Oldfield 104*, C. S. Dempster 65) beat Secondary Schools 84 (T. P. B. Smith 7-4) & 87 (J. E. Walsh 5-33) by an inns & 209 runs.

7th Match: v Otago (Dunedin) March 3, 4, 6.
Otago XII 184 (A. R. Knight 53, T. P. B. Smith 5-56) & 108 lost to Cahn's XII 437 (C. S. Dempster 200, E. A. Watts 84) by an inns & 142 runs.

8th Match: v New Zealand (Wellington) March 10, 11, 13.
New Zealand 170-5 dec (W. M. Wallace 54*) drew with Cahn's XI 163-7: rain.

9th Match: v Bay of Plenty (Rotorua) (One Day) March 15.
Bay of Plenty 233 (N. W. Bayley 76, R. Barlow 51, J. E. Walsh 5-69) drew with Cahn's XI 126-8 (H. Mudge 60*).

10th Match: v Auckland (Auckland) March 17, 18, 20.
Cahn's XII 456 (J. Hardstaff jun 84, N. Oldfield 70, V. E. Jackson 59, C. S. Dempster 56) drew with Auckland XII 270 (H. T. Pearson 76, J. E. Walsh 5-91) & 305-3 (P. E. Whitelaw 100, G. L. Weir 96).

1939: the last cricket tour to Egypt

For his eleventh annual tour to Egypt, H. M. Martineau took with him R. E. S. Wyatt (Warwicks), F. R. Brown (Surrey), T. N. Pearce (Essex), A. W. Childs-Clarke (Middx), A. P. Singleton (Worcs), D. F. Walker (Oxford), C. H. Taylor (Leics), H. R. Crouch (Surrey 2nd), R. de W. K. Winlaw (Surrey), A. G. Powell (Essex) and B. Stevens.

It is believed that this tour created a new vogue by being the first to travel by air from England. The side flew from Croydon on 31 March in an Imperial Airways Frobisher air liner. The flight to Marseilles took four hours and from there the team transferred on to a flying boat which flew via Rome and Athens, touching down at Alexandria in time for dinner. Several county players, who normally would have refused Martineau's invitation, accepted because the flight considerably reduced the time spent away from England.

Of the two important matches, the 'First Test' was a very exciting match throughout. The tourists won in the final over with three wickets in hand, Walker hitting his 60 in under 50 minutes. The 'Second Test' was quite astonishing. Egypt gained a first innings lead of 154, through a century by Hamilton, and in the end required 176 in their second innings in two hours to win – the home team sank to 50 all out, Childs-Clarke taking 4 for 15. In the other games Wyatt batted splendidly, as did Walker, and of the newcomers Singleton bowled and batted well – a most cheerful cricketer.

The team flew back to England on 29 April. It was to prove the last important English cricket tour to Egypt, though many first-class cricketers were destined to play there during the Second World War.

1939: H. M. Martineau's Team to Egypt

1st Match: v Alexandria (Alexandria)   April 3, 4.
Martineau's XI 284 (D. F. Walker 116, R. E. S. Wyatt 68) & 149-5 dec (T. N. Pearce 53) drew with Alexandria 195 (B. de Botton 70) & 106-8.

2nd Match: v R.A.F. Depot (Abuqir)   April 5, 6.
Martineau's XI 256 (D. F. Walker 100, R. E. S. Wyatt 62*) & 177-2 dec (R. E. S. Wyatt 84*) beat R.A.F. Depot 112 (Moody 51, A. P. Singleton 6-30) & 111 by 210 runs.

3rd Match: v Alexandria Area XI (Alexandria) (One Day)   April 8.
Area XI 42 (H. R. Crouch 8-20) & 115-6 lost on first innings to Martineau's XI 163-9 dec.

4th Match: v Gexira (Gezira)   April 10, 11, 12.
Martineau's XI 297 (C. H. Taylor 112, D. F. Walker 100, T. N. Pearce 57, F. R. Brown 52, J. H. Whitehead 6-109) & 219-2 dec (C. H. Taylor 114*, R. E. S. Wyatt 76) drew with Gezira 434 (R. J. Parkhouse 121, M. St. J. Packe 109, R. E. S. Yeldham 62) & 131-2 (C. P. Hamilton 51*).

5th Match: v R.A.F. Egypt (Gezira) (One Day)   April 13.
Martineau's XI 351-9 dec (R. E. S. Wyatt 113, F. R. Brown 77, B. Stevens 59) beat R.A.F. 116 (D. F. Walker 5-15) by 235 runs.

6th Match: v Army Other Ranks (Helmieh Camp) (One Day)   April 14.
Martineau's XI 297-8 dec (R. E. S. Wyatt 100*, T. N. Pearce 84) drew with Army Other Ranks 210-9 (Warwick 57).

7th Match: v United Services (Gezira)   April 15, 17.
United Services 157 (C. P. Hamilton 59, A. P. Singleton 6-21) & 172 (R. E. S. Yeldham 86, F. R. Brown 5-86) lost to Martineau's XI 380 (R. de W. K. Winlaw 101, C. H. Taylor 71, A. P. Singleton 61*) by an inns & 51 runs.

8th Match: v All Egypt (Gezira)   April 20, 21, 22.
Egypt 319 (R. J. Parkhouse 110, J. E. S. Walford 75, W. A. R. Sumner 52, F. R. Brown 8-117) & 255 (C. P. Hamilton 56) lost to Martineau's XI 363 (F. R. Brown 79, D. F. Walker 59) & 209-7 (T. N. Pearce 75*, D. F. Walker 60) by 3 wkts.

9th Match: v Victoria College (Victoria)   April 24.
Martineau's XI 304-4 dec (D. F. Walker 100, H. R. Crouch 84*, A. G. Powell 51) beat Victoria College 122 by 182 runs.

10th Match: v All Egypt (Alexandria)   April 25, 26, 27.
Martineau's XI 241 (F. R. Brown 87*, D. F. Walker 69) & 329 (C. H. Taylor 99, T. N. Pearce 76, J. E. S. Walford 5-93) beat Egypt 395 (C. P. Hamilton 113, J. K. Luard 78, W. G. Tailyour 58, H. M. Martineau 5-133) & 50 by 125 runs.

1939-40: abortive M.C.C. tour of India

In the summer of 1939, the M.C.C. selected the following team to tour India for 1939-40: A. J. Holmes (Sussex) (capt), H. T. Bartlett (Sussex), J. M. Brocklebank (Lancs), S. C. Griffith (Sussex), R. H. C. Human (Worcs), R. E. S. Wyatt (Warwicks) and the professionals Emrys Davies (Glam), H. E. Dollery (Warwicks), H. Gimblett (Som), G. H. Pope (Derbys), John Langridge (Sussex), G. S. Mobey (Surrey), M. S. Nichols (Essex), J. F. Parker (Surrey), T. P. B. Smith (Essex) and A. W. Wellard (Somerset) with Lieut-Col C. B. Rubie as manager.

The side was very much an England second team squad and probably not as strong as Lord Tennyson's team of 1937-38. War broke out before the M.C.C. party could leave England, and the tour was cancelled.

1946-47: England well beaten in first post-war tour of Australia

Within a few weeks of V.J. Day, the Australian Board of Cricket Control put out an invitation to the M.C.C. for a visit by the English team to Australia in the winter of 1946-47. Dr Evatt, a member of the Australian Government, supported this invitation in the strongest terms during a speech in London on 1 October 1945 and on 9 October the M.C.C. promised to send a team. No doubt the success of the Victory 'Tests' which were played in England between the Australian Services and England in the summer of 1945 had a lot to do with the speedy way M.C.C. agreed to make the tour. The discussion regarding the selection of the team began before Christmas 1945. The first problems seemed to involve the bowling strength, since both Farnes and Verity had died in the War. The Tests played against India in the summer of 1946 were used to a large extent as trials for the Australian visit. The eventual team was: W. R. Hammond (Gloucs) (capt), N. W. D. Yardley (Yorks) (vice-capt) and P. A. Gibb (Yorks) as the only amateurs, and A. V. Bedser (Surrey), D. C. S. Compton (Middx), W. J. Edrich (Middx), T. G. Evans (Kent), L. B. Fishlock (Surrey), J. Hardstaff (Notts), L. Hutton (Yorks), J. T. Ikin (Lancs), James Langridge (Sussex), R. Pollard (Lancs), T. P. B. Smith (Essex), W. Voce (Notts), C. Washbrook (Lancs) and D. V. P. Wright (Kent). Major R. Howard was manager and W. Ferguson acted as scorer. E. A. Bedser also travelled with the team.

The team sailed from Southampton on the R.M.S. *Stirling Castle* on 31 August. The main criticism of the team by the press was that it was too old and the names of Gimblett, Dollery, Brookes and Robertson were noted as omissions, but in retrospect it is doubtful if any or all of this quartet would have altered the outcome of the tour.

Unlike the pre-war voyages the ship did not stop, except over-night at Port Said, and the journey was accomplished in 24 days. This took the organisers by surprise and two minor additional matches were hastily added before the 'official' start of the tour at

---

1946-47: M.C.C. to Australia and New Zealand

Batting Averages

	M	I	NO	R	HS	Avge	100	c/s
L. Hutton (Yorks)	14	21	3	1267	151*	70.38	3	5
Jas Langridge (Sussex)	4	3	1	130	100	65.00	1	2
D. C. S. Compton (Middx)	19	31	4	1660	163	61.48	5	11
W. R. Hammond (Glos)	13	19	0	781	208	41.10	2	12
W. J. Edrich (Middx)	18	27	2	998	119	39.92	1	15
J. Hardstaff jun (Notts)	8	13	1	471	155	39.25	1	3
C. Washbrook (Lancs)	18	29	0	1129	133	38.93	4	6
N. W. D. Yardley (Yorks)	19	27	4	814	126	35.39	1	11
J. T. Ikin (Lancs)	20	30	6	822	102*	34.25	1	24
T. G. Evans (Kent)	16	22	6	438	101	27.37	1	29/5
L. B. Fishlock (Surrey)	10	17	1	329	57	20.56	0	5
T. P. B. Smith (Essex)	10	12	1	186	46	16.90	0	5
A. V. Bedser (Surrey)	15	22	5	264	51	15.52	0	8
P. A. Gibb (Yorks)	9	14	1	199	37*	15.30	0	10/1
W. Voce (Notts)	10	11	1	131	28	13.10	0	3
R. Pollard (Lancs)	13	9	4	49	12*	9.80	0	6
D. V. P. Wright (Kent)	15	18	5	84	20	6.46	0	5

Bowling Averages

	Balls	M	R	W	Avge	BB	5i
J. Hardstaff jun	112	1	50	3	16.66	3-24	0
D. C. S. Compton	812	18	364	17	21.41	7-36	1
N. W. D. Yardley	1859	17	477	16	29.81	3-19	0
T. P. B. Smith	2012	18	1087	32	33.96	9-121	2
D. V. P. Wright	3458	47	1916	54	35.48	7-105	3
A. V. Bedser	4040	87	1667	47	35.46	4-21	0
R. Pollard	2558	73	1021	28	36.46	4-19	0
J. T. Ikin	857	9	488	13	37.53	4-51	0
W. Voce	1781	45	801	21	38.14	6-38	1
W. J. Edrich	2072	33	1032	26	39.69	4-26	0
Jas Langridge	800	15	297	7	42.42	3-60	0

Also bowled: W. R. Hammond 24-0-8-0; B. Fishlock 8-0-3-0; P. A. Gibb 8-0-14-0; L. Hutton 168-1-132-2.

The first M.C.C. party to tour after the Second World War was the team to Australia and New Zealand in 1946-47. Here are the players as an Australian cartoonist saw them, left to right, from top: N. W. D. Yardley, T. G. Evans, T. P. B. Smith, L. Hutton, A. V. Bedser, J. Hardstaff, W. Voce, R. Pollard, W. R. Hammond, J. T. Ikin, W. J. Edrich, James Langridge, P. A. Gibb, Major R. Howard (manager), L. B. Fishlock, C. Washbrook, D. V. P. Wright, D. C. S. Compton.

Opposite *Denis Compton batting during his innings of 98 in the match against the Combined XI at Perth. G. Kessey is the wicket-keeper.*

Below *The two greatest batsmen of the 1930s were the captains of England and Australia in the first post-war Test series. Photographers gather round as Australia's Bradman (with bat) and England's Hammond inspect the Test wicket at Adelaide.*

Perth. In the two opening first-class games the bat dominated and high scoring draws were the result. M.C.C. however bowled to much greater effect in the next two important matches, very nearly winning the first and easily beating Victoria in the second. The bowling of Wright in this match raised English hopes. The matches against An Australian Eleven and New South Wales were both rained off, and after a draw with Queensland, the first Test began at Brisbane. The great debate earlier on was whether Bradman would play—the fact that he did and that he scored 187 had something to do with England's downfall, but the visitors also had the misfortune of batting twice on a rain-affected wicket, their batting collapsing in each innings, and Gibb made one or two bad blunders behind the wicket.

There was a brief respite at Gympie before the second Test at Sydney. Hammond won the toss, and though Australia were without Lindwall—ill with chicken pox—the tourists' batting was very inept against the spin of McCool and Johnson. Barnes and Bradman both hit 234 and England faced an impossible task in their innings. Edrich hit a century and most of the other English batsmen managed something, but the result was still an innings defeat. In the third Test, England gave a good account of themselves in the first innings. It was not until Tallon and Lindwall came together in Australia's second innings and added 154 for the 8th wicket that the match slipped from England's grasp and from then on it was all they could do to hang on for a draw. 343,675 people watched the game and the receipts of £44,063 were a record. There was little to choose between the two sides after each

---

1946-47: M.C.C. to Australia and New Zealand

1st Match: v Northam & Country Districts (Northam)   Oct 2, 3.
Northam 123 (T. P. B. Smith 5-55) & 71 (W. J. Edrich 6-20) lost to M.C.C. 409-6 dec (W. R. Hammond 131, D. C. S. Compton 84, L. Hutton 51) by an inns & 215 runs.

2nd Match: v Western Australian Colts (Freemantle)   Oct 7.
M.C.C. 197-4 dec (P. A. Gibb 51, L. B. Fishlock 50) drew with Colts 138-6.

3rd Match: v Western Australia (Perth)   Oct 11, 12, 14.
W. Australia 366 (D. Watt 85, M. Herbert 53) & 48-1 drew with M.C.C. 477 (W. R. Hammond 208, J. T. Ikin 66, J. Hardstaff jun 52, C. Puckett 5-126).

4th Match: v Combined XI (Perth)   Oct 17, 18, 19.
Combined XI 462 (D. Watt 157, I. W. Johnson 87) drew with M.C.C. 302 (D. C. S. Compton 98, C. Washbrook 80, N. W. D. Yardley 56).

5th Match: v South Australian Country XI (Port Pirie)   Oct 22, 23.
M.C.C. 487-6 dec (L. Hutton 164, D. C. S. Compton 100, L. B. Fishlock 98, J. Hardstaff jun 67*) beat S.A. Country XI 87 (T. P. B. Smith 5-16, D. V. P. Wright 5-40) & 92 by an inns & 308 runs.

6th Match: v South Australia (Adelaide)   Oct 25, 26, 27, 28.
M.C.C. 506-5 dec (L. Hutton 136, C. Washbrook 113, W. J. Edrich 71, D. C. S. Compton 71, N. W. D. Yardley 54*) drew with S. Australia 266 (D. G. Bradman 76, R. James 58, P. L. Ridings 57, T. P. B. Smith 5-93) & 276-8 (R. J. Craig 111, J. Mann 62*).

7th Match: v Victoria (Melbourne)   Oct 31, Nov 1, 2, 4.
M.C.C. 358 (D. C. S. Compton 143, N. W. D. Yardley 70) & 279-7 dec (L. Hutton 151*) beat Victoria 189 (A. L. Hassett 57, D. V. P. Wright 6-48) & 204 (A. L. Hassett 57, M. R. Harvey 57) by 244 runs.

8th Match: v An Australian XI (Melbourne)   Nov 8, 9, 11, 12, 13.
M.C.C. 314 (L. Hutton 71, C. Washbrook 57, W. R. Hammond 51, C. L. McCool 7-106) drew with An Australian XI 327-5 (A. R. Morris 115, D. G. Bradman 106).

9th Match: v New South Wales (Sydney)   Nov 15, 16, 18, 19.
N.S.W. 165-4 dec (A. R. Morris 81*) drew with M.C.C. 156-2 (L. Hutton 97): rain.

10th Match: v Queensland (Brisbane)   Nov 22, 23, 25, 26.
Queensland 400 (G. G. Cook 169*, R. E. Rogers 66, A. S. Young 53) & 230-6 dec (L. J. Johnson 75) drew with M.C.C. 310 (W. J. Edrich 64*, D. C. S. Compton 55, C. L. McCool 6-105) & 238-6 (C. Washbrook 124, W. J. Edrich 71).

11th Match: v Australia (Brisbane)   Nov 29, 30, Dec 2, 3, 4, 5.
Australia 645 (D. G. Bradman 187, A. L. Hassett 128, C. L. McCool 95, K. R. Miller 79, D. V. P. Wright 5-167) beat England 141 (K. R. Miller 7-60) & 172 (E. R. H. Toshack 6-82) by an inns & 332 runs.

12th Match: v Queensland Country XI (Gympie)   Dec 7, 9.
Country XI 208 (T. Allen 53, T. P. B. Smith 5-80) & 311-9 (C. G. R. Stibe 75, K. Gartrell 52*) drew with M.C.C. 282 (J. Hardstaff jun 64, L. B. Fishlock 62, T. E. Ball 5-69).

13th Match: v Australia (Sydney)   Dec 13, 14, 16, 17, 18, 19.
England 255 (W. J. Edrich 71, J. T. Ikin 60, I. W. Johnson 6-42) & 371 (W. J. Edrich 119, D. C. S. Compton 54, C. L. McCool 5-109) lost to Australia 659-8 dec (S. G. Barnes 234, D. G. Bradman 234) by an inns & 33 runs.

14th Match: v New South Wales Country XI (Newcastle)   Dec 21, 23.
M.C.C. 395 (W. R. Hammond 142, L. B. Fishlock 110, W. J. Edrich 59*, M. Hinman 5-92) & 146-6 (D. C. S. Compton 75*) drew with N.S.W. Country XI 202.

15th Match: v New South Wales Southern Districts (Canberra)   Dec 27, 28.
M.C.C. 465-8 dec (L. Hutton 133, C. Washbrook 115, D. C. S. Compton 76) drew with N.S.W. Southern Districts 11-4.

16th Match: v Victorian Country Team (Bendigo)   Dec 30.
Victorian Country 156 (T. P. B. Smith 6-43) lost to M.C.C. 200-4 (W. J. Edrich 62).

17th March: v Australia (Melbourne)   Jan 1, 2, 3, 4, 6, 7.
Australia 365 (C. L. McCool 104*, D. G. Bradman 79) & 536 (A. R. Morris 155, R. R. Lindwall 100, D. Tallon 92) drew with England 351 (W. J. Edrich 89, C. Washbrook 62, N. W. D. Yardley 61) & 310-7 (C. Washbrook 112, N. W. D. Yardley 53*).

18th Match: v Combined XI (Hobart)   Jan 10, 11, 13.
M.C.C. 278 (W. J. Edrich 82, L. B. Fishlock 52, A. V. Bedser 51) & 353-9 dec (D. C. S. Compton 124, J. Hardstaff jun 60, J. T. Ikin 50, J. Laver 5-26) drew with Combined XI 374 (K. R. Miller 70, J. Gardiner 94*, S. G. Barnes 57) & 145-2 (I. W. Johnson 80*).

19th Match: v Tasmania (Launceston)   Jan 15, 16, 17.
M.C.C. 467-5 dec (D. C. S. Compton 163, J. Hardstaff jun 155, L. Hutton 51) drew with Tasmania 103 & 129-6.

20th Match: v South Australia (Adelaide)   Jan 24, 25, 27, 28.
M.C.C. 577 (W. R. Hammond 188, Jas Langridge 100, L. Hutton 88, L. B. Fishlock 57) & 152-2 (L. Hutton 77*) drew with S. Australia 443 (R. A. Hamence 145, R. James 85, P. L. Ridings 77).

21st Match: v Australia (Adelaide)   Jan 31, Feb 1, 3, 4, 5, 6.
England 460 (D. C. S. Compton 147, L. Hutton 94, J. Hardstaff jun 67, C. Washbrook 65) & 340-8 dec (D. C. S. Compton 103*, L. Hutton 76) drew with Australia 487 (K. R. Miller 141*, A. R. Morris 122, A. L. Hassett 52) & 215-1 (A. R. Morris 124*, D. G. Bradman 56*).

22nd Match: v Victoria Country XI (Ballarat)   Feb 11, 12.
Country XI 268 (D. Brown 62) & 70-5 drew with M.C.C. 288 (P. A. Gibb 69, T. G. Evans 82, D. C. S. Compton 61).

23rd Match: v Victoria (Melbourne)   Feb 14, 15, 17, 18.
M.C.C. 355 (D. C. S. Compton 93, J. T. Ikin 71, L. B. Fishlock 51) & 118 (G. E. Tribe 6-49) drew with Victoria 327 (A. L. Hassett 126, R. N. Harvey 69, G. E. Tribe 60).

24th Match: v New South Wales (Sydney)   Feb 21, 22, 24, 25.
N.S.W. 342 (E. W. Lukeman 70, D. K. Carmody 65, T. P. B. Smith 9-121) & 262-6 dec (R. K. Kissell 80*) drew with M.C.C. 266 (D. C. S. Compton 75) & 205-3 (D. C. S. Compton 74*, L. Hutton 72).

25th Match: v Australia (Sydney)   Feb 28, March 1, 3, 4, 5.
England 280 (L. Hutton 122*, W. J. Edrich 60, R. R. Lindwall 7-63) & 186 (D. C. S. Compton 76, C. L. McCool 5-44) lost to Australia 253 (S. G. Barnes 71, A. R. Morris 57, D. V. P.Wright 7-105) & 214-5 (D. G. Bradman 63) by 5 wkts.

26th Match: v Wellington (Wellington)   March 10, 11, 12.
M.C.C. 176 (C. Washbrook 68) & 271-6 dec (C. Washbrook 133, R. McK. Murray 5-85) beat Wellington 160 (F. R. Crawford 50, W. Voce 6-38) & 73 by 214 runs.

27th Match: v Otago (Dunedin)   March 15, 17, 18.
Otago 340 (B. Sutcliffe 197) & 262-7 dec (B. Sutcliffe 128) drew with M.C.C. 385-6 dec (N. W. D. Yardley 126, J. T. Ikin 102*, T. G. Evans 101) & 216-9 (T. G. Evans 64).

28th Match: v New Zealand (Christchurch)   March 21, 22, 24, 25.
New Zealand 345-9 dec (W. A. Hadlee 116, B. Sutcliffe 58) drew with England 265-7 dec (W. R. Hammond 79, J. Cowie 6-83).

29th Match: v Auckland (Auckland)   March 28, 29.
M.C.C. 240 (D. C. S. Compton 97*) beat Auckland 85 (D. C. S. Compton 7-36) & 90 by an inns & 65 runs.

Bruce Dooland takes a low catch to dismiss Hammond off his own bowling in the third Test at Melbourne in 1946-47.

had completed an innings in the fourth Test at Adelaide, and with Compton going on to complete a century in both innings, Hammond was able to declare setting Australia 314 in 195 minutes – Bradman declined the challenge.

Fibrositis kept Hammond out of the fifth Test, Yardley leading England. Some splendid bowling by Wright gave England a first innings lead, but England were unable to press home their advantage due to the illness of Hutton, who had had to retire in the first innings. Australia won a well-fought match by five wickets and the Ashes by three matches to nil.

The M.C.C. went by flying boat to New Zealand, where four matches, including a rain-soaked Test were played. The team flew back to England calling at Bowen, Darwin, Surabaya, Singapore, Rangoon, Calcutta, Karachi, Bahrein, Basra, Cairo, Marseilles and finally Poole Harbour – the whole journey taking seven and a half days. The heavy baggage and three of the team travelled in the *Largs Castle* and did not participate in the New Zealand part of the tour.

Financially the tour was a great success with a profit of some £50,000. Each professional received £550 plus bonus, which in most cases exceeded £200.

Weak bowling and some poor fielding was the main cause of England's failure, but Hammond failed as a batsman and his captaincy came in for much adverse criticism. The two serious injuries of the tour were to Fishlock and Langridge. Hutton, Compton (after a poor start), Edrich and Washbrook were all successful batsmen – but it is only necessary to state that Yardley's 10 wickets at 37.20 runs each put him at the top of the bowling

averages, to show how the attack fared. Lindwall, Miller, Toshack and McCool all had bowling averages under 30 for Australia. Bradman easily topped the Australian batting, though Miller, Barnes and Morris each averaged over 70. All round Australia were much stronger than the English team expected and thoroughly deserved their victory.

1947-48: M.C.C. fail to win a match in West Indies

The M.C.C. sent a weak team out to the West Indies in 1947-48 and the slim chance it had of success vanished under an epidemic of illness and injury. Compton, Edrich, Hutton and Washbrook, the four principal English batsmen of the 1947 series against South Africa, declined to go, as did Bedser and Wright and indeed the England captain, Yardley.

G. O. B. Allen was brought out of virtual retirement (he had two County Championship innings for Middlesex in 1947) to lead the side, who were S. C. Griffith (Sussex), K. Cranston (Lancs), D. Brookes (Northants), H. J. Butler (Notts), T. G. Evans (Kent), J. Hardstaff (Notts), R. Howorth (Worcs), J. T. Ikin (Lancs), J. C. Laker (Surrey), W. Place (Lancs), J. D. B. Robertson (Middx), G. A. Smithson (Yorks), M. F. Tremlett (Som) and J. H. Wardle (Yorks).

The side left England aboard the s.s. *Tettela* on 23 December 1947. The voyage was a rough one and the ship docked in Bridgetown, Barbados three days late, which meant that the side had only two days in find their landlegs before the first match. Allen had strained a leg whilst on board ship and had to miss the first three games – starting an injury list that never ended. Both matches against Barbados were high scoring draws, though rain prevented a possible M.C.C. win in the second. Butler pulled a leg muscle in the first game, so for the third match, which was the first Test, England were without their captain and their principal fast bowler. West Indies reached 244 for 3 on the opening day, then rain and a brilliant spell from Laker whipped the rest out for 52. Hardstaff with 98 kept England in the game, but in their second innings West Indies greatly improved, setting England to make 395 to win on a sticky wicket – more rain arrived and the match was drawn.

Travelling on to Trinidad, the team played another high-scoring draw, the only point to note being that Hardstaff, who was again the highest scorer, tore a hamstring while fielding and was out of the side for the next month. In the return against Trinidad, Butler returned and bowled out the locals for 185, then went down with malaria. Place also joined the injury list and the team went into the second Test with only 12 fit men. Griffith, the reserve wicket-keeper, was brought into the team as a batsman and hit the first first-class hundred of his career, saving the side from collapse. West Indies found few terrors in the English bowling and in England's second innings Robertson batted grimly to prevent a home win.

Because of the injury problem, Allen cabled to England and Hutton arrived as a reinforcement for the first match against British Guiana – it was just as well, since the side was down to ten

1947-48: M.C.C. to West Indies

1st Match: v Barbados (Bridgetown)   Jan 9, 10, 12, 13.
M.C.C. 334 (R. Howorth 67*, J. D. B. Robertson 51, D. Brookes 50, E. A. V. Williams 5-73) & 260-6 (J. D. B. Robertson 90, W. Place 55) drew with Barbados 514-4 dec (A. M. Taylor 161, C. L. Walcott 120, E. D. Weekes 118*, J. D. C. Goddard 52).

2nd Match: v Barbados (Bridgetown)   Jan 15, 16, 17, 19.
Barbados 243-6 dec (G. M. Carew 81, J. Lucas 56) & 182-8 (J. C. Laker 5-76) drew with M.C.C. 358 (D. Brookes 108, J. Hardstaff jun 105).

3rd Match: v West Indies (Bridgetown)   Jan 21, 22, 23, 24, 26.
West Indies 296 (G. E. Gomez 86, J. B. Stollmeyer 78, J. C. Laker 7-103) & 351-9 dec (R. J. Christiani 99, E. A. V. Williams 72, W. Ferguson 56, R. Howorth 6-124) drew with England 253 (J. Hardstaff jun 98, J. D. B. Robertson 80) & 86-4 (J. D. B. Robertson 51*).

4th Match: v Trinidad (Port of Spain)   Jan 29, 30, 31, Feb 2.
Trinidad 481-4 dec (G. E. Gomez 178*, R. Tang Choon 103, A. G. Genteaume 101) & 101-0 dec (K. Trestrail 53*) drew with M.C.C. 418 (J. Hardstaff jun 92, K. Cranston 82, J. T. Ikin 65, T. G. Evans 53) & 80-3.

5th Match: v Trinidad (Port of Spain)   Feb 4, 5, 6, 7.
M.C.C. 305 (G. O. B. Allen 77, K. Cranston 53) & 252-6 dec (W. Place 120*) drew with Trinidad 185 & 322-7 (A. G. Ganteaume 90, D. St. E. Atkinson 83*).

6th Match: v West Indies (Port of Spain)   Feb 11, 12, 13, 14, 16.
England 362 (S. C. Griffith 140, J. C. Laker 55, W. Ferguson 5-137) & 275 (J. D. B. Robertson 133, W. Ferguson 6-92) drew with West Indies 497 (A. G. Ganteaume 112, G. M. Carew 107, F. M. M. Worrall 97, G. E. Gomez 62) & 72-3.

7th Match: v British Guiana (Georgetown)   Feb 19, 20, 21, 23.
M.C.C. 332 (L. Hutton 138, K. Cranston 73) & 191-6 dec (L. Hutton 62*, J. Trim 5-36) drew with British Guiana 296 (H. P. Bayley 113, J. C. Laker 5-74) & 76-1.

8th Match: v British Guiana (Georgetown)   Feb 25, 26, 27, 28.
No play due to rain.

9th Match: v West Indies (Georgetown)   March 3, 4, 5, 6.
West Indies 297-8 dec (F. M. M. Worrell 131*, R. J. Christiani 51) & 78-3 beat England 111 (J. D. C. Goddard 5-31) & 263 (J. Hardstaff jun 63, W. Ferguson 5-116) by 7 wkts.

10th Match: v Jamaica (Sabina Pk, Kingston)   March 15, 16, 17, 18.
Jamaica 344-7 dec (K. R. Rickards 112*, G. A. Headley 65, O. Cunningham 57, A. E. McKenzie 51) & 233-4 dec (C. Bonitto 100, J. K. Holt 87) drew with M.C.C. 278 (K. Cranston 84, J. Hardstaff jun 69) & 88-3.

11th Match: v Jamaica (Melbourne Pk, Kingston)   March 20, 22, 23, 24.
M.C.C. 313 (L. Hutton 128, S. C. Griffiths 51, I. Iffla 5-90) & 221-7 dec (J. Hardstaff jun 68) drew with Jamaica 258 (C. Bonitto 57, F. M. M. Worrell 52) & 178-3 (F. M. M. Worrell 106*).

12th Match: v West Indies (Sabina Pk, Kingston)   March 27, 29, 30, 31, April 1.
England 227 (J. D. B. Robertson 64, L. Hutton 56, H. H. H. Johnson 5-41) & 336 (W. Place 107, J. Hardstaff jun 64, L. Hutton 60, H. H. H. Johnson 5-55) lost to West Indies 490 (E. D. Weekes 141, W. Ferguson 75, K. R. Rickards 67) & 76-0 by 10 wkts.

1947-48: M.C.C. to the West Indies

Batting Averages

	M	I	NO	R	HS	Avge	100	c/s
L. Hutton (Yorks)	5	10	1	578	138	64.22	2	6
S. C. Griffith (Sussex)	6	9	2	314	140	44.85	1	5/1
J. Hardstaff jun (Notts)	8	14	0	619	105	44.21	1	4
D. Brookes (Northts)	3	5	0	182	108	36.40	1	1
W. Place (Lancs)	8	15	3	423	120*	35.25	2	1
K. Cranston (Lancs)	10	18	1	549	84	32.29	0	3
J. D. B. Robertson (Middx)	11	21	1	625	133	31.25	1	9
G. O. B. Allen (Middx)	6	11	2	262	77	29.11	0	5
R. Howorth (Worcs)	11	18	4	380	67*	27.14	0	1
J. T. Ikin (Lancs)	10	15	1	303	65	21.64	0	8
T. G. Evans (Kent)	9	15	1	300	53	21.42	0	14/3
J. C. Laker (Surrey)	8	12	2	212	55	21.20	0	4
G. A. Smithson (Yorks)	7	12	1	186	42	16.90	0	0
H. J. Butler (Notts)	4	5	3	33	15*	16.50	0	1
J. H. Wardle (Yorks)	6	8	1	77	35	11.00	0	2
M. F. Tremlett (Som)	9	13	3	80	36	8.00	0	1

Bowling Averages

	O	M	R	W	Avge	BB	5i
J. C. Laker	388.5	116	973	36	27.02	7-103	3
H. J. Butler	91	19	281	10	28.10	3-32	0
R. Howorth	518.3	149	1169	30	38.96	6-124	1
G. O. B. Allen	66	7	280	6	46.67	2-82	0
K. Cranston	247	67	651	12	54.25	4-78	0
M. F. Tremlett	281	70	700	10	70.00	3-62	0
J. H. Wardle	171.5	34	441	6	73.50	3-65	0
J. T. Ikin	231	39	685	8	85.62	3-55	0

Also bowled: J. Hardstaff jun 16-2-73-1; J. D. B. Robertson 15-3-47-0; L. Hutton 5-1-20-0; T. G. Evans 3-1-8-0; G. A. Smithson 2-0-11-0.

fit men. Hutton hit 138 in his first innings and was 62 not out when Cranston declared in the second.

For the third Test, Goddard, the West Indies captain, bowled brilliantly to dismiss England for 111 and took his side to an easy win by 7 wickets.

The final section of the tour was in Jamaica. There were two drawn matches against the colony before the fourth Test. Allen won the toss. Hutton and Robertson began with an opening stand of 129, but the rest were unable to muster another hundred and as Weekes made a splendid hundred to give West Indies a lead of 263, England had little hope of even a draw. In the event the match was lost by 10 wickets. So the tour ended without a win.

Only Laker of the M.C.C. bowlers came out of the tour with much credit, and in the Tests Robertson, Hutton and Hardstaff were the ones who really offered England much hope. For the West Indies, the emergence of Worrell and Weekes was the prime factor of the Test series.

1948-49: last man Gladwin wins Test with leg-bye in South Africa

Following the disastrous tour of 1947-48, the M.C.C. Selection and Planning Sub-Committee deliberated on the future policy regarding International tours and in August 1948 issued a report. The M.C.C. stated that they could only accept responsibility for overseas tours if the County Committees gave their whole-hearted support, if the M.C.C. were allowed to decide whether or not the status of the tour was sufficient to permit Test Matches, if the remuneration to professionals was increased to allow for the loss of possible winter earnings and if in South Africa, West Indies and India, the host country guaranteed the M.C.C. against financial loss. It was also maintained that official tours should not take place every year and to this end the proposed 1949-50 tour to India was cancelled.

For the tour to South Africa in 1948-49, the M.C.C. were able to select England's strongest side. The two major absentees were the England captain, Yardley, and Edrich. The team which left England on 7 October aboard the *Durban Castle* was F. G. Mann

1st Match: v Western Province (Cape Town) Oct 29, 30, Nov 1.
W. Province 386-4 dec (O. E. Wynne 108, O. Newton-Thompson 78, J. E. Cheetham 68*, H. G. Owen-Smith 65*) & 88-4 dec lost to M.C.C. 357-5 dec (F. G. Mann 112, J. F. Crapp 83, T. G. Evans*) & 118-1 (C. Washbrook 50*) by 9 wkts.

2nd Match: v Country Districts XI (Robertson) Nov 3, 4.
Country Districts 115 & 95 (R. O. Jenkins 6-47) lost to M.C.C. 310-5 dec (L. Hutton 81, C. H. Palmer 76*) by an inns & 100 runs.

3rd Match: v Cape Province (Cape Town) Nov 6, 8, 9.
Cape Province 225 (O. E. Wynne 105) & 323 (J. E. Cheetham 94, R. G. Draper 56, R. O. Jenkins 5-87) lost to M.C.C. 456 (L. Hutton 125, D. C. S. Compton 121, R. O. Jenkins 75*) & 93-0 (L. Hutton 62*) by 10 wkts.

4th Match: v Griqualand West (Kimberley) Nov 13, 15, 16.
M.C.C. 542-4 dec (C. Washbrook 168, D. C. S. Compton 150*, R. T. Simpson 91, A. J. Watkins, F. G. Mann 50) beat Griqualand West 258 (C. Helfrich 71, R. O. Jenkins 5-88) & 212 (D. V. P. Wright 5-61) by an inns & 72 runs.

5th Match: v Orange Free State (Bloemfontein) Nov 19, 20, 22.
M.C.C. 449-7 dec (L. Hutton 134, J. F. Crapp 127*, A. V. Bedser 77*) & 41-1 beat O.F.S. 251 (E. Warner 55, R. O. Jenkins 5-76) & 238 (R. O. Jenkins 7-94) by 9 wkts.

6th Match: v Natal (Durban) Nov 26, 27, 28.
M.C.C. 391-9 dec (D. C. S. Compton 106, J. F. Crapp 62, L. Hutton 61, C. N. McCarthy 5-110) & 129-6 (L. Hutton 78) drew with Natal 373 (O. C. Dawson 83, L. W. Payn 82, A. D. Nourse 72).

7th Match: v N-E. Transvaal (Benoni) Dec 3, 4.
N-E. Transvaal 168 (K. J. Funston 65) & 113 (R. O. Jenkins 7-55) lost to M.C.C. 484-4 dec (D. C. S. Compton 300, R. T. Simpson 130*) by an inns & 203 runs.

8th Match: v Combined Transvaal XI (Pretoria) Dec 7, 8.
M.C.C. 483-4 dec (R. T. Simpson 145, C. Washbrook 144, C. H. Palmer 69*, R. O. Jenkins 55*) drew with Combined Transvaal 151 (L. Sadler 53, R. O. Jenkins 5-71) & 140-5.

9th Match: v (Johannesburg) Dec 10, 11, 13.
M.C.C. 513-7 dec (L. Hutton 174, D. C. S. Compton 84, T. G. Evans 77*, A. J. Watkins 61, R. T. Simpson 57) drew with Transvaal 560 (D. W. Begbie 154, A. Melville 92, T. A. Harris 98).

10th Match: v South Africa (Durban) Dec 16, 17, 18, 20.
South Africa 161 & 219 (W. W. Wade 63) lost to England 253 (L. Hutton 83, D. C. S. Compton 72, N. B. F. Mann 6-59) & 128-8 (C. N. McCarthy 6-43) by 2 wkts.

11th Match: v Natal Country Districts (Ladysmith) Dec 22, 23.
Country Districts 131 & 202 (E. Eaglestone 77, M. Price-More 59) lost to M.C.C. 278-7 dec (M. F. Tremlett 108*) & 56-4 by 6 wkts.

12th Match: v South Africa (Johannesburg) Dec 27, 28, 29, 30.
England 608 (C. Washbrook 195, L. Hutton 158, D. C. S. Compton 114, J. F. Crapp 56) drew with South Africa 315 (B. Mitchell 86, W. W. Wade 85) & 270-2 (E. A. B. Rowan 156*, A. D. Nourse 56*).

13th Match: v South Africa (Cape Town) Jan 1, 3, 4, 5.
England 308 (C. Washbrook 74, A. D. B. Rowan 5-80) & 276-3 dec (L. Hutton 87, A. J. Watkins 64*, J. F. Crapp 54, D. C. S. Compton 51*) drew with South Africa (B. Mitchell 120, A. D. Nourse 112, O. E. Wynne 50, D. C. S. Compton 5-70) & 142-4.

14th Match: v Eastern Province (Port Elizabeth) Jan 8, 10, 11.
M.C.C. 450-9 dec (C. H. Palmer 116, D. C. S. Compton 108, A. J. Watkins 83) & 353-3 (J. F. Crapp 103*, F. G. Mann 80, R. T. Simpson 67, C. H. Palmer 57) drew with E. Province 397 (D. Dimbleby 87, J. H. B. Waite 80, K. G. Dimbleby 61).

15th Match: v Border (East London) Jan 16, 17, 18.
Border 156 (R. O. Jenkins 5-60) & 89 (J. A. Young 6-38) lost to M.C.C. 272-9 dec (J. F. Crapp 86, C. H. Palmer 65) by an inns & 27 runs.

16th Match: v Transvaal (Johannesburg) Jan 21, 22, 23.
M.C.C. 244-9 dec (L. Hutton 84, R. T. Simpson 54) & 40-0 drew with Transvaal 254 (B. Mitchell 60).

17th Match: v Rhodesia (Bulawayo) Jan 30, 31, Feb 1.
Rhodesia 174 & 166 drew with M.C.C. 193 (D. C. S. Compton 60, E. S. Newson 5-54) & 117-2.

18th Match: v Rhodesia (Salisbury) Feb 4, 5, 7.
M.C.C. 228 (L. Hutton 79, S. H. Martin 5-49) drew with Rhodesia 61 (A. V. Bedser 6-17) & 191-5 (C. Pretorius 75).

19th Match: v South Africa (Johannesburg) Feb 13, 14, 15, 16.
England 379 (A. J. Watkins 111, C. Washbrook 97, J. F. Crapp 51, C. N.McCarthy 5-114) & 253-7 dec (L. Hutton 123) drew with South Africa 257-9 dec (A. D. Nourse 129*, W. W. Wade 54) & 194-4 (E. A. B. Rowan 86*, K. G. Viljoen 63).

20th Match: v A Natal XI (Pietermaritzburg) Feb 19, 21, 22.
Natal XI 288 (A. D. Nourse 117, I. de Gersigny 77) & 257-6 dec (A. D. Nourse 76) drew with M.C.C. 276 (M. F. Tremlett 108, C. H. Palmer 80, D. Dinkleman 5-113) & 260-4 (D. C. S. Compton 141, M. F. Tremlett 63*).

21st Match: v Natal (Durban) Feb 25, 26, 28.
Natal 217 (J. A. Young 5-25) & 166 (D. Dowling 50, D. V. P. Wright 7-54) drew with M.C.C. 237 (R. T. Simpson 119*, L. W. Payn 5-59) & 6-0.

22nd Match: v South Africa (Port Elizabeth) March 5, 7, 8, 9.
South Africa 379 (W. W. Wade 125, B. Mitchell 99, A. D. Nourse 73) & 187-3 dec (B. Mitchell 56) lost to England 395 (F. G. Mann 136*, A. M. B. Rowan 5-167) & 174-7 by 3 wkts.

23rd Match: v Combined Universities (Cape Town) March 12, 14, 15.
M.C.C. 477 (C. Washbrook 153, D. C. S. Compton 125, M. F. Tremlett 56) beat Universities 274 (B. Crews 104, H. Birrell 56, L. Wiley 50) & 151 (D. C. S. Compton 6-62) by an inns & 52 runs.

(Middx) (capt), C. H. Palmer (Worcs), R. T. Simpson (Notts), S. C. Griffith (Sussex) and the professionals J. A. Young (Middx), R. O. Jenkins (Worcs), J. F. Crapp (Gloucs), A. J. Watkins (Glam), T. G. Evans (Kent), D. V. P. Wright (Kent), C. Gladwin (Derbys), A. V. Bedser (Surrey), M. F. Tremlett (Somerset), C. Washbrook (Lancs), L. Hutton (Yorks) and D. C. S. Compton (Middx) with Col M. A. Green as manager.

The M.C.C. did not have its customary easy start to the tour, for Western Province hit 386 for 4 and then declared. M.C.C. matched this and in the second innings Cheetham generously declared again to set M.C.C. 118 in 55 minutes, a challenge the tourists readily accepted. Natal and Transvaal also provided strong opposition and both games were high scoring draws. In between them, Compton hit his record 300 in 181 minutes at Benoni, but the bowling was exceedingly weak and not up to first-class standard.

After all the high scoring, the first Test provided a great contrast, with no individual hundreds and the bowlers generally in command. The game came to a tremendous climax when England needed two to win with two wickets left and three deliveries of the final over remaining. Gladwin actually obtained the winning run off the final ball with a leg-bye.

The second Test, at Johannesburg, was watched on the first day by a record crowd of 35,000 and they saw Hutton and Washbrook put on 359 for the first English wicket—another record. It was soon obvious however that the pitch was too easy to produce anything but a draw, so the bowlers had a thankless task. Moving straight back to Cape Town for the third Test, England batted first on an unexpectedly tricky wicket, but the home bowlers failed to exploit it to the full and though South Africa gained a lead on first innings, the absence of the left-arm spinner, N. B. F. Mann, through injury, allowed England to build a good second innings score and draw the game.

The team went up to play two matches against Rhodesia and also make a trip to the Victoria Falls, prior to the fourth Test. Although the pitch at Johannesburg had been improved a little in favour of the bowlers since the second Test, the result was another draw. The England captain declared to set South Africa 376 in 270 minutes, but the home side made no attempt to hit off the runs.

The final Test at Port Elizabeth proved the reverse of the previous game. This time Nourse declared to set England 172 in 95 minutes. England went for the runs, despite wickets falling fast and took the match with three wickets in hand.

Sailing home in the *Stirling Castle*, the team landed at South-

1948-49: M.C.C. to South Africa

Batting Averages

	M	I	NO	R	HS	Avge	100	c/s
D. C. S. Compton (Middx)	17	26	5	1781	300	84.80	8	25
L. Hutton (Yorks)	14	21	1	1477	174	73.85	5	8
R. T. Simpson (Notts)	12	19	5	788	130*	56.28	2	5
C. Washbrook (Lancs)	15	23	2	1124	195	53.52	3	4
J. F. Crapp (Glos)	14	19	3	820	127*	51.25	2	7
C. H. Palmer (Worcs)	11	18	4	478	116	34.14	1	1
C. Gladwin (Derbys)	16	16	7	289	52*	32.11	0	4
M. F. Tremlett (Som)	10	10	1	286	105	31.77	1	5
F. G. Mann (Middx)	19	24	2	673	136*	30.59	2	10
A. J. Watkins (Glam)	15	18	2	474	111	29.62	1	18
T. G. Evans (Kent)	11	14	4	288	77*	28.80	0	13/11
R. O. Jenkins (Worcs)	13	12	2	268	75*	26.80	0	6
A. V. Bedser (Surrey)	14	17	3	271	77*	19.35	0	8
J. A. Young (Middx)	14	8	4	53	22*	13.25	0	5
D. V. P. Wright (Kent)	15	11	4	91	25*	13.00	0	3
S. C. Griffith (Sussex)	10	10	2	47	13	5.87	0	21/5

Bowling Averages

	O	M	R	W	Avge	BB	5i
C. H. Palmer	30	7	64	5	12.80	3-7	0
R. O. Jenkins	408.7	65	1508	71	21.24	7-55	6
C. Gladwin	437.1	131	945	42	22.50	4-27	0
J. A. Young	430.1	123	1014	41	24.73	6-38	2
M. F. Tremlett	103	16	287	11	26.09	2-7	0
A. V. Bedser	475.1	97	1273	45	28.28	6-17	1
D. V. P. Wright	378.1	53	1544	51	30.27	7-54	2
D. C. S. Compton	275.4	40	1051	30	35.03	6-62	2
A. J. Watkins	96	12	352	4	88.00	2-16	0

Also bowled: L. Hutton 1-0-7-0; F. G. Mann 1-0-8-0.

Newlands cricket ground, Cape Town, 29 October 1948 and captain F. G. Mann leads out a strong M.C.C. side to play Western Province in the first match of the tour of South Africa, 1948-49. From left: C. Washbrook, L. Hutton, C. Gladwin, F. G. Mann, R. T. Simpson, T. G. Evans and D. C. S. Compton.

ampton on 1 April. Although the side had been undefeated on tour and won the rubber by two matches to nil, the difference between the two teams was marginal – victory by a hair's breadth by England in the first Test put South Africa at a disadvantage and Nourse took a tremendous gamble in the fifth Test, which did not pay off. The most noteworthy point on the tour was the fact that several of the Provincial teams put up great fights against the tourists – in most previous tours, only Transvaal were worthy opponents.

Hutton, Washbrook and Compton all had good records, but the surprise of the visit was the bowling of Jenkins, whose leg breaks proved most effective.

1950-51 : Australia still on top in post-war Tests

The major problem which faced both the M.C.C. and the press selectors concerning the proposed visit to Australia in 1950-51 was that of the captaincy. Both Yardley and Mann declined the invitation and after much speculation F. R. Brown was chosen – he had led England in two Tests against New Zealand in the summer of 1949, but Yardley had resumed the leadership in the initial Tests against West Indies in 1950. The other two difficulties concerned Compton, whose knee injury was making him doubtful, and Washbrook, who declined the original invitation.

The team that sailed on the *Stratheden* from Tilbury on 14 September was F. R. Brown (Northants) (capt), D. C. S. Compton (Middx), R. T. Simpson (Notts), T. E. Bailey (Essex), J. G. Dewes (Middx), D. S. Sheppard (Sussex), J. J. Warr (Middx), L. Hutton (Yorks), D. B. Close (Yorks), A. V. Bedser (Surrey), W. E. Hollies (Warwicks), D. V. P. Wright (Kent), A. J. W. McIntyre (Surrey), T. G. Evans (Kent), R. Berry (Lancs) and W. G. A. Parkhouse (Glamorgan) with Brig M. A. Green and

Brian Close, seen here bowling at Lord's in 1949, was the surprise choice for the tour to Australia in 1950-51. He was only 19 years old and already England's youngest Test player.

J. A. Nash as joint-managers. By a special arrangement C. Washbrook (Lancs) was allowed to fly out later and join the side in Australia. The two notable omissions were Edrich and Tattersall, but the press also took the selectors to task for sending so many young and inexperienced players.

Right *Freddie Brown,
M.C.C.'s captain, making a
farewell speech aboard the*
Stratheden *at Tilbury on 14
September 1950, as the team
left to tour Australia. From the
left, T. E. Bailey is talking to
J. G. Dewes, then come D. S.
Sheppard, J. J. Warr and
L. Hutton, with D. B. Close on
Brown's left.*

Below *Cyril Washbrook was
allowed to fly out later to join
the 1950-51 tour of Australia.
Here he hits Colin McCool to
the fence for four in the match
with Queensland at Brisbane.*

Below right *On the last day of
the first Test of the 1950-51
tour at Brisbane, D. V. P.
Wright snicked a ball from
Iverson into his pad, and
wicket-keeper Don Tallon
comes round to try to take the
catch.*

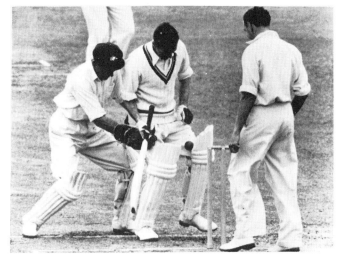

The match against Ceylon, which had had to be omitted in 1946-47, was played again, but unfortunately Hutton damaged a finger while batting and missed the first three games in Australia as a result. The team landed in Fremantle on 9 October and after two warm up games met the Western Australian team on 20 October. The match was drawn very much in favour of the visitors. A sporting declaration led to a win against South Australia, then the match against Victoria was ended by rain with the sides fairly even – the M.C.C. were captained by Compton in this match, Brown being injured, the first time an official M.C.C. team abroad had had a professional at its head. Miller hit a double century and Morris 168 for New South Wales as their score reached 509 for 3 and the M.C.C. bowling looked distinctly thin. The match however was drawn, as was the Queensland game which preceded the first Test. Hasset won the toss and batted – the luck and decision were to govern the match result, for, although England bowled quite brilliantly – Bailey, Brown,

Bedser and Wright all taking credit – and dismissed Australia on a good pitch for 228, the rains then arrived and for the rest of the match the wicket was unplayable. Brown declared at 68 for 7 and Australia collapsed to 32 for 7 in their second innings. England required 193 to win in the final innings. Hutton played a magnificent unbeaten innings of 62, but no one could stay with him and Australia won by 70 runs.

Compton was unable to play in the second Test due to his damaged knee and his absence possibly made the difference between victory and defeat.

For the second time England began by bowling out Australia cheaply, due to the efforts of Bailey and Bedser, though they had assistance from the pitch. England's batting however crumbled and only determination by Brown, Bailey and Evans produced a small first innings lead. Brown, Bailey and Bedser then dismissed Australia for 181, which left England requiring 179 to win. With three days to make the runs, England adopted the 'get them in singles' policy, which immediately gave the bowlers a psychological advantage, and apart from Hutton's 40 in 160 minutes, the English batting gradually faded away.

The return against New South Wales produced a high-scoring draw with Simpson hitting 259 and looking more like the batsman English spectators knew.

The third Test belonged to Iverson. He was an off-spin bowler, with a freakish grip, which meant that the batsman found it very difficult to tell at the moment of delivery what his intentions were. He had arrived in first-class cricket only in the previous season at the age of 34. Although playing in the first two Tests, his real worth was shown in the third. England batted first on a perfect pitch, but Miller produced an exceptional burst of fast bowling and only a moderate score of 290 was attained. Miller then went on to hit 145 not out and place Australia 136 runs in the lead. In England's second innings the wicket was taking spin and Iverson with an analysis of 19.4-8-27-6 won the match and the Ashes for Australia.

On the final day of the Test, Brown telephoned to England for two bowlers, on the grounds that Bailey and Wright were injured – Bailey had fractured his right thumb in the game and Wright tore a groin muscle. J. B. Statham and R. Tattersall, both of Lancashire, were flown out to join the side in time to play in an up-country game on 24 January.

Tattersall was drafted into the team for the fourth Test which began ten days later. Australia batted first and a double century by Morris gave them a total of 371 on a good wicket. England's batting, except for Hutton, who remained unbeaten on 156, collapsed and when Australia piled up 403 in their second innings, England needed an impossible 503 to win. Simpson made the highest score of 61, but the visitors never looked like approaching the target.

The fifth Test provided England with their first post-war victory. Brown and Bedser began by dismissing Australia for 217, then England, through Hutton and Simpson, gained a lead of 103 – a last wicket stand of 74 between Simpson and Tattersall giving England an unexpected bonus. Bedser and Wright bowled out Australia cheaply in the second innings, leaving only 95 for victory, of which Hutton made 60 – it was an appropriate end for the splendid batting the Yorkshireman had displayed throughout the tour.

The four matches in New Zealand produced three wins and were a somewhat light-hearted anti-climax to the battle against Australia.

The team flew home via Fiji, Honolulu, San Francisco and New York, the whole journey from Auckland to London Airport taking four and a half days.

England lost the series against Australia due to the lack of experienced middle order batsmen, a fact magnified by Compton's complete failure. Hutton was the best batsman on either side and Bedser the best bowler. Australia felt the lack of Bradman and relied very much on Hassett and Miller. Lindwall was not quite the menace he had been in England in 1948, but now he and Miller had Iverson to baffle any surviving batsmen.

1950-51: M.C.C. to Ceylon, Australia and New Zealand

1st Match: v Ceylon (Colombo) (One Day)   Oct 1.
M.C.C. 279-6 dec (A. J. W. McIntyre 104) drew with Ceylon 99-5.

2nd Match: v Western Australian Country XI (Northam) (One Day) Oct 14.
M.C.C. 329-5 dec (D. S. Sheppard 117, W. G. A. Parkhouse 86) drew with W. A. Country XI 113-7.

3rd Match: v Western Australian Colts XI (Perth)   Oct 16, 17.
W. A. Colts XI 103 & 117 lost to M.C.C. 369-4 dec (R. T. Simpson 109, W. G. A. Parkhouse 79, D. C. S. Compton 76, D. S. Sheppard 57) by an inns & 149 runs.*

4th Match: v Western Australia (Perth)   Oct 20, 21, 23, 24.
M.C.C. 434-9 dec (D. B. Close 108, D. C. S. Compton 106, J. G. Dewes 94) & 121-3 dec drew with W. Australia 236 (W. Langdon 60, D. K. Carmody 59, D. V. P. Wright 7-60) & 207-4 (T. Outridge 92).*

5th Match: v South Australia (Adelaide)   Oct 27, 28, 30, 31.
S. Australia 350 (R. A. Hamence 114) & 185-3 dec (L. Duldig 70, N. Dansie 64) lost to M.C.C. 351-9 dec (L. Hutton 126, R. T. Simpson 119) & 186-3 (R. T. Simpson 69, C. Washbrook 63) by 7 wkts.*

6th Match: v Victoria (Melbourne)   Nov 3, 4, 6, 8.
M.C.C. 306-9 dec (D. C. S. Compton 107) & 79-4 drew with Victoria 331 (R. Howard 139, D. T. Ring 75, T. E. Bailey 5-54).

7th Match: v New South Wales (Sydney)   Nov 10, 11, 13, 14.
N.S.W. 509-3 dec (K. R. Miller 214, A. R. Morris 168, J. W. Burke 80) & 140-2 dec (J. W. Burke 60*, J. R. Moroney 53) drew with M.C.C. 339 (L. Hutton 112, D. C. S. Compton 92, C. Washbrook 50, F. F. Johnston 6-100) & 143-2 (C. Washbrook 53*).*

8th Match: v New South Wales Country XI (Newcastle)   Nov 17, 18.
N.S.W. Country XI 169 (R. G. Beattie 69, W. E. Hollies 5-39) drew with M.C.C. 142 (J. G. Dewes 71, J. Bull 6-24).

9th Match: v New South Wales Northern Districts (Lismore)   Nov 20, 21.
M.C.C. 274 (R. T. Simpson 66, D. S. Sheppard 52, J. G. Dewes 50) drew with Northern Districts 156 & 55-2.

10th Match: v Queensland (Brisbane)   Nov 24, 25, 27, 28.
Queensland 305 (A. H. Carrigan 100, K. A. Archer 63, E. A. Toovey 58) & 5-1 drew with M.C.C. 291 (J. G. Dewes 117, C. Washbrook 81, L. J. Johnson 6-66).*

11th Match: v Australia (Brisbane)   Dec 1, 2, 4, 5.
Australia 228 (R. N. Harvey 74) & 32-7 dec beat England 68-7 dec (W. A. Johnston 5-35) & 122 (L. Hutton 62) by 70 runs.*

12th Match: v Queensland Country XI (Toowoomba)   Dec 8, 9.
M.C.C. 428-6 dec (R. T. Simpson 98, T. G. Evans 94, D. C. S. Compton 92, D. S. Sheppard 72, W. G. A. Parkhouse 57) & 294-7 dec (T. E. Bailey 63, W. G. A. Parkhouse 58) drew with Country XI 220 (T. Allen 85, D. V. P. Wright 5-52).*

13th Match: v Southern Districts of New South Wales (Canberra)   Dec 12, 13.
M. C. C. 180 (J. Robinson 5-40) & 281-3 (D. S. Sheppard 105, D. B. Close 105*, L. Hutton 54) drew with Southern Districts 164 (W. Hedditch 52*).*

14th Match: v An Australian XI (Sydney)   Dec 15, 16, 18, 19.
Australian XI 526-9 dec (J. W. Burke 128, A. R. Morris 100, K. A. Archer 81, K. R. Miller 62) drew with M.C.C. 321 (D. C. S. Compton 115, W. G. A. Parkhouse 58, A. K. Walker 5-60) & 173-3 (J. G. Dewes 66).*

15th Match: v Australia (Melbourne)   Dec 22, 23, 26, 27.
Australia 194 (A. L. Hassett 52) & 181 beat England 197 (F. R. Brown 62) & 150 by 28 runs.

16th Match: v New South Wales (Sydney)   Dec 30, Jan 1, 2, 3.
N.S.W. 333 (A. R. Morris 105, K. R. Miller 98, J. H. de Courcy 72) & 130-6 (J. R. Moroney 51*) drew with M.C.C. 553-8 dec (R. T. Simpson 259, L. Hutton 150, W. G. A. Parkhouse 92).*

17th Match: v Australia (Sydney)   Jan 5, 6, 8, 9.
England 290 (F. R. Brown 79, L. Hutton 62) & 123 (J. B. Iverson 6-27) lost to Australia 426 (K. R. Miller 145*, I. W. Johnson 77, A. L. Hassett 70) by an inns & 13 runs.

18th Match: v Tasmania (Hobart)   Jan 13, 15, 16.
Tasmania 192 & 229 (E. Rodwell 60) lost to M.C.C. 234 (C. Washbrook 61) & 188-1 (D. C. S. Compton 77, D. S. Sheppard 67*) by 9 wkts.*

19th Match: v Combined XI (Launceston)   Jan 19, 20, 22.
Combined XI 289 (G. B. Hole 105, J. Laver 59, A. V. Bedser 5-57) & 103 lost to M.C.C. 382-7 dec (D. C. S. Compton 142, C. Washbrook 112) & 13-0 by 10 wkts.

20th Match: v South Australian Country XI (Renmark)   Jan 24, 25.
S.A. Country XI 84 (R. Berry 6-36) & 124 lost to M.C.C. 233 (F. R. Brown 77, L. D. Curtiss 9-60) by an inns & 25 runs.

21st Match: v South Australia (Adelaide)   Jan 27, 29, 30, 31.
M.C.C. 211 (G. Noblet 5-56) & 220 (L. Hutton 66, S. McLean 5-68) beat S. Australia 126 & 153 (D. V. P. Wright 5-57) by 152 runs.

22nd Match: v Australia (Adelaide)   Feb 2, 3, 5, 6, 7, 8.
Australia 371 (A. R. Morris 206) & 403-8 dec (J. W. Burke 101*, K. R. Miller 99, R. N. Harvey 68) beat England 272 (L. Hutton 156*) & 228 (R. T. Simpson 61) by 274 runs.

23rd Match: v Victoria (Melbourne)   Feb 10, 12, 13, 14.
Victoria 441 (A. L. Hassett 232, D. T. Ring 74) & 234 (R. N. Harvey 56) drew with M.C.C. 414 (L. Hutton 128, T. E. Bailey 125, D. T. Ring 5-134) & 36-1.

24th Match: v Victorian Country XI (Geelong)   Feb 16, 17.
Country XI 217-7 dec (H. Heard 84) drew with M.C.C. did not bat: rain.

25th Match: v Victoria Country Districts (Euroa)   Feb 19, 20.
Country Districts 97 drew with M.C.C. 64-0: rain.

26th Match: v Australia (Melbourne)   Feb 23, 24, 26, 27, 28.
Australia 217 (A. L. Hassett 92, A. V. Bedser 5-46, F. R. Brown 5-49) & 197 (G. B. Hole 63, R. N. Harvey 52, A. V. Bedser 5-59) lost to England 320 (R. T. Simpson 156*, L. Hutton 79) & 95-2 (L. Hutton 60*) by 8 wkts.

27th Match: v Auckland (Auckland)   March 6, 7, 8.
Auckland 146 (D. V. P. Wright 5-54) & 168 (W. M. Wallace 68, R. Tattersall 5-33) lost to M.C.C. 298-7 dec (D. C. S. Compton 78, L. Hutton 69, J. G. Dewes 61) & 20-0 by 10 wkts.*

28th Match: v Otago (Dunedin)   March 10, 12.
M.C.C. 381-8 dec (C. Washbrook 147, D. S. Sheppard 75) beat Otago 83 (R. Tattersall 6-29) & 137 by an inns & 161 runs.

29th Match: v New Zealand (Christchurch)   March 17, 19, 20, 21.
New Zealand 417-8 dec (B. Sutcliffe 116, W. M. Wallace 66, J. R. Reid 50, W. A. Hadlee 50) & 46-3 drew with England 550 (T. E. Bailey 134*, R. T. Simpson 81, D. C. S. Compton 79, F. R. Brown 62, C. Washbrook 58, A. M. Moir 6-155).

30th Match: v New Zealand (Wellington)   March 24, 26, 27, 28.
New Zealand 125 (D. V. P. Wright 5-48) & 189 (V. J. Scott 60, R. Tattersall 6-44) lost to England 227 (L. Hutton 57) & 91-4 by 6 wkts.

1950-51 : M.C.C. to Ceylon, Australia and New Zealand

Batting Averages

	M	I	NO	R	HS	Avge	100	c/s
L. Hutton (Yorks)	15	25	4	1382	156*	65.80	5	18
D. C. S. Compton (Middx)	16	26	5	1095	142	52.14	4	15
R. T. Simpson (Notts)	16	28	1	1136	259	42.07	3	8
C. Washbrook (Lancs)	17	26	1	1020	147	40.80	2	6
T. E. Bailey (Essex)	11	14	4	372	134*	37.20	2	8
J. G. Dewes (Middx)	12	17	3	502	117	35.85	1	6
W. G. A. Parkhouse (Glam)	10	15	1	430	92	30.71	0	7
F. R. Brown (Northts)	13	19	2	468	79	27.52	0	11
D. B. Close (Yorks)	9	13	3	231	108*	23.10	1	9
D. S. Sheppard (Sussex)	13	20	2	415	75	23.05	0	5
T. G. Evans (Kent)	14	20	3	357	49	21.01	0	24/9
A. V. Bedser (Surrey)	13	16	3	164	42	12.61	0	10
A. J. W. McIntyre (Surrey)	7	10	2	94	32*	11.75	0	6/7
D. V. P. Wright (Kent)	14	17	6	128	45	11.63	0	2
J. B. Statham (Lancs)	5	5	1	46	18	11.50	0	0
R. Berry (Lancs)	7	6	3	32	13*	10.66	0	3
J. J. Warr (Middx)	11	13	2	100	23	9.09	0	7
W. E. Hollies (Warks)	9	9	6	19	5*	6.33	0	3
R. Tattersall (Lancs)	7	7	0	40	14	5.71	0	4

Also played in one match: E. A. Bedser (Surrey) 2.

Bowling Averages

	Balls	M	R	W	Avge	BB	5i
R. Tattersall	1472	65	562	33	17.03	6-29	3
J. B. Statham	588	18	220	11	20.00	4-17	0
A. V. Bedser	3229	75	1148	53	21.67	5-46	3
T. E. Bailey	1853	45	736	32	23.00	5-54	1
D. V. P. Wright	2590	36	1446	52	27.80	7-60	4
F. R. Brown	1796	24	853	30	28.43	5-49	1
D. B. Close	784	9	475	13	36.53	3-81	0
J. J. Warr	2122	28	915	25	36.60	4-47	0
W. E. Hollies	1688	26	858	21	40.85	4-7	0
R. Berry	997	22	479	11	43.54	3-34	0
D. C. S. Compton	826	11	490	11	44.54	3-32	0

Also bowled: E. A. Bedser 96-1-39-0; L. Hutton 24-0-11-1; C. Washbrook 36-0-33-3; R. T. Simpson 24-1-4-2.

Financially the tour was nothing like as successful as previous M.C.C. visits and the profit amounted to only £3,842 – a tenth of that produced in 1946-7 – but the rather strained atmosphere between the two sides, which had never really disappeared following the bodyline tour, seemed at last to have gone.

1951 : M.C.C. amateur team to Canada

The Canadian Cricket Association invited the M.C.C. to send an amateur team out to Canada in the summer of 1951, the hosts to pay all expenses. The object was to encourage the game, which had suffered a set-back in the 14 years since the previous visit.

The side which sailed from Liverpool on 24 July was R. W. V. Robins (Middx) (capt), M. M. Walford (Somerset), I. P. Campbell (Kent), J. R. Thompson (Warwicks), A. W. H. Mallett (Kent), A. G. Powell (Essex), G. H. Chesterton (Worcs), J. J. Warr (Middx), W. G. Keighley (Yorks), J. N. Bartlett (Sussex), A. McCorquodale (Middx), C. R. D. Rudd (Oxford U), A. H. Brodhurst (Gloucs) and Dr E. K. Scott.

All the matches were played on matting wickets, which were rather against the faster bowlers, but certainly meant that no really appalling pitches were met. The sun shone, and despite the popularity of baseball, the local press gave good coverage.

The two important fixtures were the 'Tests'. In the first at Vancouver some all-round cricket by Robins completely demolished the opposition – the captain took 9 wickets for 34 and scored 64. In the 'Second Test', Canada, due to good batting by T. L. Brierley, the pre-war Glamorgan player, were only just behind on first innings, but fell cheaply when batting a second time.

Robins returned the best bowling figures of the tour and Keighley headed the batting. The side left Canada on the *Empress of France* on 14 September.

1951 : M.C.C. to Canada

1st Match: v Quebec (Montreal)   Aug 4.
M.C.C. 144 beat Quebec 33 (J. J. Warr 6-14) by 111 runs.

2nd Match: v Ottawa Valley (Ottawa)   Aug 5.
M.C.C. 203-7 dec (W. G. Keighley 103*) drew with Ottawa Valley 114-6.

3rd Match: v Ottawa Valley (Ottawa)   Aug 6.
Ottawa Valley 69 lost to M.C.C. 429-9 (J. R. Thompson 126, W. G. Keighley 51) by 9 wkts.

4th Match: v Toronto (Toronto)   Aug 8.
M.C.C. 280-7 dec (A. W. H. Mallett 66, A. G. Powell 63*) beat Toronto 142 (B. E. F. Lowry 58) by 138 runs.

5th Match: v Hamilton & District (St Catherine's)   Aug 9.
M.C.C. 254 (M. M. Walford 91, K. Langton 5-65) beat Hamilton 132 by 122 runs.

6th Match: v South-West Ontario Cricket League (London)   Aug 10.
M.C.C. 235-5 dec (J. R. Thompson 72, M. M. Walford 55) beat Cricket League 61 by 174 runs.

7th Match: v Toronto & District (Toronto)   Aug 11.
M.C.C. 291-8 dec (R. W. V. Robins 116, B. Christen 6-87) beat Toronto 93 by 198 runs.

8th Match: v Ontario (Toronto)   Aug 12.
Ontario 97 lost to M.C.C. 193 (W. G. Keighley 102) by 5 wkts.

9th Match: v Edmonton Cricket League (Edmonton)   Aug 17.
M.C.C. 296 (J. J. Warr 86, R. W. V. Robins 69) beat Edmonton League 75 by 221 runs.

10th Match: v Alberta (Edmonton)   Aug 18.
M.C.C. 231 (J. R. Thompson 68) beat Alberta 48 by 183 runs.

11th Match: v Alberta (Edmonton)   Aug 19.
M.C.C. 319 (M. M. Walford 119, E. K. Scott 59, C. Robinson 6-84) beat Alberta 74 (R. W. V. Robins 5-12) by 245 runs.

12th Match: v B.C. Mainland League (Vancouver)   Aug 22.
M.C.C. 82 (R. Johnston 5-24) lost to Mainland League 110 by 2 wkts.

13th Match: v B.C. Mainland League (Vancouver)   Aug 23.
Mainland League 79 (R. W. V. Robins 5-16) & 91 lost to M.C.C. 270-4 dec (J. R. Thompson 65, M. M. Walford 63, W. G. Keighley 61) by an inns & 100 runs.

14th Match: v Canada (Vancouver)   Aug 24, 25.
Canada 94 (R. W. V. Robins 7-22) & 102 lost to M.C.C. 306-8 dec (M. M. Walford 86, R. W. V. Robins 64) by an inns & 110 runs.

15th Match: v Victoria & District (Victoria)   Aug 26.
M.C.C. 231 (R. W. V. Robins 65) beat Victoria 95 by 136 runs.

16th Match: v Okanagan Valley (Vernon)   Aug 29.
M.C.C. 194-7 dec (J. R. Thompson 55) beat Okanagan Valley 59 by 135 runs.

17th Match: v Calgary (Calgary)   Sept 2.
M.C.C. 243-8 dec (J. J. Warr 68*, W. G. Keighley 66) beat Calgary 61 by 182 runs.

18th Match: v A Canada XI (Calgary)   Sept 3.
A Canada XI 152 beat M.C.C. 116 (B. Christen 5-24) by 36 runs.

19th Match: v Manitoba XI (Winnipeg)   Sept 5.
M.C.C. 270-5 dec (R. W. V. Robins 70, A. H. Brodhurst 59*) beat Manitoba 91 by 179 runs.

20th Match: v Canada (Toronto)   Sept 8, 9, 10.
M.C.C. 270 (M. M. Walford 72, R. W. V. Robins 57) & 207 (J. R. Thompson 61, B. Christen 7-80) beat Canada 260 (T. L. Brierley 76) & 76 by 141 runs.

21st Match: v Montreal (Montreal)   Sept 11.
M.C.C. 260-8 dec (W. G. Keighley 70*, A. W. H. Mallett 50) drew with Montreal 121-9.

22nd Match: v West Indian (Montreal) XI (Montreal)   Sept 12.
M.C.C. 254-7 dec (R. W. V. Robins 107) beat West Indian XI 85 by 169 runs.

1951-52 : M.C.C. tour India and Pakistan

Only two of the nineteen cricketers who represented M.C.C. in Australia the previous winter arrived in Bombay aboard the *Chusan* for the tour of the Indian sub-continent. On paper therefore the party hardly represented England's second team, let alone the first. The side was N. D. Howard (Lancs) (capt), D. B. Carr (Derbys), D. V. Brennan (Yorks), R. T. Spooner (Warwicks) and the professionals T. W. Graveney (Gloucs), F. A. Lowson (Yorks), J. D. B. Robertson (Middx), A. J. Watkins (Glam), D. Kenyon (Worcs), A. E. G. Rhodes (Derbys), D. Shackleton (Hants), J. B. Statham (Lancs), M. J. Hilton (Lancs), F. Ridgway (Kent), R. Tattersall (Lancs), C. J. Poole (Notts) – the last named replaced J. T. Ikin, who was not fit enough to make the tour.

Despite the lack of famous players, the team were given a tremendous reception on landing and crowds lined the route from the docks to the Brabourne Stadium, where the team went for practice, prior to the first match. Unfortunately Poole broke a finger whilst in the nets and could not play until December.

After a high-scoring draw against a Universities XI, the team beat Western India by two wickets – a notable victory since the local side was regarded as the strongest in the country.

The first Test was staged in Delhi, where a splendid hundred by Watkins saved the team from defeat, but the tourists were without Graveney, who was ill, and Rhodes. The latter's injury proved so serious that he was sent home and E. Leadbeater of Yorkshire was flown out as a replacement.

The team moved on to Pakistan, where after a drawn match with Punjab, they met Pakistan in the first 'Unofficial Test'. Scoring was painfully slow and it was soon obvious that there would be no definite outcome to the match. A promising 16-year-old, Hanif Mohammad, opened the batting for the home eleven. In the second 'Unofficial Test', England collapsed on coir matting, Fazal Mahmood taking 6 for 40, and though Statham and Shackleton bowled exceptionally well and Graveney bolstered up the second innings with a century, Pakistan won by 4 wickets. The party returned to India for the second Test against that country and after two first innings each of which easily exceeded 400, Ridgway and Watkins suddenly surprised themselves by dismissing India for 208 in the second innings. Time however did not allow England to get the reward they deserved.

In the third Test, England were without Lowson, who damaged a finger, and Poole was brought into the side. The batting was depressingly slow – about 35 runs per hour – and the match was drawn, long before the end. Hilton and Tattersall bowled out India on the first day of the fourth Test for 121 – the only time in Tests that the Lancashire spinners really proved their worth. Watkins batted well and when India went cheaply in the second innings, England won by 8 wickets.

Both Central Zone and South Zone were beaten with ease, so

The end of England's first innings in the third Test match in Calcutta on the M.C.C. tour of India, Pakistan and Ceylon in 1951-52. Leadbeater is run out attempting a second run off Mankad. Leadbeater had been flown out as a replacement.

England came to the fifth Test with more confidence than for the previous internationals. The captain however went down with pleurisy and Carr led England for the first time. The tourists made a fair start, reaching 224 for 5 at the close of the first day. The death of George VI meant the cancellation of the second day,

---

1951-52: M.C.C. to India, Pakistan and Ceylon

1st Match: v University of India (Bombay)   Oct 5, 6, 7.
M.C.C. 340 (T. W. Graveney 101, J. D. B. Robertson 58, H. T. Dani 5-79) & 40-0 drew with University 375 (P. Roy 89, R. B. Kenny 86*, H. T. Dani 66).

2nd Match: v Western India (Ahmedabad)   Oct 9, 10, 11.
W. India 164 (G. Kishenchand 65) & 139 (D. K. Gaekwad 66*) lost to M.C.C. 192 (T. W. Graveney 62, J. M. Patel 5-40) & 112-8 (S. Nyalchand 5-36) by 2 wkts.

3rd Match: v Holkar (Indore)   Oct 13, 14, 15.
Holkar 291 (B. B. Nimbalkar 63, H. G. Gaekwad 62*, C. T. Sarwate 59) & 142-5 (C. T. Sarwate 56*) drew with M.C.C. 329 (J. D. B. Robertson 131, F. A. Lowson 70).

4th Match: v Northern India (Amritsar)   Oct 20, 21, 22.
M.C.C. 340 (F. A. Lowson 138, T. W. Graveney 79, M. K. Rajdhan 6-72) & 173-4 (J. D. B. Robertson 105) drew with N. India 209 (L. Amarnath 97*, D. Shackleton 5-36).

5th Match: v National Defence Academy (Dehra Dun) (One Day)   Oct 26.
N.D.A. 80 (A. E. G. Rhodes 5-22) lost to M.C.C. 87-1 (A. J. Watkins 59) by 9 wkts.*

6th Match: v Services XI (Dehra Dun)   Oct 28, 29, 30.
Services XI 167 & 175 (H. R. Adhikari 64) drew with M.C.C. 338-4 dec (T. W. Graveney 101, R. T. Spooner 90, N. D. Howard 51) & 4-0.

7th Match: v India (New Delhi)   Nov 2, 3, 4, 6, 7.
England 203 (J. D. B. Robertson 50, S. G. Shinde 6-91) & 368-6 (A. J. Watkins 137*, D. B. Carr 76, F. A. Lowson 68) drew with India 418-6 dec (V. S. Hazare 164*, V. M. Merchant 154).

8th Match: v Punjab C.A. (Sialkot)   Nov 10, 11, 12.
Punjab C.A. 364 (Nazar Mohammad 140, Agha Ahmad Raza 52) & 114-6 dec drew with M.C.C. 229 (D. B. Carr 63, Fazal Mahmood 5-58) & 50-1.

9th Match: v Pakistan (Lahore)   Nov 15, 16, 17, 18.
M.C.C. 254 (J. D. B. Robertson 61, Khan Mohammad 5-84) & 368-1 (R. T. Spooner 168*, T. W. Graveney 109*, J. D. B. Robertson 70) drew with Pakistan 428-8 dec (Maqsood Ahmad 137*, M. E. Z. Ghazali 86, Nazar Mohammad 66).

10th Match: v Universities XI (Lahore)   Nov 20, 21.
Universities 88 & 245-2 dec (Shakoor Ahmad 104, Shujayuddin 112*) drew with M.C.C. 133-3 dec (D. Kenyon 70*) & 54-1.*

11th Match: v Bahawalpur-Karachi (Bahawalpur)   Nov 24, 25, 26.
Bahawalpur 348-9 dec (Imtiaz Ahmed 99, Hanif Mohammad 71, Wazir Mohammad 67) drew with M.C.C. 123 & 131-3 (J. D. B. Robertson 50*).

12th Match: v Pakistan (Karachi)   Nov 29, 30, Dec 1, 2.
M.C.C. 123 (Fazal Mahmood 6-40) & 291 (T. W. Graveney 123, Khan Mohammad 5-88) lost to Pakistan 130 & 288-6 (Hanif Mohammad 64, A. H. Kardar 50*) by 4 wkts.

13th Match: v Bombay (Bombay)   Dec 8, 9, 10.
M.C.C. 338 (D. Kenyon 95, F. A. Lowson 76, R. V. Divecha 6-74) & 126-3 (F. A. Lowson 71*) drew with Bombay C.A. 291 (R. S. Modi 86, S. W. Sohoni 58*).

14th Match: v India (Bombay)   Dec 14, 15, 16, 18, 19.
India 485-9 dec (V. S. Hazare 155, P. Roy 140, C. D. Gopinath 50*) & 208 drew with England 456 (T. W. Graveney 175, A. J. Watkins 80) & 55-2.

15th Match: v Maharashtra (Poona)   Dec 21, 22, 23.
Maharashtra 249 (M. R. Rege 133) & 124-2 (H. T. Dani 72*) drew with M.C.C. 410 (F. A. Lowson 76, D. Kenyon 76, D. V. Brennan 67*, D. Shackleton 66, C. J. Poole 50, D. G. Chowdhury 5-124).

16th Match: v Bengal (Calcutta)   Dec 26, 27, 28.
Bengal 188 (C. S. Nayudu 57, R. Tattersall 7-58) & 134 (N. Chatterjee 59) lost to M.C.C. 342-8 dec (A. J. Watkins 113*) by an inns & 20 runs.

17th Match: v India (Calcutta)   Dec 30, 31, Jan 1, 3, 4.
England 342 (A. J. Watkins 68, C. J. Poole 55, R. T. Spooner 71) & 252-5 dec (R. T. Spooner 92, C. J. Poole 69*) drew with India 344 (D. G. Phadkar 115, M. H. Mankad 59) & 103-0 (M. H. Mankad 71*).

18th Match: v East Zone (Jamshedpur)   Jan 6, 7, 8.
M.C.C. 370-5 dec (J. D. B. Robertson 183, D. B. Carr 66*, A. J. Watkins 63) & 20-1 beat East Zone 158 (B. Frank 98*, D. Shackleton 5-64) & 228 (B. Frank 75) by 9 wkts.

19th Match: v India (Kanpur)   Jan 12, 13, 14.
India 121 (R. Tattersall 6-48) & 157 (H. R. Adhikari 60, M. J. Hilton 5-61) lost to England 203 (A. J. Watkins 66, Ghulam Ahmed 5-70) & 76-2 by 8 wkts.

20th Match: v Central Zone (Nagpur)   Jan 20, 21, 22.
Central Zone 134 & 196 (C. T. Sarwate 54) lost to M.C.C. 296 (C. J. Poole 87, D. Kenyon 59, C. T. Sarwate 6-107) & 38-1 by 9 wkts.

21st Match: v Hyderabad (Hyderabad)   Jan 26, 27, 28.
Hyderabad 320 (Ali Hussain 95, E. B. Aibara 76, M. V. Bobjee 66) & 82-3 drew with M.C.C. 441-8 dec (D. Kenyon 112, T. W. Graveney 96, C. J. Poole 79, E. Leadbeater 63*, Ghulam Ahmed 5-123).

22nd Match: v South Zone (Bangalore)   Feb 1, 2, 3.
South Zone 217 (L. T. Adisesh 69) & 221 (M. Kannaiyaram 56*, M. J. Hilton 5-44) lost to M.C.C. 335-9 dec (F. A. Lowson 98, R. T. Spooner 63, D. B. Carr 56, T. D. Krishna 5-93) & 104-1 (F. A. Lowson 57*) by 9 wkts.

23rd Match: v India (Madras)   Feb 6, 8, 9, 10.
England 266 (J. D. B. Robertson 77, R. T. Spooner 66, M. H. Mankad 8-55) & 183 (J. D. B. Robertson 56) lost to India 457-9 dec (P. R. Umrigar 130*, P. Roy 111, D. G. Phadkar 61) by an inns & 8 runs.

24th Match: v Commonwealth XI (Colombo)   Feb 16, 17, 18.
Commonwealth XI 517 (C. I. Gunesekara 135, K. R. Miller 106, R. N. Harvey 74) beat M.C.C. 103 & 155 by an inns & 259 runs.

25th Match: v Ceylon (Colombo)   Feb 22, 23, 24.
Ceylon 58 & 179 (E. Leadbeater 5-41) lost to M.C.C. 270-4 dec (T. W. Graveney 102*, R. T. Spooner 57, D. Kenyon 52) by an inns & 33 runs.

26th Match: v Central Province XI (Kandy)   Feb 27, 28.
Central Province 165 (T. B. Werapitiya 57) & 106 (E. Leadbeater 6-35) lost to M.C.C. 300 (T. W. Graveney 120) by an inns & 29 runs.

27th Match: v Galle Gymkhana Club (Galle)   March 2, 3.
M.C.C. 187 (R. B. Wijesinghe 5-72) & 106-4 beat Galle 75 (M. J. Hilton 6-28) & 217 (B. R. Heyn 61) by 6 wkts.

Batting Averages

	M	I	NO	R	HS	Avge	100	c/s
T. W. Graveney (Glos)	19	32	7	1393	175	55.72	6	4
C. J. Poole (Notts)	11	13	2	491	87	44.63	0	4
F. A. Lowson (Yorks)	16	28	5	1016	138	44.17	1	5
J. D. B. Robertson (Middx)	19	31	3	1173	183	41.89	3	12
A. J. Watkins (Glam)	19	25	2	872	137*	37.91	2	19
R. T. Spooner (Warks)	17	26	2	886	168*	36.91	1	20/4
E. Leadbeater (Yorks)	8	7	2	176	63*	35.20	0	5
D. B. Carr (Derby)	18	22	3	579	76	30.47	0	18
D. Kenyon (Worcs)	17	29	4	733	112	29.32	1	2
A. E. G. Rhodes (Derby)	3	3	1	55	45	27.50	0	0
D. Shackleton (Hants)	16	20	3	306	66	18.00	0	4
N. D. Howard (Lancs)	15	21	1	335	51	16.75	0	11
D. V. Brennan (Yorks)	13	15	4	166	67*	15.09	0	21/8
J. B. Statham (Lancs)	15	16	4	162	27	13.50	0	5
M. J. Hilton (Lancs)	15	14	1	173	47	13.30	0	9
F. Ridgway (Kent)	16	17	8	114	24	12.66	0	14
R. Tattersall (Lancs)	16	18	11	82	32*	11.71	0	6

Bowling Averages

	O	M	R	W	Avge	BB	5i
J. D. B. Robertson	106	31	263	14	18.78	3-9	0
J. B. Statham	369.5	106	807	40	20.17	4-9	0
M. J. Hilton	412.5	159	906	41	22.09	5-44	2
D. Shackleton	484.1	125	1184	51	23.21	5-36	2
F. Ridgway	409	87	1068	41	26.04	4-20	0
R. Tattersall	546.3	157	1284	49	26.20	7-58	2
A. E. G. Rhodes	73.2	17	225	8	28.12	4-100	0
T. W. Graveney	42.4	7	182	6	30.33	4-67	0
D. B. Carr	246.3	43	819	23	35.60	4-37	0
E. Leadbeater	198.1	45	692	20	34.60	5-41	1
C. J. Poole	23	4	72	2	36.00	1-8	0
A. J. Watkins	425.2	111	969	25	38.76	3-20	0

Also bowled: R. T. Spooner 3-0-17-0; N. D. Howard 6-0-29-1; D. Kenyon 1-0-9-0; F. A. Lowson 2-0-16-0.

but on the third Mankad removed the last five batsmen for 42 runs. Umrigar and Roy hit hundreds for India and though England did better in their second innings, the match was won by India with an innings to spare.

The team travelled from Madras to Colombo for a four-match visit to Ceylon. In the first match they met a strong Commonwealth Eleven, which included the Australians Harvey and Miller. The tourists were completely outplayed. The umpiring in the matches in Ceylon was not all that could be desired and Statham, after having many appeals turned down, clean bowled the last batsman, breaking the leg-stump in the process. 'That was bloody close, wasn't it?' he asked the umpire.

The batsman of the tour was Graveney, but in the Tests Watkins did remarkably well. Lowson scored runs in the ordinary games but did not appear to have the temperament for Test cricket, whilst Kenyon had a very poor time. Ridgway and Statham were the best of the faster bowlers–for some reason Howard neglected Shackleton–Tattersall worked hard, but Hilton disappointed.

Mankad had a great series and was the outstanding figure of the Tests.

1953-54: Hutton the first professional to captain M.C.C. touring party

For the home series against India in 1952, the selectors broke with tradition and appointed a professional–Len Hutton–as captain of England. There was no M.C.C. tour overseas in the winter of 1952-53, but in 1953-54, after Hutton had won back the Ashes in the summer, he was the automatic choice to lead the M.C.C. in the West Indies.

The tour ended as the most controversial and unhappy venture since the Bodyline Tour, but it began amicably enough, the team flying out to Bermuda for three preliminary matches. The side

which left England on 14 December was L. Hutton (Yorks) (capt), T. E. Bailey (Essex), D. C. S. Compton (Middx), P. B. H. May (Surrey), T. W. Graveney (Gloucs), T. G. Evans (Kent), W. Watson (Yorks), J. H. Wardle (Yorks), F. S. Trueman (Yorks), J. C. Laker (Surrey), G. A. R. Lock (Surrey), A. E. Moss (Middx), R. T. Spooner (Warwicks), K. G. Suttle (Sussex), J. B. Statham (Lancs) and C. H. Palmer (Leics), as a player-manager. This was the first time the full strength of England had toured West Indies and the only absentee of note was A. V. Bedser.

Leaving the tranquility of Bermuda, the M.C.C. travelled to Jamaica, trouncing the island team by an innings. Watson hit an excellent hundred, but the main reason for the success was the fast bowling of Statham and Trueman, who made the ball lift alarmingly on the hard wicket. In the return, Jamaica batted poorly in their first innings, but Holt made 152 in the second innings and the game was drawn.

England picked four fast bowlers for the first Test at Sabina Park and then found the pitch was a docile one. West Indies hit

1st Match: v Combined Bermuda XI (Hamilton)   Dec 16, 17.
Combined XI 73 & 104 (J. C. Laker 5-35) lost to M.C.C. 205 (J. C. Laker 67, T. W. Graveney 52) by an inns & 28 runs.

2nd Match: v All Bermuda (Hamilton)   Dec 20, 21, 22.
M.C.C. 148 (E. Woods 5-49) & 166-6 dec drew with Bermuda 133 (G. A. R. Lock 8-54) & 90-6.

3rd Match: v Bermuda (Hamilton)   Dec 23, 24, 26.
Bermuda 133 (G. A. R. Lock 7-35) drew with M.C.C. 135-1 (L. Hutton 67, W. Watson 55*).

4th Match: v Combined Parishes (Innswood, Jam.)   Dec 30, 31.
Parishes 168 (M. C. Frederick 85) & 89-3 drew with M.C.C. 275-4 dec (T. E. Bailey 78, D. C. S. Compton 73).

5th Match: v Jamaica (Kingston)   Jan 2, 3, 5, 6.
Jamaica 266 (K. R. Rickards 75, M. C. Frederick 66) & 170 (F. S. Trueman 5-45) lost to M.C.C. 457-7 dec (W. Watson 161, T. W. Graveney 82, D. C. S. Compton 56) by an inns & 21 runs.

6th Match: v Jamaica (Melbourne Pk, Kingston)   Jan 8, 9, 11, 12.
Jamaica 187 (M. C. Frederick 58) & 328-4 dec (J. K. Holt 152, A. F. Rae 53, G. A. Headley 53*) drew with M.C.C. 286 (P. B. H. May 124) & 34-1.

7th Match: v West Indies (Sabina Pk, Kingston)   Jan 15, 16, 18, 19, 20, 21.
West Indies 417 (J. K. Holt 95, C. L. Walcott 65, J. B. Stollmeyer 60, E. D. Weekes 55, C. A. McWatt 54) & 209-6 dec (E. D. Weekes 90*) beat England 170 & 316 (W. Watson 116, P. B. H. May 69, L. Hutton 56, E. S. M. Kentish 5-49) by 140 runs.

8th Match: v Leeward Is (Antigua)   Jan 25, 26.
Leewards 38 (J. H. Wardle 5-7) & 167 (D. C. S. Compton 5-50) lost to M.C.C. 261 (L. Hutton 82, T. W. Graveney 50) by an inns & 56 runs.

9th Match: v Barbados (Bridgetown)   Jan 29, 30, Feb 1, 2, 3.
Barbados 389 (D. St. E. Atkinson 151) & 179 (G. A. R. Lock 5-57) lost to M.C.C. 373 (K. G. Suttle 96, L. Hutton 59*, P. B. H. May 57, W. Watson 53) & 196-9 (K. G. Suttle 62, J. D. C. Goodard 5-43) by 1 wkt.

10th Match: v West Indies (Bridgetown)   Feb 6, 8, 9, 10, 11, 12.
West Indies 383 dec (C. L. Walcott 220, B. H. Pairaudeau 71, D. St. E. Atkinson 53) & 292-2 dec (J. K. Holt 166, F. M. M. Worrell 76*) beat England 181 (L. Hutton 72) & 313 (D. C. S. Compton 93, L. Hutton 77, T. W. Graveney 64*, P. B. H. May 62) by 181 runs.

11th Match: v British Guiana (Georgetown)   Feb 17, 18, 19, 20.
M.C.C. 607 (W. Watson 257, T. W. Graveney 231) beat British Guiana 262 (R. J. Christiani 75, J. H. Wardle 6-77) & 247 (R. J. Christiani 82) by an inns & 98 runs.

12th Match: v West Indies (Georgetown)   Feb 24, 25, 26, 27, March 1, 2.
England 435 (L. Hutton 169, D. C. S. Compton 64, S. Ramadhin 6-113) & 75-1 beat West Indies 251 (E. D. Weekes 94, C. A. McWatt 54) & 256 (J. K. Holt 64) by 9 wkts.

13th Match: v Windward Is (St George's, Grenada)   March 6, 8.
M.C.C. 205-7 dec (L. Hutton 82) & 177-3 (P. B. H. May 93*, J. H. Wardle 66) drew with Windwards 194 (I. Neverson 90*, F. S. Trueman 7-69).

14th Match: v Trinidad (Port of Spain)   March 10, 11, 12, 13, 15.
Trinidad 329 (G. E. Gomez 91, J. B. Stollmeyer 89) & 232 (N. Asgarali 65) lost to M.C.C. 331-8 dec (W. Watson 141, C. H. Palmer 87) & 233-3 (D. C. S. Compton 90*, T. E. Bailey 90) by 7 wkts.

15th Match: v West Indies (Port of Spain)   March 17, 18, 19, 20, 22, 23.
West Indies 681-8 dec (E. D. Weekes 206, F. M. M. Worrell 167, C. L. Walcott 124, D. St. E. Atkinson 74) & 212-4 dec (F. M. M. Worrell 56, D. St. E. Atkinson 53, C. L. Walcott 51*) drew with England 537 (P. B. H. May 135, D. C. S. Compton 133, T. W. Graveney 92) & 98-3.

16th Match v Jamaica Colts & Country XI (Montego Bay)   March 26, 27.
M.C.C. 135 (T. E. Bailey 55) drew with Combined XI 97-6: rain.

17th Match: v West Indies (Sabina Pk, Kingston)   March 30, 31, Apr 1, 2, 3.
West Indies 139 (C. L. Walcott 50, T. E. Bailey 7-34) & 346 (C. L. Walcott 116, J. B. Stollmeyer 64) lost to England 414 (L. Hutton 205, J. H. Wardle 66) & 72-1 by 9 wkts.

The four Yorkshiremen on the 1953-54 M.C.C. tour of the West Indies. From left : Willie Watson, Fred Trueman, Johnny Wardle and the captain, Len Hutton.

Left *The second Test match on the 1953-54 tour, and the second won by the West Indies. Tom Graveney, on-driving Sonny Ramadhin at the Kensington Oval, Barbados, scored 64 not out.*

Below *The England team being presented to the Governor, Sir Alfred Savage, before the start of the third Test against the West Indies in 1953-54. The players are L. Hutton, T. E. Bailey, D. C. S. Compton, J. C. Laker, J. H. Wardle, G. A. R. Lock, W. Watson, J. B. Statham, P. B. H. May, T. G. Evans, T. W. Graveney, K. C. Suttle.*

1953-54: M.C.C. to the West Indies

Batting Averages

	M	I	NO	R	HS	Avge	100	c/s
L. Hutton (Yorks)	8	12	2	780	205	78.00	2	3
W. Watson (Yorks)	9	16	3	892	257	68.61	4	4
T. W. Graveney (Glos)	8	14	3	617	231	56.09	1	14
T. E. Bailey (Essex)	8	11	4	346	90	49.42	0	3
D. C. S. Compton (Middx)	10	14	1	630	133	48.46	1	7
K. G. Suttle (Sussex)	4	7	1	251	96	41.83	0	3
P. B. H. May (Surrey)	10	18	2	630	135	39.37	2	0
C. H. Palmer (Leics)	3	4	0	142	87	35.50	0	0
J. H. Wardle (Yorks)	5	5	0	130	66	26.00	0	5
J. C. Laker (Surrey)	7	9	1	123	33	15.37	0	4
F. S. Trueman (Yorks)	8	9	3	81	20	13.50	0	7
R. T. Spooner (Warks)	5	8	1	93	28	13.28	0	4/3
G. A. R. Lock (Surrey)	9	12	2	105	40*	10.50	0	6
A. E. Moss (Middx)	5	6	2	39	16	9.75	0	2
T. G. Evans (Kent)	6	8	0	72	28	9.00	0	9/1
J. B. Statham (Lancs)	5	6	2	28	10*	7.00	0	2

Bowling Averages

	O	M	R	W	Avge	BB	5i
J. B. Statham	194.5	35	541	22	24.59	4-35	0
A. E. Moss	161.5	38	490	18	27.22	4-47	0
T. E. Bailey	251.5	79	611	22	27.77	7-34	1
J. H. Wardle	240.3	77	569	18	31.61	6-77	1
F. S. Trueman	319.4	81	909	27	33.66	5-45	1
J. C. Laker	330.5	113	756	22	34.36	4-47	0
G. A. R. Lock	486.1	157	1178	28	42.07	5-57	1
D. C. S. Compton	81.4	16	325	6	54.16	2-40	0

Also bowled: C. H. Palmer 22-13-33-0; T. W. Graveney 16-6-71-0; L. Hutton 6-0-43-0.

417, whereas the tourists were muddled by Ramadhin and Valentine, falling for 170. Stollmeyer did not enforce the follow on, an action that produced some ugly demonstrations by the crowd. When West Indies batted a second time Lock was no-balled for throwing, which upset some of the English players. England were eventually set 457 to make in 570 minutes. By the close on the fifth day, the total had reached 233 for 2. The crowd was becoming more and more critical of Stollmeyer and the umpires were also under extreme pressure – attacks, though not of a serious nature, were made on the wife and son of one umpire. As it was England collapsed on the sixth day and West Indies won by a large margin.

A two-day game was played in the Leewards, before the team moved to Barbados. England won a dramatic game against the island team, but the umpires again no-balled Lock for throwing. West Indies outplayed England in the second Test; Hutton's concentration was upset by the crowd's barracking. The English batting in fact was quite dreadful in the first innings and the tourists reached the low point of their travels.

Beating British Guiana with ease gave England some confidence for the third Test, which had to be won. Hutton called correctly and he played a masterly innings to give England a total of 435. The West Indies' first innings was marred by the riot which erupted when McWatt was run out. Suddenly the air was filled with flying bottles and broken beer crates. The English outfielders ran into the centre of the pitch and mounted police arrived. It was suggested that Hutton call the team in, but he refused and gradually calm was restored – Wardle helped to break the tension with some of his clowning. A police cordon was required around the umpire's house for the rest of the game. England enforced the follow on and won the game by 9 wickets.

Injuries kept Valentine, Gomez and Evans out of the fourth Test, also Statham pulled a rib muscle after nine overs and was out for the rest of the tour. None of this had much bearing on the match which was a very high-scoring draw. It seemed impossible to complete games on the jute-matting of Port of Spain. The only disagreements in the match were the English players' complaints on several umpiring decisions. Hutton also had a few words to say to Trueman regarding his behaviour on the field.

The deciding Test took place at Sabina Park. West Indies elected to bat and on what seemed a perfect wicket suddenly found themselves all out for 139, Bailey produced the bowling performance of his career, taking 7 for 34. Hutton then played another incredible innings, being at the wicket just under nine hours and making 205. West Indies did better in their second innings, but

the tourists won by 9 wickets and managed to draw the series.

The M.C.C. team came in for a lot of criticism for not hiding their displeasure at some of the umpiring decisions and dramatic gestures together with untactful remarks by the players did not help to calm the volatile crowds, but despite all the uproar, which the press in some cases blew up out of all proportion, the relations between the two teams were fairly harmonious, which certainly helped matters.

The two batsmen of the side were Hutton and Compton, whilst Statham and Bailey stood out as the best bowlers. Trueman was much too erratic.

Walcott, Weekes and Worrell remained the best home batsmen, though a 17-year-old Sobers looked a promising all-rounder.

1954-55: the speed of Tyson shatters Australia

Hutton, who had won the Ashes for England in 1953 at home, led the M.C.C. to Australia in 1954-55, with the task of retaining them.

The team, which was selected on 27 July was L. Hutton (Yorks) (capt), P. B. H. May (Surrey) (vice-capt), R. T. Simpson (Notts), W. J. Edrich (Middx), T. E. Bailey (Essex), M. C. Cowdrey (Kent), D. C. S. Compton (Middx), A. V. Bedser (Surrey), T. G. Evans (Kent), J. H. Wardle (Yorks), J. B. Statham (Lancs), T. W. Graveney (Gloucs), R. Appleyard (Yorks), J. McConnon (Glam), P. J. Loader (Surrey), F. H. Tyson (Northants) and K. V. Andrew (Northants). The manager was C. G. Howard and the baggage-master G. Duckworth, the old Lancashire wicket-keeper. The players omitted most noted by the press were Trueman, Lock and Laker.

Of this original selection the only doubt was Compton. In the end he travelled later by air, and J. V. Wilson (Yorks) was added to the party. Also included was H. W. Dalton as masseur, the first time such an official had been sent.

Leaving Tilbury on the s.s. *Orsova*, the side arrived at Perth

1954-55: M.C.C. to Ceylon, Australia and New Zealand

Batting Averages

	M	I	NO	R	HS	Avge	100	c/s
D. C. S. Compton (Middx)	11	16	2	799	182	57.07	3	3
L. Hutton (Yorks)	15	25	2	1059	145*	46.04	2	6
T. W. Graveney (Glos)	15	22	3	855	134	45.00	4	20
P. B. H. May (Surrey)	18	29	3	1096	129	42.15	4	16
M. C. Cowdrey (Kent)	17	31	1	1019	110	33.96	3	13
T. E. Bailey (Essex)	15	21	2	551	88	29.00	0	7
R. T. Simpson (Notts)	16	27	3	644	136	26.83	1	5
F. H. Tyson (Northants)	14	20	4	286	62*	17.87	0	3
J. V. Wilson (Yorks)	11	19	2	301	72	17.70	0	10
J. H. Wardle (Yorks)	18	23	3	341	63	17.05	0	9
W. J. Edrich (Middx)	11	18	0	293	88	16.27	0	5
J. McConnon (Glam)	5	7	1	85	22	14.16	0	2
T. G. Evans (Kent)	13	20	2	244	40	13.55	0	34/7
J. B. Statham (Lancs)	13	14	4	132	25	13.20	0	6
R. Appleyard (Yorks)	13	17	9	82	19*	10.25	0	8
A. V. Bedser (Surrey)	7	11	2	85	30	9.44	0	3
P. J. Loader (Surrey)	11	13	2	90	22	8.18	0	6
K. V. Andrew (Northts)	8	11	2	71	28*	7.88	0	16/2

Bowling Averages

	Balls	M	R	W	Avge	BB	5i
R. Appleyard	1962	82	656	44	14.90	6-21	2
J. B. Statham	2445	69	916	54	16.96	6-23	2
F. H. Tyson	2764	65	1140	64	17.81	7-27	4
P. J. Loader	1902	42	817	41	19.92	6-22	1
J. V. Wilson	183	0	100	5	20.00	2-1	0
J. H. Wardle	3153	135	1166	57	20.45	5-42	3
T. E. Bailey	1898	49	769	36	21.36	4-53	0
A. V. Bedser	1655	33	659	24	27.45	5-57	1
J. McConnon	601	18	267	8	33.37	2-37	0
D. C. S. Compton	101	1	101	2	50.50	1-21	0

Also bowled: T. W. Graveney 102-3-47-1; M. C. Cowdrey 68-1-71-1; W. J. Edrich 64-2-53-0; L. Hutton 6-0-2-1; R. T. Simpson 28-1-5-2.
C. G. Howard played in one non-first-class match.

Above *Trevor Bailey in typical obdurate mood quietly playing a ball from Ray Lindwall during the second Test in Sydney of the 1954-55 tour of Australia.*

Left *England wicket-keeper Keith Andrew runs out Australia's Graeme Hole in the first Test of the 1954-55 Australian tour at Brisbane.*

on 7 October – there had been the usual one-day game in Colombo.

The team won the first three first-class matches, though only a bright knock by Compton, who had just arrived, saved the side at Adelaide. The three wins were followed by three draws.

The first Test was lost because Hutton gambled and put in Australia. The home side replied to this impudence by hitting 601 for 8 and then declaring. Hutton had thought the battery of four fast bowlers – Statham, Tyson, Bailey and Bedser – would break through. The problem was that about ten catches were dropped and Morris and Harvey both hit centuries. The England batting, which lacked Compton, who was injured fielding, collapsed twice to Lindwall, Miller and later the spin of Benaud and Johnson. Australia won by an innings with a day to spare.

In the second Test Morris won the toss and put England in. Splendid bowling all round dismissed the tourists for 154, but Bailey and Tyson made certain that Australia did not obtain a commanding lead and May hit a century in England's second innings, so that the home side required 223 for victory. It was not an unreasonable target, but Statham and Tyson bowled in great style, making the ball get up nastily, and with only Harvey really defying them, the English pacemen won the game by 38 runs. One interesting note on the match was the dropping of Bedser. This caused quite a stir, but was justified.

After an up-country game, the teams met at Melbourne for the third Test. Hutton decided to bat on winning the toss, only to see Cowdrey play a lone role in the England innings. Miller, who had missed the previous Test through injury, bowled with great fire,

dismissing Hutton, Edrich and Compton for 14 runs. Statham and Tyson retaliated and Australia had a first innings lead of only 40. England's batting was stronger in the second innings, with May playing a good innings of 91, and Australia required 240 to win. As in the second Test Tyson and Statham swept right through them. This time even Harvey did not survive. The receipts for the match were a record £47,933.

On the holiday trip to Tasmania McConnon broke the little finger of his right hand and returned to England. Back on the mainland, South Australia were beaten by an innings and 143 runs, which was a pleasant prelude to the fourth Test. Australia were without Lindwall, but on the first day it was so hot, no one was keen to field. Australia batted and England wilted. The home team hit 323 and the tourists methodically plodded to 341 in 541 minutes, so it looked a certain draw. Hutton however brought on Appleyard after Statham had bowled two overs in Australia's second innings and this unexpected move produced three quick wickets, after which Tyson and Statham dealt with the remainder and England, though Miller grabbed three wickets, won at a canter. Thus the Ashes were retained.

The worst storms in fifty years ruined the fifth Test and it was drawn, though England were well on top.

The four matches in New Zealand included two Tests, both of which England won and in the second, the home side were dismissed for a record low of 26. The tourists flew home via the United States arriving in London on 5 April.

The Australian critics berated their team, describing it as worse than the 1912 side which went to England, when most of the best players of the day refused to go.

Tyson and Statham were the cricketers of the tour – Tyson was regarded as the fastest Englishman to visit Australia since Larwood. Hutton led the team ably and managed his bowlers well, but his batting was much more defensive than previously. Cowdrey and May were the two young successes in the batting line-up, though Graveney also made a big impression.

One of the problems Australia faced was that of the captaincy, and many felt that Miller ought to have been preferred to Johnson, but Australia also suffered from a large crop of injuries, which must be taken into account.

1954-55: M.C.C. to Ceylon, Australia and New Zealand

1st Match: v Ceylon (Colombo) (One Day)   Sept 30.
M.C.C. 178-8 dec (M. C. Cowdrey 66) drew with Ceylon 101-4.*

2nd Match: v Western Australian Country XI (Bunbury)   Oct 11, 12.
M.C.C. 344-5 dec (W. J. Edrich 129, L. Hutton 59, T. W. Graveney 58) drew with Country XI 116 (J. McConnon 5-30) & 128-6.

3rd Match: v Western Australia (Perth)   Oct 15, 16, 18, 19.
W. Australia 103 (J. B. Statham 6-23) & 255 (K. D. Meuleman 109, D. K. Carmody 75) lost to M.C.C. 321 (L. Hutton 145) & 40-3 by 7 wkts.*

4th Match: v Combined XI (Perth)   Oct 22, 23, 25.
Combined XI 86 & 163 lost to M.C.C. 311 (P. B. H. May 129) by an inns & 62 runs.

5th Match: v South Australia (Adelaide)   Oct 29, 30, Nov 1, 2.
M.C.C. 246 (D. C. S. Compton 113, J. W. Wilson 5-81) & 181 (L. Hutton 98) beat S. Australia 254 (L. E. Favell 84, F. H. Tyson 5-62) & 152 (R. Appleyard 5-46) by 21 runs.

6th Match: v An Australian XI (Melbourne)   Nov 5, 6, 8, 9, 10.
M.C.C. 205 (R. T. Simpson 74, I. W. Johnson 6-66) drew with Australian XI 167-7.

7th Match: v New South Wales (Sydney)   Nov 12, 13, 15, 16.
M.C.C. 252 (M. C. Cowdrey 110, L. Hutton 102) & 327 (M. C. Cowdrey 103, L. Hutton 87) drew with N.S.W. 382 (W. J. Watson 155, K. R. Miller 86) & 78-2.

8th Match: v Queensland (Brisbane)   Nov 19, 20, 22, 23.
M.C.C. 304 (R. T. Simpson 136, D. C. S. Compton 110) & 288 (P. B. H. May 77, D. C. S. Compton 69, T. E. Bailey 51) drew with Queensland 288 & 25-2.*

9th Match: v Australia (Brisbane)   Nov 26, 27, 29, 30, Dec 1.
Australia 601-8 dec (R. N. Harvey 162, A. R.Morris 153, R. R. Lindwall 64*, G. B. Hole 57) beat England 190 (T. E. Bailey 88) & 257 (W. J. Edrich 88) by an inns & 154 runs.

10th Match: v Queensland Country XI (Rockingham)   Dec 4, 6.
M.C.C. 317 (W. J. Edrich 74, P. B. H. May 69, J. V. Wilson 61, D. Watt 5-56) beat Qld Country XI 95 & 210 (W. M. Brown 78, R. Appleyard 7-51) by an inns & 12 runs.

11th Match: v Prime Minister's XI (Canberra) (One Day)   Dec 8
M.C.C. 278-7 dec (P. B. H. May 101, T. W. Graveney 56) beat Prime Minister's XI 247 (R. Benaud 113) by 31 runs.

12th Match: v Victoria (Melbourne)   Dec 10, 11, 13, 14.
M.C.C. 312 (M. C. Cowdrey 79, T. E. Bailey 60) & 236-5 dec (P. B. H. May 105, M. C. Cowdrey 54) drew with Victoria 277 (R. N. Harvey 59, F. H. Tyson 6-68) & 88-3.*

13th Match: v Australia (Sydney)   Dec 17, 18, 20, 21, 22.
England 154 & 296 (P. B. H. May 104, M. C. Cowdrey 54) beat Australia 228 & 184 (R. N. Harvey 92*, F. H. Tyson 6-85) by 38 runs.

14th Match: v N.S.W. Northern Districts XI (Newcastle)   Dec 27, 28, 29.
Districts 211 (R. McDonald 63, J. H. Wardle 6-36) & 246 (R. Wotton 52, R. Appleyard 5-59) lost to M.C.C. 438 (P. B. H. May 157, T. G. Evans 69, D. C. S. Compton 60, J. Bull 5-80) & 20-1 by 9 wkts.

15th Match: v Australia (Melbourne) Dec 31, Jan 1, 3, 4, 5.
England 191 (M. C. Cowdrey 102) & 279 (P. B. H. May 91, W. A. Johnston 5-85) beat Australia 231 (J. B. Statham 5-60) & 111 (F. H. Tyson 7-27) by 128 runs.

16th Match: v Combined XI (Hobart)   Jan 8, 10, 11.
Combined XI 221 (R. N. Harvey 82, E. Rodwell 70) & 184-6 dec (R. Benaud 68) drew with M.C.C. 242 (T. E. Bailey 53) & 99-2.*

17th Match: v Tasmania (Launceston)   Jan 13, 14, 15.
M.C.C. 427-7 dec (T. W. Graveney 134, J. H. Wardle 63, J. V. Wilson 62, L. Hutton 61) & 133-6 dec beat Tasmania 117 (P. J. Loader 6-22) & 200 (J. Maddox 62*) by 243 runs.*

18th Match: v South Australian Country XI (Mount Gambier)   Jan 18, 19.
M.C.C. 328 (R. T. Simpson 106, P. B. H. May 82, D. C. S. Compton 53) beat S.A. Country XI 106 (R. Appleyard 6-26) & 45 (J. B. Statham 6-3) by an inns & 177 runs.

19th Match: v South Australia (Adelaide)   Jan 21, 22, 24.
S. Australia 185 (G. R. Langley 53) & 123 lost to M.C.C. 451 (D. C. S. Compton 182, P. B. H. May 114, M. C. Cowdrey 64) by an inns & 143 runs.

20th Match: v Australia (Adelaide)   Jan 28, 29, 31, Feb 1, 2.
Australia 323 (L. V. Maddocks 69) & 111 lost to England 341 (L. Hutton 80, M. C. Cowdrey 79) & 97-5 by 5 wkts.

21st Match: v Victoria Country XI (Yallourn)   Feb 5, 7.
Country XI 182 (W. Young 56, J. H. Wardle 5-46) & 99 (J. H. Wardle 7-45) lost to M.C.C. 307-8 dec (L. Hutton 75, R. T. Simpson 59, T. W. Graveney 50) by an inns & 26.

22nd Match: v Victoria (Melbourne)   Feb 11, 12, 14, 15.
Victoria 113 drew with M.C.C. 90-1: rain.

23rd Match: v New South Wales (Sydney)   Feb 18, 19, 21, 22.
N.S.W. 172 (B. C. Booth 74, A. V. Bedser 5-57) & 314-8 dec (R. B. Simpson 98, K. R. Miller 71, J. W. Burke 62, R. Benaud 57, J. H. Wardle 5-118) beat M.C.C. 172 & 269 (L. Hutton) by 45 runs.*

24th Match: v Australia (Sydney)   Feb 25, 26, 28, March 1, 2, 3.
England 371-7 dec (T. W. Graveney 111, D. C. S. Compton 84, P. B. H. May 79, T. E. Bailey 72) drew with Australia 221 (C. C. McDonald 72, J. H. Wardle 5-79) & 118-6.

25th Match: v Canterbury (Christchurch)   March 5, 7, 8.
Canterbury 140 & 206 (J. G. Leggat 99) lost to M.C.C. 302 (T. W. Graveney 101, F. H. Tyson 62) & 45-3 by 7 wkts.*

26th Match: v New Zealand (Dunedin)   March 11, 12, 14, 15, 16.
New Zealand 125 (B. Sutcliffe 74) & 132 lost to England 209-8 dec & 49-2 by 8 wkts.

27th Match: v Wellington (Wellington)   March 19, 21, 22.
M.C.C. 207 (T. W. Graveney 102) & 201 (J. R. Reid 5-56) beat Wellington 127 (J. H. Wardle 5-42) & 94 (R. Appleyard 6-21) by 187 runs.

28th Match: v New Zealand (Auckland)   March 25, 26, 28.
New Zealand 200 (J. R. Reid 73) & 26 (R. Appleyard 4-7) lost to England 246 (L. Hutton 53, A. M. Moir 5-62) by an inns & 20 runs.

1955-56: umpiring decisions provoke 'incident' in Pakistan

The M.C.C. dispatched what was described as an 'A' team to Pakistan for a series of sixteen matches in the winter of 1955-56. The party which sailed from Liverpool on 3 December aboard the s.s. *Circassia* was D. B. Carr (Derbys) (capt), W. H. H. Sutcliffe (Yorks), P. E. Richardson (Worcs), A. J. Watkins (Glam), K. F. Barrington (Surrey), G. A. R. Lock (Surrey), D. B. Close (Yorks), M. J. Cowan (Yorks), A. E. Moss (Middx), J. M. Parks (Sussex), P. J. Sainsbury (Hants), H. W. Stephenson (Somerset), R. Swetman (Surrey), F. J. Titmus (Middx), M. Tompkin (Leics) and the manager C. G. Howard. P. J. Loader had to withdraw due to unfitness and Lock took his place.

The side was a very young one, only Watkins, Stephenson and Tompkin being over 20, but no official Test Matches were in the programme, which was designed to assist in the growth of cricket in Pakistan.

The tour opened in Karachi on 26 December and the team performed well in both matches played in that city, winning one and having the best of a draw. Rain ruined the match at Hyderabad, but the tourists beat the Amir of Bahawalpur's Eleven by an innings. Both victories were the results of good bowling by Lock. A dull draw against the Universities preceded the first 'Unofficial Test', which was remarkably boring–about 30,000 watched the third day's play, when in 5½ hours just 107 runs were scored. M.C.C. dropped several catches which did not improve the remote possibility of a definite finish. Travelling to East Pakistan, the team were beaten in the second 'Unofficial Test' by an innings, Fazal Mahmood and Khan Mohammad using the matting wicket to full advantage and the visitors' batting disintegrating twice. Cowan, the M.C.C. fast bowler, strained his back just before the game and was flown home a few days later– N. I. Thomson of Sussex came as a replacement. After the defeat, two successive innings' victories were achieved, Lock taking 20 wickets in the two matches.

The M.C.C. needed to win the third 'Unofficial Test' to save the series, but despite an injury to Fazal, Pakistan won by seven wickets, with the slow left-arm spin of Kardar causing the batsmen much anguish.

An incident in this match caused much upset at the time and

1955-56: M.C.C. to Pakistan

Batting Averages

	M	I	NO	R	HS	Avge	100	c/s
P. E. Richardson (Worcs)	11	16	1	650	105	43.33	2	5
K. F. Barrington (Surrey)	12	17	2	586	87	39.06	0	6
D. B. Close (Yorks)	12	20	1	684	92	36.00	0	12
F. J. Titmus (Middx)	11	16	1	457	72	30.46	0	8
M. Tompkin (Leics)	11	16	1	334	85	22.26	0	2
R. Swetman (Surrey)	8	11	2	197	45	21.88	0	16/5
P. J. Sainsbury (Hants)	9	11	5	130	32	21.66	0	5
D. B. Carr (Derbys)	11	17	2	310	61	20.66	0	9
A. J. Watkins (Glam)	11	15	1	256	59	18.28	0	10
G. A. R. Lock (Surrey)	11	15	2	237	62*	18.23	0	9
H. W. Stephenson (Som)	8	10	2	122	39	15.25	0	13
W. H. H. Sutcliffe (Yorks)	10	14	1	173	58	13.30	0	5
J. M. Parks (Sussex)	10	15	0	198	52	13.20	0	3
M. J. Cowan (Yorks)	4	3	2	8	6	8.00	0	1
A. E. Moss (Middx)	11	13	4	41	14	4.55	0	1
N. I. Thomson (Sussex)	4	5	1	9	7	2.25	0	2

Bowling Averages

	O	M	R	W	Avge	BB	5i
G. A. R. Lock	557	296	869	81	10.72	8-17	10
P. J. Sainsbury	184.4	90	268	16	16.75	3-10	0
A. E. Moss	318	92	717	41	17.48	5-25	1
N. I. Thomson	88.5	25	215	11	19.54	4-59	0
F. J. Titmus	323.2	124	651	28	23.25	4-50	0
M. J. Cowan	71.5	19	133	5	26.60	3-76	0
D. B. Close	145	58	313	11	28.45	2-40	0
D. B. Carr	32	16	86	3	28.66	2-19	0
K. F. Barrington	28.1	9	69	2	34.50	1-3	0
A. J. Watkins	145	62	282	7	40.28	2-30	0

Also bowled: J. M. Parks 6-1-39-1; P. E. Richardson 4-1-19-1; W. H. H. Sutcliffe 12.4-4-26-3; R. Swetman 2-0-10-1.

The M.C.C. 'A' team which toured Pakistan in 1955-56. The captain D. B. Carr is seated centre, with the manager C. G. Howard on his left and W. H. H. Sutcliffe on his right. Behind are M. Tompkin, P. J. Sainsbury, M. J. Cowan, D. B. Close, H. W. Stephenson, F. J. Titmus, G. A. R. Lock, J. M. Parks, R. Swetman, A. E. Moss, K. F. Barrington, A. J. Watkins, P. E. Richardson.

the stage was reached where M.C.C. offered to recall the team. On the first day there were four lbw decisions against M.C.C. batsmen and some undiplomatic comments by the tourists. On the evening of the third day of the match, some of the M.C.C. team proceeded to pour cold water over Idris Begh, one of the umpires, in the way students might act on a Rag Night. The press naturally went to town on the story. The President of M.C.C., Lord Alexander, cabled the Pakistan cricket authorities and offered to cancel the rest of the tour, at the same time paying Pakistan compensation for any lost revenue. The incident however was papered over and the three remaining games completed, though in the final 'Unofficial Test', which M.C.C. won by 2 wickets, Imtiaz Ahmed accused the M.C.C. players of abusing the umpires and the tour ended on rather a sour note.

The team flew home to London on 16 March and on 20 March M.C.C. at Lord's issued a prepared statement on the incidents. The M.C.C. laid the blame for throwing a bucket of water over the umpire directly on D. B. Carr, the captain, who was present at the incident.

The feature of the tour was the splendid bowling of Lock. Richardson and Close dominated the disappointing batting.

1955-56: Swanton takes team to the West Indies and Bermuda

The first major tour since the Second World War not under the auspices of the M.C.C., left Heathrow Airport on 5 March 1956 under the managership of E. W. Swanton. The team was M. C.

1st Match: v Barbados Schools XI (Bridgetown) (One Day)   March 12.
Schools XI 183-4 dec (R. Brancker 83*) lost to Swanton's XI 191-5 (M. J. Stewart 54) by 5 wkts.

2nd Match: v Barbados (Bridgetown)   March 15, 16, 17, 19.
Barbados 522-8 dec (C. C. Hunte 151, N. E. Marshall 100, D. St. E. Atkinson 77) beat Swanton's XI 262 (G. Goonesena 62, G. H. G. Doggart 54, M. C. Cowdrey 50, Holder 5-50) & 248 (M. J. Stewart 68) by an inns & 12 runs.

3rd Match: v Barbados (Bridgetown)   March 21, 22, 23, 24.
Swanton's XI 488 (T. W. Graveney 154, G. H. Doggart 55, M. J. Stewart 63, G. Goonesena 52) & 95-4 drew with Barbados 288 (C. B. Williams 133) & 328-7 dec (C. L. Walcott 130, C. C. Hunte 95).

4th Match: v South Trinidad (Point-a-Pierre)   March 28, 29.
Swanton's XI 326-9 dec (A. C. D. Ingleby-Mackenzie 108, R. C. M. Kimpton 69, M. J. Stewart 55) drew with S. Trinidad 212-9 (Oliver 79, Sampath 69, F. H. Tyson 5-16).

5th Match: v Trinidad (Port of Spain)   March 31, April 2, 3.
Swanton's XI 259 (T. W. Graveney 117) & 152 beat Trinidad 94 (F. H. Tyson 5-28) & 293 (G. E. Gomez 88, D. Ramsamooj 52, F. H. Tyson 5-50) by 24 runs.

6th Match: v West Indies XI (Port of Spain)   April 6, 7, 9, 10, 11.
Swanton's XI 277 (A. S. M. Oakman 71, S. Ramadhin 5-68) & 221 lost to West Indies XI 392 (E. D. Weekes 89, G. St. A. Sobers 71) & 107-2 (C. C. Hunte 55*) by 8 wkts.

7th Match: v Bermuda XI (Hamilton) (One Day)   April 15.
Swanton's XI 134 beat Bermuda XI 77 by 57 runs.

Cowdrey (Kent) (capt), G. H. G. Doggart (Sussex), J. J. Warr (Middx), T. W. Graveney (Gloucs), F. H. Tyson (Northants), D. E. Blake (Hants), A. C. D. Ingleby-Mackenzie (Hants), G. Goonesena (Notts), A. S. M. Oakman (Sussex), M. J. Stewart (Surrey), Swaranjit Singh (Warwicks) and R. G. Marlar (Sussex), and R. C. M. Kimpton (Worcs) joined the side in Barbados.

Although the tourists lost the first match against Barbados, in the second game Graveney hit a century, and due to the bowling of Warr and Goonesena, the tourists enforced the follow on. Walcott then made a hundred which ensured a draw.

Going on to Trinidad, the tourists beat the island side—Graveney hit another century—but were defeated by a West Indies XI. Ramadhin bowled with great skill and Sobers hit a splendid 71.

The tour ended in Bermuda with a one-day match against the local side. Graveney was the star of the batting, though Stewart also performed well and Goonesena was the leading all-rounder. Tyson headed the bowling with 26 wickets at 15.65 runs each.

1956-57: South Africa's Endean out 'handled ball' in Test

The sixteen players under the managership of F. R. Brown who left England bound for South Africa aboard the *Edinburgh Castle* were P. B. H. May (Surrey) (capt), D. J. Insole (Essex), T. E. Bailey (Essex), P. E. Richardson (Worcs), M. C. Cowdrey (Kent), A. S. M. Oakman (Sussex), D. C. S. Compton (Middx), J. M. Parks (Sussex), T. G. Evans (Kent), B. Taylor (Essex), J. H. Wardle (Yorks), J. B. Statham (Lancs), F. H. Tyson (Northants), P. J. Loader (Surrey), G. A. R. Lock (Surrey) and J. C. Laker (Surrey). The two notable omissions were Graveney and Trueman, otherwise the team was as strong as could be collected.

The tourists began the visit in a blaze of glory, Boland, Western Province, Eastern Province, Orange Free State, Rhodesia (twice) providing six consecutive innings victories. Wardle, who played in four of the six matches took 33 wickets, while May hit four centuries.

As had happened on previous tours, Transvaal provided the M.C.C. with stiffer opposition. Heine and Adcock put the visitors' batting in perspective and a win was achieved by just 3 wickets. The M.C.C. then met Tayfield at Pretoria and collapsed twice. Wardle bowled well, but could not prevent the first defeat of an M.C.C. side in South Africa since 1930-31. Two drawn matches brought the team to Johannesburg for the first Test. There was tremendous interest in the match, over 100,000 attending the five days—a new record—but the batting was dread-

1st Match: v Boland & S.W. Districts (Paarl)   Oct 23, 24.
M.C.C. 385-8 dec (A. S. M. Oakman 87, D. C. S. Compton 75, P. B. H. May 68) beat Boland 149 & 109 by an inns & 127 runs.

2nd Match: v Western Province (Cape Town)   Oct 26, 27, 29, 30.
W. Province 129 (J. B. Statham 5-26) & 129 (J. C. Laker 6-47) lost to M.C.C. 334 (P. B. H. May 162, A. S. M. Oakman 63, E. R. H. Fuller 6-83) by an inns & 76 runs.

3rd Match: v Eastern Province (Port Elizabeth)   Nov 3, 5.
E. Province 105 (J. H. Wardle 5-30) & 59 (G. A. R. Lock 6-14) lost to M.C.C. 365 (P. B. H. May 118, D. J. Insole 118, A. H. McKinnon 5-159) by an inns & 201 runs.

4th Match: v Orange Free State (Bloemfontein)   Nov 9, 10.
M.C.C. 420-4 dec (M. C. Cowdrey 173, A. S. M. Oakman 150) beat O.F.S. 71 (J. H. Wardle 6-16) & 181 (J. H. Wardle 8-80) by an inns & 168 runs.

5th Match: v Rhodesia (Bulawayo)   Nov 17, 18, 19.
Rhodesia 192 (P. N. F. Mansell 50) & 129 (G. A. R. Lock 5-12) lost to M.C.C. 407-7 dec (P. B. H. May 124*, P. E. Richardson 100, D. J. Insole 67) by an inns & 86 runs.

6th Match: v Rhodesia (Salisbury)   Nov 23, 24, 25.
M.C.C. 501 (P. B. H. May 206, T. E. Bailey 110, T. G. Evans 50, G. B. Lawrence 6-104) beat Rhodesia 57 (P. J. Loader 7-28) & 152 by an inns & 292 runs.

7th Match: v Transvaal (Johannesburg)   Nov 30, Dec 1, 3, 4.
Transvaal 212 (W. R. Endean 81) & 130 lost to M.C.C. 279 (M. C. Cowdrey 84, D. C. S. Compton 72, P. S. Heine 5-86) & 67-7 by 3 wkts.

8th Match: v South African XI (Pretoria)   Dec 7, 8, 10, 11.
South African XI 138 & 116 (K. J. Funston 55, J. H. Wardle 6-30) beat M.C.C. 107 (H. J. Tayfield 6-36) & 109 (H. J. Tayfield 6-47) by 38 runs.

9th Match: v Natal (Durban)   Dec 14, 15, 17, 18.
M.C.C. 307 (D. J. Insole 116, P. B. H. May 107) & 150-7 dec drew with Natal 209 (T. L. Goddard 89, J. C. Laker 5-53) & 90-7.

10th Match: v North-Eastern Transvaal (Benoni)   Dec 20, 21, 22.
N.E. Transvaal 125 drew with M.C.C. 148-2 (D. C. S. Compton 71*, P. E. Richardson 52).

11th Match: v South Africa (Johannesburg)   Dec 24, 26, 27, 28, 29.
England 268 (P. E. Richardson 117, M. C. Cowdrey 59) & 150 beat South Africa 215 & 72 (T. E. Bailey 5-20) by 131 runs.

12th Match: v South Africa (Cape Town)   Jan 1, 2, 3, 4, 5.
England 369 (M. C. Cowdrey 101, T. G. Evans 62, D. C. S. Compton 58, H. J. Tayfield 5-130) & 220-6 dec (D. C. S. Compton 64, M. C. Cowdrey 61) beat South Africa 205 (J. H. Wardle 5-53) & 72 (J. H. Wardle 7-36) by 312 runs.

13th Match: v Country Districts XI (Queenstown)   Jan 8, 9.
Country Districts 50 (P. J. Loader 5-14) & 115 lost to M.C.C. 275-6 dec (P. B. H. May 91, D. J. Insole 70) by an inns & 110 runs.

14th Match: v Border (East London)   Jan 11, 12.
M.C.C. 400-8 dec (T. E. Bailey 162, P. B. H. May 79, M. C. Cowdrey 62, W. R. Chalmers 5-133) beat Border 78 & 104 by an inns & 218 runs.

15th Match: v Natal (Pietermaritzburg)   Jan 18, 19, 21, 22.
M.C.C. 293 (D. C. S. Compton 101, M. C. Cowdrey 76, T. L. Goddard 5-65) & 122-6 dec drew with Natal 163 & 185-5.

16th Match: v South Africa (Durban)   Jan 25, 26, 28, 29, 30.
England 218 (T. E. Bailey 80, P. E. Richardson 68) & 254 (D. J. Insole 110*, H. J. Tayfield 8-69) drew with South Africa 283 (R. A. McLean 100, T. L. Goddard 69, J. H. Wardle 5-61) & 142-6.

17th Match: v Transvaal (Johannesburg)   Feb 1, 2, 4, 5.
Transvaal 232 drew with M.C.C. 594-8 (D. J. Insole 192, D. C. S. Compton 131, P. B. H. May 73, B. Taylor 65, F. H. Tyson 5*).

18th Match: v Griqualand West (Kimberley)   Feb 8, 9, 11.
M.C.C. 310 (P. E. Richardson 83, D. J. Insole 53, M. C. Cowdrey 52) beat Griqualand West 76 (J. H. Wardle 7-20) & 187 (R. A. Evans 110) by an inns & 47 runs.

19th Match: v South Africa (Johannesburg)   Feb 15, 16, 18, 19, 20.
South Africa 340 (R. A. McLean 93, T. L. Goddard 67, J. H. B. Waite 61) & 142 beat England 251 (P. B. H. May 61) & 214 (D. J. Insole 68, M. C. Cowdrey 55, H. J. Tayfield 9-113) by 17 runs.

20th Match: v Western Province (Cape Town)   Feb 22, 23, 25, 26.
M.C.C. 335 (P. B. H. May 116, C. B. van Ryneveld 5-95) & 186-8 dec (P. B. H. May 79, E. R. H. Fuller 5-26) drew with W. Province 257 (G. A. S. Innes 75, J. H. Ferrandi 52*, C. B. van Ryneveld 50, G. A. R. Lock 5-69) & 176-8 (J. H. Ferrandi 60, G. A. R. Lock 5-75).

21st Match: v South Africa (Port Elizabeth)   March 1, 2, 4, 5.
South Africa 164 (W. R. Endean 70) & 134 (F. H. Tyson 6-40) beat England 110 & 130 (H. J. Tayfield 6-78) by 58 runs.

22nd Match: v Combined Universities (Cape Town)   March 9, 11, 12.
Combined Universities 142 & 165 (G. D. Varnals 53) lost to M.C.C. 335 (T. G. Evans 80, M. C. Cowdrey 72, D. C. S. Compton 51, D. B. Pithey 5-100) by an inns & 28 runs.

fully slow. The bowlers received some help from the wicket; England, batting first plodded to 45 in the 2½ hours before lunch on the first day and the tempo never increased. England won the game due to some great bowling by Bailey and Statham in the final innings, when South Africa, needing 204 to win, fell for 72.

The second Test began directly after the first and followed the same slow tempo and the same result, when by coincidence England bowled out South Africa in their final innings for 72 yet again—Wardle took 7 for 36. Endean was adjudged out 'handled ball' in this match, the first instance in Test cricket.

Some more pedestrian batting was featured in the third Test. This time South Africa required 190 to win in the fourth innings with 250 minutes left – when the final hour arrived 83 were needed, but it was all too much.

Cautious batting remained the order of the day in the fourth Test, but for the first time South Africa won the toss and batted first. McLean hit a lucky 93 and a total of 340 was reached. The home team kept a firm grip on the match from then on and the bowling of Tayfield, who was chaired off the field at the end of play, won the game for South Africa.

South Africa needed to win the fifth Test to square the rubber. England were unfortunate in that their two best bowlers, Statham and Wardle, could not play due to injury. The most controversial feature of the match was the pitch, which had been relaid only three months before. This provided a great many shooters, especially as the match wore on, and Tyson had easily his best return of the tour. England, though, batted very feebly and it was the lack of runs in the end that lost them the match, rather than the absence of Statham and Wardle. Heine and Adcock proved the tourists' downfall in the first innings, then Tayfield delivered

1956-57: M.C.C. to South Africa

Batting Averages

	M	I	NO	R	HS	Avge	100	c/s
P. B. H. May (Surrey)	16	24	1	1270	206	55.21	6	4
D. J. Insole (Essex)	18	25	4	996	192	47.42	4	24
M. C. Cowdrey (Kent)	18	27	1	1035	173	39.80	2	28
D. C. S. Compton (Middx)	14	22	1	792	131	37.71	2	7
T. E. Bailey (Essex)	16	25	2	703	162	30.56	2	10
P. E. Richardson (Worcs)	17	26	0	789	117	30.34	2	2
A. S. M. Oakman (Sussex)	14	19	0	534	150	28.10	1	16
F. H. Tyson (Northts)	13	17	5	294	55*	24.50	0	4
T. G. Evans (Kent)	12	19	1	354	80	19.67	0	31/9
B. Taylor (Essex)	11	13	0	249	65	19.15	0	12/6
G. A. R. Lock (Surrey)	14	18	4	229	39	16.35	0	11
J. H. Wardle (Yorks)	14	18	3	207	37	13.80	0	11
J. C. Laker (Surrey)	14	16	6	79	17	7.90	0	3
J. B. Statham Lancs	12	12	6	42	12*	7.00	0	5
P. J. Loader (Surrey)	15	16	2	81	13	5.78	0	5

Also played in one match: F. R. Brown (Northants) 0; J. M. Parks (Sussex) 4.

Bowling Averages

	O	M	R	W	Avge	BB	5i
J. H. Wardle	380.3	94	1103	90	12.25	8-80	8
G. A. R. Lock	352.7	120	833	56	14.87	6-14	4
T. E. Bailey	254.5	76	461	29	15.89	5-20	1
P. J. Loader	316	76	751	46	16.32	7-28	1
J. B. Statham	233.2	40	607	36	16.86	5-26	1
F. H. Tyson	254.3	65	636	37	17.18	6-40	1
J. C. Laker	387.7	122	875	50	17.50	6-47	2
D. C. S. Compton	16.2	1	73	3	24.33	2-43	0

Also bowled: A. S. M. Oakman 15-4-48-0; F. R. Brown 9-2-26-0; T. G. Evans 1-0-8-0.

---

the *coup de grâce*. The run-rate reached a new all-time low for Test cricket, with 122 being hit on the third day in 290 minutes.

South Africa therefore drew the series and deserved to do so. Of the English batsmen, Insole proved what rugged determination can do and headed the Test averages. Richardson also did well, but the rest did nothing to improve their reputations – May was brilliant in the ordinary matches, but failed in the Tests, as did Compton. Cowdrey found Tayfield too much for him. Parks developed eye trouble and was sent home – it was not necessary to send a replacement, though, with hindsight, Graveney ought to have gone.

Wardle's left-handed off-breaks and googlies were the basis of the English attack, Laker however disappointed. Tyson was not the fast bowler he had been in Australia and Statham, except at the end, was the best of the quicker bowlers.

South Africa suffered from the injury which kept McGlew out of four Tests, but Goddard batted well and Tayfield bowled in tremendous form.

Record crowds watched the tourists' matches. The M.C.C. share of the receipts from the matches was about £60,000, which meant a profit of £26,500.

1956-57: silver jubilee visit to India

The purpose of the visit to India with its two matches was to celebrate the silver jubilee of the Bengal Cricket Association and the team flew out from London on Boxing Day 1956 and returned by air on 11 January. The party was W. J. Edrich (Middx) (capt), R. T. Simpson (Notts), W. Watson (Yorks), A. V. Bedser (Surrey), T. W. Graveney (Gloucs), C. L. McCool (Somerset), F. S. Trueman (Yorks), A. E. Moss (Middx), A. Wharton (Lancs), B. Dooland (Notts), G. E. Tribe (Northants) and T. L. Livingston (Northants) with C. G. Howard as manager.

The team played two matches, losing one and winning one. Graveney's hundreds in the second match came in fine style as the batting of the official England side struggled in South Africa.

The spin of Ghulam Ahmed and Mankad proved decisive in the first game, whilst Tribe was the most effective visiting bowler.

1956-57: C. G. Howard's Team to India

1st Match: v Chief Minister's XI (Calcutta)   Dec 30, 31, Jan 1, 2.
Chief Minister's XI 149 and 378-8 dec (N. Contractor 157, V. S. Hazare 60, L. Armanath 59) beat Howard's Team 227-9 dec (W. J. Edrich 58) and 158 by 142 runs.

2nd Match: v President's XI (Bombay)   Jan 5, 6, 7, 8.
Howard's Team 319 (T. W. Graveney 153) and 313-7 dec (T. W. Graveney 120, W. J. Edrich 58) beat President's XI 171 (P. R. Umrigar 57) and 309 (P. R. Umrigar 100) by 152 runs.

1956-57: Duke of Norfolk's team to Jamaica

At the invitation of the Jamaican Cricket Association, the Duke of Norfolk took a team out to the island in the early months of 1957.

The side consisted of E. D. R. Eagar (Hants) (capt), J. J. Warr (Middx), D. E. Blake (Hants), T. W. Graveney (Gloucs), T. Greenhough (Lancs), A. C. D. Ingleby-Mackenzie (Hants), R. E. Marshall (Hants), A. E. Moss (Middx), D. V. Smith (Sussex), G. E. Tribe (Northants), W. Watson (Yorks), D. V. P. Wright (Kent), D. Barrick (Northants) and Lord Cobham (Worcs).

The three major matches were against the Jamaica team and the tourists won two, with the other drawn. Tribe was the best bowler of the side and took 45 wickets at a cost of 17.91 runs each. The batting laurels went to Marshall and Watson. Smith also played some impressive innings. Blake, the wicket-keeper, broke an arm and Ingleby-Mackenzie took over the stumping duty in the second half of the tour.

The best batting for Jamaica came from O. G. Smith who hit two centuries and a 50 in the first-class matches. Kentish was the most effective of the home bowlers but only appeared in one match.

The team returned home on 7 April. The Jamaican authorities had guaranteed the necessary £10,000 required to pay for the tour – happily the receipts from the matches, which proved most popular, just about covered this sum.

1956-57: Duke of Norfolk's Team to Jamaica

1st Match: v St Mary (Prospect St Mary)   Feb 22, 23.
Norfolk's XI 168 (W. Watson 77) & 214-1 dec (R. E. Marshall 106*, D. V. Smith 60) beat St Mary 98 & 187 (Pottinger 61, D. V. P. Wright 7-31) by 97 runs.

2nd Match: v Country Districts (Chedwyn Park)   Feb 25, 26.
Country Districts 232-9 dec drew with Norfolk's XI 363-8 (R. E. Marshall 87, W. Watson 76, G. E. Tribe 66).

3rd Match: v Jamaica Next XI (Sabina Park)   Feb 27, 28, March 1.
Norfolk's XI 334-5 dec (R. E. Marshall 95, T. W. Graveney 90, W. Watson 55*) & 185-7 dec (D. V. Smith 72) drew with Jamaica Next XI 222-9 dec & 185-5 (G. Smith 64).

4th Match: v All Jamaica (Sabina Park)   March 2, 4, 5.
Jamaica 327 (N. L. Bonitto 129, J. K. Holt jun 71, G. E. Tribe 5-95) & 326-5 dec (E. D. McMorris 114) drew with Norfolk's XI 379 (T. W. Graveney 92, D. E. Blake 62, R. Gilchrist 5-110) & 222-7.

5th Match: v St Elizabeth (Monymusk)   March 7, 8.
St Elizabeth 121 & 134-5 drew with Norfolk's XI 248-8 dec (R. E. Marshall 128).

6th Match: v Cornwall XVI (Montego Bay)   March 9, 11.
Cornwall 116-13 dec (A. E. Moss 6-36) & 94-10 drew with Norfolk's XI 232 (D. V. Smith 55, A. C. D. Ingleby-Mackenzie 53, Lord Cobham 50).

7th Match: v Combined Estates (Frome)   March 12, 13.
Combined Estates 127 (G. E. Tribe 6-41) & 110 (G. E. Tribe 5-48) lost to Norfolk's XI 258-9 dec (R. E. Marshall 100, D. V. Smith 62) by an inns & 21 runs.

8th Match: v Jamaica (Malbourne Park)   March 15, 16, 18, 19.
Jamaica 330-9 dec (O. G. Smith 118, A. E. Moss 5-84) & 178 (J. K. Holt jun 93*) lost to Norfolk's XI 218 (W. Watson 71*, T. W. Graveney 51, E. S. Kentish 5-36) & 291-7 (R. E. Marshall 97, D. Barrick 66) by 3 wkts.

9th Match: v Jamaica (Sabina Park)   March 21, 22, 23, 25, 26.
Jamaica 261 (O. G. Smith 118, E. D. McMorris 58) & 321 (D. T. Dewdney 7-55) & 348-3 (T. W. Graveney 83*, R. E. Marshall 82, D. V. Smith 68, W. Watson 54*) by 7 wkts. [J. K. Holt jun 55, G. E. Tribe 6-83) lost to Norfolk's XI 235 (D. T. Dewdney 7-55)]

10th Match: v Combined Parishes (St Antonio)   March 28.
Norfolk's XI 267 (R. E. Marshall 69) drew with Combined Parishes 93-4.

1957-58: first tour of Tanganyika, Kenya and Uganda

Due to the enthusiasm of Mr A. Davies of the Kenya Kongonis Club, the M.C.C. were persuaded to take a team out to East Africa for the first time in 1957-58.

The party flew from England on Boxing Day 1957 and went direct to Dar-es-Salaam, where the first match was staged on 28 December. The team was F. R. Brown (Northants) (capt), S. C. Griffith (Sussex) (vice-capt/manager), J. A. Bailey (Essex), G. W. Cook (Kent), G. H. G. Doggart (Sussex), A. C. D. Ingleby-Mackenzie (Hants), C. J. M. Kenny (Essex), P. E. Richardson (Worcs), R. V. C. Robins (Middx), D. R. W. Silk (Somerset), M. J. K. Smith (Warwicks), J. J. Warr (Middx) and W. R. Watkins (Middx) as baggage master.

Tanganyika held the tourists to a close draw, but the English side was still recovering from the journey. After the single game in Dar-es-Salaam, the side went to Mombasa and then on to Nairobi, where the Kongonis managed to inflict the sole defeat on the M.C.C., after Brown had set them 212 to win at 80 per hour. Prodger hit an excellent unbeaten hundred.

The final leg of the tour was in Kampala against Uganda, where the tourists proved too good for the locals.

The tour was a great success and just reward for those who organised it. Doggart found he could make runs on the matting wickets and was the best bat; Robins just headed the bowling, but Brown, Bailey and Warr were also most useful.

The team returned to England by air on 21 January.

1957-58: M.C.C. to East Africa

1st Match: v Tanganyika (Dar-es-Salaam)   Dec 28, 29.
Tanganyika 167-7 dec (R. D. Patel 56) & 91-7 dec drew with M.C.C. 95 (Mohmedhussein 5-17) & 146-7.

2nd Match: v Coast XI (Mombasa)   Dec 31, Jan 1.
Coast XI 120 & 80 lost to M.C.C. 164 & 37-0 by 10 wkts.

3rd Match: v Kenya Kongonis (Nairobi)   Jan 4, 5.
M.C.C. 340-7 dec (M. J. K. Smith 80, A. C. D. Ingleby-Mackenzie 76) & 115-5 dec (G. W. Cook 53) lost to Kenya Kongonis 245 (P. R. Morris 73, P. Prodger 52, G. L. Krauss 50*) & 212-3 (P. Prodger 115, D. W. Dawson 62*) by 7 wkts.

4th Match: v Kongonis' President's XI (Nyeri) (One Day)   Jan 8.
M.C.C. 195 (F. R. Brown 87) beat President's XI 87 by 108 runs.

5th Match: v H. L. Hunter's XI (Rift Valley) (One Day)   Jan 10.
M.C.C. 291-3 dec (G. H. G. Doggart 110*) drew with H. L. Hunter's XI 173-5.

6th Match: v Kenya C.A. (Nairobi)   Jan 11, 12.
M.C.C. 219 (G. H. G. Doggart 103, D. R. W. Silk 51) & 161-3 dec (D. R. Silk 62) drew with Kenya C.A. 131 & 151-5 (Gursaran Singh 59).

7th Match: v C. O. Oates' XI (Eldoret) (One Day)   Jan 14.
M.C.C. 263-9 dec (M. J. K. Smith 89) drew with C. O. Oates' XI 181-6 (D. W. Dawson 54).

8th Match: v Kongonis Festival XII (Nairobi) (One Day) Jan 16.
M.C.C. 302-9 dec (P. E. Richardson 131) drew with Festival XII 194-8 (D. Lee 59).

9th Match: v Uganda (Kampala)   Jan 18, 19.
Uganda 122 & 143 (J. A. Boucher 51) lost to M.C.C. 263 (M. J. K. Smith 63, A. C. D. Ingleby-Mackenzie 57) & 6-0 by 10 wkts.

1958-59: May's side disappoints against Australian 'throwers'

The team selected to visit Australia for 1958-59 was announced at the end of July: P. B. H. May (Surrey) (capt), T. E. Bailey (Essex), M. C. Cowdrey (Kent), T. G. Evans (Kent), T. W. Graveney (Gloucs), J. C. Laker (Surrey), P. J. Loader (Surrey), G. A. R. Lock (Surrey), C. A. Milton (Gloucs), P. E. Richardson (Worcs), J. B. Statham (Lancs), R. Subba Row (Northants), R. Swetman (Surrey), F. S. Trueman (Yorks), F. H. Tyson

---

1958-59: M.C.C. to Ceylon, Australia and New Zealand

1st Match: v Ceylon (Colombo) (One Day)   Oct 5.
Ceylon 47-6; rain stopped play.

2nd Match: v Board of Control President's XI (Colombo)   Oct 6.
No play due to rain.

3rd Match: v Western Australia (Perth)   Oct 17, 18, 20, 21.
M.C.C. 351 (T. W. Graveney 177*, P. B. H. May 60) & 146-4 dec (M. C. Cowdrey 65*) drew with W. Australia 221 (R. B. Simpson 60) & 124-3 (J. W. Rutherford 77*).

4th Match: v Combined XI (Perth)   Oct 24, 25, 27, 28.
M.C.C. 349 (P. B. H. May 113, M. C. Cowdrey 78, T. G. Evans 55, B. Strauss 5-99) & 257-4 (M. C. Cowdrey 100*, T. E. Bailey 71*, F. S. Trueman 53) drew with Combined XI 260 (N. C. O'Neill 104).

5th Match: v South Australia (Adelaide)   Oct 31, Nov 2, 3.
S. Australia 165 (J. C. Laker 5-31) & 194 (J. C. Laker 5-70) lost to M.C.C. 245 (P. E. Richardson 88, J. W. Martin 7-110) & 115-1 (C. A. Milton 63*) by 9 wkts.

6th Match: v Victoria (Melbourne)   Nov 7, 8, 10, 11.
M.C.C. 396 (C. A. Milton 116, R. Subba Row 83) & 149-3 dec (T. W. Graveney 78*) beat Victoria 252 (I. R. Huntington 73, C. C. McDonald 54, J. B. Statham 7-47) & 206 (C. C. McDonald 62, G. A. R. Lock 6-74) by 87 runs.

7th Match: v New South Wales (Sydney)   Nov 14, 15, 17, 18.
N.S.W. 391-7 dec (R. N. Harvey 149, J. W. Burke 104, N. C. O'Neill 84) drew with M.C.C. 177 (R. Benaud 5-48) & 356-6 (P. E. Richardson 87, C. A. Milton 81, T. W. Graveney 59, R. Swetman 52).

8th Match: v Australian XI (Sydney)   Nov 21, 22, 24, 25.
M.C.C. 319 (P. B. H. May 140, T. W. Graveney 70) & 257-3 dec (P. B. H. May 114, R. Subba Row 68*, P. E. Richardson 52) beat Australian XI 128 & 103 (G. A. R. Lock 6-29) by 345 runs.

9th Match: v Queensland (Brisbane)   Nov 28, 29, Dec 1, 2.
M.C.C. 151 (R. Subba Row 51, R. R. Lindwall 5-57) & 71-4 drew with Queensland 210.

10th Match: v Australia (Brisbane)   Dec 5, 6, 8, 9, 10.
England 134 & 198 (T. E. Bailey 68) lost to Australia 186 & 147-2 (N. C. O'Neill 71*) by 8 wkts.

11th Match: v Tasmania (Hobart)   Dec 13, 15, 16.
M.C.C. 229-7 dec (P. B. H. May 80, P. E. Richardson 56) drew with Tasmania 94-4 (R. Stokes 54*).

12th Match: v Combined XI (Launceston)   Dec 18, 19, 20.
M.C.C. 384-9 dec (C. A. Milton 85, P. B. H. May 80, M. C. Cowdrey 72, T. Cowley 5-92) & 162-4 (T. W. Graveney 52) drew with Combined XI 241 (C. C. McDonald 104).

13th Match: v South Australia (Adelaide)   Dec 24, 26, 27, 29.
M.C.C. 276 (T. W. Graveney 54) & 195-9 dec (R. Swetman 76, B. Hurn 5-62) drew with S. Australia 223 (J. Lill 86, F. S. Trueman 5-46) & 138-9 (L. E. Favell 52).

14th Match: v Australia (Melbourne)   Dec 31, Jan 1, 2, 4, 5.
England 259 (P. B. H. May 113, A. K. Davidson 6-64) & 87 (I. Meckiff 6-38) lost to Australia 308 (R. N. Harvey 167, J. B. Statham 7-57) & 42-2 by 8 wkts.

15th Match: v Australia (Sydney)   Jan 9, 10, 12, 13, 14, 15.
England 219 (R. Benaud 5-83) & 287-7 dec (M. C. Cowdrey 100*, P. B. H. May 92) drew with Australia 357 (N. C. O'Neill 77, A. K. Davidson 71, K. D. Mackay 57, L. E. Favell 54, J. C. Laker 5-107) & 54-2.

16th Match: v Victoria (Melbourne)   Jan 17, 19, 20, 21.
Victoria 286 (J. H. Shaw 94, C. N. Crompton 73, F. S. Trueman 5-42) & 180 (C. N. Crompton 64) lost to M.C.C. 313 (W. Watson 141, M. C. Cowdrey 85) & 156-1 (P. E. Richardson 65) by 9 wkts.

17th Match: v New South Wales (Sydney)   Jan 23, 24, 26, 27.
N.S.W. 215 (R. N. Harvey 92) & 44-0 drew with M.C.C. 303 (P. B. H. May 136, T. E. Bailey 54, R. Benaud 5-83).

18th Match: v Australia (Adelaide)   Jan 30, 31, Feb 2, 3, 4, 5.
Australia 476 (C. C. McDonald 170, J. W. Burke 66, N. C. O'Neill 56) & 36-0 beat England 240 (M. C. Cowdrey 84, R. Benaud 5-91) & 270 (P. B. H. May 59, T. W. Graveney 53*) by 10 wkts.

19th Match: v Victorian Country XI (Wangaratta) (One Day)   Feb 7.
Country XI 31 (P. J. Loader 5-17) lost to M.C.C. 308-8 (P. B. H. May 56, T. W. Graveney 50, J. B. Mortimore 50*) by 9 wkts.

20th Match: v Southern New South Wales (Wagga Wagga) (One Day)   Feb 9.
Southern N.S.W. 117 lost to M.C.C. 260-8 (P. E. Richardson 77, W. Watson 63) by 7 wkts.

21st Match: v Prime Minister's XI (Canberra) (One Day)   Feb 10.
Prime Minister's XI 288-7 dec (A. R. Morris 79, B. James 88) lost to M.C.C. 332 (M. C. Cowdrey 101, E. R. Dexter 76) by 4 wkts.

22nd Match: v Australia (Melbourne)   Feb 13, 14, 15, 17, 18.
England 205 (P. E. Richardson 68) & 214 (T. W. Graveney 54) lost to Australia 351 (C. C. McDonald 133, A. T. W. Grout 74, R. Benaud 64) & 69-1 (C. C. Mc-Donald 51*) by 9 wkts.

23rd Match: v Otago (Dunedin)   Feb 21, 23, 24.
Otago 70 (F. S. Trueman 5-34) & 157 (F. S. Trueman 8-45) lost to M.C.C. 321 (M. C. Cowdrey 115, P. B. H. May 97) by an inns & 94 runs.

24th Match: v New Zealand (Christchurch)   Feb 27, 28, March 2.
England 374 (E. R. Dexter 141, P. B. H. May 71) beat New Zealand 142 (G. A. R. Lock 5-31) & 133 (J. W. Guy 56, G. A. R. Lock 6-53) by an inns & 99 runs.

25th Match: v Wellington (Wellington)   March 6, 7.
M.C.C. 511-9 dec (M. C. Cowdrey 117, P. E. Richardson 111, W. Watson 106, T. W. Graveney 91) beat Wellington 127 & 173 (R. A. Vance 53) by an inns & 211 runs.

26th Match: v Northern & Central Districts (Hamilton)   March 10, 11, 12.
M.C.C. 198 (T. W. Graveney 108, D. D. Beard 6-34) & 73-0 drew with Districts 185.

27th Match: v New Zealand (Auckland)   March 14, 16, 17, 18.
New Zealand 181 (B. Sutcliffe 61) drew with England 311-7 (P. B. H. May 124*, P. E. Richardson 67).

(Northants), J. H. Wardle (Yorks) and W. Watson (Leics), with F. R. Brown as manager, E. D. R. Eagar as assistant manaager and G. Duckworth as baggage-master. Prior to the announcement of the side, Wardle and Laker had stated that they did not wish to tour, but amid a lot of press comment, both altered their minds.

The newspapers were well pleased with the final composition of the squad and could only bemoan the omission of Dexter. Soon after the team had been made public however, the Yorkshire Committee sacked Wardle due to his being at loggerheads with the county captain. Wardle wrote a series of articles in the *Daily Mail* which served to add fuel to the explosive situation and the M.C.C. withdrew his invitation.

The team of 16 players instead of 17 therefore sailed off on the s.s. *Iberia* bound for Fremantle. The traditional match in Colombo was ruined by rain. Watson, who had injured a knee on shipboard, was flown to Perth for treatment.

After drawing both matches in Perth, the side went to Adelaide, where South Australia were beaten due to the spin of Laker and Lock, and then to Melbourne where Statham and Lock removed the opposition. When An Australian Eleven was convincingly beaten at Sydney, May hitting a hundred in each innings, England looked favourites to win the first Test. Trueman could not play owing to back trouble, but it was feeble batting that let England down.

Bailey batted 458 minutes to make 68 to try to save England but it was a vain attempt as O'Neill hit a splendid not out 71 to bring Australia victory by 8 wickets. Owing to an injury to Subba Row, Mortimore was flown out to reinforce the team. Watson was given a full trial in the two Tasmanian matches which followed the first Test and seemed fit.

The second Test was fairly even on the first innings, due to a century from May, but the left-arm fast bowler Meckiff shattered the English second innings with 6 for 38 and Australia won by 8 wickets. The success of Meckiff increased the already large press campaign against his bowling action and indeed against that of J. W. Burke, the Australian opening bat and occasional bowler, and Slater of Western Australia, who played in the third Test. England had to stop Australia winning this game and with Meckiff breaking down allied to some better batting by May and Cowdrey, the game was drawn. May took the unusual step of playing E. R. Dexter in the match, despite the fact that he had not played in a match and had just flown in from England.

In the fourth Test, knowing England had to win, May put Australia in and saw McDonald and Burke put on 171 before the first wicket fell. Laker could not play and England had the fast trio of Tyson, Truman and Statham, but they made little impression. When the tourists batted, Benaud's spin proved to be the key to the Ashes and England, after being forced to follow on,

Above *The third Test match at Sydney on the 1958-59 M.C.C. tour of Australia. Roy Swetman is caught by 'Slasher' Mackay at forward short leg for 41 off Richie Benaud. The other fielders are Neil Harvey, Wally Grout and Alan Davidson.*

Left *Another victim for Benaud's leg trap. England opener Arthur Milton caught by Alan Davidson for 8 in the second innings of the third Test at Sydney in 1958-59. Grout and Mackay are the other fielders.*

1958-59: M.C.C. to Ceylon, Australia and New Zealand

Batting Averages

	M	I	NO	R	HS	Avge	100	c/s
P. B. H. May (Surrey)	17	26	2	1512	140	63.00	6	5
T. W. Graveney (Gloucs)	19	30	4	1229	177*	47.26	2	18
M. C. Cowdrey (Kent)	20	31	5	1209	117	46.50	4	23
R. Subba Row (Northts)	10	15	3	414	83	34.50	0	2
W. Watson (Leics)	12	18	1	554	141	32.58	2	4
C. A. Milton (Gloucs)	12	24	3	658	116	31.33	1	11
P. E. Richardson (Worcs)	18	30	0	886	111	29.53	1	4
T. E. Bailey (Essex)	13	22	3	501	71*	26.36	0	5
R. Swetman (Surrey)	15	21	5	415	76	25.93	0	24/3
E. R. Dexter (Sussex)	12	17	1	330	141	20.62	1	1
J. B. Statham (Lancs)	9	12	5	131	36*	18.71	0	4
F. S. Trueman (Yorks)	17	21	2	312	53	16.42	0	16
J. B. Mortimore (Gloucs)	12	12	2	151	44*	15.10	0	4
T. G. Evans (Kent)	7	10	0	124	55	12.40	0	8/3
G. A. R. Lock (Surrey)	15	18	1	191	44	11.23	0	9
J. C. Laker (Surrey)	10	13	3	107	22*	10.70	0	1
P. J. Loader (Surrey)	8	10	7	31	11*	10.33	0	1
F. H. Tyson (Northts)	16	17	2	149	33	9.93	0	2

Bowling Averages

	Balls	M	R	W	Avge	BB	5i
J. C. Laker	2257	63	655	38	17.23	5-31	3
F. S. Trueman	2723	61	1067	57	18.71	8-45	4
P. J. Loader	1359	30	507	26	19.50	4-23	0
J. B. Statham	1665	30	549	28	19.60	7-47	2
G. A. R. Lock	3682	118	1328	57	23.29	6-29	4
F. H. Tyson	2490	70	934	37	25.24	4-40	0
J. B. Mortimore	1643	62	537	20	26.85	4-30	0
E. R. Dexter	653	17	265	9	29.44	3-11	0
T. E. Bailey	1448	31	516	10	51.60	3-35	0
T. W. Graveney	162	1	107	1	107.00	1-39	0

Also bowled: M. C. Cowdrey 51-0-42-1; C. A. Milton 32-1-33-0; R. Subba Row 12-1-7-0.

only just avoided the ignominy of an innings defeat.

A car accident involving Loader and Statham prevented either playing in the fifth Test. Watson was also injured, so England entered the match with little prospect of saving their self-respect. The batting again fell to pieces and Australia gained a first innings lead of 146. Lindwall created a new record in the second innings by taking his 217th Test wicket and beating the 216 taken by Grimmett. England managed to avoid an innings defeat, but not by very much.

The team went off to New Zealand, where life was much simpler, and after beating Otago by an innings, they won by the same margin in the first Test against New Zealand and against Wellington. Rain marred the remaining two matches. The team then flew back to England via the United States.

With England losing the series against Australia by four matches to nil, it was difficult to find the individual successes of the tour. It was quite apparent that Tyson was 'over the hill' and that Bailey and Evans were no longer the players of old. Statham and Laker were the only bowlers to command much respect in the Tests. The batting was very poor, the contrast between the Test averages of the two sides being very marked. Australia had seven batsmen averaging over 25, England had three.

In mitigation, it must be admitted that the tourists suffered from more than the usual crop of injuries and there was the continued controversy over Australia's bowlers with 'throwing' actions – but the two leading Australian wicket-takers were Benaud and Davidson, about whose action there was no debate.

1958-59: M.C.C. tour of Brazil and Argentina

The team which arrived by air in Rio de Janeiro on 21 December 1958 was G. H. G. Doggart (Sussex) (capt), D. B. Carr (Derbys) (vice-capt), J. A. Bailey (Essex), P. I. Bedford (Middx), M. H. Bushby (Kent), C. B. Howland (Cambridge U), A. C. D. Ingleby-Mackenzie (Hants), R. V. C. Robins (Middx), D. M. Sayer (Kent), D. R. W. Silk (Somerset), M. J. K. Smith (Warwicks) and O. S. Wheatley (Warwicks). Originally E. R. Dexter was selected, but he was sent to reinforce M.C.C. in Australia and Sayer took

his place. M. J. Bear joined the team in the Argentine, where he was coaching.

Four matches were played in Brazil, two being against the Brazil C.A., but the opposition proved rather weak and even the fact that the games were played on matting made little difference.

In the Argentine the two important three-day matches were the 'Tests'. At Hurlingham in the 'First Test', Argentine showed some fight and batting first reached 120 for 1, but Wheatley then took control. In the 'Second Test' Ingleby-Mackenzie broke a finger and Argentine made a good start, before a double century by Mike Smith put the visitors in a strong position.

The speed of Sayer and spin of Bedford were too good for the home sides, whose field placings and general tactics were not very sophisticated. It was hoped however that the tour would help to improve cricket in both Brazil and the Argentine.

1958-59: M.C.C. to South America

1st Match: v Brazil (Niteroi) (One Day) Dec 23.
M.C.C. 20-2: rain stopped play.

2nd Match: v Brazil C.A. (Niteroi) Dec 24, 26.
M.C.C. 223-4 dec (M. J. K. Smith 81) & 239-8 dec (A. C. D. Ingleby-Mackenzie 109, M. J. K. Smith 61) beat Brazil C.A. 72 & 66 by 324 runs.

3rd Match: v Brazil C.A. (Pirituba) Dec 27, 28.
M.C.C. 338-6 dec (G. H. G. Doggart 97, D. R. W. Silk 93, A. C. D. Ingleby-Mackenzie 60, M. H. Bushby 52) & 56-1 dec beat Brazil C.A. 125 (T. M. Spitteler 62) & 74 by 195 runs.

4th Match: v Sao Paulo (Pirituba) Dec 30.
Sao Paulo 41 lost to M.C.C. 42-2.

5th Match: v Argentine C.A. Colts XVI (Hurlingham) One Day Jan 2.
M.C.C. 290-4 dec (G. H. G. Doggart 81, M. H. Bushby 56, D. R. W. Silk 53, A. C. D. Ingleby-Mackenzie 52) drew with Colts XVI 42-13 (J. A. Bailey 6-14).

6th Match: v Argentine C.A. (Lomas) Jan 3, 4.
M.C.C. 145-7 dec (D. R. W. Silk 56) & 170-2 dec (M. J. K. Smith 56, G. H. G. Doggart 53*) beat Argentine C.A. 16 (J. A. Bailey 5-11) & 136 by 163 runs.

7th Match: v Argentine C.A. (Belgrano) Jan 6, 7.
M.C.C. 423-7 dec (D. R. W. Silk 150, M. H. Bushby 84, G. H. G. Doggart 79, D. B. Carr 66) beat Argentine C.A. 203 (E. McCrea-Steele 59, P. I. Bedford 7-64) & 119.

8th Match: v Argentine C.A. (Hurlingham) Jan 9, 10, 11.
Argentine C.A. 188 (C. D. Ayling 86, O. S. Wheatley 5-39) & 195 (P. I. Bedford 5-73) lost to M.C.C. 363 (D. B. Carr 144, M. H. Bushby 70) & 21-0 by 10 wkts.

9th Match: v Northern Camps XV (Venado Tuerto) (One Day) Jan 13.
M.C.C. 235 (G. H. G. Doggart 141) beat Northern Camps XV 89 (J. A. Bailey 6-16, R. V. C. Robins 5-31) by 146 runs.

10th Match: v Argentine C.A. (Belgrano) Jan 15, 16, 17.
M.C.C. 410-6 dec (M. J. K. Smith 216, D. B. Carr 91) beat Argentine C.A. 81 & 112 (P. I. Bedford 5-25) by an inns & 217 runs.

11th Match: v Argentine C.A. (Belgrano) (One Day) Jan 17.
M.C.C. 270-1 dec (M. J. Bear 115*, D. R. W. Silk 100*) beat Argentine C.A. 103 by 167 runs.

1959: M.C.C. find Philadelphia in sad decline

In the second half of the 1959 summer, a team of amateurs made a 25-match tour of North America under the auspices of the M.C.C. The team was D. R. W. Silk (Somerset) (capt), J. R. Thompson (Warwicks) (vice-capt/manager), J. F. Pretlove (Kent), J. A. Bailey (Essex), D. J. Mordaunt (Sussex), P. I. Bedford (Middx), M. H. Bushby (Kent), D. J. Green (Derbys), A. C. Smith (Warwicks), J. D. Piachaud (Hants), R. M. Prideaux (Cambridge U), C. B. Howland (Cambridge U) and R. W. Barber (Lancs).

Most of the matches on the tour were of one-day duration, and having got used to the matting wickets in the first few fixtures, the tourists soon settled down.

The most important match of the visit was the three-day game with Canada – the 'Test Match'. In this game Prideaux hit a well-judged century and some devastating bowling by Piachaud ended any hopes the Canadians might have entertained.

The final matches were played in the United States, but the M.C.C. found the former famous centre of Philadelphia was only a shadow of the days before 1914.

1959-60: successful tour of the West Indies and Honduras

The team which the M.C.C. selected for the West Indies surprised many of the press by its youthful appearance. Evans, the principal English wicket-keeper since the war, had retired. Neither Lock nor Laker was included and Bailey was also dropped. The team which sailed on the *Camito* on 8 December 1959 was P. B. H. May (Surrey) (capt), F. S. Trueman (Yorks), J. B. Statham (Lancs), A. E. Moss (Middx), M. C. Cowdrey (Kent), D. A. Allen (Gloucs), K. V. Andrew (Northants), K. F. Barrington (Surrey), E. R. Dexter (Sussex), T. Greenhough (Lancs), R. Illingworth (Yorks), G. Pullar (Lancs), M. J. K. Smith (Warwicks), R. Subba Row (Northants) and R. Swetman (Surrey), with R. W. V. Robins as manager.

The critics raised few queries, except that Close and Parks might have been included and possibly Taylor of Yorkshire. The failure in Australia and the number of new faces meant that the press did not give the team much hope of beating the West Indies.

The tour commenced at Grenada with a 10-wicket win over the Windwards, but any hopes raised by this victory were soon dashed in Bridgetown where Barbados hit 533 for 5 and declared, then dismissed M.C.C. cheaply, forcing them to follow on and eventually defeating them by 10 wickets. Nurse hit a double century and Sobers 154. The formidable fast bowler Griffith caused the visiting batsmen most trouble.

The first Test followed four days later. Statham could not play due to an injury received in the previous match. The wicket was absolutely plumb and when May won the toss, England batted stoutly—only May of the batsmen failed, while Barrington and Dexter hit hundreds. West Indies did not begin their innings until lunch on the third day and England reduced them to 114 for 3. At this point Worrell joined Sobers in a partnership which lasted from 4.50 on Friday to 11.40 on Tuesday and added 399 runs—a record for West Indies in Test Matches. Needless to say the match was drawn.

Moving on to Trinidad, where the Port of Spain wicket was now turf for the first time, England beat the local side twice, before tackling West Indies in the second Test. May won the toss and somehow England survived a barrage of bumpers and short-pitched deliveries from Hall and Watson to reach 382—Barrington and Smith hit hundreds, but May again failed. Both Hall and Watson were cautioned by the umpires for excessive use of the short-pitched delivery. On the third day West Indies collapsed in a quite unexpected fashion in the face of Trueman and Statham. Eight wickets went down for 98, at which point the crowd—a record 29,000—erupted. Bottles began to fly, followed by beer cans and a vast assortment of missiles. The playing area was filled with a seething mass—the players marooned on the pitch. Eventually the combined efforts of the fire brigade, mounted police and riot squad restored order. No further play was possible that day, but after a break on Sunday, the match resumed on Monday and continued in comparative peace. Kanhai scored a great century in West Indies second innings, but England's commanding lead was too much and the tourists won by 256 runs. The total attendance for the match was a record 98,000.

The third Test played at Sabina Park, Kingston, was most exciting, in that the initiative swung from one side to the other

1959-60: Surrey tour Rhodesia

Shortly after the close of the 1959 English season, a party of Surrey cricketers travelled to Rhodesia for a two-match tour. Some fine leg-spin bowling by Mansell gave Rhodesia a victory by 2 runs in the first game and in the second Surrey, batting first, collapsed to the opening bowler, Partridge. Edrich hit a century in the second innings, but the tourists were lucky to avoid a second defeat. The team which went out was W. S. Surridge (capt), J. H. Edrich, K. F. Barrington, D. G. W. Fletcher, A. V. Bedser, R. Swetman, G. A. R. Lock, M. J. Stewart, T. H. Clark, E. A. Bedser, A. J. W. McIntyre, P. J. Loader and B. Constable.

1959-60: M.C.C. to the West Indies

1st Match: v Windward Islands (Grenada)   Dec 21, 22, 23.
Windward Is 89 (T. Greenhough 6-32) & 69 (F. S. Trueman 5-22) lost to M.C.C. 121 (T. Redhead 5-39) & 39-0 by 10 wkts.

2nd Match: v Barbados Colts (Bridgetown)   Dec 26, 28.
M.C.C. 323-7 dec (M. J. K. Smith 102, M. C. Cowdrey 56, K. F. Barrington 55) drew with Colts 222 (W. Greenidge 61).

3rd Match: v Barbados (Bridgetown)   Dec 30, 31, Jan 1, 2.
Barbados 533-5 dec (S. M. Nurse 213, G. St. A. Sobers 154, C. C. Hunte 69) & 58-0 beat M.C.C. 238 (K. F. Barrington 79) & 352 (K. F. Barrington 79, R. Illingworth 72, P. B. H. May 69).

4th Match: v West Indies (Bridgetown)   Jan 6, 7, 8, 9, 11, 12.
England 482 (E. R. Dexter 136*, K. F. Barrington 128, G. Pullar 65) & 71-0 drew with West Indies 563-8 dec (G. St. A. Sobers 226, F. M. M. Worrell 197*).

5th Match: v Trinidad (Port of Spain)   Jan 15, 16, 18, 19.
Trinidad 301-9 dec (M. C. Carew 102*, B. A. Davis 62, A. Corneal 54) & 131-6 dec lost to M.C.C. 171-9 dec (C. K. Singh 5-57) & 262-4 (R. Subba Row 73, E. R. Dexter 69*) by 6 wkts.

6th Match: v Trinidad (Point-a-Pierre)   Jan 21, 22, 23.
M.C.C. 337-9 dec (M. C. Cowdrey 173, G. Pullar 68) & 2-0 beat Trinidad 166 (D. A. Allen 7-33) & 172 (M. C. Carew 70) by 10 wkts.

7th Match: v West Indies (Port of Spain)   Jan 28, 29, 30, Feb 1, 2, 3.
England 382 (K. F. Barrington 121, M. J. K. Smith 108, E. R. Dexter 77) & 230-9 dec beat West Indies 112 (F. S. Trueman 5-35) & 244 (R. B. Kanhai 110) by 256 runs.

8th Match: v Jamaica Colts (Sabina Park, Kingston)   Feb 6, 8.
M.C.C. 306-9 dec (R. Swetman 100, G. Pullar 84) drew with Colts 295 (E. H. Griffith 177, P. E. Taylor 56, T. Greenhough 5-91).

9th Match: v Jamaica (Malbourne Park, Kingston)   Feb 10, 11, 12, 13.
Jamaica 374 (E. D. McMorris 104, F. M. M. Worrell 75, R. G. Scarlett 72*) & 202-7 (E. D. McMorris 74, R. G. Scarlett 59) drew with M.C.C. 525-6 dec (P. B. H. May 124, M. J. K. Smith 111, R. Subba Row 92, E. R. Dexter 75).

10th Match: v West Indies (Sabina Park, Kingston)   Feb 17, 18, 19, 20, 22, 23.
England 277 (M. C. Cowdrey 114, W. W. Hall 7-69) & 305 (M. C. Cowdrey 97, G. Pullar 66) drew with West Indies 353 (G. St. A. Sobers 147, E. D. McMorris 73, S. M. Nurse 70) & 175-6 (R. B. Kanhai 57).

11th Match: v Leeward Islands (Antigua)   Feb 25, 26, 27.
Leeward Is 296 (O. Williams 84, D. Michael 64) & 199-3 (L. Harris 89*, D. Michael 58*) drew with M.C.C. 456-5 dec (M. C. Cowdrey 115, R. Subba Row 110, E. R. Dexter 107).

12th Match: v British Guiana (Georgetown)   March 2, 3, 4, 5.
British Guiana 375-6 dec (B. F. Butcher 123, C. L. Walcott 83, G. Gibbs 78) & 67-2 drew with M.C.C. 494 (M. C. Cowdrey 139, G. Pullar 141, M. J. K. Smith 97).

13th Match: v West Indies (Georgetown)   March 9, 10, 11, 12, 14, 15.
England 295 (M. C. Cowdrey 65, D. A. Allen 55, W. W. Hall 6-90) & 334-8 (E. R. Dexter 110, R. Subba Row 100) drew with West Indies 402-8 dec (G. St. A. Sobers 145, R. B. Kanhai 55).

14th Match: v Berbice (Berbice)   March 18, 19, 21.
Berbice 387-2 dec (J. S. Solomon 201*, B. F. Butcher 131*) drew with M.C.C. 641-6 (J. M. Parks 183, K. F. Barrington 103, R. Illingworth 100, G. Pullar 65, R. Subba Row 58*, E. R. Dexter 54, M. J. K. Smith 50).

15th Match: v West Indies (Port of Spain)   March 25, 26, 28, 29, 30, 31.
England 393 (M. C. Cowdrey 119, E. R. Dexter 76, K. F. Barrington 69) & 350-7 dec J. M. Parks 101*, M. J. K. Smith 96, G. Pullar 54) drew with West Indies 338-8 dec (G. St. A. Sobers 92, C. C. Hunte 72*, C. L. Walcott 53) & 209-5 (F. M. M. Worrell 61).

16th Match: v Governor's XI (Belize) (One Day)   April 2.
M.C.C. 278-8 dec (D. A. Allen 55*) beat Governor's XI 60.

17th Match: v All Honduras XI (Belize)   April 4.
M.C.C. 277 (R. Subba Row 58) beat All Honduras 114.

Above *The two captains, F. C. M. 'Gerry' Alexander of the West Indies and Peter May of England going out to toss up before the second Test at Port of Spain, West Indies, in 1959-60.*

Above left *Clearing up the mess at the Queen's Park Oval, Port of Spain, Trinidad, after the bottle-throwing riot on 30 January 1960, during the second Test between the West Indies and England. A record 29,000 crowd erupted when the West Indies collapsed.*

and the outcome was in doubt almost to the last. May again won the toss and batted, but Hall's fast deliveries proved too much for everyone but Cowdrey, who made 114 and played one of the best innings of his long career. West Indies began strongly, with a Sobers century and fifties by McMorris and Nurse, but England fought back to remove the last seven wickets for 24 runs. Cowdrey again played magnificently in England's second innings to make the highest score of 97. West Indies were set 230 to win in 245 minutes, on a wicket that helped the bowlers. The home team went for the runs, but gave up finally when six wickets had gone and the match was drawn. May refused to permit Kanhai to use a runner in this last innings—which produced some controversy, but in the end it was discovered that May was in the wrong.

Georgetown, British Guiana, was the scene of the fourth Test. A week before it, May's health broke down and it was announced that he had been unwell for some time, not having recovered from an operation in the summer. He was flown back to England and Cowdrey took over the leadership. Hall once more caused problems in England's first innings, but slow batting by West Indies allied to very defensive tactics on the part of Cowdrey made a draw almost certain before the home innings had progressed far – Sobers spent 420 minutes on his 145. Subba Row, who had come into the England team for May, chipped a knuckle bone in England's second innings, but the game gradually petered out. Statham received the news that his son was dangerously ill and he left for home directly after the game. Parks, the Sussex bats-

1959-60: M.C.C. to the West Indies

Batting Averages

		M	I	NO	R	HS	Avge	100	c/s
M. C. Cowdrey	(Kent)	11	18	2	1014	173	63.37	5	4
E. R. Dexter	(Sussex)	12	18	2	908	136*	56.75	3	3
R. Subba Row	(Norths)	9	14	3	598	110	54.36	2	4
G. Pullar	(Lancs)	11	18	2	777	141	48.56	1	1
K. F. Barrington	(Surrey)	12	19	1	830	128	46.11	3	7
M. J. K. Smith	(Warks)	13	19	2	649	111	38.17	2	5
P. B. H. May	(Surrey)	9	12	0	389	124	32.41	1	1
D. A. Allen	(Gloucs)	9	12	5	199	55	28.42	0	3
R. Illingworth	(Yorks)	12	16	2	353	100	25.21	1	3
R. Swetman	(Surrey)	9	12	1	177	45	16.09	0	9/2
J. B. Statham	(Lancs)	8	8	3	78	20*	15.60	0	1
T. Greenhough	(Lancs)	6	4	3	15	8*	15.00	0	1
F. S. Trueman	(Yorks)	10	13	2	153	37	13.90	0	11
K. V. Andrew	(Norths)	4	1	0	4	4	4.00	0	7/5
A. E. Moss	(Middx)	8	5	1	15	5*	3.75	0	0

Also played in two matches: J. M. Parks (Sussex) 183, 43, 101* (ct 1, st 2).

Bowling Averages

		O	M	R	W	Avge	BB	5i
F. S. Trueman		342.3	86	883	37	23.86	5-22	2
D. A. Allen		305	94	639	23	27.78	7-33	1
T. Greenhough		182	43	590	21	28.09	6-32	1
J. B. Statham		213	57	493	15	32.86	3-42	0
K. F. Barrington		238.4	64	619	17	36.41	3-42	0
R. Subba Row		53	7	169	4	42.25	2-50	0
A. E. Moss		251	57	687	13	52.84	3-21	0
E. R. Dexter		192.4	36	637	11	57.90	2-7	0
R. Illingworth		365	107	781	11	71.00	2-46	0

Also bowled: M. C. Cowdrey 3-0-36-0; G. Pullar 1-0-1-1; M. J. K. Smith 2-0-22-0; R. Swetman 1-0-10-0.

man, came out as a reinforcement and hit 183 against Berbice in the match following the Test.

England only required to draw the fifth Test to win the series and this they managed to do, Cowdrey making a century in the first innings and Parks one in the second.

The tour ended with two one-day matches in Honduras – about 4,000 turned out to watch each game, which were of an exhibition nature.

Despite the riot in Trinidad and the problems of bouncers, the visit was most successful, the relationship between the two sides amicable and record crowds with record receipts and profits were the order of the day.

The problem of throwing, which had been so evident in Australia, was now common in the West Indies but the umpires were reluctant to enforce the law, though in general the standard of umpiring was much better than on the previous visit.

Cowdrey was the outstanding bat and opened the England innings with Pullar, who was most consistent. Dexter played well, but Barrington suffered very much from the bouncers. Trueman and Statham proved an outstanding partnership, but the spinners had a poor time. Sobers stood head and shoulders above the rest of the West Indies batsmen.

1960-61: young M.C.C. party fly out to New Zealand

The M.C.C. sent a young team out to New Zealand in the winter of 1960-61 under the captaincy of D. R. W. Silk (Somerset), the rest of the side being W. Watson (Leics) (vice-capt), D. A. Allen (Gloucs), R. W. Barber (Lancs), J. D. F. Larter (Northants), J. T. Murray (Middx), D. E. V. Padgett (Yorks), J. M. Parks (Sussex), R. M. Prideaux (Kent), W. E. Russell (Middx), D. M. Sayer (Kent), D. R. Smith (Gloucs), W. J. Stewart (Warwicks) and D. Wilson (Yorks). The manager was a New Zealander, J. H. Phillipps, who had managed two New Zealand teams in England. The object of the tour was to visit as many centres as possible and this made the travelling quite a major feature of the tour. In addition the team were billeted out with various families at each stop for economic reasons, which tended to go against the building up of team spirit.

The team travelled from England by air, the first major M.C.C. side to do so on the outward journey, though several had flown home.

Prior to the first 'Unofficial Test', the only difficulty the side faced was at Christchurch, where the M.C.C. were required to make 190 in 215 minutes. Watson hit a brilliant 106 in 161 minutes, but the rest of the batting failed and the tourists won by only one wicket.

In the 'First Test', both sides declared their first innings closed, before Barber and Allen dismissed New Zealand cheaply in the second innings, leaving M.C.C. 145 minutes to make 206. 100 came in 77 minutes, but after Prideaux went, wickets fell and the team opted for a draw. Watson led the M.C.C. side in this and in the 'Second Test', which was won by New Zealand due to

1960-61: M.C.C. to New Zealand

1st Match: v Auckland (Auckland) Dec 24, 26, 27.
Auckland 261 (W. B. Norman 52*) & 193-9 dec drew with M.C.C. 241 (R. W. Barber 68, W. J. Stewart 64) & 156-6 (R. M. Prideaux 68).

2nd Match: v Hawke's Bay & Southern Hawke's Bay (Napier) Dec 28, 29.
Hawke's Bay 124 & 60-9 drew with M.C.C. 249 (W. Watson 88, W. E. Russell 59, D. E. V. Padgett 55).

3rd Match: v Wellington (Wellington) Dec 31, Jan 2.
Wellington 68 & 158 lost to M.C.C. 317 (R. M. Prideaux 160) by an inns & 91 runs.

4th Match: v Marlborough (Blenheim) Jan 4, 5.
Marlborough 188 (R. Sheridan 62) & 104 (R. Sheridan 54) lost to M.C.C. 396 (D. R. Smith 82, R. W. Barber 75, W. E. Russell 72) by an inns & 104 runs.

5th Match: v Canterbury (Christchurch) Jan 7, 9, 10.
Canterbury 287 (P. G. Z. Harris 108, R. W. Barber 5-85) & 190 (R. C. Motz 65) lost to M.C.C. 288-3 dec (W. E. Russell 111, R. M. Prideaux 90) & 190-9 (W. Watson 106, M. E. Chapple 5-56) by 1 wkt.

6th Match: v New Zealand Colts (Ashburton) Jan 11, 12.
Colts 272-6 dec (B. F. Yuile 75*, I. A. Hartland 62, B. F. Hastings 59) drew with M.C.C. 340-6 (J. T. Murray 80*, D. R. Smith 73*, R. W. Barber 52).

7th Match: v Otago (Dunedin) Jan 13, 14, 16.
Otago 349-6 dec (S. M. McGregor 86, R. E. Long 71, J. W. D'Arcy 62, B. Sutcliffe 59*) & 75-3 drew with M.C.C. 203 (J. M. Parks 92*).

8th Match: v Central Otago (Alexandria) (One Day) Jan 17.
Central Otago 74 & 100-4 lost to M.C.C. 152-7 dec (W. J. Stewart 50) by 9 wkts.

9th Match: v New Zealand (Dunedin) Jan 20, 21, 23, 24.
New Zealand 313-7 dec (P. G. Z. Harris 78, J. T. Sparling 75) & 169 (R. C. Motz 60, R. W. Barber 5-86) drew with M.C.C. 277-5 dec (J. M. Parks 82, R. M. Prideaux 63) & 167-7 (R. M. Prideaux 76).

10th Match: v South Island M.A. XI (Timaru) Jan 25, 26.
South Island M.A. XI 83 (D. Wilson 6-37) & 99 (D. A. Allen 5-40) lost to M.C.C. 202 (D. R. Smith 55) by an inns & 20 runs.

11th Match: v Central Districts (Wanganui) Jan 28, 30, 31.
M.C.C. 376-7 dec (D. E. V. Padgett 129, D. R. W. Silk 81) & 142-2 dec (W. J. Stewart 71*, R. M. Prideaux 63) drew with Central Districts 231-8 dec (D. N. Macleod 59, J. D. F. Larter 5-56) & 278-8 (I. B. Leggat 56).

12th Match: v New Zealand (Wellington) Feb 3, 4, 6, 7.
New Zealand 148 & 228 (J. R. Reid 83, J. T. Sparling 60) beat M.C.C. 111 (R. C. Motz 5-34) & 132 (J. C. Alabaster 5-71) by 133 runs.

13th Match: v Hutt Valley (Lower Hutt) Feb 8, 9.
M.C.C. 215 (D. R. W. Silk 54, W. Watson 53) & 151-2 dec (W. E. Russell 69*) beat Hutt Valley 118-4 dec (J. R. Reid 67*) & 118 by 130 runs.

14th Match: v Manawatu-Wairarapa (Palmerston North) Feb 10, 11.
M.C.C. 286-9 dec (D. E. V. Padgett 78, R. M. Prideaux 58) & 126-2 dec (W. E. Russell 62*) beat Manawatu-Wairarapa 151 (K. Percy 50, D. Wilson 5-18) & 189 by 72 runs.

15th Match: v Bay of Plenty-Thames Valley (Tauranga) Feb 14, 15.
M.C.C. 297-6 dec (W. Watson 114, D. E. V. Padgett 60) beat Bay of Plenty-Thames Valley 147 (D. A. Allen 6-39) & 129 (R. W. Barber 5-42) by an inns & 21 runs.

16th Match: v Northern Districts (Hamilton) Feb 16, 17, 18.
M.C.C. 366-5 dec (D. E. V. Padgett 125*, J. M. Parks 85, W. J. Stewart 61) & 24-2 beat Northern Districts 119 & 270 (E. C. Petrie 57*, G. R. Satherley 52) by 8 wkts.

17th Match: v Northland (Whangarei) Feb 21, 22.
Northland 124 & 153-8 dec (D. A. Allen 6-89) lost to M.C.C. 219-4 dec (J. M. Parks 107*) & 60-2 by 8 wkts.

18th Match: v Governor-General's XI (Auckland) Feb 24, 25, 27.
M.C.C. 227 (J. M. Parks 57) & 277 (D. A. Allen 50) beat Governor-General's XI 252 (B. Sutcliffe 74) & 227 (R. W. Barber 7-89) by 25 runs.

19th Match: v Taranaki, Wangarui & Rangitikei (New Plymouth) Feb 28, March 1.
Taranaki 125 (D. A. Allen 8-24) & 69 (D. A. Allen 7-12) lost to M.C.C. 161 (J. M. Parks 53, J. F. Jones 5-45) & 35-1 by 9 wkts.

20th Match: v Nelson (Nelson) March 3, 4.
M.C.C. 332-6 dec (R. W. Barber 102, R. M. Prideaux 88) drew with Nelson 114-7.

21st Match: v Buller & West Coast (Westport) March 6.
No play due to rain.

22nd Match: v New Zealand (Christchurch) March 10, 11, 13, 14.
M.C.C. 223 (W. Watson 61, D. E. V. Padgett 54) & 45-1 drew with New Zealand 249-8 dec (J. C. Alabaster 57*).

```
1960-61: M.C.C. to New Zealand and Malaya
```

Batting Averages

	M	I	NO	R	HS	Avge	100	c/s
R. M. Prideaux (Kent)	10	18	2	710	160	44.37	1	11
D. E. V. Padgett (Yorks)	8	13	2	446	129	40.54	2	5
W. J. Stewart (Warks)	7	12	3	354	71*	39.44	0	2
W. Watson (Leics)	7	10	1	339	106	37.66	1	5
J. M. Parks (Sussex)	8	13	2	411	92*	37.36	0	8/1
D. A. Allen (Gloucs)	7	7	3	130	50	32.50	0	1
D. R. W. Silk (Som)	6	6	0	190	81	31.66	0	2
W. E. Russell (Middx)	8	14	1	330	111	25.38	1	9
R. W. Barber (Lancs)	10	16	2	316	68	22.57	0	6
J. T. Murray (Middx)	8	11	4	108	25	15.42	0	23/7
D. R. Smith (Gloucs)	10	12	1	142	48*	12.90	0	4
D. Wilson (Yorks)	5	7	1	54	23	9.00	0	3
J. D. F. Larter (Northts)	9	8	5	14	5	4.66	0	1
D. M. Sayer (Kent)	7	6	1	13	7	2.60	0	2

Bowling Averages

	O	M	R	W	Avge	BB	5i
J. D. F. Larter	241.2	77	534	36	14.83	5-56	1
D. A. Allen	223	102	404	19	21.26	4-44	0
R. W. Barber	381.3	90	1070	45	23.77	7-89	3
D. Wilson	169.4	54	402	15	26.80	3-37	0
D. R. Smith	386.3	96	874	32	27.31	4-38	0
D. M. Sayer	169.1	45	363	11	33.00	3-30	0

Also bowled: J. T. Murray 4-1-23-0; W. E. Russell 18-5-73-1; D. R. W. Silk 30-7-119-1. M. J. Bear (Essex) played in one non-first-class match.

Alabaster exploiting the worn wicket with his leg breaks in the final innings.

The great match of the tour was against the Governor-General's Eleven, led by Lord Cobham – a record 27,000 watched the second day's play. The M.C.C. won, thanks to the leg-breaks of Barber, who took 7 for 89 in the last innings. The 'Third Test' was the final match of the tour. Larter, the tourists' fast bowler, could not play owing to appendicitis after the first day, but in fact rain cut short the game, which was drawn.

The team suffered from a large number of injuries. Silk injured his hand early on, whilst Stewart was hampered by a troublesome knee injury.

Prideaux was the outstanding batsman, though Padgett did well in the later matches and Watson was a tower of strength. The batting of Russell, Parks and Barber disappointed. The bowling was not as good as hoped. Larter did not really look hostile and Sayer was mediocre. Allen easily headed the bowling table in all matches, but in the first-class games, the variable Barber was more successful if more expensive.

Financially the tour produced a deficit of £1,527.

1961: Surridge takes a team to Bermuda

Under the sponsorship of the Bermuda Cricket Association, the following team left England by air on 8 July 1961 for a three-week tour of the colony: W. S. Surridge (Surrey) (capt), K. C. Bates, K. Cranston (Lancs), M. P. Murray (Middx), J. K. Hall (Surrey), J. K. E. Slack (Cambridge U), W. Murray Wood (Kent), J. C. L. Gover, G. P. S. Delisle (Middx), C. B. R. Fetherstonhaugh (Devon), I. R. Lomax (Wilts), T. W. Graveney (Worcs), A. C. Revill (Leics) and M. J. Osborne.

The innings of the tour was by Graveney, who hit 205 not out in under 300 minutes against Bermuda in the 'First Test' – he also hit 104 in 150 minutes in the 'Second Test' and ended the tour with an average of 86.75. The other batsmen found the matting on concrete wickets a bit of a problem.

The best bowler was Hall, whose fast bowling picked up 33 wickets at 12.66. Surridge split a finger in the second match and was not very effective.

Fetherstonhaugh proved an excellent wicket keeper and also batted with confidence. The best of the home players was Sheridan Raynor who scored a splendid century off the tourists' attack.

1961-62: F. R. Brown's tour of East Africa

Under the leadership of F. R. Brown (Northants), the following went on a four-week tour of East Africa in the autumn of 1961: R. E. Marshall (Hants), R. A. Gale (Middx), W. E. Alley (Somerset), P. M. Walker (Glam), J. B. Mortimore (Gloucs), A. C. D. Ingleby-Mackenzie (Hants), D. J. Shepherd (Glam), L. A. Johnson (Northants), J. K. Hall (Surrey), P. J. Loader (Surrey), R. I. Jefferson (Surrey), P. B. Wight (Somerset) and D. W. Dawson.

The three important matches were those against Kenya, Tanganyika and Uganda. Each of these was won, the closest being that in Nairobi, where Brown's bowling proved very effective and a good innings by Alley took the tourists to a four-wicket victory.

```
1961-62: F. R. Brown's Team to East Africa
```

1st Match: v Governor's XI (Nairobi)   Oct 20.
Brown's XI 269 (W. E. Alley 70, R. A. Gale 64) drew with Governor's XI 136-7.

2nd Match: v Kenya (Nairobi)   Oct 21, 22, 23.
Kenya 167 (Jarman 51, F. R. Brown 6-51) & 205 (W. E. Alley 4-16) lost to Brown's XI 201 (R. E. Marshall 72) & 172-6 (W. E. Alley 82, Daljit Singh 5-60) by 4 wkts.

3rd Match: v Lt-col W. E. Merrill's XI (Eldoret)   Oct 24.
Brown's XI 243 drew with Merrill's XI 153-8.

4th Match: v H. A. Collins' XI (Nakuru)   Oct 25, 26.
Collins' XI 184-9 dec (R. K. Semti 55) & 156-6 dec drew with Brown's XI 131-3 dec & 118-8.

5th Match: v Tanganyika (Dar-es-Salaam)   Oct 28, 29, 30.
Brown's XI 280 (R. E. Marshall 93, W. E. Alley 73, Tashkent Patel 7-75) & 184-7 dec beat Tanganyika 153 & 100 by 211 runs.

6th Match: Nov 4, 5, 6.
No play due to rain.

7th Match: v Kenya Kongonis (Nairobi)   Nov 8, 9.
Brown's XI 217-9 dec (Saunders 5-65) beat Kenya Kongonis 144 on first inns by 73 runs.

8th Match: v Uganda (Kampala)   Nov 11, 12, 13.
Brown's XI 208-6 dec (R. E. Marshall 100) beat Uganda 90 & 96 by an inns & 22 runs.*

1961-62: England beat Pakistan and lose to India

The M.C.C. followed a pattern which had been established for two or three previous major tours by announcing the names of a list of possibles (this time numbering 29) for the visit to the Indian sub-continent. No less than eight of those asked stated they were not available and as seven of the eight were certainties if England wished to field the strongest possible team in the Tests, this meant that the eventual side was little better than M.C.C. 'A'. The eight who declined were D. B. Close, M. C. Cowdrey, J. H. Edrich, J. A. Flavell, P. B. H. May, J. B. Statham, R. Subba Row and F. S. Trueman. Among those who refused were the two most likely captains, May and Cowdrey. The team which left England by air on 8 October was E. R. Dexter (Sussex) (capt), M. J. K. Smith (Warwicks) (vice-capt), D. A. Allen (Gloucs), R. W. Barber (Lancs), K. F. Barrington (Surrey), A. Brown (Kent), B. R. Knight (Essex), G. A. R. Lock (Surrey), G. Millman (Notts), J. T. Murray (Middx), P. H. Parfitt (Middx), G. Pullar (Lancs), P. E. Richardson (Kent), W. E. Russell (Middx), D. R. Smith (Gloucs) and D. W. White (Hants), with T. N. Pearce (manager) and H. W. Dalton (masseur). The only omission commented upon in the press was that of Titmus.

Since India arranged to tour West Indies in February, March and April, the original tour programme had to be changed, which caused some oddities.

After two matches at Rawalpindi and Lyallpur, the first Test v Pakistan took place at Lahore. England were without Lock, but

1961-62: M.C.C. to India, Pakistan and Ceylon

1st Match: v President's XI (Rawalpindi) Oct 13, 14, 15.
President's XI 208 & 195-8 dec (Mushtaq Mohammad 102*, G. A. R. Lock 5-53) drew with M.C.C. 197 (Javed Akhtar 7-56) & 154-7 (W. E. Russell 72).

2nd Match: v Governor's XI (Lyallpur) Oct 17, 18, 19.
M.C.C. 252 (K. F. Barrington 55, Afaq Hussain 6-89) & 106 (G. Pullar 53, A. D'Souza 7-33) beat Governor's XI 119 & 210 (Shakoor Ahmed 60, Mahmood Hussain 50, D. A. Allen 7-67) by 29 runs.

3rd Match: v Pakistan (Lahore) Oct 21, 22, 24, 25, 26.
Pakistan 387-9 dec (Javed Burki 138, Mushtaq Mohammad 76, Saeed Ahmed 74) & 200 lost to England 380 (K. F. Barrington 139, M. J. K. Smith 99) & 209-5 (E. R. Dexter 66*) by 5 wkts.

4th Match: v Combined Universities (Poona) Oct 28, 29, 30.
Universities 346-9 dec (A. G. Milkha Singh 74, H. Gore 54, S. P. Gaekwad 53) & 67-3 drew with M.C.C. 417 (K. F. Barrington 149*, J. T. Murray 74, G. Pullar 64, N. Vishwanath 6-161).

5th Match: v West Zone (Ahmedabad) Nov 3, 4, 5.
M.C.C. 272-7 dec (G. Pullar 104) & 167-5 dec (P. H. Parfitt 58) drew with West Zone 211 (V. H. Bhosle 62*, D. R. Smith 5-58) & 159-5 (R. F. Surti 51*).

6th Match: v Bombay (Bombay) Nov 7, 8, 9.
M.C.C. 286-5 dec (R. W. Barber 71, M. J. K. Smith 56, J. T. Murray 51*) & 125-1 dec drew with Bombay 224 (S. G. Adhikari 87) & 137-7.

7th Match: v India (Bombay) Nov 11, 12, 14, 15, 16.
England 500-8 dec (K. F. Barrington 151*, E. R. Dexter 85, G. Pullar 83, P. E. Richardson 71) & 184-5 dec (K. F. Barrington 52*) drew with India 390 (S. A. Durani 71, C. G. Borde 69, V. L. Manjrekar 68, M. L. Jaisimha 56) & 180-5 (V. L. Manjrekar 84, M. L. Jaisimha 51).

8th Match: v President's XI (Hyderabad) Nov 18, 19, 20.
President's XI 281-5 dec (Nawab of Pataudi 70, R. F. Surti 69, P. Roy 65) & 163-5 dec (A. L. Apte 76*) lost to M.C.C. 261 (M. J. K. Smith 89, R. W. Barber 54) & 184-6 (P. H. Parfitt 84) by 4 wkts.

9th Match: v Rajasthan (Jaipur) Nov 22, 23, 24.
Rajasthan 268 (S. A. Durani 124, D. R. Smith 6-47) & 155-6 dec drew with M.C.C. 222-6 dec (K. F. Barrington 91) & 86-2.

10th Match: v Central Zone (Nagpur) Nov 26, 27, 28.
M.C.C. 405-3 dec (P. H. Parfitt 166*, W. E. Russell 101, P. E. Richardson 58) & 58-3 drew with Central Zone 234 (M. Sharma 68, K. Rungta 52) & 235-6 dec (Suryavir Singh 112).

11th Match: v India (Kanpur) Dec 1, 2, 3, 5, 6.
India 467-8 dec (P. R. Umrigar 147*, V. L. Manjrekar 96, M. L. Jaisimha 70) drew with England 244 (R. W. Barber 69*, S. P. Gupte 5-90) & 497-5 (K. F. Barrington 172, E. R. Dexter 126*, G. Pullar 119).

12th Match: v North Zone (Jullundur) Dec 8, 9, 10.
North Zone 152 (V. L. Mehra 56) & 145 (V. L. Mehra 53) lost to M.C.C. 256-9 dec (E. R. Dexter 72, V. M. Muddiah 6-71) & 42-1 by 9 wkts.

13th Match: v India (New Delhi) Dec 13, 14, 16, 17, 18.
India 466 (V. L. Manjrekar 189*, M. L. Jaisimha 127) drew with England 256-3 (K. F. Barrington 113*, G. Pullar 89).

14th Match: v East Zone (Cuttack) Dec 22, 23, 24.
M.C.C. 261-4 dec (K. F. Barrington 80*, P. E. Richardson 59) & 277-5 (P. E. Richardson 147) drew with East Zone 263-8 dec (R. B. Kenny 70, M. P. Barua 66).

15th Match: v Services XI (Calcutta) Dec 26, 27, 28.
M.C.C. 339-9 dec (P. H. Parfitt 112, R. W. Barber 58, E. R. Dexter 58) beat Services XI 172 (V. K. Dandekar 69, D. W. White 5-42) & 130 by an inns & 37 runs.

16th Match: v India (Calcutta) Dec 30, 31, Jan 1, 3, 4.
India 380 (C. G. Borde 68, Nawab of Pataudi 64, V. L. Mehra 62, D. A. Allen 5-67) & 252 (C. G. Borde 61) beat England 212 (P. E. Richardson 62, E. R. Dexter 57, S. A. Durani 5-47) & 233 (E. R. Dexter 62) by 187 runs.

17th Match: v South Zone (Bangalore) Jan 6, 7, 8.
M.C.C. 193 (M. J. K. Smith 57, E. A. S. Prasanna 6-56) & 192-2 dec (M. J. K. Smith 67*, G. Pullar 52) beat South Zone 132 & 216 (S. Nazareth 65, A. V. Jaganath 52).

18th Match: v India (Madras) Jan 10, 11, 13, 14, 15.
India 428 (Nawab of Pataudi 103, N. J. Contractor 86, F. M. Engineer 65, R. G. Nadkarni 63) & 190 (V. L. Manjrekar 85, G. A. R. Lock 6-65) beat England 281 (M. J. K. Smith 73, S. A. Durani 6-105) & 209 by 128 runs.

19th Match: v Pakistan (Dacca) Jan 19, 20, 21, 23, 24.
Pakistan 393-7 dec (Javed Burki 140, Hanif Mohammad 111, Saeed Ahmed 69) & 216 (Hanif Mohammad 104, Alim-ud-Din 50, D. A. Allen 5-30) drew with England 439 (G. Pullar 165, R. W. Barber 86, K. F. Barrington 84) & 38-0.

20th Match: v Combined XI (Bahawalpur) Jan 26, 27, 28.
M.C.C. 114 (Fazal Mahmood 6-28) & 69-0 drew with Combined XI 162 (Asif Ahmed 58).

21st Match: v Pakistan (Karachi) Feb 2, 3, 4, 6, 7.
Pakistan 253 (Alim-ud-Din 109, Hanif Mohammad 67) & 404-8 (Hanif Mohammad 89, Imtiaz Ahmed 86, Alim-ud-Din 53) drew with England 507 (E. R. Dexter 205, P. H. Parfitt 111, G. Pullar 60, A. D'Souza 5-112).

22nd Match: v Ceylon C.A. (Colombo) Feb 10, 11.
M.C.C. 257 (E. R. Dexter 74, P. H. Parfitt 73, P. E. Richardson 52, I. Gunasekera 5-61) & 159 (N. Chanmugam 5-43) drew with Ceylon C.A. 235 (H. I. K. Fernando 79, E. R. Dexter 5-112) & 20-0.

23rd Match: v Up-Country XI (Radella) Feb 13, 14.
Up-Country XI 204 (G. Goonesena 68, A. S. Brown 6-38) & 93 (G. A. R. Lock 5-22) lost to M.C.C. 290 (M. J. K. Smith 85, G. A. R. Lock 74) & 10-0 by 10 wkts.

24th Match: v Ceylon (Colombo) Feb 16, 17, 18.
Ceylon 210 (C. N. Lafir 84) & 144 (E. R. Dexter 5-51) lost to M.C.C. 284 (K. F. Barrington 93, P. H. Parfitt 50) & 72-2 by 8 wkts.

Brown, Barber and Allen managed to dismiss Pakistan cheaply in their second innings to leave England 250 minutes to make 208 – a fine display by Dexter, in his first Test as captain, won the game.

Three drawn matches were played before England switched opponents and met India. England piled up 500 before Dexter declared and as India made 390, a draw became the obvious outcome, though Dexter made a sporting declaration which was ignored.

In the second Test against India progress was slow due in part to the unruly crowd, who flashed mirrors in the eyes of the batsmen and threw missiles at the fieldsmen. Fires and fights kept breaking out. This was all to India's disadvantage, since the home side bowled England out cheaply and enforced the follow on. In the second innings however Pullar, Barrington and Dexter made hundreds and the game was drawn. Rain ruined the third Test, the final two days being washed out. The batting was slow however and without the rain the match would probably have been drawn anyway. The Nawab of Pataudi (son of the old England and India Test player) made his debut for India in this game.

India won the toss and the game in the fourth Test at Calcutta. Solid batting gave the home side 380 on the first innings, then England fell to Durani and Borde. Allen and Lock struck back, but on a spinners' wicket England never looked like making the 421 needed for victory and a succession of nine England v India draws was broken.

In complete contrast to the usual method set by Test captains when leading in the series with one match to go, Contractor in the fifth Test won the toss and scored freely, his example was followed by the Nawab, whose hundred came in 155 minutes. India scored their total of 428 at not much under a run per minute, but dropped catches helped their cause. The English batsmen were not so fluent and battled against the spin of Durani and Borde. The match was won by India just after lunch on the fifth day.

Travelling to East Pakistan, England played the second Test against Pakistan at Dacca. The home team were not inspired by India and the Test was probably the most boring on record – Hanif batted about 15 hours for 215 runs in his two innings. England were somewhat quicker, but with about two days to go a draw seemed the only result conceivable.

Barrington could not play in the third Test at Karachi and White had to retire after opening the English bowling, due to a pulled muscle. Neither problem had much bearing on the out-

1961-62: M.C.C. to India, Pakistan and Ceylon

Batting Averages

	M	I	NO	R	HS	Avge	100	c/s
K. F. Barrington (Surrey)	17	26	7	1329	172	69.94	5	12
E. R. Dexter (Sussex)	17	27	5	1053	205	47.86	2	15
G. Pullar (Lancs)	17	25	1	1046	165	43.58	3	5
P. H. Parfitt (Middx)	17	29	4	1043	166*	41.72	3	23
P. E. Richardson (Kent)	17	30	3	1003	147	37.14	1	11
M. J. K. Smith (Warks)	17	29	6	789	99	34.30	0	12
R. W. Barber (Lancs)	18	23	4	637	86	33.52	0	9
W. E. Russell (Middx)	12	21	3	603	101	33.50	1	6
J. T. Murray (Middx)	11	15	3	278	74	23.16	0	14/3
B. R. Knight (Essex)	16	20	3	380	39*	22.35	0	11
A. Brown (Kent)	11	7	5	39	12*	19.50	0	7
D. A. Allen (Gloucs)	16	15	2	233	40	17.92	0	6
G. A. R. Lock (Surrey)	15	17	5	182	49	15.16	0	20
G. Millman (Notts)	14	18	6	177	36*	14.75	0	23/8
D. R. Smith (Gloucs)	13	11	3	114	34	14.25	0	6
D. W. White (Hants)	12	9	1	54	15	6.75	0	3

Also played in two matches: J. G. Binks (Yorks) 12, 0 (ct 7, st 1).

Bowling Averages

	O	M	R	W	Avge	BB	5i
D. W. White	225	52	635	32	19.84	5-42	1
A. Brown	237	61	586	25	23.44	4-13	0
G. A. R. Lock	695.3	287	1406	59	23.83	6-65	2
D. R. Smith	348	81	859	36	23.86	6-47	2
B. R. Knight	365	95	1024	39	26.25	4-7	0
W. E. Russell	79	30	165	6	27.50	3-25	0
D. A. Allen	719.3	272	1427	50	28.54	7-67	3
P. H. Parfitt	114	30	340	11	30.90	3-50	0
E. R. Dexter	327	89	805	24	33.54	5-51	1
K. F. Barrington	112	27	323	9	35.88	2-3	0
R. W. Barber	438.1	92	1384	35	39.54	4-66	0

Also bowled: J. T. Murray 7-2-18-2; G. Pullar 14-6-37-1; P. E. Richardson 20-9-48-3; M. J. K. Smith 12-4-17-2.

come of the game which England would have won if dropped catches had not occurred—the immobile Hanif was missed twice. Dexter hit a double century, but even he took 500 minutes over the task.

The tour ended with a three-match visit to Ceylon.

With England fielding almost a second team, the results of the tour were much as expected. Dexter and Barrington were the best batsmen, and of the younger players, Parfitt proved the most effective. Lock and Allen were the hardest worked and most deserving of the bowlers—England really missed a pair of fast bowlers.

Murray, the wicket-keeper, was taken ill and went home. Binks was flown out as a replacement, but with Millman keeping well was not required very much.

The tour proved very popular and about 1,200,000 watched the eight Tests.

1962: Gloucestershire tour Bermuda

In April 1962, the Gloucestershire County Team made a three-week tour of Bermuda. The team was: C. T. M. Pugh (capt), D. R. Smith, J. B. Mortimore, A. S. Brown, D. M. Young, C. A. Milton, D. A. Allen, B. J. Meyer, A. Dindar, F. J. Andrews, D. Carpenter, C. Cook and D. G. A'Court.

The most important game against 'Pick of Bermuda' was drawn after three declarations—it was limited to two days. Brown was the most effective bowler on the tour, whilst Pugh and Mortimore were the best batsmen.

1962: Gloucestershire to Bermuda

1st Match: v Devonshire R.C. (Devonshire R.C.)   April 10.
Gloucs 253 (D. R. Smith 86, D. M. Young 69, C. Ford 6-63) lost to Devonshire 256-7 (C. Dill 76) by 3 wkts.*

2nd Match: v Western Counties (Somerset C.C.)   April 12.
Western Counties 196 (W. Wilson 77) beat Gloucs 124 by 72 runs.

3rd Match: v Bermuda C.A. (National Sports Club)   April 17.
Gloucs 204-5 dec (D. M. Young 61, C. T. M. Pugh 51) beat Bermuda C.A. 56 (A. S Brown 8-32) by 148 runs.

4th Match: v Pond Hill Stars (Somerset C.C.)   April 19.
Pond Hill Stars 114 (A. S. Brown 6-48) beat Gloucs 89 by 25 runs.

5th Match: v Somers Isles Cricket League (Devonshire R.C.)   April 21.
Somers Isles 264-8 dec (F. Nisbett 87, E. Pitcher 69) drew with Gloucs 205-3 (C. T. M. Pugh 125).*

6th Match: v Somerset C.C. (Somerset C.C.)   April 22.
Somerset C.C. 250-5 dec (N. L. Hazel 85, A. S. Bean 79) drew with Gloucs 134-6 (C. A. Milton 56, J. B. Mortimore 53).*

7th Match: v National Sports Club (National S.C.)   April 24.
Gloucs 256-7 dec (J. B. Mortimore 69, A. S. Brown 54) beat National S.C. 81 by 175 runs.

8th Match: v Eastern Counties (National S.C.)   April 26.
Gloucs 258-6 dec (J. B. Mortimore 111, A. Dindar 56) beat Eastern Counties 89 by 169 runs.

9th Match: v Pick of Bermuda (Devonshire R.C.)   April 28, 29.
Pick of Bermuda 271-6 dec & 222-5 dec (C. W. Smith 63) drew with Gloucs 278-8 dec (D. A. Allen 96) & 159-5.

1962-63: Dexter's side draw series with Australia

The team to tour Australia in 1962-63 was E. R. Dexter (Sussex) (capt), M. C. Cowdrey (Kent) (vice-capt), D. A. Allen (Gloucs), K. F. Barrington (Surrey), L. J. Coldwell (Worcs), T. W. Graveney (Gloucs), R. Illingworth (Yorks), B. R. Knight (Essex), J. D. F. Larter (Northants), J. T. Murray (Middx), P. H. Parfitt (Middx), G. Pullar (Lancs), the Rev D. S. Sheppard (Sussex),

A. C. Smith (Warwicks), J. B. Statham (Lancs), F. J. Titmus (Middx) and F. S. Trueman (Yorks), with the Duke of Norfolk as manager, A. V. Bedser as his assistant, W. R. Watkins as scorer, and S. Cowan as masseur. Announced in August, there were no alterations when the side flew to Aden on 27 September and then sailed on the *Canberra*, via Colombo to Fremantle.

The press were on the whole unable to improve on the selectors' choice, but wondered if the side could bowl out Australia as Trueman and Statham were moving into the veteran class for effective fast bowlers.

Although the team beat Western Australia in the first first-class match, the batting failed in the second game and a Combined Eleven won by 10 wickets. R. B. Simpson hit 109 and 66 not out for the victors. After a series of draws, New South Wales inflicted an innings defeat on the tourists. R. B. Simpson made another hundred and Benaud took 7 for 18 in the M.C.C.'s second innings. The prospects for England were now looking decidedly nasty.

Australia had all the best of the first Test and Benaud was happy to declare with only 4 second innings wickets down to set England 378 in 360 minutes. Dexter batted exceptionally well, as he had in the first innings, but England were fighting to save the game when stumps were drawn. The second Test proved a tremendous tussle—Dexter again batted in good form and Trueman and Statham managed to dismiss Australia twice for reasonable totals. England required 234 to win in the final innings and a century from Sheppard produced a win by 7 wickets, Australia dropping some vital catches.

The team went to Tasmania for the break between the second and third Tests and overwhelmed the Combined Eleven at Launceston, who were dismissed for 77 and 57. The third Test took place at Sydney. Graveney was too ill to play and Parfitt re-appeared, having taken Graveney's place in the first Test. The difference between the two teams on first innings was minimal, but Davidson produced a great opening spell at the start of England's second innings and the tourists never recovered, leaving Australia the simple task of making 65 to win, which they did with a day and a half to spare.

Australia decided to play safe in the fourth Test and both sides seemed too frightened of losing to make a real attempt to win, though Australia were handicapped when Davidson broke down early in the England first innings. As it was England needed 356 to win at 89 an hour when the final innings began. Barrington

---

1962-63: M.C.C. to Ceylon, Australia and New Zealand

Batting Averages

	M	I	NO	R	HS	Avge	100	c/s
K. F. Barrington (Surrey)	17	27	5	1763	219*	80.13	6	17
M. C. Cowdrey (Kent)	16	29	5	1380	307	57.50	3	10
T. W. Graveney (Worcs)	11	18	4	737	185	52.64	2	13
B. R. Knight (Essex)	12	19	5	675	125	48.21	2	4
E. R. Dexter (Sussex)	16	27	1	1107	102	42.57	1	14
F. J. Titmus (Middx)	16	21	6	595	137*	39.66	1	10
Rev D. S. Sheppard								
(Sussex)	16	28	0	1074	113	38.35	1	11
G. Pullar (Lancs)	10	19	1	564	132	31.33	1	0
A. C. Smith (Warks)	13	16	5	330	69*	30.00	0	37/1
P. H. Parfitt (Middx)	14	22	2	525	131*	26.25	1	14
R. Illingworth (Yorks)	12	16	3	329	65*	25.30	0	10
D. A. Allen (Gloucs)	9	9	3	119	32*	19.83	0	5
F. S. Trueman (Yorks)	12	14	0	194	38	13.85	0	9
J. T. Murray (Middx)	7	9	4	69	24*	13.80	0	11/1
J. B. Statham (Lancs)	9	11	2	96	30	10.66	0	6
L. J. Coldwell (Worcs)	9	8	4	14	4	3.50	0	6
J. D. F. Larter (Northts)	10	3	1	6	4*	3.00	0	3

Bowling Averages

	Balls	M	R	W	Avge	BB	5i
F. S. Trueman	2563	54	1020	55	18.54	7-75	4
D. A. Allen	2322	89	690	29	23.79	5-43	2
J. D. F. Larter	2123	49	938	39	24.05	4-24	0
F. J. Titmus	3939	134	1399	49	28.55	7-79	2
J. B. Statham	2325	34	1043	33	31.60	4-49	0
B. R. Knight	1558	38	691	20	34.55	3-32	0
K. F. Barrington	1212	27	653	17	38.41	3-32	0
L. J. Coldwell	1979	48	821	21	39.09	6-49	1
R. Illingworth	1793	56	709	17	41.70	4-34	0
E. R. Dexter	1656	26	759	18	42.16	4-8	0

Also bowled: T. W. Graveney 72-2-36-2; G. Pullar 72-0-38-0.

Above *The M.C.C. party after their arrival at Fremantle on board the liner* Canberra *for the Australian tour of 1962-63. Back: P. H. Parfitt, A. C. Smith, F. J. Titmus, J. D. F. Larter, B. R. Knight, T. W. Graveney, L. J. Coldwell, the Rev D. S. Sheppard, A. V. Bedser (assistant manager). Front: J. T. Murray, G. Pullar, D. A. Allen, E. R. Dexter (captain), J. B. Statham, the Duke of Norfolk, R. Illingworth, F. S. Trueman, M. C. Cowdrey, K. F. Barrington.*

Left *The first day of the first Test at Brisbane on the 1962-63 tour. Bill Lawry caught for 5 by Alan Smith off Fred Trueman. The other batsman is Bobby Simpson.*

Below *England captain Ted Dexter caught by Simpson for 47 from the bowling of Norman O'Neill in the final Test of the 1962-63 tour. Barrington is the non-striker.*

1st Match: v Ceylon (Colombo)   Oct 3.
M.C.C. 181-8 dec (D. S. Shephard 73) drew with Ceylon 152-8 (C. I. Gunesekara 76, R. Illingworth 5-59).

2nd Match: v Western Australia Country XI (Kalgoorlie)   Oct 16, 17.
M.C.C. 247-7 dec (G. Pullar 102) & 314-8 (J. T. Murray 102, D. S. Sheppard 59) drew with W.A. Country XI 212 (L. Campbell 66).

3rd Match: v Western Australia (Perth)   Oct 19, 20, 22.
M.C.C. 303 (F. J. Titmus 88, E. R. Dexter 76) & 49-0 beat W. Australia 77 & 274 (K. Gartrell 72, M. Vernon 68) by 10 wkts.

4th Match: v Combined XI (Perth)   Oct 26, 27, 29, 30.
M.C.C. 157 (B. R. Knight 65*) & 270 (D. S. Sheppard 92, E. R. Dexter 60, D. E. Hoare 5-60) lost to Combined XI 317 (R. B. Simpson 109, J. Parker 55, W. M. Lawry 52, D. A. Allen 5-76) & 115-0 (R. B. Simpson 66*) by 10 wkts.

5th Match: v South Australia (Adelaide)   Nov 2, 3, 5, 6.
S. Australia 335 (J. Lill 87, I. McLachlan 53) & 283-7 dec (G. St. A. Sobers 99) drew with M.C.C. 508-9 dec (F. J. Titmus 137, K. F. Barrington 104, T. W. Graveney 99, B. R. Knight 55, A. C. Smith 55, N. J. N. Hawke 6-130) & 95-1 (G. Pullar 56).

6th Match: v Australian XI (Melbourne)   Nov 9, 10, 12, 13.
M.C.C. 633-7 dec (K. F. Barrington 219*, B. R. Knight 108, E. R. Dexter 102, M. C. Cowdrey 88) & 68-5 dec drew with Australian XI 451 (R. B. Simpson 130, B. K. Shepherd 114, I. M. McLachlan 55, R. N. Harvey 51) & 201-4 (B. K. Shepherd 91*, I. M. McLachlan 68).

7th Match: v New South Wales Country XI (Griffith)   Nov 14.
N.S.W. Country XI 186-6 dec (M. Rudd 82) lost to M.C.C. 187-3 (G. Pullar 77*, E. R. Dexter 76*) by 7 wkts.

8th Match: v New South Wales (Sydney)   Nov 16, 17, 19.
M.C.C. 348 (G. Pullar 132, M. C. Cowdrey 50) & 104 (R. Benaud 7-18) lost to N,S,W, 532-6 dec (N. C. O'Neill 143, R. B. Simpson 110, R. N. Harvey 63, R. G. Flockton 62*, A. K. Davidson 55) by an inns & 80 runs.

9th Match: v Queensland (Brisbane)   Nov 23, 24, 26, 27.
Queensland 433-7 dec (K. D. Mackay 114, S. C. Trimble 95, G. M. Bizzell 59, A. T. W. Grout 56) & 94-7 drew with M.C.C. 581-6 dec (K. F. Barrington 183*, D. S. Sheppard 94, B. R. Knight 81, E. R. Dexter 80, T. W. Graveney 52).

10th Match: v Queensland Country XI (Toowoomba)   Nov 28.
Qld Country XI 202 4 dec (I B Oxenford 66, W. Brown 56*) lost to M.C.C. 204-3 (P. H. Parfitt 128*) by 7 wkts.

11th Match: v Australia (Brisbane)   Nov 30, Dec 1, 3, 4, 5.
Australia 404 (B. C. Booth 112, K. D. Mackay 86*, R. Benaud 51, R. B. Simpson 50) & 362-4 dec (W. M. Lawry 98, R. B. Simpson 71, R. N. Harvey 57, N. C. O'Neill 56) drew with England 389 (P. H. Parfitt 80, K. F. Barrington 78, E. R. Dexter 70, R. Benaud 6-115) & 278-6 (E. R. Dexter 99, G. Pullar 56, D. S. Sheppard 53).

12th Match: v Queensland Country XI (Townsville)   Dec 7, 8.
Qld Country XI 165 & 138 (D. A. Allen 5-57) lost to M.C.C. 423-9 dec (T. W. Graveney 118, P. H. Parfitt 98, D. S. Sheppard 67, R. Illingworth 58) by an inns & 120 runs.

13th Match: v Victorian Country XII (Bendigo)   Dec 10, 11.
Victorian Country XII 110 & 159-4 (F. Watts 63) drew with M.C.C. 360-8 dec (M. C. Cowdrey 111, K. F. Barrington 90, T. W. Graveney 59*).

14th Match: v Victorian Country XII (Shepparton)   Dec 12.
Victorian Country XII 191-6 dec lost to M.C.C. 196-5 (G. Pullar 51) by 6 wkts.

15th Match: v Victoria (Melbourne)   Dec 14, 15, 17, 18.
Victoria 340 (W. M. Lawry 177, N. L. West 70) & 175 (L. J. Caldwell 6-49) lost to M.C.C. 336 (G. Pullar 91, R. Illingworth 50) & 180-5 (M. C. Cowdrey 63, D. S. Sheppard 50) by 5 wkts.

16th Match: v South Australian Country XI (Port Lincoln)   Dec 20.
S.A. Country XI 55 lost to M.C.C. 56-0 by 10 wkts.

17th Match: v South Australia (Adelaide)   Dec 23, 24, 26, 27.
M.C.C. 586-5 dec (M. C. Cowdrey 307, T. W. Graveney 122*, D. S. Sheppard 81, K. F. Barrington 52) & 167-6 dec (K. F. Barrington 52*) drew with S. Australia 450 (L. E. Favell 120, G. St. A. Sobers 89, H. N. Dansie 64, I. M. McLachlan 62, J. C. Lill 55) & 113-4 (G. St. A. Sobers 75*).

18th Match: v Australia (Melbourne)   Dec 29, 31, Jan 1, 2, 3.
Australia 316 (W. M. Lawry 52) & 248 (B. C. Booth 103, W. M. Lawry 57, F. S. Trueman 5-62) lost to England 331 (M. C. Cowdrey 113, E. R. Dexter 93, A. K. Davidson 6-75) & 237-3 (D. S. Sheppard 113, M. C. Cowdrey 58*, E. R. Dexter 52) by 7 wkts.

19th Match: v Combined XI (Launceston)   Jan 4, 5, 7.
M.C.C. 331-7 dec (D. S. Sheppard 82, K. F. Barrington 73, B. R. Knight 68, R. Illingworth 65*) & 116-1 (D. S. Sheppard 67) beat Combined XI 77 & 57 by 313 runs.

20th Match: v Tasmania (Hobart)   Jan 8, 9.
Tasmania 203 (R. Stokes 82) & 181-6 (R. Stokes 76*) drew with M.C.C. 324 (P. H. Parfitt 121, G. Pullar 63, J. O'Brien 7-73).

21st Match: v Australia (Sydney)   Jan 11, 12, 14, 15.
England 279 (M. C. Cowdrey 85, G. Pullar 53, R. B. Simpson 5-57) & 104 (A. K. Davidson 5-25) lost to Australia 319 (R. B. Simpson 91, B. K. Shepherd 71*, R. N. Harvey 64, F. J. Titmus 7-79) & 67-2 by 8 wkts.

22nd Match: v New South Country XI (Newcastle)   Jan 18, 19, 20.
M.C.C. 319 (B. R. Knight 73, G. Pullar 53) & 190-4 dec (E. R. Dexter 71*) beat N,S,W, Country XI 203 (D. Dives 71) ? 161 (D. A. Allen 5-38) by 145 runs.

23rd Match: v Australia (Adelaide)   Jan 25, 26, 28, 29, 30.
Australia 393 (R. N. Harvey 154, N. C. O'Neill 110) & 293 (B. C. Booth 77, R. B. Simpson 71) drew with England 331 (K. F. Barrington 63, E. R. Dexter 61, F. J. Titmus 59*, G. D. McKenzie 5-89) & 223-4 (K. F. Barrington 132*).

24th Match: v Victoria (Melbourne)   Feb 1, 2, 4, 5.
M.C.C. 375 (T. W. Graveney 185, I. Meckiff 5-93) & 218-5 dec (E. R. Dexter 70, K. F. Barrington 66) drew with Victoria 307 (J. Potter 106, D. A. Allen 5-43) & 188-9 (R. M. Cowper 51).

25th Match: v Prime Minister's XI (Canberra) (One Day)   Feb 6.
M.C.C. 253-7 dec (D. S. Sheppard 72) beat Prime Minister's XI 250 (R. Benaud 68, D. A. Allen 5-68) by 3 runs.

26th Match: v New South Wales Country XI (Dubbo)   Feb 8, 9.
N.S.W. Country XI 137 & 227-5 (I. Drake 101) drew with M.C.C. 451-8 dec (T. W. Graveney 106, M. C. Cowdrey 97, D. S. Sheppard 93, B. R. Knight 70).

27th Match: v New South Wales Country XI (Tamworth)   Feb 11, 12.
N.S.W. Country XI 109 (B. Weissel 51) & 222 lost to M.C.C. 322-6 dec (E. R. Dexter 87, B. R. Knight 62, R. Illingworth 62*) & 10-0 by 10 wkts.

28th Match: v Australia (Sydney)   Feb 15, 16, 18, 19, 20.
England 321 (K. F. Barrington 101) & 268-8 dec (K. F. Barrington 94, D. S. Sheppard 68, M. C. Cowdrey 53) drew with Australia 349 (P. J. P. Burge 103, N. C. O'Neill 73, R. Benaud 57, F. J. Titmus 5-103) & 152-4 (P. J. P. Burge 52*).

29th Match: v New Zealand (Auckland)   Feb 22, 23, 25, 26.
England 562-7 dec (P. H. Parfitt 131*, K. F. Barrington 126, B. R. Knight 125, M. C. Cowdrey 86) beat New Zealand 258 (B. W. Yuile 64, R. C. Motz 60, J. R. Reid 59) & 89 by an inns & 215 runs.

30th Match: v New Zealand (Wellington)   March 1, 2, 4.
New Zealand 194 (R. W. Blair 64*) & 187 (W. R. Playle 65) lost to England 428-8 dec (M. C. Cowdrey 128*, K. F. Barrington 76, A. C. Smith 69*) by an inns & 47 runs.

31st Match: v Otago Invitation XI (Dunedin)   March 8, 9, 11.
Otago 116 (F. S. Trueman 5-19) & 170 (F. S. Trueman 6-64) lost to M.C.C. 296-9 dec (D. S. Sheppard 76, M. C. Cowdrey 60, P. H. Parfitt 54) by an inns & 10 runs.

32nd Match: v New Zealand (Christchurch)   March 15, 16, 18, 19.
New Zealand 266 (J. R. Reid 74, F. S. Trueman 7-75) & 159 (J. R. Reid 100) lost to England 253 & 173-3 by 7 wkts.

made certain that England could not lose, hitting an excellent hundred.

The fifth and last Test, which ought to have been the climax of the tour, with each side having won one match so far, turned out to be a very poor affair and the crowd could not be blamed for their barracking. Dexter won the toss and England spent the first day making 195 for 5. Australia gained a small lead on first innings and later, with Sheppard, Cowdrey and Barrington all making runs, Dexter declared to set Australia 241 in 240 minutes. Four wickets went down for 70 when Lawry took control and amid slow hand clapping and boos batted out time.

Going on to New Zealand, the tourists played two Tests straight away and won both by an innings. The third and final Test was won by 7 wickets and the side flew home with at least some credit.

The chief memory of the tour was the poor English fielding. The best English batting came from Barrington, Dexter and Cowdrey. In the bowling Titmus proved well worth his place, which was surprising, since he was expected to play second fiddle to Allen when the tour began. Trueman bowled much better than his critics forecast, but Statham was not so good as previously. Larter was too inaccurate to make much of a contribution and little was seen of Coldwell or Knight in the important games. Murray lost the wicket-keeping position to Smith.

Simpson was the dominant Australian batsman, neither Lawry nor O'Neill being quite as good as feared. Davidson and McKenzie led the Australian attack—Benaud, after a brilliant start, falling away.

1963-64: M.C.C. tour of Tanganyika, Kenya, Uganda

Following the path of F. R. Brown's tour two years before, the M.C.C. sent the following side to East Africa in the autumn of 1963: M. J. K. Smith (Warwicks) (capt), W. Watson (Leics) (player-manager), P. H. Parfitt (Middx), M. J. Stewart (Surrey), C. Milburn (Northants), J. B. Mortimore (Gloucs), R. J. Langridge (Sussex), R. N. S. Hobbs (Essex), T. W. Cartwright (Warwicks), L. A. Johnson (Northants), J. D. F. Larter (Northants) and I. J. Jones (Glamorgan).

The team, which was of good first-class county standard, was obviously too strong for the opposition. All the matches were played on jute matting rather than coir, which meant that life was easier for the batsmen. The most important match of the tour was against an East African Invitation Eleven at Kampala, but the tourists found little difficulty in winning by an innings. The only game that was at all close was the match against the Kenya Kongonis. Smith set the locals 298 to win. Shuttleworth and Giles put on 83 for the last wicket and were within 11 of victory, when Shuttleworth was run out.

A young local batsman who impressed the tourists was Basharat – better known now as the Notts cricketer, B. Hassan.

The tour was not a financial success, the attendances in Nairobi being much lower than expected.

1963-64: all five Tests drawn in India

Following the complaints regarding the over-long tour to the Indian sub-continent in 1961-62, the M.C.C. experimented with an eight-week tour to India alone, consisting of ten matches only, five of which were Tests.

Before selecting the team, the M.C.C. drew up a list of no less than 36 possible players and asked each if he were available. The team eventually announced was M. C. Cowdrey (Kent) (capt), M. J. K. Smith (Warwicks) (vice-capt), K. F. Barrington (Surrey), J. G. Binks (Yorks), J. B. Bolus (Notts), J. H. Edrich (Surrey), I. J. Jones (Glamorgan), B. R. Knight (Essex), J. D. F. Larter (Northants), J. B. Mortimore (Gloucs), J. M. Parks (Sussex), J. S. E. Price (Middx), P. J. Sharpe (Yorks), F. J. Titmus (Middx) and D. Wilson (Yorks) with D. G. Clark as manager. The side was much better than the one of 1961-62, though lacking Dexter, Trueman and Close, a trio which had featured strongly in the home Tests of 1963.

A few weeks after the team had been announced, Cowdrey stated he was not fit, owing to an arm injury and M. J. Stewart of Surrey was included, with M. J. K. Smith taking over as captain.

Flying to India, the tour began at Bangalore, where a high-scoring draw was played. In the second game however the local side – South Zone – proved very vulnerable to spin and a combination of Titmus, Wilson and Barrington was too much for them.

India scored 457 for seven in the first Test and the only effective English bowler was Titmus, but slow scoring after a bright first day made a draw certain. England had four players who were taken ill during the match, which did not help the tourists' cause.

In the match after the first Test, Barrington had the misfortune to break a finger, and Smith cabled home for some reinforcements – M. C. Cowdrey and P. H. Parfitt were dispatched but did not arrive in time for the second Test. England went into the game in dire straits, since Edrich, Sharpe and Mortimore were all on the sick list, so both wicket-keepers had to be played. At tea-time on the first day Stewart fell ill and the match continued with only ten men in the English camp. India totally failed to take advantage of the situation and some splendid all-round cricket by the English ten easily saved the day.

England had twelve fit men for the third Test, Cowdrey and Parfitt having arrived. Price produced his best performance to dismiss India for 241, but England in reply struggled. Cowdrey with a slow hundred managed to get a small first innings lead, but loss of time due to rain put any question of a definite decision out of court.

Cowdrey hit another century in the fourth Test and England gained a lead of over a hundred. Kunderan however insured India against defeat and on the last day the Nawab hit a double century, but it was purely academic.

The pitch for the last Test at Kanpur was completely dead and the twenty-two players merely went through the motions for the statutory five days. Knight and Parfitt hit hundreds for England and Nadkarni gave an exhibition display on the final day. The

1963-64: M.C.C. to India

Batting Averages

	M	I	NO	R	HS	Avge	100	c/s
K. F. Barrington (Surrey)	4	4	1	336	108	112.00	1	2
M. C. Cowdrey (Kent)	4	5	2	315	151	105.00	2	5
P. H. Parfitt (Middx)	5	7	3	351	121	87.75	1	2
J. H. Edrich (Surrey)	6	8	1	386	150	55.14	1	1
P. J. Sharpe (Yorks)	6	10	2	434	86	54.25	0	4
M. J. K. Smith (Warks)	8	11	4	376	75*	53.71	0	4
J. B. Bolus (Notts)	9	15	0	752	113	50.13	1	4
M. J. Stewart (Surrey)	5	5	0	223	119	44.60	1	3
J. M. Parks (Sussex)	8	10	3	271	52	38.71	0	11/2
D. Wilson (Yorks)	9	8	2	203	112	33.83	1	1
F. J. Titmus (Middx)	7	8	3	164	84*	32.80	0	5
B. R. Knight (Essex)	8	10	1	276	127	30.66	1	1
J. B. Mortimore (Gloucs)	6	6	1	143	73*	28.60	0	7
J. G. Binks (Yorks)	6	5	0	121	55	24.20	0	13/1
J. S. E. Price (Middx)	7	4	1	34	32	11.33	0	3
J. D. F. Larter (Northts)	7	4	1	12	10	4.00	0	2

Also played in 5 matches: I. J. Jones (Glam) 5.

Bowling Averages

	O	M	R	W	Avge	BB	5i
K. F. Barrington	39.3	8	131	7	18.71	3-11	0
F. J. Titmus	474.5	178	1000	36	27.77	6-73	2
J. S. E. Price	184.1	34	569	17	33.47	5-73	1
J. D. F. Larter	151.3	27	477	14	34.07	2-22	0
J. B. Mortimore	308.2	123	603	16	37.68	5-75	1
D. Wilson	302	117	569	13	43.76	4-28	0
B. R. Knight	147.2	27	493	11	44.81	3-24	0
I. J. Jones	124	19	417	9	46.33	3-59	0
P. H. Parfitt	145	51	402	8	50.25	2-71	0

Also bowled: J. B. Bolus 17-4-63-2; J. M. Parks 14-1-95-1; M. J. K. Smith 14-0-60-0; M. J. Stewart 7-0-42-0; J. H. Edrich 5-1-27-0; M. C. Cowdrey 5-0-34-0; P. J. Sharpe 2-1-4-0; J. G. Binks 2-0-16-0.

(Kent), T. E. Bailey (Essex), E. R. Dexter (Sussex), F. S. Trueman (Yorks), T. W. Graveney (Worcs), P. E. Richardson (Kent), J. T. Murray (Middx), R. E. Marshall (Hants), A. C. D. Ingleby-Mackenzie (Hants), A. T. Castell (Hants), K. E. Palmer (Somerset) and R. N. S. Hobbs (Essex).

The tour commenced with two minor games and then the three matches against Jamaica followed. Compton celebrated his return to first-class cricket with a century in the first match against Jamaica, but the tourists' bowling was none too effective and Jamaica declared in both innings with only 5 and 4 wickets lost.

In the second match Worrell, the Jamaican captain, declared to set the visitors 377 in 420 minutes. Dexter hit a brilliant hundred in 67 minutes and Graveney also reached a hundred to bring the Cavaliers victory by 4 wickets. Some good leg-break bowling by Hobbs dismissed the home team twice in the third match and with another hundred from Dexter, the Cavaliers won by 5 wickets.

The tour was most enjoyable, but was of little interest to the public, less than 1,000 watching each day's play.

1964: Yorkshire tour North America and Bermuda

After the 1964 English season, the Yorkshire side travelled to North America for a three-week tour. Sponsored by various organisations and guaranteed by the cricket authorities in Canada, United States and Bermuda, the team, under the management of R. A. Roberts, flew from London on 18 September to New York. The side was D. B. Close (capt), J. H. Hampshire, D. E. V. Padgett, R. A. Hutton, P. J. Sharpe, R. Illingworth, J. G. Binks, F. S. Trueman, D. Wilson and M. Ryan—because of illness A. G. Nicholson could not go and G. St. A. Sobers, the West Indies Test cricketer, was co-opted for the latter matches.

The first two matches in New York were in fact against West Indian elevens who played cricket to a fairly high standard. Visits were made to Toronto and British Columbia, then down to

---

last match was one of three declarations against North Zone, but the result was another draw and the England party flew home.

All five Tests had been drawn and to some extent England deserve credit for achieving this, for the side was decimated by injury and illness. The best English bowler was Titmus, whose off-spin proved the one really effective weapon in the attack, though Price improved as the tour went on. Cowdrey's technique was too good for the Indian bowlers and Smith batted well, but most of the younger element did little to improve their standing, though Bolus played some determined knocks.

On the Indian wickets however it was very difficult to assess a player's true value and even from the Indian press came cries that the pitches must be altered if Indian cricket was to survive.

1963-64: Compton takes Cavaliers to Jamaica

Whilst the M.C.C. team struggled against doped pitches and illness in India, the 'International Cavaliers Cricket Club' travelled to Jamaica for a five-match tour of that island. The team which was entirely composed of English county cricketers was: D. C. S. Compton (Middx) (capt), J. C. Laker (Essex), T. G. Evans

1963-64: Cavaliers to Jamaica

1st Match: v Combined Parishes (Montego Bay) (One Day) Jan 6.
Combined Parishes 164 lost to Cavaliers 166-6 (E. R. Dexter 55) by 4 wkts.

2nd Match: v Colts & Country XI (Monymusk) Jan 7, 8.
Cavaliers 211 (R. E. Marshall 51, R. G. Scarlett 6-59) & 102-2 drew with Colts & Country XI 239 (G. Robinson 57, R. Grandison 56).

3rd Match: v Jamaica (Kingston) Jan 9, 10, 11.
Jamaica 254-5 dec (E. Griffith 146) & 202-4 dec (H. Reid 101*, E. D. McMorris 60) drew with Cavaliers 238-7 dec (D. C. S. Compton 103) & 216-8 (J. T. Murray 60, E. R. Dexter 58).

4th Match: v Jamaica (Kingston) Jan 15, 16, 17, 18.
Jamaica 279 (L. A. King 75, R. N. S. Hobbs 5-69) & 260-6 dec (M. L. C. Foster 136*) lost to Cavaliers 163 (T. E. Bailey 76) & 377-6 (E. R. Dexter 176, T. W. Graveney 108*) by 4 wkts.

5th Match: v Jamaica (Kingston) Jan 22, 23, 24, 25.
Jamaica 185 (E. D. McMorris 103*) & 246 (E. Griffith 63) lost to Cavaliers 297-6 dec (E. R. Dexter 120, J. T. Murray 68) & 135-5 (P. E. Richardson 84) by 5 wkts.

1964: Yorkshire to North America and Bermuda

1st Match: v New York Combined Leagues (Mount Vernon) Sept 19
Yorkshire 217-8 dec (D. B. Close 76) drew with Combined Leagues 176-4 (King 56).

2nd Match: v New York Combined Leagues (Randall's Island) Sept 20.
Yorkshire 125 (Larrier 6-41) beat Combined Leagues 56 (F. S. Trueman 6-21) by 69 runs.

3rd Match: v British Commonwealth C.C. (Washington) Sept 21.
Yorkshire 350 (R. Illingworth 103, J. G. Binks 69, D. Wilson 62) beat British Commonwealth C.C. 46 by 304 runs.

4th Match: v Toronto C.C. (Toronto) Sept 23.
Yorkshire 251-6 dec (D. E. V. Padgett 77, G. Boycott 75) drew with Toronto 94-5.

5th Match: v Ontario XI (Toronto) Sept 24.
Yorkshire 189-6 dec (J. H. Hampshire 54, R. Illingworth 51) drew with Ontario 114-2 (A. Khan 52*).

6th Match: Alberta (Calgary) Sept 25.
No play due to rain.

7th Match: v British Columbia (Vancouver) Sept 26.
Yorkshire 246 (J. H. Hampshire 76) beat British Columbia 88 by 158 runs.

8th Match: v Southern California (Hollywood) Sept 27.
Yorkshire 251 (D. E. V. Padgett 50) beat Southern California 77 (R. Illingworth 4-17) by 174 runs.

9th Match: v Southern California (Hollywood) Sept 28.
Yorkshire 326-9 dec (R. Illingworth 144) beat Southern California 65 (D. Wilson 6-11)

10th Match: v St George's C.C. (Hamilton) Oct 1.
St George 48 lost to Yorkshire 322-8 (G. St. A. Sobers 117, G. Boycott 108) by 5 wkts.

11th Match: v Somerset C.C. (Hamilton) Oct 3.
Yorkshire 172 beat Somerset C.C. 141 by 31 runs.

12th Match: v Bermuda (Hamilton) Oct 4.
Yorkshire 255 (P. J. Sharpe 114*) beat Bermuda 65 by 190 runs.

13th Match: v Pick of the Leagues (Hamilton) Oct 6.
Pick of the Leagues 69 lost to Yorkshire 167 (G. St. A. Sobers 77).

Hollywood, before the major matches played in Bermuda. Here the bowling of Trueman and Sobers was too much for the locals, but the matches were well attended, at least 10,000 watching each day.

The team arrived back in England on 8 October.

1964-65: Cavaliers visit the West Indies

Having toured Jamaica the previous winter, the Cavaliers repeated the visit in 1964-65, but included Barbados on the itinerary. The team was: T. E. Bailey (Essex) (capt), M. C. Cowdrey (Kent), T. G. Evans (Kent), K. W. R. Fletcher (Essex), G. Goonesena (Notts), J. H. Hampshire (Yorks), R. G. A. Headley (Worcs), A. C. D. Ingleby-Mackenzie (Hants), B. R. Knight (Essex), A. P. E. Knott (Kent), J. C. Laker (Essex), R. E. Marshall (Hants), P. E. Richardson (Kent), F. S. Trueman (Yorks) and D. W. White (Hants).

Jamaica were dismissed by Laker for 214 in the first innings of the initial first-class match and though the Cavaliers declared soon after getting a first innings lead, the match was drawn. The Cavaliers fell cheaply to Hall and Sobers in the return game and were easily beaten.

Both matches in Barbados were drawn, though in the first the Cavaliers were forced to follow on and had to rely on some good batting by Richardson and Cowdrey for their second innings recovery.

1964-65: Cavaliers to West Indies

1st Match: v Eastern Zone (St Mary, Jamaica) (One Day)   Jan 27.
Cavaliers 295-6 dec (R. G. A. Headley 69, J. H. Hampshire 52, P. E. Richardson 51) drew with Eastern Zone 132-3.

2nd Match: v Jamaica Colts (St Ann's Bay)   Jan 29, 30.
Cavaliers 312-8 dec (B. R. Knight 133, K. W. R. Fletcher 75) & 132-5 (R. E. Marshall 66) drew with Colts 241 (L. Chambers 65).

3rd Match: v Jamaica (Montego Bay)   Feb 4, 5, 6.
Jamaica 214 (H. Bennett 64, J. C. Laker 5-54) & 249-4 dec (R. Pinnock 67*, M. L. C. Foster 61) drew with Cavaliers 250-4 dec (M. C. Cowdrey 77*, R. G. A. Headley 76, P. E. Richardson 54) & 122-3 (R. G. A. Headley 74*).

4th Match: v Central Zone (Mandeville)   Feb 10, 11.
Central Zone 144 (R. G. A. Headley 6-38) & 112 (G. Goonesena 6-38) lost to Cavaliers 237-9 dec & 22-1.

5th Match: v Jamaica (Kingston)   Feb 13, 15, 16.
Jamaica 332 (G. St. A. Sobers 114, E. D. A. McMorris 61, F. S. Trueman 5-78) & 242-6 dec (C. C. Hunte 78, E. H. C. Griffith 61) beat Cavaliers 189 (J. H. Hampshire 55) & 176 (K. W. R. Fletcher 78) by 209 runs.

6th Match: v Barbados (Bridgetown)   Feb 20, 22, 23.
Barbados 333-4 dec (M. R. Bynoe 110, S. M. Nurse 100, G. St. A. Sobers 52) & 222-4 (P. D. Lashley 90) drew with Cavaliers 152 & 326-4 dec (P. E. Richardson 114, M. C. Cowdrey 95).

7th Match: v Barbados (Bridgetown)   Feb 25, 26, 27.
Cavaliers 264-5 dec (P. E. Richardson 73*, B. R. Knight 68) & 266-9 dec (B. R. Knight 110, A. P. E. Knott 66) drew with Barbados 270-3 dec (R. Brancker 125*, P. D. Lashley 113*) & 241-7 (R. Bradshaw 57, K. D. Boyce 55).

1964-65: champions Worcestershire go on world tour

The Champion County of 1964, Worcestershire, undertook a tour of 15 matches, commencing in Kenya and ending in Los Angeles, which involved a journey round the world. Under the managership of J. Lister, the players were D. Kenyon (capt), T. W. Graveney, B. L. d'Oliveira, R. G. A. Headley, M. J. Horton, D. N. F. Slade, D. W. Richardson, R. Booth, N. Gifford, J. A.

1964-65: Worcestershire to Africa, Asia and N. America

1st Match: v Kenya (Nairobi)   Feb 13, 14, 15.
Worcestershire 353 (B. L. d'Oliveira 162) & 282-8 dec (T. W. Graveney 92, D. Kenyon 82, B. L. d'Oliveira 53) drew with Kenya 354-4 dec (Narendra Patel 127, Akhil Lakhani 122) & 139-5 (Charanjive 50).

2nd Match: v Rhodesia (Bulawayo)   Feb 20, 21, 22.
Worcestershire 277 (B. L. d'Oliveira 73, D. N. F. Slade 64, G. B. Lawrence 6-61) & 161-5 dec (D. Kenyon 63) beat Rhodesia 82 (L. J. Coldwell 5-18) & 160 (G. B. Lawrence 60*, L. J. Coldwell 5-26) by 196 runs.*

3rd Match: v Country Districts (Que Que)   Feb 24, 25.
Worcestershire 348-6 dec (R. G. A. Headley 178, B. L. d'Oliveira 51) & 56-3 dec beat Country Districts 169-6 dec (E. Butcher 51) & 150 (N. Gifford 5-54) by 85 runs.

4th Match: v Rhodesia (Salisbury)   Feb 27, 28, March 1.
Rhodesia 235 (A. J. Pithey 98) & 344-4 dec (R. A. Gripper 116, A. J. Pithey 68, K. C. Bland 62, J. D. McPhun 61) beat Worcestershire 308-6 dec (T. W. Graveney 136*, D. N. F. Slade 58) & 115 (V. E. J. Dickinson 5-44, J. H. du Preez 5-36) by 156 runs.*

5th Match: v Calcutta (Ballygunge)   March 5, 6.
Calcutta 166 (C. V. Gadkari 90) & 188-6 (J. M. Wilson 68) drew with Worcestershire 445-6 dec (T. W. Graveney 104, B. L. d'Oliveira 104, R. G. A. Headley 102, D. W. Richardson 58).

6th Match: v Chief Minister's XI (Eden Gardens, Calcutta)   March 9, 10.
Chief Minister's XI 240-9 dec (P. Roy 58) & 127-5 dec (R. Saxsena 69) drew with Worcestershire 215.

7th Match: v Malaysia (Singapore)   March 13, 14.
Worcestershire 254-9 dec (T. W. Graveney 161, Way 5-57) & 131-3 dec beat Malaysia 101 (B. L. d'Oliveira 7-31) & 135 (J. Jeremiah 54, N. Gifford 7-38) by 149 runs.

8th Match: v Singapore (Singapore) (One Day)   March 15.
Worcestershire 252-4 dec (T. W. Graveney 92, M. J. Horton 69) drew with Singapore 71-2.

9th Match: v Selangor State XI (Kuala Lumpur) (One Day)   March 19.
Worcestershire 296-3 dec (M. J. Horton 127, R. G. A. Headley 107) drew with Selangor 69-4.*

10th Match: v Malaysia (Kuala Lumpur)   March 20, 21.
Worcestershire 310-7 dec (T. W. Graveney 58, B. L. d'Oliveira 55, D. Kenyon 54) beat Malaysia 119 (N. Gifford 7-56) & 74 (L. J. Coldwell 6-46) by an inns & 117 runs.

11th Match: v Royal Bangkok Sports Club (Bangkok) (One Day)   March 24.
Worcestershire 242-8 dec (B. L. d'Oliveira 117) beat Royal Bangkok S.C. 62 (L. J. Coldwell 5-24) by 180 runs.

12th Match: v Hong Kong League President's XI (Hong Kong)   March 26.
Worcestershire 282 (T. W. Graveney 116) beat President's XI 102 by 180 runs.

13th Match: v Hong Kong (Kowloon)   March 27, 28.
Hong Kong 150 (J. Fawcett 58, B. L. d'Oliveira 5-51) & 108 (B. L. d'Oliveira 5-21) lost to Worcestershire 359 (T. W. Graveney 132, D. N. F. Slade 51, Daniels 5-90) by an inns & 101 runs.

14th Match: v Honolulu (Honolulu)   March 30.
Worcestershire 184-5 dec (T. W. Graveney 85) beat Honolulu 48 by 136 runs.*

15th Match: v South California C.A. (Hollywood).   April 3.
No play due to rain.

Flavell, B. M. Brain and L. J. Coldwell. Although only twelve players were taken, happily there were no serious injuries and no need to co-opt any additional men.

Kenya batted very well in the opening match and were able to declare with four wickets down, after obtaining a lead on first innings, but in the end the target of 282 in 180 minutes was too large for the home side and the game was drawn.

Each side won one match in the two games against Rhodesia. Coldwell dismissed Rhodesia quickly in the first game, but in the second Worcester collapsed before the spinners in their second innings.

Two minor matches were played in India—both draws—before the team went on to Singapore and Malaysia. Rain unfortunately marred several matches as it did the final match in Hollywood, which was completely washed out.

Graveney hit well over 1,000 runs on the tour, easily the best record, and Coldwell returned the best bowling figures.

1964-65: M.C.C. tour of South America

A Committee under the chairmanship of Lord Luke raised the funds to finance the 1964-65 M.C.C. team to South America where it was felt that some additional stimulus to the game was required, following the M.C.C. tour of 1958-59. As the M.C.C.

1964-65: M.C.C. to South America

1st Match: v Rio (Niteroi) (One Day)   Dec 7.
M.C.C. 312-5 dec (C. Gibson 70, R. A. Gale 58) beat Rio 98 (A. R. Duff 5-38) by 214 runs.

2nd Match: v Brazil C.A. (Niteroi)   Dec 9, 10.
M.C.C. 272-5 dec (C. Gibson 58, A. R. Lewis 58, R. A. Gale 50) & 94-4 dec beat Brazil 216-9 dec (G. Thompson 61, M. Corbett 52) & 95 by 55 runs.*

3rd Match: v Brazil C.A. XI (Sao Paulo)   Dec 12, 13.
M.C.C. 278-8 dec (R. A. Hutton 60) & 74-1 dec (R. C. Kerslake 51) drew with Brazil 55 (A. R. Duff 6-18).

4th Match: v R. G. Holland's XI (Sao Paulo) (One Day)   Dec 15.
M.C.C. 297-5 dec (A. R. Duff 77, R. C. White 71, R. I. Jefferson 52) beat R. G. Holland's XI 101 by 196 runs.*

5th Match: v E. Huddart's XI (Sao Paulo) (One Day)   Dec 16.
M.C.C. 234-7 dec (R. A. Hutton 72, R. C. Kerslake 57) beat E. Huddart's XI 54 (P. I. Bedford 5-16) by 180 runs.

6th Match: v Chile C.A. XI (Santiago) (One Day)   Dec 19.
M.C.C. 279-4 dec (A. R. Lewis 87, R. A. Hutton 84) beat Chile 99 by 180 runs.

7th Match: v Chile (Santiago) (One Day)   Dec 20.
M.C.C. 337-4 dec (R. C. Kerslake 63, J. D. Martin 62, A. C. Smith 59, A. R. Duff 54) beat Chile 133 by 204 runs.

8th Match: v Chile (Vina del Mar) (One Day)   Dec 21.
M.C.C. 323 (D. J. Mordaunt 75, A. R. Lewis 66) beat Chile 89 (A. R. Duff 4-27) by 234 runs.

9th Match: v Argentine C.A. Colts XII (Belgrano) (One Day)   Dec 24.
M.C.C. 287-4 dec (R. C. White 64, R. A. Gale 62, C. Gibson 51) beat Colts XII 146 (P. I. Bedford 6-54) by 141 runs.*

10th Match: v Argentine C.A. XI (Lomas)   Dec 26, 27.
M.C.C. 403 (R. C. White 108, R. A. Gale 79, A. R. Lewis 59, P. I. Bedford 51, M. Lacey 5-119) beat Argentine 90 (R. I. Jefferson 6-27) & 82 by an inns & 231 runs.

11th Match: v Veterans XI (San Isidro) (One Day)   Dec 29.
Veterans 69 lost to M.C.C. 70-3 by 7 wkts.

12th Match: v Argentine XII (Hurlingham)   Dec 30, 31.
M.C.C. 355 (D. J. Mordaunt 63, A. R. Lewis 55, A. C. Smith 51 & 42-4 dec beat Argentine XII 63 & 124 (P. I. Bedford 6-50) by 210 runs.

13th Match: v Argentine XI (Belgrano)   Jan 1, 2, 3.
Argentine 156 (G. Paine 85) & 160 (P. I. Bedford 5-50) lost to M.C.C. 476-8 dec (R. A. Gale 132, A. R. Lewis 110, R. A. Hutton 94, R. C. White 85) by an inns & 160 runs.

14th Match: v Northern Camps (Venado Tuerto)   (One Day)   Jan 5.
M.C.C. 252 (P. I. Bedford 51, D. J. Mordaunt 51) beat Northern Camps 172 (A. R. Duff 7-36) by 80 runs.

15th Match: v Argentine (Hurlingham)   Jan 8, 9, 10.
Argentine 71 & 101 (R. A. Hutton 6-24) lost to M.C.C. 490 (D. J. Mordaunt 122, R. A. Gale 98, A. R. Duff 58) by an inns & 318 runs.

had not intended to make another tour before 1968, private finance was required for this additional visit.

The team which left England by air on 7 December was: A. C. Smith (Warwicks) (capt), P. I. Bedford (Middx), A. R. Duff (Worcs), R. A. Gale (Middx), C. Gibson (M.C.C.), M. G. Griffith (Sussex), R. A. Hutton (Yorks), R. I. Jefferson (Surrey), R. C. Kerslake (Somerset), A. R. Lewis (Glamorgan), D. J. Mordaunt (Sussex), R. C. White (Gloucs) and J. D. Martin (Somerset).

The first four matches were played in Brazil, where cricket seemed to be gradually dying, no new players coming along to replace the old stagers. Cricket was also very limited in Chile where three matches took place and the major games were reserved for the Argentine. The three 'Tests' however provided the M.C.C. with three large victories, but there was no doubt that the Argentine had some good young players, who needed more coaching to improve their standard.

The M.C.C. left South America on 12 January. Gale headed the batting table, but Mordaunt, Hutton and Lewis were not far behind. The two spinners Duff and Bedford captured most wickets.

1964-65: M.C.C. undefeated in South Africa

With E. R. Dexter announcing that he was intending to stand as a candidate in the forthcoming General Election and M. C. Cowdrey stating he was not available, the M.C.C. chose M. J. K. Smith (Warwickshire) to lead the side to South Africa. The

Graeme Pollock out and a wicket for John Price in the final Test of the 1964-65 tour of South Africa. Jim Parks took the diving catch behind the wicket.

remainder of the team was K. F. Barrington (Surrey), G. Boycott (Yorks), T. W. Cartwright (Warwicks), R. W. Barber (Warwicks), J. M. Parks (Sussex), P. H. Parfitt (Middx), J. T. Murray (Middx), J. M. Brearley (Middx), N. I. Thomson (Sussex), D. J. Brown (Warwicks), F. J. Titmus (Middx), R. N. S. Hobbs (Essex), D. A. Allen (Gloucs), J. S. E. Price (Middx) and E. R. Dexter, who failed in his attempt to get into Parliament and joined the side as vice-captain.

The critics were worried about the batting in the absence of Cowdrey, Russell, Graveney and Stewart. The selection of Brearley in preference to the last three noted was bitterly criticised.

Travelling to South Africa by air for the first time, the M.C.C. began the tour with two matches in Rhodesia. The early matches all produced wins, or draws in the tourists' favour–even the usually formidable Transvaal side was beaten by an innings.

In the first Test at Durban, Smith was fortunate to win the toss and see his team reach 485 for 5 declared, for the wicket soon began to take spin and the South Africans were bemused by Allen and Titmus. England won by an innings.

Following two more innings victories, Smith again won the toss in the second Test. Barber, Dexter and Barrington mastered the home bowling and a total of 531 was reached. South Africa still could not tackle Titmus and Allen with any certainty and were forced to follow on. A great century by Bland, who used his feet to the spinners prevented England going two up in the series.

It was South Africa's turn to bat first and exceed 500 in the third Test. Slow scoring however meant that England had no chance of winning, even before they began to bat, and the game meandered to a tame draw. There was a great hullabaloo in this game on the subject of batsmen 'walking' if they thought a catch had been taken and the umpire seemed uncertain. In this match Barlow of South Africa stood his ground, while Barrington 'walked'. The former went on to 138.

The match against Border, which was won by 9 wickets, saw a

1st Match: v Matabeleland XI (Bulawayo) Oct 21, 22.
Matabeleland 133 & 144 (F. J. Titmus 7-58) lost to M.C.C. 253-9 dec (M. J. K. Smith 60, P. H. Parfitt 55) & 28-0 by 10 wkts.

2nd Match: v Rhodesia (Salisbury) Oct 24, 25, 26, 27.
Rhodesia 281 (K. C. Bland 66, A. J. Pithey 65) & 225 (N. Frangos 82) lost to M.C.C. 298 (P. H. Parfitt 82, K. F. Barrington 74) & 209-5 (R. W. Barber 108) by 5 wkts.

3rd Match: v South African Colts (Benoni) Oct 30, 31, Nov 2.
Colts 398 (N. Rosendorff 83, B. A. Richards 63, N. S. Crookes 60, J. T. Botten 57, M. J. Macaulay 55*) & 161 (F. J. Titmus 5-71) drew with M.C.C. 267 (J. M. Brearley 68) & 241-8 (G. Boycott 53, E. R. Dexter 50, N. S. Crookes 5-102).

4th Match: v Transvaal Country Districts (Vereeniging) Nov 3, 4.
M.C.C. 337-5 dec (J. M. Brearley 102, M. J. K. Smith 102) drew with Transvaal 107 & 271 (P. S. Heine 108, R. N. S. Hobbs 5-146).

5th Match: v Transvaal (Johannesburg) Nov 6, 7, 9.
Transvaal 125 & 257 (I. R. Fullerton 92) lost to M.C.C. 464-9 dec (K. F. Barrington 169, M. J. K. Smith 124, R. W. Barber 59, P. S. Heine 5-110) by an inns & 82 runs.

6th Match: v Natal (Durban) Nov 13, 14, 16, 17.
Natal 360-9 dec (G. D. Varnals 111, R. Dumbrill 68, N. I. Thompson 5-58) & 102 lost to M.C.C. 445 (J. M. Parks 80*, P. H. Parfitt 74, D. J. Brown 69, E. R. Dexter 59) & 19-0 by 10 wkts.

7th Match: v Eastern Province (Port Elizabeth) Nov 20, 21, 23.
M.C.C. 447-7 dec (G. Boycott 193*, M. J. K. Smith 153) beat E. Province 133 (F. J. Titmus 5-32) & 164 (F. J. Titmus 5-38).

8th Match: v Western Province (Cape Town) Nov 27, 28, 30, Dec 1.
M.C.C. 441 (K. F. Barrington 169*, G. Boycott 106) & 228-6 dec (K. F. Barrington 82, J. M. Brearley 64) drew with W. Province 357 (P. L. van der Merwe 121, L. J. Weinstein 53) & 158-8.

9th Match: v South Africa (Durban) Dec 4, 5, 7, 8.
England 485-5 dec (K. F. Barrington 148*, J. M. Parks 108*, R. W. Barber 74, G. Boycott 73) beat South Africa 155 (D. A. Allen 5-41) & 226 (K. C. Bland 68, F. J. Titmus 5-66) by an inns & 104 runs.

10th Match: v South African Universities (Pietermaritzburg) Dec 12, 14, 15.
Universities 114 (K. F. Barrington 5-29) & 130 (E. V. Chatterton 54) lost to M.C.C. 356 (G. Boycott 81, J. T. Murray 81, M. J. K. Smith 76, P. H. Parfitt 50, R. S. Steyn 5-84) by an inns & 112 runs.

11th Match: v North-Eastern Transvaal (Pretoria) Dec 18, 19, 21.
N.E. Transvaal 204 & 135 lost to M.C.C. 350 (J. T. Murray 142, F. J. Titmus 65, G. G. Hall 6-145) by an inns & 11 runs.

12th Match: v South Africa (Johannesburg) Dec 23, 24, 26, 28, 29.
England 531 (E. R. Dexter 172, K. F. Barrington 121, R. W. Barber 97, P. H. Parfitt 52, P. M. Pollock 5-129) drew with South Africa 317 (A. J. Pithey 85, E. J. Barlow 71) & 336-6 (K. C. Bland 144*, R. G. Pollock 55, T. L. Goddard 50).

13th Match: v South Africa (Cape Town) Jan 1, 2, 4, 5, 6.
South Africa 501-7 dec (A. J. Pithey 154, E. J. Barlow 138, K. C. Bland 78) & 346 (E. J. Barlow 78, R. G. Pollock 73, K. C. Bland 64, D. T. Lindsay 50) drew with England 442 (M. J. K. Smith 121, E. R. Dexter 61, J. M. Parks 59, R. W. Barber 58, H. D. Bromfield 5-88) and 15-0.

14th Match: v Border (East London) Jan 9, 11, 12.
Border 215 (W. S. Farrer 66, R. W. Barber 6-67) & 244 (H. M. Ackerman 108, C. P. Wilkins 65) lost to M.C.C. 407-5 dec (T. W. Cartwright 111*, E. R. Dexter 110, G. Boycott 56) & 54-1 by 9 wkts.

15th Match: v Orange Free State (Bloemfontein) Jan 15, 16, 18.
O.F.S. 170 & 171-9 dec (R. van der Poll) lost to M.C.C. 199-7 dec (J. M. Parks 89, G. Boycott 73, M. J. Macaulay 7-58) & 143-3 by 7 wkts.

16th Match: v South Africa (Johannesburg) Jan 22, 23, 25, 26, 27.
South Africa 390-6 dec (E. J. Barlow 96, A. J. Pithey 95, J. H. B. Waite 64, T. L. Goddard 60, K. C. Bland 55) & 307-3 dec (T. L. Goddard 112, R. G. Pollock 65*) drew with England 384 (P. H. Parfitt 122*, K. F. Barrington 93, R. W. Barber 61) & 153-6 (G. Boycott 76*).

17th Match: v Griqualand West (Kimberley) Jan 29, 30, Feb 1.
Griqualand West 140 (C. W. Symcox 62) & 107 (K. F. Barrington 7-40) lost to M.C.C. 226 & 24-0 by 10 wkts.

18th Match: v Invitation XI (Cape Town) Feb 5, 6, 8, 9.
Invitation XI 437 (K. C. Bland 116, D. Gamsy 88, R. K. Muzzell 70, J. T. Botten 53, P. L. van der Merwe 50, T. W. Cartwright 5-107) & 316-7 dec (R. G. Pollock 91, K. C. Bland 67, D. Gamsy 55, R. K. Muzzell 52) drew with M.C.C. 326 (G. Boycott 114, T. W. Cartwright 53*) & 205-7 (M. J. K. Smith 78*).

19th Match: v South Africa (Port Elizabeth) Feb 12, 13, 15, 16, 17.
South Africa 502 (R. G. Pollock 138, E. J. Barlow 69, P. L. van der Merwe 66, T. L. Goddard 61) & 178-4 dec (R. G. Pollock 77*) drew with England 435 (G. Boycott 117, K. F. Barrington 72) & 29-1.

Batting Averages

		M	I	NO	R	HS	Avge	100	c/s
K. F. Barrington	(Surrey)	13	18	5	1128	169*	86.76	4	7
M. J. K. Smith	(Warks)	14	17	2	877	153	58.46	3	21
G. Boycott	(Yorks)	15	25	5	1135	193*	56.75	4	7
T. W. Cartwright	(Warks)	8	10	4	293	111*	48.83	1	6
E. R. Dexter	(Sussex)	13	19	2	791	172	46.52	2	11
R. W. Barber	(Warks)	11	14	1	595	108	45.76	1	14
J. M. Parks	(Sussex)	12	17	3	524	108*	37.42	1	21/3
P. H. Parfitt	(Middx)	15	20	1	708	122*	37.26	1	22
J. T. Murray	(Middx)	10	14	3	398	142	36.18	1	23/8
J. M. Brearley	(Middx)	12	19	3	406	68	25.37	0	12
N. I. Thomson	(Sussex)	13	13	5	167	39	20.87	0	7
D. J. Brown	(Warks)	10	9	2	141	69	20.14	0	2
F. J. Titmus	(Middx)	10	12	3	156	65	17.33	0	6
R. N. S. Hobbs	(Essex)	9	7	2	72	36	14.40	0	6
D. A. Allen	(Gloucs)	11	11	1	95	38*	9.50	0	4
J. S. E. Price	(Middx)	10	8	2	26	10	4.33	0	2

Played in one match: K. E. Palmer (Som) 10.

Bowling Averages

	O	M	R	W	Avge	BB	5i
K. F. Barrington	73.1	23	174	24	7.25	7-40	2
D. A. Allen	506.4	182	921	38	24.23	5-41	1
F. J. Titmus	593.1	188	1240	51	24.31	5-32	4
D. J. Brown	256.1	67	637	23	27.69	4-42	0
R. W. Barber	187	44	605	21	28.80	6-67	1
J. S. E. Price	287	71	789	27	29.22	4-42	0
R. N. S. Hobbs	316	103	796	27	29.48	3-24	0
N. I. Thomson	492.2	170	1034	35	29.54	5-58	1
T. W. Cartwright	366.3	141	817	25	32.68	5-107	1
G. Boycott	94	24	262	8	32.75	3-47	0
E. R. Dexter	91	14	307	4	76.75	1-32	0
P. H. Parfitt	83	25	198	2	99.00	1-9	0
K. E. Palmer	63	8	189	1	189.00	1-113	0

Also bowled: M. J. K. Smith 11-1-43-0.

bowlers however and the game was another draw—in an attempt at the impossible, South Africa made a sporting declaration in their second innings, but rain ended the match.

The touring team therefore ended the campaign undefeated, which surprised many of their detractors. In the closing stages they were also handicapped by injuries to Price, Cartwright and Brown, so their performance was certainly meritorious. Dexter batted better for not being captain and Barrington performed well throughout. Boycott came good in the last two Tests, but Brearley failed sadly. The faster bowlers achieved little and most of the work of prising out the opposition rested with Titmus and Allen.

Both the attendance figures and match receipts showed a drop compared with the previous M.C.C. visit.

1965-66: England and Australia draw Test series

The party selected to go to Australia in 1965-66 was: M. J. K. Smith (Warwicks) (capt), M. C. Cowdrey (Kent) (vice-capt), D. A. Allen (Gloucs), R. W. Barber (Warwicks), K. F. Barrington (Surrey), G. Boycott (Yorks), D. J. Brown (Warwicks), J. H. Edrich (Surrey), K. Higgs (Lancs), I. J. Jones (Glamorgan), J. D. F. Larter (Northants), J. T. Murray (Middx), P. H. Parfitt (Middx), J. M. Parks (Sussex), W. E. Russell (Middx), F. J. Titmus (Middx), S. C. Griffith (manager), J. T. Ikin (manager's assistant), J. Jennings (physiotherapist). The obvious absentees were Dexter and Statham and in fact the fast bowling department looked weak, since both Larter and Jones were unlikely to withstand the rigours of the tour.

For the first time the M.C.C. team flew all the way to Australia by jet, though with a stopover in Colombo.

The first two major matches of the tour were in Perth. In the first game, after declarations, a nine-run win was achieved, but the bowling on both sides was rather thin. The bowling again struggled in the second game. Higgs and Jones were very wayward and three declarations still resulted in a draw. In Adelaide

young batsman—Ackerman—hit a brilliant hundred. He later played for Northants. South Africa had all the best of the fourth Test, but failed to win. For some unknown reason Smith put the home team in to bat, but he was saved from the consequences of his folly by, first, three expensive blunders on the part of wicket-keeper Waite, second, by rain which cut over three hours off the playing time and third, by Boycott who defied the bowlers in the final innings.

South Africa needed to win the fifth Test to save the series and they began quite splendidly with 502 in just under two days. Dour batting by Boycott and Barrington frustrated the home

Cowdrey put South Australia in on a damp pitch and, appreciating this, Larter, Allen and Brown shot out the opposition for 103. Although batting better in the second innings, South Australia lost by 6 wickets and things were looking up for the tourists. The match against Victoria provided that State with its first victory against M.C.C. since the war. Both the tourists' bowling and batting failed in the first innings and though improving in the second, due to Barrington who hit 158 and took 4 for 24, it was too late. Some very consistent batting–no less than seven of the team made fifties, produced victory over New South Wales and there was more high scoring in the drawn game with Queensland, though the sick list was mounting, both Cowdrey and Barber being indisposed.

Rain decided the first Test, half of the first day and all of the second disappearing, and it was not until the fourth day that Australia declared the first innings of the match closed at 443 for 6. The match headed gently for a draw.

A generous declaration by State captain Favell gave the M.C.C. a win over South Australia. The bat dominated the second Test– England's attack was suspect in the absence of both Brown and Higgs and though Jones, Knight and Allen removed Australia for 358, they struggled in the second innings and another draw emerged. England won the toss in the third Test and Barber and

Boycott gave the tourists a great start with a partnership of 234. The second wicket did not fall until 303 and on a pitch which was worsening Brown bowled splendidly to dismiss Australia; the follow on was enforced and this time Titmus and Allen went straight through the home batting to bring England an innings victory. The holiday matches in Tasmania were played prior to the fourth Test, in which England were completely outplayed. McKenzie and Hawke demolished the English batting, then Simpson and Lawry opened with a partnership of 244.

The fifth Test ought to have been an exciting struggle, each side having won one game. England batted, and though both openers fell quickly, Barrington hit a sparkling hundred, which seemed to set the tempo for the match, but somehow the lower order English batsmen dragged their feet and when Australia batted, the over rate was so painfully slow that the game wound methodically down. It was a feeble end to what was, on the whole, a good tour.

The first New Zealand Test gave England a bit of a jolt, but at the close the home team were fighting to save themselves. Rain ruined the second Test, but the third was just plain dull–England required 204 to win in 270 minutes but never looked likely to approach the modest target. The team flew home via Hong Kong, where two one-day matches were played.

1965-66: M.C.C. to Australia and New Zealand and Ceylon and Hong Kong

1st Match: v Ceylon C.S. President's XI (Colombo) (One Day)   Oct 19.
M.C.C. 198-6 dec (R. W. Barber 64*) drew with President's XI 156-6.

2nd Match: v Ceylon (Colombo) (One Day)   Oct 20.
M.C.C. 127 (N. Chanmugam 5-26) drew with Ceylon 77-1 (R. Reid 54*): rain.

3rd Match: v Western Australia Country XI (Moora) (One Day)   Oct 27.
M.C.C. 232-7 dec (J. H. Edrich 66) beat W.A. Country XI 150 (J. McCormack 64, R. W. Barber 5-64) by 82 runs.

4th Match: v Western Australia (Perth)   Oct 29, 30, Nov 1, 2.
M.C.C. 447-5 dec (R. W. Barber 126, J. M. Parks 107*, M. J. K. Smith 67*) & 156-5 dec beat W. Australia 303-9 dec (P. C. Kelly 119, D. Chadwick 52*, I. J. Jones 5-59) & 291 (M. Vernon 118, P. C. Kelly 108*) by 9 runs.

5th Match: v Combined XI (Perth)   Nov 5, 6, 8, 9.
M.C.C. 379-5 dec (M. J. K. Smith 112*, J. H. Edrich 92, F. J. Titmus 69) & 205-4 dec (R. W. Barber 113) drew with Combined XI 231-5 dec (R. M. Cowper 89, P. J. P. Burge 52) & 322-6 (R. M. Cowper 122*, P. J. P. Burge 50).

6th Match: v South Australia (Adelaide)   Nov 12, 13, 15, 16.
S. Australia 103 & 364 (L. E. Favell 96, A. B. Shiell 83, L. Marks 67, B. N. Jarman 61) lost to M.C.C. 310 (G. Boycott 94, K. F. Barrington 69, J. H. Edrich 61, D. J. Sincock 5-113) & 158-4 (K. F. Barrington 51) by 6 wkts.

7th Match: v Victoria Country Districts (Hamilton) (One Day)   Nov 17.
Country Districts 167-6 (J. Kerr 50*) lost to M.C.C. 264 (J. M. Parks 75, W. E. Russell 50) by 6 wkts.

8th Match: v Victoria (Melbourne)   Nov 19, 20, 22, 23.
Victoria 384-7 dec (W. M. Lawry 153, D. R. Cowper 60*, G. D. Watson 59*, I. R. Redpath 53) & 165 (W. M. Lawry 61) beat M.C.C. 211 & 306 (K. F. Barrington 158, M. C. Cowdrey 52) by 32 runs.

9th Match: v Victoria Country XI (Euroa)   Nov 24.
No play due to rain.

10th Match: v New South Wales (Sydney)   Nov 26, 27, 29, 30.
M.C.C. 527-6 dec (W. E. Russell 93, R. W. Barber 90, F. J. Titmus 80*, M. C. Cowdrey 63, J. M. Parks 63, D. A. Allen 54*) & 2-1 beat New South Wales 288 (K. D. Walters 129, B. C. Booth 80) & 240 (G. Thomas 56, F. J. Titmus 5-45) by 9 wkts.

11th Match: v Queensland (Brisbane)   Dec 3, 4, 6, 7.
M.C.C. 452-5 dec (J. H. Edrich 133, W. E. Russell 110, K. F. Barrington 80*, F. J. Titmus 51*) & 123-2 dec (J. H. Edrich 68*) drew with Queensland 222 (P. J. P. Burge 114*) & 315-8 (T. R. Veivers 74, D. Bull 64, P. J. P. Burge 60).

12th Match: v Queensland Country Districts XI (Beaudesert) (One Day)   Dec 8.
Country Districts 152-7 dec (G. Jennings 77) lost to M.C.C. 159-3 by 7 wkts.

13th Match: v Australia (Brisbane)   Dec 10, 11, 13, 14, 15.
Australia 443-6 dec (W. M. Lawry 166, K. D. Walters 155, T. R. Veivers 56*) drew with England 280 (F. J. Titmus 60, K. F. Barrington 53, J.M. Parks 52, P. I. Philpott 5-90) & 186-3 (G. Boycott 59*).

14th Match: v Prime Minister's XI (Canberra) (One Day)   Dec 17.
Prime Minister's XI 288-7 dec (A. P. Sheahan 79, J. W. Burke 60) lost to M.C.C. 289-8 (G. Boycott 95, M. C. Cowdrey 52, M. J. K. Smith 51*) by 2 wkts.

15th Match: v N.S.W. Country Districts XI (Bathurst) (One Day) Dec 18
Country Districts XI 221 (K. F. Barrington 6-92) lost to M.C.C. 256-6 (J. H. Edrich 67*, K. F. Barrington 61) by 5 wkts.

16th Match: v N.S.W. Country Districts XI (Albury) (One Day)   Dec 20.
Country Districts XI 190 (G. Stacey 56*) lost to M.C.C. 253-5 (M. J. K. Smith 81, J. H. Edrich 76) by 5 wkts.

17th Match: v South Australia Country Districts XI (Mount Gambier) (One Day)   Dec 22
Country Districts 176-6 dec lost to M.C.C. 223-2 (G. Boycott 99, P. H. Parfitt 52*) by 8 wkts.

18th Match: v South Australia (Adelaide)   Dec 23, 24, 27, 28.
S. Australia 459-7 dec (A. B. Shiell 202*, B. N. Jarman 70, I. M. Chappell 59) & 253-4 dec (I. M. Chappell 113*) lost to M.C.C. 444 (J. T. Murray 110, M. J. K. Smith 108, B. R. Knight 79, K. F. Barrington 63) & 270-4 (R. W. Barber 77, M. C. Cowdrey 63*, G. Boycott 58) by 6 wkts.

19th Match: v Australia (Melbourne)   Dec 30, 31, Jan 1, 3, 4.
Australia 358 (R. M. Cowper 99, W. M. Lawry 88, R. B. Simpson 59) & 426 (P. J. P. Burge 120, K. D. Walters 115, W. M. Lawry 78, R. B. Simpson 67) drew with England 558 (J. H. Edrich 109, M. C. Cowdrey 104, K. F. Barrington 63, J. M. Parks 71, F. J. Titmus 56*, G. Boycott 51, G. D. McKenzie 5-134) & 5-0.

20th Match: v Australia (Sydney)   Jan 7, 8, 10, 11, 12.
England 488 (R. W. Barber 185, J. H. Edrich 103, G. Boycott 84, D. A. Allen 50*, N. J. Hawke 7-105) beat Australia 221 (R. M. Cowper 60, G. Thomas 51, D. J. Brown 5-63) & 174 by an inns & 93 runs.

21st Match: v Northern N.S.W. Country Districts XI (Newcastle)   Jan 14, 15, 17.
Country Districts XI 334 (C. Baker 101, K. M. Hill 98) & 126 lost to M.C.C. 449 (M. J. K. Smith 164, F. J. Titmus 114) & 13-0 by 10 wkts.

22nd Match: v Tasmania (Launceston)   Jan 19, 20, 21.
M.C.C. 371-9 dec (M. J. K. Smith 96, J. M. Parks 91, M. C. Cowdrey 63) & 289-7 (M. C. Cowdrey 108, J. M. Parks 58, B. R. Knight 51*) drew with Tasmania 322 (B. Richardson 112, B. Patterson 67*).

23rd Match: v Combined XI (Hobart)   Jan 22, 24, 25.
Combined XI 199 (R. M. Cowper 53, F. J. Titmus 6-65) & 271-1 (R. M. Cowper 143*, W. M. Lawry 126*) drew with M.C.C. 471-9 dec (G. Boycott 156, J. T. Murray 83, M. C. Cowdrey 70, K. Hooper 5-106).

24th Match: v Australia (Adelaide)   Jan 28, 29, 31, Feb 1.
England 241 (K. F. Barrington 60, G. D. McKenzie 6-48) & 266 (K. F. Barrington 102, F. J. Titmus 53, N. J. N. Hawke 5-54) lost to Australia 516 (R. B. Simpson 225, W. M. Lawry 119, I. J. Jones 6-118) by an inns & 9 runs.

25th Match: v New South Wales (Sydney)   Feb 4, 5, 7, 8.
New South Wales 488 (G. Thomas 129, R. B. Simpson 123, K. D. Walters 57) drew with M.C.C. 329 (P. H. Parfitt 87) & 472-6 (W. E. Russell 101*, B. R. Knight 94, G. Boycott 77, R. W. Barber 75, M. J. K. Smith 64).

26th Match: v Australia (Melbourne)   Feb 11, 12, 14, 15, 16.
England 485-9 dec (K. F. Barrington 115, J. M. Parks 89, J. H. Edrich 85, M. C. Cowdrey 79) & 69-3 drew with Australia 543-8 dec (R. M. Cowper 307, W. M. Lawry 108, K. D. Walters 60).

27th Match: v President's XI (Wellington)   Feb 19, 21, 22.
President's XI 237 (R. W. Morgan 72*, M. J. F. Shrimpton 58, D. A. Allen 5-96) & 188-7 drew with M.C.C. 359-6 dec (P. H. Parfitt 121, M. J. K. Smith 78, G. Boycott 51).

28th Match: v New Zealand (Christchurch)   Feb 25, 26, 28, March 1.
England 342 (D. A. Allen 88, P. H. Parfitt 54, M. J. K. Smith 54) & 201-5 dec (M. J. K. Smith 87) drew with New Zealand 347 (B. E. Congdon 104, R. C. Motz 58, E. C. Petrie 55) & 48-8.

29th Match: v New Zealand (Dunedin)   March 4, 5, 7, 8.
New Zealand 192 (R. C. Motz 57) & 147-9 drew with England 254-8 dec (M. C. Cowdrey 89*, J. T. Murray 50).

30th Match: v New Zealand (Auckland)   March 11, 12, 14, 15.
New Zealand 296 (B. W. Sinclair 114, B. E. Congdon 64, D. A. Allen 5-123) & 129 drew with England 222 (M. C. Cowdrey 59, W. E. Russell 56) & 159-4.

31st Match: v President's XI (Hong Kong) (One Day)   March 18.
M.C.C. 149-7 (C. Metcalfe 5-41): rain stopped play.

32nd Match: v Hong Kong (Kowloon) (One Day)   March 19.
M.C.C. 266-6 dec (G. Boycott 108, W. E. Russell 59) beat Hong Kong 193 (D. Coffey 88) by 73 runs.

1965-66: M.C.C. to Ceylon, Australia and New Zealand

Batting Averages

	M	I	NO	R	HS	Avge	100	c/s
K. F. Barrington (Surrey)	11	17	3	946	158	67.57	3	10
F. J. Titmus (Middx)	10	12	4	528	80*	66.00	0	7
J. M. Parks (Sussex)	12	18	6	771	107*	64.25	1	32/6
M. C. Cowdrey (Kent)	16	26	6	1076	108	53.80	2	12
R. W. Barber (Warks)	13	22	2	1001	185	50.05	3	10
M. J. K. Smith (Warks)	17	28	5	1079	112*	46.91	2	28
W. E. Russell (Middx)	12	20	4	709	110	44.31	2	7
J. H. Edrich (Surrey)	16	25	1	1060	133	44.16	3	6
B. R. Knight (Essex)	9	13	3	426	94	42.60	0	6
G. Boycott (Yorks)	13	21	2	784	156	41.26	1	6
D. A. Allen (Gloucs)	15	15	6	285	88	31.66	0	9
J. T. Murray (Middx)	9	11	1	305	110	30.50	1	17/3
P. H. Parfitt (Middx)	12	21	2	565	121	29.73	1	12
D. J. Brown (Warks)	11	13	1	157	44	13.08	0	1
K. Higgs (Lancs)	14	10	6	38	12*	9.50	0	5
I. J. Jones (Glam)	14	10	2	30	16	3.75	0	4
J. D. F. Larter (Northts)	5	3	0	7	4	2.33	0	4

Bowling Averages

	Balls	M	R	W	Avge	BB	5i
W. E. Russell	56	1	36	3	12.00	3-20	0
K. F. Barrington	260	1	149	6	24.83	4-24	0
K. Higgs	3279	100	1214	44	27.39	4-5	0
D. J. Brown	2134	49	1026	35	29.31	5-63	1
I. J. Jones	3093	74	1473	48	30.68	6-118	2
F. J. Titmus	3363	90	1109	36	30.81	6-65	2
D. A. Allen	4546	186	1594	47	33.91	5-96	2
J. D. F. Larter	794	12	411	12	34.25	4-49	0
B. R. Knight	1728	55	658	19	34.63	4-84	0
P. H. Parfitt	662	20	325	7	46.42	2-5	0
G. Boycott	594	25	285	4	71.25	2-32	0
R. W. Barber	1409	8	873	10	87.30	2-33	0

Also bowled: M. C. Cowdrey 8-0-7-0; J. H. Edrich 6-0-6-0; J. T. Murray 24-0-19-0; J. M. Parks 48-4-17-1; M. J. K. Smith 24-0-9-0.

Above *A vociferous Australian appeal for leg before wicket against England skipper Mike Smith in the first Test of the 1965-66 Australian tour at Brisbane. Bob Cowper and Wally Grout seem confident but the verdict was no.*

Below *Bob Barber out at last. A tired Barber bowled by Neil Hawke after scoring 185 in the third Test at Sydney, an innings which was the basis of an innings victory for the tourists.*

The main problem, which was forecast by the critics, was the fitness of the fast bowlers. In the event Larter spent most of his time recovering from strains, Brown was also injury prone and B. R. Knight (Essex) was in fact flown in to make good the party just before the first Test. The third fast man, Jones, improved as the tour progressed, but his habit of running on to the wicket was frowned on by the umpires and he was actually barred from further bowling in one match. Higgs, also, suffered illness which lost him many opportunities.

Boycott and Barber prospered as opening partners to some extent, but Boycott had the unfortunate habit of making the bowling look twice what it was. Barrington and Edrich both did well, as did Cowdrey. Parks should have been played just as a batsman, since he was worth a place in the Test side, but his keeping left something to be desired.

Smith refused to give Barber's leg spin a proper chance and this left the slow bowling very poor, since Titmus was right out of sorts.

For Australia Simpson and Lawry were absolute reliability and Walters was very promising. Hawke and McKenzie, the two principal bowlers, both suffered injuries which was inconsiderate, since Australia had no replacements.

1965-66: champions Worcestershire go to Jamaica

Sponsored by Carreras of Jamaica Ltd, Worcestershire, the 1965 County Champions, made a short tour of Jamaica in the spring of 1966. Unfortunately all the matches were drawn, as they were arranged for two days only, except for the one first-class game. The team flew to Jamaica via New York and the first game commenced on 18 March on the West Indies Sugar Company ground, but rain cut into the match.

In the first-class game, Sobers captained the local side and hit a scintillating century to save his side from defeat.

The touring party was D. Kenyon (capt), M. J. Horton, R. G. A. Headley, B. L. d'Oliveira, D. W. Richardson, J. A.

Ormrod, R. Booth, D. N. F. Slade, B. M. Brain, L. J. Coldwell, J. A. Flavell, N. Gifford. T. W. Graveney had to stand down at the last minute owing to his wife's illness.

1966-67: first M.C.C. under-25 tour goes to Pakistan

The side which M.C.C. sent to Pakistan in 1966-67 was a new experiment for English cricket, in that selection was confined to players under 25. In format the programme followed that of the 1963-64 tour to India, with a heavy list of fixtures crammed into a few weeks. This imposed a severe strain on cricketers unused to living in Pakistan.

The team was J. M. Brearley (Middx) (capt), D. J. Brown (Warwicks) (vice-capt), R. N. Abberley (Warwicks), D. L. Amiss (Warwicks), G. G. Arnold (Surrey), M. Bissex (Gloucs), K. W. R. Fletcher (Essex), R. N. S. Hobbs (Essex), R. A. Hutton (Yorks), A. P. E. Knott (Kent), J. A. Ormrod (Worcs), P. I. Pocock (Surrey), D. L. Underwood (Kent) and A. R. Windows (Gloucs) with L. E. G. Ames as manager.

Playing their opening match at Hyderabad, the M.C.C. began with a win against Southern Zone. Brown bowled splendidly and Brearley and Amiss carried the batting. Victory was also achieved in the second game, but Abberley, who hit 92, damaged a finger and as he would be unable to play in the next few weeks was flown home, M. A. Buss taking his place.

The 'First Test' at Lahore was a high-scoring draw. Pakistan made little effort to make runs, Mushtaq taking 323 minutes over his hundred, whilst Majid spent 190 minutes over reaching fifty. Fletcher batted well and relatively quickly for M.C.C., but there was never even a remote possibility of a definite outcome to the game, after Pakistan's first innings had been declared closed at 429 for 6.

The match against Northern Zone was noteworthy for Brearley's triple century – M.C.C. hit 514 for 4 on the first day in 5½ hours play and in terms of speed both the total and Brearley's 312 not out were new records in Pakistan. Hobbs, Hutton and Fletcher then bowled the opposition out twice to provide an innings victory. The next game produced another win with a hundred from Amiss, but some of the M.C.C. batsmen were unable to fathom Intikhab Alam, the young leg-spinner who later played many years with Surrey.

Brearley hit a double century in the 'Second Test', but his chief partner Amiss was lucky to reach three figures, being dropped several times. The match was interrupted by rain and though Brearley enforced the follow on and Mushtaq was injured, Asif Iqbal hit a marvellous hundred to save the match for Pakistan.

The 'Third Test' followed immediately. The M.C.C. were hit by illness and injury and not at their best. Pakistan gained a first innings lead of 37, but three run outs in their second innings together with a series of bumpers meant that they were unable to capitalise on their advantage and M.C.C. were set 255 in 220 minutes. Brearley decided not to attempt to win and the game was drawn.

Brearley, Amiss and Fletcher all batted well on the tour – England made a great discovery in Knott, and Hobbs and Pocock showed much promise in the spin department, so the tour was certainly successful from England's future. For Pakistan Asif was a great captain and Majid a most promising bat. Wasim Bari as a wicket-keeper batsman also impressed.

1966-67: Arabs tour Barbados

A strong side of Arabs made a seven-match tour of Barbados in January 1967. The party consisted of A. C. D. Ingleby-Mackenzie (Hants) (capt), C. A. Fry (Northants), A. H. Barker (Oxford U), H. C. Blofeld (Cambridge U), A. R. Duff (Worcs), G. P. S. Delisle (Middx), I. R. Lomax, S. G. Metcalfe (Oxford U),

1st Match: v Pickwick (Kensington Oval)   Jan 7.
Arabs 227-9 dec (S. G. Metcalfe 73, A. R. Duff 56*) beat Pickwick 178 (A. Taylor 65) by 49 runs.

2nd Match: v E. De C. Weekes' XI (Kensington Oval)   Jan 8.
E. De C. Weekes' XI 114 (J. D. Piachaud 5-40) & 104-5 lost to Arabs 239 (H. C. Blofeld 50) by 8 wkts.

3rd Match: v Combined Barbados Schools (Harrison College)   Jan 10, 11.
Schools 180 (J. D. Piachaud 6-56) & 156-9 dec drew with Arabs 198 (A. H. Barker 65) & 66-7.

4th Match: v Lodge School Past & Present (St John)   Jan 12.
Arabs 225-9 dec (G. P. S. Delisle 62) lost to Lodge School 260-8 (G. Hutchinson 82, A. Bethell 67) by 5 wkts.

5th Match: v Carlton-Maple (Black Rock)   Jan 13.
Arabs 136 (G. Sealy 5-37) lost to Carlton-Maple 182-9 (C. Burnham 60) by 5 wkts.

6th Match: v Wanderers (Bridgetown)   Jan 15.
Wanderers 191 (J. D. Piachaud 5-60) beat Arabs 80 (R. Edwards 7-33) by 111 runs.

7th Match: v Police (Queen's Park)   Jan 16.
Police 206-7 dec lost to Arabs 220-7 (C. A. Fry 67) by 3 wkts.

8th Match: v Empire-Spartan (Queen's Park)   Jan 18.
Arabs 78 (A. Howard 5-26) lost to Empire-Spartan 91-7 by 4 wkts.

9th Match: v President's XI (Kensington Oval)   Jan 20, 21, 22.
Arabs 97-9 dec & 143 beat President's XI 133 (J. D. Piachaud 6-45) & 81 (K. E. Walters 7-27) by 26 runs.

J. D. Piachaud (Hants), P. D. Hill-Wood, S. H. Parker-Bowles, D. Perrett, P. Wigan and K. E. Walters (Barbados). The last-named played due to some last minute withdrawals from the original side.

The outstanding player of the tour was Piachaud and his off-breaks captured 38 wickets at 12.7 each. Metcalfe was the most successful bat, though Duff also played well. Ingleby-Mackenzie was taken ill and missed three games.

The major match of the tour was the three-day game against a President's XI, which included Gordon Greenidge, P. D. Lashley and other West Indian cricketers of note. Rain badly affected the wicket and the Arabs won a low scoring match by 26 runs.

1967: M.C.C. visit North America for Canadian Centenniel

On 21 July 1967 the M.C.C. side left London for Canada to help celebrate the Canadian Centenniel Year. The team was D. R. W. Silk (Somerset) (capt), R. A. Gale (Middx), R. C. Kerslake (Somerset), D. Bennett (Middx), J. P. Fellows-Smith (Northants), G. N. S. Ridley (Kent), E. A. Clark (Middx), J. D. Piachaud (Kent), D. J. Mordaunt (Sussex), A. R. Duff (Worcs), R. Aldridge, C. J. Saunders (Oxford U), A. E. Moss (Middx) and the old West Indian batsman, Everton Weekes.

The most serious cricket was played in the first ten days in Ottawa, when six one-day games were followed by the 'Test Match' against Canada. The spin of Piachaud and Ridley proved too much for the home side in this match and a century from Gale together with 99 by Fellows-Smith produced an innings victory for the tourists.

After visiting the West Coast of Canada the side went, via Toronto, to the United States for five matches and had a hard fight in the match against Staten Island, but most of the games were more in the nature of exhibition matches and no defeats were met.

Bennett had an outstanding tour with the bat and all the bowlers returned good figures, Weekes played some innings reminiscent of his best days. In addition the old West Indian Test player acted as wicket keeper when injury early on the tour meant that Saunders was forced to miss some of the matches. Bennett easily topped the batting averages whilst Moss was the leading bowler.

1967: M.C.C. to North America

1st Match: v Manitoba (Ottawa)   July 22.
M.C.C. 223-6 dec (R. A. Gale 103, J. P. Fellows-Smith 52*) beat Manitoba 36 by 187 runs.

2nd Match: v Ontario (Ottawa)   July 23.
M.C.C. 178-7 dec drew with Ontario 98-7.

3rd Match: v British Columbia (Ottawa)   July 24.
M.C.C. 200-5 dec (D. Bennett 69*, R. C. Kerslake 69) beat British Columbia 53 (G. N. S. Ridley 5-15) by 147 runs.

4th Match: v Saskatchewan (Ottawa)   July 25.
M.C.C. 203-4 dec (D. J. Mordaunt 72, R. A. Gale 64) beat Saskatchewan 74 (J. D. Piachaud 5-32) by 129 runs.

5th Match: v Quebec (Ottawa)   July 26.
Quebec 55 lost to M.C.C. 56-2 by 8 wkts.

6th Match: v Alberta (Ottawa)   July 27.
M.C.C. 185-7 dec (D. R. W. Silk 67) beat Alberta 58 by 127 runs.

7th Match: v Canada (Ottawa)   July 29, 30, 31.
Canada 161 (V. K. Taylor 50, J. D. Piachaud 5-22) & 172 (J. D. Piachaud 8-86) lost to M.C.C. 355 (R. A. Gale 102, J. P. Fellows-Smith 99, D. Bennett 51) by an inns & 22 runs.

8th Match: v Saskatchewan (Regina)   Aug 5.
M.C.C. 178-5 dec beat Saskatchewan 58 by 120 runs.

9th Match: v Alberta (Edmonton)   Aug 7.
Alberta 92 lost to M.C.C. 94-1 (E. D. Weekes 54*) by 9 wkts.

10th Match: v British Columbia Mainland League (Vancouver)   Aug 10.
B.C. Mainland League 51 (D. J. Mordaunt 5-11) lost to M.C.C. 52-0 by 10 wkts.

11th Match: v British Columbia Mainland League (Vancouver)   Aug 11.
M.C.C. 215-6 dec (D. Bennett 117*) beat B.C. Mainland League 82 by 133 runs.

12th Match: v British Columbia C.A. (Vancouver)   Aug 12.
M.C.C. 209-7 dec (R. A. Gale 112) beat British Columbia C.A. 137 by 72 runs.

13th Match: v Victoria (Vancouver)   Aug 13.
M.C.C. 233-6 dec (G. N. S. Ridley 82, R. C. Kerslake 58) beat Victoria 115 (D. J. Mordaunt 6-36) by 118 runs.

14th Match: v Quebec C.A. (Montreal)   Aug 18.
M.C.C. 189-1 dec (R. A. Gale 112*, D. R. W. Silk 51) drew with Quebec C.A. 32-1.

15th Match: v Quebec C.A. (Montreal)   Aug 19.
Quebec C.A. 158 (E. Braithwaite 56, J. D. Piachaud 5-63) lost to M.C.C. 162-6 (R. A. Gale 56) by 4 wkts.

16th Match: v Hamilton & District League (Toronto)   Aug 20.
M.C.C. 177-7 dec (D. Bennett 61, E. A. Clark 52) beat Hamilton 86 (A. E. Moss 5-6) by 91 runs.

17th Match: v South Ontario C.A. (London)   Aug 23.
M.C.C. 216-3 dec (D. Bennett 103*, E. A. Clark 66) beat South Ontario 77 (A. R. Duff 5-33) by 139 runs.

18th Match: v J. Benson's XI (Toronto)   Aug 25.
M.C.C. 155-5 dec beat J. Benson's XI 60 by 95 runs.

19th Match: v Toronto (Toronto)   Aug 26.
M.C.C. 240-3 dec (E. A. Clark 90, E. D. Weekes 53*) beat Toronto 128 by 112 runs.

20th Match: v Toronto & District C.C. (Toronto)   Aug 27.
Toronto 10-1: rain stopped play.

21st Match: v British Commonwealth in Washington (Washington)   Aug 30.
M.C.C. 182-7 dec (D. Bennett 71) beat British Commonwealth 115 (J. D. Piachaud 5-5) by 67 runs.

22nd Match: v U.S.C.A. Southern Zone (Washington)   Aug 31.
M.C.C. 177-5 dec (G. N. S. Ridley 66, E. A. Clark 50) beat Southern Zone 34 (A. E. Moss 5-9, J. D. Piachaud 5-10) by 143 runs.

23rd Match: v Philadelphia C.C. (Philadelphia)   Sept 2.
M.C.C. 211-6 dec (D. J. Mordaunt 59*, E. A. Clark 59) beat Philadelphia 77 by 134 runs.

24th Match: v Staten Island C.C. (Staten Island)   Sept 3.
M.C.C. 184-9 dec (L. Mullings 5-32) drew with Staten Island 125-8.

25th Match: v New York Inter-state League (New York)   Sept 4.
M.C.C. 140-8 dec beat New York League 53 (A. E. Moss 6-14) by 87 runs.

1967-68: England win despite another riot in the West Indies

On the eve of the final Test against Pakistan at the Oval in August 1967, Brian Close, the England captain for all six home Tests of that summer, was censured for alleged unfair play, whilst leading Yorkshire against Warwickshire. This led to him being sacked as captain of the M.C.C. team to West Indies – an appointment which had been made by the selectors some time previously. The controversy divided cricket followers into two camps and was described as 'one of the unhappiest ten days in the game's history'. Close's crime was that of 'time-wasting' on the final afternoon of the Warwickshire match to prevent Yorkshire being defeated.

Above *The M.C.C. party for the West Indies in 1967-68 at London Airport. From the front: manager L. E. G. Ames, A. P. E. Knott, R. N. S. Hobbs, M. C. Cowdrey (captain), B. L. d'Oliveira, F. J. Titmus (behind bat), J. H. Edrich (pointing), T. W. Graveney, D. J. Brown, J. M. Parks, C. Milburn, P. I. Pocock, K. F. Barrington, G. Boycott, J. A. Snow, K. Higgs, I. J. Jones.*

Left *The fifth Test in the 1967-68 tour of the West Indies. Tom Graveney is out after turning a ball from Lance Gibbs which ricochetted off Gary Sobers (right) to be caught be wicket-keeper Murray.*

Close's replacement as captain was Colin Cowdrey, who had therefore at last been promoted to the captaincy, after years as vice-captain, in most unpleasant circumstances.

The full touring party was M. C. Cowdrey (Kent) (capt), F. J. Titmus (Middx) (vice-capt), K. F. Barrington (Surrey), G. Boycott (Yorks), D. J. Brown (Warwicks), B. L. d'Oliveira (Worcs), J. H. Edrich (Surrey), T. W. Graveney (Worcs), K. Higgs (Lancs), R. N. S. Hobbs (Essex), I. J. Jones (Glamorgan), A. P. E. Knott (Kent), C. Milburn (Northants), J. M. Parks (Sussex), P. I. Pocock (Surrey), J. A. Snow (Sussex) and

L. E. G. Ames as manager. Aside from the absence of Close, the main criticism was the absence of Lock and Underwood and the fact that Brown was preferred to Arnold. In passing it should be mentioned that M. J. K. Smith had announced his retirement and was not in the running for the captaincy.

The tour opened in Barbados and after a Colts game a high scoring match against the island side was played. The team then went straight on to Trinidad and were outplayed by the locals, being lucky to draw the game. The first Test was held at Port of Spain where England's solid batting hit 568 – Barrington and Graveney

1967-68: M.C.C. to West Indies

1st Match: v Barbados Colts (Bridgetown)   Dec 30, Jan 1.
M.C.C. 199-6 dec (A. P. E. Knott 69, F. J. Titmus 63*) & 63-5 drew with Colts 290-4 dec (G. A. Greenidge 116*).

2nd Match: v President's XI (Bridgetown)   Jan 3, 4, 5, 6.
President's XI 435-9 dec (C. A. Davis 158*, G. S. Camacho 85, D. L. Murray 63, K. F. Barrington 5-99) & 116-1 dec (R. C. Fredericks 64*) drew with M.C.C. 365 (M. C. Cowdrey 139, G. Boycott 135) & 94-2 (K. F. Barrington 53*).

3rd Match: v Trinidad (Port of Spain)   Jan 9, 10, 11, 12.
Trinidad 321 (R. de Souza 86, C. A. Davis 68) & 204-3 dec (M. C. Carew 90*, C. A. Davis 62) drew with M.C.C. 207 (W. V. Rodriguez 6-51) & 188-6 (J. H. Edrich 67).

4th Match: v Trinidad Colts (Point-a-Pierre)   Jan 15, 16.
M.C.C. 400-6 dec (C. Milburn 139, J. M. Parks 67) drew with Colts 121 (R. N. S. Hobbs 6-59) & 119-4.

5th Match: v West Indies (Port of Spain)   Jan 19, 20, 22, 23, 24.
England 568 (K. F. Barrington 143, T. W. Graveney 118, M. C. Cowdrey 72, G. Boycott 68, C. C. Griffith 5-69) drew with West Indies 363 (C. H. Lloyd 118, R. B. Kanhai 85) & 243-8 (B. F. Butcher 52).

6th Match: v Jamaica Colts (Montego Bay)   Jan 27, 29.
M.C.C. 116 (W. Taylor 5-34) & 71-1 (J. H. Edrich 53*) drew with Colts 216 (L. Dyer 64, R. N. S. Hobbs 7-97).

7th Match: v Jamaica (Kingston)   Jan 31, Feb 1, 2, 3.
M.C.C. 135 (B. Wellington 6-23) & 343-6 dec (M. C. Cowdrey 107, J. H. Edrich 98, B. L. d'Oliveira 68*) beat Jamaica 98 (J. A. Snow 5-36) & 206 by 174 runs.

8th Match: v West Indies (Kingston)   Feb 8, 9, 10, 12, 13.
England 376 (M. C. Cowdrey 101, J. H. Edrich 96, K. F. Barrington 63) & 68-8 drew with West Indies 143 (J. A. Snow 7-49) & 391-9 dec (G. St. A. Sobers 113*, S. M. Nurse 73).

9th Match: v Leeward Islands (Antigua)   Feb 15, 16, 17.
Leeward Is 144 & 323-8 dec (L. Sergeant 127, E. Gilbert 58*) drew with M.C.C. 362-4 dec (G. Boycott 165, K. F. Barrington 100*) & 8-0.

10th Match: v Barbados (Bridgetown)   Feb 22, 23, 24, 26.
M.C.C. 578-5 dec (G. Boycott 243, J. H. Edrich 73, K. F. Barrington 69*, C. Milburn 68, B. L. d'Oliveira 66) drew with Barbados 276 (S. M. Nurse 144, P. I. Pocock 5-84) & 161-5 (M. R. Bynoe 64*, G. St. A. Sobers 56).

11th Match: v West Indies (Bridgetown)   Feb 29, March 1, 2, 4, 5.
West Indies 348 (B. F. Butcher 86, G. St. A. Sobers 68, G. S. Camacho 57, J. A. Snow 5-86) & 284-6 (C. H. Lloyd 113*, B. F. Butcher 60) drew with England 449 (J. H. Edrich 146, G. Boycott 90, T. W. Graveney 55, B. L. d'Oliveira 51).

12th Match: v Windward Islands (St Lucia)   March 8, 9, 11.
M.C.C. 215 & 34-3 drew with Windward Is 165 (I. Shillingford 69, R. N. S. Hobbs 5-50).

13th Match: v West Indies (Port of Spain)   March 14, 15, 16, 18, 19.
West Indies 526-7 dec (R. B. Kanhai 153, S. M. Nurse 136, G. S. Camacho 87) & 92-2 dec lost to England 404 (M. C. Cowdrey 148, A. P. E. Knott 69*, G. Boycott 62, B. F. Butcher 5-34) & 215-3 (G. Boycott 80*, M. C. Cowdrey 71) by 7 wkts.

14th Match: v Guyana (Georgetown)   March 21, 22, 23.
Guyana 163 (C. H. Lloyd 63) & 160 (R. C. Fredericks 57, P. I. Pocock 6-57) lost to M.C.C. 207 (G. Boycott 60) & 119-0 (J. H. Edrich 60*, G. Boycott 50*) by 10 wkts.

15th Match: v Guyana Colts (Georgetown) (One Day)   March 25.
Colts 162-7 dec (G. A. R. Lock 5-36) lost to M.C.C. 183-4 (K. F. Barrington 58) by 6 wkts.

16th Match: v West Indies (Georgetown)   March 28, 29, 30, April 1, 2, 3.
West Indies 414 (G. St. A. Sobers 152, R. B. Kanhai 150) & 264 (G. St. A. Sobers 95*, J. A. Snow 6-60) drew with England 371 (G. Boycott 116, G. A. R. Lock 89, M. C. Cowdrey 59) & 206-9 (M. C. Cowdrey 82, A. P. E. Knott 73*, L. R. Gibbs 6-60).

1967-68: M.C.C. to the West Indies

Batting Averages

	M	I	NO	R	HS	Avge	100	c/s
A. P. E. Knott (Kent)	7	10	7	267	73*	89.00	0	17/3
G. Boycott (Yorks)	11	16	2	1154	243	82.42	4	2
M. C. Cowdrey (Kent)	9	15	1	871	148	62.21	4	11
J. H. Edrich (Surrey)	10	17	1	739	146	46.18	1	5
K. F. Barrington (Surrey)	11	16	3	591	143	45.46	2	6
B. L. d'Oliveira (Worcs)	11	16	6	401	68*	40.10	0	5
T. W. Graveney (Worcs)	11	17	2	389	118	25.93	1	17
G. A. R. Lock (Leics)	3	4	0	98	89	24.50	0	2
C. Milburn (Norths)	6	9	0	186	68	20.66	0	7
K. Higgs (Lancs)	6	5	0	91	42	18.20	0	2
D. J. Brown (Warks)	6	8	1	108	41	15.42	0	2
R. N. S. Hobbs (Essex)	5	4	0	46	40	11.50	0	3
I. J. Jones (Glam)	9	9	5	43	21	10.75	0	3
F. J. Titmus (Middx)	5	6	0	60	19	10.00	0	2
J. M. Parks (Sussex)	8	10	0	99	42	9.90	0	15
J. A. Snow (Sussex)	7	7	0	51	37	7.28	0	1
P. I. Pocock (Surrey)	7	7	2	27	13	5.40	0	7

Bowling Averages

	O	M	R	W	Avge	BB	5i
R. N. S. Hobbs	107.4	21	333	19	17.52	5-50	1
J. A. Snow	271.1	64	739	37	19.97	7-49	4
K. Higgs	167	41	361	15	24.06	4-40	0
P. I. Pocock	273	89	654	22	29.72	6-57	2
I. J. Jones	299.2	54	920	25	36.80	3-27	0
D. J. Brown	204	39	595	16	37.18	3-27	0
G. A. R. Lock	97	18	274	7	39.14	3-62	0
K. F. Barrington	193	33	636	13	48.92	5-99	1
B. L. d'Oliveira	226	65	542	11	49.27	2-14	0
F. J. Titmus	164.4	50	420	8	52.50	3-93	0

Also bowled: G. Boycott 13.3-5-27-2; T. W. Graveney 4-2-3-0; C. Milburn 3-2-7-0; M. C. Cowdrey 1-0-1-0.

West Indies had all the best of the fifth Test. Kanhai and Sobers hit centuries and England had Lock to thank for reaching a satisfactory total. The spin bowler batted 150 minutes to make 89, his highest score in first-class cricket. On the final day, England needed 308 to win, but collapsed to 41 for 5 against the spin bowling of Gibbs. All seemed lost, but Cowdrey and Knott shared in a partnership of 127 that saved the game, England having one wicket to fall when the stumps were drawn.

The tour was a huge success from England's viewpoint and from the viewpoint of diplomacy, since several problems which might have got out of hand were kept in perspective. England returned home undefeated.

Cowdrey and Boycott took the honours in the batting and Snow was the leading bowler—England now had a fast bowler who was better than his West Indian counterpart and the home side were therefore reluctant to indulge in a bumper war.

The sad note in the tour was the injury to Titmus, who lost four toes in a boating accident shortly before the third Test. Lock was flown in as a replacement, being dispatched from Western Australia, where he was wintering.

For the West Indies, Hall and Griffiths, the famous fast bowlers, were no longer to be feared and the bowling revolved around Sobers and Gibbs. The most promising of the younger element was a bespectacled left-hander—Clive Lloyd.

---

made hundreds. West Indies however had to rely on Lloyd and were unable to avoid the follow on. In the final session of play Sobers and Hall managed to save the side from an innings defeat.

Jamaica was the scene of M.C.C.'s first victory, when on a difficult wicket Snow shattered the Jamaican batting in their first innings and just managed to bring M.C.C. a win in extra time by taking the final wicket when the tailenders proved troublesome.

England had all the best of the second Test. Cowdrey batted in splendid form and assisted by Edrich and Barrington gave England a substantial first innings total, which looked larger when Snow put the West Indies batting to rout with figures of 7 for 49. West Indies followed on. Again the batting failed and the score stood at 204 for 5 when the umpire gave Butcher out caught at the wicket. This correct decision was not acceptable to the crowd and a bottle-throwing riot commenced. This upset the English players and West Indies, through Sobers, saved the match. The third Test also ended in a draw. Although West Indies batted first, England still achieved a first innings lead, with Edrich and Boycott giving the side an opening partnership of 172, but Lloyd hit a hundred in the West Indian second innings and there was no hope of a definite finish.

A fatal declaration by Sobers, made on the strength of some good bowling in the first innings by Butcher, gave England victory with three minutes to spare in the fourth Test.

1967-68: International Eleven tour Africa and Asia

Though entitled an International Eleven, the side which toured parts of Africa and Asia in the early months of 1968 was composed entirely of English County cricketers, so presumably the title was describing the extent of the tour rather than its individuals. The team, managed by J. Lister, was M. J. Stewart (Surrey) (capt), D. L. Amiss (Warwicks), G. G. Arnold (Surrey), J. Birkinshaw (Leics), M. H. Denness (Kent), K. W. R. Fletcher (Essex), G. Goonesena (Notts), A. W. Greig (Sussex), Khalid Ibadulla (Warwicks), H. Latchman (Middx), H. J. Rhodes (Derbys), K. G. Suttle (Sussex), R. W. Tolchard (Leics) and D. L. Underwood (Kent).

The party arrived back in England on 10 April. The most impressive young player on the tour was R. W. Tolchard, the wicket-keeper.

1967-68: champions Warwickshire visit Kenya and Uganda

The Warwickshire county cricketers, complete with a plane load of supporters, toured East Africa in the autumn of 1967, playing eight matches. The team was M. J. K. Smith (capt), T. W. Cartwright, D. L. Amiss, J. A. Jameson, Khalid Ibadulla, R. N. Abberley, A. C. Smith, R. B. Edmonds, L. R. Gibbs, D. J. Brown and J. M. Allan.

The most important match was against an Invitation Eleven at Mombasa. Warwickshire obtained a large lead on the first innings, but rain and a not out innings of 86 by R. D. Patel saved the local side. The two other three-day matches were against Uganda and Kenya. In both these games rain prevented a completion.

C. S. Elliott, the old Derbyshire cricketer, travelled with the team as umpire.

1967-68: Warwickshire to Uganda and Kenya

1st Match: v Kampala C.C. (Kampala)   Sept 28.
Warwickshire 232-4 dec (J. A. Jameson 102) drew with Kampala C.C. 178-5 (Bowles 52, de Souza 52).

2nd Match: v African XI (Logogo Stadium)   Sept 29.
African XI 133-8 dec drew with Warwickshire 86-3.

3rd Match: v Uganda (Kampala)   Sept 30, Oct 1, 2.
Uganda 205 (Lawrence 67, Bhasker 66) drew with Warwickshire 342-6 (D. L. Amiss 126, T. W. Cartwright 93).*

4th Match: v Invitation XI (Eldoret)   Oct 4.
Warwickshire 216 (D. L. Amiss 67, M. J. K. Smith 57, Patel 6-61) beat Invitation XI 91 (R. B. Edmonds 5-21) by 125 runs.

5th Match: v Rift Valley (Nakuru)   Oct 6.
Warwickshire 233-6 dec (R. N. Abberley 85, D. L. Amiss 59) drew with Rift Valley 182-8.

6th Match: v Kenya Kongonis (Nairobi)   Oct 7, 8, 9.
Kongonis 156 (T. W. Cartwright 6-55) & 302 (Tongue 137, M. J. K. Smith 81) drew with Warwickshire 199 (D. L. Amiss 61, R. N. Abberley 56) & 214-7 (J. A. Jameson 96, Khalid Ibadulla 74).

7th Match: v Invitation XI (Mombasa)   Oct 14, 15, 16.
Invitation XI 116 (Babla 56) & 206-8 (R. D. Patel 86, A. C. Smith 5-37) drew with Warwickshire 413-7 dec (J. A. Jameson 76, M. J. K. Smith 73, Khalid Ibadulla 62, T. W. Cartwright 57*, W. J. Stewart 52).*

8th Match: v Nyeri (Nyeri)   Oct 19.
Warwickshire 149-9 dec (M. J. K. Smith 54) beat Nyeri 107 by 42 runs.

9th Match: v Kenya (Nairobi)   Oct 21, 22, 23.
Warwickshire 368-9 dec (T. W. Cartwright 123, Khalid Ibadulla 79, M. J. K. Smith 63) & 58-1 drew with Kenya 255-9 dec (Virendra 82, Jawahirshah 74, A. C. Smith 5-66).

1968-69: the d'Oliveira affair— then riots in Pakistan

The d'Oliveira affair was the dominant feature of the sporting press in the last weeks of the 1968 summer. The M.C.C. were programmed to tour South Africa in the winter of 1968-69 and announced the following team: M. C. Cowdrey (Kent) (capt), T. W. Graveney (Gloucs) (vice-capt), K. F. Barrington (Surrey), G. Boycott (Yorks), D. J. Brown (Warwicks), T. W. Cartwright (Warwicks), R. M. H. Cottam (Hants), J. H. Edrich (Surrey), K. W. R. Fletcher (Essex), A. P. E. Knott (Kent), J. T. Murray (Middx), R. M. Prideaux (Northants), P. I. Pocock (Surrey), J. A. Snow (Sussex), D. L. Underwood (Kent). The main criticism was the absence of Milburn. Cartwright was pronounced unfit after the selection was made public and d'Oliveira

---

1967-68: International XI to Africa and Asia

1st Match: v Sir Ernest Beoku-Betts' XI (Freetown)   Jan 19, 20.
Beoku-Betts XI 63 (G. Goonesena 6-23) & 102 lost to International XI 379-5 dec (D. L. Amiss 120, M. H. Denness 110, K. Ibadulla 55) by an inns & 214 runs.

2nd Match: v Sierra Leone Selection Trust Ltd (Yengema) (One Day)   Jan 21.
Sierra Leone 50 (H. C. Latchman 5-9) lost to International XI 51-1 by 9 wkts.

3rd Match: v University of Sierra Leone (Njala) (One Day)   Jan 24.
International XI 275-5 dec (M. J. Stewart 73, M. H. Denness 63, A. W. Greig 63) beat University 29 by 246 runs.

4th Match: v Sierra Leone (Freetown)   Jan 26, 27.
Sierra Leone 117 (M. Turay 53) & 100 (A. W. Greig 6-36) lost to International XI 335-8 dec (D. L. Amiss 118) by an inns & 118 runs.

5th Match: v Uganda (Kampala)   Feb 3, 4, 5.
Uganda 228 (Davda 55, Mushtaq 53) & 115 lost to International XI 325 (K. Ibadulla 88, J. Birkenshaw 69, K. W. R. Fletcher 67, R. W. Tolchard 54) & 22-2 by 8 wkts.

6th Match: v Rift Valley Invitation XI (Nakura) (One Day)   Feb 7.
International XI 275-8 dec (M. H. Denness 107) drew with Rift Valley 147-8.

7th Match: v East African Conference XI (Nairobi)   Feb 9, 10, 11.
International XI 306 (J. Birkenshaw 97, D. Pringle 5-97) & 187 (K. W. R. Fletcher 50, J. Birkenshaw 50, D. Pringle 5-67) drew with East African XI 231 (P. Upendra 79) & 206-9 (V. Noordin 56).

8th Match: v Pakistan Board of Control XI (Karachi)   Feb 16, 17, 18, 19.
International XI 182 (K. G. Suttle 79, Saeed Ahmed 5-39) & 351-7 dec (K. W. R. Fletcher 108, J. Birkenshaw 59, A. W. Greig 54) beat Board of Control XI 246 (Javed Burki 58) & 244 (Saeed Ahmed 97, Mohammed Ilyas 50) by 43 runs.*

9th Match: v Indian XI (Bombay)   Feb 23, 24, 25, 26.
International XI 255 (D. L. Amiss 109) & 314-7 dec (K. W. R. Fletcher 107, K. G. Suttle 66, K. Ibadulla 55, S. Venkataraghavan 5-80) beat Indian XI 138 & 249 (V. Bhosle 69) by 182 runs.*

10th Match: v Chief Minister's XI (Madras)   Feb 29, March 1, 2, 3.
International XI 360 (K. Ibadulla 107, A. W. Greig 106, D. L. Amiss 67, V. V. Kumar 5-113) & 205-5 dec beat Chief Minister's XI 164 (D. L. Underwood 6-41) & 111 by 290 runs.

11th Match: v Ceylon President's XI (Colombo)   March 5, 6, 7.
International XI 179 (K. G. Suttle 63, Abu Fuard 6-31) & 155-2 dec (K. W. R. Fletcher 82, K. G. Suttle 59) beat President's XI 42 (D. L. Underwood 8-10) & 98 (D. L. Underwood 7-33) by 194 runs.*

12th Match: v Ceylon Government Service C.A. (Kandy)   March 9, 10.
Ceylon G.S.C.A. 200 (D. P. de Silva 50) drew with International XI 322-9 (H. C. Latchman 62*, H. J. Rhodes 54, T. B. Kehelgamuwa 6-67).*

13th Match: v Singapore (Singapore)   March 17, 18.
International XI 307-7 dec (M. J. Stewart 66, G. Goohesena 55) beat Singapore 67 (D. L. Underwood 7-30) & 35 by an inns & 205 runs.

14th Match: v Combined Services (Singapore) (One Day)   March 19.
International XI 190 beat Combined Services 81 by 109 runs.

15th Match: v Malacca C.A. (Malacca)   March 21, 22.
Malacca C.A. 67 & 23-7 drew with International XI 211 (M. H. Denness 57).

16th Match: v Negri Sembilan H.H. Invitation XI (Seremban)   March 23, 24.
Invitation XI 85 (D. L. Underwood 8-19) drew with International XI 122-1 (K. G. Suttle 54).*

17th Match: v M.C.A. Patron's XI (Penang)   March 26, 27.
Patron's XI 101 & 41 (G. G. Arnold 6-7) lost to International XI 235-3 dec (K. W. R. Fletcher 121) by inns & 93 runs.*

18th Match: v M.C.A. President's XI (Kuala Lumpur)   March 30, 31.
President's XI 54 (D. L. Underwood 6-12) & 83 (D. L. Underwood 5-28) lost to International XI 225 (Dr A. E. Delilkan 7-71) by an inns & 88 runs.

19th Match: v Royal Bangkok Sports Club (Bangkok) (One Day)   April 3.
International XI 267-5 dec (D. L. Amiss 82, M. J. Stewart 51) drew with Royal Bangkok S.C. 117-7.

20th Match: v Hong Kong C.A. President's XI (Hong Kong) (One Day)   April 5.
International XI 233-8 dec (K. G. Suttle 61, M. J. Stewart 57, K. Ibadulla 56) beat President's XI 74 (H. J. Rhodes 5-16) by 159 runs.

21st Match: v Hong Kong League XI (Kowloon)   April 6, 7.
International XI 353 (K. Ibadulla 70, M. H. Denness 52, J. Murphy 5-65) beat Hong Kong League XI 66 & 73 by an inns & 214 runs.

The tour began in Sierra Leone, which was new ground for an English touring side of any importance. The four matches played there did not tax the tourists too much, for though cricket seemed to flourish in Freetown the standard was not very high. In Kenya however the tourists had to struggle to prevent defeat at the hands of an East African XI, and the last pair survived for 12 minutes to save the game. In Pakistan Fletcher hit a century which enabled a declaration to take place, setting the local side 288 to make at 52 per hour. The spin of Goonesena however proved too much for them and victory was obtained by 43 runs.

In India another victory was obtained after Stewart declared at Bombay and again at Madras. Brilliant bowling by Underwood, who used a damp wicket to its best advantage, gave the tourists an easy win in Colombo. The team travelled on to Singapore and Malaysia, before stops in Thailand and finally Hong Kong.

1968-69: M.C.C. to Ceylon and Pakistan

1968-69: M.C.C. to Ceylon and Pakistan

1st Match: v Ceylon Board XI (Colombo) (Limited Over) Jan 25.
M.C.C. 236-6 lost to Board XI 234-7 (R. Fernando 58, B. Reid 57) on faster scoring rate.

2nd Match: v Ceylon Board XI (Colombo) (Limited Over) Jan 26.
M.C.C. 192-5 (J. H. Edrich 51) beat Board's XI 174 (H. I. Fernando 65) by 18 runs.

3rd Match: v Central Province XI (Kandy) (Limited Over) Jan 28.
M.C.C. 246-6 (R. M. Prideaux 69, J. T. Murray 55*) beat Central Province 185 (S. Rajaratnam 50) by 61 runs.

4th Match: v Ceylon (Colombo) Jan 30, 31, Feb 1.
Ceylon 283-9 dec (A. Tennekoon 101) & 118-0 (R. Fernando 59*, B. Reid 50*) drew with M.C.C. 406-4 dec (J. H. Edrich 177, T. W. Graveney 106, K. W. R. Fletcher 81).

5th Match: v Board of Control XI (Bahawalpur) Feb 5, 6, 7.
Board XI 262-7 dec (Salah-ud-Din 77, Aftab Gul 50) & 173-8 dec (Aftab Gul 55, D. L. Underwood 6-40) drew with M.C.C. 218-8 dec (A. P. E. Knott 80) & 126-4.

6th Match: v Central Zone (Lyallpur) Feb 8, 9, 10.
Central Zone 198-7 dec (Mohammad Ilyas 55) & 170-8 dec (Hanif Mohammad 50, R. M. H. Cottam 5-35) drew with M.C.C. 198-6 dec (B. L. d'Oliveira 102*) & 61-0.

7th Match: v West Pakistan Governor's XI (Sahiwal) Feb 15, 16, 17.
Governor's XI 87-1: rain ended play.

8th Match: v Pakistan (Lahore) Feb 21, 22, 23, 24.
England 306 (M. C. Cowdrey 100, J. H. Edrich 54, A. P. E. Knott 52) & 225-9 dec (K. W. R. Fletcher 83) drew with Pakistan 209 (Asif Iqbal 70) & 203-5 (M. J. Khan 68).

9th Match: v Pakistan (Dacca) Feb 28, March 1, 2, 3.
Pakistan 246 (Mushtaq Mohammad 52) & 195-6 dec (D. L. Underwood 5-94) drew with England 274 (B. L. d'Oliveira 114*) & 33-0.

10th Match: v Pakistan (Karachi) March 6, 7, 8.
England 502-7 (C. Milburn 139, T. W. Graveney 105, A. P. E. Knott 96*): match terminated due to riots.

1968-69: M.C.C. to Ceylon and Pakistan

Batting Averages

	M	I	NO	R	HS	Avge	100	c/s
C. Milburn (Northts)	1	1	0	139	139	139.00	1	0
B. L. d'Oliveira (Worcs)	6	6	3	281	114*	93.66	2	7
A. P. E. Knott (Kent)	7	6	2	273	96*	68.25	0	7/5
J. H. Edrich (Surrey)	6	8	1	377	177	53.85	1	0
T. W. Graveney (Worcs)	6	6	0	317	106	52.83	2	1
K. W. R. Fletcher (Essex)	6	8	1	298	83	42.57	0	6
D. J. Brown (Warks)	6	4	2	80	44*	40.00	0	1
M. C. Cowdrey (Kent)	7	8	1	228	100	32.57	1	2
R. M. H. Cottam (Hants)	4	3	2	20	12*	20.00	0	3
R. M. Prideaux (Northts)	6	9	2	109	25*	15.57	0	2
J. A. Snow (Sussex)	6	4	2	27	9*	13.50	0	1
D. L. Underwood (Kent)	6	4	0	35	22	8.75	0	1
J. T. Murray (Middx)	3	3	0	16	8	5.33	0	4/1
P. I. Pocock (Surrey)	5	4	0	15	12	3.75	0	4
R. N. S. Hobbs (Essex)	2			did not bat				1

Bowling Averages

	O	M	R	W	Avge	BB	5i
D. L. Underwood	189	71	380	20	19.00	6-40	2
R. M. H. Cottam	158.3	44	371	16	23.18	5-35	1
B. L. d'Oliveira	62	16	133	5	26.60	3-9	0
J. A. Snow	110	24	294	10	29.40	4-70	0
D. J. Brown	117	27	304	8	38.00	3-43	0
P. I. Pocock	127	32	355	8	44.37	2-61	0

Also bowled: M. C. Cowdrey 1-0-6-0; R. M. Prideaux 3-2-9-0; T. W. Graveney 6-0-11-0; K. W. R. Fletcher 21-2-102-1; R. N. S. Hobbs 20-3-71-2.

was chosen to replace him. The South African Government stated that they could not accept d'Oliveira, a Cape Coloured, as a member of the touring party and the M.C.C. therefore cancelled the tour. The South African Government blamed 'political forces' for the selection of d'Oliveira on the grounds that Cartwright was picked as a bowler and had been replaced by d'Oliveira, who was primarily a batsman.

It was proposed that the M.C.C. should make a tour of India, Pakistan and Ceylon, but on financial grounds the visit to India had to be cancelled – Mrs Gandhi refused to release the £20,000 foreign exchange that the tour required.

The party eventually left London on 21 January 1969. The team showed two more alterations to the original, Barrington and Boycott being replaced by C. Milburn (Northants) and R. N. S. Hobbs (Essex). The four initial matches were played in Ceylon, the major one being the three-day game against Ceylon, which was drawn on a placid wicket. The contrast between Ceylon and Pakistan was alarming. The latter country was in a state of political upheaval. The first Test in Lahore was played in or around a continuous riot. Somehow Cowdrey managed to score a century amid the general confusion and but for Asif, Pakistan would have been in a very parlous condition – he hit 70 out of 206. Cowdrey set Pakistan 300 minutes to make 323 but they fell well short. The match over-rate was deplorable.

Going straight to Dacca for the second Test, the M.C.C. found the city's law and order had completely broken down. Police and military had withdrawn leaving the city in the hands of the left-wing students, who tended to use the match as a focal point for their grievances. As can be imagined this did not make for a very pleasant atmosphere for any cricket match. Snow and Brown dismissed Pakistan for 246 and then a great innings from d'Oliveira saved England. On a difficult pitch Pakistan were in danger of collapsing in their second innings, but Mushtaq, Saeed and Majid held fast and the game was drawn. The third Test began three days later in Karachi, but before the England first innings could be completed rioting ended the match and the tourists hurriedly left for England. The credit for surviving so long in such chaotic conditions belongs to Ames, the manager, who through all the problems remained calm.

The M.C.C. party leave London airport in January 1969 for the tour of Ceylon and Pakistan. This tour was arranged after the cancellation of the South African tour due to the inclusion in the party of Basil d'Oliveira (seen at the foot of the steps behind captain Cowdrey). In the event the tour of Pakistan was truncated by rioting.

1968-69: weak side tours South Africa

R. J. McAlpine captained the following side which made a 3½-week tour of South Africa in February and March 1969: R. A. Gale (Middx), R. V. C. Robins (Middx), M. O. C. Sturt (Middx), A. E. Moss (Middx), I. R. Lomax (Wilts), E. J. Lane-Fox (Oxon), A. R. B. Neame (M.C.C.), S. G. Metcalfe (Oxford U), P. L. B. Stoddart (Bucks), B. C. G. Wilenkin (Cambridge U), T. B. L. Coghlan (Cambridge U), E. Arundel (M.C.C.), J. Hurn (Wilts), N. Style and D. C. Wing.

The first two games were in Salisbury and in both the tourists were lucky to get away with draws. The Rhodesian Currie Cup players took the English bowling apart in both games.

There followed five matches in Johannesburg, with the tourists decisively beaten in three. Moss provided the team with its first victory at White River in N.E. Transvaal, when he returned the curious bowling analysis of 19-12-15-2.

Of the two games played in Swaziland, one was rained off entirely and the other drawn in an interesting state.

In the final match Robins took 5 for 56, whilst Lomax hit 59 and victory was obtained by 3 wickets. Syd Buller accompanied the side as umpire.

1968-69: R. J. McAlpine's Team to South Africa

1st Match: v President's XI (Salisbury)   Feb 16.
President's XI 333-6 dec (S. Robertson 108, A. J. Pithy 92, K. C. Bland 42) drew with McAlpine's XI 184-8 (S. G. Metcalfe 60).

2nd Match: v Stragglers C.C. (Salisbury)   Feb 17.
McAlpine's XI 247-7 dec (R. A. Gale 101, E. Lane Fox 59, M. Shacklock 5-97) lost to Stragglers C.C. 251-3 (J. Clarke 127*, P. R. Carlstein 64) by 7 wkts.

3rd Match: v Staggerers C.C. (Johannesburg)   Feb 19, 20.
Staggerers 182 (B. Pfaff 77) & 170-6 dec beat McAlpine's XI 155-8 dec & 103 by 94 runs.

4th Match: v Country Club (Johannesburg)   Feb 22.
McAlpine's XI 177-9 dec lost to Country Club 180-4 by 6 wkts.

5th Match: v Vagabonds (Johannesburg)   Feb 23.
McAlpine's XI 203-9 dec (N. Style 71) drew with Vagabonds 171-9 (W. Kerr 73).

6th Match: v Wanderers (Johannesburg)   Feb 24.
McAlpine's XI 169 (E. Lane Fox 67) lost to Wanderers 173-5 (W. Kerr 62) by 5 wkts.

7th Match: v Wilfred Isaac's XI (Johannesburg)   Feb 25.
Isaac's XI 168-4 dec drew with McAlpine's XI 112-8 (E. Lane Fox 60).

8th Match: v White River (White River)   Feb 26.
McAlpine's XI 127 (B. C. G. Wilenkin 74) beat White River 88 (A. R. B. Neame 7-51) by 39 runs.

9th Match: v Swaziland (Usutu)   March 1.
McAlpine's XI 202-5 dec (R. A. Gale 91) drew with Swaziland 169-6.

10th Match: v Swaziland (Usutu)   March 2.
No play due to rain.

11th Match: v Hilton College (Hilton)   March 4.
McAlpine's XI 218-2 dec (I. R. Lomax 116*, B. C. G. Wilenkin 73) beat Hilton College 100 (R. V. C. Robins 7-45) by 118 runs.

12th Match: v Grasshoppers (Pietermaritzburg)   March 5.
Grasshoppers 215-7 dec (L. Lund 82) lost to McAlpine's XI 217-5 (S. G. Metcalfe 84, A. R. B. Neame 71) by 5 wkts.

13th Match: v Kookaburras (Mount Egdecombe)   March 7.
McAlpine's XI 95 lost to Kookaburras 101-2 (A. McLeod 53*) by 8 wkts.

14th Match: v Crickets (Kloof)   March 8.
Crickets 146 (A. R. B. Neame 5-35) drew with McAlpine's XI 128-9 (R. A. Gale 50).

15th Match: v Inanda (Johannesburg)   March 9.
Inanda 161 (R. V. C. Robins 5-56) lost to McAlpine's XI 163-7 (I. R. Lomax 59) by 3 wkts.

1969-70: Duke of Norfolk's team to the West Indies

Sponsored partly by Gillette Industries, the Duke of Norfolk managed a team to the West Indies in February and March 1970. The full side was M. C. Cowdrey (Kent) (capt), J. Birkenshaw (Leics), the Earl of Cottenham, M. H. Denness (Kent), M. J. Edwards (Surrey), A. W. Greig (Sussex), M. G. Griffith (Sussex), R. N. S. Hobbs (Essex), B. Leadbeater (Yorks), C. M. Old (Yorks), P. J. Sharpe (Yorks), D. L. Underwood (Kent), A. Ward (Derbyshire). The Duke of Norfolk accompanied the side as did E. W. Swanton and C. S. Elliott (umpire).

The team flew straight to Barbados and after a few days acclimatisation, went on to St Lucia for a series of three matches. The major game, a three-day fixture with the Windward Islands, was rained off on the last day but saw Cowdrey in fine form and Underwood return figures of 18-10-19-3. A crowd of some 6,000 turned out in Dominica for the next game, which the visitors won by 8 runs. Going on to Trinidad via St Vincent, the tourists were beaten by Trinidad, for whom Inshan Ali took 12 for 153. The final leg of the tour was in Barbados, where the island fielded a young side and lost by an innings. The tour was a success and particularly appreciated in the various Windward Islands.

1969-70: Duke of Norfolk's XI to West Indies

1st Match: v St Lucia (St Lucia) (One Day)   Feb 25.
Norfolk's XI 185-4 dec (A. W. Greig 55*, B. Leadbeater 53*) drew with St Lucia 98-7.

2nd Match: v St Lucia (St Lucia) (Limited Over)   Feb 26.
Norfolk's XI 163-7 beat St Lucia 131-8 by 32 runs.

3rd Match: v Windward Islands (St Lucia)   Feb 27, 28, March 1.
Norfolk's XI 220 (M. C. Cowdrey 81, P. J. Sharpe 64) & 116-1 (M. H. Denness 53*) drew with Windward Is 193 (H. Williams 54, R. N. S. Hobbs 6-82).

4th Match: v Dominica (Roseau) (Limited Over)   March 2.
Norfolk's XI 191 beat Dominica 183 (I. Shillingford 57, G. C. Shillingford 53) by 8 runs.

5th Match: v St Vincent (St Vincent) (Limited Over)   March 3.
Norfolk's XI 251-8 (M. H. Denness 58) beat St Vincent 106.

6th Match: v Trinidad (Port of Spain)   March 6, 7, 8, 9.
Norfolk's XI 150 (Inshan Ali 8-58) & 297 (J. Birkenshaw 64, M. C. Cowdrey 57*) lost to Trinidad 252 (H. Ramoutar 56) & 199-2 (C. A. Davis 96*, O. Durity 60) by 8 wkts.

7th Match: v Tobago (Shaw Park) (Limited Over)   March 11.
Norfolk's XI 206 (M. H. Denness 83, M. J. Edwards 55) beat Tobago 106 by 100 runs.

8th Match: v Barbados (Bridgetown)   March 14, 15, 16.
Barbados 208 (D. A. J. Holford 67, N. Clarke 51) & 192 lost to Norfolk's XI 452 (P. J. Sharpe 84, M. C. Cowdrey 83, J. Birkenshaw 78, A. W. Greig 65) by an inns & 52 runs.

9th Match: v Barbados (Bridgetown) (Limited Over)   March 18.
Norfolk's XI 172-8 (B. Leadbetter 80*, A. W. Greig 54) lost to Barbados 175-2 (P. D. Lashley 102*) by 8 wkts.

1969-70: champions Glamorgan tour Bermuda and West Indies

To celebrate the winning of the 1969 County Championship, Glamorgan, sponsored by Rizla Ltd, made a six-match tour of the West Indies in April 1970. The team was managed by P. B. Clift, the county coach, and the party consisted of A. R. Lewis (capt), A. Jones, R. C. Davis, K. J. Lyons, B. A. Davis, P. M. Walker, E. W. Jones, M. A. Nash, A. E. Cordle, D. L. Williams, D. J. Shepherd, G. C. Kingston, O. S. Wheatley and D. W. Lewis. The County found the West Indian opposition stronger than

---

1969-70: Glamorgan to West Indies

1st Match: v St George's C.C. (Bermuda)   April 1, 2.
St George's 163 (W. Pitcher 55) and 175 beat Glamorgan 142 (W. Pitcher 5-28) & 164 by 32 runs.

2nd Match: v St Kitts (Basseterre)   April 4, 5, 6.
Glamorgan 279 (A. Jones 86, R. C. Davis 61) & 158-3 dec (B. A. Davis 88*) drew with St Kitts 181 (P. M. Walker 5-43) & 220-9 (L. Sargeant 105).

3rd Match: v Windward Islands (Roseau)   April 7, 8, 9.
Windward Is 302 (N. Phillip 96, T. M. Findlay 51) & 173-4 dec (V. Elwin 59) drew with Glamorgan 268-8 dec (E. W. Jones 64) & 125-3.

4th Match: v Grenada (St George's, Grenada)   April 11, 12.
Glamorgan 153-5 dec & 103-1 dec (A. Jones 53) drew with Grenada 152-7 dec & 88-8.

5th Match: v Trinidad Colts (Brechin Castle) (Limited Over)   April 15.
Glamorgan 156-7 beat Colts 131-9 by 25 runs.

6th Match: v Trinidad (Port of Spain)   April 17, 18, 19.
Glamorgan 272 (A. Jones 114, Inshan Ali 5-44) & 96 lost to Trinidad 242 & 127-5 by 5 wkts.

expected and the only victory came against the Colts in Trinidad – the attendances of the two matches played on this island were badly affected by the Black Power movement, which was causing much political unrest. As with the Duke of Norfolk's side, the left-arm spinner Inshan Ali worried the Welshmen, who were easily beaten by Trinidad. The other first-class match was drawn, though Phillip for the Windward Islands hit 96 very quick runs and E. W. Jones also batted well.

1969-70: M.C.C. tour Ceylon and Far East

It was intended to tour Uganda, Zambia and Kenya, but these three countries all took umbrage at the proposed visit of South Africa to England and cancelled the arrangements. The M.C.C. therefore, for the second successive winter, were forced to replan and the team were welcomed in Ceylon, Malaysia, Singapore, Thailand and Hong Kong instead. The tourists were A. R. Lewis (Glamorgan) (capt), A. C. Smith (Warwicks) (player-manager), G. G. Arnold (Surrey), W. Blenkiron (Warwicks), G. Boycott (Yorks), K. W. R. Fletcher (Essex), R. M. C. Gilliat (Hants), J. H. Hampshire (Yorks), A. Jones (Glamorgan), P. I. Pocock (Surrey), G. R. J. Roope (Surrey), D. J. Shepherd (Glamorgan), R. W. Taylor (Derbys), D. Wilson (Yorks) and J. S. Buller as umpire.

About 10,000 attended the first day of the opening match in Colombo and saw Ceylon take a first innings lead against the tourists, but a century by Alan Jones redressed the balance and Wilson's left-arm spin did the rest. The tourists combined coaching with playing in matches and found an unexpected enthusiasm for the game in Malaysia and Singapore. The team went to Bangkok, where the game was kept alive by a group of dedicated cricketers, and to Hong Kong.

The team flew back home after the final game on 15 March.

1969-70: M.C.C. to Ceylon and Far East

1st Match: v Ceylon (Colombo) Feb 20, 21, 22, 23.
M.C.C. 132 & 302-7 dec (A. Jones, Sahabandu 5-86) beat Ceylon 134 (D. Wilson 6-35) & 127 (D. Wilson 8-36) by 173 runs.

2nd Match: v Yang Di Pertuan Besar's XI (Seremban) Feb 26, 27.
M.C.C. 305-8 dec (J. H. Hampshire 67, R. M. C. Gilliat 66, G. Boycott 60, C. Navaratnam 5-90) drew with Besar's XI 110 & 163-7.

3rd Match: v Singapore (Singapore) Feb 28, March 1.
M.C.C. 315-3 dec (G. Boycott 149*, K. W. R. Fletcher 96*, A. Jones 67) beat Singapore 178 (W. Dougan 60) & 122 (D. Wilson 6-45) by 121 runs.

4th Match: v Malaysian President's XI (Ipoh) March 3, 4.
M.C.C. 272-6 dec (G. Boycott 147*, J. H. Hampshire 55*, A. Jones 53) & 25-1 dec beat President's XI 61 & 73 by 163 runs.

5th Match: v Malaysia (Kuala Lumpur) March 7, 8.
M.C.C. 345-4 dec (R. M. C. Gilliat 109, A. R. Lewis 74, G. Boycott 66*) & 110-2 dec (K. W. R. Fletcher 50*) beat Malaysia 102 & 113 by 240 runs.

6th Match: v Royal Bangkok Sports Club (Bangkok) March 11.
M.C.C. 223-1 dec (G. Boycott 116, A. Jones 102*) beat Royal Bangkok S.C. 52 (D. J. Shepherd 5-16) by 171 runs.

7th Match: v Hong Kong President's XI (Hong Kong) March 14.
M.C.C. 204 (D. Wilson 57) beat President's XI 140 (D. Wilson 6-58) by 64 runs.

8th Match: v Hong Kong (Kowloon) March 15.
M.C.C. 190-0 dec (A. Jones 104*, G. Boycott 79*) drew with Hong Kong 125-5.

1970-71: Illingworth's team regain the Ashes

Following the cancellation of the South African visit to England in the summer of 1970, a series was arranged against a Rest of the World Team. In so far as the M.C.C. proposed to visit Australia

in the winter of 1970-71, the major point in these matches was that Illingworth led the English side in place of Cowdrey, who had been injured. During the 1970 season the press, when not occupied with the South African 'Ban the Tour' news, concerned itself about the prospective captaincy of M.C.C. in Australia – the lobbies were divided between Cowdrey as captain and Illingworth as his number two, or vice-versa. The first announcement from Lord's however was that D. G. Clark would manage the side. Later the M.C.C. announced that Illingworth would be captain and the full team was: R. Illingworth (Leics) (capt), M. C. Cowdrey (Kent) (vice-capt), G. Boycott (Yorks), B. L. d'Oliveira (Worcs), J. H. Edrich (Surrey), K. W. R. Fletcher (Essex), J. H. Hampshire (Yorks), B. W. Luckhurst (Kent), P. Lever (Lancs), J. A. Snow (Sussex), K. Shuttleworth (Lancs), A. Ward (Derbys), D. Wilson (Yorks), D. L. Underwood (Kent), A. P. E. Knott (Kent) and R. W. Taylor (Derbys), with B. Thomas as assistant to D. G. Clark.

The critics questioned the absence of A. W. Greig, R. N. S. Hobbs and M. H. Denness, and were worried about the lack of good fielders.

The team flew from London on 18 October, but in view of complaints of 'jet-lag' by some recent tour managers, the first game did not commence until the 28 October, when a one-day affair was won by 10 wickets. The feature of the matches prior to the first Test was the inability of the tourists to dismiss the opposition cheaply. South Australia hit 649 for 9 declared, in the initial first-class match, but they were much aided by a double century from the South African Barry Richards. Against Victoria the M.C.C. collapsed in front of A. L. Thomson, a relatively unknown fast bowler, and then Victoria scored over 300 before declaring. New South Wales declared with 410 on the board, whilst Queensland hit 360. The M.C.C. attack was not helped by a foot injury to Ward, which ended the tour for him after the fifth match. R. G. D. Willis, the young Surrey fast bowler, was flown out as a replacement.

The team therefore began the first Test rather on the defensive. Australia batted first and with Stackpole making a double century the home team reached 433. England however batted with remarkable consistency to obtain a lead of 31 and Australia struggled in their second innings; in fact England might have forced a win if the over rate had not been so slow.

Western Australia, led by Lock, had all the best of a drawn match before the second Test, the first England had ever played

---

1970-71: M.C.C. to Australia and New Zealand

Batting Averages

	M	I	NO	R	HS	Avge	100	c/s
G. Boycott (Yorks)	12	22	6	1535	173	95.93	6	6
J. H. Edrich (Surrey)	14	25	5	1136	130	56.80	3	8
B. W. Luckhurst (Kent)	11	20	3	954	135	56.11	4	11
B. L. d'Oliveira (Worcs)	13	20	3	870	162*	51.17	4	6
A. P. E. Knott (Kent)	12	17	5	539	101	44.91	1	24/4
J. H. Hampshire (Yorks)	10	17	3	463	156*	33.07	1	6
R. Illingworth (Leics)	14	21	4	537	53	31.58	0	6
K. W. R. Fletcher (Essex)	12	21	1	602	80	30.10	0	10
M. C. Cowdrey (Kent)	11	18	1	511	101	30.05	1	3
J. A. Snow (Sussex)	10	10	1	150	38	16.66	0	2
R. W. Taylor (Derbys)	5	6	0	98	31	16.33	0	14/5
P. Lever (Lancs)	13	13	1	188	64	15.66	0	6
R. G. D. Willis (Surrey)	9	8	3	74	27	14.80	0	4
D. Wilson (Yorks)	6	3	0	35	19	11.66	0	3
K. Shuttleworth (Lancs)	9	10	2	88	24	11.00	0	3
A. Ward (Derbys)	2	3	1	15	8*	7.50	0	0
D. L. Underwood (Kent)	13	14	7	41	13*	5.85	0	11

Bowling Averages

	O	M	R	W	Avge	BB	5i
D. L. Underwood	422	110	1123	43	26.11	6-12	3
J. A. Snow	306.5	57	1021	38	26.86	7-40	2
R. G. D. Willis	182	29	738	23	32.08	4-81	0
K. Shuttleworth	188.5	23	662	17	38.94	5-47	1
P. Lever	311.2	48	951	23	41.34	4-17	0
A. Ward	38.5	3	166	4	41.50	2-25	0
M. C. Cowdrey	24	0	127	3	42.33	2-46	0
R. Illingworth	284	71	883	20	44.15	3-39	0
K. W. R. Fletcher	40.3	2	232	5	46.40	3-43	0
B. L. d'Oliveira	192	34	569	12	47.41	2-15	0
D. Wilson	120.7	19	406	8	50.75	3-32	0

Also bowled: G. Boycott 4.4-0-31-1; J. H. Hampshire 9-0-53-0; B. W. Luckhurst 2-0-6-0.

at Perth. This match, which saw a maiden hundred by Greg Chappell, was another draw. Illingworth set Australia 245 to make in 145 minutes on the final day and it was a challenge completely ignored by Lawry, who spent an hour making six runs.

Another match of declarations and ultimately a draw was played against South Australia, after which the tourists went to Tasmania before the third Test at Melbourne. Three days of almost continuous rain caused this to be the first Test in Australia between the two countries to be abandoned entirely due to the weather, but the Australian Board and the English officials in Australia agreed to play a one-day game on what should have been the last day of the Test and to reschedule the remaining fixtures to insert an additional Test.

The fourth Test at Sydney began four days after the hastily arranged one-day international. England batted first and after making a modest 332 went on to dominate the game completely. Snow bowled brilliantly, when no other fast bowler could get anything out of the wicket and Boycott batted in his best form to make the highest score in both England innings – 77 and 142 not out. Of the Australians only Lawry mastered the tourists' attack and with grim determination remained unbeaten after 255 minutes, seeing all ten wickets fall. England won by the large margin of 299 runs. Aside from the victory over Tasmania, it was the first first-class win of the tour.

Bad behaviour by the crowd marred the fifth Test, which was drawn in Australia's favour due to poor English catching, Cowdrey being the main culprit. Both Thomson and Snow bowled bouncers, but only the latter was warned by the umpires. Play on the last day was rather pointless, but made even more so by more unruly demonstrations by the spectators, who booed and slow hand-clapped. Luckhurst, who hit a century in England's first innings, broke a finger.

The sixth Test followed directly after the fifth and though Illingworth was in a position to enforce Australia to follow on, he did not do so as the pitch eased in the later stages of the match – the last day was pretty pointless. The seventh Test began after an interval of nine days and two one-day games. Australia gained an 80-run lead on first innings, but Snow was again warned against bowling bumpers. The crowd became restive and Illingworth actually led the England team off the field, only resuming when the umpires threatened to award the match to Australia by default. The English batting in the second innings improved greatly on the first and Australia needed 223 on a pitch which aided the bowlers. Stackpole put up a lone fight and England won by 62 runs, thus taking the series two matches to nil.

The tour ended with five matches in New Zealand, including two Tests, one of which was won by England and the other drawn.

Illingworth thoroughly deserved the success he achieved, for he welded the team into a very competent unit. England's bowling relied very much on Snow, and the batting laurels went to Boycott, Edrich and Luckhurst. Illingworth and d'Oliveira also had good tours, but Underwood should have done better in the Tests. Cowdrey was a shadow of his former self, the loss of the leadership seeming too much for him.

Australia had a poor time, only Lawry really living up to his reputation, though Lillee and O'Keeffe looked good prospects.

1970-71: M.C.C. to Australia and New Zealand

1st Match: v South Australia Country XI (Port Pirie)   Oct 28.
Country XI 146-9 dec (J. Kernahan 54*) lost to M.C.C. 148-0 (B. W. Luckhurst 82*, G. Boycott 64*) by 10 wkts.

2nd Match: v South Australia (Adelaide)   Oct 30, 31, Nov 1, 2.
M.C.C. 451-9 dec (G. Boycott 173, K. W. R. Fletcher 70, J. H. Edrich 63, J. H. Hampshire 52) & 235-4 (B. L. d'Oliveira 103*, K. W. R. Fletcher 80) drew with S. Australia 649-9 dec (B. A. Richards 224, I. M. Chappell 93, J. P. Causby 68, K. G. Cunningham 65, G. S. Chappell 57).

3rd Match: v Victoria Country XI (Horsham)   Nov 4.
Country XI 152-8 dec lost to M.C.C. 153-3 (J. H. Edrich 57) by 7 wkts.

4th Match: v Victoria (Melbourne)   Nov 6, 7, 8, 9.
M.C.C. 142 (A. L. Thomson 6-80) & 341 (M. C. Cowdrey 101) lost to Victoria 304-8 dec (A. P. Sheahan 71, I. R. Redpath 68) & 180-4 (A. P. Sheahan 58*, I. R. Redpath 57) by 6 wkts.

5th Match: v New South Wales (Sydney)   Nov 13, 14, 15, 16.
N.S.W. 410-5 dec (K. D. Walters 201*, G. R. Davies 57, K. J. O'Keeffe 55*, A. J. Turner 50) drew with M.C.C. 204 (K. J. O'Keeffe 6-69) & 325-1 (B. W. Luckhurst 135, G. Boycott 129*, K. W. R. Fletcher 51*).

6th Match: v Queensland Country XI (Warwick)   Nov 18.
Country XI 89 lost to M.C.C. 300 (B. L. d'Oliveira 105, M. C. Cowdrey 53) on first innings.

7th Match: v Queensland (Brisbane)   Nov 21, 22, 23, 24.
Queensland 360 (S. C. Trimble 177, R. F. Surti 83) drew with M.C.C. 418-4 (G. Boycott 124*, J. H. Edrich 120, K. W. R. Fletcher 77).

8th Match: v Queensland Country XI (Redlands Bay)   Nov 25.
Country XI 142 lost to M.C.C. 155-3 (R. Illingworth 52*) by 7 wkts.

9th Match: v Australia (Brisbane)   Nov 27, 28, 29, Dec 1, 2.
Australia 433 (K. R. Stackpole 207, K. D. Walters 112, J. A. Snow 6-114) & 214 (W. M. Lawry 84, K. Shuttleworth 5-47) drew with England 464 (J. H. Edrich 79, B. W. Luckhurst 74, A. P. E. Knott 73, B. L. d'Oliveira 57) & 39-1.

10th Match: v Western Australia (Perth)   Dec 5, 6, 7, 8.
W. Australia 257-5 dec (R. J. Inverarity 93, R. Edwards 56) & 285 (A. L. Mann 110) drew with M.C.C. 258-3 dec (G. Boycott 126, B. W. Luckhurst 111) & 256-6 (J. H. Edrich 70, B. W. Luckhurst 60).

11th Match: v Western Australia Country XI (Narrogin)   Dec 9.
Country XI 150-2 dec (T. Waldron 58*, P. Silinger 50) lost to M.C.C. 163-5 (K. W. R. Fletcher 66) by 5 wkts.

12th Match: v Australia (Perth)   Dec 11, 12, 13, 15, 16.
England 397 (B. W. Luckhurst 131, G. Boycott 70) & 287-6 dec (J. H. Edrich 115*, G. Boycott 50) drew with Australia 440 (I. R. Redpath 171, G. S. Chappell 108, I. M. Chappell 50) & 100-3.

13th Match: v South Australia (Adelaide)   Dec 18, 19, 20, 21.
S. Australia 297-2 dec (B. A. Richards 146, A. J. Woodcock 119*) & 338-7 dec (G. S. Chappell 102, K. G. Cunningham 60, A. J. Woodcock 52) drew with M.C.C. 238 (M. C. Cowdrey 57) & 336-8 (B. L. d'Oliveira 162*, G. Boycott 92).

14th Match: v Tasmania (Hobart)   Dec 23, 24, 26.
M.C.C. 316-4 dec (J. H. Hampshire 156*, J. H. Edrich 52) & 72-1 beat Tasmania 164 (P. Roberts 77) & 223 (K. Ibadulla 51) by 9 wkts.

15th Match: v Combined XI (Launceston)   Dec 27, 28, 29.
M.C.C. 184-4 (G. Boycott 74, M. C. Cowdrey 66) drew Combined XI did not bat: rain.

16th Match: v Australia (Melbourne)   Dec 31, Jan 1, 2.
No play due to rain.

17th Match: v Australians (Melbourne) (Limited Over)   Jan 5.
M.C.C. 190 (J. H. Edrich 82) lost to Australians 191-5 (I. M. Chappell 60) by 5 wkts.

18th Match: v New South Wales Country XI (Wagga Wagga)   Jan 7.
Country XI 117 lost to M.C.C. 241-4 (G. Boycott 76, B. W. Luckhurst 62) by 9 wkts.

19th Match: v Australia (Sydney)   Jan 9, 10, 12, 13, 14.
England 332 (G. Boycott 77, J. H. Edrich 55) & 319-5 dec (G. Boycott 142*, B. L. d'Oliveira 56, R. Illingworth 53) beat Australia 236 (I. R. Redpath 64, K. D. Walters 55) & 116 (W. M. Lawry 60*, J. A. Snow 7-40) by 299 runs.

20th Match: v Northern New South Wales (Newcastle)   Jan 16, 17, 18.
M.C.C. 355-6 dec (B. W. Luckhurst 124, K. W. R. Fletcher 122, R. Illingworth 55*) & 322-4 (J. H. Hampshire 122, M. C. Cowdrey 70) drew with Northern N.S.W. 171 (D. Wilson 7-62).

21st Match: v Australia (Melbourne)   Jan 21, 22, 23, 25, 26.
Australia 493-9 dec (I. M. Chappell 111, R. W. Marsh 92*, I. R. Redpath 72, W. M. Lawry 56, K. D. Walters 55) & 169-4 dec drew with England 392 (B. L. d'Oliveira 117, B. W. Luckhurst 109) & 161-0 (G. Boycott 76*, J. H. Edrich 74*).

22nd Match: v Australia (Adelaide)   Jan 29, 30, Feb 1, 2, 3.
England 470 (J. H. Edrich 130, K. W. R. Fletcher 80, G. Boycott 58, J. H. Hampshire 55, D. K. Lillee 5-84) & 233-4 dec (G. Boycott 119*) drew with Australia 235 (K. R. Stackpole 87) & 328-3 (K. R. Stackpole 136, I. M. Chappell 104).

23td Match: v Southern New South Wales (Canberra)   Feb 6.
No play due to rain.

24th Match: v Western Australia (Sydney) (Limited Over)   Feb 8.
M.C.C. 152 (B. L. d'Oliveira 54) drew with W. Australia 24-2.

25th Match: v New South Wales Country XI (Parkes)   Feb 9.
Country XI 116 (D. Wilson 5-50) lost to M.C.C. 184-7 (R. W. Taylor 77) by 7 wkts.

26th Match: v Australia (Sydney)   Feb 12, 13, 14, 16, 17.
England 184 & 302 (J. H. Edrich 57, J. H. Edrich 59) beat Australia 264 (G. S. Chappell 65, I. R. Redpath 59) & 160 (K. R. Stackpole 67) by 62 runs.

27th Match: v Wellington (Wellington) (Limited Over)   Feb 20.
Wellington 188 beat M.C.C. 165 by 23 runs.

28th Match: v Otago (Dunedin) (Limited Over)   Feb 21.
M.C.C. 167 beat Otago 144-7 by 23 runs.

29th Match: v New Zealand (Christchurch)   Feb 25, 26, 27, March 1.
New Zealand 65 (D. L. Underwood 6-12) & 254 (G. M. Turner 76, B. E. Congdon 55, D. L. Underwood 6-85) lost to England 231 (B. L. d'Oliveira 100) & 89-2 (J. H. Hampshire 51*) by 8 wkts.

30th Match: v Central Districts (Palmerston North) (Limited Over)   March 3.
Central Districts 208-6 lost to M.C.C. 209-6 (B. W. Luckhurst 85) by 4 wkts.

31st Match: v New Zealand (Auckland)   March 6, 7, 8, 9.
England 321 (A. P. E. Knott 101, P. Lever 64, B. L. d'Oliveira 58, M. C. Cowdrey 54, R. S. Cunis 6-76) & 237 (A. P. E. Knott 96) drew with New Zealand 313-7 dec (M. G. Burgess 104, G. M. Turner 65, G. T. Dowling 53, D. L. Underwood 5-108) & 40-0.

1971-72: Gloucestershire win 'Tests' in Zambia

The Gloucestershire County side at the invitation of the Zambia Cricket Union undertook a three-week tour of that country in October 1971. The team which flew from Heathrow on 5 October was A. S. Brown (capt), C. A. Milton, G. G. M. Wiltshire, D. R. Shepherd, J. Davey, J. H. Shackleton, J. C. Foat, J. P. Sullivan, R. B. Nicholls, Sadiq Mohammad, Zaheer Abbas and two Glamorgan players, D. J. Shepherd and R. C. Davis, together with G. W. Parker as manager.

The 'First Test' against Zambia began on 8 October and the local side hit up 355 in their first innings, but Milton, Zaheer and Davis all scored heavily to put Gloucester in the lead and Don Shepherd bowled the Zambians out cheaply in the second innings, in time to allow the tourists to win by 5 wickets. Unfortunately Brown was taken ill after this match and Don Shepherd led the team for the rest of the visit.

In the 'Second Test' two innings of note by Zaheer made certain of victory, whilst in the 'Third' Sadiq held the batting together with 124 out of a total of 250.

Cricket did not appear to be played in Zambian schools and was kept going by expatriates and Asians.

1971-72: Gloucestershire in Zambia

1st Match: v Zambia (Lusaka)   Oct 8, 9, 10.
Zambia 355 (B. Ellis 87, D. C. Patel 58) & 145 lost to Gloucs 335 (Zaheer Abbas 117, R. C. Davis 73, C. A. Milton 70) & 169-5 by 5 wkts.

2nd Match: v Livingstone (Bharat Grd) (Limited Over)   Oct 14.
Gloucs 238-4 (Zaheer Abbas 88, Sadiq Mohammad 67) drew with Livingstone 130-7.*

3rd Match: v Zambia (Kitwe)   Oct 16, 17, 18.
Zambia 123 (R. C. Davis 6-27) & 169 (R. C. Davis 5-62) lost to Gloucs 225-6 dec (Zaheer Abbas 60) & 68-2 (Zaheer Abbas 55) by 8 wkts.*

4th Match: v Copperbelt XI (Kitwe)   Oct 20, 21.
Gloucs 218 (J. C. Foat 64, R. B. Nicholls 55) & 204-2 dec drew with Copperbelt XI 196-9 dec (R. Goodchild 71) & 187-7.

5th Match: v Zambia (Lusaka)   Oct 23, 24, 25.
Zambia 203 & 122 lost to Gloucs 250 (Sadiq Mohammad 124, G. Rees 5-93, P. G. Nana 5-102) & 70-4 by 6 wkts.

1972-73: Kent lose one-day matches in West Indies

The John Player League Champions of 1972, Kent, were invited to tour the West Indies with the object of playing a series of one-day matches based on the John Player Rules.

The team flew from London on 4 January and after a single day's recovery period, were beaten by Jamaica by 33 runs. Boyce hit a splendid 72 in the return match the following day, but again Jamaica proved the winners.

Flying on to Trinidad, the county side beat the Under-25s, but failed against the full island side.

Barbados also beat Kent twice and the tour ended in Guyana where two more defeats were suffered.

The touring party was B. W. Luckhurst (capt), G. W. Johnson, R. B. Elms, D. A. Laycock, J. N. Graham, R. A. Woolmer, D. Nicholls, A. G. E. Ealham and J. N. Shepherd; B. Dudleston (Leics), K. D. Boyce (Essex) and J. M. Brearley (Middx) as guest players; and C. Lewis, county coach, L. E. G. Ames, county manager, and M. C. Cowdrey, who joined the side in Trinidad.

The games in Guyana and the smaller islands were watched by large crowds and in every way except the actual results the tour was successful. It was really expecting too much of the visitors to produce their best form against strong opposition in so short a time – the whole trip only lasted 18 days.

1972-73: Kent to West Indies

1st Match: v Jamaica (Kingston) (Limited Over)   Jan 6.
Jamaica 181-7 (M. L. C. Foster 67) beat Kent 149 by 32 runs.*

2nd Match: v Jamaica (Kingston) (Limited Over)   Jan 7.
Kent 193-9 (K. D. Boyce 72) lost to Jamaica 195-6 by 4 wkts.

3rd Match: v Trinidad Under 25 XI (Brechin Castle) (Limited Over)   Jan 9.
Kent 167 beat Under 25 XI 131 by 36 runs.

4th Match: v Trinidad (Port of Spain) (Limited Over)   Jan 11.
Kent 143 lost to Trinidad 144-6 by 4 wkts.

5th Match: v Tobago (Tobago) (Limited Over)   Jan 12.
Kent 182 beat Tobago 115 by 67 runs.

6th Match: v Barbados (Bridgetown) (Limited Over)   Jan 13.
Barbados 173-8 (G. A. Greenidge 97) beat Kent 160 by 13 runs.

7th Match: v Barbados (Bridgetown) (Limited Over)   Jan 14.
Barbados 169-8 beat Kent 132 by 37 runs.

8th Match: v St Lucia (St Lucia) (Limited Over)   Jan 15.
Kent 187 beat St Lucia 100 by 87 runs.

9th Match: v Antigua (Antigua) (Limited Over)   Jan 16.
Kent 235-6 (J. M. Brearley 82, K. D. Boyce 52) beat Antigua 205 (I. V. A. Richards 63, B. D. Julien 5-20) by 30 runs.*

10th Match: v Guyana (Berbice) (Limited Over)   Jan 18.
Guyana 197-9 beat Kent 160 (J. N. Shepherd 57) by 37 runs.*

11th Match: v Guyana (Georgetown) (Limited Over)   Jan 20.
Guyana 226-6 (A. I. Kallicharran 67, C. H. Lloyd 51) beat Kent 164-8 by 62 runs.

1972-73: D. H. Robins' tour of South Africa

The problems of flying straight from England and playing cricket against first-class players without any preliminary practice or warm-up games were quite apparent on this tour, in which the team organised by D. H. Robins, the old Warwickshire cricketer, played Eastern Province and Western Province in two first-class games within a week of arrival and lost both.

The full touring party was: D. J. Brown (Warwicks) (capt), C. T. Radley (Middx), J. T. Murray (Middx), R. G. D. Willis (Warwicks), F. C. Hayes (Lancs), M. J. Smith (Middx), J. H. Hampshire (Yorks), R. D. V. Knight (Gloucs), D. P. Hughes (Lancs), R. N. S. Hobbs (Essex), D. R. Turner (Hants), J. K.

1972-73: Derrick Robins' Team to South Africa

1st Match: v Eastern Province (Port Elizabeth)   Jan 1, 2, 3.
Robins XI 306-4 dec (C. T. Radley 125, M. J. Smith 116) & 135 (J. T. Murray 58, R. Hanley 6-34) lost to E. Province 218 (S. J. Bezuidenhout 54) & 224-4 (S. J. Bezuidenhout 97, C. P. Wilkins 58) by 6 wkts.

2nd Match: v Western Province (Cape Town)   Jan 5, 6, 8.
W. Province 371-2 dec (E. J. Barlow 147, O. J. A. Snyman 133, J. R. Cheetham 54) & 175-2 dec (O. J. A. Snyman 70, C. A. Gie 62*) beat Robins XI 234 (J. H. Hampshire 65, F. C. Hayes 50, M. H. Bowditch 5-31) & 191 (F. C. Hayes 59) by 121 runs.*

3rd Match: v O.F.S. & Griqualand West (Bloemfontein) (Limited Over)   Jan 10.
Robins XI 312-6 (J. H. Hampshire 105, D. R. Turner 88) beat Combined XI 269-7 (M. J. Doherty 68, S. D. Bruce 52) by 43 runs.*

4th Match: v Transvaal (Johannesburg)   Jan 12, 13, 14.
Robins XI 344-9 dec (M. J. Smith 113, F. C. Hayes 75) & 199-4 dec (C. T. Radley 102) drew with Transvaal 275-6 dec (A. Bacher 147, S. J. Cook 64) & 188-8.

5th Match: v Northern Transvaal (Pretoria) (Limited Over)   Jan 17.
Robins XI 241-9 (F. C. Hayes 66, M. J. Smith 53) beat N. Transvaal 220 (D. Lindsay 92) by 21 runs.

6th Match: v Natal (Durban)   Jan 19, 20, 21.
Natal 180-8 dec (R. G. D. Willis 6-26) & 227-8 dec (A. Bruyns 65, H. R. Fotheringham 61) lost to Robins XI 250-9 dec (M. J. Smith 62, C. T. Radley 59) & 160-6 (C. T. Radley 53) by 4 wkts.

7th Match: v Border (East London) (Limited Over)   Jan 24.
Robins XI 213 (J. H. Hampshire 67) beat Border 106 (R. N. S. Hobbs 5-28) by 107 runs.

8th Match: v Combined B Section XI (Pretoria)   Jan 26, 27, 28.
Robins XI 237 (C. T. Radley 80, J. T. Murray 64) & 200-5 dec (J. T. Murray 63, J. H. Hampshire 56*) drew with Combined XI 208-8 dec (A. A. During 66*, H. R. Fotheringham 51) & 85-4.*

9th Match: v Invitation XI (Johannesburg)   Feb 2, 3, 5, 6.
Invitation XI 387-9 dec (B. A. Richards 100, A. Bruyns 97, B. L. Irvine 53) beat Robins XI 118 & 152 by an inns & 117 runs.

10th Match: v Invitation XI (Johannesburg) (Limited Over)   Feb 6.
Robins XI 146 lost to Invitation XI 147-9 (M. J. Procter 58) by 1 wkt.

1972-73: D. H. Robins' Team to South Africa

Batting Averages

		M	I	NO	R	HS	Avge	100	c/s
C. T. Radley	(Middx)	6	12	0	554	125	46.16	2	7
J. T. Murray	(Middx)	5	8	1	245	64	35.00	0	14
R. G. D. Willis	(Warks)	5	5	3	69	34	34.50	0	2
F. C. Hayes	(Lancs)	6	11	2	304	75	33.77	0	1
M. J. Smith	(Middx)	6	12	0	380	116	31.66	2	1
J. H. Hampshire	(Yorks)	6	12	2	258	65	25.80	0	2
A. Long	(Surrey)	1	2	0	44	29	22.00	0	1
R. D. V. Knight	(Gloucs)	5	10	0	188	44	18.80	0	5
D. P. Hughes	(Lancs)	5	9	0	159	44	17.66	0	0
R. N. S. Hobbs	(Essex)	3	3	1	30	17*	15.00	0	3
D. R. Turner	(Hants)	3	5	0	70	24	14.00	0	0
J. K. Lever	(Essex)	5	8	3	39	13	7.80	0	2
A. S. Brown	(Gloucs)	2	4	0	29	18	7.25	0	1
P. J. Lewington	(Warks)	3	3	2	7	5*	7.00	0	1
D. J. Brown	(Warks)	3	4	0	13	8	3.25	0	1
R. D. Jackman	(Surrey)	1	2	0	5	5	2.50	0	1
P. Willey	(Northts)	1	1	0	2	2	2.00	0	0

Bowling Averages

	O	M	R	W	Avge	BB	5i
P. Willey	15	5	36	4	9.00	4-36	0
J. H. Hampshire	6	4	13	1	13.00	1-13	0
J. K. Lever	147	41	348	16	21.75	3-20	0
R. N. S. Hobbs	98.2	18	325	10	32.50	4-55	0
R. G. D. Willis	131.2	31	358	11	32.54	6-26	1
D. P. Hughes	103.1	27	393	10	39.30	3-34	0
D. J. Brown	68.4	16	209	4	52.25	2-45	0
A. S. Brown	44	6	176	3	58.66	2-72	0
R. D. Jackman	17	3	66	1	66.00	1-66	0
P. J. Lewington	76	13	279	4	69.75	2-56	0
R. D. V. Knight	59	12	194	2	97.00	1-14	0

1972-73: Oxford and Cambridge Universities to Malaysia and Singapore

1st Match: v Singapore C.C. (Singapore).
Oxbridge 268-8 dec (P. D. Johnson 67) beat Singapore C.C. 122 by 146 runs.

2nd Match: v Civil Service (Singapore).
Oxbridge 251-8 dec (A. K. C. Jones 79, H. K. Steele 50) beat Civil Service 69 (R. J. Hadley 5-21) by 182 runs.

3rd Match: v Singapore C.A. (Singapore).
Singapore C.A. 251-8 dec (Chaturvedi 82, Tessensohn 59) & 156-9 dec (Jaya 61) drew with Oxbirdge 182-5 dec (M. J. J. Faber 52) & 187-8 (P. Hodson 50).

4th Match: v ANZUK Forces (Singapore).
Oxbridge 241 (P. C. H. Jones 50, Casey 6-88) beat ANZUK Forces 115 by 126 runs.

5th Match: v Johore (Johore).
Oxbridge 244 (H. K. Steele 56, de Silva 5-72) & 152-2 dec (M. J. J. Faber 62, P. D. Johnson 55*) drew with Johore 157 & 154-6 (Toh Choo Beng 59).

6th Match: v Malacca (Malacca).
Malacca 78 (C. B. Hamblin 5-32) & 85 (P. H. Edmonds 6-8) lost to Oxbridge 192-8 dec by an inns & 29 runs.

7th Match: v Perak (Perak).
Perak 33 (R. J. Hadley 5-3) & 70 (P. H. Edmonds 5-7) lost to Oxbridge 171-6 dec (J. M. Ward 52*) by an inns & 68 runs.

8th Match: v Penang (Penang).
Penang 105 & 79 lost to Oxbridge 224-3 dec (M. J. Heal 64, P. D. Johnson 60*, A. K. C. Jones 56) by an inns & 40 runs.

9th Match: v Negri Sembilan (Negri Sembilan).
Negri Sembilan 189 (Bala Kandjah 60, H. K. Steele 6-63) & 113 lost to Oxbridge 130 (Navaratnam 5-24) & 173-4 by 6 wkts.

10th Match: v Malaysia C.A. (Kuala Lumpur).
Oxbridge 257 (P. D. Johnson 74) & 276-9 dec (M. G. Heal 90, H. K. Steele 51) beat Malaysia C.A. 217 (Koo Kim Kuang 57, Ranjit Singh 50) & 86 (P. H. Edmonds 5-33) by 230 runs.

Lever (Essex), P. J. Lewington (Warwicks), P. Willey (Northants) and A. Long (Surrey). A. S. Brown was sent for after the second match when Willey was injured. J. D. Bannister travelled as manager, J. Jennings as physiotherapist and Brian Johnston as press officer.

After the initial defeats, the tourists almost beat Transvaal and then obtained their first first-class victory over Natal, winning off the last ball.

The most important match was virtually a 'Test Match' at Johannesburg and because of injuries, the tourists called in R. D. Jackman, the Rhodesian and Surrey cricketer, but even so South Africa (styled Invitation Section A XI) won by an innings. B. A. Richards hit a brilliant hundred and with Procter and Barlow in the attack, the tourists' batting crumbled. Over 16,000 watched the second day's play.

Radley headed the first-class averages, whilst Lever was easily the best bowler.

1972-73: Oxford and Cambridge tour Malaysia

Professor J. W. Linnett arranged a ten-match tour of Malaysia and Singapore by a combined team of 14 cricketers who represented Oxford or Cambridge University in 1972. The side was P. C. H. Jones (capt), A. K. C. Jones, S. C. Corlett, M. J. J. Faber, C. B. Hamelin, M. G. Heal and J. M. Ward of Oxford; and from Cambridge P. H. Edmonds, R. J. Hadley, P. Hodson, P. D. Johnson, M. P. Kendall, H. K. Steele and C. R. V. Taylor. Peter Wheatley acted as manager.

The pace attack of Hadley and Corlett proved too good for most of the opposition and against Perak Hadley returned figures of 5-3-3-5. The leading batsman was Johnson who hit three memorable fifties.

The reason for the tour was to try and improve cricket in Malaysia, but only in Johore was any coaching done. The tour which took place in July and August lasted four weeks and involved 10 matches, none of which was lost.

The hospitality received throughout the tour was almost overwhelming and the grateful players found they were hard put to keep match fit.

1972-73: the M.C.C. tour to India, Pakistan and Sri Lanka

The problem of the captaincy of major M.C.C. tours continued to tax the selectors in the summer of 1972; Illingworth who led England against Australia through that season declined the leadership of the winter tour. M. J. K. Smith was then offered the post and declined. In the end the captaincy was given to A. R. Lewis, the only other contender of any standing being J. M. Brearley. The full side, announced in September, was A. R. Lewis (Glamorgan) (capt), M. H. Denness (Kent) (vice-capt), D. L. Amiss (Warwicks), G. G. Arnold (Surrey), J. Birkenshaw (Leics), R. M. H. Cottam (Northants), K. W. R. Fletcher (Essex), N. Gifford (Worcs), A. W. Greig (Sussex), A. P. E. Knott (Kent), C. M. Old (Yorks), P. I. Pocock (Surrey), G. R. J. Roope (Surrey), R. W. Tolchard (Leics), D. L. Underwood (Kent) and B. Wood (Lancs), with D. B. Carr as manager. Both G. Boycott and J. A. Snow refused invitations to tour.

The team flew into Bombay on 30 November and after a rest travelled on to Hyderabad for the opening match. Arnold, Pocock and Wood were already indisposed with stomach upsets, but the game was a tame draw. Another draw was played at Indore, after Central Zone had decided not to attempt the sporting chance of 216 in 140 minutes. A third game of declarations was acted out before the first Test in Delhi. Some great bowling by Arnold dismissed India for 173. Only Greig of the English batsmen could however master Chandrasekhar and England's lead amounted to just 27 runs. The English spinners, Underwood and Pocock, ran through the Indian second innings, which left the tourists needing 207 for victory. Lewis and Greig, though kept in check by the spin of Bedi, took England to a 7-wicket win. The second Test followed directly after. Again the scoring was low, but this time the Indian bowlers, Chandrasekhar and Bedi, held the upper hand and evened the series to one match each.

Away from the excitement of the Tests, the tourists played another drawn match of declarations – the Nawab of Pataudi (now playing as M. A. Khan) hit a hundred, as did Knott and Fletcher.

Fletcher continued to bat well in the third Test and was unlucky to be 97 not out when the English innings ended, Chandrasekhar once more caused the damage. M. A. Khan hit the

1972-73: M.C.C. to Pakistan, India and Sri Lanka

1st Match: v Board President's XI (Hyderabad)   Dec 5, 6, 7.
President's XI 317-5 dec (S. M. Gavaskar 86, A. V. Mankad 60*, R. D. Parkar 59, C. P. S. Chauhan 53) & 84-2 (C. P. S. Chauhan 56*) drew with M.C.C. 321-7 dec (M. H. Denness 95, D. L. Amiss 81).

2nd Match: v Central Zone (Indore)   Dec 9, 10, 11.
M.C.C. 261-9 dec (B. Wood 117) & 209-4 dec (K. W. R. Fletcher 56, G. R. J. Roope 50) drew with Central Zone 255-3 dec (Suryaveer Singh 102, S. A. Durani 81*) & 114-4 (P. Sharma 51*).

3rd Match: v North Zone (Amritsar)   Dec 15, 16, 17.
M.C.C. 285-3 dec (K. W. R. Fletcher 120*, G. R. J. Roope 68, B. Wood 54) & 123-4 dec (A. W. Greig 54) drew with North Zone 166-7 dec (Madan Lal 66, M. Amarnath 51, R. M. H. Cottam 5-19) & 147-8.

4th Match: v India (New Delhi)   Dec 20, 21, 23, 24, 25.
India 173 (S. Abid Ali 58, G. G. Arnold 6-45) & 233 (E. D. Solkar 75, F. M. Engineer 63) lost to England 200 (A. W. Greig 68*, B. S. Chandrasekhar 8-79) & 208-4 (A. R. Lewis 70*) by 6 wkts.

5th Match: v India (Calcutta)   Dec 30, 31, Jan 1, 3, 4.
India 210 (F. M. Engineer 75) & 155 (S. A. Durani 53, A. W. Greig 5-24) beat England 174 (B. S. Chandrasekhar 5-65) & 163 (A. W. Greig 67, B. S. Bedi 5-63) by 28 runs.

6th Match: v South Zone (Bangalore)   Jan 6, 7, 8.
South Zone 274-5 dec (M. A. K. Pataudi 100*, B. P. Patel 93) & 214-7 dec (K. Jayantilal 103*) drew with M.C.C. 299-5 dec (A. P. E. Knott 156, K. W. R. Fletcher 100*) & 104-1.

7th Match: v India (Madras)   Jan 12, 13, 14, 15, 16.
England 242 (K. W. R. Fletcher 97*, B. S. Chandrasekhar 6-90) & 159 (M. H. Denness 76) lost to India 316 (M. A. K. Pataudi 73) & 86-6 by 4 wkts.

8th Match: v East Zone (Jamshedpur)   Jan 20, 21, 22.
M.C.C. 306-5 dec (G. R. J. Roope 125, R. W. Tolchard 70) & 99-4 dec drew with East Zone 148 (A. Roy 70, R. M. H. Cottam 5-25) & 176-8.

9th Match: v India (Kanpur)   Jan 25, 27, 28, 29, 30.
India 357 (A. L. Wadekar 90, S. M. Gavaskar 69, M. A. K. Pataudi 54) & 186-6 (G. R. Viswanath 75*) drew with England 397 (A. R. Lewis 125, J. Birkenshaw 64, K. W. R. Fletcher 58).

10th Match: v West Zone (Ahmedabad)   Feb 2, 3, 4.
M.C.C. 279-5 dec (G. R. J. Roope 130, D. L. Amiss 63) & 208-9 dec (R. W. Tolchard 51*, P. K. Shivalkar 6-77) drew with West Zone 218-4 dec (A. V. Mankad 54, H. S. Kanitkar 53*, C. P. S. Chauhan 51) & 194-4 (K. D. Ghavri 79*, H. S. Kanitkar 72*).

11th Match: v India (Bombay)   Feb 6, 7, 8, 10, 11.
India 448 (F. M. Engineer 121, G. R. Viswanath 113, A. L. Wadekar 87, S. A. Durani 73) & 244-5 dec (S. M. Gavaskar 67, F. M. Engineer 66) drew with England 480 (A. W. Greig 148, K. W. R. Fletcher 113, A. P. E. Knott 56, B. S. Chandrasekhar 5-135) & 67-2.

12th Match: v Central Province (Kandy) (Limited Over)   Feb 14.
M.C.C. 273-8 (D. L. Amiss 55, M. H. Denness 53, A. W. Greig 63) beat Central Province 107 by 166 runs.

13th Match: v Sri Lanka (Colombo)   Feb 16, 17, 18.
Sri Lanka 86 & 200 lost to M.C.C. 163 (A. W. Greig 61, D. S. de Silva 5-40) & 127-3 (D. L. Amiss 51*) by 7 wkts.

14th Match: v Governor's XI (Peshawar)   Feb 24, 25, 26.
No play: rain.

15th Match: v Pakistan (Lahore)   March 2, 3, 4, 6, 7.
England 355 (D. L. Amiss 112, K. W. R. Fletcher 55, M. H. Denness 50) & 306-7 dec (A. R. Lewis 74, M. H. Denness 68, A. W. Greig 72) drew with Pakistan 422 (Sadiq Mohammad 119, Asif Iqbal 102, Mushtaq Mohammad 66) & 124-3 (Talat Ali 57).

16th Match: v President's XI (Rawalpindi)   March 9, 10, 11, 12, 13.
President's XI 216-8 dec (Aftab Baluch 50) & 88 (N. Gifford 6-30) lost to M.C.C. 147 (Mohammad Nazir 5-49) & 158-6 (D. L. Amiss 62*) by 4 wkts.

17th Match: v Pakistan (Hyderabad)   March 16, 17, 18, 20, 21.
England 487 (D. L. Amiss 158, K. W. R. Fletcher 78, A. P. E. Knott 71) & 218-6 (A. W. Greig 64, A. P. E. Knott 63*) drew with Pakistan 569-9 dec (Mushtaq Mohammad 157, Intikhab Alam 138, Asif Iqbal 68, P. I. Pocock 5-169).

18th Match: v Pakistan (Karachi)   March 24, 25, 27, 28, 29.
Pakistan 445-6 dec (Majid Khan 99, Mushtaq Mohammad 99, Sadiq Mohammad 89, Intikhab Alam 61) & 199 (N. Gifford 5-55, J. Birkenshaw 5-57) drew with England 386 (D. L. Amiss 99, A. R. Lewis 88, K. W. R. Fletcher 54) & 30-1.

highest score for India, who batted much more solidly than the visitors and gained a useful first innings lead. England collapsed to the spinners in their second innings, but they made India struggle for the 86 required in the final innings and six wickets went down before India won.

The fourth Test saw higher scoring. India, now leading 2 to 1 in the series, were interested only in a draw and the two first innings were not completed until the final morning of the match.

The same pattern was evident in the fifth Test. Engineer and Viswanath made hundreds for India, as did Fletcher and Greig for England and the game slid to a draw.

The defeated England side went on to Sri Lanka for two matches before commencing the series against Pakistan. The one first-class match before the first Test was totally washed out. In the Test itself, England began with a century partnership from Amiss and Denness, but the batting fell away at the end with the last five wickets going for 25 runs. Asif Iqbal and Sadiq hit hundreds to give Pakistan a lead and though England had a few hiccups in their second innings, the match was drawn.

Pakistan had a chance of winning the second Test, but stout batting by Greig and Knott in the second innings after 5 wickets had gone down for 77, saved the visitors.

The M.C.C. party leaving for the tour to India, Pakistan and Sri Lanka in 1972-73. From left at front: K. W. R. Fletcher, A. P. E. Knott, D. B. Carr (manager), A. R. Lewis (captain), B. Wood, D. L. Amiss, D. L. Underwood, M. H. Denness, R. W. Tolchard. On the steps is B. W. Thomas and behind G. G. Arnold and J. Birkenshaw, P. I. Pocock and G. R. J. Roope, C. M. Old and R. M. H. Cottam, A. W. Greig and N. Gifford.

1972-73: M.C.C. to India, Sri Lanka and Pakistan

Batting Averages

	M	I	NO	R	HS	Avge	100	*c/s
K. W. R. Fletcher (Essex)	14	22	5	881	120*	51.82	3	15
A. W. Greig (Sussex)	13	21	3	826	148	45.88	1	16
D. L. Amiss (Warks)	12	23	4	861	158	45.31	2	5
R. W. Tolchard (Leics)	7	9	4	221	70	44.20	0	15
A. P. E. Knott (Kent)	13	20	3	666	156	39.17	1	23/2
M. H. Denness (Kent)	14	23	1	706	95	32.09	0	9
J. Birkenshaw (Leics)	10	15	2	393	64	30.23	0	8
A. R. Lewis (Glam)	12	18	2	483	125	30.18	1	1
G. R. J. Roope (Surrey)	12	20	2	532	130	29.55	2	16
C. M. Old (Yorks)	8	13	5	208	42	26.00	0	6
B. Wood (Lancs)	11	20	2	465	117	25.83	1	4
N. Gifford (Worcs)	7	6	3	71	24	23.66	0	4
G. G. Arnold (Surrey)	12	13	2	176	45	16.00	0	0
D. L. Underwood (Kent)	10	8	4	55	20*	13.75	0	4
R. M. H. Cottam (Northts)	9	5	1	25	13	6.25	0	0
P. I. Pocock (Surrey)	12	14	3	60	33	5.45	0	5

Bowling Averages

	O	M	R	W	Avge	BB	5i
B. Wood	20	5	49	3	16.33	2-10	0
R. M. H. Cottam	212	61	508	28	18.14	5-19	2
N. Gifford	290.4	106	568	24	23.67	6-30	2
A. W. Greig	329.1	89	759	29	26.17	5-24	1
G. G. Arnold	341.3	87	842	29	29.03	6-45	1
C. M. Old	206.2	47	555	17	32.64	4-43	0
P. I. Pocock	471.2	117	1234	37	33.35	5-169	1
D. L. Underwood	442.5	164	934	26	35.92	4-56	0
J. Birkenshaw	347.1	75	1032	25	41.28	5-57	1
K. W. R. Fletcher	29	4	125	2	62.50	1-12	0
G. R. J. Roope	48	15	110	1	110.00	1-10	0

Also bowled: D. L. Amiss 3-0-13-0; M. H. Denness 1-0-7-0; A. P. E. Knott 4-0-29-0.

Rioting and crowds invading the pitch were the feature of the third Test, which like its predecessors ended in a draw. The bowling of Gifford and Birkenshaw, whose spin dismissed Pakistan for 199 on the last day was outstanding.

The great successes of the tour were Greig and Fletcher. Greig really mastered the Indian spinners and his bowling and fielding combined to make him the best all-rounder in the English team. Lewis also came out of his ordeal well, both as batsman and captain. Old looked most promising, even on the slow wickets, and learnt a lot from Arnold. Amiss did well in Pakistan, but struggled in India. Knott was rather disappointing.

In India the great players were the spinners Chandrasekhar and Bedi, but Pakistan had five really notable men: Majid, Asif Iqbal, Sadiq, Mushtaq and Intikhab.

1973-74: D. H. Robins' second tour to South Africa

D. H. Robins took a second team to South Africa in the autumn of 1973. Mindful of the previous year's record, he recruited a stronger side: D. B. Close (Somerset) (capt), Younis Ahmed (Surrey), J. H. Edrich (Surrey), B. C. Francis (Essex), R. A. Woolmer (Kent), G. R. J. Roope (Surrey), M. J. Smith (Middx), J. T. Murray (Middx), J. N. Shepherd (Kent), J. K. Lever (Essex), G. W. Johnson (Kent), P. G. Lee (Lancs), J. W. Gleeson (Australia), J. A. Snow (Sussex), R. W. Tolchard (Leics) and R. E. East (Essex). L. E. G. Ames travelled as manager and J. Jennings as physiotherapist.

The team flew from London on 15 October and created history in the first match of the tour by playing against an African XI in Soweto. The three major games of the tour however were the 'Tests' against the South African Invitation XI. The 'First Test' took place at Cape Town and the tourists arrived there with a good record, having beaten two Provincial sides and drawn with two more. In the 'Test' the visitors gained a first innings lead and came close to winning, but the task of making 238 in 180 minutes proved a little too steep, especially when rain interrupted.

The 'Second Test' was a high-scoring draw. Edrich hit 170, but Richards for South Africa managed 180—any hopes of a definite finish were removed by a four-hour stoppage for rain.

In the 'Third Test' South Africa dominated throughout and won by an innings. Gleeson was unfit, which was a serious blow to the tourists and Barlow, after being dropped, went on to make 211. Snow was not selected for this 'Test' for disciplinary reasons.

Younis Ahmed and Edrich headed the batting averages, whilst Gleeson topped the bowling table. The tour was regarded as a major breakthrough in sport, since both Younis of Pakistan and Shepherd of the West Indies were among the visiting team.

1973-74: Derrick Robins' Team to South Africa

1st Match: v African XI (Soweto) (One Day) Oct 20.
Robins XI 359 (G. R. J. Roope 110, J. H. Edrich 108) beat African XI 137 (J. W. Gleeson 7-33) by 222 runs.

2nd Match: v Orange Free State (Bloemfontein) (Limited Over) Oct 23.
Robins XI 243-9 (J. H. Edrich 79, J. N. Shepherd 54) beat O.F.S. 120-7 (R. East 52*) on faster scoring rate.

3rd Match: v Griqualand West (Kimberley) (Limited Over) Oct 24.
Robins XI 197-6 (G. W. Johnson 65, B. C. Francis 65) beat Griqualand West 112-7 by 85 runs.

4th Match: v Western Province (Cape Town) Oct 26, 27, 28.
W. Province 286-4 dec (H. M. Ackerman 179*, F. S. Goldstein 54) & 149-5 drew with Robins XI 375-4 dec (B. C. Francis 194, J. H. Edrich 118).

5th Match: v Border (East London) (Limited Over) Oct 31.
Robins XI 274-4 (D. B. Close 72, Younis Ahmed 61, M. J. Smith 56) beat Border 152 (J. W. Gleeson 5-32) by 122 runs.

6th Match: v Natal (Durban) Nov 2, 3, 5.
Robins XI 222-8 dec (G. W. Johnson 57) & 98-2 dec drew with Natal 134-7 dec & 32-0.

7th Match: v Northern Transvaal (Pretoria) (Limited Over) Nov 7.
N. Transvaal 202-8 (K. D. Verdoorn 80) lost to Robins XI 203-4 (B. C. Francis 106, M. J. Smith 54) by 6 wkts.

8th Match: v Transvaal (Johannesburg) Nov 9, 10, 12.
Transvaal 217-9 dec & 199 lost to Robins XI 303-6 dec (Younis Ahmed 123) & 116-2 by 8 wkts.

9th Match: v Eastern Province (Port Elizabeth) Nov 16, 17, 19.
E. Province 123 (A. M. Short 58) & 206 (C. P. Wilkins 51) lost to Robins XI 261 (R. A. Woolmer 83, Younis Ahmed 80) & 69-2 by 8 wkts.

10th Match: v African XI (New Brighton) Nov 22.
No play due to rain.

11th Match: v South African Invitation XI (Cape Town) Nov 23, 24, 26, 27.
Invitation XI 278 (H. M. Ackerman 76, E. J. Barlow 61) & 287-8 dec (B. A. Richards 81, H. M. Ackerman 56, E. J. Barlow 54, J. K. Lever 5-62) drew with Robins XI 329 (B. C. Francis 87, G. R. J. Roope 65) & 142-5.

12th Match: v South African Invitation XI (Durban) Nov 30, Dec 1, 3, 4.
Robins XI 383-9 dec (J. H. Edrich 170, J. T. Murray 59, D. B. Close 50) & 39-0 drew with Invitation XI 454 (B. A. Richards 180, A. J. S. Smith 81, V. A. P. van der Bijl 50*).

13th Match: v South African Invitation XI (Johannesburg) Dec 7, 8, 10, 11.
Robins XI 227-9 dec (G. R. J. Roope 60, J. N. Shepherd 53) & 218 lost to Invitation XI 528-8 dec (E. J. Barlow 211, B. L. Irvine 125, M. J. Procter 54, J. K. Lever 6-117) by an inns & 83 runs.

14th Match: v South African Invitation XI (Johannesburg) (Limited Over) Dec 12.
Robins XI 201-9 beat Invitation XI 198 (H. M. Ackerman 65) by 3 runs.

1973-74: D. H. Robins' Team to South Africa

Batting Averages

	M	I	NO	R	HS	Avge	100	c/s
Younis Ahmed (Surrey)	6	10	3	351	123	50.14	1	3
J. H. Edrich (Surrey)	6	10	1	441	170	49.00	2	1
B. C. Francis (Essex)	6	11	2	411	194	45.66	1	2
R. A. Woolmer (Kent)	6	7	1	229	83	38.16	0	5
G. R. J. Roope (Surrey)	7	10	1	293	75	32.55	0	6
M. J. Smith (Middx)	3	5	0	149	44	29.80	0	1
J. T. Murray (Middx)	4	5	0	146	59	29.20	0	9
D. B. Close (Som)	7	11	3	200	50	25.00	0	8
J. N. Shepherd (Kent)	7	7	0	169	53	24.14	0	4
J. K. Lever (Essex)	6	4	3	20	9*	20.00	0	2
G. W. Johnson (Kent)	3	6	1	96	57	19.20	0	3
P. G. Lee (Lancs)	3	3	2	19	11	19.00	0	0
J. W. Gleeson (NSW)	4	2	0	10	7	5.00	0	3
J. A. Snow (Sussex)	5	3	0	6	6	2.00	0	0
R. W. Tolchard (Leics)	3	3	3	75	40*	—	0	6/1
R. E. East (Essex)	1	1	1	15	15*	—	0	0

Bowling Averages

	O	M	R	W	Avge	BB	5i
J. W. Gleeson	134	47	361	18	20.05	4-59	0
J. A. Snow	168.1	38	411	18	22.83	4-52	0
J. K. Lever	197.2	41	528	20	26.40	6-117	2
J. N. Shepherd	208	45	566	15	37.73	4-54	0
R. A. Woolmer	106	22	315	9	35.00	3-60	0
P. G. Lee	69.2	13	244	5	48.80	2-17	0
G. R. J. Roope	14	0	56	1	56.00	1-21	0
D. B. Close	47	9	184	2	92.00	1-0	0

Also bowled: G. W. Johnson 23-10-36-0; Younis Ahmed 8-1-33-0; R. E. East 9-2-13-0; M. J. Smith 3-1-7-0.

1973-74: M.C.C. tour of Kenya, Zambia and Tanzania

Under the managership of J. A. Bailey, the following team toured East Africa in January 1974: J. M. Brearley (Middx) (capt), J. A. Bailey (Essex) (vice-capt), D. L. Acfield (Essex), R. W. Barber (Warwicks), T. W. Cartwright (Somerset), L. J. Champniss (Bucks), E. A. Clark (Middx), N. J. Cosh (Surrey), A. L. Dixon (Kent), M. G. Griffith (Sussex), J. L. Hutton, R. D. V. Knight (Gloucs), D. R. Owen-Thomas (Surrey) and P. H. Parfitt (Middx).

The programme on the visit was too tightly arranged, which meant that the players could not give of their best, but the party went through without defeat.

The important match of the tour was against East Africa, when some good bowling by Cartwright proved too much for the local side. Knight was the best batsman in this match as indeed he was throughout the tour, except on two wet wickets. Barber suffered an injured hand, but batted well on occasion, as did Parfitt. Cartwright was easily the best bowler, his 35 wickets costing 11.20 each.

The best of the local players were almost without exception Asians, Jawahir Shah being the most notable figure.

It was to be hoped that the tour helped to boost cricket in the three countries visited.

1973-74: M.C.C. to East Africa

1st Match: v Zambia (Lusaka)   Dec 29, 30.
M.C.C. 118 (M. Pardor 5-45) & 166-7 dec (E. A. Clark 53*) drew with Zambia 153 & 62-8.

2nd Match: v Zambia (Kitwe)   Dec 31, Jan 1.
Zambia 158 & 95 lost to M.C.C. 136-6 dec (R. W. Barber 50) & 118-5 by 5 wkts.

3rd Match: v Tanzania (Dar-es-Salaam)   Jan 4, 6.
M.C.C. 275 (P. H. Parfitt 53) & 216-6 dec (J. M. Brearley 66) drew with Tanzania 306 (Pranlal 69, Tapu 64) & 103-2.

4th Match: v Moshi (Moshi) (Limited Over)   Jan 7.
M.C.C. 306-7 (M. G. Griffith 96, R. W. Barber 64, P. H. Parfitt 64) beat Moshi 123-6 by 183 runs.

5th Match: v Kenya Coast XI (Mombasa) (Limited over)   Jan 10.
M.C.C. 272-2 (R. D. V. Knight 137*, E. A. Clark 56*) beat Kenya 236-7 by 36 runs.

6th Match: v Kenya (Mombasa)   Jan 11, 12, 13.
Kenya 276 (Narendra 95, Jahawir 64) & 218-6 dec (Jagoo 72) drew with M.C.C. 221 (R. W. Barber 99, Mehmood 6-33) & 133-4.

7th Match: v Kenya & Uganda XI (Nairobi)   Jan 15, 16.
Combined XI 101 (D. L. Acfield 5-22) & 112 lost to M.C.C. 177-6 dec (E. A. Clark 63) & 37-1 by 9 wkts.

8th Match: v East Africa (Nairobi)   Jan 18, 19, 20.
M.C.C. 300 (P. H. Parfitt 83, R. D. V. Knight 78) & 208-7 dec (R. D. V. Knight 51*) beat East Africa 169 (Jagoo Shah 53, T. W. Cartwright 5-53) & 102 (T. W. Cartwright 5-30) by 237 runs.

1973-74: England draw Test series in West Indies

The saga of the English captaincy continued to be a subject of debate through 1973. The defeat of England by West Indies in England in the summer of 1973 signalled the end of Illingworth as England's leader. Lewis, who had led M.C.C. to India the previous winter, had retired due to injury and the succession therefore fell to Denness, the vice-captain in India. The full touring party was M. H. Denness (Kent) (capt), A. W. Greig (Sussex) (vice-capt), D. L. Amiss (Warwicks), G. G. Arnold (Surrey), J. Birkenshaw (Leics), G. Boycott (Yorks), K. W. R. Fletcher (Essex), F. C. Hayes (Lancs), M. Hendrick (Derbys), J. A. Jameson (Warwicks), A. P. E. Knott (Kent), C. M. Old (Yorks), P. I. Pocock (Surrey), R. W. Taylor (Derbys), D. L. Underwood (Kent), R. G. D. Willis (Warwicks) and the manager D. B. Carr. The outstanding omission was that of Snow, but he had had a great deal of injury in the last year or so and it was felt not worth risking him. In Old, Hendrick and Willis the team had three 24-year-old players who looked to be capable of taxing the opposition.

1973-74: M.C.C. to the West Indies

Batting Averages

	M	I	NO	R	HS	Avge	100	c/s
D. L. Amiss (Warks)	9	16	1	1120	262*	74.66	5	3
G. Boycott (Yorks)	10	16	3	960	261*	73.84	3	3
A. W. Greig (Sussex)	9	14	1	665	148	51.15	3	12
K. W. R. Fletcher (Essex)	10	16	3	564	129*	43.38	2	9
M. H. Denness (Kent)	10	17	2	504	67	33.60	0	5
J. Birkenshaw (Leics)	5	6	2	127	53*	31.75	0	2
F. C. Hayes (Lancs)	9	16	2	444	88	31.71	0	8
R. G. D. Willis (Warks)	6	6	5	30	10*	30.00	0	8
A. P. E. Knott (Kent)	10	17	1	474	87	29.62	0	14
J. A. Jameson (Warks)	7	13	0	325	91	25.00	0	5
R. W. Taylor (Derby)	3	3	0	69	65	23.00	0	5/1
M. Hendrick (Derby)	5	5	3	29	16	14.50	0	2
D. L. Underwood (Kent)	7	10	3	100	24	14.28	0	5
G. G. Arnold (Surrey)	8	10	2	101	25	12.62	0	2
C. M. Old (Yorks)	6	10	0	122	53	12.20	0	2
P. I. Pocock (Surrey)	7	11	0	77	23	7.00	0	3

Bowling Averages

	O	M	R	W	Avge	BB	5i
J. A. Jameson	35	10	74	4	18.50	2-25	0
K. W. R. Fletcher	20.5	4	63	3	21.00	2-25	0
A. W. Greig	277.1	57	766	30	25.53	8-86	3
M. Hendrick	108.2	21	320	12	26.66	4-38	0
J. Birkenshaw	165.5	35	467	16	29.18	6-101	1
R. G. D. Willis	140	27	526	15	35.06	4-91	0
P. I. Pocock	326.3	79	844	19	44.42	5-110	1
D. L. Underwood	263.5	88	573	12	47.75	2-48	0
G. G. Arnold	174.3	40	611	12	50.91	5-44	1
C. M. Old	135.4	28	459	9	51.00	3-56	0

Also bowled: G. Boycott 9-1-33-1; F. C. Hayes 0.2-0-4-0.

The M.C.C. party for the West Indies reporting at Lord's on the last day of 1973-74. From the front: M. H. Denness (captain), A. P. E. Knott, R. W. Taylor, K. W. R. Fletcher, J. Birkenshaw, D. L. Amiss, F. C. Hayes, D. L. Underwood, J. A. Jameson, G. G. Arnold, P. I. Pocock, C. M. Old, M. Hendrick, R. G. D. Willis, A. W. Greig.

The team flew from London on 11 January direct to Barbados and opened the tour with two minor matches in St Lucia, before taking on the President's XI. A great opening partnership of 252 by Boycott and Amiss, the former going on to 261 not out, gave the tourists a bright start. Arnold then took five wickets to dismiss the opposition for 164, but from then on matters did not go right and the game was drawn. On a very slow pitch, the match against Trinidad, which came next in the programme, was a very dull affair.

The first Test began at Port of Spain on 2 February and England had a terrible time for the first half as West Indies swept to a first innings lead of 261. Boycott and Amiss however began the second innings with a stand of 209 and the score rose to 315 for 1, but Gibbs then took a hand and the score tumbled to 392 all out. West Indies had no problem in knocking off the 132 required to win.

Amiss saved the second Test when all seemed lost. Again England had an enormous deficit on first innings – 230 – and going in again lost their 7th wicket at 271. Amiss however would not be moved and aided by the tail enders, notably Old, held out. The Warwickshire batsman made 262 not out.

M.C.C. however suffered a humiliating defeat at the hands of Barbados, just before the third Test, which was a repeat of the second, except that Fletcher and Knott were England's savours,

though it must be admitted that Gibbs the off-spinner could not bowl in the second England innings. No less than 99 no-balls were called in this match. On the third day a record crowd watched the game and so many clamoured for admittance that security broke down outside the ground. Happily the spectators behaved splendidly in the circumstances and play was hardly disrupted at all.

England got off to a good start in the fourth Test, making 448 in their first innings, with a century by Greig, but rain then washed out most of the remaining time. Sobers, although chosen, did not turn up for the match, and his place was given to Foster.

England had to win the final Test to save the series, but they failed to gain a lead on first innings, despite some magnificent bowling by Greig who reduced West Indies from 224 for 2 to 305 all out. Boycott then held England together in the second innings, as indeed he had done in the first, so that West Indies required 226 to win and over a day to make the runs. Greig actually opened the bowling with off-breaks and the West Indian batsmen seemed to lose their nerve as the game edged on with either team able to win – in the end it was England's by 26 runs.

England therefore, perhaps unjustly, drew the series one match each. Greig was the player of the series, but he was also responsible for the one major incident of the tour, when he fielded the final ball of the day in the first Test and ran out Kallicharran, who thought play was over and was walking to the pavilion. The authorities in fact over-ruled the umpire and allowed Kallicharran to continue on the next day, which resulted in vast press lectures on the authority of the umpires and the Laws.

Denness did not have a very good tour, seeming to be out of his depth, both as captain and batsman. Amiss played well and looked much better than in England. The fast bowlers were of no consequence and for what wickets they could get England relied on the spinners – at least in the Tests.

Rowe and Fredericks were the outstanding home batsmen, and the days of Sobers, Kanhai and Lloyd appeared over.

1973-74: Arabs' second tour to Barbados

In January 1974, the Arabs made a second major tour to Barbados. The team, which contained mainly first-class cricketers, was A. R. Lewis (Glamorgan) (capt), R. C. Kinkead-Weekes (Oxford U), S. G. Metcalfe (Oxford U), Earl of Cottenham, C. A. Fry (Northants), R. C. Daniels, M. J. J. Faber (Oxford U), R. J. Priestley, J. R. T. Barclay (Sussex), J. W. O. Allerton (Oxford U), T. J. Mottram (Hants), R. A. Hutton (Yorks), J. M. M. Hooper (Surrey), J. O. Trumper and I. A. Balding.

The tour began with an easy win over the Windward Islands, but were quickly brought down to earth by Clyde Walcott's XI in the second game. The highest innings was 121 by Daniels, made on a difficult wicket against the Wanderers in a match which was won in the penultimate over – Faber had the misfortune to break a finger whilst batting.

The only three-day game was against the President's XI. Lewis scored two innings of 80 and 85, but was unable to prevent defeat by 7 wickets. The best bowler on the tour was Mottram, and Lewis was the leading batsman. Daniels broke a finger, which got in the way of a quicker ball from Griffith in the sixth match.

1974-75: Lillee and Thomson destroy England in Australia

The team selected to go to Australia in 1974-75 was M. H. Denness (Kent) (capt), J. H. Edrich (Surrey) (vice-capt), D. L. Amiss (Warwicks), G. G. Arnold (Surrey), G. Boycott (Yorks), K. W. R. Fletcher (Essex), A. W. Greig (Sussex), M. Hendrick (Derbys), A. P. E. Knott (Kent), P. Lever (Lancs), D. Lloyd (Lancs), C. M. Old (Yorks), R. W. Taylor (Derbys), F. J. Titmus (Middx), D. L. Underwood (Kent) and R. G. D. Willis (Warwicks), with A. V. Bedser as manager, A. C. Smith as his assistant and B. W. Thomas as physiotherapist. For the first time for several years, the captaincy remained unchanged for two successive major tours. The critics attacked the inclusion of five faster bowlers and felt a batsman should have replaced Hendrick.

In fact the emergence of a great pair of Australian fast bowlers – Lillee and Thomson – governed the destiny of the Ashes, but of course in August 1974, the English selectors were not to know that, though it was forcefully pointed out that of the six selectors only two were really familiar with cricket in Australia. The team did not leave England however before controversy enveloped it. Boycott withdrew on the ground that he was not yet fit enough mentally to return to Test cricket. The England captain deposed in favour of Denness two years previously, Illingworth, then leapt into print with the headline BOYCOTT QUITS FRED KARNO'S ARMY. Illingworth attacked Denness's captaincy and the non-selection of Snow. Greig also criticised the selection

in an interview. B. W. Luckhurst was chosen by the selectors to fill Boycott's place.

The tour opened with a one-day game at Port Lincoln, before the first first-class match against South Australia, when M.C.C. had the better of a draw and were handicapped by Old straining his knee. The tourists had all the best of a draw against Victoria, and might have won if Titmus had been allowed to bowl earlier. Some good off-spin bowling by Greig won the game against New South Wales and an all-round performance produced a victory in the next first-class match against Queensland. So to the first Test. Australia won the toss and batted, but on a moderate wicket had to thank Ian Chappell for a total of 309. Then the fast but erratic Thomson rattled all the England batsmen except Greig, who fought through to the only century of the match. England were 44 behind on first innings. Ian Chappell declared in the second innings to set the visitors 333 in 400 minutes, but it was really a

1974-75: M.C.C. to Australia and New Zealand

Batting Averages

	M	I	NO	R	HS	Avge	100	c/s
M. H. Denness (Kent)	15	25	4	1136	188	54.09	3	10
K. W. R. Fletcher (Essex)	16	22	3	919	216	48.36	2	18
D. L. Amiss (Warks)	15	23	2	983	164*	46.80	3	12
A. W. Greig (Sussex)	14	22	2	934	167*	46.70	2	19
A. P. E. Knott (Kent)	14	21	4	723	106*	42.52	1	44/2
J. H. Edrich (Surrey)	13	19	4	576	70	38.40	0	9
D. Lloyd (Lancs)	11	18	1	534	80	31.41	0	9
R. W. Taylor (Derby)	6	5	2	89	27*	29.66	0	11/1
B. W. Luckhurst (Kent)	10	17	1	415	116	25.93	1	13
M. C. Cowdrey (Kent)	7	12	1	284	78	25.81	0	4
C. M. Old (Yorks)	12	15	3	286	48	23.83	0	e8
D. L. Underwood (Kent)	14	14	3	209	33	19.00	0	2
F. J. Titmus (Middx)	9	13	1	174	61	14.50	0	4
M. Hendrick (Derby)	8	9	4	62	24*	12.40	0	7
R. G. D. Willis (Warks)	9	15	6	108	21	12.00	0	5
P. Lever (Lancs)	10	4	1	35	14	11.66	0	6
G. G. Arnold (Surrey)	12	10	2	34	14	4.25	0	3

Also played in two matches B. Wood (Lancs) 0, 33 (ct 3); in one match A. C. Smith (Warks) 15.

Bowling Averages

	O	M	R	W	Avge	BB	5i
D. L. Underwood	412.3	102	1214	48	25.29	7-113	2
C. M. Old	206.7	25	871	33	26.39	7-59	1
A. W. Greig	367.2	63	1421	50	28.42	5-51	3
M. Hendrick	160.3	26	582	19	30.63	5-68	1
R. G. D. Willis	223.7	29	811	26	31.19	5-61	1
P. Lever	228.4	21	923	27	34.18	6-38	1
F. J. Titmus	258.3	50	771	21	36.71	3-61	0
G. G. Arnold	331.3	51	1136	30	37.86	5-86	1

Also bowled: M. C. Cowdrey 4-0-27-2; K. W. R. Fletcher 6-0-45-0; D. Lloyd 6.6-2-25-2; B. W. Luckhurst 1-0-1-1; B. Wood 4-0-19-0.

The M.C.C. party for Australia in 1974-75 at London airport. Back: K. W. R. Fletcher, B. W. Luckhurst, G. G. Arnold, D. L. Amiss, D. Lloyd, R. W. Taylor. Centre: F. J. Titmus, D. L. Underwood, C. M. Old, A. W. Greig, R. G. D. Willis, M. Hendrick, P. Lever. Front: B. W. Thomas (physiotherapist), A. V. Bedser (manager), M. H. Denness (captain), J. H. Edrich, A. P. E. Knott, A. C. Smith (assistant manager).

Left *Tony Greig fought hard on the disastrous M.C.C. tour of 1974-75, and put himself in line for the England captaincy. Here he off-drives in the fourth Test. Walters, Greg Chappell and Ian Chappell are the slips.*

Below left *Australia won the Ashes in the fourth Test at Sydney on the 1974-75 tour. Greg Chappell (right) caught the last man Geoff Arnold (left) with five minutes remaining. Wicket-keeper Rodney Marsh rushes to congratulate Australian skipper Ian Chappell.*

Below *Lillee and Thomson destroyed England in the 1974-75 series of Tests in Australia. This is Jeff Thomson flat out in the fourth Test. Amiss is the non-striker.*

question of survival – and England failed. Thomson took 6 for 46. Amiss batted with a broken thumb, Edrich with a broken hand. The weakened batting collapsed against Western Australia when set 298 to win in 245 minutes. The selectors flew out Cowdrey as reinforcement.

The second Test was a disaster for England, who disintegrated when put into bat on the first day and lost the match by 9 wickets. Thomson again proved the destroyer, though England's injury list was frightening – Amiss and Edrich were joined by Lever and Hendrick.

The third Test proved a great contrast to the two previous defeats. The England batting was no better, but the bowling, despite the absence of Hendrick, who played but retired after $2\frac{1}{2}$ overs, kept the Australian batting very much in check. It was a nail-biting draw, with Australia wanting 8 to win with 2 wickets in hand when time was called.

Between the third and fourth Tests, a One-day International was played, but proved of little interest, only 18,977 attending the game, which England won with ease.

The first headline of the fourth Test was that the England captain stood down, due to lack of form; Edrich took over. This did not, however, have the desired effect on the batting and as England's bowlers failed miserably, the match and the Ashes were lost. A Sydney record of 178,027 people attended the match.

M.C.C. went off to Tasmania to recuperate and came back to beat New South Wales, but this improvement did not last as far as the fifth Test. Denness, who returned to the side, put Australia in on a damp pitch and Underwood got England off to a great start, as the home side floundered to 84 for 5, but the tail wagged furiously and the total rose to 304. England were shot out by Lillee and Thomson for 172 and although Thomson was absent injured in the second innings only a determined Knott put up much resistance. Australia won by 163 runs.

Against all the odds England fought back in the sixth Test, in which nearly everything went right for the tourists. Lever bowled Australia out for 152, Denness and Fletcher hit centuries and despite Greg Chappell's hundred in the second innings, England did not need to bat twice. It should be stated that Thomson was unfit for the match.

In New Zealand England played two Tests, winning the first by an innings but having the second rained off. The tourists ended their programme with two pleasant matches in Hong Kong.

The series belonged to Lillee and Thomson, the latter a new-comer to English players, but the former known in England in 1972. It was the combination of the two that was lethal.

On the England side Greig and Knott were the batting suc-cesses – going in at 6 and 7! Of the bowlers Willis was the best but went rapidly downhill after the third Test, due to injury. Under-wood also did well, having matured. The England fielding was far poorer than the Australian and though Denness's captaincy had improved on his West Indian performance, it still left something to be desired.

1st Match: v South Australia Country XI (Port Lincoln) (One Day)   Oct 30.
Country XI 7-1 drew with M.C.C. – rain.

2nd Match: v South Australia (Adelaide)   Nov 1, 2, 3, 4.
S. Australia 247 (J. Nash 67, M. Hendricks 57) & 320 (I. M. Chappell 78, G. J. Cosier 65, M. Hendrick 5-68) drew with M.C.C. 349-9 dec (J. H. Edrich 58, A. W. Greig 54, T. J. Jenner 5-110) & 82-3.

3rd Match: v Victoria Country XI (Warrnambool) (One Day)   Nov 6.
M.C.C. 158-4 dec (B. W. Luckhurst 94) drew with Country XI 83-5.

4th Match: v Victoria (Melbourne)   Nov 8, 9, 10, 11.
Victoria 293-8 dec (W. L. Stillman 61, R. J. Bight 53) & 174-8 drew with M.C.C. 392-9 dec (D. L. Amiss 152, B. W. Luckhurst 116).

5th Match: v Capital Territory Country XI (Canberra) (One Day)   Nov 13.
M.C.C. 159-2 dec (D. Lloyd 66, J. H. Edrich 51 ret) drew with Country XI 58-1.

6th Match: v New South Wales (Sydney)   Nov 15, 16, 17, 18.
N.S.W. 338 (I. C. Davis 91, A. Turner 72, G. J. Gilmour 59*, R. B. McCosker 52) & 174 (R. B. McCosker 56, Greig 5-55) lost to M.C.C. 332-7 dec (K. W. R. Fletcher 79, A. W. Greig 70) & 181-4 (D. Lloyd 80, K. W. R. Fletcher 57*) by 6 wkts.

7th Match: v Queensland Country XI (Nambour)   Nov 20.
No play due to rain.

8th Match: v Queensland (Brisbane)   Nov 22, 23, 24, 25.
M.C.C. 258 & 175 (G. Dymock 5-48) beat Queensland 226 (G. S. Chappell 122) & 161 (G. S. Chappell 51) by 46 runs.

9th Match: v South-East Queensland (Southport) (One Day)   Nov 26.
S-E Queensland 52 (A. W. Greig 5-1) lost to M.C.C. 53-0 by 10 wkts.

10th Match: v Australia (Brisbane)   Nov 29, 30, Dec 1, 3, 4.
Australia 309 (I. M. Chappell 90, G. S. Chappell 58) & 288-5 dec (G. S. Chappell 71, K. D. Walters 62*, R. Edwards 53) beat England 265 (A. W. Greig 110) & 166 (J. R. Thomson 6-46) by 166 runs.

11th Match: v Western Australia (Perth)   Dec 7, 8, 9, 10.
W. Australia 265-8 dec (W. J. Edwards 50) & 346-5 dec (R. J. Inverarity 99, G. D. Watson 86*, R. S. Langer 62*) beat M.C.C. 314-5 dec (A. W. Greig 167*, A. P. E. Knott 62) & 177 (A. W. Greig 57, R. G. Paulsen 7-41) by 120 runs.

12th Match: v Western Australia Country XI (Geraldton) (One Day)   Dec 11.
M.C.C. 214-6 dec (B. W. Luckhurst 76) drew with Country XI 153-9.*

13th Match: v Australia (Perth)   Dec 13, 14, 15, 17.
England 208 (A. P. E. Knott 51) & 293 (F. J. Titmus 61, J. R. Thomson 5-93) lost to Australia 481 (R. Edwards 115, K. D. Walters 103, G. S. Chappell 62) & 23-1 by 9 wkts.

14th Match: v South Australia (Adelaide)   Dec 21, 22, 23.
S. Australia 270-6 dec (G. J. Cosier 75, A. J. Woodcock 62, D. L. Underwood 5-58) & 222-6 dec (R. Drewer 61) drew with M.C.C. 277-2 dec (M. H. Denness 88*, M. C. Cowdrey 78, D. L. Amiss 73) & 210-6 (D. L. Amiss 57).

15th Match: v Australia (Melbourne)   Dec 26, 27, 28, 30, 31.
England 242 (A. P. E. Knott 52) & 244 (D. L. Amiss 90, A. W. Greig 60) drew with Australia 241 (I. R. Redpath 55, R. G. D. Willis 5-61) & 238-8 (G. S. Chappell 61).

16th Match: v Australia (Melbourne) (Limited Over)   Jan 1.
Australia 190 lost to England 191-7.

17th Match: v Australia (Sydney)   Jan 4, 5, 6, 8, 9.
Australia 405 (G. S. Chappell 84, R. B. McCosker 80, G. G. Arnold 5-86) & 289-4 dec (G. S. Chappell 144, I. R. Redpath 105) beat England 295 (A. P. E. Knott 82, J. H. Edrich 50) & 228 (A. W. Greig 54) by 171 runs.

18th Match: v Tasmania (Hobart)   Jan 11, 12, 13.
M.C.C. 204-4 dec (B. W. Luckhurst 59) drew with Tasmania 189-5 (J. S. Wilkinson 79, S. J. Howard 69).

19th Match: v Tasmania (Launceston)   Jan 14, 15, 16.
Tasmania 164 & 105 lost to M.C.C. 341-4 dec (M. H. Denness 157*, B. W. Luckhurst 74) by an inns & 72 runs.

20th Match: v New South Wales (Sydney)   Jan 18, 19, 20.
M.C.C. 315-5 dec (M. H. Denness 99, K. W. R. Fletcher 85, D. Lloyd 51, D. L. Amiss 52) & 266-7 dec (D. L. Amiss 124, A. P. E. Knott 79) beat N.S.W. 157 (Old 7-59) & 237 (D. J. Colley 90) by 187 runs.

21st Match: v Australia (Adelaide)   Jan 25, 26, 27, 29, 30.
Australia 304 (T. J. Jenner 74, K. D. Walters 55, D. L. Underwood 7-113) & 272-5 dec (K. D. Walters 71*, R. W. Marsh 55, I. R. Redpath 52) beat England 172 (M. H. Denness 51) & 241 (A. P. E. Knott 106*, K. W. R. Fletcher 63) by 163 runs.

22nd Match: v Northern New South Wales (Newcastle)   Feb 1, 2, 3.
Northern N.S.W. 251-5 dec (C. Baker 73*, O. Bush 63) & 270-6 dec (G. R. Davies 82, R. Haworth 65*, O. Bush 50) lost to M.C.C. 281-5 dec (D. L. Amiss 74, J. H. Edrich 66*, B. W. Luckhurst 50) & 242-6 (M. C. Cowdrey 85, B. W. Luckhurst 50) by 4 wkts.

23rd Match: v New Zealand (Melbourne) (Limited Over)   Feb 5.
New Zealand 262-8 beat M.C.C. 196 (A. W. Greig 79) by 66 runs.

24th Match: v Australia (Melbourne)   Feb 8, 9, 10, 12, 13.
Australia 152 (I. M. Chappell 65, P. Lever 6-38) & 373 (G. S. Chappell 102, I. R. Redpath 83, R. B. McCosker 76, I. M. Chappell 50) lost to England 529 (M. H. Denness 188, K. W. R. Fletcher 146, A. W. Greig 89, J. H. Edrich 70, M. H. N. Walker 8-143) by an inns & 4 runs.

25th Match: v Wellington (Wellington)   Feb 15, 16, 17.
M.C.C. 218 (A. P. E. Knott 56) & 52-1 drew with Wellington 188-6 dec (J. F. M. Morrison 80, G. A. Newdick 57).

26th Match: v New Zealand (Auckland)   Feb 20, 21, 22, 23, 25.
England 593-6 dec (K. W. R. Fletcher 216, M. H. Denness 181, J. H. Edrich 64, A. W. Greig 51) beat New Zealand 326 (J. M. Parker 121, J. F. M. Morrison 58, K. J. Wadsworth 58, A. W. Greig 5-98) & 184 (J. F. M. Morrison 58, G. P. Howarth 51*, A. W. Greig 5-51) by an inns & 83 runs.

27th Match: v New Zealand (Christchurch)   Feb 28, March 1, 2, 3, 4, 5.
New Zealand 342 (G. M. Turner 98, K. J. Wadsworth 58) drew with England 272-2 (D. L. Amiss 164*, M. H. Denness 59*).

28th Match: v New Zealand (Dunedin) Limited Over)   March 8.
M.C.C. 136 drew with New Zealand 15-0.

29th Match: v New Zealand (Wellington) (Limited Over)   March 9.
New Zealand 227 (B. E. Congdon 101) drew with M.C.C. 35-1.

30th Match: v Hong Kong President's XI (Hong Kong) (One Day)   March 12.
M.C.C. 239-3 dec (K. W. R. Fletcher 103) beat President's XI 155 by 84 runs.

31st Match: v Hong Kong (Hong Kong) (One Day)   March 13.
M.C.C. 234-3 dec (D. L. Amiss 101, B. Wood 68) beat Hong Kong 132 by 102 runs.

1974-75: English Counties XI tour of the West Indies

The following side visited Trinidad and Barbados in February 1975: J. H. Hampshire (Yorks) (capt), J. Birkenshaw (Leics), R. O. Butcher (Middx), R. E. East (Essex), F. C. Hayes (Lancs), D. P. Hughes (Lancs), P. G. Lee (Lancs), J. K. Lever (Essex), A. G. Nicholson (Yorks), D. W. Randall (Notts), G. Sharp (Northants), B. Wood (Lancs) and R. C. S. Titchener-Barratt (player-manager), with T. W. Spencer (umpire) and E. Solomon (scorer). Unfortunately Hughes had to return home due to a family bereavement and Wood was summoned to New Zealand to assist the M.C.C. team, so the team was unexpectedly depleted, S. A. Gomes was co-opted as a replacement.

The side drew all their important matches, but won all three one-day games. The batting and fielding was good, but the attack was not strong enough to overcome the opposition. The matches were poorly attended and there was little interest in the visit.

1974-75: English Counties XI to West Indies

1st Match: v Trinidad Under 23 (Queen's Park)   Feb 5, 6.
English XI 181-9 dec (J. H. Hampshire 52) & 173-4 dec (B. Wood 54) drew with Trinidad 133 & 72-4.*

2nd Match: v Trinidad (Queen's Park)   Feb 8, 9, 10.
Trinidad 274-5 dec (L. Gomes 103, S. A. Gomes 56) & 161 drew with English XI 240 (B. Wood 77) & 74-3.*

3rd Match: v Barbados (Bridgetown)   Feb 14, 15, 16.
English XI 222 (D. W. Randall 60) & 149-6 dec drew with Barbados 140-5 dec & 76-2.

4th Match: v Barbados (Bridgetown)   Feb 18, 19, 20.
Barbados 131 (W. Ashby 52, R. E. East 5-25) & 174 (R. C. S. Titchener-Barratt 5-25) drew with English XI 216-8 dec (S. A. Gomes 104) & 15-1.*

5th Match: v British High Commission XI (Bridgetown) (Limited Over)   Feb 21.
English XI 251-6 dec (J. H. Hampshire 134, D. W. Randall 92) beat High Commission XI 174-8 (C. L. King 53) by 77 runs.

6th Match: v Texaco (Brighton St Michael) (Limited Over)
English XI 175-6 (J. H. Hampshire 50) beat Texaco 92 by 83 runs.*

7th Match: v St Catherines (East Pt, St Phillip) (Limited Over)
English XI 164-9 beat St Catherines 160-9 by 4 runs.

1974-75: D. H. Robins' third tour to South Africa

The combination taken out by D. H. Robins in 1974-75 was not as powerful as the 1973-74 team and failed to win any of the first-class matches, but was more successful in the one-day games.

The team was D. B. Close (Somerset) (capt), B. C. Francis (Essex), J. F. Steele (Leics), F. C. Hayes (Lancs), J. H. Hampshire (Yorks), R. W. Tolchard (Leics), J. N. Shepherd (Kent), S. Turner (Essex), E. E. Hemmings (Warwicks), S. J. Rouse (Warwicks), G. A. Greenidge (Sussex), C. T. Radley (Middx), Younis Ahmed (Surrey), J. Lyon (Lancs), T. J. Jenner (Australia), M. H. N. Walker (Australia), F. M. Francke (Sri Lanka) and

```
1974-75: D. H. Robins' Team to South Africa

1st Match: v Natal (Durban)   Feb 28, March 1, 3.
Natal 257 (D. Bestall 105) & 172-7 dec (A. J. S. Smith 70) drew with Robins XI 164 &
220-6 (J. F. Steele 84, F. C. Hayes 69).

2nd Match: v Eastern Province (Port Elizabeth)   March 7, 8, 10.
Robins XI 232-6 dec (C. T. Radley 64, J. N. Shepherd 50*) & 280-7 dec (C. T. Radley
91, S. J. Rouse 53) lost to E. Province 254-6 dec (R. G. Pollock 103) & 260-5 (R. G.
Pollock 167*) by 5 wkts.

3rd Match: v African XI (Soweto) (Limited Over)   March 12.
Robins XI 286-6 (F. C. Hayes 132, R. W. Tolchard 79) beat African XI 154 by 132 runs.

4th Match: v Transvaal (Johannesburg)   March 14, 15, 17.
Robins XI 309-3 dec (B. C. Francis 96, Younis Ahmed 72, C. T. Radley 66) & 210-8 dec
(D. R. Neilson 5-83) drew with Transvaal 283-7 dec (W. van der Linden 87, B. L.
Irvine 68, C. E. B. Rice 50*) & 149-2.

5th Match: v African XI (Langa) (Limited Over)   March 19.
Robins XI 230-9 (S. J. Rouse 58, C. T. Radley 52) beat African XI 120 by 110 runs.

6th Match: v Western Province (Cape Town)   March 21, 22, 24, 25.
W. Province 231 (F. S. Goldstein 73, E. J. Barlow 69) & 206 (R. E. T. Morris 69) drew
with Robins XI 295-6 dec (F. C. Hayes 66, R. W. Tolchard 55) & 99-5.

7th Match: v President's XI (Cape Town)   March 28, 29, 31.
President's XI 371 (E. J. Barlow 155, B. A. Richards 58, A. W. Greig 5-33) & 265-4 dec
(R. G. Pollock 95, D. Bestall 57*) beat Robins XI 183 (P. P. Henwood 5-41) & 193
(T. J. Jenner 57, V. A. P. van der Bijl 5-44) by 260 runs.

8th Match: v President's XI (Cape Town) (Limited Over)   April 1.
Robins XI 160 lost to President's XI 162-5 (B. A. Richards 63) by 5 wkts.
```

```
1974-75: D. H. Robins Team to West Indies

1st Match: v Carlton Club (Black Rock)   Oct 22.
Carlton Club 157-7 beat Robins' XI 122 by 35 runs.

2nd Match: v Empire C.C. (Bank Hall)   Oct 24.
Robins' XI 156-7 lost to Empire C.C. 157-4 (C. King 55*) by 6 wkts.

3rd Match: v St Lucia (Castries)   Nov 3, 4, 5.
Robins' XI 349-4 dec (R. W. Tolchard 135, J. A. Jameson 94) beat St Lucia 82 & 254
(R. Depres 83, Mushtaq Mohammad 5-52) by an inns & 13 runs.

4th Match: v St Vincent (Kingstown)   Nov 7.
Robins' XI 135 beat St Vincent 78 by 57 runs.

5th Match: v Sr Vincent (Kingstown)   Nov 8.
St Vincent 109 lost to Robins' XI 111-4 by 6 wkts.

6th Match: v Dominica (Roseau)   Nov 12, 13, 14.
Robins' XI 359 (Mushtaq Mohammad 136, J. A. Jameson 84) beat Dominica 146
(G. W. Johnson 6-18) & 143 (J. Lawrence 57) by an inns & 70 runs.

7th Match: v Dominica (Roseau)   Nov 14.
Robins' XI 162 beat Dominica 150 by 12 runs.

8th Match: v Montserrat (Plymouth)   Nov 16.
Robins' XI 192 (J. A. Jameson 54) beat Montserrat 54 by 138 runs.

9th Match: v St Kitts (Basseterre)   Nov 17, 18.
St Kitts 96 & 57-5 drew with Robins' XI 191-4 dec (Mushtaq Mohammad 94*).

10th Match: v Leeward Is (St Johns)   Nov 23, 24, 25.
Leewards 181 & 295-5 drew with Robins' XI 327-8 dec (R. W. Tolchard 61, Mushtaq
Mohammad 56, J. A. Jameson 56).

11th Match: v Barbados (Kensington Oval)   Nov 30.
Barbados 124 beat Robins' XI 70 by 54 runs.

12th Match: v Barbados (Kensington Oval)   Dec 1.
Robins' XI 192-8 (J. A. Jameson 54) lost to Barbados 193-7 (P. D. Lashley 83) by
3 wkts.
```

A. W. Greig (Sussex) – Greig joined the team after being with the M.C.C. in Australia.

The most important match was against the President's XI at Cape Town, when two excellent innings by Barlow and R. G. Pollock combined with the bowling of Van der Bijl to defeat the tourists by 260 runs. R. G. Pollock was also in fine form for Eastern Province, scoring centuries in both innings. As on the previous visit the tourists played one-day matches against African sides.

1974-75: D. H. Robins' Team to South Africa

Batting Averages

	M	I	NO	R	HS	Avge	100	c/s
Younis Ahmed (Surrey)	2	4	1	155	72*	51.66	0	2
J. N. Shepherd (Kent)	5	8	3	233	50*	46.60	0	4
A. W. Greig (Sussex)	2	4	1	126	45	42.00	0	1
C. T. Radley (Middx)	4	8	0	316	91	39.50	0	5
F. M. Francke (Queensland)	3	3	2	38	21	38.00	0	1
T. J. Jenner (S. Austr)	3	4	1	106	57	35.33	0	1
D. B. Close (Som)	5	10	4	199	36*	33.16	0	4
J. F. Steele (Leics)	2	4	0	128	84	32.00	0	3
B. C. Francis (Essex)	3	6	0	187	95	31.16	0	0
F. C. Hayes (Lancs)	5	10	0	285	69	28.50	0	2
S. Turner (Essex)	4	6	2	90	33	22.50	0	0
S. J. Rouse (Warks)	3	4	1	62	53	20.66	0	2
M. H. N. Walker (Victoria)	3	3	1	32	12*	16.00	0	1
R. W. Tolchard (Leics)	4	7	0	108	55	15.42	0	11/1
E. E. Hemmings (Warks)	2	1	0	12	12	12.00	0	0
J. H. Hampshire (Yorks)	3	4	0	20	11	5.00	0	1

J. Lyon (Lancs) (ct 2, st 1) & G. A. Greenidge (Sussex) played in one match, but did not bat.

Bowling Averages

	O	M	R	W	Avge	BB	5i
A. W. Greig	57	9	187	10	18.70	5-33	1
J. F. Steele	53.1	11	158	7	22.57	3-30	0
M. H. N. Walker	116.1	26	306	12	25.50	4-59	0
J. N. Shepherd	142.5	27	467	14	33.35	3-57	0
E. E. Hemmings	41	7	141	4	35.25	3-32	0
S. Turner	91	15	273	7	39.00	2-45	0
T. J. Jenner	75	12	266	6	44.33	2-26	0
F. M. Francke	45	9	189	3	63.00	2-71	0
S. J. Rouse	64.3	11	269	4	67.25	1-29	0

Also bowled: D. B. Close 9-0-53-0.

1974-75: D. H. Robins' tour to the West Indies

The following team made a short tour of the West Indies in 1974-75: J. A. Jameson (Warwicks) (capt), D. L. Bairstow (Yorks), R. M. H. Cottam (Northants), B. Dudleston (Leics), P. H. Edmonds (Middx), M. J. Harris (Notts), G. W. Johnson (Kent), Mushtaq Mohammad (Northants), P. I. Pocock (Surrey), S. J. Rouse (Warwicks), P. J. Sainsbury (Hants), J. N. Shepherd (Kent), M. J. Smith (Middx), R. W. Tolchard (Leics) and S. Turner (Essex), with L. E. G. Ames as manager, D. Bennett as assistant manager and J. A. Jennings as physiotherapist.

Three weeks before the team left England the governments of Guyana and Trinidad & Tobago announced that the side would not be permitted to tour those countries due to Mr Robins connections with South Africa; it was also incorrectly reported that Mushtaq had been barred from joining the tour by the Pakistan Cricket Board for the same reasons. Mr Robins wrote to the two governments explaining his views, but neither would reverse its decision and the team, which flew out on 16 October, confined its matches to the Leeward Islands and Barbados.

The major match of the tour – a three-day game against Barbados was not started because of rain and two limited overs games were played there. Rain also marred several other fixtures. Mushtaq and G. W. Johnson played well on the tour.

1975-76: D. H. Robins' fourth tour to South Africa

In taking his fourth team to South Africa in successive years, D. H. Robins originally intended to include only players under the age of 25, but it was not possible to produce a strong enough side with this limitation and some more experienced players were added to the party. The full team was D. Lloyd (Lancs) (capt), G. A. Cope (Yorks), P. Carrick (Yorks), P. G. Lee (Lancs), D. W. Randall (Notts), P. A. Slocombe (Somerset), D. S. Steele (Northants), F. C. Hayes (Lancs), M. Hendrick (Derby), R. W. Tolchard (Leics), G. P. Howarth (Surrey), T. M. Chappell (Australia), J. R. Douglas (Australia), D. F. Whatmore (Australia) and G. B. Troup (New Zealand). F. J. Titmus joined the team later, when both Hendrick and Cope dropped out with injuries.

The war in Angola overshadowed the tour, as did the internal cricketing events in South Africa, when the three bodies governing white, black and coloured cricket in the country merged into one – unfortunately a selected 'mixed' team which was to have played the tourists never materialised due to squabbles.

The visitors played four first-class matches, winning two and losing two, though the game against Natal was desperately close and the tourists, set 164 to win on a spinners' wicket, failed by only 3 runs. Steele batted well, averaging 60 in all matches.

The team was managed by K. F. Barrington, whose guidance proved invaluable to the younger members.

1975-76: the first M.C.C. tour to West Africa

At the invitation of the West Africa Cricket Conference and with financial assistance from various businesses in the area, the M.C.C. sent for the first time a team to West Africa in the winter

of 1975-76. The side was: E. A. Clark (Middx) (capt), R. W. Barber (Warwicks) (vice-capt), J. G. Lofting (player-manager), J. R. T. Barclay (Sussex), L. J. Champniss (Bucks), T. M. Cordaroy (Middx), G. F. Goddard (Scotland), A. J. Good (Lancs), J. M. M. Hooper (Surrey), R. Julian (Leics), R. D. V. Knight (Gloucs), M. D. Mence (Berks), D. Nicholls (Kent) and D. C. Wing. M. C. Cowdrey agreed to join the tour halfway through, as Knight had to return to England.

The tour began in Gambia, where both matches were won. The tourists flew on to Sierra Leone where the first three-day game was played against West Africa. It was a fairly even match until the home side, requiring 241 to win in the final innings, collapsed to the fast bowling of Good. There were two matches in Ghana before the 'Second Test' against West Africa was played in Nigeria. Wing completely demolished the West Africans in their first innings and the tourists won with ease.

1976: tourists find standard in Canada dropping

The tour which D. H. Robins made to Canada in September and October 1976 played 15 one-day matches. The tourists found that the standard of cricket in the country had fallen compared with that of 1967 when the last major English side visited Canada.

The team was P. H. Parfitt (Middx) (capt), P. J. Sainsbury (Hants) (vice-capt), C. W. J. Athey (Yorks), J. R. T. Barclay (Sussex), P. R. Downton (Kent), M. W. Gatting (Middx), I. J. Gould (Middx), D. I. Gower (Leics), D. R. Gurr (Somerset), G. W. Humpage (Warwicks), V. J. Marks (Somerset), A. S. Patel (Middx), S. P. Perryman (Warwicks), R. L. Savage (Warwicks) and C. J. Tavare (Kent), with D. Bennett as manager.

The visit was marred by demonstrations against the team, organised under the impression that the side was from South Africa—in fact few if any of the tourists had been with D. H. Robins on tours there, so the demonstrators were confused.

The best match was against Edmonton, where the tourists just managed to win by 10 runs, but generally they were too strong.

1976-77: successful tour of India and the Centenary Test

The leading English cricketers had a rest in the winter of 1975-76 and after the mauling by Thomson and Lillee in the 1974-75 series under Denness, which was followed by an innings defeat at the hands of Australia in England in the First Test of 1975, the captaincy was given to A. W. Greig—not that this improved the English record, for they went down 3 matches to nil in the 1976 home series against the West Indies. The selectors however kept their faith in Greig and the full party to go to India in 1976-77 was A. W. Greig (Sussex) (capt), J. M. Brearley (Middx) (vice-capt),

Below *The M.C.C. party for the tour of India and Sri Lanka in 1976-77, which culminated in the Centenary Test in Melbourne on the way home. Back: R. W. Tolchard, G. D. Barlow, R. A. Woolmer, G. Mill, C. M. Old, R. G. D. Willis, M. W. W. Selvey, J. K. Lever, D. L. Amiss, G. A. Cope, D. W. Randall. Front: B. W. Thomas (physiotherapist), K. W. R. Fletcher, A. P. E. Knott, A. W. Greig (captain), J. M. Brearley, D. L. Underwood, K. F. Barrington (manager).*

Bottom left *John Lever bowling in the second Test in Calcutta. Lever figured in the dispute about his use of Vaseline, allegedly to keep the shine on the ball.*

Bottom right *Tony Greig is chaired by his team after the third Test in Madras which ensured an England win in the series. He and Brearley have their stumps.*

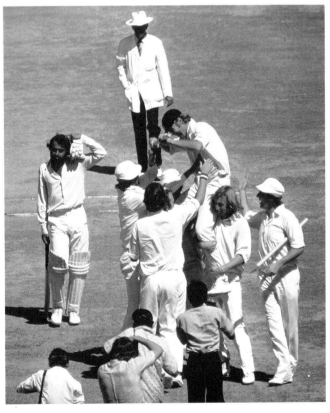

Above *The two teams for the Centenary Test, Melbourne, 1977. Back: D. L. Amiss, D. W. Hookes, R. A. Woolmer, G. J. Gilmour, J. K. Lever, R. G. D. Willis, G. J. Cosier, C. M. Old, R. D. Robinson, D. G. Barlow, R. J. Bright, I. C. Davis, D. W. Randall. Front: K. W. R. Fletcher, M. H. N. Walker, A. P. E. Knott, R. W. Marsh, A. W. Greig, G. S. Chappell, J. M. Brearley, K. D. Walters, D. L. Underwood, D. K. Lillee.*

Left *Action from the Centenary Test, Melbourne, 1977. Brearley about to be caught by Hookes in the gully off Lillee.*

Below *The hero of the Centenary Test, Derek Randall, hooking for four. He scored a brilliant 174.*

D. L. Amiss (Warwicks), G. D. Barlow (Middx), G. A. Cope (Yorks), K. W. R. Fletcher (Essex), A. P. E. Knott (Kent), J. K. Lever (Essex), G. Miller (Derbys), C. M. Old (Yorks), D. W. Randall (Notts), M. W. W. Selvey (Middx), R. W. Tolchard (Leics), D. L. Underwood (Kent), R. G. D. Willis (Warwicks) and R. A. Woolmer (Kent) with K. F. Barrington as manager. Those who were not included were Boycott, who still shunned Test cricket, Snow, whose fitness had caused him to miss two of the five Tests in 1976, Steele, who was most unlucky not to get a place and Willey, Hendrick and Gooch, who also just missed selection.

The tour was basically to India, but in order to celebrate the centenary of the first Test in 1877, the team were to go to Australia at the end of the programme and play a 'Centenary Test'.

Flying to India, the tourists began their fixtures with a drawn match against West Zone, in which Brearley, Fletcher and Greig all made hundreds. In the draw against Central Zone Barlow and Knott hit centuries, and the high scoring continued through all the early matches; the bowlers did not quite do enough to remove the opposition, but all the games ended with M.C.C. on top.

In the first Test, England began painfully, losing 4 for 65, but Amiss, Knott and Lever came to the rescue to build a reasonable total. Lever then celebrated his Test debut by bowling India out and the home team followed on 259 in arrears. Underwood did the rest and England unexpectedly won by an innings. The second Test was played on a difficult wicket, with the bowlers in charge. Hard fought innings by Tolchard and Greig, who batted with a high temperature, put England over 150 ahead on the first

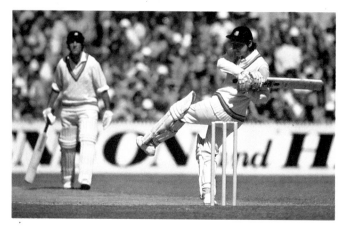

innings and India could do little in their second attempt, so that the tourists went two up in the series.

India's batting failed again in the third Test and England won a low scoring game by 200 runs. This match was the scene of the 'Vaseline' incident. Lever used strips of gauze coated with vaseline to prevent sweat running into his eyes, but the umpires maintained that the vaseline was used to keep the shine on the ball.

India batted better in the fourth Test and as Chandrasekhar exploited the wearing pitch to its full in England's first innings and Bedi continued the treatment in the second England innings, the home side won by 140 runs.

1976-77: M.C.C. to India, Sri Lanka and Australia

1st Match: v West Zone (Poona)   Nov 29, 30, Dec 1.
West Zone 257 (R. B. Bhalekar 66, E. D. Solkar 57, R. G. D. Willis 5-24) & 82-3 drew with M.C.C. 585-5 dec (J. M. Brearley 202, A. W. Greig 162*, K. W. R. Fletcher 118, R. W. Tolchard 67).

2nd Match: v Central Zone (Jaipur)   Dec 3, 4, 5.
M.C.C. 260-3 dec (G. D. Barlow 113, D. L. Amiss 60) & 155-1 dec (A. P. E. Knott 108*) drew with Central Zone 169-8 dec (A. P. Deshpande 64) & 120-5.

3rd Match: v Board President's XI (Ahmedabad)   Dec 7, 8, 9.
M.C.C. 289-5 dec (G. D. Barlow 102, D. L. Amiss 51, G. Miller 51*) & 127-4 dec (J. M. Brearley 59) drew with President's XI 213-5 dec (P. Sharma 111, A. V. Mankad 51*) & 144-6.

4th Match: v North Zone (Jullundur)   Dec 12, 13, 14.
M.C.C. 389-6 dec (C. M. Old 109*, J. M. Brearley 65, R. A. Woolmer 57, A. W. Greig 53) & 161-5 dec (C. M. Old 54*) drew with North Zone 210-8 dec & 126-3.

5th Match: v India (New Delhi)   Dec 17, 18, 19, 21, 22.
England 381 (D. L. Amiss 179, A. P. E. Knott 75, J. K. Lever 53) beat India 122 (J. K. Lever 7-46) & 234 (S. M. Gavaskar 71) by an inns & 25 runs.

6th Match: v East Zone (Gauhati)   Dec 27, 28, 29.
M.C.C. 213-6 dec (D. W. Randall 55, R. W. Tolchard 53) & 143-8 dec (G. D. Barlow 61) drew with East Zone 147 (R. Mukherjee 62, R. G. D. Willis 5-29) & 137-7.

7th Match: v India (Calcutta)   Jan 1, 2, 4, 5, 6.
India 155 (R. G. D. Willis 5-27) & 181 (B. P. Patel 56) lost to England 321 (A. W. Greig 103, R. W. Tolchard 67, C. M. Old 52, B. S. Bedi 5-110) & 16-0 by 10 wkts.

8th Match: v Combined Universities & Under 22 XI (Nagpur)   Jan 8, 9, 10.
M.C.C. 237-4 dec (J. M. Brearley 76*, D. L. Amiss 56) & 131-8 dec beat Combined XI 121 (G. A. Cope 6-41) & 104 by 143 runs.

9th Match: v India (Madras)   Jan 14, 15, 16, 18, 19.
England 262 (J. M. Brearley 59, A. W. Greig 54) & 185-9 dec (B. S. Chandrasekhar 5-50) beat India 164 (J. K. Lever 5-59) & 83 by 200 runs.

10th Match: v South Zone (Hyderabad)   Jan 22, 23, 24.
South Zone 228-7 dec (S. Abid Ali 63) & 107-2 (M. V. Narasimha Rao 64*) drew with M.C.C. 401-9 dec (D. W. Randall 142, D. L. Amiss 138).

11th Match: v India (Bangalore)   Jan 28, 29, 30, Feb 1, 2.
India 253 (S. Amarnath 63, S. M. H. Kirmani 52, R. G. D. Willis 6-53) & 259-9 dec (G. R. Viswanath 79*, S. M. Gavaskar 50) beat England 195 (D. L. Amiss 82, B. S. Chandrasekhar 6-76) & 177 (A. P. E. Knott 81*, B. S. Bedi 6-71) by 140 runs.

12th Match: v Bombay (Indore)   Feb 5, 6, 7.
M.C.C. 308-4 dec (J. M. Brearley 79, K. W. R. Fletcher 65*, D. W. Randall 61*, R. A. Woolmer 60) & 112-2 dec (G. Miller 52) drew with Bombay 201-7 dec (V. Mohanraj 76) & 97-5.

13th Match: v India (Bombay)   Feb 11, 12, 14, 15, 16.
India 338 (S. M. Gavaskar 108, B. P. Patel 83) & 192 (S. Amarnath 63, D. L. Underwood 5-84) drew with England 317 (J. M. Brearley 91, A. W. Greig 76, D. L. Amiss 50) & 152-7 (K. W. R. Fletcher 58, K. D. Ghavri 5-33).

14th Match: v Sri Lanka (Colombo) (Limited Over)   Feb 20.
M.C.C. 201-6 (R. A. Woolmer 63) beat Sri Lanka 178-7 (B. Warnapura 58) by 23 runs.

15th Match: v Sri Lanka Board President's XI (Galle)   Feb 22, 23.
President's XI 238 (J. Woutersz 53*, G. A. Cope 5-64) drew with M.C.C. 154-3 (J. M. Brearley 81*).

16th Match: v Sri Lanka (Colombo)   Feb 25, 26, 27, 28.
M.C.C. 360-6 dec (G. D. Barlow 118, A. W. Greig 59*, G. Miller 56) & 99-3 drew with Sri Lanka 151 & 210-6 (A. P. B. Tennekoon 97, B. Warnapura 69).

17th Match: v Sri Lanka (Colombo) (Limited Over)   March 2.
M.C.C. 123 lost to Sri Lanka 124-7 by 3 wkts.

18th Match: v Western Australia (Perth)   March 5, 6, 7.
W. Australia 326-8 dec (C. S. Serjeant 101*, R. W. Marsh 59) & 218-4 dec (R. S. Langer 83, R. I. Charlesworth 69) drew with M.C.C. 244-9 dec (J. M. Brearley 61, G. D. Barlow 60, G. Miller 56) & 239-8 (J. M. Brearley 58).

19th Match: v Australia (Melbourne)   March 12, 13, 14, 16, 17.
Australia 138 & 419-9 dec (R. W. Marsh 110*, I. C. Davis 68, K. D. Walters 66, D. W. Hookes 56) beat England 95 (D. K. Lillee 6-26) & 417 (D. W. Randall 174, D. L. Amiss 64, D. K. Lillee 5-139) by 45 runs.

1976-77: M.C.C. to India, Sri Lanka and Australia

Batting Averages

		M	I	NO	R	HS	Avge	100	c/s
G. D. Barlow	(Middx)	9	13	2	562	118	51.09	3	3
J. M. Brearley	(Middx)	14	20	2	888	202	49.33	1	14
D. L. Amiss	(Warks)	12	20	1	868	179	45.67	2	5
R. W. Tolchard	(Leics)	9	14	6	352	67	44.00	0	15
A. W. Greig	(Sussex)	13	20	2	705	162*	39.16	2	16
D. W. Randall	(Notts)	15	24	3	822	174	39.14	2	9
A. P. E. Knott	(Kent)	12	19	4	563	108*	37.53	1	30/2
G. Miller	(Derby)	10	11	2	325	56	36.11	0	5
K. W. R. Fletcher	(Essex)	10	16	3	356	118	27.38	1	9
C. M. Old	(Yorks)	12	17	5	325	109*	27.03	1	6
R. A. Woolmer	(Kent)	11	20	0	498	60	24.90	0	7
J. K. Lever	(Essex)	12	14	2	165	53	13.75	0	6
D. L. Underwood	(Kent)	10	10	1	94	23	10.44	0	9
R. G. D. Willis	(Warks)	11	10	4	62	37	10.33	0	5
G. A. Cope	(Yorks)	7	3	3	43	27*	—	0	3
M. W. W. Selvey	(Middx)	9	4	4	56	28*	—	0	3

Bowling Averages

	Balls	M	R	W	Avge	BB	5i
D. L. Underwood	2369	145	741	44	16.84	5-84	1
J. K. Lever	2128	62	898	53	16.94	7-46	2
G. A. Cope	1626	96	506	26	19.46	6-41	1
R. G. D. Willis	1656	41	740	37	20.00	6-53	4
C. M. Old	1494	52	624	28	22.28	4-104	0
G. Miller	776	44	314	10	31.40	4-54	0
M. W. W. Selvey	1252	53	616	19	32.42	3-81	0
A. W. Greig	1272	36	639	15	42.60	3-64	0
R. A. Woolmer	626	22	299	7	42.71	2-14	0
K. W. R. Fletcher	90	4	55	1	55.00	1-8	0

Also bowled: D. L. Amiss 12-0-21-0; G. D. Barlow 6-0-2-0; D. W. Randall 30-1-14-0.

set 463 to win. It seemed an impossible task, but an inspired performance by Randall, who hit 174, took England to within 45 runs of Australia and thus gave the supporters of both teams something about which to enthuse.

The tour of India was a great success for Greig, not only as a batsman but as a captain, and for once the English visitors managed to conquer the irritating ailments which usually sink most of the team. The English bowling of Underwood, who was at last really effective away from home, Willis, in short spells, and Lever, caused the Indian batsmen to struggle nearly all the time. The English batting was however unreliable and Knott was often required to make up for the deficiencies higher up. The fielding was very good, except in the last Test. The Indian spinners were not as destructive as expected, but perhaps this was due to the fact that India played three Tests against New Zealand immediately before the England series.

The moves to set up the World Series 'Super Tests' were being made in the spring of 1977, but it was not until May that the general public in England realised the extent of the plans.

1976-77: M.C.C. tour of Bangladesh

At the invitation of the Bangladesh Cricket Control Board, M.C.C. sent out a team for a brief tour in the winter of 1976-77. The side, which arrived by air on 29 December, was E. A. Clark (Middx) (capt), J. R. T. Barclay (Sussex), A. R. Duff (Worcs), J. M. M. Hooper (Surrey), M. D. Mence (Berks), M. E. J. C. Norman (Leics), J. D. Piachaud (Oxford), N. F. M. Popplewell (Hants), B. Taylor (Essex), D. R. Owen-Thomas (Surrey), M. J. Vernon (Gloucs), R. C. Kinkead-Weekes (Middx), D. C. Wing (Cambs) and J. G. Lofting as player-manager.

There were three two-day matches, two of which were drawn and one three-day 'Test' against Bangladesh. The home team won the toss and batted very slowly to reach 266 for 9 declared. M.C.C. attacked from the start of their innings, with Barclay making a splendid 65, but the only hope of a definite result was for M.C.C. to dismiss Bangladesh cheaply in their second innings. This they failed to do and the game was drawn. The attendance for the three days was about 90,000.

The fifth Test was very even. India ought to have scored more since the tourists dropped a number of catches, but these second lives were not used to the full. England began their last innings 214 in 245 minutes, but could only reach 152 for 7.

Having finished the tour of India, the team flew to Sri Lanka where four matches were played and then on to Australia for the Centenary Test. They had one game in Perth against Western Australia, in which the home side had the best of a draw, but because of travel difficulties, the M.C.C. arrived only the day before the match.

The Centenary Test, which was played in Melbourne before a gathering of most of the old England-Australia Test cricketers and in the presence of the Queen, commenced on 12 March. The first two innings went entirely the way of the bowlers, with Australia dismissed for 138 and England for only 95. Australia fell to 187 for 5 in their second innings, but Marsh hit a hundred and with fifties from Davis, Hookes and Walters, England were

1976-77: M.C.C. to Bangladesh

1st Match: v North Zone (Rajahahi)   Dec 31, Jan 1.
North Zone 119 & 185-7 dec (Raqibul 73) drew with M.C.C. 123-1 dec (J. R. T. Barclay 60, M. E. J. C. Norman 55) & 39-4.*

2nd Match: v East Zone (Chittagong)   Jan 3, 4.
East Zone 162 (Ashraful 68) & 74 (J. D. Piachaud 6-24) lost to M.C.C. 296-6 dec (J. M. M. Hooper 68, J. R. T. Barclay 60, N. F. M. Popplewell 55*) by an inns & 60 runs.*

3rd Match: v Bangladesh (Dacca)   Jan 7, 8, 9.
Bangladesh 266-9 dec (Yousuf Babu 78) & 152-6 drew with M.C.C. 347 (M. D. Mence 75, E. A. Clark 74, J. R. T. Barclay 65).*

4th Match: v South Zone (Jessore)   Jan 11, 12.
M.C.C. 204-5 dec (R. C. Kinkead-Weekes 68, E. A. Clark 60) & 117-4 dec drew with South Zone 203-9 dec (Raqibul 66) & 72-2.*

1977-78: D. H. Robins' tour of the Far East

Rain affected many of the matches on this tour to Malaysia, Singapore, Hong Kong and Sri Lanka. The team was M. H. Denness (Essex) (capt), M. J. Smith (Middx), P. Carrick (Yorks), C. S. Cowdrey (Kent), J. E. Emburey (Middx), D. I. Gower (Leics), D. R. Gurr (Somerset), G. P. Howarth (Surrey), Intikhab Alam (Surrey), K. B. S. Jarvis (Kent), J. K. Lever (Essex), H. Pilling (Lancs), R. W. Tolchard (Leics), P. Willey (Northants) and J. G. Wright (Derbys), with J. Lister as manager.

The team flew to Singapore and had two days in which to get acclimatised before going to Seremban for the first match. The tourists were well in control when at lunch on the second day rain flooded the ground and ended the game. The tourists were too good for most of the opposition and it was a pity that both the matches that might have extended them – in Sri Lanka – were drawn because of rain. Spin bowling reigned supreme throughout the tour, with Intikhab, Emburey and Willey prospering.

Gower batted in tremendous form in Hong Kong and in his innings of 114 v Combined Services hit no fewer than 10 fours and 5 sixes. The matches in Sri Lanka were watched by large crowds – in the first match there the gates were closed with 15,000 present, and it was a pity that such enthusiasm was not rewarded by better weather in the three-day matches.

1977-78: Derrick Robins' Team to Far East

1st Match: v H. R. H. Yang Di-Pertaun Besar's XI (Seremban)   Sept 20, 21.
Besar's XI 54 & 67-8 drew with Robins XI 208-4 dec (D. I. Gower 105).

2nd Match: v Singapore C.A. (Singapore) (Limited Over)   Sept 24.
Robins XI 194-6 beat Singapore 100-9 by 94 runs.

3rd Match: v Singapore C.C. (Singapore) (One Day)   Sept 25.
Robins XI 200-4 dec (C. S. Cowdrey 59) beat Singapore 110 by 90 runs.*

4th Match: v Combined Services (Hong Kong) (One Day)   Sept 29.
Robins XI 306-3 dec (D. I. Gower 114, M. J. Smith 80, H. Pilling 74) beat Combined Services 140 by 166 runs.

5th Match: v Ted Wilson's President's XI (Hong Kong) (One Day)   Oct 1.
Robins XI 195-5 dec (R. W. Tolchard 65, P. Willey 64) beat President's XI 84 by 119 runs.

6th Match: v Hong Kong (Kowloon) (One Day)   Oct 2.
Robins XI 167 drew with Hong Kong 94-9.

7th Match: v Penang Sports Club (Penang) (One Day)   Oct 4.
Robins XI 158-4 dec (J. G. Wright 82) beat Penang 63 by 95 runs.*

8th Match: v Royal Australian Air Force XII (Penang) (One Day)   Oct 5.
Robins XI 196-4 dec (C. S. Cowdrey 63, R. W. Tolchard 54) drew with R.A.A.F. 49-10.*

9th Match: v Malaysian President's XI (Padang)   Oct 9, 10.
Robins XI 197 (C. S. Cowdrey 72) drew with President's XI 25-2.

10th Match: v Sri Lanka Board President's XI (Colombo) (Limited Over)   Oct 12.
President's XI 121-9 lost to Robins XI 122-3 by 7 wkts.

11th Match: v Galle District XI (Galle) (Limited Over)   Oct 13.
Robins XI 199-6 (P. Willey 82, G. P. Howarth 50) beat Galle 119-5 by 80 runs.

12th Match: v President's XI (Kandy)   Oct 15, 16, 17.
President's XI 117 (R. Dias 49, P. Willey 5-3) & 107-3 drew with Robins XI 183 (R. W. Tolchard 52, J. Woutersz 5-25).

13th Match: v Sri Lanka Board President's XI (Colombo)   Oct 21, 22, 23.
President's XI 206-6 dec (B. Warnapura 100) drew with Robins XI 107-2 (D. I. Gower 59).*

1977-78: England tour of Pakistan and New Zealand

The Kerry Packer saga ran unabated through the English summer of 1977 and England, led by Brearley, had little difficulty in crushing an Australian side preoccupied by other matters. Boycott announced that he was now available for Test Matches and the England selectors put him back in the team. The England team (the T.C.C.B. had suggested that Test Match tours should be sent out under the title 'England', rather than 'M.C.C.') for the tour of Pakistan and New Zealand was selected as follows: J. M. Brearley (Middx) (capt), G. Boycott (Yorks) (vice-capt), I. T. Botham (Somerset), G. A. Cope (Yorks), P. R. Downton

1977-78: England to Pakistan and New Zealand

1st Match: v B.C.C.P. Patron's XI (Rawalpindi)   Nov 30, Dec 1, 2.
Patron's XI 151 (Shafiq Ahmed 52, G. Miller 6-62) & 118-6 drew with England 64-9 dec (Liaqat Ali 5-23) & 32-1.

2nd Match: v United Bank XI (Faisalabad)   Dec 4, 5, 6.
England 284-1 dec (G. Boycott 123, B. C. Rose 110*) & 165-3 dec (G. R. J. Roope 102*) drew with United Bank 210-4 dec (Sadiq Mohammad 53, Nasir Valika 53*) & 58-2.*

3rd Match: v N.W. Frontier Governor's XI (Peshawar)   Dec 8, 9, 10.
England 285-3 dec (G. Boycott 115, G. R. J. Roope 63*, J. M. Brearley 57) & 122-3 dec (D. W. Randall 57) beat Governor's XI 127 & 68 by 212 runs.*

4th Match: v Pakistan (Lahore)   Dec 14, 15, 16, 18, 19.
Pakistan 407-9 dec (Haroon Rashid 122, Mudassar Nazar 114, Javed Miandad 71) & 106-3 drew with Endland 288 (G. Miller 98*, G. Boycott 63).

5th Match: v Pakistan (Sahiwal) (Limited Overs)   Dec 23.
Pakistan 208-6 (Javed Miandad 77) lost to England 212-7 (B. C. Rose 54) by 3 wkts.

6th Match: v Habib Bank XI (Lahore) (Limited Overs)   Dec 28.
England 166-7 (G. Boycott 56) beat Habib Bank 103-7 by 65 runs.

7th Match: v Pakistan (Sialkot) (Limited Over)   Dec 30.
Pakistan 151 lost to England 152-4 (D. W. Randall 51) by 6 wkts.*

8th Match: v Pakistan (Hyderabad)   Jan 2, 3, 4, 6, 7.
Pakistan 275 (Haroon Rashid 108, Javed Miandad 88*) & 259-4 (Mudassar Nazar 66, Javed Miandad 61*) drew with England 191 (G. Boycott 79, Qadir 6-44) & 186-1 (G. Boycott 100*, J. M. Brearley 74).

9th Match: v Punjab XI (Bahawalpur)   Jan 9, 10, 11.
Punjab XI 217-9 dec (Mohsin Khan 97) & 193-9 drew with England 334-5 dec (D. W. Randall 87, G. R. J. Roope 85, B. C. Rose 72).*

10th Match: v Pakistan (Lahore) (Limited Over)   Jan 13.
Pakistan 158-6 (Mohsin Khan 51) beat England 122 by 36 runs.*

11th Match: v Sind XI (Karachi) (Limited Over)   Jan 15.
England 141-5 (M. W. Gatting 59) lost to Sind 142-7 (Mohsin Khan 59) by 3 wkts.

12th Match: v Pakistan (Karachi)   Jan 18, 19, 20, 22, 23.
England 266 (G. R. J. Roope 56, G. Boycott 56, D. W. Randall 55) drew with Pakistan 281 (Mudassar Nazar 76, P. H. Edmonds 7-66).

13th Match: v Auckland (Auckland)   Jan 27, 28, 29.
England 210 & 208-3 dec (B. C. Rose 107) drew with Auckland 182-4 dec (M. G. Burgess 74) & 114-3 (R. J. Kasper 61*).*

14th Match: v Northern Districts (Hamilton) (Limited Over)   Jan 30.
England 164-9 beat Northern Districts 83-3 on faster scoring rate.

15th Match: v Central Districts (New Plymouth)   Feb 1, 2, 3.
England 296-6 dec (M. W. Gatting 66, G. R. J. Roope 55, C. M. Old 55) & 104 (D. R. O'Sullivan 5-14) tied with Central Districts 198 & 202.

16th Match: v Canterbury (Christchurch)   Feb 5, 6, 7.
England 173 (C. M. Old 51, R. J. Hadlee 5-50) & 230-4 dec (I. T. Botham 126) drew with Canterbury 144 (P. G. Coman 51) & 142-5 (R. J. Hadlee 56).*

17th Match: v New Zealand (Wellington)   Feb 10, 11, 12, 14, 15.
New Zealand 228 (J. G. Wright 55, C. M. Old 6-54) & 123 (R. G. D. Willis 5-32) beat England 215 (G. Boycott 77) & 64 (R. J. Hadlee 6-26) by 72 runs.

18th Match: v Otago (Dunedin)   Feb 17, 18, 19.
Otago 130 (J. K. Lever 5-59) & 146 (I. T. Botham 7-58) lost to England 195 & 82-4 by 6 wkts.

19th Match: v Young New Zealand (Temuka)   Feb 20, 21, 22.
England 310 (D. W. Randall 104) beat Young N.Z. 139 (G. Miller 6-71) & 148 by an inns & 23 runs.

20th Match: v New Zealand (Christchurch)   Feb 24, 25, 26, 28, March 1.
England 418 (I. T. Botham 103, G. Miller 89, G. R. J. Roope 50, P. H. Edmonds 50) & 96-4 dec beat New Zealand 235 (R. W. Anderson 62, J. M. Parker 53*, I. T. Botham 5-73) & 105 by 174 runs.

21st Match: v New Zealand (Auckland)   March 4, 5, 6, 8, 9, 10.
New Zealand 315 (G. P. Howarth 122, G. N. Edwards 55, M. G. Burgess 50, I. T. Botham 5-109) & 382-8 (G. P. Howarth 102, R. W. Anderson 55, G. N. Edwards 54) drew with England 429 (C. T. Radley 158, G. R. J. Roope 68, G. Boycott 54, I. T. Botham 53, S. L. Boock 5-67).

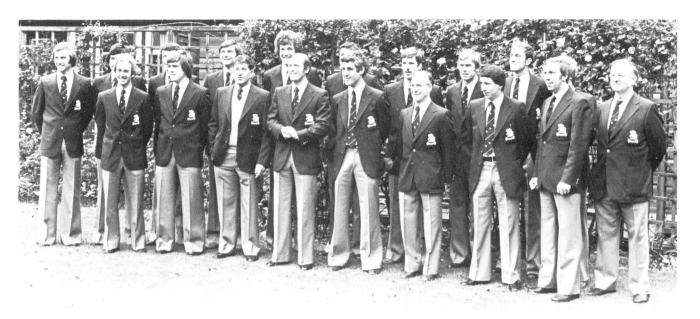

The England party for Pakistan in 1977-78. From left: J. K. Lever, G. Miller (partly obscured), R. W. Taylor, G. R. J. Roope (half-hidden), M. W. Gatting, C. M. Old, K. F. Barrington (manager), R. G. D. Willis, G. Boycott, M. Hendrick (almost hidden), J. M. Brearley, I. T. Botham, B. W. Thomas (physiotherapist), B. C. Rose, D. W. Randall, P. H. Edmonds, G. A. Cope, P. R. Downton (completely hidden), G. Saulez (scorer).

(Kent), P. H. Edmonds (Middx), M. W. Gatting (Middx), M. Hendrick (Derbys), J. K. Lever (Essex), G. Miller (Derbys), C. M. Old (Yorks), D. W. Randall (Notts), G. R. J. Roope (Surrey), B. C. Rose (Somerset), R. W. Taylor (Derbys) and R. G. D. Willis (Warwicks), with K. F. Barrington as Manager and B. W. Thomas as physiotherapist.

The players who had signed contracts for the Kerry Packer organisation, A. W. Greig, A. P. E. Knott, R. A. Woolmer, J. A. Snow, D. L. Underwood and D. L. Amiss, were not considered, which in effect meant that the English First Eleven lost four or five of its members.

It is worth nothing that each member of the England touring

party was paid £5,000, plus £100 for each previous M.C.C. tour. The payment for the 1976-77 tour had been £3,000.

The team flew from England on 24 November and the initial first-class match was begun on 30 November. After two draws, victory was achieved at Peshawar, immediately prior to the first Test. Like England, Pakistan were badly affected by players signing for the Packer organisation – Asif, Mushtaq, Imran, Majid and Zaheer were all playing in Australia – and the home team were fortunate that two young players, Mudassar and Haroon, hit hundreds for them. Pakistan had the better of a drawn game, but politically motivated riots on the second and third days marred the match. England won two one-day Internationals, before the second Test at Hyderabad. Pakistan again had much the better of a draw, and might have won, but Wasim Bari did not risk declaring until it was too late to dangle a carrot in front of the visiting batsmen.

Pakistan managed to win the last one-day International. In a minor game directly after it Brearley broke his arm and thus Boycott led England into the third Test. C. T. Radley (Middx) joined the team to replace Brearley. Kerry Packer released Mushtaq, Zaheer and Imran prior to the game and they arrived ready to represent Pakistan, but if they had been selected for the Pakistan side, England would have refused to play and thus ended the series. So Pakistan did without the three and a very dull plodding match was painfully enacted. The umpires pulled up stumps an hour before the end to save any further misery. That was therefore the end of the three-match series against Pakistan – three draws, and the England team flew off to New Zealand for a Test Match series of three.

The tour opened in Auckland too soon after the England arrival and the tourists had the worse of a draw. There was an exciting tie against Central Districts. With the scores level the last home batsman attempted a wild swipe at Willis and was bowled.

The first Test took place at Wellington and New Zealand created history by beating England for the first time – after 47 previous matches. The end of the first two innings left New Zealand with a 13-run advantage, but Willis then dismissed the home team for 123, leaving England requiring only 137 to win. The tourists capitulated before Richard Hadlee, who took 6 for 26, and New Zealand won by 72 runs.

The defeat was avenged in the second Test. Botham hit his maiden Test hundred and then returned the best bowling figures of the New Zealand first innings with 5 for 73 as England gained a handsome lead of 183. England went on to win by 174 runs.

The third Test was a high-scoring draw on an excellent wicket. In general the batting was too slow, neither side being too keen on losing the series, which was as a result drawn one match each.

1977-78: England to Pakistan and New Zealand

Batting Averages

	M	I	NO	R	HS	Avge	100	c/s
G. Boycott (Yorks)	13	20	3	867	123*	51.00	3	4
I. T. Botham (Som)	9	12	4	397	126*	49.62	2	7
G. R. J. Roope (Surrey)	14	19	4	725	102*	48.33	1	19
J. M. Brearley (Middx)	6	9	3	252	74	42.00	0	6
G. Miller (Derby)	13	17	3	468	98*	33.42	0	11
B. C. Rose (Som)	12	19	3	508	110*	31.75	2	8
C. T. Radley (Middx)	7	11	0	312	158	28.36	1	4
D. W. Randall (Notts)	14	21	0	589	104	28.04	1	7
R. W. Taylor (Derby)	11	13	2	236	45	21.45	0	20/1
M. W. Gatting (Middx)	8	12	2	177	66	17.70	0	7
C. M. Old (Yorks)	10	12	1	191	55	17.36	0	6
G. A. Cope (Yorks)	6	5	1	60	22	15.00	0	1
J. K. Lever (Essex)	8	8	2	65	33*	10.83	0	4
R. G. D. Willis (Warks)	11	11	6	50	14	10.00	0	3
P. H. Edmonds (Middx)	12	11	0	104	50	9.45	0	23
M. Hendrick (Derby)	7	6	2	33	15*	8.25	0	1
P. R. Downton (Kent)	4	2	0	9	9	4.50	0	11

Bowling Averages

	O	M	R	W	Avge	BB	5i
R. G. D. Willis	241.6	58	658	39	16.87	5-32	1
C. M. Old	176.3	56	488	28	17.42	6-54	1
I. T. Botham	210.4	41	691	35	19.74	7-58	3
J. K. Lever	192.3	40	576	29	19.86	5-59	1
G. Miller	249.2	51	880	38	23.15	6-62	2
P. H. Edmonds	337	85	834	33	25.27	7-66	1
M. Hendrick	128.5	28	288	10	28.80	2-20	0
G. A. Cope	161	40	455	14	32.50	3-102	0
M. W. Gatting	20.7	3	71	2	35.50	1-0	0

Also bowled: G. Boycott 4-0-5-0; D. W. Randall 2-0-3-0; G. R. J. Roope 3-0-19-0.

The twin tour could not be regarded as a success for England. The batting was too brittle. The one real bonus of the visit was the form of Botham, who made a great impact as both batsman and bowler. Roope and Randall were great fieldsmen, but hardly worth their places as batsmen. Rose was another failure and lost his Test place. Willis was the best bowler, though Old also could point to some good performances.

1977-78: the Minor Counties tour to Kenya

A representative team of the Minor Counties made their first overseas tour to Kenya, flying from London on 9 January 1978 to Nairobi. The team was D. Bailey (Ches) (capt), M. J. Ikin (Staffs), M. D. Nurton (Oxfords), N. A. Riddell (Durham), B. G. Collins (Herts), K. V. Jones (Beds), G. Wallen (Devon), P. H. Jones (Suffolk), M. Beaty (Cumberland), P. J. Kippax (Northumberland), P. N. Gill (Staffs), J. S. Wilkinson (Durham), D. I. Yeabsley (Devon) and R. Entwistle (Cumberland), with C. G. Howard as manager.

The first match was lost, but the side quickly learnt from this, and adapting well to the matting wickets won the other five matches. Unfortunately the three-day game with East African C.C. was washed out without a ball being bowled.

The tour was entirely successful and most enjoyable, the standard of cricket being very fair, but almost wholly confined to the Asian community.

1977-78: Minor Counties Team to Kenya

1st Match: v Kenya C.A. Chairman's XI (Nairobi) Jan 11.
Minor Counties 241-6 dec (R. Entwistle 66) lost to Kenya C.A. 242-5 (Rehman 139, Jawahir 52) by 5 wkts.*

2nd Match: v Kenya C.A. (Nairobi) Jan 13, 14, 15.
Minor Counties 344-7 dec (M. D. Nurton 83, P. J. Kippax 89, D. Bailey 59) & 153-3 dec (R. Entwistle 64) beat Kenya C.A. 178 (Jawahir 75, B. G. Collins 5-52) & 226 (Charantive 67, Nasoor 59) by 93 runs.

3rd Match: v Rift Valley (Nakuru) Jan 17.
Minor Counties 221-7 dec (M. J. Ikin 94, K. V. Jones 66) beat Rift Valley 118 (Shah 67) by 103 runs.

4th Match: v East African C.C. (Impala Gymkhana) Jan 19.
East African C.C. 121-7 lost to Minor Counties 125-2 (D. Bailey 58) by 8 wkts.*

5th Match: v East Africa C.C. Jan 20, 21, 22.
No play: Rain.

6th Match: v Mombasa Sports (Mombasa) Jan 28.
Minor Counties 311-9 (R. Entwistle 62, M. J. Ikin 67, P. N. Gill 67, N. A. Riddell 53) beat Mombasa Sports 141-9 by 170 runs.

7th Match: v Kenya Kongonis (Nairobi) Jan 29.
Minor Counties 247-7 (P. J. Kippax 76, R. Entwistle 54) beat Kenya Kongonis 97 (M. J. Ikin 5-27) by 150 runs.

1978-79: second M.C.C. tour of Bangladesh

The M.C.C. made their second tour to Bangladesh in December 1978 and January 1979. The team was: E. A. Clark (Middx) (capt), B. L. Reed (Hants), A. R. Duff (Worcs), S. Dyson (M.C.C.), C. A. Fry (Hants), C. B. Hamblin (Oxford U), C. C. Hunte (West Indies), J. A. Jameson (Warwicks), P. J. Levington (Berks), W. G. Merry (Herts), H. K. More (Scotland), N. J. W. Stewart (Berks), K. Taylor (Yorks) and C. L. Toole. B. L. Reed acted as manager.

The three 'Tests' against Bangladesh were all drawn, two of them in favour of the tourists. The visitors received an enthusiastic welcome everywhere and it was estimated that 200,000 people watched 13 days of cricket.

1978-79: M.C.C. to Bangladesh

1st Match: v C.C.B. President's XI (Jessore) Dec 29, 30.
President's XI 210-8 dec (Shafiqul 51) & 52-3 dec drew with M.C.C. 166 & 5-2.

2nd Match: v Bangladesh (Mymensingh) Jan 1.
Bangladesh 104-9 lost to M.C.C. 106-0 (J. A. Jameson 61) by 10 wkts.*

3rd Match: v Bangladesh (Rajshahi) (Limited Over) Jan 3, 4, 5.
M.C.C. 247 (J. A. Jameson 59, Nazrul 5-70) & 114-1 dec (C. C. Hunte 55) drew with Bangladesh 173 & 104-2.*

4th Match: v Bangladesh (Chittagong) Jan 7, 8, 9.
M.C.C. 303-8 dec (C. C. Hunte 89, H. K. More 60) & 105-3 dec (C. C. Hunte 53) drew with Bangladesh 192 (Shafiqul 73, W. G. Merry 5-45) & 97-7.

5th Match: v Bangladesh (Dacca) (Limited Over) Jan 10.
M.C.C. 155-7 beat Bangladesh 84 (C. L. Toole 5-6) by 71 runs.

6th Match: v Bangladesh (Dacca) Jan 11, 12, 13.
M.C.C. 210 (E. A. Clark 71) & 172-4 dec (C. C. Hunte 60) drew with Bangladesh 152 (N. J. W. Stewart 5-44) & 147-8.

1978-79: England easily beat Australia in 'Packer' tour

The 1978-79 series against Australia was played in competition with the World Series Cricket matches organised by Kerry Packer's companies. The English team therefore lacked Underwood, Knott, Amiss and Greig, but for the Australians matters were much more serious – of the seventeen who toured England in the summer of 1977, only two played in the 1978-79 series against England. The press, which was in the main anti-Packer, maintained that the 1977 Australians were second rate and most would have been discarded anyway. This theory, however, was totally demolished a year later when the opposing factions sank their differences and all the major pro-Packer Australians resumed their places in the official Test team.

Returning however to the summer of 1978, when the English selectors were picking the side to go to Australia, the problem initially was yet again the captaincy. Brearley had proved himself the ideal captain, but his performance as a batsman was not up to Test standard, so the newspapers had a field day on the old question of whether a captain is worth his place on his leadership alone. With all the disasters attributed to captains in the past, the selectors thought the answer was 'Yes'. The full team was J. M. Brearley (Middx) (capt), R. G. D. Willis (Warwicks) (vice-capt), I. T. Botham (Somerset), G. Boycott (Yorks),

---

1978-79: England to Australia

Batting Averages

	M	I	NO	R	HS	Avge	100	c/s
D. W. Randall (Notts)	10	18	2	763	150	47.68	2	6
R. W. Tolchard (Leics)	3	5	1	142	72	35.50	0	13
J. M. Brearley (Middx)	11	21	5	538	116*	33.62	1	11
D. I. Gower (Leics)	12	20	1	623	102	32.78	1	7
G. Boycott (Yorks)	12	23	3	533	90*	26.65	0	5
G. Miller (Derby)	11	18	3	398	68*	26.53	0	5
I. T. Botham (Som)	9	14	0	361	74	25.78	0	14
G. A. Gooch (Essex)	13	23	1	514	74	23.36	0	13
R. W. Taylor (Derby)	10	15	2	230	97	17.69	0	35/6
P. H. Edmonds (Middx)	7	9	2	115	38*	16.42	0	8
C. M. Old (Yorks)	6	6	1	81	40	16.20	0	2
C. T. Radley (Middx)	6	9	0	138	60	15.33	0	2
R. G. D. Willis (Warks)	10	13	4	115	21*	12.77	0	3
J. E. Emburey (Middx)	9	12	2	101	42	10.10	0	9
J. K. Lever (Essex)	6	7	0	67	28	9.57	0	0
M. Hendrick (Derby)	8	12	4	68	20	8.50	0	6

Bowling Averages

	O	M	R	W	Avge	BB	5i
M. Hendrick	185.4	40	399	28	14.25	5-11	1
G. Miller	277.1	74	607	36	16.86	6-56	2
J. E. Emburey	261.1	73	563	31	18.16	5-67	1
I. T. Botham	239.3	44	848	44	19.27	5-51	2
R. G. D. Willis	210.3	34	696	34	20.47	5-44	1
C. M. Old	138	24	452	21	21.52	6-42	1
J. K. Lever	119.1	18	377	13	29.00	4-28	0
P. H. Edmonds	147	34	397	11	36.09	5-52	1
G. A. Gooch	26	2	80	1	80.00	1-16	0

Also bowled: G. Boycott 3-0-11-0; D. W. Randall 2-0-9-0; C. T. Radley 1-0-4-0.

Above *England in Australia, 1978-79, taken before the fourth Test at Sydney. Back: D. W. Randall, C. T. Radley, J. K. Lever, G. Miller, I. T. Botham, P. H. Edmonds, M. Hendrick, J. E. Emburey, G. A. Gooch, D. I. Gower, R. W. Tolchard, G. Saulez (scorer). Front: B. W. Thomas (physiotherapist), G. Boycott, R. G. D. Willis, J. M. Brearley (captain), D. J. Insole (manager), R. W. Taylor, C. M. Old, K. F. Barrington (assistant manager).*

Right *The second Test of the 1978-79 Australian tour. Maclean about to be caught by Gooch off Miller.*

P. H. Edmonds (Middx), J. E. Emburey (Middx), G. A. Gooch (Essex), D. I. Gower (Leics), M. Hendrick (Derbys), J. K. Lever (Essex), G. Miller (Derbys), C. M. Old (Yorks), C. T. Radley (Middx), D. W. Randall (Notts), R. W. Taylor (Derbys) and R. W. Tolchard (Leics) with D. J. Insole as manager, K. F. Barrington as his assistant and B. W. Thomas as physiotherapist. The critics, apart from wondering if Tavare might have been picked, or Bairstow as reserve wicket-keeper, agreed with the selectors, and the team flew out on 24 October. The only query was Botham, who had injured himself at a farewell party, but he was expected to be fit before the first Test.

England had a surprise start to the tour when the batting collapsed twice against South Australia and the visitors were beaten, a young fast bowler, R. M. Hogg, causing the downfall. No other cloud however disturbed the party's progress to the first Test, when Australia had a terrible first two days – England obtaining a first innings lead of 170 – and though the home side

made a much better fight in their second attempt, England won by 7 wickets.

Boycott and Gower in contrasting styles saved the England batting in the second Test. Willis dismissed Australia cheaply and England went on to win by 166 runs. Against all the predictions, Australia won the third Test. Hogg bowled exceptionally well to remove England twice and Wood and Darling produced the runs for Australia. The home team looked like squaring the rubber in the fourth Test, when they again brushed aside the English batting and, through Darling and Border, obtained a first innings advantage of 142. Randall and Brearley happily returned to form in the England second innings and Australia required 205 to win in 265 minutes. The spinners, Miller and Emburey, took command, bringing England victory by 93 runs.

The trip to Tasmania and two one-day Internationals took place before the fifth Test, when the teams were even on first innings, but after Australia had taken six England second innings

wickets for 132, Miller and Taylor more than doubled the score, then Australia fell to Willis and Hendrick and lost by 205 runs.

Australia had some consolation in winning two one-day Internationals, but England found little difficulty in crowning the tour with victory in the sixth Test Match.

Owing to the counter-attractions of World Series Cricket, the interest in the 'official' Tests was much lower than usual and attendances at most games were very low. With Australia fielding virtually a second eleven, it was impossible to make any sound judgements on the performances of the English players. Gower and Randall easily topped the Test batting averages, but only because of the moderate achievements of the rest—Boycott and Brearley averaged 21.91 and 16.72 respectively and the other specialist batsman, Gooch, managed 22.36. The arguments over the Yorkshire captaincy obviously distracted Boycott from his run-making. The batting survived because of the strength of the all-rounders, Botham and Miller. Hendrick and Miller led the bowling table, but the outstanding man of the series was Hogg for Australia who took 41 wickets at 12.85 each.

The team were fortunate regarding injuries, the only serious one being to Tolchard—Bairstow was flown out to replace him, but scarcely played.

1978-79: England to Australia

1st Match: v South Australia Country XI (Renmark) (One Day)   Nov 1.
England 199-4 dec (C. T. Radley 64) drew with S.A. Country XI 137-6.

2nd Match: v South Australia (Adelaide)   Nov 3, 4, 5, 6.
S. Australia 311 (J. E. Nash 124) & 149 (I. R. McLean 52, P. H. Edmonds 5-52) beat England 232 (D. I. Gower 73, G. Boycott 62) & 196 (D. I. Gower 50) by 32 runs.

3rd Match: v Victoria Country XI (Leongatha) (One Day)   Nov 8.
England 130-8 dec beat Victoria Country XI 59 (J. E. Emburey 5-10) by 71 runs.

4th Match: v Victoria (Melbourne)   Nov 10, 11, 12, 13.
Victoria 254 (J. K. Moss 73) & 33-0 drew with England 241-8 dec (J. M. Brearley 116, D. W. Randall 63).

5th Match: v Capital Territory XI (Canberra) (Limited Over)   Nov 15.
England 255-2 (G. Boycott 123, R. W. Tolchard 108) beat Capital Territory 76 by 179 runs.*

6th Match: v New South Wales (Sydney)   Nov 17, 18, 19, 20.
England 374 (D. W. Randall 110, G. A. Gooch 66, I. T. Botham 56) & 4-0 beat N.S.W. 165 (J. Dyson 67, G. Miller 6-56) & 210 (A. M. Hilditch 93, I. T. Botham 5-51) by 10 wkts.

7th Match: v Queensland Country XI (Bundaberg) (Limited Over)   Nov 22.
England 259-5 (R. W. Tolchard 74, J. M. Brearley 59) beat Qld Country XI 127 by 132 runs.

8th Match: v Queensland (Brisbane)   Nov 24, 25, 26, 27.
Queensland 172 & 289 (J. A. Maclean 94, I. T. Botham 5-70) lost to England 254 (J. M. Brearley 75*, D. W. Randall 66) & 208-4 (G. Boycott 60) by 6 wkts.

9th Match: v Australia   Dec 1, 2, 3, 5, 6.
Australia 116 & 339 (K. J. Hughes 129, G. N. Yallop 102) lost to England 286 (D. W. Randall 75, R. M. Hogg 6-74) & 170-3 (D. W. Randall 74*) by 7 wkts.

10th Match: v Western Australia (Perth)   Dec 9, 10, 11.
England 144 (R. W. Tolchard 61*) & 126 (B. Yardley 5-54) beat W. Australia 52 (M. Hendrick 5-11) & 78 by 140 runs.

11th Match: v Western Australia Country XI (Albany) (Limited Over)   Dec 13.
England 208-4 (G. A. Gooch 112) beat W.A. Country XI 139 (R. Miguel 51, P. H. Edmonds 6-53) by 69 runs.

12th Match: v Australia (Perth)   Dec 15, 16, 17, 19, 20.
England 309 (D. I. Gower 102, G. Boycott 77, R. M. Hogg 5-65) & 208 (R. M. Hogg 5-57) beat Australia 190 (P. M. Toohey 81*, R. G. D. Willis 5-44) & 161 (G. M. Wood 64) by 166 runs.

13th Match: v South Australia (Adelaide)   Dec 22, 23, 24.
S. Australia 241-7 dec (B. L. Causby 87, R. J. Parker 51) & 231-6 dec (R. K. Blewett 51) drew with England 234-5 dec (R. W. Tolchard 72, C. T. Radley 60) & 238-9 (G. Miller 68*, G. A. Gooch 64).

14th Match: v Australia (Melbourne)   Dec 29, 30, Jan 1, 2, 3.
Australia 258 (G. M. Wood 100) & 167 beat England 143 (R. M. Hogg 5-30) & 179 (R. M. Hogg 5-36) by 103 runs.

15th Match: v Australia (Sydney)   Jan 6, 7, 8, 10, 11.
England 152 (I. T. Botham 59, A. G. Hurst 5-28) & 346 (D. W. Randall 150, J. M. Brearley 53, J. D. Higgs 5-148) beat Australia 294 (W. M. Darling 91, A. R. Border 60*) & 111 by 93 runs.

16th Match: v Australia (Sydney) (Limited Over)   Jan 13.
Australia 17-1 drew with England did not bat.

17th Match: v Northern New South Wales (Newcastle)   Jan 14, 15, 16.
Northern N.S.W. 223-9 dec (J. Gardner 59, C. Beatty 62) & 166 (C. Evans 64) lost to England 163 & 230-1 (G. Boycott 117, C. T. Radley 55*, J. M. Brearley 50) by 9 wkts.*

18th Match: v Tasmania (Launceston) (Limited Over)   Jan 18.
England 240-8 (I. T. Botham 61, D. W. Randall 60) beat Tasmania 77 by 163 runs.

19th Match: v Tasmania (Hobart)   Jan 19, 20, 21.
Tasmania 105 (C. M. Old 6-42) & 118-4 drew with England 210-5 dec (G. Boycott 90*).

20th Match: v Australia (Melbourne) (Limited Over)   Jan 24.
Australia 101 lost to England 102-3 by 7 wkts.

21st Match: v Australia (Adelaide)   Jan 27, 28, 29, 31, Feb 1.
England 169 (I. T. Botham 74) & 360 (R. W. Taylor 97, G. Miller 64) beat Australia 164 & 160 by 205 runs.

22nd Match: v Tasmania (Melbourne) (Limited Over)   Feb 3.
Tasmania 131-6 lost to England 134-7 by 3 wkts.

23rd Match: v Australia (Melbourne) (Limited Over)   Feb 4.
England 212-6 (D. I. Gower 101) lost to Australia 215-6 (P. M. Toohey 54*, K. J. Hughes 50) by 4 wkts.*

24th Match: v Geelong & District (Geelong) (Limited Over)   Feb 6.
England 165-9 beat Geelong 100-9 by 48 runs.

25th Match: v Australia (Melbourne) (Limited Over)   Feb 7.
England 94 lost to Australia 95-4 by 6 wkts.

26th Match: v Australia (Sydney)   Feb 10, 11, 12, 14.
Australia 198 (G. N. Yallop 121) & 143 (B. Yardley 61*, G. Miller 5-44) lost to England 308 (G. A. Gooch 74, D. I. Gower 65) & 35-1 by 9 wkts.

1978-79: D. H. Robins' tour to South America, including Colombia

In February and March 1979, D. H. Robins took his team to South America and broke new ground in visiting Colombia as well as Peru, Brazil, Chile and Argentina.

The team was C. S. Cowdrey (Kent) (capt), C. W. J. Athey (Yorks), N. E. Briers (Leics), R. G. L. Cheatle (Sussex), I. J. Gould (Middx), T. A. Lloyd (Warwicks), D. N. Patel (Worcs), S. P. Perryman (Warwicks), G. B. Stevenson (Yorks), L. B. Taylor (Leics), K. P. Tomlins (Middx) and J. P. Whiteley (Yorks).

All thirteen of the matches played were won, including the most important, which was the single 'Test' match played against Argentina.

P. H. Parfitt travelled as manager and H. Blofeld as assistant manager.

The full results of the tour have not been published.

1979-80: D. H. Robins' under-23 team to Australia and New Zealand

D. H. Robins confined his team to players under 23 for his six-week tour of Australia and New Zealand in February and March 1980. The team was C. S. Cowdrey (Kent) (capt), C. W. J. Athey (Yorks), K. J. Barnett (Derbys), N. G. B. Cook (Leics), K. E. Cooper (Notts), A. L. Jones (Glamorgan), C. Maynard (Warwicks), W. G. Merry (Middx), G. J. Parsons (Leics), D. N. Patel (Worcs), A. C. S. Pigott (Sussex), C. J. Richards (Surrey), G. C. Small (Warwicks), K. Sharp (Yorks) and R. G. Williams (Northants). B. Simmons travelled as manager, H. C. Blofeld as P.R.O. and L. E. G. Ames as 'vice-chairman'.

The strength of the team was in its spin attack of Patel, Williams and Cook, which coped successfully with most opposition batsmen, the two defeats being against North Tasmania, when the batting failed, and against Otago Minor Association, who were bowled out for 85 by Cooper in their first innings, but came back to win by 7 wickets through a century from Blakely. Both first-class matches were drawn – rain prematurely ended the first and in the second against Young New Zealand, Cowdrey declared to set the opposition 223 at about 5 runs an over.

1979-80: Derrick Robins' Team to Australia and New Zealand

1st Match: v New South Wales Colts (Sydney) (Limited Over)   Feb 17.
N.S.W. Colts 98-9 (C. W. J. Athey 5-14) lost to Robins XI 100-5 by 5 wkts.

2nd Match: v New South Wales Colts (Sydney)   Feb 18, 19.
Robins XI 169 (D. N. Patel 52) & 155-7 dec drew with N.S.W. Colts 93-8 dec (N. G. B. Cook 5-17) & 220-8.

3rd Match: v North-Western Tasmania (Devonport)   Feb 24, 25.
N.W. Tasmania 223-6 dec & 125-4 dec drew with Robins XI 129-7 dec & 125-8.

4th Match: v North Tasmania (Launceston) (Limited Over)   Feb 27.
Robins XI 241 (C. W. J. Athey 56) beat N. Tasmania 146 by 95 runs.

5th Match: v North Tasmania (Launceston) (Limited Over)   Feb 28.
Robins XI 102 lost to N. Tasmania 104-1 by 9 wkts.

6th Match: v Tasmanian C.A. (Hobart)   March 4, 5.
Robins XI 256-5 dec (K. Sharp 102*, K. J. Barnet 61) & 140-4 dec (C. S. Cowdrey 50*) drew with Tasmanian C.A. 163-7 dec & 136-6 (B. F. Davison 87*).

7th Match: v Otago Minor Association (Alexandra)   March 8, 9.
Robins XI 171-9 dec & 146-5 dec lost to Otago M.A. 85 (K. E. Cooper 6-32) & 234-3 (J. Blakely 124*) by 7 wkts.

8th Match: v Canterbury Minor Association (Ashburton)   March 11, 12.
Robins XI 173 (C. S. Cowdrey 60*) drew with Canterbury M.A. 88-1.

9th Match: v Marlborough (Blenheim) (One Day)   March 14.
Robins XI 181-8 dec beat Marlborough 138 by 43 runs.

10th Match: v Nelson (Nelson)   March 15, 16.
Nelson 147-9 dec & 274-5 dec (G. N. Edwards 144*, M. H. Toynbee 65) lost to Robins XI 184-7 dec (C. W. J. Athey 69) & 238-5 (C. W. J. Athey 73) by 5 wkts.

11th Match: v Manawatu (Palmerston North) (Limited Over)   March 18.
Manawatu 122 lost to Robins XI 123-0 (K. Sharp 69*, C. W. J. Athey 49*) by 10 wkts.

12th Match: v Hawke's Bay & Wairarapa (Napier)   March 19, 20.
Robins XI 232-5 dec (K. J. Barnett 81, R. G. Williams 52*) & 106-4 beat Hawke's Bay & W. 108 & 228 (Thompson 77) by 6 wkts.

13th Match: v Northern Districts (Hamilton)   March 22, 23, 24.
N. Districts 218-9 dec (D. N. Patel 5-69) & 226-3 (J. G. Gibson 65, J. M. Parker 60*, C. M. Kuggeleijn 50) drew with Robins XI 318-8 dec (K. Sharp 106, C. Maynard 57*).

14th Match: v Thames Valley Invitation XI (Ngatea)   March 25, 26.
Thames Valley 172 (K. Puna 77*) & 95 (R. G. Williams 5-34) lost to Robins XI 321-8 dec (R. G. Williams 157*, C. Maynard 50*) by an inns & 54 runs.

15th Match: v Young New Zealand (Auckland)   March 28, 29, 30.
Robins XI 223 (D. N. Patel 105, M. C. Snedden 5-41) & 300-4 dec (C. W. J. Athey 116, K. Sharp 82, D. N. Patel 54) drew with Young N.Z. 301-8 dec (I. D. Smith 72, M. C. Snedden 69) & 160-6 (J. A. Rutherford 75).

1979-80: England tour Australia with the West Indies

On 30 May 1979, the World Series Cricket organisation announced that agreement had been reached with the Australian Board of Control and that as a result the W.S.C. cricket programme would cease and the players contracted to that programme paid off. The result of this agreement was a hastily arranged tournament of one-day Internationals and Test Matches in Australia for the winter of 1979-80, with both England and West Indies touring there. The English schedule was a total of 20 matches in Australia of which nine were one-day Internationals and three were Test Matches.

England selected the following for the tour: J. M. Brearley (Middx) (capt), D. L. Bairstow (Yorks), I. T. Botham (Somerset), G. Boycott (Yorks), G. R. Dilley (Kent), G. A. Gooch (Essex), D. I. Gower (Leics), M. Hendrick (Derbys), W. Larkins (Northants), J. K. Lever (Essex), G. Miller (Derbys), D. W. Randall (Notts), R. W. Taylor (Derbys), D. L. Underwood (Kent), P. Willey (Northants), R. G. D. Willis (Warwicks). A. V. Bedser

The England party for the 1979-80 tour of Australia, in which a triangular one-day tournament took place with the West Indies as the third team. Back: G. B. Stevenson, P. Willey, J. E. Emburey, G. Saulez (scorer), G. R. Dilley, I. T. Botham, J. K. Lever. Centre: D. W. Randall, D. L. Bairstow, D. I. Gower, G. A. Gooch, W. Larkins, R. W. Taylor. Front: B. W. Thomas (physiotherapist), D. L. Underwood, R. G. D. Willis, A. V. Bedser (manager), J. M. Brearley, G. Boycott, K. F. Barrington (assistant manager).

went as manager. Old declined the invitation on medical grounds and the only omission of any note was Edmonds. Underwood was the sole W.S.C. player to be selected.

The side flew from London on 4 November and their arrival in Australia was greeted with cat-calls from the local press. The English authorities were unhappy about quite a number of points regarding the one-day rules and also the proposed floodlit matches: questions such as the proposed fines for slow over-rates, the use of a white ball, the number of bumpers to be allowed per over, whether the tourists would have to pay the cost of organising practice sessions under floodlight and a number of others. These problems were built up on by the Australian press and Brearley, in particular, came in for heavy attack, which spilt over from the press into the crowds at the matches. The bitter rivalry between W.S.C. and the I.C.C. could not be eradicated overnight.

Of the three Tests played in this confused fixture list, the first, at Perth, which was staged a month after the tour began, will always be remembered for Lillee's aluminium bat, which he attempted to use in the first innings – the argument held up play for ten minutes, after which he reverted to a traditional type. England held their own for the first half of the game, but in the final innings only Boycott held out as his colleagues were dismissed cheaply and Australia won by 138 runs. In the second Test, both sides struggled in their first innings on a damp wicket, but again England's second innings was a one-man-band – Gower – and though Underwood took three Australian wickets cheaply when the home side needed 216 to win Greg Chappell and Hughes steered them to victory.

With the series of three already decided, England went to Melbourne for the third Test. Brearley won the toss and Gooch and Boycott gave the tourists a great start with a partnership of 116, then the middle batting surrendered with a squeak. Australia built up a lead of 171 and although Botham hit a marvellous hundred, Australia wanted a mere 103 to win – the final margin was 8 wickets. The contrast between the five to one Test series in 1978-79 and the three to nil defeat was sharp indeed. The English authorities cried that the series was not 'for the Ashes', a statement which ranked with the famous remark that W.S.C. matches would be granted 'first-class' status if Mr Packer had played ball.

The other section of the tour concerned the one-day Internationals between Australia, England and West Indies. In the preliminary matches, England performed the best, winning 5 out of 8. West Indies came second and thus the final was between those two, which was a terrible blow to the organisers, since the

absence of Australia badly affected the attendance. Three dropped catches lost England the first match of the three to decide the champion country and as West Indies won the second with ease – Greenidge and Richards batting in top form – a third game was not required and West Indies took the crown.

The English side's batting was never very satisfactory. Randall was tried as an opener, but this experiment failed. Gower, who had looked so good the previous year, was not at all sound in the middle order, save for his 98 at Sydney. Willey, who performed well in one-day games, failed miserably in the Tests with 35 runs in 6 innings. Even Botham failed, except in the final Test, and later in India.

From Australia England flew to India for a special Test to celebrate the Golden Jubilee of the Indian Board of Cricket Control. The game was Botham's. He took 13 wickets and hit the only hundred of the match winning the game for England single-

1979-80: England to Australia and India

Batting Averages

	M	I	NO	R	HS	Avge	100	c/s
G. A. Gooch (Essex)	7	14	3	639	115	58.09	1	9
G. Boycott (Yorks)	8	15	4	599	110	54.45	2	3
G. Miller (Derby)	4	6	2	203	71	50.75	0	3
I. T. Botham (Som)	6	10	1	331	119*	36.77	2	5
G. R. Dilley (Kent)	5	6	3	101	38*	33.66	0	2
G. B. Stevenson (Yorks)	4	5	2	91	33	30.33	0	0
J. M. Brearley (Middx)	7	11	1	302	81	30.20	0	5
P. Willey (Northts)	8	12	3	269	101*	29.88	1	3
D. I. Gower (Leics)	9	15	2	354	98*	27.23	0	6
D. W. Randall (Notts)	6	10	0	250	97	25.00	0	3
R. W. Taylor (Derby)	8	11	1	227	47*	22.70	0	29/1
W. Larkins (Northts)	6	10	1	190	90	21.11	0	3
J. E. Emburey (Middx)	3	4	0	71	50	17.75	0	2
J. K. Lever (Essex)	7	7	2	75	22	15.00	0	4
D. L. Underwood (Kent)	6	8	0	88	43	11.00	0	5
D. L. Bairstow (Yorks)	2	2	0	13	12	6.50	0	2
R. G. D. Willis (Warks)	4	6	0	21	11	3.50	0	0
M. Hendrick (Derby)	1	1	0	1	1	1.00	0	0

Bowling Averages

	O	M	R	W	Avge	BB	5i
I. T. Botham	242	81	532	34	15.64	7-48	4
D. L. Underwood	260	81	609	25	24.36	7-66	1
G. B. Stevenson	87	13	307	11	27.90	4-44	0
G. R. Dilley	88.1	11	243	7	34.71	3-40	0
G. A. Gooch	43	13	113	3	37.66	2-16	0
J. K. Lever	235.5	55	622	16	38.87	4-111	0
J. E. Emburey	111.2	25	282	7	40.28	3-80	0
P. Willey	111	18	332	7	47.42	3-68	3
G. Miller	106	20	268	5	53.60	2-47	0
R. G. D. Willis	113	30	252	3	84.00	1-26	0

Also bowled: G. Boycott 4-0-19-0; M. Hendrick 4-1-14-0; W. Larkins 6-0-15-0.

Above *England players (Brearley and Taylor facing) make a concerted but unsuccessful appeal for leg before wicket against McCosker in the second Test match at Sydney on the 1979-80 tour.*

Above right *The one-day grand final at Melbourne between England and the West Indies at Melbourne. Bairstow survives a run-out attempt as Holding dives for the ball and wicket-keeper Deryck Murray watches.*

Right *The England party went from Australia to India to play a Golden Jubilee Test match against the home country in February 1980. The Indian captain Sunil Gavaskar caught behind by Taylor off Botham in the second innings.*

Right *One-day evening matches were a feature of the 1979-80 Australian tour. The sunset, clouds and floodlights make a dramatic backdrop for this match at Sydney.*

Far right *The Golden Jubilee Test match in India was a personal triumph for Ian Botham, who produced the greatest all-round performance in Test history—an innings of 114 and bowling analyses of 6-58 and 7-48.*

handed. The rest of the team were still shell-shocked from the junketings in Australia.

The whole tour was best forgotten. Botham enhanced his reputation and Gooch improved. Miller and Hendrick were both injured, which adversely affected the bowling, Embury and G. B. Stevenson (Yorkshire) being flown out as replacements. Willis had a lean time and ended the tour by only being first change, instead of opening the bowling.

For Australia, Greg Chappell was outstanding. Lillee worried England most, but Dymock headed the Test bowling table. Hogg was slain by the West Indians and Thomson was of little account.

1979-80: M.C.C. to Australia and India

1st Match: v Queensland (Brisbane)   Nov 12, 13, 14.
England 176 (D. W. Randall 97, C. G. Rackemann 5-25) & 226-5 dec (G. Miller 57*, P. Willey 57*, D. I. Gower 50) drew with Queensland 219-9 dec (T. V. Hohns 62, M. F. Kent 58) & 97-1.

2nd Match: v Northern New South Wales (Newcastle) (Limited Over)   Nov 17.
Northern N.S.W. 133 (C. Beatty 67) lost to England 136-1 (G. Boycott 78) by 9 wkts.

3rd Match: v Northern New South Wales (Newcastle) (Limited Over)   Nov 18.
England 213-7 (J. M. Brearley 67, W. Larkins 51) beat Northern N.S.W. 181-7 (G. G. Geise 58*) by 32 runs.

4th Match: v Combined Universities (Adelaide)   Nov 22, 23, 24, 25.
England 179 (D. W. Randall 97, C. G. Rackemann 6-78) & 411-8 dec (G. A. Gooch 124, I. T. Botham 76, R. W. Taylor 66*) drew with Universities 168 (C. Beatty 53, D. L. Underwood 8-41) & 227-5 (D. M. Wellham 95, P. J. Davies 57).

5th Match: v West Indies (Sydney) (Limited Over)   Nov 28.
England 211-8 (P. Willey 58*) beat West Indies 196 (L. G. Rowe 60) by 2 runs.

6th Match: v Tasmania (Hobart)   Nov 30, Dec 1, 2.
England 214-3 dec (G. Boycott 101*, G. A. Gooch 51) & 135-1 dec (G. A. Gooch 70*, D. I. Gower 53) beat Tasmania 71-3 dec & 178 (R. L. Knight 74, D. L. Underwood 7-66).

7th Match: v South Australia (Adelaide)   Dec 4, 5, 6.
England 252-2 dec (G. Boycott 110, J. M. Brearley 81) & 227-7 dec (G. Miller 71, G. Boycott 63*) drew with South Australia 226-4 dec (J. J. Crowe 78*) & 181-3 (W. M. Darling 75*, J. J. Crowe 55).

8th Match: v Australia (Melbourne) (Limited Over)   Dec 8.
Australia 207-9 (G. S. Chappell 92) lost to England 209-7 (G. Boycott 68) by 3 wkts.

9th Match: v Australia (Sydney) (Limited Over)   Dec 11.
England 264-7 (G. Boycott 105, P. Willey 64) beat Australia 192 (T. J. Laughlin 74) by 72 runs.

10th Match: v Australia (Perth)   Dec 14, 15, 16, 18, 19.
Australia 244 (K. J. Hughes 99, I. T. Botham 6-78) & 337 (A. R. Border 115, J. M. Wiener 58, I. T. Botham 5-98) beat England 228 (J. M. Brearley 64) & 215 (G. Boycott 99*, G. Dymock 6-34) by 138 runs.

11th Match: v West Indies (Brisbane) (Limited Over)   Dec 23.
England 217-8 (G. Boycott 68, D. I. Gower 59) lost to West Indies 218-1 (C. G. Greenidge 85*, I. V. A. Richards 85*) by 9 wkts.

12th Match: v Australia (Sydney) (Limited Over)   Dec 26.
Australia 194-6 (I. M. Chappell 60*, G. S. Chappell 52) lost to England 195-6 (G. Boycott 86*, P. Willey 51) by 4 wkts.

13th Match: v Queensland (Brisbane)   Dec 28, 29, 30, 31.
England 324 (G. A. Gooch 115, J. E. Embury 50) & 274-8 dec (P. Willey 101*, G. A. Gooch 53) beat Queensland 237 (W. R. Broad 53, A. D. Parker 52*, M. G. Morgan 50) & 223 by 138 runs.

14th Match: v Australia (Sydney)   Jan 4, 5, 6, 8.
England 123 & 237 (D. I. Gower 98*) lost to Australia 145 & 219-4 (G. S. Chappell 98*) by 6 wkts.

15th Match: v West Indies (Melbourne)   Jan 12.
No play: rain.

16th Match: v Australia (Sydney) (Limited Over)   Jan 14.
Australia 163 lost to England 164-8 (G. A. Gooch 69) by 2 wkts.

17th Match: v West Indies (Adelaide) (Limited Over)   Jan 16.
West Indies 246-5 (I. V. A. Richards 88, A. I. Kallicharran 57, C. G. Greenidge 50) beat England 139 (A. M. E. Roberts 5-22) by 107 runs.

18th Match: v West Indies (Melbourne) (Limited Over)   Jan 20.
West Indies 215-8 (C. G. Greenidge 80) beat England 213-7 (P. Willey 51) by 2 runs.

19th Match: v West Indies (Limited Over)   Jan 22.
England 208-8 (G. Boycott 63) lost to West Indies 209-2 (C. G. Greenidge 98*, I. V. A. Richards 65) by 8 wkts.

20th Match: v New South Wales (Canberra)   Jan 27, 28, 29.
New South Wales 212-7 dec (K. D. Walters 62) & 243-2 dec (A. M. J. Hilditch 78, T. M. Chappell 70*) lost to England 203 & 254-2 (W. Larkins 90, G. A. Gooch 73*, G. Boycott 51) by 8 wkts.

21st Match: v Australia (Melbourne)   Feb 1, 2, 3, 5, 6.
England 306 (G. A. Gooch 99, J. M. Brearley 60*, D. K. Lillee 6-60) & 273 (I. T. Botham 119*, G. A. Gooch 51, D. K. Lillee 5-78) lost to Australia 477 (G. S. Chappell 114, I. M. Chappell 75, B. M. Laird 74, A. R. Border 63) & 103-2 by 8 wkts.

22nd Match: v India (Bombay)   Feb 15, 17, 18, 19.
India 242 (I. T. Botham 6-58) & 149 (I. T. Botham 7-48) lost to England 296 (I. T. Botham 114, K. D. Ghavri 5-52) & 98-0 by 10 wkts.

1980-81: England well beaten in tour of the West Indies

The selectors delayed announcing the English team for West Indies until 15 September, due to a small extent to the injuries of Willey, Dilley, Edmonds and Botham, though whether anyone could forecast the fitness of those four three months ahead – the tour did not commence until January – seemed unlikely. The team was I. T. Botham (Somerset) (capt), R. G. D. Willis (Warwicks) (vice-capt), D. L. Bairstow (Yorks), G. Boycott (Yorks), R. O. Butcher (Middx), G. R. Dilley (Kent), P. R. Downton (Middx), J. E. Embury (Middx), M. W. Gatting (Middx), G. A. Gooch (Essex), D. I. Gower (Leics), G. Miller (Derbys), C. M. Old (Yorks), B. C. Rose (Somerset), G. B. Stevenson (Yorks), P. Willey (Northants). A. C. Smith was appointed manager with K. F. Barrington as his assistant, and B. W. Thomas as physiotherapist.

The team left England on 15 January and the tour opened in Trinidad on 23 January, where England had little difficulty in beating a Young West Indian XI. The four-day game against the Windwards was washed out by rain and replaced by two one-day matches, both of which England won, but they were unlucky to lose the first one-day International by just two runs. Rain ruined the first-class game at Port of Spain, just prior to the first Test. In this England were completely outplayed; the fast brigade of Roberts, Holding, Croft and Garner blasted their way through the English batting – Boycott alone achieved a fifty – but the England attack without Willis's old power was soon blunted and the West Indies made a big score.

The Warwickshire bowler had broken down in Trinidad and Jackman was sent as a replacement. The arrival of Jackman coincided with the Guyanan section of the tour. Politics then took over and on 26 February the Guyana Government decided to expel Jackman on the grounds that he had played cricket in South Africa. The authorities at Lord's countered by refusing to play the second Test, due to commence on 28 February. The English team flew to Barbados as the various West Indian Governments took stock of the situation. The tour was in the balance. On 4 March, the Governments concerned agreed that the tour should continue and the scheduled one-day match against Barbados began as planned the next day. In the meanwhile, Rose, who had eye trouble, was flown home and Athey of Yorkshire arrived to take his place.

England won the one-day game, but drew with Barbados, prior to the third Test at Bridgetown. Once more the tourists were outplayed. Clive Lloyd hit a century in the first innings and Richards one in the second – the English batting wilted before the fast bowlers, except that Gooch fought splendidly in the second innings. The defeat was by 298 runs.

The match was marred by the sudden death of Barrington, the assistant manager, on the second evening.

The fourth Test was the first staged at St John's, Antigua. England saved the game due to rain and an unbeaten hundred from Boycott in the second innings, after they had been nearly 200 behind on the first innings.

The last leg of the tour took the team to Jamaica where they first met the island side. The game was drawn, but the team did well enough to obtain a first innings lead – if they had played two spinners, there might have been a chance of victory.

The final game of the visit was the fifth Test. Lloyd put England in but his gamble only half worked, as Boycott and Gooch gave their team a good start – the other batsmen failed miserably however and West Indies gained their customary large first innings lead. The England second innings slumped to 32 for 3 and a loss seemed likely, but Gower and Willey put on a hundred for the fourth wicket and the match was drawn. England thus fought back well in the last two Tests, to save some honour.

West Indies won the series by two matches to nil and there could be no doubt that they were the better team. The idea of saddling Botham with the captaincy was obvious madness and the great all-rounder proved it by his performances – his Test batting average was 10.42.

The advocates of Botham as captain were quick to point out that the atmosphere between the teams, in the English team itself and even in the crowds – for once there were no riots – was excellent and Botham deserved his credit for this. It did not seem to occur to these advocates that the serene atmosphere was due to the fact that the West Indies were never even remotely in danger of losing a single Test.

The successes in the English side were Gooch and Gower and for West Indies Holding and Croft, though Richards did all that was expected of him and the old maestro, Lloyd, flourished once more.

Below *The England party in Barbados for the third Test of the tour of the West Indies, 1980-81. Back : D. L. Bairstow, R. D. Jackman, M. W. Gatting, C. W. J. Athey, G. B. Stevenson, G. R. Dilley, J. E. Emburey, P. Willey, D. I. Gower, P. R. Downton, R. O. Butcher, G. Saulez (scorer). Front : B. W. Thomas (physiotherapist), G. A. Gooch, G. Miller, I. T. Botham, A. C. Smith (manager), G. Boycott, C. M. Old, K. F. Barrington (assistant manager). It was during this match that Ken Barrington died.*

Bottom left *Colin Croft was one of the most successful in a battery of fast bowlers which the West Indies used to destroy the English batting in the 1980-81 tour of the West Indies.*

Bottom right *David Gower was one of the few English batsmen on the 1980-81 tour of the West Indies to return with his reputation undiminished. He appears to be enjoying this sweep to fine leg.*

Action from the first Test of the 1980-81 West Indies tour. Michael Holding takes his 100th Test wicket as Brian Rose is caught behind by Deryck Murray.

1980-81: England to West Indies

1st Match: v Young West Indies (Pointe-a-Pierre)   Jan 23, 24, 25, 26.
England 483-6 dec (D. I. Gower 187, M. W. Gatting 94, G. Boycott 87, R. A. Harper 5-142) & 208-5 dec (G. Boycott 87) beat Young West Indies 320 (P. J. Dujon 105*) & 181 (G. Miller 6-70) by 190 runs.

2nd Match: v Windward Is (Arnos Vale)   Jan 30, 31, Feb 1, 2.
No play.

3rd Match: v Windward Is (Arnos Vale) (Limited Over)   Feb 1.
England 165-9 beat Windward Is 150-9 by 15 runs.

4th Match: v Windward Is (Arnos Vale) (Limited Over)   Feb 2.
Windward Is 183 (L. John 56) lost to England 184-4 (G. Boycott 85*, G. A. Gooch 50) by 6 wkts.

5th Match: v West Indies (Arnos Vale) (Limited Over)   Feb 4.
West Indies 127 (E. H. Mattis 62) beat England 125 (I. T. Botham 60) by 2 runs.

6th Match: v Trinidad & Tobago (Port of Spain)   Feb 7, 8, 9, 10.
England 355 (G. A. Gooch 117, D. I. Gower 77, G. Boycott 70) drew with Trinidad & Tobago 392-8 (H. A. Gomes 75, D. L. Murray 75, T. Cuffy 61, R. Nanaan 66*).

7th Match: v West Indies (Port of Spain)   Feb 13, 14, 16, 17, 18.
West Indies 426-9 dec (D. L. Haynes 96, C. G. Greenidge 84, C. H. Lloyd 64, A. M. E. Roberts 50*, J. E. Emburey 5-124) beat England 178 (C. E. H. Croft 5-40) & 169 (G. Boycott 70) by an inns & 79 runs.

8th Match: v Guyana (Georgetown)   Feb 21, 22, 23, 24.
No play.

9th Match: v Guyana (Georgetown)   Feb 24.
No play.

10th Match: v Guyana (Georgetown)   Feb 25.
No play.

11th Match: v West Indies (Berbice) (Limited Over)   Feb 26.
England 137 lost to West Indies 138-4 by 6 wkts.

12th Match: v West Indies (Georgetown)   Feb 28, March 1, 2, 4, 5. Cancelled.

13th Match: v Barbados (Bridgetown) (Limited Over)   March 5.
England 207-6 (G. A. Gooch 84) beat Barbados 196 (G. N. Reifer 55) by 11 runs.

14th Match: v Barbados (Bridgetown)   March 7, 8, 9, 10.
England 298 (G. Boycott 77) & 219-6 drew with Barbados 334 (C. L. King 76, J. E. Emburey 5-92).

15th Match: v West Indies (Bridgetown)   March 13, 14, 15, 17, 18.
West Indies 265 (C. H. Lloyd 100, H. A. Gomes 58) & 379-7 dec (I. V. A. Richards 182*, C. H. Lloyd 66) beat England 122 & 224 (G. A. Gooch 116, D. I. Gower 54) by 298 runs.

16th Match: v Leeward Is (Plymouth)   March 21, 22, 23, 24.
Leeward Is 161 (A. L. Kelly 72, G. R. Dilly 5-48, G. B. Stevenson 5-50) & 263 (S. I. Williams 62, V. A. Amory 56) lost to England 251 (G. Miller 91*, G. Boycott 72) & 174-5 (R. O. Butcher 77*) by 5 wkts.

17th Match: v West Indies (St Johns)   March 27, 28, 29, 31, April 1.
England 271 (P. Willey 102, C. E. H. Croft 6-74) & 234-3 (G. Boycott 104*, G. A. Gooch 83) drew with West Indies 468-9 dec (I. V. A. Richards 114, C. G. Greenidge 63, C. H. Lloyd 58, M. A. Holding 58*).

18th Match: v Jamaica (Kingston)   April 4, 5, 6, 7.
England 413 (G. Boycott 98, M. W. Gatting 93) & 294-8 dec (G. A. Gooch 122, R. O. Butcher 51) drew with Jamaica 368 (L. G. Rowe 116, M. C. Neita 67, R. A. Austin 62, J. E. Emburey 6-92).

19th Match: v West Indies (Kingston)   April 10, 11, 12, 14, 15.
England 285 (G. A. Gooch 153, M. A. Holding 5-56) & 302-6 dec (D. I. Gower 154*, P. Willey 67) drew with West Indies 442 (C. H. Lloyd 95, H. A. Gomes 90*, D. L. Haynes 84, C. G. Greenidge 62).

1980-81: England to the West Indies

Batting Averages

		M	I	NO	R	HS	Avge	100	c/s
G. A. Gooch	(Essex)	7	13	0	777	153	59.76	4	4
D. I. Gower	(Leics)	8	14	1	726	187	55.84	2	4
G. Boycott	(Yorks)	9	17	2	818	104*	54.53	1	2
P. Willey	(Northts)	7	13	5	383	102*	47.87	1	0
G. Miller	(Derby)	4	7	3	151	91*	37.75	0	4
R. O. Butcher	(Middx)	7	13	2	385	77*	35.00	0	7
M. W. Gatting	(Middx)	5	9	0	268	94	29.77	0	3
C. W. J. Athey	(Yorks)	4	8	0	121	41	15.12	0	1
I. T. Botham	(Som)	8	14	0	197	40	14.07	0	8
B. C. Rose	(Som)	3	5	0	69	43	13.80	0	0
D. L. Bairstow	(Yorks)	4	7	2	64	26*	12.80	0	9/1
R. D. Jackman	(Surrey)	5	7	2	47	17	9.40	0	0
J. E. Emburey	(Middx)	7	10	2	74	34	9.25	0	3
P. R. Downton	(Middx)	6	9	1	67	26*	8.37	0	11/3
G. R. Dilley	(Kent)	7	8	4	26	15*	6.50	0	0
C. M. Old	(Yorks)	4	4	0	13	8	3.25	0	5
G. B. Stevenson	(Yorks)	4	4	0	6	3	1.50	0	0

Bowling Averages

	O	M	R	W	Avge	BB	5i
G. Miller	109.2	29	299	14	21.35	6-70	1
R. D. Jackman	136.2	29	380	12	31.66	4-68	0
I. T. Botham	224.2	43	790	23	34.34	4-77	0
G. R. Dilley	212.2	44	733	20	36.65	5-48	1
G. B. Stevenson	88	16	337	9	37.44	5-50	1
J. E. Emburey	300.4	95	675	18	37.50	6-92	3
P. Willey	110	28	269	7	38.42	3-29	0
C. M. Old	62.3	14	208	5	41.60	3-60	0

Also bowled: G. Boycott 3-2-5-0; M. W. Gatting 3-1-10-0; G. A. Gooch 42-14-108-1.

1980-81: Middlesex tour of Zimbabwe

The Middlesex team went on a six-match tour of Zimbabwe in September and October 1980 with the following side: J. M. Brearley (capt), R. O. Butcher, N. G. Cowans, P. R. Downton, J. E. Emburey, M. W. Gatting, I. J. Gould, S. P. Hughes, R. J. Maru, W. G. Merry, C. T. Radley, M. W. W. Selvey, W. N. Slack and K. P. Tomlins, with as manager, D. Bennett.

The County had the better of the three limited overs games, but the three first-class fixtures were very even. Gatting had a splendid time with the bat and never failed, but the bowlers found things more difficult.

In the first game the visitors declared to set Zimbabwe 282 to win, but after losing some quick wickets, they settled for a draw. In the victory by Zimbabwe, Heron defied the bowlers with an excellent 66. In the final match, the highest innings was the fourth, but Zimbabwe's total of 333 fell 83 short of victory.

1980-81: Leicestershire tour of Zimbabwe

In March 1981, Leicester followed Middlesex's footsteps and played a series of matches in Zimbabwe. Owing to the fact that Gower was with England in the West Indies and Davison and Clift were absent, the county co-opted two non-Leicester men. The full team was R. W. Tolchard (capt), J. P. Agnew, J. C. Balderstone, T. J. Boon, P. Booth, N. E. Briers, R. A. Cobb, N. G. B. Cook, G. Forster, J. H. Hampshire (Yorks), G. J. Parsons, D. S. Steele (Derbys), L. B. Taylor and D. A. Wenlock, with D. Tebbitt as manager.

The chief point of interest was the third first-class game which was drawn with the scores level, Cook being run out on the last ball. Rain seriously affected the first three-day match.

The best innings of the tour belonged to J. H. Hampshire, who scored 112 in the final match.

1981-82: England lose to India— and the first Test for Sri Lanka

The problem of the captaincy continued to exercise the minds of the selectors at the beginning of the 1981 English season and eventually Botham resigned to allow Brearley to be re-appointed, but the latter made it clear that he did not wish to go to India. The critics were divided between Fletcher of Essex or Barclay of Sussex as tour captain. On 30 August Fletcher was appointed.

The full team was announced on 8 September as K. W. R. Fletcher (Essex) (capt), R. G. D. Willis (Warwicks) (vice-capt), P. J. W. Allott (Lancs), I. T. Botham (Somerset), G. Boycott (Yorks), G. Cook (Northants), G. R. Dilley (Kent), J. E. Emburey (Middx), M. W. Gatting (Middx), G. A. Gooch (Essex), D. I. Gower (Leics), J. K. Lever (Essex), C. J. Richards (Surrey), C. J. Tavare (Kent), R. W. Taylor (Derbys) and D. L. Underwood (Kent), with R. Subba Row as manager and B. W. Thomas as physiotherapist. There were no outstanding omissions.

Above *The England party to tour India in 1981-82, photographed at Lord's before their departure. Back: M. W. Gatting, G. Cook, D. I. Gower, J. E. Emburey, G. R. Dilley, P. J. W. Allot, C. J. Tavare, C. J. Richards, G. Saulez (scorer). Front: B. M. Thomas (physiotherapist), J. K. Lever, R. W. Taylor, D. L. Underwood, K. W. R. Fletcher (captain), R. G. D. Willis, I. T. Botham, G. A. Gooch, R. Subba Row (manager).*

Right *The first Test in Bombay of the 1981-82 tour of India. Vengsarkar snicks Dilley and Botham juggles with the ball at second slip. It was eventually held by Tavare at first slip.*

Within a few weeks, the anti-South African lobby were attacking the inclusion of Boycott and Cook on the tour and the stage was reached where the Indian Government appeared to be adamant that unless these two withdrew, the tour was off. The T.C.C.B. refused to omit the two players and the bargaining and posturing continued for about three weeks. Less than a week before the team was scheduled to depart, the Indian Government allowed the tour to go ahead and the party set out on 5 November.

Even when the side landed, the Communist Party in India called for a boycott of the Tests, but the anti-tour faction soon evaporated.

Following a warm-up match in Bombay, the tourists played a high-scoring match at Pune, which looked like a draw until Botham hit 98 in 73 minutes and gave England victory by 6 wickets. Scoring was much harder in the second match with spin predominating. Underwood had a field day and the tourists won a second match. There was a draw in Baroda, but a victory in the first one-day International.

The first Test was staged at Bombay. India struggled to 179 in their first innings, but Doshi dismissed England for 166. In the final innings the tourists required 241 to win – against all predictions, the batting surrendered to the Indian seamers and the home

country won by the large margin of 138 runs. The English officials complained about the umpiring.

In the second Test England batted with care and with Gavaskar also being careful for 708 minutes, the match drifted to a draw. The game was marred by a breach of etiquette on the part of the English captain, who showed his disgust at being dismissed by knocking over the stumps. England were without Willis in this match, due to a stomach upset. The tourists batting collapsed in the match against the North Zone, but redeemed itself in the second innings.

A splendid 88 by Vengsarkar gave India her first win in a limited-overs match, played just prior to the third Test. England objected to one of the umpires appointed for this game and the appointment was altered.

With Boycott intent on beating the record for the most runs in Test cricket, England crawled to 190 for 1 on the first day of the third Test. The Indian batsmen also broke records by adding century partnerships for the 8th and 9th wickets – the game staggered to a draw. Fletcher then made some pointed remarks about England's slow scoring: Boycott took umbrage. The scoring however did not improve in the fourth Test, though wickets fell faster and Fletcher declared to set India 306 in 360 minutes – bad

1981-82: England to India and Sri Lanka

Batting Averages

	M	I	NO	R	HS	Avge	100	c/s
G. Boycott (Yorks)	8	14	5	701	105	77.88	2	3
I. T. Botham · (Som)	11	15	1	760	142	54.28	2	7
G. A. Gooch (Essex)	13	21	3	967	127	53.72	2	10
D. I. Gower (Leics)	13	18	3	755	94	50.33	0	7
C. J. Richards (Surrey)	6	6	4	97	46	48.50	0	11/1
K. W. R. Fletcher (Essex)	13	18	6	581	108	48.41	1	9
G. Cook (Northts)	7	10	1	372	104*	41.33	2	5
C. J. Tavare (Kent)	13	19	0	761	149	40.05	1	10
M. W. Gatting (Middx)	12	14	1	509	127	39.15	2	5
G. R. Dilley (Kent)	10	11	2	204	52	22.66	0	3
R. W. Taylor (Derbys)	11	10	2	132	40	16.50	0	27/1
D. L. Underwood (Kent)	11	10	5	74	22*	14.80	0	3
R. G. D. Willis (Warks)	10	6	3	26	13	8.66	0	3
J. E. Emburey (Middx)	12	12	2	79	33	7.90	0	5
J. K. Lever (Essex)	8	5	0	36	16	7.20	0	2
P. J. W. Allott (Lancs)	7	5	1	22	9*	5.50	0	3

Bowling Averages

	O	M	R	W	Avge	BB	5i
D. I. Gower	5	2	6	1	6.00	1-1	0
G. Cook	6.5	1	21	2	10.50	2-18	0
D. L. Underwood	385.3	150	784	34	23.05	6-64	3
J. E. Emburey	380.1	98	1063	42	25.30	6-33	1
R. G. D. Willis	242.1	63	687	24	28.62	4-35	0
J. K. Lever	214	45	664	20	33.20	5-100	1
I. T. Botham	317.2	64	928	25	37.12	5-61	1
M. W. Gatting	11	1	40	1	40.00	1-16	0
P. J. W. Allott	181.4	39	601	15	40.06	5-54	2
G. R. Dilley	210.2	29	767	15	51.13	3-93	0
K. W. R. Fletcher	29	2	121	2	60.50	1-6	0
G. A. Gooch	58.1	14	150	2	75.00	2-12	0

Also bowled: C. J. Richards 2-1-5-0; C. J. Tavare 4-0-18-0; R. W. Taylor 2-0-6-0.

light cut 70 minutes off this and Gavaskar took care of the rest.

Following the match Boycott flew home. He complained of stomach trouble and felt it impossible to continue. News of the forthcoming pirate tour to South Africa had not yet leaked out.

Dropped catches assisted India in the Madras Test, on the first day, and on the second India actually continued throughout the day without losing a wicket. Viswanath and Yashpal added 217. Botham for several overs kept up a barrage of derisive gestures and remarks at the batsmen – totally uncalled-for behaviour. The match was drawn.

England again complained about an umpire appointed for the deciding one-day International – but India went on to win the match and the series.

Rain interrupted the final Test, and though Botham hit a well-judged hundred, there was never a great deal of hope that a definite decision would occur, so India won the rubber one match to nil.

The better side won and England could not really lay all the blame on the umpires. Botham and Gower had a good tour, whilst Gooch improved after a tentative start. Allott also looked a better bowler, but his partner Dilley was a disappointment. In the spin department Doshi and Shastri had the edge on Underwood and Emburey.

The tourists went on to Sri Lanka, where, after a drawn three-day game, they played two limited-overs matches and then the inaugural Test against Sri Lanka. The newcomers did well up to the halfway stage, but Emburey bowled them out cheaply in the second innings and Tavare delivered the final punch with an innings of 85. There was a final game for the benefit of the baggage-man and the side arrived back in England on 24 February.

1981-82: S.A.B. English team in South Africa

The official England team landed at Gatwick airport from their tour of India and Sri Lanka. Four days later twelve England cricketers arrived at Johannesburg and the news of the English tour to South Africa hit the headlines.

The team was G. A. Gooch (Essex) (capt), J. E. Emburey (Middx), J. K. Lever (Essex), D. L. Underwood (Kent), G. Boycott (Yorks), D. L. Amiss (Warwicks), A. P. E. Knott (Kent), M. Hendrick (Derbys), W. Larkins (Northants), P. Willey (Northants), C. M. Old (Yorks) and L. B. Taylor (Leics) – three players already playing in South Africa, G. W. Humpage (Warwicks), R. A. Woolmer (Kent) and A. Sidebottom (Yorks), joined the side in the following week or so. Only the absence of Botham and Willis deprived the side of being as strong as any which could be fielded by the official England eleven.

The first reaction to the tour came from India, who threatened to cancel their proposed visit to England if any of the tourists were chosen for England. Northants allegedly demanded the withdrawal of the players' county registrations and Michael Foot, the leader of the Labour Party, demanded that the Government condemn the tourists and their action – the government refused to do this.

The fixtures began with a two-day warm-up game which was drawn. In the first one-day International Gooch hit a superb hundred, but the combination of Richards, Cook and Pollock proved too much for the tourists' attack and South Africa won fairly comfortably.

The three-day match against Western Province proved a disastrous one for the visitors – Lever broke down in his first over and then Emburey fractured his thumb, putting himself out of the rest of the tour and worse seriously weakening the tourists' spin attack. The tourists were set 249 in 240 minutes, but reached 225 for 8 when stumps were drawn.

In the 'First Test', South Africa got off to a good start, making 277 for 1 on the opening day. The English side collapsed before van der Bijl and though Gooch hit a good century when they followed on, South Africa won the game.

In the second one-day International about 14,000 watched South Africa win – van der Bijl was too accurate for the visiting batsmen and their attack was weak, since Old could not play.

The 'Second Test' saw some excellent bowling from Lever, only Kirsten showing much resistance to him, but rain reduced play and the game drifted to a draw. Procter could not captain South Africa, who were led by Richards. Rain also interferred with the third one-day International, producing an exciting finish with the tourists needing 4 off the last over – they could make only two. Rain also ruined the last match, the 'Third Test', but the English team had all the better of a draw. The T.C.C.B. announced prior to this game that the tourists would be banned from Test cricket for three years.

Although they did not win a match, the team was not outclassed and if the tour had been prolonged might well have beaten South Africa.

1981-82: S.A.B. Team to South Africa

1st Match: v S.A. Under 25 (Pretoria) March 3, 4.
S.A.B. XI 152-7 dec (A. P. Kuiper 5-22) & 32-2 drew with S.A. Under 25 XI 170-8 dec.

2nd Match: v South Africa (Port Elizabeth) (Limited Over) March 6.
S.A.B. XI 240-5 (G. A. Gooch 114, D. L. Amiss 71*) lost to South Africa 244-3 (S. J. Cook 82, B. A. Richards 62, R. G. Pollock 57*) by 7 wkts.

3rd Match: v Western Province (Cape Town) March 8, 9, 10.
W. Province 263-8 dec (A. P. Kuiper 90) & 204-7 dec (P. N. Kirsten 67*) drew with S.A.B. XI 219 (G. A. Gooch 64, D. L. Amiss 52) & 225-8 (G. Boycott 95).

4th Match: v South Africa (Johannesburg) March 12, 13, 14, 15.
South Africa 400-7 dec (S. J. Cook 114, P. N. Kirsten 88, B. A. Richards 66, R. G. Pollock 64*) & 37-2 beat S.A.B. XI 150 (D. L. Amiss 66*, V. A. P. van der Bijl 5-25) & 283 (G. A. Gooch 109, V. A. P. van der Bijl 5-79) by 8 wkts.

5th Match: v South Africa (Durban) (Limited Over) March 17.
South Africa 231-6 beat S.A.B. XI 152 by 79 runs.

6th Match: v South Africa (Cape Town) March 19, 20, 21, 22.
S.A.B. XI 223 (G. A. Gooch 83) & 249-3 dec (W. Larkins 95, D. L. Amiss 73*, G. A. Gooch 68) drew with South Africa 235 (P. N. Kirsten 114, J. K. Lever 6-86) & 38-0.

7th Match: v South Africa (Johannesburg) (Limited Over) March 24.
South Africa 243-5 (S. J. Cook 62, C. E. B. Rice 58*, A. P. Kuiper 54) beat S.A.B. XI 111-7 on faster scoring rate.

8th Match: v South Africa (Durban) March 26, 27, 28, 29.
South Africa 181-9 dec (A. J. Kourie 50*, L. B. Taylor 5-61) & 143-2 (S. J. Cook 50*) drew with S.A.B. XI 311-8 dec (R. A. Woolmer 100, D. L. Amiss 50, V. A. P. van der Bijl 5-97).

Index of touring cricketers

A complete list follows of the cricketers involved in the tours included in this book. Players selected for the tour to India in 1939-40 are included although the War prevented the tour taking place. The principal destination of each tour is shown in brackets after the season. The abbreviations are as follows:

A   Australia
AA   Africa and Asia
Ar   Argentine
B   Bermuda
Ba   Barbados
Bg   Bangladesh
C   Canada
Ce   Ceylon
E   Egypt
EA   East Africa
FE   Far East
I   India
J   Jamaica
K   Kenya
M   Malaysia
NA   North America
NZ   New Zealand
P   Pakistan
R   Rhodesia
SA   South Africa
SAm   South America
US   United States
W   West Indies
WA   West Africa
Wo   World Tour
Z   Zimbabwe
Za   Zambia
* denotes played in emergency.

Abberley, R. N. 1966-67(P); 1967-68(EA)
Abel, R. 1887-88(A); 1888-89(SA); 1891-92(A)
Absolom, C. A. 1878-79(A)
A'Court, D. G. 1962(B)
Agnew, J. P. 1980-81(Z)
Ainsworth, J. L. 1898(NA)
Akers-Douglas, I. S. 1929(E)
Albertini, W. R. 1937-38(SAm)
Alexander, G. 1882-83(A)*
Allan, J. M. 1967-68(EA)
Allen, D. A. 1959-60(W); 1960-61(NZ); 1961-62(I); 1962(B); 1962-63(A); 1964-65(SA); 1965-66(A)
Allen, G. O. B. 1926-27(SAm); 1932-33(J); 1936-37(A); 1947-48(W)
Allerton, J. W. O. 1973-74(Ba)
Alley, W. E. 1961-62(EA)
Allom, M. J. C. 1927-28(J); 1929-30(NZ); 1930-31(NZ)
Allott, P. J. W. 1981-82(I)
Ames, L. E. G. 1928-29(A); 1929-30(W); 1932-33(A); 1934-35(W); 1936-37(A); 1938-39(SA)
Amiss, D. L. 1966-67(P); 1967-68(AA); 1967-68(EA); 1972-73(I); 1973-74(W); 1974-75(A); 1981-82(SA)
Anderson, G. 1863-64(A)
Anderson, J. O. 1911-12(Ar)*
Andrew, F. J. 1962(B)
Andrew, K. V. 1954-55(A); 1959-60(W)
Appleby, A. 1872(NA)
Appleyard, R. 1954-44(A)
Arbuthnot, L. G. 1901-02(W)

Arkwright, H. A. 1895(NA)
Archer, A. G. 1898-99(SA)
Armitage, E. L. 1935(E)
Armitage, T. 1876-77(A)
Arnold, E. G. 1903-04(A)
Arnold, G. G. 1966-67(P); 1967-68(AA); 1969-70(FE); 1972-73(I); 1973-74(W); 1974-75(A)
Arnott, T. 1924(US); 1926-27(J); 1927-28(J); 1929-30(Ar); 1934-35(W)*
Arundell, E. R. 1968-69(SA)
Aspinall, J. B. 1902-03(I)
Astill, W. E. 1924-25(SA); 1925-26(W); 1926-27(I); 1927-28(J); 1928-29(J); 1929-30(W); 1931-32(J); 1938-39(NZ)
Athey, C. W. J. 1979-80(A); 1980-81(I)
Atkinson-Clark, J. C. 1936(E)
Attewell, W. 1884-85(A); 1887-88(A); 1891-92(A)
Awdry, C. E. 1932(E); 1933(E)
Ayres, G. W. 1891-92(SA)

Bailey, D. 1977-78(K)
Bailey, J. A. 1957-58(EA); 1958-59(SAm); 1959(NA)
Bailey, T. E. 1950-51(A); 1953-54(W); 1954-55(A); 1956-57(SA); 1958-59(A); 1963-64(J); 1964-65(W)
Bainbridge, H. W. 1886(NA)
Bagnall, H. F. 1931-32(J)
Baird, H. H. C. 1911-12(Ar)
Bairstow, D. L. 1974-75(W); 1978-79(A); 1979-80(A); 1980-81(W)
Baker, H. Z. 1903(NA)
Baker, W. W. 1938(E)*
Bakewell, A. H. 1933-34(I)
Balderstone, J. C. 1980-81(Z)
Balding, I. A. 1973-74(Ba)
Ball, D. C. S. 1938(E)
Barber, R. W. 1959(NA); 1960-61(NZ); 1961-62(I); 1964-65(SA); 1965-66(A); 1975-76(WA)
Barber, W. 1935-36(NZ)
Barclay, J. R. T. 1973-74(Ba); 1975-76(WA); 1976-77(Bg)
Bardswell, G. R. 1894(NA); 1896-97(W)
Barker, A. H. 1966-67(Ba)
Barker, M. M. 1894-95(W)
Barlow, G. D. 1976-77(I)
Barlow, R. G. 1881-82(A); 1882-83(A); 1886-87(A)
Barnes, S. F. 1901-02(A); 1907-08(A); 1911-12(A); 1913-14(A)
Barnes, W. 1879(NA); 1882-83(A); 1884-85(A); 1886-87(A)
Barnett, C. J. 1933-34(I); 1936-37(A)
Barnett, K. J. 1979-80(A)
Barratt, F. 1929-30(NZ)
Barrick, D. 1956-57(J)
Barrington, K. F. 1955-56(P); 1959-60(R); 1959-60(W); 1961-62(I); 1962-63(A); 1963-64(I); 1964-65(SA); 1965-66(A); 1967-68(W)
Bartlett, H. T. 1938-39(SA); 1939-40(I)
Bartlett, J. N. 1951(C)
Bartley, E. L. D. 1924-25(SA)
Barton, V. A. 1891-92(SA)

Bateman-Champain, H. F. 1889-90(I)*
Bates, K. C. 1961(B)
Bates, W. 1879(NA); 1881-82(A); 1882-83(A); 1884-85(A); 1886-87(A); 1887-88(A)
Bathurst, L. C. V. 1894(NA)
Baxter, A. D. 1935-36(NZ)
Bean, G. 1891-92(A)
Bear, M. J. 1958-59(SAm); 1960-61(NZ)*
Beaumont, J. 1887-88(A)
Beaty, M. 1977-78(K)
Bedford, P. I. 1958-59(SAm); 1959(NA); 1964-65(SAm)
Bedser, A. V. 1946-47(A); 1948-49(SA); 1950-51(A); 1954-55(A); 1956-57(I); 1959-60(R); 1962-63(A)
Bedser, E. A. 1950-51(A); 1959-60(R)
Beeson, N. W. 1938-39(J)
Beldam, C. A. 1896-97(W)
Bell, J. 1968-69(SA)
Bell, R. M. 1909(E)
Bell, T. M. 1961-62(EA)*
Bellamy, — 1904-05(W)*
Belle, B. H. 1938-39(J)
Benka, H. F. 1938(E)
Bennett, C. T. 1925-26(W)
Bennett, G. 1861-62(A)
Bennett, R. A. 1897(NA); 1901-02(W)
Benson, E. T. 1929-30(NZ)
Berens, R. 1894-95(W); 1896-97(W); 1898(NA)
Berry, R. 1950-51(A)
Beton, S. 1904-05(W)*
Biggs, L. M. 1902-03(I)*
Binks, J. G. 1961-62(I): 1963-64(I); 1964(NA)
Bird, M. C. 1909-10(SA); 1911-12(Ar); 1913-14(SA)
Birkenshaw, J. 1967-68(AA); 1969-70(W); 1972-73(I); 1973-74(W); 1974-75(W)
Bissex, M. 1966-67(P)
Blake, D. E. 1955-56(W); 1956-57(J)
Blaker, R. N. R. 1901-02(W)
Blenkiron, W. 1969-70(FE)
Bligh, Hon Ivo F. W. 1882-83(A)
Block, S. A. 1929(E)
Blofeld, H. C. 1966-67(Ba)
Blois, D. 1938(E)*
Blunt, R. C. 1933(NA)
Blythe, C. 1907-08(A); 1909-10(SA); 1901-02(A); 1903(NA); 1905-06(SA)
Board, J. H. 1897-98(A); 1898-99(SA); 1905-06(SA)
Bohlen F. H. 1907(NA)*
Bolitho, W. E. T. 1885(NA)
Bolton, L. H. 1938(E)*
Bolus, J. B. 1963-64(I)
Bond, F. 1922-23(SA)*
Bonham-Carter, H. 1889-90(I)*
Bonnor, R. E. 1907(NA)
Boon, T. J. 1980-81(Z)
Booth, M. W. 1913-14(SA)
Booth, P. 1980-81(Z)
Booth, R. 1964-65(Wo); 1965-66(W)
Bosanquet, B. J. T. 1898(NA); 1899(NA); 1901(NA); 1901-02(W); 1902-03(NZ); 1903-04(A)
Botham, I. T. 1977-78(P); 1978-79(A); 1979-80(A); 1980-81(W); 1981-82(I)
Boult, F. H. 1873-74(A)
Bourke, Capt the Hon M. A. 1896-97(W)*
Bowden, M. P. 1887-88(A); 1888-89(SA)
Bowes, W. E. 1932-33(A); 1935-36(J)
Bowley, E. H. 1924-25(SA); 1929-30(NZ); 1931-32(J)
Boyce, K. D. 1972-73(W)

Boycott, G. 1964(NA); 1964-65(SA); 1965-66(A); 1967-68(W); 1969-70(FE); 1970-71(A); 1973-74(W); 1977-78(P); 1978-79(A); 1979-80(A); 1980-81(W); 1981-82(I); 1981-82(SA)
Boyes, G. S. 1926-27(I)
Brackley, Lord 1904-05(W); 1909(E)
Bradley, W. M. 1902-03(NA)
Brain, B. M. 1964-65(Wo); 1965-66(J)
Brand, Hon D. F. 1922-23(NZ)
Brann, G. 1887-88(A); 1891-92(A); 1899(NA)
Branston, G. T. 1906-07(NZ); 1907(NA); 1909(E)
Braund, L. C. 1901-02(A); 1903-04(A); 1907-08(A)
Bray, E. H. 1898(NA)
Brearley, J. M. 1964-65(SA); 1966-67(P); 1972-73(W); 1976-77(I); 1977-78(P); 1978-79(A); 1979-80(A); 1980-81(Z)
Brennan, D. V. 1951-52(I)
Briers, N. E. 1980-81(Z)
Briggs, J. 1884-85(A); 1886-87(A); 1887-88(A); 1888-89(SA); 1891-92(A); 1894-95(A); 1897-98(A)
Brinckman, Sir T. E. W. 1937-38(SAm)
Brocklebank, J. M. 1937(C); 1939-40(I)
Brocklebank, T. A. L. 1920(NA); 1924(US)
Brockwell, W. 1891-92(SA); 1894-95(A)
Brodhurst, A. H. 1938-39(J); 1951(C)
Bromley-Davenport, H. R. 1894-95(W); 1895-96(W); 1896-97(W); 1898-99(SA)
Brooke, R. H. J. 1933(E)
Brookes, D. 1947-48(W)
Brooks, R. C. 1920(NA)
Brown, A. 1961-62(I)
Brown, A. S. 1962(B); 1971-72(Za); 1972-73(SA)
Brown, D. J. 1964-65(SA); 1965-66(A); 1966-67(P); 1967-68(W); 1967-68(EA); 1968-69(P); 1972-73(SA)
Brown, F. R. 1932-33(A); 1934(E); 1936(E); 1939(E); 1950-51(A); 1956-57(SA); 1957-58(EA); 1961-62(EA)
Brown, G. 1910-11(W); 1922-23(SA); 1926-27(I); 1931-32(J)
Brown, J. T. 1894-95(A)
Browning, F. H. 1907(NA)
Bruen, H. 1885(NA)
Bryan, J. L. 1924-25(A)
Buckenham, C. P. 1909-10(SA)
Buckland, E. H. 1886(NA)
Buckley, C. F. S. 1936(E)
Bull, F. G. 1897(NA)
Burn, R. C. W. 1904-05(W); 1905(NA)
Burnham, G. Le Roy 1923(C)
Burns, W. B. 1906-07(NZ)
Burnup, C. J. 1898(NA); 1902-03(NZ); 1903(NA)
Burrows, M. B. 1920(NA)
Burton, D. C. F. 1910-11(W); 1912-13(W)
Burton, D. S. G. 1910-11(W)
Bush, F. W. 1894-95(W); 1896-97(W)
Bush, J. A. 1873-74(A)
Bushby, M. H. 1958-59(SAm); 1959(NA)
Buss, M. A. 1966-67(P)
Butcher, R. O. 1974-75(W); 1980-81(W); 1980-81(Z)
Butler, H. J. 1947-48(W)

Butt, H. R.   1895-96(SA)
Butterworth, R. E. C.   1936-37(Ce)

Caesar, J.   1859(NA); 1863-64(A)
Caffyn, W.   1859(NA); 1861-62(A);
  1863-64(A)
Cahn, Sir J.   1928-29(J);
  1929-30(Ar); 1933(NA);
  1936-37(Ce); 1938-39(NZ)
Campbell, I. P.   1951(C)
Cameron, J. H.   1938-39(J)
Carpenter, D.   1962(B)
Carpenter, R.   1859(NA); 1863-64(A)
Carr, A. W.   1922-23(SA)
Carr, D. B.   1951-52(I); 1955-56(P);
  1958-59(SAm)
Carrick, P.   1975-76(SA);
  1977-78(FE)
Cartwright, G. H. M.   1920(NA)
Cartwright, T. W.   1963-64(EA);
  1964-65(SA); 1967-68(EA)
Castell, A. T.   1963-64(J)
Cawley, A.   1938-39(J)*
Cawston, E.   1934(E); 1936(E)
Champniss, L. J.   1975-76(WA)
Chapman, A. P. F.   1922-23(NZ);
  1924-25(A); 1928-29(A);
  1930-31(SA); 1931-32(J); 1938(E)
Chappell, T. M.   1975-76(SA)
Charleston, —   1887-88(A)*
Charlwood, H. R. J.   1868(NA);
  1876-77(A)
Chatterton, W.   1891-92(SA)
Chester, F.   1937-38(SAm)(ump)
Chesterton, G. H.   1951(C)
Chichester-Constable, R. C. J.
  1926-27(I)
Childs-Clarke, A. W.   1936(E);
  1937(E); 1938(E); 1939(E)
Chinnery, H. B.   1897(NA);
  1902-03(I)
Clark, E. A.   1975-76(WA);
  1976-77(Bg); 1978-79(Bg)
Clark, E. W.   1927-28(J); 1933-34(I)
Clark, T. H.   1959-60(R)
Clarke, A.   1863-64(A)
Clarke, J.   1886-87(A)*
Clayton, F. G. H.   1902-03(I)
Close, D. B.   1950-51(A);
  1955-56(P); 1964(NA);
  1973-74(SA); 1974-75(SA)
Cobb, A. R.   1885(NA); 1886(NA)
Cobb, R. A.   1980-81(Z)
Cobbett, M. R.   1882-83(A)*
Coen, S. K.   1927-28(SA)*
Coghlan, T. B. L.   1968-69(SA)
Coldwell, L. J.   1962-63(A);
  1964-65(Wo); 1965-66(J)
Cole, T. G. O.   1904-05(W)
Collins, B. G.   1977-78(K)
Collins, G. C.   1925-26(W)
Collins, L. G. A.   1907(NA)
Collins, L. P.   1907(NA)
Collins, P.   1913(US)
Colman, G. R. R.   1913(US)
Compton, D. C. S.   1946-47(A);
  1948-49(SA); 1950-51(A);
  1953-54(W); 1954-55(A);
  1956-57(SA); 1963-64(J)
Constable, B.   1959-60(R)
Cook, C.   1962(B)
Cook, G.   1981-82(I)
Cook, G. W.   1957-58(EA)
Cook, N. G. B.   1979-80(A);
  1980-81(Z)
Cooper, K. E.   1979-80(A)
Cope, G. A.   1975-76(SA);
  1976-77(I); 1977-78(P)
Copson, W. H.   1936-37(A)
Cordaroy, T. M.   1975-76(WA)
Cordle, A. E.   1969-70(W)
Corlett, S. C.   1972-73(M)
Cornford, W. L.   1929-30(NZ)
Cornwallis, O. W.   1923(C)
Cottam, R. M. H.   1968-69(P);
  1972-73(I); 1974-75(W)
Cottenham, Earl of   1969-70(W);

1973-74(Ba)
Cottrell, C. E.   1886(NA)
Coventry, Hon C. J.   1888-89(SA)
Covington, F. E.   1937-38(SAm)
Cowan, M. J.   1955-56(P)
Cowans, N. G.   1980-81(Z)
Cowdrey, C. S.   1977-78(FE);
  1979-80(A)
Cowdrey, M. C.   1954-55(A);
  1955-56(W); 1956-57(SA);
  1958-59(A); 1959-60(W);
  1962-63(A); 1963-64(I);
  1964-65(W); 1965-66(A);
  1967-68(W); 1968-69(P);
  1969-70(W); 1970-71(A);
  1972-73(W); 1974-75(A);
  1975-76(WA)
Cranston, K.   1947-48(W); 1961(B)
Crapp, J. F.   1948-49(SA)
Crawford, J. N.   1905-06(SA);
  1907-08(A)
Crawford, V. F. S.   1901(NA)
Crawley, L. G.   1925-26(W)
Creese, W. H.   1913-14(E)
Crisp, R. J.   1936-37(Ce)
Critchley-Salmonson, H. R. S.
  1929-30(Ar)
Crouch, H. R.   1939(C)
Curwen, C. A. F.   1938(E)
Curwen, W. J. H.   1906-07(NZ);
  1911-12(A)*
Curzon, Hon A. M.   1889-90(I)
Cuthbertson, G. B.   1924(US)
Cuttell, W. R.   1898-99(SA)

Dacre, C. C. R.   1931-32(J)
Daft, R.   1879(NA)
Dales, H. L.   1925-26(W)
Daniel, R. C.   1973-74(Ba)
Dalmeny, Lord   1931(E)
Dashwood, T. H. K.   1901-02(W)
Davenport, J. A.   1901-02(W)
Davey, J.   1971-72(Za)
Davidson, H. K.   1938-39(J)*
Davies, Emrys   1939-40(I)
Davis, B. A.   1969-70(W)
Davis, R. C.   1969-70(W);
  1971-72(Za)
Dawson, D. W.   1961-62(EA)
Dawson, E. W.   1927-28(SA)
  1928-29(J); 1929-30(NZ);
  1932(E); 1933(E)
Dawson, J. M.   1894-95(W);
  1896-97(M)
Deed, J. A.   1937(E)
Delisle, G. P. S.   1961(B);
  1966-67(Ba)
de Little, E. R.   1889-90(I)
Dempster, C. S.   1936-37(Ce);
  1938-39(NZ)
Denness, M. H.   1967-68(AA);
  1969-70(NA); 1972-73(I);
  1973-74(W); 1974-75(A);
  1977-78(FE)
Denton, D.   1905-06(SA);
  1909-10(SA)
de Soysa, G. R. J.   1938-39(J)
de Trafford, C. E.   1894(NA);
  1906-07(NZ); 1911-12(Ar)
Dewes, J. G.   1950-51(A)
Dexter, E. R.   1958-59(A);
  1959-60(W); 1961-62(I);
  1962-63(A); 1963-64(J);
  1964-65(SA)
Difford, I. D.   1905-06(SA)*;
  1913-14(SA)*
Dilley, G. R.   1979-80(A);
  1980-81(W); 1981-82(I)
Dillon, E. W.   1901-02(W);
  1903(NA)
Dindar, A.   1962(B)
Diver, A. J. D.   1859(NA)
Dixon, E. J. H.   1938-39(J)
Dobson, B. P.   1909(E); 1912-13(W);
  1913(US)
Docker, G. A. M.   1912-13(W)
Docker, L. C.   1887-88(A)

Dods, H. W.   1937-38(SAm)
Doggart, G. H. G.   1955-56(W);
  1957-58(EA); 1958-59(SAm)
d'Oliveira, B. L.   1964-65(Wo);
  1965-66(J); 1967-68(W);
  1968-69(P); 1970-71(A)
Doll, M. H. C.   1912-13(W)
Dollery, H. E.   1939-40(I)
Dolphin, A.   1920-21(A); 1926-27(I)*
Dooland, B.   1956-57(I)
Douglas, J. R.   1975-76(SA)
Douglas, J. W. H. T.   1906-07(NZ);
  1907(NA); 1911-12(A);
  1913-14(SA); 1920-21(A);
  1924-25(A)
Downton, P. R.   1977-78(P);
  1980-81(W); 1980-81(Z)
Dowson, E. M.   1901(NA);
  1901-02(W); 1902-03(NZ)
Druce, N. F.   1895(NA); 1897-98(A)
Drummond, A. V.   1909(E)
Drummond, G. H.   1903-04(A)*;
  1904-05(W)
Ducat, A.   1929-30(NZ)*
Duckworth, G.   1928-29(A);
  1930-31(SA); 1932-33(A);
  1936-37(A)
Dudleston, B.   1974-75(W)
Duff, A. R.   1964-65(SAm);
  1966-67(Ba); 1976-77(Bg);
  1978-79(Bg)
Duleepsinhji, K. S.   1929-30(NZ)
Durlacher, E. O.   1927-28(W)*
Durston, F. J.   1928-29(J);
  1937-38(SAm)
Dyson, A. H.   1938-39(NZ)
Dyson, S.   1978-79(Bg)

Eagar, E. D. R.   1956-57(J)
Ealham, A. G. E.   1972-73(W)
Earle, G. F.   1924(US); 1926-27(I);
  1929-30(NZ); 1932(E); 1933(E);
  1934(E)
East, R. E.   1973-74(SA);
  1974-75(W)
Eastman, L. C.   1937-38(SAm)
Ebden, C. H. M.   1904-05(W);
  1909(E)
Eckersley, P. T.   1926-27(I);
  1927-28(J); 1929-30(Ar)
Edmonds, P. H.   1972-73(M);
  1974-75(W); 1977-78(P);
  1978-79(A)
Edmonds, R. B.   1967-68(EA)
Edrich, J. H.   1959-60(R);
  1963-64(I); 1965-66(A);
  1967-68(W); 1968-69(P);
  1970-71(A); 1973-74(SA);
  1974-75(A)
Edrich, W. J.   1937-38(I);
  1946-47(A); 1954-55(A); 1956-57(I)
Edwards, M. J.   1969-70(W)
Eiloart, C. H.   1913(US)
Emburey, J. E.   1977-78(FE);
  1978-79(A); 1979-80(A);
  1980-81(W); 1980-81(Z);
  1981-82(I); 1981-82(SA)
Elliott, G.   1896-97(W)
Elliott, H.   1927-28(SA); 1933-34(I)
Elms, R. B.   1972-73(W)
Emmett, T.   1876-77(A); 1878-79(A);
  1879(NA); 1881-82(A)
Enthoven, H. J.   1937(C)
Entwistle, R.   1977-78(K)
Evans, R. E.   1938(E)
Evans, T. G.   1946-47(A);
  1947-48(W); 1948-49(SA);
  1950-51(A); 1953-54(W);
  1954-55(A); 1956-57(SA);
  1958-59(A); 1963-64(J);
  1964-65(W)
Eyre, C. H.   1905(NA)

Faber, M. J. J.   1972-73(M);
  1973-74(Ba)
Fabian, A. H.   1938-39(J)
Fagg, A. E.   1936-37(A)

Fairbairn, S. G.   1912-13(W)
Falcon, M.   1913(US)
Fane, F. L.   1901-02(W);
  1902-03(NZ); 1905-06(SA);
  1907-08(A); 1909-10(W)
Farnes, K.   1934-35(W); 1936-37(A);
  1938-39(SA)
Farrimond, W.   1930-31(SA);
  1934-35(W)
Fetherstonhaugh, C. B. R.   1961(B)
Fender, P. G. H.   1920-21(A);
  1922-23(SA); 1926-27(J)
Ferris, J. J.   1891-92(SA)
Fielder, A.   1903-04(A); 1907-08(A)
Findlay, W.   1911-12(Ar)
Fisher, H.   1935-36(J)
Fishlock, L. B.   1936-37(A);
  1946-47(A)
Fitzgerald, R. A.   1872(NA)
Flavell, J. A.   1964-65(Wo); 1965-66(J)
Fletcher, D. G. W.   1959-60(R)
Fletcher, K. W. R.   1964-65(W);
  1966-67(P); 1967-68(AA);
  1968-69(P); 1969-70(FE);
  1970-71(A); 1972-73(I);
  1973-74(W); 1974-75(A);
  1976-77(I); 1981-82(I)
Flood, C. W.   1929-30(Ar)
Flowers, W.   1884-85(A); 1886-87(A)
Foat, J. C.   1971-72(Za)
Foley, C. P.   1904-05(W)
Foljambe, G. A. T.   1892-93(I)
Forbes, D. W. A. W.   1937(C)
Ford, C. G.   1934(E); 1935(E)
Ford, F. G. J.   1894-95(A)
Ford, N. M.   1937(C)
Forster, G.   1980-81(Z)
Fortescue, Rev A. T.   1886(NA)
Foster, F. R.   1911-12(A)
Foster, R. E.   1903-04(A)
Fothergill, A. J.   1889-90(SA)
Fowler, R. St. L.   1920(NA); 1923(C)
Fox, R. H.   1906-07(NZ)
Frames, A. S.   1924-25(SA)*
Francis, B. C.   1973-74(SA);
  1974-75(SA)
Francis, C. K.   1872(NA)
Francke, F. M.   1974-75(SA)
Franklin, H. W. F.   1931(E)
Frazer, J. E.   1923(C)
Freeman, A. P.   1922-23(NZ);
  1924-25(A); 1927-28(SA);
  1928-29(A)
Freeman, G.   1868(NA)
Fry, C. A.   1966-67(Ba);
  1973-74(Ba); 1978-79(Bg)
Fry, C. B.   1896-97(SA)
Fulcher, E. J.   1911-12(Ar)

Gale, R. A.   1961-62(EA);
  1964-65(SAm); 1968-69(SA)
Gardom, W. D.   1926-27(SAm)*
Garnett, H. G.   1901-02(A)
Gatting, M. W.   1977-78(P);
  1980-81(W); 1980-81(Z);
  1981-82(I)
Gaussen, H. L.   1910-11(W)
Gay, L. H.   1894-95(A)
Geary, G.   1924-25(SA); 1926-27(I);
  1927-28(SA); 1928-29(A);
  1931-32(J)
Gibb, P. A.   1933(NA); 1935-36(J);
  1937-38(I); 1938-39(SA);
  1946-47(A)
Gibbs, J. A.   1892-93(I)
Gibbs, L. R.   1967-68(EA)
Gibson, A. B. E.   1889-90(I);
  1892-93(I)
Gibson, C.   1964-65(SAm)
Gibson, C. H.   1922-23(NZ)
Gibson, K. L.   1909(E)
Gifford, N.   1964-65(W); 1965-66(J);
  1972-73(I)
Gilbert, W. R.   1873-74(A)
Gill, P. N.   1977-78(K)
Gillespie, J. V.   1937(E)
Gilliat, R. M. C.   1969-70(FE)

Gilligan, A. E. R. 1922-23(SA); 1924-25(A); 1926-27(I)
Gilligan, A. H. H. 1924(US); 1924-25(A); 1929-30(NZ)
Gillingham, Rev F. H. 1926-27(J)
Gimblett, H. 1939-40(I)
Gladwin, C. 1948-49(SA)
Gleeson, J. W. 1973-74(SA)
Goddard, G. F. 1975-76(WA)
Goddard, T. W. J. 1930-31(SA); 1938-39(SA)
Godsell, R. T. 1905(NA)
Goldie, K. O. 1907(NA)
Goldney, G. H. H. 1889-90(I)
Gomes, S. A. 1974-75(W)
Gooch, G. A. 1978-79(A); 1979-80(A); 1980-81(W); 1981-82(I); 1981-82(SA)
Good, A. J. 1975-76(WA)
Goodway, C. C. 1936-37(Ce); 1938-39(NZ)
Goonesena, G. 1955-56(W); 1964-65(W); 1967-68(AA)
Gough-Calthorpe, F. S. 1922-23(NZ); 1925-26(W); 1929-30(W)
Gould, I. J. 1980-81(Z)
Gover, A. V. 1937-38(I)
Gover, J. C. L. 1961(B)
Gower, D. I. 1977-78(FE); 1978-79(A); 1979-80(A); 1980-81(W); 1981-82(I)
Grace, E. M. 1863-64(A)
Grace, G. F. 1873-74(A)
Grace, W. G. 1872(NA); 1873-74(A); 1891-92(A)
Graham, J. N. 1972-73(W)
Graveney, T. W. 1951-52(I); 1953-54(W); 1954-55(A); 1955-56(W); 1956-57(J); 1956-57(I); 1958-59(I); 1961(B); 1962-63(A); 1963-64(J); 1964-65(Wo); 1967-68(W); 1968-69(P)
Green, D. J. 1959(NA)
Green, L. 1926-27(J); 1929-30(Ar)
Green, S. V. 1901-02(A)*
Greenhough, T. 1956-57(J); 1959-60(W)
Greenidge, G. A. 1974-75(SA)
Greenway, C. E. 1913(US)
Greenwood, A. 1873-74(A); 1876-77(A)
Gregory, R. J. 1933-34(I)
Greig, A. W. 1967-68(AA); 1969-70(W); 1972-73(I); 1973-74(W); 1974-75(A); 1974-75(SA); 1976-77(I)
Grell, E. L. G. N. 1910-11(W)*
Grieve, B. A. F. 1888-89(SA)
Griffith, G. 1861-62(A); 1868(NA)
Griffith, M. G. 1964-65(SAm); 1969-70(W)
Griffith, S. C. 1935-36(NZ); 1939-40(I); 1947-48(W); 1948-49(SA); 1957-58(EA)
Grundy, J. 1859(NA)
Guise, J. L. 1934(E)
Gunn, G. 1907-08(A); 1911-12(A); 1929-30(W)
Gunn, J. R. 1901-02(A); 1929-30(Ar)
Gunn, W. 1886-87(A)
Gurr, D. R. 1977-78(FE)

Hadingham, A. W. G. 1935(E)
Hadley, R. J. 1972-73(M)
Hadow, W. H. 1872(NA)
Haig, N. 1929-30(W)
Haigh, S. 1898-99(SA); 1905-06(SA)
Hall, J. B. 1936-37(Ce)
Hall, J. K. 1961(B); 1961-62(EA)
Hamblin, C. B. 1972-73(M); 1978-79(Bg)
Hammond, W. R. 1925-26(W); 1927-28(SA); 1928-29(A); 1930-31(SA); 1932-33(A);

1934-35(W); 1936-37(A); 1938-39(SA); 1946-47(A)
Hampshire, J. H. 1964(NA); 1964-65(W); 1969-70(FE); 1970-71(A); 1972-73(W); 1974-75(W); 1974-75(SA); 1980-81(Z)
Handfield-Jones, R. M. 1930(E)
Handford, S. 1886(NA)*
Hann, L. H. 1938(E)*
Harbord, W. E. 1934(E); 1934-35(W)
Hardstaff, J., sen 1907-08(A); 1929-30(W)ump
Hardstaff, J., jun 1935-36(NZ); 1936-37(I); 1937-38(I); 1938-39(NZ); 1946-47(A); 1947-48(W)
Hargreave, S. 1902-03(NZ)
Hargreaves, H. 1924(US)
Harris, Lord 1872(NA); 1878-79(A)
Harris, M. J. 1974-75(W)
Harrison, W. E. 1901(NA)
Harrison, W. P. 1906-07(NZ)
Hartley, J. C. 1895(NA); 1905-06(SA); 1922-23(NZ); 1923(C)
Hatfeild, C. E. 1911-12(Ar); 1913(US)
Hawke, Lord 1887-88(A); 1889-90(I)*; 1891(NA); 1892-93(I); 1894(NA); 1895-96(SA); 1896-97(SA); 1898-99(SA); 1911-12(Ar)
Hayes, E. G. 1904-05(W); 1905-06(SA); 1907-08(A)
Hayes, F. C. 1972-73(SA); 1973-74(W); 1974-75(W); 1974-75(SA); 1975-76(SA)
Hayward, D. L. 1961(B)*
Hayward, T. 1859(NA); 1863-64(A)
Hayward, T. W. 1895-96(SA); 1897-98(A); 1901-02(A); 1903-04(A)
Hazel, N. L. 1961(B)*
Hazlerigg, A. G. 1935(E)
Head, J. R. 1896-97(W)
Headlam, C. 1902-03(I)
Headley, R. G. A. 1964-65(Wo); 1964-65(W); 1965-66(J)
Heal, M. G. 1972-73(M)
Heane, G. F. H. 1929-30(Ar); 1933(NA); 1938-39(NZ)
Hearne, A. 1891-92(A); 1903(US)
Hearne, F. 1888-89(SA)
Hearne, G. F. 1884-85(A)*
Hearne, G. G. 1891-92(SA)
Hearne, J. T. 1891-92(SA); 1897-98(A)
Hearne, J. W. 1910-11(W); 1911-12(A); 1913-14(SA); 1920-21(A); 1924-25(A)
Hearne, T. 1861-62(A)
Heath, L. 1910-11(W)*
Hemingway, W. McG. 1895(NA); 1897(NA)
Hemmings, E. E. 1974-75(SA)
Henderson, R. 1884-85(A)*
Hendren, E. H. 1920-21(A); 1924-25(A); 1928-29(A); 1929-30(SA); 1930-31(SA); 1934-35(W)
Hendrick, M. 1973-74(W); 1974-75(A); 1975-76(SA); 1977-78(P); 1978-79(A); 1979-80(A); 1981-82(SA)
Henley, F. A. H. 1905(NA)
Hermon, J. V. 1932(E)
Heseltine, C. 1892-93(I); 1895-96(SA); 1896-97(W)
Hesketh-Pritchard, H. V. 1904-05(W); 1907(NA)
Hewett, H. T. 1891(NA); 1895-96(SA)
Hickson, G. A. S. 1924(US)
Higgs, K. 1965-66(A); 1967-68(W)
Hilder, A. L. 1926-27(J); 1927-28(J); 1928-29(J); 1932(E)

Hill, A. 1876-77(A)
Hill, A. E. L. 1923(C); 1932(E)
Hill, A. J. L. 1892-93(I); 1894(NA); 1896-97(SA); 1911-12(Ar)
Hill, M. Ll. 1926-27(I)
Hill, V. T. 1895(NA); 1898(NA)
Hilliard, H. 1889-90(I)*
Hill-Wood, C. K. H. 1929(E); 1930(E)
Hill-Wood, P. D. 1966-67(Ba)
Hill-Wood, W. W. H. 1922-23(NZ)
Hillyard, G. W. 1891(NA); 1894(NA)
Hilton, M. J. 1951-52(I)
Hine-Haycock, T. R. 1885(NA); 1886(NA)
Hirst, G. H. 1897-98(A); 1903-04(A)
Hitch, J. W. 1911-12(A); 1920-21(A)
Hobbs, J. B. 1907-08(A); 1909-10(SA); 1911-12(A); 1913-14(SA); 1920-21(A); 1924-25(A); 1928-29(A)
Hobbs, R. N. S. 1963-64(EA); 1963-64(J); 1964-65(SA); 1966-67(P); 1967-68(W); 1968-69(P); 1969-70(W); 1972-73(SA)
Hodson, P. 1972-73(M)
Hollies, W. E. 1934-35(W); 1950-51(I)
Hollins, A. M. 1901(NA)
Hollins, F. H. 1901-02(W); 1902-03(I); 1923(C)
Holloway, B. H. 1910-11(W)
Holmes, A. J. 1938-39(SA); 1939-40(I)
Holmes, E. R. T. 1926-27(J); 1934-35(W); 1935-36(NZ)
Holmes, P. 1924-25(SA); 1925-26(W); 1927-28(SA)
Hone, L. 1878-79(A)
Hooper, J. M. M. 1973-74(Ba); 1975-76(WA); 1976-77(Bg)
Hopley, F. J. V. 1905(NA)
Hornby, A. H. 1902-03(I)
Hornby, A. N. 1872(NA); 1878-79(A)
Horner, C. E. 1885(NA)
Hornsby, J. H. J. 1889-90(I); 1891(NA); 1892-93(I)
Horton, M. J. 1964-65(Wo); 1965-66(J)
Hosie, A. L. 1937-38(I)*
Howard, C. G. 1954-55(A)
Howard, N. D. 1951-52(I)
Howard, R. 1936-37(A)*
Howarth, G. P. 1975-76(SA); 1977-78(FE)
Howell, H. 1920-21(A); 1924-25(A)
Howorth, R. 1947-48(W)
Howland, C. B. 1958-59(SAm); 1959(NA)
Hubble, J. C. 1927-28(SA)*
Hughes, D. P. 1972-73(SA); 1974-75(W)
Hughes, J. S. 1923(C)
Hughes, S. P. 1980-81(Z)
Hughes, — 1889-90(I)*
Huish, F. H. 1903(NA)
Human, J. H. 1933-34(I); 1935-36(NZ)
Human, R. H. C. 1939-40(I)
Humpage, G. W. 1981-82(SA)
Humphrey, R. 1873-74(A)
Humphrey, T. 1868(NA)
Humphreys, E. 1912-13(W)
Humphreys, W. A. 1894-95(A)
Humphries, J. 1907-08(A)
Hunte, C. C. 1978-79(Bg)
Hunter, J. 1884-85(A)
Hunter, K. O. 1905(NA)
Hurn, J. 1968-69(SA)
Huskinson, G. N. B. 1933(E)
Hutchings, K. L. 1903(NA); 1907-08(A)
Hutton, L. 1935-36(J); 1938-39(SA); 1946-47(A); 1947-48(W);

1948-49(SA); 1950-51(A); 1953-54(W); 1954-55(A)
Hutton, R. A. 1964(NA); 1964-65(SAm); 1966-67(P); 1973-74(Ba)

Ibadulla, K. 1967-68(AA); 1967-68(EA)
Iddison, R. 1861-62(A)
Iddon, J. 1928-29(J); 1934-35(W)
Ikin, J. T. 1946-47(A); 1947-48(W)
Ikin, M. J. 1977-78(K)
Illingworth, R. 1959-60(W); 1962-63(A); 1964(NA); 1970-71(A)
Ingleby-Mackenzie, A. C. D. 1955-56(W); 1956-57(J); 1957-58(EA); 1958-59(SAm); 1961-62(EA); 1963-64(J); 1964-65(W); 1966-67(Ba)
Insole, D. J. 1956-57(SA)
Intikhab Alam 1977-78(FE)
Iremonger, J. 1911-12(A)
Irwin, P. H. 1924(US)
Isaacs, W. J. H. 1937(E)
Isherwood, L. C. R. 1926-27(SAm); 1929(E)

Jackman, R. D. 1972-73(SA); 1980-81(W)
Jackson, F. S. 1892-93(I)
Jackson, G. R. 1926-27(SAm); 1927-28(SA)
Jackson, J. 1859(NA); 1863-64(A)
Jackson, V. E. 1938-39(NZ)
Jameson, J. A. 1967-68(EA); 1973-74(W); 1974-75(W); 1978-79(Bg)
Jameson, T. O. 1924-25(SA); 1925-26(W); 1926-27(SAm); 1937-38(I)
Jaques, A. 1912-13(W)
Jardine, D. R. 1920(NAm); 1928-29(A); 1932-33(A); 1933-34(I)
Jarvis, K. B. S. 1977-78(FE)
Jefferson, R. I. 1961-62(EA); 1964-65(SAm)
Jenkins, R. O. 1948-49(SA)
Jenner, T. J. 1974-75(SA)
Jessop, G. L. 1897(NA); 1899(NA); 1901-02(A)
Jewell, M. F. S. 1926-27(SAm)
John, A. 1889-90(I)*
Johnson, G. W. 1972-73(W); 1973-74(W); 1974-75(W)
Johnson, L. A. 1961-62(EA); 1963-64(EA)
Johnson, P. D. 1972-73(M)
Johnson, P. R. 1901(NA); 1902-03(NZ); 1906-07(NZ)
Johnston, A. C. 1929(E); 1930(E)
Jones, A. 1969-70(W); 1969-70(FE)
Jones, A. K. C. 1972-73(M)
Jones, A. L. 1979-80(A)
Jones, A. O. 1901-02(A); 1907-08(A)
Jones, E. W. 1969-70(W)
Jones, I. J. 1963-64(EA); 1963-64(I); 1965-66(A); 1967-68(W)
Jones, K. V. 1977-78(K)
Jones, P. C. H. 1972-73(M)
Jones, P. H. 1977-78(K)
Judd, A. K. 1927-28(J); 1933(E); 1935(E)
Julian, R. 1975-76(WA)
Jupp, H. 1868(NA); 1873-74(A); 1876-77(A)
Jupp, V. W. C. 1922-23(SA)

Kaye, M. A. C. P. 1938-39(J)
Keighley, W. G. 1951(C)
Kemp-Welch, G. D. 1927-28(J); 1931(E); 1931-32(J)
Kendall, M. P. 1972-73(M)
Kennedy, A. S. 1922-23(SA); 1924-25(SA)
Kenny, C. J. M. 1957-58(EA)

Kenyon, D. 1951-52(I); 1964-65(Wo); 1965-66(J)
Kerr, F. W. 1889-90(I)
Kershaw, F. 1902-03(I)
Kerslake, R. C. 1964-65(SAm)
Key, K. J. 1886(NA); 1891(NA); 1902-03(I)
Kilner, R. 1924-25(A); 1925-26(W)
Kimpton, R. C. M. 1938-39(J); 1955-56(W)
Kingston, G. C. 1969-70(W)
Kinkead-Weekes, R. C. 1973-74(Ba); 1976-77(Bg)
Kinneir, S. 1911-12(A)
Kippax, P. J. 1977-78(K)
Kirk, H. 1898(NA)
Knight, A. E. 1903-04(A)
Knight, B. R. 1961-62(I); 1962-63(I); 1963-64(I); 1964-65(W); 1965-66(A)
Knight, R. D. V. 1972-73(SA); 1975-76(WA)
Knott, A. P. E. 1964-65(W); 1966-67(P); 1967-68(W); 1968-69(P); 1970-71(A); 1972-73(I); 1973-74(W); 1974-75(A); 1976-77(I); 1981-82(SA)
Knott, C. H. 1929(E); 1930(E); 1931(E); 1933(E); 1934(E); 1936(E)

Lagden, Sir G. Y. 1905-06(SA)*
Laker, J. C. 1947-48(W); 1953-54(W); 1956-57(SA); 1958-59(A); 1963-64(J); 1964-65(W)
Landale, F. B. 1924(US)
Lane-Fox, E. J. 1968-69(SA)
Langridge, Jas. 1933-34(I); 1935-36(NZ); 1937-38(I); 1946-47(A)
Langridge, John R. 1939-40(I)
Langridge, R. J. 1963-64(EA)
Larkins, W. 1979-80(A); 1981-82(SA)
Larter, J. D. F. 1960-61(NZ); 1962-63(A); 1963-64(EA); 1963-64(I); 1965-66(A)
Larwood, H. 1928-29(A); 1932-33(A)
Latchman, H. 1967-68(AA)
Lawrence, C. 1861-62(A)
Lawson, M. P. L. 1937(E)*
Lawson-Smith, E. M. 1889-90(I)
Laycock, D. A. 1972-73(W)
Leadbeater, B. 1969-70(W)
Leadbeater, E. 1951-52(I)
Leaney, E. 1891-92(SA)
Leatham, A. E. 1889-90(I); 1892-93(I); 1896-97(W); 1902-03(NZ)
Lee, E. C. 1898(NA); 1901-02(W); 1920(NA)
Lee, G. M. 1927-28(J)
Lee, H. W. 1930-31(SA)*
Lee, P. G. 1973-74(SA); 1974-75(W); 1975-76(SA)
Lees, W. S. 1905-06(SA)
Legard, A. R. 1935(E)
Legge, G. B. 1927-28(SA); 1929-30(NZ)
Leigh, R. 1896-97(W)
Leigh-Barratt, R. 1894-95(W); 1896-97(W)
Leslie, C. F. H. 1882-83(A)
Lever, J. K. 1972-73(SA); 1973-74(SA); 1974-75(W); 1976-77(I); 1977-78(P); 1977-78(FE); 1978-79(A); 1979-80(A); 1981-82(I); 1981-82(SA)
Lever, P. 1970-71(A); 1974-75(A)
Leveson-Gower, H. D. G. 1896-97(W); 1897(NA); 1905-06(SA); 1909-10(SA)
Carlton Levick, T. H. 1926-27(SAm)
Levett, W. H. V. 1933-34(I)

Lewington, P. J. 1972-73(SA); 1978-79(Bg)
Lewis, A. R. 1964-65(SAm); 1969-70(W); 1969-70(FE); 1972-73(I); 1973-74(Ba)
Lewis, D. W. 1969-70(W)
Lewis, R. P. 1896-97(W)
Leyland, M. 1926-27(I)*; 1928-29(A); 1930-31(SA); 1932-33(A); 1934-35(W); 1935-36(J); 1936-37(A)
Liddelow, G. 1910-11(W)*
Lilley, A. F. A. 1901-02(A); 1903-04(A)
Lilley, B. 1928-29(J)
Lillywhite, Jas, jun 1868(NA); 1873-74(A); 1876-77(A); 1881-82(A); 1884-85(A); 1886-87(A)
Lillywhite, John 1859(NA)
Lindsay, W. O'B. 1931(E)
Livingston, L. 1956-57(I)
Livock, G. E. 1934(E)
Livsey, W. H. 1922-23(SA)
Llewellyn, G. C. B. 1899(NA)
Lloyd, D. 1974-75(A); 1975-76(SE)
Lloyd, F. O. G. 1929(E); 1930(E)
Loader, P. J. 1954-55(A); 1956-57(SA); 1958-59(A); 1959-60(R); 1961-62(EA)
Lock, G. A. R. 1953-54(W); 1955-56(P); 1956-57(SA); 1958-59(A); 1959-60(R); 1961-62(I); 1967-68(W)
Lock, H. C. 1926-27(J)
Lockwood, E. 1879(NA)
Lockwood, W. 1894-95(A)
Lockyer, T. 1859(NA); 1863-64(A)
Lofting, J. G. 1975-76(WA); 1976-77(Bg)
Lohmann, G. A. 1886-87(A); 1887-88(A); 1891-92(A); 1895-96(SA)
Lomax, I. R. 1961(B); 1966-67(Ba); 1968-69(SA)
Long, A. 1972-73(SA)
Lowndes, W. G. L. F. 1930(E); 1931(E); 1932(E)
Lowe, W. W. 1895(NA)
Lowry, T. C. 1920(NA); 1922-23(NZ); 1924(US)
Lowson, F. A. 1951-52(I)
Lubbock, A. 1872(NA)
Lubbock, E. 1872(NA)
Lucas, A. P. 1878-79(A)
Lucas, R. S. 1894(NA); 1894-95(W)
Luckhurst, B. W. 1970-71(A); 1972-73(W); 1974-75(A)
Lumb, E. 1887-88(A)*
Lush, J. G. 1938-39(NZ)
Luther, A. C. G. 1909(E)
Lyon, B. H. 1936-37(Ce)
Lyon, J. 1974-75(SA)
Lyons, K. J. 1969-70(W)
Lyttelton, Hon C. J. (Lord Cobham) 1935-36(NZ); 1956-57(J)

McAlpine, K. 1891(NA); 1894(NA)
McAlpine, R. J. 1968-69(SA)
McArthur, K. 1887-88(A)*; 1891-92(A)*
Macaulay, G. G. 1922-23(SA)
MacBryan, J. C. W. 1924-25(SA)
McConnon, J. E. 1954-55(A)
McCool, C. L. 1956-57(I)
McCorkell, N. 1937-38(I)
McCormick, E. J. 1887-88(A)*
McCorquodale, A. 1951(C)
McDonell, H. C. 1905(NA)
McGahey, C. P. 1901-02(A)
MacGregor, G. 1891-92(A); 1907(NA)
McIntyre, A. J. W. 1950-51(A); 1959-60(R)
McIntyre, Martin 1873-74(A)
Mackinnon, F. A. 1878-79(A)
MacLaren, A. C. 1894-95(A);

1897-98(A); 1899(NA); 1901-02(A); 1911-12(Ar); 1922-23(NZ)
Maclean, G. A. 1896-97(W)*
MacLean, J. F. 1922-23(NZ)
Maclean, M. F. 1892-93(I)
McMaster, J. E. P. 1888-89(SA)
Magill, M. D. P. 1938-39(J)
Mailey, A. A. 1938(E)*
Makepeace, J. W. H. 1920-21(A)
Mallet, V. A. L. 1926-27(SAm)*
Mallett, A. W. H. 1951(C)
Mann, E. W. 1905(NA)
Mann, F. G. 1948-49(SA)
Mann, F. T. 1922-23(SA)
Marlar, R. G. 1955-56(W)
Marley, R. C. 1938-39(J)*
Marriott, C. S. 1924-25(SA); 1933-34(I)
Marriott, H. H. 1895(NA); 1897(NA)
Marryat, G. 1901(NA)*
Marshall, J. 1863-64(A)*
Marshall, R. E. 1956-57(J); 1961-62(EA); 1963-64(J); 1964-65(W)
Marshall, R. L. 1894-95(W)
Martin, F. 1891-92(SA)
Martin, J. D. 1964-65(SAm)
Martineau, H. M. 1929(E); 1930(E); 1931(E); 1932(E); 1933(E); 1934(E); 1935(E); 1936(E); 1937(E); 1938(E); 1939(E)
Maru, R. J. 1980-81(Z)
Mason, J. R. 1897-98(A); 1903(NA)
Masterman, J. C. 1923(C); 1930(E); 1931(E); 1937(C)
Maul, H. C. 1878-79(A)
Maxwell, C. R. N. 1933(NA); 1936-37(Ce); 1938-39(NZ)
Maxwell, Capt — 1889-90(I)*
May, P. B. H. 1953-54(W); 1954-55(A); 1956-57(SA); 1958-59(A); 1959-60(W)
May, P. R. 1906-07(NZ)
Mayhew, J. F. N. 1930(E)
Maynard, C. 1979-80(A)
Mead, C. P. 1911-12(A); 1913-14(SA); 1922-23(SA); 1927-28(J); 1928-29(A)
Melle, B. G. von B. 1913(US)
Mence, M. D. 1975-76(WA); 1976-77(Bg)
Mendl, D. F. 1934(E)
Mendl, J. F. 1937(C)
Mercer, J. 1926-27(I); 1928-29(J)
Merry, W. G. 1978-79(Bg); 1979-80(A); 1980-81(Z)
Metcalfe, E. J. 1909(E); 1913(US); 1920(NA); 1924(US)
Metcalfe, S. G. 1966-67(Ba); 1968-69(SA); 1973-74(Ba)
Meyer, B. J. 1962(B)
Midwinter, W. E. 1881-82(A)
Milburn, C. 1963-64(EA); 1967-68(W); 1968-69(P)
Miles, H. P. 1926-27(SAm)
Miller, A. M. 1895-96(SA)
Miller, G. 1976-77(I); 1977-78(P); 1978-79(A); 1979-80(A); 1980-81(W)
Milles, Hon H. A. 1891(NAm)
Milligan, F. W. 1895(NAm); 1898-99(SA)
Millman, G. 1961-62(I)
Mitchell, A. 1933-34(I); 1935-36(J)
Mitchell, F. 1895(NA); 1898(NA); 1898-99(SA); 1901(NA)
Mitchell-Innes, N. S. 1935-36(NZ)
Mitchell, T. B. 1932-33(A)
Milton, C. A. 1958-59(W); 1962(B); 1971-72(Za)
Mobey, G. S. 1939-40(I)
Moon, L. J. 1905(NA); 1905-06(SA)
Moore, D. N. 1931(E)
Moorhouse, C. 1909(E)
Mordaunt, D. J. 1959(NA); 1964-65(SAm)

Mordaunt, G. J. 1894(NA)
More, H. K. 1978-79(Bg)
More, R. E. 1901(NA)
Morkel, D. P. B. 1933(NA); 1936-37(Ce)
Morley, F. 1879(NA); 1882-83(A)
Morris, H. M. 1926-27(J)
Morrison, J. S. F. 1920(NA)
Mortimore, J. B. 1958-59(A); 1961-62(EA); 1962(B); 1963-64(EA); 1963-64(I)
Mortimer, W. 1895(NA)
Mortlock, W. 1861-62(A)
Mottram, T. J. 1973-74(Ba)
Moss, A. E. 1953-54(W); 1955-56(P); 1956-57(J); 1956-57(I); 1959-60(W); 1968-69(SA)
Moss, J. 1904-05(W)
Mudge, H. 1936-37(Ce); 1938-39(NZ)
Mudie, W. 1861-62(A)
Mulholland, Hon H. G. H. 1913(US)
Munt, H. R. 1929-30(Ar); 1933(NA)
Murdoch, W. L. 1891-92(SA)
Murray, J. T. 1960-61(NZ); 1961-62(I); 1962-63(A); 1963-64(J); 1964-65(SA); 1965-66(A); 1968-69(P); 1972-73(SA); 1973-74(SA)
Murray, M. P. 1961(B)
Murray, S. L. 1889-90(I)*
Murray-Wood, W. 1938-39(J); 1961(B)

Mushtaq Mohammad 1974-75(W)

Napier, G. G. 1905(NA)
Nash, M. A. 1969-70(W)
Neame, A. R. B. 1968-69(SA)
Nettlefold, E. P. 1937(E)*
Neve, J. T. 1937(E)
Newham, W. 1887-88(A)
Newman, F. C. W. 1928-29(J); 1929-30(Ar); 1933(NA)
Newman, G. C. 1937(C)
Newton, A. E. 1885(NA); 1887-88(A)
Nevinson, J. H. 1931(E); 1937(E)
Nicholas, F. W. H. 1924-25(SA); 1928-29(J); 1929-30(Ar)
Nicholls, D. 1972-73(W); 1975-76(WA)
Nicholls, R. B. 1971-72(Za)
Nichols, M. S. 1928-29(J); 1929-30(NZ); 1931-32(J); 1933-34(I); 1939-40(I)
Nicholson, A. G. 1974-75(W)
Norfolk, Duke of 1956-57(J)
Norman, M. E. J. C. 1976-77(Bg)
Nurton, M. D. 1977-78(K)

Oakman, A. S. M. 1955-56(W); 1956-57(SA)
O'Brien, T. C. 1887-88(A); 1895-96(SA)
O'Connor, J. 1926-27(J); 1928-29(J); 1929-30(W)
Old, C. M. 1969-70(W); 1972-73(I); 1973-74(W); 1974-75(A); 1976-77(I); 1977-78(P); 1978-79(A); 1980-81(W); 1981-82(SA)
Oldfield, N. 1938-39(NZ)
Ormrod, J. A. 1965-66(J); 1966-67(P)
Osborne, M. J. 1961(B)
Oscroft, W. 1873-74(A); 1879(NA)
Ottaway, C. J. 1872(NA)
Oughton, A. T. 1962(B)*
Owen-Thomas, D. R. 1976-77(Bg)

Padgett, D. E. V. 1960-61(NZ); 1964(NA)
Page, C. C. 1906-07(NZ)
Page, R. 1935(E)
Paine, G. A. E. 1934-35(W)
Palairet, R. C. N. 1896-97(W)
Palmer, C. H. 1948-49(SA); 1953-54(W)

Palmer, K. E. 1963-64(J); 1964-65(SA)*
Parfitt, P. H. 1961-62(I); 1962-63(A); 1963-64(EA); 1963-64(I); 1964-65(SA); 1965-66(A)
Parker, C. W. L. 1924-25(SA)
Parker, J. F. 1939-40(I)
Parker, J. P. 1926-27(J)
Parker-Bowles, S. H. 1966-67(Ba)
Parkhouse, W. G. A. 1950-51(A)
Parkin, C. H. 1920-21(A)
Parkin, I. U. 1901(NA)
Parks, J. H. 1935-36(NZ); 1937-38(I)
Parks, J. M. 1955-56(P); 1956-57(SA); 1959-60(W); 1960-61(NZ); 1963-64(I); 1964-65(SA); 1965-66(A); 1967-68(W)
Parr, G. 1859(NA); 1863-64(A)
Parsons, G. J. 1979-80(A); 1980-81(Z)
Parsons, J. H. 1926-27(I)
Pataudi, Nawab of 1932-33(A)
Patel, D. N. 1979-80(A)
Patiala, Maharajah of 1926-27(I)*; 1933-34(I)*
Patten, M. 1923(C)
Payne, M. W. 1905(NA)
Paynter, E. 1932-33(A); 1938-39(SA)
Peach, H. A. 1928-29(J)
Pearce, T. N. 1939(E)
Peate, E. 1881-82(A)
Peebles, I. A. R. 1927-28(SA); 1930(E); 1930-31(SA); 1932(E); 1933(NA); 1936-37(Ce); 1937-38(I)
Peel, R. 1884-85(A); 1887-88(A); 1891-92(A); 1894-95(A)
Penn, E. F. 1898(NA)
Penn, F. 1878-79(A)
Perks, R. T. D. 1938-39(SA)
Perrett, D. S. 1966-67(Ba)
Philipson, H. 1889-90(I); 1891-92(A); 1894-95(A)
Phillips, F. A. 1895(NA)
Phillips, J. 1887-88(A)*
Phillipson, W. E. 1938-39(NZ)
Piachaud, J. D. 1959(NA); 1966-67(Ba); 1976-77(Bg)
Pickering, F. P. U. 1872(NA)
Pigott, A. C. S. 1979-80(A)
Pilkington, T. A. 1926-27(SAm)
Pilling, H. 1977-78(FE)
Pilling, R. 1881-82(A); 1887-88(A)
Pinder, G. 1879(NA)
Place, W. 1947-48(W)
Pocock, P. I. 1966-67(P); 1967-68(W); 1968-69(P); 1969-70(FE); 1972-73(I); 1973-74(W); 1974-75(W)
Pollard, R. 1946-47(A)
Ponsonby, R. 1909-10(SA)*
Poole, C. J. 1951-52(I)
Pooley, E. 1868(NA); 1876-77(A)
Pope, G. H. 1937-38(I); 1939-40(I)
Popplewell, N. F. M. 1976-77(Bg)
Pougher, A. D. 1887-88(A); 1891-92(SA)
Powell, A. G. 1935-36(NZ); 1937(C); 1937(C); 1938(E); 1939(E); 1951(C)
Powell, V. 1968-69(SA)
Powys-Keck, H. J. 1902-03(I); 1904-05(W)
Preston, J. M. 1887-88(A)
Pretlove, J. F. 1959(NA)
Price, J. S. E. 1963-64(I); 1964-65(SA)
Price, W. F. F. 1929-30(W); 1937-38(SAm)
Prideaux, R. M. 1959(NA); 1960-61(NZ); 1968-69(P)
Priestley, A. 1894(W); 1896-97(W); 1897-98(A)*; 1899(NA); 1901(NA)
Priestley, R. J. 1973-74(Ba)

Pullar, G. 1959-60(W); 1961-62(I); 1962-63(A)

Quaife, William 1901-02(A)

Radcliffe, O. G. 1891-92(A)
Radley, C. T. 1972-73(SA); 1974-75(SA); 1977-78(P); 1978-79(A); 1980-81(Z)
Randall, D. W. 1974-75(W); 1975-76(SA); 1976-77(I); 1977-78(P); 1978-79(A); 1979-80(A)
Ranjitsinhji, K. S. 1897-98(A); 1899(NA)
Raphael, R. H. 1902-03(NZ)*; 1902-03(I)
Rawlin, J. T. 1887-88(A)
Rawlinson, Capt — 1889-90(I)
Read, H. D. 1933(E); 1935-36(NZ)
Read, J. M. 1884-85(A); 1886-87(A); 1887-88(A); 1888-89(SA); 1891-92(A)
Read, W. W. 1882-83(A); 1887-88(A); 1891-92(SA)
Reddick, T. B. 1933(NA); 1936-37(Ce)
Reed, B. L. 1979-80(Bg)
Relf, A. E. 1903-04(A); 1905-06(SA); 1912-13(W); 1913-14(SA)
Relf, R. R. 1913-14(SA)*
Revill, A. C. 1961(B)
Rhodes, A. E. G. 1951-52(I)
Rhodes, H. J. 1967-68(A)
Rhodes, S. D. 1929-30(Ar); 1933(NA); 1936-37(Ce)
Rhodes, W. 1903-04(A); 1907-08(A); 1909-10(A); 1911-12(A); 1913-14(SA); 1920-21(A); 1929-30(W)
Richards, C. J. 1979-80(A); 1981-82(I)
Richardson, D. W. 1964-65(Wo); 1964-65(W); 1965-66(J)
Richardson, P. E. 1955-56(P); 1956-57(SA); 1957-58(EA); 1958-59(A); 1961-62(I); 1963-64(J)
Richardson, T. 1894-95(A); 1897-98(A)
Richmond, T. L. 1929-30(SAm)
Ricketts, G. W. 1891(NA)
Riddell, N. A. 1977-78(K)
Ridgway, F. 1951-52(I)
Ridley, J. N. 1902-03(I)
Rimington, Capt M. F. 1892-93(I)*
Ritchie, D. M. 1923(C)
Roberts, D. 1920(NA); 1937(E)
Roberts, J. H. 1888-89(SA)
Robertson, J. D. B. 1947-48(W); 1951-52(I)
Robins, R. V. C. 1957-58(EA); 1958-59(SAm); 1968-69(SA)
Robins, R. W. V. 1929-30(Ar); 1933(NA); 1936-37(A); 1951(C)
Robinson, A. G. 1901-02(W)
Robinson, C. D. 1895(NA)
Robinson, D. C. 1927-28(J)
Robinson, E. P. 1935-36(J)
Robinson, J. S. 1892-93(I); 1894(NA)
Robson, C. 1899(NA); 1901-02(A)
Roebeck, St G. M. de 1896-97(W)*
Roller, W. E. 1885(NA); 1886(NA)
Rome, D. A. M. 1935(E); 1936(E); 1937(E)
Romilly, Lord 1923(C)
Roope, G. R. J. 1969-70(FE); 1972-73(I); 1973-74(SA); 1977-78(P)
Root, C. F. 1925-26(W)
Rose, B. C. 1977-78(P); 1980-81(W)
Rose, W. M. 1872(NA)
Rotherham, H. 1886(NA)
Rought-Rought, D. C. 1938(E)
Rouse, S. J. 1974-75(SA); 1974-75(W)
Rowbotham, J. 1868(NA)

Rowland, C. A. 1929-30(Ar)
Royle, V. P. F. A. 1878-79(A)
Rudd, C. R. D. 1951(C)
Russell, C. A. G. 1920-21(A); 1922-23(SA); 1924-25(SA)
Russell, W. E. 1960-61(NZ); 1961-62(I); 1965-66(A)
Ryan, M. 1964(NA)

Sadiq Mohammad 1971-72(Za)
Sainsbury, P. J. 1955-56(P); 1974-75(W)
Sanders, E. J. 1885(NA); 1886(NA)
Sandham, A. 1922-23(SA); 1924-25(A); 1926-27(I); 1928-29(J); 1929-30(W); 1930-31(SA); 1938-38(SAm)
Santall, F. R. 1937-38(SAm)
Sarel, W. G. M. 1913(US)
Sayer, D. M. 1958-59(SAm); 1960-61(NZ)
Schultz, S. S. 1878-79(A)
Schwarz, R. O. 1901(NA); 1907(NA)
Scott, E. K. 1951(C)
Scott, P. A. 1892-93(I)*
Scott, R. P. 1938(E)*
Scott, R. P. 1929(E); 1930(E)
Scott-Chad, G. N. 1931-32(J)
Scotton, W. H. 1881-82(A); 1884-85(A); 1886-87(A)
Seabrook, F. J. 1927-28(J)
Selby, J. 1876-77(A); 1879(NA); 1881-82(A)
Sellar, K. A. 1936(E); 1937(C)
Selvey, M. W. W. 1976-77(I); 1980-81(Z)
Sevier, W. W. 1889-90(I)*
Sewell, C. O. H. 1898(NA)
Sewell, R. P. 1894-95(W)
Sewell, T. 1861-62(A)
Seymour, J. 1903(NA)
Shackleton, D. 1951-52(I)
Shackleton, J. H. 1971-72(Za)
Shand, F. L. 1889-90(I); 1892-93(I)*
Sharp, G. 1974-75(W)
Sharp, K. 1979-80(A)
Sharpe, J. W. 1891-92(A)
Sharpe, P. J. 1963-64(I); 1964(NA); 1969-70(W)
Shaw, A. 1868(NA); 1876-77(A); 1879(NA); 1881-82(A); 1884-85(A); 1886-87(A)
Shaw, G. 1928-29(J)
Shaw, W. 1886-87(A)*
Shepherd, D. J. 1961-62(EA); 1969-70(W); 1969-70(FE); 1971-72(Za)
Shepherd, D. R. 1971-72(Za)
Shepherd, J. N. 1972-73(W); 1973-74(SA); 1974-75(SA); 1974-75(W)
Sheppard, D. S. 1950-51(A); 1962-63(A)
Shermerdine, G. O. 1920(NA)
Sherring, — 1892-93(I)*
Sherwin, M. 1886-87(A)
Shrewsbury, A. 1879(NA); 1881-82(A); 1884-85(A); 1886-87(A); 1887-88(A)
Shuttleworth, K. 1970-71(A)
Sidebottom, A. 1981-82(SA)
Silk, D. R. W. 1957-58(EA); 1958-59(SAm); 1959(NA); 1960-61(NZ)
Simpson, C. 1910-11(W)*
Simpson, R. T. 1948-49(SA); 1950-51(A); 1954-55(A); 1956-57(I)
Simpson-Hayward, G. H. T. 1902-03(I); 1904-05(W); 1906-07(NZ); 1907(NA); 1909(E); 1909-10(SA)
Sims, J. M. 1935-36(NZ); 1936-37(A); 1937-38(SAm)
Singh, S. 1955-56(W)
Singleton, A. P. 1937(C); 1939(E)
Skene, R. W. 1929(E)

Skinner, A. C. 1888-89(SA)
Skinner, W. R. 1937-38(SAm)
Slack, J. K. E. 1961(B)
Slack, W. N. 1980-81(Z)
Slade, D. N. F. 1964-65(W); 1965-66(J)
Slocombe, P. A. 1975-76(SA)
Smailes, T. F. 1935-36(J)
Small, G. C. 1979-80(A)
Smith, A. C. 1959(NA); 1962-63(A); 1964-65(SAm); 1967-68(EA); 1969-70(FE)
Smith, A. E. C. 1938(E)
Smith, C. A. 1887-88(A); 1888-89(SA)
Smith, C. I. J. 1934-35(W)
Smith, D. 1935-36(NZ)
Smith, D. R. 1960-61(NZ); 1961-62(I); 1962(B)
Smith, D. V. 1956-57(J)
Smith, E. J. 1911-12(A); 1913-14(SA); 1925-26(W)
Smith, John (Cambs) 1868(NA)
Smith, M. J. 1972-73(SA); 1973-74(SA); 1974-75(W); 1977-78(FE)
Smith, M. J. K. 1957-58(EA); 1958-59(SAm); 1959-60(W); 1961-62(I); 1963-64(EA); 1963-64(I); 1964-65(SA); 1965-66(J); 1967-68(EA)
Smith, S. G. 1910-11(W); 1912-13(W)
Smith, T. P. B. 1937-38(I); 1938-39(NZ); 1939-40(I); 1946-47(A)
Smith, W. C. 1912-13(W)
Smithson, G. A. 1947-48(W)
Smith-Turberville, H. S. 1894-95(W)
Snooke, S. J. 1907(NA)
Snow, J. A. 1967-68(W); 1968-69(P); 1970-71(A); 1973-74(SA)
Sobers, G. St. A. 1964(NA)
Solbe, E. P. 1933(NA)
Somerset, A. P. F. C. 1910-11(W); 1912-13(W)
Somerset, A. W. F. 1904-05(W); 1910-11(W); 1912-13(W)
Southerton, J. 1873-74(A); 1876-77(A)
Spooner, R. T. 1951-52(I); 1953-54(W)
Stanley, H. T. 1896-97(W)
Stanning, J. 1902-03(NZ)
Stanyforth, R. T. 1926-27(SAm); 1927-28(SA); 1929-30(W); 1932(E)
Staples, S. J. 1927-28(SA); 1928-29(A)
Statham, J. B. 1950-51(A); 1951-52(I); 1953-54(W); 1954-55(A); 1956-57(SA); 1958-59(A); 1959-60(W); 1962-63(A)
Steel, A. G. 1882-83(A)
Steele, D. S. 1975-76(SA); 1980-81(Z)
Steele, H. K. 1972-73(M)
Steele, J. F. 1974-75(SA)
Stephenson, E. 1861-62(A)
Stephenson, H. H. 1859(NA); 1861-62(A)
Stephenson, H. W. 1955-56(P)
Stevens, B. 1939(E)
Stevens, G. T. S. 1922-23(SA); 1927-28(SA); 1929-30(W); 1931-32(J)
Stevenson, G. B. 1979-80(A); 1980-81(W)
Stewart, H. C. 1903(NA)
Stewart, M. J. 1955-56(W); 1959-60(R); 1960-61(NZ); 1963-64(EA); 1963-64(I); 1967-68(AA)
Stewart, N. J. W. 1978-79(Bg)
Stocks, F. W. 1897(NA)

Stoddart, A. E.   1887-88(A);
  1891-92(A); 1894-95(A);
  1896-97(W); 1897-98(A); 1899(NA)
Stoddart, P. L. B.   1968-69(SA)
Stone, C. C.   1896-97(W)
Storer, W.   1897-98(A)
Stow, V. A. S.   1905(NA)
Street, G. B.   1922-23(SA)
Strudwick, H.   1903-04(A);
  1909-10(SA); 1911-12(A);
  1913-14(A); 1920-21(A);
  1924-25(A)
Studd, C. T.   1882-83(A)
Studd, G. B.   1882-83(A)
Studd, R. A.   1895(NA)
Sturdy, R. G.   1938-39(J)
Sturt, M. O. C.   1968-69(SA)
Style, N.   1968-69(SA)
Subba Row, R.   1958-59(A);
  1959-60(W)
Sullivan, D.   1926-27(J); 1927-28(J)
Sullivan, J. P.   1971-72(Za)
Summers, G. F.   1933(NA);
  1936-37(Ce)
Surridge, W. S.   1959-60(R); 1961(B)
Sutcliffe, H.   1924-25(A);
  1927-28(SA); 1928-29(A);
  1932-33(A); 1935-36(I)
Sutcliffe, W. H. H.   1955-56(P)
Suttle, K. G.   1953-54(W);
  1967-68(AA)
Swan, H. D.   1922-23(NZ);
  1929-30(Ar)
Swanton, E. W.   1933(NA);
  1955-56(W)
Swetman, R.   1955-56(P);
  1958-59(A); 1959-60(R);
  1959-60(W)

Tapling, T. K.   1889-90(I)
Tarrant, G.   1863-64(A); 1868(NA)
Tate, M. W.   1924-25(A);
  1926-27(I); 1928-29(A);
  1930-31(SA); 1932-33(A);
  1937-38(SAm)
Tattersall, R.   1950-51(A);
  1951-52(I)
Tavare, C. J.   1981-82(I)
Taylor, B.   1956-57(SA);
  1976-77(Bg)
Taylor, C. H.   1937(C); 1939(E)
Taylor, C. R. V.   1972-73(M)
Taylor, K.   1978-79(Bg)
Taylor, L. B.   1980-81(Z);
  1981-82(SA)
Taylor, R. W.   1969-70(FE);
  1970-71(A); 1973-74(W);
  1974-75(A); 1977-78(P);
  1978-79(A); 1979-80(A); 1981-82(I)
Taylor, T. L.   1902-03(NZ)
Tennyson, A.   1926-27(J)*
Tennyson, Hon L. H.   1913-14(SA);
  1924-25(SA); 1925-26(W);
  1926-27(J); 1927-28(J); 1928-29(J);
  1931-32(J); 1937-38(I)
Thomas, E.   1889-90(I)
Thompson, C. E.   1923(C)
Thompson, G. J.   1902-03(NZ);
  1904-05(W); 1909-10(NA)
Thompson, J. R.   1951(C); 1959(NA)
Thomson, N. I.   1955-56(P);
  1964-65(SA)
Thorley, J. J.   1924(US)
Thornton, A. J.   1885(NA)
Thornton, Rev R. T.   1885(NA)
Throwley, Lord   1891(NA)
Titchener-Barrett, R. C. S.
  1974-75(W)
Tinley, R. C.   1863-64(A)
Titchmarsh, C. H.   1922-23(NZ)
Titmus, F. J.   1955-56(P);
  1962-63(I); 1963-64(I);
  1964-65(SA); 1965-66(A);
  1967-68(W); 1974-75(A);
  1975-76(SA)
Tolchard, R. W.   1967-68(AA);
  1972-73(I); 1973-74(SA);

1974-75(SA); 1974-75(W);
  1975-76(SA); 1976-77(I);
  1977-78(FE); 1978-79(A);
  1980-81(Z)
Tomkinson, J. E.   1902-03(I)
Tomlins, K. P.   1980-81(Z)
Tompkin, M.   1955-56(P)
Tonge, J. N.   1897(NA)
Toole, C. L.   1978-79(Bg)
Torrens, A. A.   1906-07(NZ)
Townsend, C. L.   1899(NA)
Townsend, D. C. H.   1934-35(W);
  1936(E)
Townsend, L. F.   1929-30(W);
  1933-34(I)
Tremlett, M. F.   1947-48(W);
  1948-49(SA)
Tribe, G. E.   1956-57(J); 1956-57(I)
Trott, A. E.   1898-99(SA);
  1902-03(NZ)
Troughton, L. H. W.   1911-12(Ar)
Troup, G. B.   1975-76(SA)
Trueman, F. S.   1953-54(W);
  1956-57(I); 1958-59(A);
  1959-60(W); 1962-63(A);
  1963-64(J); 1964(NA); 1964-65(W)
Trumper, J. O.   1973-74(Ba)
Tudor, C. L. St. J.   1913(US)
Tufnell, N. C.   1906-07(NZ);
  1909-10(SA); 1911-12(Ar)
Turnbull, M. J. L.   1929-30(NZ);
  1930-31(SA)
Turner, C.   1935-36(J)
Turner, D. R.   1972-73(SA)
Turner, J. A.   1885(NA); 1886(NA)
Turner, N. F.   1937(E)
Turner, S.   1974-75(SA);
  1974-75(W)
Twisleton-Wykeham-Fiennes, Hon
  E. E.   1898-99(SA)*
Tyldesley, G. E.   1924-25(SA);
  1926-27(J); 1927-28(SA);
  1928-29(A)
Tyldesley, H.   1922-23(NZ)
Tyldesley, J. T.   1898-99(SA);
  1901-02(A); 1903-04(A)
Tyldesley, R. K.   1924-25(A)
Tylecote, E. F. S.   1882-83(A)
Tyler, A. W.   1933(E)
Tyler, E. J.   1895-96(SA)
Tyson, F. H.   1954-55(A);
  1955-56(W); 1956-57(SA);
  1958-59(A)

Ulyett, G.   1876-77(A); 1878-79(A);
  1879(A); 1881-82(A); 1884-85(A);
  1887-88(A); 1888-89(A)
Underwood, D. L.   1966-67(P);
  1967-68(AA); 1968-69(P);
  1969-70(W); 1970-71(A);
  1972-73(I); 1973-74(W);
  1974-75(A); 1976-77(I);
  1979-80(A); 1981-82(I);
  1981-82(SA)
Unwin, F. St. G.   1938(E)

Valentine, B. H.   1931-32(J);
  1933(E) 1933-34(I); 1935(E);
  1938(E); 1938-39(SA)
Vaulkhard, D. H.   1928-29(J)
Vere-Hodge, N.   1937(E)
Verity, H.   1932-33(A); 1933:34(I);
  1935-36(I); 1936-37(A);
  1938-39(SA)
Vernon, G. F.   1882-83(A);
  1887-88(A); 1889-90(I); 1892-93(I)
Vernon, M. J.   1976-77(Bg)
Vine, J.   1911-12(A)
Vizard, R. D.   1889-90(I)*
Voce, W.   1929-30(W); 1930-31(SA);
  1932-33(A); 1936-37(A);
  1946-47(A)
Von Donop, Maj P. G.   1889-90(I)*

Waddington, A.   1920-21(A)
Wade, T. H.   1936-37(A)*
Wainwright, E.   1897-98(A)

Wakefield, W. H.   1894-95(W);
  1896-97(W)
Walford, M. M.   1938-39(J); 1951(C)
Walker, D. F.   1939(E)
Walker, J. G.   1889-90(I)
Walker, M. H. N.   1974-75(SA)
Walker, P. M.   1961-62(EA);
  1969-70(W)
Wallen, G.   1977-78(K)
Walsh, J. E.   1936-37(Ce);
  1938-39(NZ)
Walters, C. F.   1931-32(J);
  1933-34(I)
Walters, F. H.   1887-88(A)*
Walters, K. W.   1966-67(Ba)
Ward, A. (Derbys)   1969-70(W);
  1970-71(A)
Ward, A. (Lancs)   1894-95(A)
Ward, J. M.   1972-73(M)
Wardle, J. H.   1947-48(W);
  1953-54(W); 1954-55(A);
  1956-57(SA)
Warner, P. F.   1896-97(W);
  1897(NA); 1898(NA); 1898-99(SA);
  1902-03(NZ); 1903-04(A);
  1904-05(SA); 1911-12(A);
  1926-27(NA)
Warner, R. S. A.   1898(NA)
Warr, J. J.   1950-51(A); 1951(C);
  1955-56(W); 1956-57(J);
  1957-58(EA)
Washbrook, C.   1946-47(A);
  1948-49(SA); 1950-51(A)
Waterfield, J. E.   1889-90(I)*
Watkins, A. J.   1948-49(SA);
  1951-52(I); 1955-56(P)
Watkins, W. R.   1957-58(EA)
Watson, F. B.   1925-26(W)
Watson, Hon R. B.   1905(NA)*
Watson, W.   1953-54(W);
  1956-57(J); 1956-57(I); 1958-59(A);
  1960-61(NZ); 1963-64(EA)
Watts, E. A.   1937-38(SAm);
  1938-39(NZ)
Weatherby, J. H.   1894-95(W)
Webbe, A. J.   1878-79(A)
Weber, O.   1896-97(W)*
Weigall, G. J. V.   1903(NA);
  1926-27(SAm); 1927-28(J)
Welch, W. M.   1936(E)
Wellard, A. W.   1937-38(I);
  1939-40(I)
Wells, G.   1861-62(A)
Welman, F. T.   1886(NA)
Wenlock, D. A.   1980-81(Z)
Werner, R. H.   1937(E)*
Wharton, A.   1956-57(I)
Whatman, A. D.   1896-97(W);
  1897(NA); 1901-02(W);
  1902-03(NZ)
Whatmore, D. F.   1975-76(SA)
Wheatley, O. S.   1958-59(SAm);
  1969-70(W)
Wheatherly, R. E.   1938-39(J)
Whitby, H. O.   1885(NAm)
Whitcombe, D. M. P.   1913(US)
White, A. H.   1924(US)
White, D. W.   1961-62(I);
  1964-65(W)
White, J. C.   1926-27(SAm);
  1928-29(A); 1930-31(SA)
White, R. C.   1964-65(SAm)
Whitfield, G. S.   1903-04(A)*
Whittington, T. A. L.   1910-11(W);
  1912-13(W)
Whitwell, W. F.   1894(NA)
Whysall, W. W.   1924-25(A);
  1928-29(J)
Wickham, R. W.   1896-97(W)
Wigan, P.   1966-67(Ba)
Wight, P. B.   1961-62(EA)
Wilcox, D. R.   1934(E); 1935(E);
  1936(E); 1937(E); 1938(E)
Wilenkin, B. C. G.   1968-69(SA)
Wilkinson, W. A. C.   1922-23(NZ)
Wilkinson, L. L.   1938-39(SA)
Wilkinson, J. S.   1977-78(K)

Willey, P.   1972-73(SA);
  1977-78(FE); 1979-80(A);
  1980-81(W); 1981-82(SA)
Williams, D.   1961-62(EA)*
Williams, D. L.   1969-70(W)
Williams, E. S. B.   1931(E)
Williams, F.   1887-88(A)*
Williams, J. N.   1902-03(NZ)*
Williams, P. F. C.   1906-07(NZ)*
Williams, R. A.   1902-03(NZ)*;
  1902-03(I)
Williams, R. G.   1979-80(A)
Williams, W.   1896-97(W)
Willis, R. G. D.   1970-71(A);
  1972-73(SA); 1973-74(W);
  1974-75(A); 1976-77(I);
  1977-78(P); 1978-79(A);
  1979-80(A); 1980-81(W);
  1981-82(I)
Wills, G. S.   1932(E)
Willsher, E.   1868(NA)
Wilson, C. E. M.   1895(NA);
  1898-99(SA)
Wilson, D.   1960-61(NZ);
  1963-64(I); 1964(NA);
  1969-70(FE); 1970-71(A)
Wilson, D. C.   1938-39(J)
Wilson, E. R.   1901(NA); 1901-02(W);
  1911-12(Ar); 1920-21(A);
Wilson, G.   1922-23(NZ)
Wilson, J. V.   1954-55(SA)
Wiltshire, G. G. M.   1971-72(Za)
Windows, A. R.   1966-67(P)
Wing, D. C.   1968-69(SA);
  1975-76(WA); 1976-77(Bg)
Winlaw, R. de W. K.   1939(E)
Winter, G. E.   1898(NA)
Wisden, J.   1859(NA)
Wolfe, G.   1938-39(NZ)
Wood, A.   1935-36(J); 1937-38(SAm)
Wood, B.   1972-73(I); 1974-75(A);
  1974-75(W)
Wood, G. E. C.   1929(E)
Wood, H.   1888-89(SA); 1891-92(SA)
Wood, R.   1886-87(A)*
Woods, S. M. J.   1891(NA);
  1895-96(SA); 1896-97(W);
  1899(NA); 1901-02(A)*
Woolley, F. E.   1909-10(A);
  1911-12(A); 1913-14(SA);
  1920-21(A); 1922-23(SA);
  1924-25(A); 1929-30(NZ)
Woolmer, R. A.   1972-73(W);
  1973-74(SA); 1976-77(I);
  1981-82(SA)
Worthington, T. S.   1929-30(NZ);
  1936-37(A); 1937-38(I)
Wreford-Brown, C.   1891(NA)
Wright, C. W.   1891(NA);
  1892-93(I); 1894(NA); 1895-96(SA)
Wright, D. V. P.   1938-39(SA);
  1946-47(A); 1948-49(SA);
  1950-51(A); 1956-57(J)
Wright, H. F.   1892-93(I)
Wright, J. G.   1977-78(FE)
Wyatt, R. E. S.   1926-27(I);
  1927-28(SA); 1929-30(W);
  1930-31(SA); 1932-33(A);
  1934-35(W); 1936(E); 1936-37(A);
  1937-38(SAm); 1939(E); 1939-40(I)
Wykes, N. G.   1937(C)
Wyld, H. J.   1905(NA)
Wynyard, E. G.   1904-05(W);
  1905-06(W); 1906-07(NZ);
  1907(NA); 1909(E); 1909-10(SA);
  1920(NA); 1923(C)

Yardley, N. W. D.   1937-38(I);
  1938-39(SA); 1946-47(A)
Yeabsley, D. I.   1977-78(K)
Young, H. I.   1910-11(W)
Young, J. A.   1948-49(SA)
Young, R. A.   1907-08(A)
Younis Ahmed   1973-74(SA);
  1974-75(SA)

Zaheer Abbas   1971-72(Za)

Photographic acknowledgements
BBC Hulton Picture Library: 41, 63 top, 63 below, 70, 73, 78, 79, 82 below, 90, 92 below, 97, 99, 103 below, 110, 123 top; Central Press Photos: 83, 94 below, 101 below, 112 below, 113, 114, 117 top, 123 centre, 123 below, 127, 129 top, 129 below, 135 left, 135 right, 140 top, 140 below left, 145, 151 below, 162; Mary Evans Picture Library: 10, 12 below, 43; Patrick Eagar: title-spread, 164, 165, 169, 170, 173, 175, 176, 177, 178, 179, 181, 182, 184; Keystone Press Agency: 118 top, 118 left, 118 right, 121, 125 top, 125 below, 132 top, 132 below, 140 below right, 148 top, 148 below, 151 top, 154, 160; Hamlyn Group Picture Library: 112 top; Hamlyn Group–Trent Bridge Cricket Ground: 9, 11, 12 top, 13, 16, 18, 20, 21, 22, 25, 27, 28, 32, 37, 39, 40, 42, 46, 56, 57, 65, 84, 87 below, 101 top, 105; Sport and General Press Agency: 117 below; Trent Bridge Cricket Ground: 52, 59 top, 59 below, 74, 82 top, 87 top, 92 top, 94 top, 103 top.